ENCYCLOPEDIA
OF
AMERICAN
FOLKLIFE

Volume 4

ENCYCLOPEDIA OF AMERICAN FOLKLIFE

Volume 4

SIMON J. BRONNER, editor

M.E.Sharpe
Armonk, New York
London, England

M.E. Sharpe, Inc.
80 Business Park Drive
Armonk, NY 10504

© 2006 by M.E. Sharpe, Inc.

Library of Congress Cataloging-in-Publication Data

Encyclopedia of American folklife / Simon Bronner, editor.
p. cm.
Includes bibliographical references and indexes.
ISBN-13: 978-0-7656-8052-5 (hc : alk. paper)
ISBN-10: 0-7656-8052-1 (hc : alk. paper)
1. Folklore—United States—Encyclopedias. 2. United States—Social life and customs—
Encyclopedias. I. Bronner, Simon J.

GR105+
398.0973'03—dc22   2005032119

Cover images, clockwise from top left corner, by Getty Images and the following: Gianluigi Guercia;
Justin Ide; Stephen Chernin/Stringer; Regis Martin; Mark Wilson; David McNew; Mark Wilson;
Robert Nickelsberg/Time & Life Pictures; Mario Tama; Frank Driggs Collection/Hulton Archive.

Printed and bound in the United States

The paper used in this publication meets the minimum requirements of
American National Standard for Information Sciences—Permanence of
Paper for Printed Library Materials,
ANSI Z 39.48.1984.

BM (c) 10 9 8 7 6 5 4 3 2 1

Publisher: Myron E. Sharpe
Vice President and Editorial Director: Patricia Kolb
Vice President and Production Director: Carmen Chetti
Executive Editor and Manager of Reference: Todd Hallman
Development Editor: Jeffrey Hacker
Program Coordinator: Cathleen Prisco
Production Editor: Jennifer Morettini
Text Design: Carmen Chetti
Cover Design: Jesse Sanchez

Contents

~~~~ ~~~~

vi   Contents

Topic Finder

Amish, Nebraska
Amish, Old Order
Baptists, Old Regular
Buddhists
Carpatho-Rusyn Communities
Catholic Charismatics
Catholics
Christmas
Church of the Brethren
Communal Societies
Cults and Rumor-Panics, Satanic
Dance, Liturgical
Easter
Eastern Orthodox Christians
Gospel Music
Grottoes
Gullah or Geechee Communities
Hare Krishna
Hasidim and Misnagidim (Haredim)
Healing, Faith
Hindus
Hutterites
Jewish Communities
Jews, Crypto- and Protestant Millennialism
Love Feast
Lutherans
Mennonites
Mennonites, Reformed
Mennonites, Wenger
Millennialists
Molokans
Montagnard-Dega Communities
Mormon Fundamentalists
Mormons
Muslims
Old German Baptist Brethren
Old Order River Brethren
Pentecostals
Quakers
Religion
Senegalese Communities
Serbian and Montenegrin Communities
Shakers
Shrines and Crosses, Roadside
Sikhs
Snake-Handling Sects
Spiritualists

Tibetans
Wiccans

Sports and Games
Bodybuilders and Weight Lifters
Boston
Chicago
Cockfighting
Des Moines
Detroit
Gamblers and Gambling
Games, Drinking
Games and Toys
Little League Baseball and Youth Sports
    Organizations
Martial Artists
New York City
Saint Louis
Skateboarders
Sports Teams
Thanksgiving
Wrestling, Professional

States, Territories, and Commonwealths
Alaska
American Samoa
Guam
Hawaiians, Native
Pennsylvania Culture Region
Puerto Rican Communities
Texas

Theories and Disciplines
Communication
Community and Group
Context
Feminism
Folk Society
Folklife and Folk Culture
Folklore
Folklorists
Function and Functionalism
Geography
History and Heritage
Material Culture
Men and Masculinity
Nationalism

ENCYCLOPEDIA
OF
AMERICAN
FOLKLIFE

Volume 4

S

SADDLES AND SADDLE MAKING

In the United States, there are two major types of saddles made for riding horses, generally referred to as English and western. English saddle traditions are European in origin (not necessarily from England). English saddles are relatively small and light, little more than a seat for the rider. In the United States, they are usually made of hemlock-tanned leather, which cannot be stamped very easily; thus, the aesthetic qualities of English saddles lie in their overall form and finish rather than decoration, and, of course, in their usefulness. English saddles exist in a number of specialized forms, including racing and dressage saddles. While there are many mass-produced English saddles available, saddles for such elite events as polo matches and show jumping championships are likely to be handmade by saddle makers who specialize in specific forms.

Western stock saddles, by contrast, are large and heavy, developed for use by cowboys and ranchers. The western saddle is the predominant saddle type throughout the western United States and Canada. By the mid-twentieth century, it was becoming increasingly popular in the East as well, largely due to the influence of western movies and television shows. The western saddle is a specialized piece of occupational equipment, meant for extended periods of heavy riding and for cattle herding and roping. Its origins can be traced to the Mexican *vaquero* (cowboy) saddle of the 1700s. It has large skirts, a deep seat, and a horn for roping. It is a complicated and time-consuming object to put together, consisting of sixty or more parts and requiring dozens of specialized tools. At its core is the saddle tree, which in modern saddles consists of four wooden parts and a metal horn, all tightly covered with rawhide. Saddle trees are usually made by specialists who make them as their full-time occupation. The saddle maker assembles and shapes the various components of the saddle on the tree. The underside of the saddle is padded with sheepskin, but most other parts are leather. The parts are stitched, tied, or laced together.

Historical and Social Background

Western saddles have roots in the *vaquero* traditions that emerged in Mexico in the sixteenth century as adaptations of Spanish and Moorish horse culture. After the Mexican-American War (1846–1848), when Mexico ceded its northern region to the United States, much of the occupational lore of *vaqueros* was adopted by American ranchers. This included techniques for handling horses, cattle, and sheep, the construction and layout of ranches, occupational folk speech, recreational and celebratory events such as rodeo, as well as saddle making and other crafts. As the ranching industry spread north from Texas and the Southwest during the nineteenth century, all these traditions spread with it. Most of them continue in altered and localized forms to the present day. Although many of the simpler crafts associated with ranching are carried out by cowboys in their spare time (making tack from rawhide or horsehair, for example), the center of ranching-related crafts has always been the saddle shop. Saddle shops make and sell not only saddles but also bridles, ropes, and all kinds of tack; soft leather goods such as chaps and vests; cowboy boots and hats; bits and spurs; miscellaneous leather goods such as belts, billfolds, photo albums, and brief cases; and decorative items such as belt buckles and jewelry.

Large saddle shops existed in Mexico by the sixteenth century, employing many saddle and harness makers, leather carvers, apprentices, and specialists in related crafts such as silver engraving. All saddles and other products produced in a shop bore its stamp, no matter who actually did the work. This atelier system still exists in large saddle shops throughout Mexico, the United States, and Canada. In addition, cowboys and others sell crafts to the shop or they work on consignment.

By the mid- to late nineteenth century, regional variations in saddle forms had developed throughout the American West, most notably in Texas, California, and the Great Basin. Texas saddles were larger and heavier than other western saddles: skirts were large, heavy, square, and lined with sheepskin, and riggings (the assemblage of hardware, straps, and cinches that holds the saddle on the back of the horse) were double, with both front and rear cinches. California saddles were smaller and lighter, with rounded skirts and large *tapaderos* (stirrup covers), and "center fire" (single) riggings. By the end of the nineteenth century, distinct regional forms had evolved from these earlier forms in the Northern Plains and the Northwest, and most western saddles had developed large swells under the horns to hold the rider's thighs more firmly in place. Great Basin "buckaroo" saddles, by contrast, have retained "archaic" nineteenth-century forms, most notably having "slick forks," which means there are no swells under the horn. In the twentieth century, regional variations in saddle form became less important, as most large saddle shops would make saddles in any form the customer specified; at the same time, many specialized forms of rodeo and show saddles developed, which were adapted not to regions but to the specific uses of the saddle.

Craft

The decoration of leather has always been integral to the saddle maker's craft, going back to seventeenth-century Mexico. This includes the carving and stamping of leather, as well as the use of engraved silver and other minor aspects such as lacing and the quilting of padded seats. Leatherwork patterns vary from basketwork and other geometric designs to intricately carved flowers, wildlife, or scenes of rodeo and ranch life. Floral motifs are by far the most common, generally in interlocking, scroll-like patterns with roots in Mexico and, ultimately, in the Islamic civilization of Moorish Spain. All western saddles have bilateral tripartite symmetry; designs on one side must be mirror images of designs on the other side.

Western saddles are made with oak-tanned leather, which is easy to carve and stamp. The leather has to be dampened to the proper consistency. Leather-carving techniques vary, but the process generally starts by drawing a pattern lightly on the leather with a pencil, then carving the outline with a specialized tool known as a swivel knife. Details are then filled in with leather stamps, metal bolts with designs on one end, which are pounded into leather with rawhide mallets, so that the leather is pressed down but not cut. Some stamps have specific designs such as flower centers; some serve to model, shade, or provide background. Leatherworkers can vary the impact of a specific stamp according to the angle and amount of force used. Smaller swivel knives are sometimes used as well, to fill in details.

The amount of carving can vary from relatively sparse—creased borders, basket-weave patterns, or single flowers in the corners of the skirt—to saddles completely covered with finely detailed, intricate decorations. The use of fancy carved saddles by wealthy ranchers or in parades goes back to the seventeenth century, but in the twentieth century these saddles have become more abundant, commissioned for Hollywood stars, for use in festivals such as the Rose Bowl Parade, or as rodeo trophies.

Distinct regional traditions of leatherwork,

silver engraving, and other decorative elements emerged during the nineteenth century throughout the West and have persisted, albeit with many changes, to the present. A knowledgeable observer may be able to determine the approximate place and date of origin of a saddle by the type, size, and arrangement of flowers and other motifs on the leather. Oak leaf and acorn designs, for example, are associated with the Southwest. Parade saddles from California or Nevada may display large quantities of engraved silver; Great Plains saddles tend to use much less. Regional styles of decoration have often derived from well-known individual saddle shops, such as Porter's of Arizona, Visalia of California, or King's of Wyoming.

Like many traditional crafts, saddle making has been affected by mass production. Although saddles were mass-produced in St. Louis shortly after the Civil War, large-scale mass production did not take place until after World War II. Mass-produced saddles took over the market for less-expensive pleasure-riding saddles in the 1950s, driving many saddle makers out of business. Most cowboys continue to use handmade saddles if they can afford them, because they are more durable and dependable than factory saddles and can be made with the specific needs of rider and horse in mind. One impact of the loss of the low-end market, however, was the growth of a market for "art saddles" in the second half of the twentieth century.

The best-known and most influential creator of art saddles has been Don King, founder of King's Saddlery in Sheridan, Wyoming. In his youth, King traveled widely around the West with his father, an itinerant cowboy, working in saddle shops and learning a variety of regional leather-carving styles. Setting up his own shop in Sheridan after World War II, King was soon producing trophy saddles for the major national rodeo organizations. He developed an ornate and distinctive leather-carving style on these saddles, consisting of small and finely detailed wild roses arranged in intricate, scroll-like, seemingly three-dimensional patterns. Through a combination of innovation, artistry, and business acumen, King's

Saddlery had become one of the largest and best-known saddleries in the West by the 1970s, and many saddle makers were coming to Sheridan to apprentice with King and learn from his style. In the 1980s, King began to make a series of saddles and other objects covered with increasingly small and innovative flowers in elaborate patterns. Such saddles are not made for riding, although they are as well built and durable as any cowboy saddle. King displays his saddles in museums and galleries, and sells them to elite clients including the British and Saudi Arabian royal families, and several presidents.

By the end of the century, Sheridan had become the center of western saddle making, home to dozens of saddle makers and leatherworkers. Most of these craftspeople have developed distinctive variants of the Sheridan style, which has become a highly marketable commodity, and aim their work ultimately at an upscale "art" market. At the same time, many saddle makers continue to produce less-expensive custom saddles for working cowboys.

The most notable development in saddle making in the late twentieth and early twenty-first centuries has been the emergence of art and collectors markets. Saddles and other craft objects from prestigious older saddle shops such as Visalia of California, Garcia of Nevada, and Myres of Texas command exorbitant prices and are proudly displayed in museums and private collections; the same is true of well-known contemporary shops such as King's Saddlery or Holes Saddlery in Idaho. In 1989, Don King opened a museum behind his saddlery that displays hundreds of western saddles, thousands of tools, and hundreds of related craft objects such as bits, spurs, and handmade tack, along with western paintings in the manner of Frederick Remington and Charles Russell, Plains Indian crafts such as beaded moccasins, silver-mounted rifles, and many other examples of regional art and memorabilia. King's Saddlery Museum exemplifies a western regional art market, a "taste culture" that characterizes many museums, galleries, and private art collections around the West.

The emergence of the art and collectibles

markets, along with the continued vitality of regional horse cultures, ensures the vitality of saddle making as a twenty-first century craft, at once traditional and dynamic.

Timothy H. Evans

See also: Animals; Cowboys; Craft; Folk Art; Great Plains Indians; Great Plains Region; Material Culture; Rocky Mountain Cultural Region.

Sources

Beatie, Russel H. *Saddles.* Norman: University of Oklahoma Press, 1981.

Dary, David. *Cowboy Culture: A Saga of Five Centuries.* New York: Knopf, 1981.

Evans, Timothy H. *King of the Western Saddle: The Sheridan Saddle and the Art of Don King.* Jackson: University Press of Mississippi, 1998.

Rice, Lee M., and Glenn R. Vernam. *They Saddled the West.* Centreville, MD: Cornell Maritime Press, 1975.

Salaman, R.A. *Dictionary of Leather-Working Tools, c. 1700–1950.* New York: Macmillan, 1985.

SAILORS

The term "sailor" once called to mind a specific image: a lively young man, wiry and tanned from climbing about a square-rigged sailing vessel on a transoceanic voyage. Ideas about who can be considered a sailor, though, have broadened since the days of the great age of sail, when the word signified a person employed on one of thousands of the commercial vessels that carried the world's trade goods and passengers from continent to continent. In the twenty-first century, the word takes in a wide swath of mariners, young and old, male and female, who perform work or seek recreation on the water. Yachtsmen on the East Coast, cadets on sail training vessels, vacationers aboard Maine windjammers or massive cruise ships, navy and coast guard personnel, and racing teams, among countless others, all claim the designation of "sailor."

Despite vast differences in ethnicity, region, class, and reasons for voyaging, those who ply the waters do share in common traditions with those who go to sea. They take part in seafaring customs that can be traced to ancient times, applying the same principles and vying with the same forces of nature as did those who went before. They adopt rituals, expressions, and beliefs that are common to mariners everywhere, while displaying regional and occupational variations. Though steeped in tradition, seagoing occupations have changed in the past century to adapt to the mechanization of the commercial fleet, the containerization of cargo, and the growing recreational and educational uses that ships now serve.

Customs from the Age of Sail

Although the imposing square-rigged vessels that reached the peak of their development in the mid-nineteenth century had gradually fallen out of use by the early twentieth century, the customs and lore familiar to sailors who worked aboard them has remained not only alive, but also remarkably consistent despite technological and social change. Many of the customs of sailors under sail power—such as naming traditions, a predilection toward orderliness, and beliefs about signs of danger—made a nearly seamless transition to steam- and then diesel-powered vessels, and are found today aboard military, cruise, and cargo vessels. Other behaviors specific to sail technology have survived on the many varieties of modern sailing vessels: sail training ships; sailing vessels offering educational programs; passenger-carrying vessels such as windjammers and day-sailing vessels; and the hundreds of thousands of privately owned yachts and small boats scattered around the nation's waterways.

Voyages today are generally shorter and safer than in the age of sail. Electronics, engine power, and satellite technology have significantly improved communication, navigation, speed, and comfort. But the strongest influences on a sailor's life remain unchanged. Tides, winds, and currents exert a great deal of force on any vessel. Weather is volatile and, at times, powerfully destructive. A vessel at sea becomes an isolated island, cut off from support ashore. Space is confined and privacy at a premium. Mariners depend on the competence of the crew and the cooperation of the entire company, requiring clear communication

Sailors on a navy ship take part in an old "crossing the line" (equator) ritual that includes the King Neptune's Court ceremony. In a kind of initiation folk drama, "pollywogs" pay homage to the royal court of King Neptune, his queen (in a wig and women's clothing), and the sea spirit Davy Jones. *(Simon Bronner)*

and designation of responsibility. Boredom is a frequent companion, brought on by monotonous duty routines and unchanging scenery. For these reasons and many others, the lore associated with sailors and mariners in general has been well preserved, well recorded, and, though remarkably consistent over time, voluminous and constantly growing. The practice of sailing, in and of itself, also encourages traditional behaviors and the passing along of vital information in memorable form; the fragile position of a vessel floating amid hostile elements does not reward experimentation or improvisation. Established behaviors, tried and true, are openly preferred over innovations.

Merchant Crews

As the cargo-carrying, square-rigged ships fell out of use in the early twentieth century, many career mariners became concerned that society as a whole would lose desirable characteristics developed by service at sea. Sailing on a commercial vessel was, for many young men, a coming-of-age experience as well as an occupation, and was a vehicle for the transmission of values such as duty, brotherhood, courage, and cooperation. Beginning in the 1930s, a new form of large sailing vessel began to appear: reconditioned merchant ships fitted out with extra bunks and designated as "sail training vessels." Sometimes government sponsored and sometimes independently owned, these ships turned a sailor's life on its head. No longer were young men paid to go to sea; now they could be expected to pay for the privilege of working aboard a sailing ship. Personal development, not commerce, became the primary reason to undertake a voyage.

Sail training vessels became a repository for the older sea folklife still being gathered from the dying merchant trade. The communities of cadets and crew they created fostered the preservation of the more colorful, "salty" expressions of professional sailors: chanteys and sea songs, art works, weather lore, and stories. At the same time, other forms of traditional behavior continued without the official sanction of the folk-revival adherents of sailors' lore, often passed down by officers and captains of sail training vessels who in their younger years were members of merchant crews. This less picturesque lore included jokes, pranks, hazing rituals, and practical information vital to the safe operation of the vessel. Thousands of young people were exposed to all types of sailors' folklife in a demanding educational setting, and were encouraged to adopt its use in order to fit in and gain the respect of the officers. Doubtless many of these cadets went on to become the captains of recreational sailing vessels, small boat owners, or frequent passengers aboard such vessels, spreading the lore they had been taught to other crew members and passengers. The influence of the early sail training era is still felt today, as these programs continue to proliferate, and every coastal city seeks its own "tall ship" as a goodwill ambassador.

Beliefs, Names, and Jonahs

Beliefs make up a large portion of the folk expressions of sailors. Almost no facet of the mariner's trade is without its attendant customs and beliefs, intended to ward off bad luck or to court good fortune. Customs to protect vessels arose during ancient times, when oceans were seen as the home of animated forces that could protect or destroy any vessel. From the design, construction, and naming of a new vessel to its launching and operation at sea, beliefs influence the behavior of everyone concerned with the venture. In the age of the clipper ships, figureheads (decorative carvings mounted on the bows of ships) were designed and built to function as the "eyes" of the ship, always watching for the safest path. A bare-breasted female figurehead was believed to calm wild seas. These figureheads, often depicting dramatic characters, also gave the vessel a strong

identity; the custom survives today in navy submarine crests, which feature mascot animals.

During vessel construction, a coin is often placed under the main mast as payment to the spirits for a safe career. A sip of whiskey is consumed by shipbuilders after they install the last hull plank, called the "whiskey plank." Whiskey appeared at a new vessel's christening, though in present times a substitute of champagne or wine is preferred. In any case, a libation offering to the gods is still thought to bring favor upon a vessel—so much so that when the newly built schooner *Amistad* was launched at Mystic Seaport, Connecticut, in 2002, a plan to christen her with plain water was met with protest and dismay by the ship's builders.

Naming conventions are affected by belief as well. A preference for feminine or masculine names varies by time and place. Humble family names have been popular in the fishing trades, as they are thought not to anger jealous deities. Some taboos warn against ever changing the name of a vessel.

Persons, things, and actions that bring bad luck on a voyage are called "Jonahs," particularly in the fishing trades. The name probably derives from the biblical story of Jonah, who fled from God on a ship to Tarshish. God brought a great tempest that almost destroyed the vessel, and the sailors cast lots to determine who had brought such evil upon the ship. The lot fell to Jonah, and the sailors, to prevent further misfortune, cast him into the sea. Once Jonah was overboard, the waters turned calm (Jon. 1:1–16).

Jonahs are observed aboard today's vessels, as they were in the past. Black suitcases, pigs, women, clergymen, bananas, checkerboards, rabbits, blue objects, and many other seemingly innocuous items have been identified as Jonahs. Actions such as sailing on a Friday (particularly Friday the thirteenth), whistling, hanging a coil of rope without recoiling it, or laying a hatch cover upside down on deck are cause for fear of bad luck. In many cases, practical reasons to avoid a taboo action are easy to find: an open hatchway and a cover lying on the deck both present hazards, and rehanging an uncoiled rope could cause it to tangle when paying out again. In other cases, Jonahs arise by correlation, as when an unusual sight or event is followed by an accident.

Jonahs are reinforced when experience seems to lend them credulity, as Sebastian Junger describes in the best-selling book and hit movie *The Perfect Storm* (1998 and 2000). A number of Gloucester fishermen attributed the loss of the fishing vessel *Andrea Gail* to the blue crates she was carrying. Beliefs allow sailors to feel some sense of control over the environment and are maintained today with a cautious skepticism that honors the experiences of mariners past. Having the temerity to flout belief, though, has become a badge of courage in recent times. During World War II, aboard the British submarine *Osiris*, whose number was S13, daring sailors vied for the chance to dive at 1300 hours on Friday the thirteenth.

Hazing, Rituals, and Celebrations

Hazing is a common practice aboard modern-day sailing vessels, as it was in the past. Fools' errands, such as sending an inexperienced sailor or "green hand" to "polish the gold spike in the keel" or "fetch red oil for the port light and green oil for the starboard light" (all nonexistent), served to emphasize the need for comprehensive knowledge of equipment and nomenclature. Ignorance or carelessness could create danger for everyone aboard. By ridiculing the green hand, experienced mariners signal that status on a vessel is reached through skill and acquired practical knowledge, not by pedigree or shoreside education. To throw off the wrong line at the wrong time could send men falling to their deaths; to misread a compass could cause the ship to run aground.

Though voyages today are shorter than in the past, rituals and celebrations are still an important marker of milestones. "Crossing the Line" ceremonies, found in merchant vessels for centuries, have expanded into the cruise trade as entertainment. During such events, those who are crossing an important boundary go through a comic haz-

ing ritual and receive a new title. Crossing the international date line, for example, confers membership in the Order of the Golden Dragon; venturing into the arctic circle, the Order of the Bluenose; and crossing the equator, the Sons of Neptune. Other customs that have been observed include the British merchant marine's Dead Horse ceremony in the age of sail, celebrating the paying off of debt owed for advanced wages, and that of writing the first ship's log entry of the new year in verse, still practiced aboard U.S. military vessels.

Singing and Storytelling

Sea music is a well-known expression of sailor culture. The colorful, rhythmic chanteys of the age of sail functioned chiefly as work songs. By singing along in call-and-response, sailors coordinated the labor needed to hoist heavy sails, march slowly around a capstan to raise an anchor, or pump out a leaking ship. Singing chanteys at work indicated a slightly undermanned vessel; crews needed careful coordination to get tasks done with fewer men. Since the decline of commercial sailing vessels, there has been a folk revival of sea chanteys as entertainment, commonly heard in pubs as drinking songs. Indeed, the popular taste for chanteys saved a number of the songs from being lost to history, although their origin as work songs was often forgotten. In recent years, singing chanteys at work for educational purposes has become a part of programs aboard sail training vessels, on historic reproduction vessels such as the Hudson River Sloop *Clearwater*, and in the commercial passenger schooner trade. In addition to the old songs, new single-pull chanteys are continually emerging on board passenger schooners. These short bursts of song provide enough warning for two or more people to give a concentrated pull on a very tight line, such as a sheet for controlling sails. Simple hollers such as "Two-six, *heave*!," "Me whatnots are caught in the *block*," and "One, two, three o'clock, four o'clock, *rock*" have proven to have great utility even in a commercial context. Crews aboard passenger schooners, made up mostly of college-age men and women, also carry on a tradition of bawdy fo'c'sle (forecastle) songs, adapted from old sea songs and modern-day rugby songs.

The "sailor's yarn" of lore is alive and well in the form of personal narrative, usually called a "sea story." Sea stories typically describe accidents or near misses and serve to illustrate the disastrous consequences of ineptitude, the bravery or quick thinking of the teller, or the unpredictability of events at sea. They may be second- or thirdhand, relating cautionary tales of events that befell other vessels. A frequent theme in sea stories is the failure of electronic equipment, such as the loss of a Global Positioning System (GPS) after a lightning strike. Stories like these assert a continuing need for old-fashioned seamanship despite advances in technology.

Though the age of merchant sail has passed, the sheer number of people who experienced it and the practical utility of its folklife ensured that much of the occupational culture of pre-industrial sailors would not be lost. Students, passengers, and cadets continue to live and work aboard sailing vessels in the United States, inevitably bringing their own mix of experience and art to bear on the traditional body of lore. And yet, because of the demanding nature of working within the ocean element and the strongly imparted culture of the sea passed down from senior officers to green hands, the lore of sailors of 150 years ago is still very much in use today. Should one of them step onto the deck of a modern sail training vessel, the presence of women and the lack of cargo would be the most noticeable differences; the songs, stories, and pastimes would be much the same.

Michelle Moon

See also: Cape Cod; Occupational Folklife; Rituals and Rites; San Diego; Soldiers.

Sources

Bassett, Fletcher S. *Legends and Superstitions of the Sea and of Sailors in All Lands and at All Times.* 1885. Reprint, Detroit: Singing Tree Press, 1971.

Beck, Horace P. *Folklore and the Sea.* 1973. Reprint, Mystic, CT: Mystic Seaport Museum, 1996.

Carlson, Patricia Ann, ed. *The Literature and Lore of the Sea.* Amsterdam: Rodopi, 1986.

Gilmore, Janet C. *The World of the Oregon Fishboat: A Study in Maritime Folklife.* Ann Arbor, MI: UMI Research Press, 1986.

Healey, James C. *Foc's'le and Glory-Hole: A Study of the Merchant Seaman and His Occupation.* New York: Greenwood, 1969.

Lovette, Leland P. *Naval Customs Traditions and Usage.* 3rd ed. Annapolis, MD: U.S. Naval Institute, 1939.

Morgan, Douglas. *What Do You Do with a Drunken Sailor? Unexpurgated Sea Chanties.* Pomfret, CT: Swordsmith, 2002.

Richardson, Keith P. "Polliwogs and Shellbacks: An Analysis of the Equator Crossing Ritual." *Western Folklore* 36 (1977): 154–59.

Shay, Frank. *American Sea Songs and Chanteys.* New York: W.W. Norton, 1948.

———. *A Sailor's Treasury.* New York: W.W. Norton, 1951.

Taylor, David A. *Documenting Maritime Folklife: An Introductory Guide.* Washington, DC: Library of Congress, 1992.

SAINT LOUIS

St. Louis is Missouri's largest metropolitan area and historically the urban area people most readily associate with the state. It often is viewed as a historical and cultural crossroads of America, an image reinforced by its geographic location south of the point where the Missouri and Illinois rivers join the Mississippi River. Its metropolitan area extends for seven thousand square miles and as of 2000 includes around two and a half million people. Residents identify themselves in various ways, based on traditions, customs, a sensitivity concerning past glories, and ethnic composition. Founded in 1764 by the merchant Pierre Laclède and his assistant, Auguste Chouteau, St. Louis was named for the canonized king of France, Louis IX, and began its Euro-American urban history as a Mississippi River town in Spanish territory. Centuries prior to that, the area was the center of a massive and sprawling Woodlands Indian trade network, with a population of more than twenty thousand. (The area came to be called "Cahokia" for another group of Native Americans who moved to the area around 1600.) These

The Louisiana Purchase Exposition of 1904, or the St. Louis World's Fair, is regarded to this day as a symbol of the city's "golden age." Artifacts of the exposition are treasured; local legends and family tales associated with the event abound. *(Brown Brothers)*

Woodlands people had created a mound-building society (flourished 700–1500 C.E.) that left dozens of earth mounds throughout the region—hence St. Louis's nineteenth-century nickname, Mound City.

Passing through both French and Spanish hands prior to becoming part of the United States in the Louisiana Purchase of 1803, St. Louis developed as a multicultural city of immigrants and migrants, many of whom either passed through on their way west or stayed on to help supply the travelers. Although a number of cities have adopted the sobriquet of "gateway," St. Louis is universally recognized as the Gateway to the West, symbolized by the dedication of the Gate-way Arch, designed by Eero Saarinen, along the Mississippi River waterfront in 1965.

Ethnicity

Spanish and French influence on the city's society and culture was dominant in the eighteenth century, but British American ways took hold after the Revolutionary War and particularly after the Louisiana Purchase. American settlers, largely from the mercantile East and the midwestern frontier, came in droves. Following the overall trend in both the East and the Midwest, Irish and German immigration characterized nineteenth-century St. Louis. By the late nineteenth century, Italian and African American settlement had become significant, and the twentieth century brought significant numbers from dozens of other nations. Greek, Lebanese, Serbian, Bosnian, Chinese, Filipino, Vietnamese, and Hispanic peoples populated the metropolitan areas from the late nineteenth century through the twentieth century, along with an ongoing influx of Irish, Germans, and African Americans. All of these groups brought their religious, familial, and regional customs with them. The individual and blended traditions of all these groups characterize the St. Louis cultural environment in the twenty-first century.

St. Louis boasts ethnic festivals throughout the year, but perhaps the most visible are the two St. Patrick's Day celebrations in the region (one formalized in downtown St. Louis, the other a parish-communal celebration in the Irish enclave of Dogtown), Soulard's Mardi Gras celebration (reputed to be the second largest in the United States), and the Annie Malone Parade celebrating the African American community. More identifiable ethnic celebrations include the Hill Day celebration in that Italian American neighborhood, as well as the traditional Italian *festas* of San Sebastiano and Santa Rosalia. Generally, however, celebrations among Catholic, Orthodox Lutheran, Jewish, and Islamic religious groups in St. Louis tend to be less public and more community based. Accordingly, those traditions exert strong societal influences over the area's politics and culture. A prominent civic event in St. Louis derives from a tradition inspired by New Orleans's Mardi Gras festivities—a celebration of corporate and civic power known as the Veiled Prophet (VP) celebration. The event has been held annually from 1878 to the present but has taken a more overtly patriotic form as the city's Fourth of July celebration since 1995.

Foodways

St. Louisans' identification with food ranges from the high brow to the low brow, from the proud to the self-conscious. The attitude toward food is a broad reflection of the overall civic identity, which is to say ambivalent. Although the city has strong ethnic and cultural foodway traditions, residents take pride in the breadth and quality of restaurants in the region. One curious fact of restaurant culture in St. Louis is the conception of a family restaurant as a bar and grill, perhaps deriving from the strong German brewing tradition in the region.

On the high-brow end would be the city's Italian food, concentrated in the Italian enclave called the Hill. The Hill is a residential neighborhood of shotgun houses with excellent Italian restaurants on nearly every corner. One of the signature foods of St. Louis is toasted ravioli, which tradition holds was created accidentally when an Italian chef dropped some ravioli in a deep-fat-frying pan. St. Louis thin-crust pizza also originated on the Hill, and its most famous provider, Imo's, is both beloved and reviled among residents. One of the characteristic features of St. Louis thin-crust pizza is the use of provel cheese, a blend of provolone and American cheese. As with many things St. Louisan, the thin-crust pizza is set up for comparison with a Chicago counterpart (in this case, the Chicago deep-dish pizza). For more than a century, St. Louisans have evinced a strong communal rivalry (if not sense of inferiority) to the economic, industrial, cultural, and artistic institutions of the larger and more influential metropolis in the Midwest, Chicago.

Other signature foods in St. Louis include frozen custard (especially that served at Ted Drewes), gooey butter cake (found in all St. Louis bakeries), and local versions of the two diner foods scrapple and slingers. St. Louis scrapple is made with pancake batter, with sausage, onions, and spices inside; slingers (associated with the Eat-Rite diner) are a confabulation of eggs, potatoes, meat, cheese, and onions, covered with chili.

Speech

St. Louisans take pride in their subtle variation of a midwestern accent. Linguistically, St. Louis is a "speech island" that fits into the North or North Midland dialect area, although the rest of Missouri tends to fit into the South or South Midland dialect area. The outsider may not notice the local accent unless it is explicitly demonstrated. A primary component is the pronunciation of an "ah" sound for words containing "or" (or their equivalents). The common example is Interstate 44, which runs east and west through the south side of the city. St. Louisans delight in explaining to outsiders that the thoroughfare is called "Farty Far." Other characteristic features of the St. Louis accent include an intrusive "r" in words made with "wash" to form a "warsh" sound; "s" and "z" alternates in "greasy" and "sink"; a long "o" sound for the last syllable in "potato" and "tomato"; and the substitution of a long "o" for the "oo" sound in "tour." Soft drinks are sodas, a St. Louis migrant from the countryside is a "hoosier" (derogatory term), and an addressed group of people is "guys," "you guys," or even "youse guys," instead of the more Southern "y'all."

Legacy of the Louisiana Purchase Exposition

If outsiders are to understand the St. Louisan identity, it is essential to recognize the impact of the Louisiana Purchase Exposition, also known as the 1904 World's Fair, or simply, the Fair. The city still looks back on the Fair as the symbol of its golden age, when "the world came to St. Louis." Accordingly, a host of local legends are associated with the exposition: that the gigantic axle of the huge Ferris wheel lies buried in the city's Forest Park (the site of the Fair); or that Dogtown received its name because tribal Filipinos displayed at the Fair snatched dogs from this nearby neighborhood for their meals (they did not); or that ice cream in a waffle cone, the hot dog on a bun, the hamburger, and iced tea all were invented at the Fair (they were not). Collecting and displaying artifacts from the Fair, ranging from souvenir postcards to architectural elements of the Fair's buildings, are some of the ways St. Louisans connect to the glory days. Family tales with an association with the Fair are ram-

pant, from purported genealogical connections to organizers and officials to stories of ancestors married on the grounds (often on the Ferris wheel). Businesses still tap into exposition folklore, such as the popular 1904 World's Fair Doughnuts. No other event in St. Louis-area history—not the flight of Charles Lindbergh (financed by St. Louis businessmen), not the Lewis and Clark expedition, not even the building of the Gateway Arch—has generated as many stories and as much vicarious collecting as the Fair.

Music

Many outsiders think of St. Louis as a music town, probably based on the classic song by a non–St. Louisan, W.C. Handy, "St. Louis Blues" (1914). Indeed the city does have a long and vibrant musical heritage. The most famous ragtime composer, Scott Joplin, lived, played, and flourished in St. Louis; his home there is now a national landmark. The stories associated with three classic blues ballads—"Staggerlee," "Duncan and Brady," and "Frankie and Johnny"—are said to have occurred in St. Louis, and many of the giants of the blues have left their footprints in the city's performance halls—even if many stayed only shortly, on their way to Chicago or Kansas City.

Henry Townsend, a 1985 National Heritage Fellow, has lived and played the blues in St. Louis since the 1920s, one of the few who came and stayed. Ike and Tina Turner, Oliver Sain, and Johnnie Johnson are other prominent St. Louis blues and fusion artists. Chuck Berry of rock 'n' roll fame had his start in St. Louis and lives there still, and the hip-hop star Nelly is the most recent St. Louis musician to make a mark nationally.

Sports and Festivals

St. Louis is known as a sports town—baseball primarily—and has an active fan culture with informal social gatherings and neighborhood bars devoted to cheering the hometown Cardinals. The opening-day pep rally has been a long-standing tradition in the city. St. Louis has been home to teams from the four major professional sports (baseball, football, basketball, and hockey) almost as long as there have been leagues. The local faithful idolize winning teams in all sports, but the baseball team remains the chief grist of local legend and the centerpiece of civic identity. The typical folklore generated from sports in St. Louis tends to be the personal-experience narrative—being at Busch Stadium in 1998 when Mark McGwire hit his record-breaking sixty-second home run of the season or attending the celebrations downtown when the Cardinals won a World Series.

While sports venues often act as public celebrations of city pride, street festivals are also important to residents as expressions of ethnic and community identity. Annual ethnic celebrations such as the St. Patrick's Day parade are outlets for many heritage groups. The Festival of African and African American Music puts the spotlight on traditional gospel and dance groups, and the Strassenfest features German food, crafts, and music. Fair St. Louis is the city's massive Fourth of July celebration on the grounds of the Gateway Arch, complete with fireworks and an air show. Building on the city's blues roots, the Big Muddy Blues Festival in September brings national acts to the city as well as featuring homegrown talent. The four-day St. Louis Storytelling Festival, established in 1980, is a showcase for local tale-tellers and often has themes related to the city's pioneer and ethnic past. Concerned with preserving St. Louis traditions, organizations such as the International Folklore Federation and the Missouri Historical Society have active programs to document and conserve the city's folklife.

John B. Wolford

See also: Folk Festivals; German Communities; Sports Teams.

Sources

Brown, Cecil. *Stagolee Shot Billy*. Cambridge, MA: Harvard University Press, 2003.

Ehrlich, Walter. *Zion in the Valley: The Jewish Community of St. Louis.* Vol. 2, *The Twentieth Century*. Columbia: University of Missouri Press, 2002.

Faherty, William Barnaby. *The Irish in St. Louis: An Un-matched Celtic Community*. Columbia: University of Missouri Press, 2001.

Golenbock, Peter. *The Spirit of St. Louis: A History of the St. Louis Cardinals and Browns*. New York: Harper-Entertainment, 2001.

Mormino, Gary R. *Immigrants on the Hill: Italian-Americans in St. Louis, 1882–1982*. Urbana: University of Illinois Press, 1986.

Morris, Ann, ed. *Lift Every Voice and Sing: St. Louis African Americans in the Twentieth Century*. Columbia: University of Missouri Press, 1999.

Primm, James Neal. *Lion of the Valley: St. Louis, Missouri, 1764–1980*. 3rd ed. St. Louis: Missouri Historical Society Press, 1998.

Spencer, Thomas M. *The St. Louis Veiled Prophet Celebration: Power on Parade, 1877–1995*. Columbia: University of Missouri Press, 2000.

SAMOA

See American Samoa

SAN DIEGO

San Diego is the second-largest city in California (after Los Angeles), with 1.2 million people residing in the city proper, 2.9 million people in San Diego County, and another 1.2 million in the sister city of Tijuana, Mexico, just south of the border. This makes San Diego one of the largest metropolitan areas in North America and a place of diverse folk practices based on ethnicity, historical experience, language, and neighborhood traditions. Its folklife, often associated in the public imagination with an ethnic mix of Mexican and Native American cultures, has since the twentieth century entailed a wider diversity of national and language groups. The area's most conspicuous occupational folklife today derives from naval operations, but a long heritage of ranching has also left a strong imprint.

Historical Background

The area that is now called San Diego historically is the territory of the Kumeyaay people, a Yuman-speaking group (also known as Southern Diegueño, Mission Indian). Also in the area were

Decorations marking Día de los Muertos (Day of the Dead) proliferate in San Diego as the November holiday approaches. This colorful scene from an *ofrenda*, an altar to honor the memory of ancestors, was created by artist Mary Lou Valencia. *(Courtesy of Jana Fortier)*

Uto-Aztecan–speaking groups known as Luiseño and Cupeño. San Diego may be Kumeyaay homeland, but it was also part of the Spanish colonial empire. In 1542, Juan Rodríguez Cabrillo sailed into the San Diego Bay and claimed the land for Spain. In 1769, Gaspar de Portolá established the first military post on Presidio Hill in what is now San Diego's Old Town district. On the same day, Franciscan friar Junipero Serra founded the first of his twenty-one California missions, San Diego de Alcala. Later in 1769, the Spanish ship *San Carlos* arrived with the cattle that established the area's chief product, cowhides. By 1820, Kumeyaay and Mestizos worked as *vaqueros* (from the Spanish *vaca*, "cow": "cow-workers"), with fourteen hundred Native Americans in residence and fifteen thousand head of cattle maintained at the local California missions.

The ranch hands who maintained herds of cattle provided the hard labor for elite Spanish ranch owners and toiled under extremely harsh conditions. Out of this colonial style of ranching evolved today's modern ranches in San Diego County. *Vaqueros* derive from Spanish and Mexican traditions, but Euro-American cattle ranching also had an influence on modern ranches. Contemporary cattle workers in San Diego County may identify themselves as cowboys, *vaqueros*, or "buckaroos" (an Anglicized form of *vaquero*), depending on their style of saddles, blankets, girthing gear, reins, ropes, spurs, hats, boots, clothing, and working methods. While local boot makers, saddlers, and rawhide braiders create fine gear, ranch hands continue these arts as well. In addition, ballads, cowboy poetry, folk songs, and western acoustic music complete the folk and traditional arts that reflect what is locally called *los Califorñios* culture.

After about 1840, Yankee, European, African American, and Asian settlers trickled into California, joining the local Castilian, *mestizo* (mixed-race persons of indigenous and Spanish parentage), and Native American communities. After California and the American Southwest became part of the United States in 1848 (with the signing of the Treaty of Guadalupe Hidalgo), even more immigrants arrived in the San Diego region. In 1860, the city's population numbered only 731; within ten years it jumped to 2,300; and by the turn of the century reached approximately 18,000.

Settlers of African American ancestry were part of the early migrant traditions. For example, a black prospector named Fred Coleman discovered placer gold near present-day Julian in 1870, setting off a local "gold fever." In addition, Jewish settlers owned businesses such as restaurants, banks, tailor shops, and general merchandise stores. A number of groups identified themselves according to religious traditions. The various houses of worship in 1870 included Baptist, Presbyterian, Methodist, Unitarian, Roman Catholic, and Episcopalian churches. Such facilities, as well as Japanese American Associations, introduced at the turn of the century, were important for cohesiveness and developing connections between home and neighborhood.

Ethnic and Environmental Diversity

The contemporary folklife of San Diego is a product not only of cultural influences, but also of the environment. The city is located in a temperate region of the Pacific Coast near mesas, deserts, mountains, and forests, each of which is home to different folk occupations. In the mountain valleys live *vaqueros*, the descendents of America's first cowboys, who continue to herd cattle on local ranches. In the deserts live many of San Diego's eighteen Native American tribal groups, including tradition bearers who weave baskets, perform dances, and pass on stories. Along the coast, sea chantey singers congregate and give performances to tourists. All in all, the rich natural environment provides the materials necessary to produce folk dance, music, and crafts, putting a unique stamp on San Diego's folklife.

Folk cultural activities in this array sometimes compete alongside one another. For this reason, San Diego can be described as a "heterotopia," or a mix of cultural groups living in the same space but with different opportunities for public expression. Activities in the well-known tourist areas of the city, such as Old Town and Balboa Park, have more visibility than folk activities in new immigrant neighborhoods, generally carried out in more private settings such as temples and mosques.

About one-third of householders in San Diego speak a language other than English at home, and 21.5 percent of the population is foreign born. New immigrants come primarily from Mexico, with significant numbers from Asia (the Philippines, China, Japan, Korea, India), Great Britain, Russia, and the Middle East (Iraq, Iran, Somalia, Ethiopia). Most of the new immigrant populations have a sense of contributing to the city's mixed folklife and of helping to create an emergent tradition of multiculturalism.

The many signs of cultural diversity include performances of the *veena* from India, a seven-stringed, large-bodied wooden instrument. The bridge is placed on the flat top of the body of the *veena* and the neck attached to the stem is usually carved with a figure such as the head of a dragon. It is played by sitting cross-legged on the floor and holding the instrument in front. It is strongly associated with the playing of songs in Hindi but has appealed to a diverse audience in San Diego. Contemporary Japanese cultural traditions seen in San Diego include dances such as the *bon odori*, a Buddhist celebration to honor departed relatives and friends, *taiko* drumming, bonsai gardening, tea ceremony demonstrations, and ikebana (flower arranging). Classes in these arts often draw students from a variety of ethnic backgrounds.

Together with the native Kumeyaay, indigenous migrants from other parts of North America (Navajo, Zuni, Dakota, Yaqui, Apache) have made contributions to San Diego's rich folklife. Today the tradition bearers in these communities continue Native cultural traditions through dance, music, and craft production. Some of the Kumeyaay's cultural activities include the making of water jars, cooking vessels, digging sticks, acorn storage baskets, fishing nets, balls and sticks for the field hockey-like game of shinny, and bone gambling-game pieces, as well as tattooing and basket weaving. Kumeyaay weavers make coiled baskets from juncus (a sharp-stemmed reed), pine needles, deergrass, willow, fan palm, and yucca. Basket patterns are created with dyes from materials such as walnuts, elderberry, or even rusty metal. In addition to crafts, Kumeyaay perform dances and allegorical songs, of which the Bird Songs are the best-known.

San Diego's regional and cultural ties are complex. Although it shares with much of the Southwest a warm climate and a major Mexican and Native American presence, San Diego is often portrayed as distinct from the rest of the region. The uncertain regional identity is due in part to its image as an oceanfront tourist zone that attracts surfers, snorkelers, swimmers, sailors, divers, and beach vollyeballers. The distinctive speech (e.g., "dude," "wipeout," "awesome") and dress (e.g., flip-flops, bleached hair, and tropical shirts) of surfing culture have spread far beyond their coastal California roots. Still, with a long history of colorful characters and an oral tradition of some of the biggest waves in the world, San Diego remains one of the great centers of the surfing world. One of the legendary locations in San Diego for big waves and adventurers who rode them is called the Tijuana Sloughs at Imperial Beach. As far back as the early 1940s, surfers such as Allen "Dempsey" Holder, Charlie Wright, and Emil Sigler attained folk-hero status by braving the surf there.

Cultural Conservation and Folklife Programming

As evidenced in local festival performances, San Diego folklife is closely intertwined with cultural tourism. Through its grant programs, the City of San Diego Commission for Arts and Culture supports festivals and neighborhood art programs that address the needs of folk and traditional artists. Approximately 140 folk and traditional arts groups are listed with the commission. One hundred named neighborhoods make up San Diego's City of Villages development plan and are often used as a basis for situating artisans, cultural festivals, and neighborhood arts projects. For example, the Linda Vista Multicultural Festival draws on that neighborhood's diversity of immigrant groups to host a yearly cultural event featuring Hmong needlework, Ghanaian High Life music, Brazilian drumming, Mexican *folklorico* dance groups, Yaqui cultural dance, and Filipino folk dance.

San Diego held the Panama California International Exposition in 1915 at Balboa Stadium, and today many cultural institutions continue to promote area folk artists and folklife in the twelve-hundred-acre Balboa Park. The House of Pacific Relations is a collection of twenty-nine national folklife groups that hold programs featuring traditional costumes, arts, crafts, ethnic foods, folk dance, and music on a weekly basis; more than two dozen nations from Europe, Asia, and North and South America are represented. The San Diego Museum of Man sponsors a variety of events, including a fair, special exhibitions, demonstrations, and lectures, as well as publications, devoted to folklife issues. The Mingei International Museum focuses on traditional and contemporary folk art, craft, and design from around the world; the name derives from the Japanese words for "all people" (*min*) and "art" (*gei*). The WorldBeat Cultural Center promotes indigenous cultures of the world through music, art, and education. The Centro Cultural de la Raza is dedicated to promoting Chicano, Mexican, and Native American art and culture.

Throughout the city, other organizations work to promote the local folklife. A schedule of performances is available from various organizations, such as San Diego Folk Heritage, Voz Alta, a group dedicated mostly to Latino art, and the City of San Diego Art + Sol events calendar. In the center of the city, Old Town San Diego State Historic Park uses a cultural tourism approach to portray life in the Mexican and early American period of 1821 to 1872. Folk musicians such as mariachi bands, minstrels, and sea chantey singers serenade visitors. Museums in the park display customary nineteenth-century San Diego folklife, and shops sell items such as soap, tobacco, gingham, and Native American arts.

The future of San Diego folklife will be shaped by its diverse neighborhoods and cultural traditions. It will be found in its urban shrines, memorial walls, gospel music, Christmas lights, Día de los Muertos (Mexican Day of the Dead) accoutrements, the sacred Catholic images of carved *santos*, or saints' figures, *corona* wreaths, Muslim rap, black storytelling, and the grunion run, a recreational fishing event unique to San Diego and Baja California.

Jana Fortier

See also: Chicano and Mexican Communities; Sailors; Southwestern Indians.

Sources

Clayton, Lawrence, Jim Hoy, and Jerald Underwood. *Vaqueros, Cowboys, and Buckaroos: The Genesis and Life of the Mounted North American Herders.* Austin: University of Texas Press, 2001.

Kwiatkowska, Barbara J. "Introduction to the Musical Culture of the Diegueño Indians from San Diego County Reservations in California." *Canadian Folk Music Bulletin* 24 (1990): 14–21.

Lee, Melicent. *Indians of the Oaks.* San Diego: San Diego Museum of Man, 1989.

Stein, Lou. *San Diego County Place Names.* San Diego: Tofua, 1975.

Toelken, Barre. "Folklore and Reality in the American West." In *Sense of Place: American Regional Cultures*, ed. Barbara Allen and Thomas Schlereth, 14–27. Lexington: University Press of Kentucky, 1990.

SAN FRANCISCO BAY AREA

One of the most ethnically and culturally diverse regions of the United States, the San Francisco Bay Area, by the Pacific Coast in northern California, is home to a population of approximately eight million. The region includes the nine counties that surround the bay: San Francisco, San Mateo, Santa Clara, Alameda, Marin, Contra Costa, Solano, Napa, and Sonoma. Three large cities—San Francisco, Oakland, and San Jose—dominate this metropolitan area, which locals refer to as "the Bay Area" with no additional qualifier. At the same time, San Francisco is known locally as simply "the City," a nickname that suggests its symbolic preeminence.

Issues of everyday life that enter folklore in the Bay Area include traffic, especially for commuters contending with any of the five bridges over the bay, and the astronomical cost of real estate. More significantly, the sheer natural beauty of the region and a temperate climate throughout the year encourage outdoor activities, health consciousness, and a keen environmental awareness. The roots of local environmentalism run deep: Oakland is home to Lake Merritt, the oldest wildlife refuge in North America (1870), and San Francisco is the home base of the Sierra Club, founded by John Muir in 1892—to name just two early examples. In the twenty-first century, an extensive local network of national, state, and regional parks encourage outdoor recreation and raise awareness about environmental concerns. Community programs throughout the region promote recycling, composting, organic gardening, and carpooling.

Ethnic Diversity

Besides environmentalism, the key factor that shapes Bay Area folklife is the ethnic diversity of

Food is an integral part of San Francisco folklife. Seafood, such as the crab at Fisherman's Wharf, is abundant; ethnic eateries reflect the diversity of the community at large; and sourdough bread is a staple. *(San Francisco History Center, San Francisco Public Library)*

this region. The precise demographics vary from county to county, but the importance of ethnic identity is everywhere evident. Place names, in particular, recall the nearly seventy-five years of Spanish and Mexican rule, as well as the California Native Americans who first peopled the region.

The original inhabitants of the Bay Area were mostly Ohlone and Coast Miwoks, who established villages around the shores of the bay and survived principally through hunting, fishing, and gathering. Spanish colonizers arrived in 1776, founding a *presidio* (fort) and a mission, San Francisco de Asís (for which San Francisco's Mission District is named)—the sixth in the system of twenty-one Franciscan missions that would eventually run the length of California. In the decades that followed, most of the native population of coastal California was brought—often brutally—under the sway of these missions. Spanish rule over Alta California lasted until 1821, when Mexico won its independence. Afterward, a series of Mexican governors ruled the region and settlement began in earnest, with the governors granting large tracts of land—*ranchos*—to retired soldiers.

In the early 1840s, the first overland party of American settlers arrived in California, and in 1848, Mexico ceded California to the United States as part of the Treaty of Guadalupe Hidalgo, which ended the Mexican-American War. Soon after the signing of this treaty, word spread that gold had been discovered at Sutter's Mill, and the California gold rush was on. More than one hundred thousand fortune seekers—the so-called forty-niners—poured into the area, by land and by sea, drastically transforming the entire region and decimating the Native American population, which had already diminished significantly under the mission system. In two years, San Francisco's population grew from five hundred to twenty-five thousand, and the city established itself as a vital port and financial center.

Beginning most dramatically with the gold rush and continuing with the transcontinental railroad, agriculture and, most recently, the high-tech industry, economic opportunity has drawn people to the Bay Area from all over the world. The lure of gold brought adventurers from the East Coast. Through the second half of the nineteenth century—both during and after the gold rush—thousands of European immigrants came to San Francisco, particularly Irish, Italians, French, and Germans, as well as eastern Europeans. Large numbers of Chinese immigrants came also, establishing San Francisco's Chinatown. Later, during World War II, African Americans from the South came to work in Oakland's shipyards. And throughout the twentieth century, Mexican and Central American immigrants significantly expanded the local Latino population. In recent years, immigrants have also flocked to the Bay Area from eastern Europe, the Middle East, and Asia Minor. "Little Kabul" in Fremont, for example, is home to the largest Afghan American community in the United States.

Its West Coast location has also made San Francisco an important destination for immigrants from around the Pacific Rim, especially since the end of the Vietnam War. Daly City and Vallejo, for example, now have large Filipino populations, while San Jose boasts one of the nation's largest Vietnamese communities. South Asians have also come to the Bay Area in large numbers, most recently in response to the demands of the high-tech industry. The Chinese and Japanese communities first established in the nineteenth century still have a significant presence.

As immigrants settled in, they established mutual assistance associations, social clubs, and cultural organizations. And as their needs changed, many of these groups turned their attention to the preservation and promotion of ethnic folkways. One of many possible examples is San Francisco's Slavonic Cultural Center, which traces its roots to the Slavonic Mutual and Benevolent Society, begun in 1857 as a fraternal organization for Slavic immigrants. In the late 1970s, the organization moved into a permanent space and reinvented its mission. Today, the Slavonic Cultural Center is a focal point for Balkan music, dance, and culture in the Bay Area, sponsoring instrumental ensembles, a choir, an oral history project, a performance series, and an annual festival.

What is significant about ethnic diversity in the Bay Area is not just its variety, but also its depth. For any ethnic category and genre, one is likely to find not just a single organization or practitioner, but many. Bay Area folklife is particularly marked by expressions of ethnic identity, which are visible in community organizations, festivals, performances, and everyday practice. A review of two genres—foodways and dance—reflects the richness and complexity of Bay Area folklife.

Foodways

While it is difficult to identify any one dish as a local specialty—with the possible exception of sourdough bread, which today is produced primarily by commercial and artisan bakeries—food is taken very seriously in the Bay Area. Local foodways have been shaped primarily by diverse cultural and culinary influences and by the ready availability of fresh local ingredients. These influences are perhaps most visible in restaurant cooking, but they also form the foundation of local foodways on a more general scale. The emergence of so-called California cuisine began with Alice Waters's innovative restaurant, Chez Panisse, located in Berkeley's "Gourmet Ghetto," and this style of cooking has been embraced by many other chefs and establishments.

Waters's emphasis on fresh, seasonal, local produce speaks to environmental as well as culinary concerns and has sparked a broader trend in local foodways, including the emergence of small-scale organic farms and an emphasis on sustainable farming practices. These farmers supply the needs of local chefs and—through specialty groceries, a network of weekly farmers' markets, and local farm stands—make these products generally available. In addition, some specialty farmers seek out and raise lesser-known or "heirloom" varieties of fruits and vegetables, and many home gardeners are doing the same.

At the same time, the cultural diversity of the Bay Area is an equally important influence on local foodways. Its most obvious and accessible expression is the vast array of ethnic eateries. Anything you crave can be found here in abundance and variety—from Mexican, to Afghan, to Tibetan, to Hawaiian, to Peruvian, to Basque, to Senegalese cuisine, and everything in between. San Francisco alone boasts more than two hundred Chinese restaurants. A dense local economy supports the diversity of foodways, and community members as well as local "foodies" can track down needed ingredients in specialty groceries.

Two local organizations are especially noteworthy in the area of foodways. COPIA, the American Center for Wine, Food and the Arts, is a museum and educational center in Napa devoted to exploring American foodways and associated arts. The organization offers regular tastings of local wines and sponsors food demonstrations, garden tours, exhibits, and other cultural events that focus on food practices. The second food-related organization has a specific ethnic focus: Kagami Kai, located in San Francisco, is dedicated to presenting and preserving the traditional art of *mochi* pounding to audiences in the Japanese American community and beyond. To the accompaniment of *taiko* drumming, group members use wooden mallets and pestles to pound hot glutinous rice into sticky rice taffy, or *mochi*. Kagami Kai performs at local festivals and cultural events throughout the year.

Dance

Folk dance thrives in the Bay Area, and the range and depth of these traditions richly illustrate local cultural diversity and ethnic pride, as well as the vitality of local folklife. One catalog of local folk artists lists more than three hundred dance groups, ranging from African American stepping and Brazilian samba to Hawaiian hula, Punjabi bhangra, Cambodian classical dance, Chinese lion dance, Irish step dancing, powwow dancing, English morris, and many more. Large- and small-scale dance troupes may be seen performing in ethnic parades and festivals, public and private, throughout the region. Many perform primarily within their own communities, but some have become quasi-professional organizations—such as Ballet Afsaneh (dances of the Silk Road), De Rompe y Raja (Afro-Peruvian dance), and Diamano Coura Senegalese Dance Company.

Notable among the venues that present ethnic dance is the Traditional Arts Program at the California Academy of Sciences, which has documented local folklife since 1983. Its public programs focus on artistic expression and ethnic diversity in the Bay Area, with presentations ranging from cooking demonstrations, crafts workshops, and ethnographic films to performances of theater, martial arts, and storytelling—as well as music and dance. Also noteworthy is World Arts West, which sponsors San Francisco's annual Ethnic Dance Festival, showcasing two dozen local troupes every June, and runs People Like Me, an arts education program focusing on ethnic dance. In addition, ethnic music and dance are featured on mainstream stages such as University of California, Berkeley's Cal Performances series, which suggests the broad appeal of such programming in this region.

Besides featuring performances, the Bay Area offers abundant opportunities for participation in a similarly diverse range of dance traditions. Dance classes of all kinds are widely available, and numerous organizations offer regular evening dances of various sorts to perpetuate traditions. One can go contra dancing several nights a week in the Bay Area—or easily find somewhere to take part in Cajun, salsa, tango, Scottish, hula, West African, Israeli, or belly dance, among many others. Of particular note is Ashkenaz Music & Dance Community Center in Berkeley, where people of all ages and backgrounds dance every night to live music—again, from diverse traditions. The annual San Francisco Free Folk Festival, sponsored by the San Francisco Folk Music Club, features a weekend of dance and music workshops and performances every June, as well as an annual summer camp.

Local Identities

Most residents of the Bay Area would acknowledge a sense of overall Bay Area identity, yet there are striking differences among the various locales that make up this region. For example, San Francisco's freewheeling, "anything goes" flavor dates back to the days of the Barbary Coast, a red-light district adjacent to the city's waterfront that was home to saloons, brothels, gambling halls, and the less-than-savory characters who peopled them. The city's bohemian reputation was further enhanced by the beatnik and hippie eras of the 1950s and 1960s, and by the visibility of the local gay subculture. At the same time, the city is an important banking center—dating from the many financial institutions that arose in the wake of the gold rush.

Berkeley, home of the University of California, takes the countercultural mind-set a step further: the town has a reputation—born in the free speech and civil rights movements of the 1960s—for being aggressively progressive, ardently environmental, and proudly eccentric. "The People's Republic of Berkeley" now both celebrates and mocks its own image with an annual "How Berkeley Can You Be?" parade, featuring such tongue-in-cheek entries as the NIMBY Brigade, the Goddess of Berserkocracy, and Young Republicans for Heterosexuality.

Other parts of the Bay Area have their own cultural microclimates that reflect demographic differences. Silicon Valley, roughly contiguous with Santa Clara and San Mateo Counties, was once known as "The Valley of Heart's Delight" because in its fertile soil grew almost endless orchards of fruit and nut trees. By 1998, only forty-five hundred acres of orchard remained. Silicon Valley today is a place of youth and ideas, with an emphasis on innovation and pride in being ahead of the technology curve. In contrast, the Bay Area's northern counties have remained more rural and agricultural; the wine country of the Napa and Sonoma Valleys, for example, is particularly well known.

Jennifer Michael

See also: Chinatowns; Chinese Communities; Gay San Francisco; Japanese Communities.

Sources

Fracchia, Charles A. *City by the Bay: A History of Modern San Francisco, 1945–Present.* Los Angeles: Heritage Media, 1997.

Nugent, Walter. *Into the West: The Story of Its People.* New York: Vintage Books, 2001.

Richards, Rand. *Historic San Francisco: A Concise History and Guide.* San Francisco: Heritage House, 1991.

Starr, Kevin, and Richard J. Orsi, eds. *Rooted in Barbarous Soil: People, Culture, and Community in Gold Rush California.* Berkeley: University of California Press, 2000.

Stryker, Susan, and Jim Van Buskirk. *Gay by the Bay: A History of Queer Culture in the San Francisco Bay Area.* San Francisco: Chronicle Books, 1996.

Traditional Arts Program, California Academy of Sciences. www.calacademy.org/research/anthropology/tap/index.htm.

Turner, Tom. *Sierra Club: 100 Years of Protecting Nature.* New York: Abrams, in association with the Sierra Club, 1991.

Yung, Judy. *Unbound Feet: A Social History of Chinese Women in San Francisco.* Berkeley: University of California Press, 1995.

SANTA FE

Santa Fe is the political capital of New Mexico and arguably the cultural capital of the entire Spanish Southwest. Officially called La Villa Real de Santa Fe de San Francisco de Asis (Royal City of the Holy Faith of St. Francis of Assisi), it is located in the north central part of the state. It is also called the City Different, not least because of its long and distinctive history marked by colonial conquest, native revolt, and reconquest. Associated with its colonial past is its claim of holding the oldest statue of the Virgin Mary to which a constant public devotion has been maintained. Another distinction of Santa Fe is its standing as the oldest capital city in the United States, officially founded in 1609. A local joke has it that the Palace of the Governors had a leak in the roof before the Pilgrims landed at Plymouth Rock. Situated seven thousand feet above sea level at the base of the Sangre de Cristo Mountains (the southernmost segment of the Rockies), it is also the highest state capital in the United States. In folklife, Santa Fe is significant for its local fiestas, Spanish and Native American folk crafts and arts marketplace, and foodways.

The name of Santa Fe indicates the early presence of Spaniards, yet its earlier inhabitants called it the "dancing ground of the sun." There is archaeological evidence of Paleo Indian (15000–12000 B.C.E.), Archaic Indian (8000 B.C.E.), and early Pueblo occupations in the form of spear points, arrowheads, pit houses, pottery, and other artifacts found in the town. Native Americans, however, abandoned the site by the late fourteenth century, making it an ideal locale for the

Santa Fe's Indian Market, held annually in August, features the work of craftsmen representing more than one hundred tribes. Jewelry, pottery, blankets, and rugs are perennially popular with buyers. Santa Fe is the center of native, Hispanic, and regional expressive art in the American Southwest. *(Simon Bronner)*

second Spanish capital in New Mexico. In 1821, Mexico, which included the lands of what is now the American Southwest, declared independence from Spain and the Santa Fe trade began. The fabled Santa Fe Trail stretched from Franklin, Missouri, through what is now Kansas, Colorado, and Oklahoma before dipping south to Watrous, New Mexico, and then north from San Juan del Vado to Santa Fe. After the Mexican-American War in 1848, Mexico ceded its northern lands to the United States, thus forming America's Southwest region. The trail brought American adventurers, traders, and health seekers until 1880, when the railroad reached Santa Fe and the use of the trail for stagecoaches and wagons sharply declined. Historical legends of the Old West can still be heard when mention is made of the trail, and visitors flock to it along a historic trail administered by the National Park Service. As a result of the settlement and migration history in Santa Fe, residents often refer to three main ethnic influences of Indian (Native American), Hispanic, and "Anglo." The latter term refers less to British Americans than to anyone who is not Native American or Hispanic, including African and Asian Americans. In the twentieth century, the city attracted a jnumber of Italian, French, Syrian, Chinese, and Tibetan immigrants, although the largest foreign-born population is from Mexico. Some 12 percent of today's sixty-six thousand residents are foreign born, and about half of those entered the city since 1990. Those trends are largely responsible for Santa Fe's significant population growth and increased diversity since the late twentieth century.

Fiestas

The background of fiestas associated with Santa Fe dates back to the seventeenth century, at the time of Spanish colonization. Droughts were devastating and common, as were epidemics of European diseases, which were particularly destructive to the indigenous populations. The Spaniards exploited the labor of Native Americans and fought among themselves over it. Finally in 1680, after five years of planning, many Pueblos and other Native Americans united and carried out the only successful indigenous revolt on the North American continent and the only successful native revolt against the Spaniards anywhere in their vast empire.

In 1692, Governor Diego De Vargas returned to Santa Fe with about one hundred soldiers, promising to restore a revered statue of the Spanish patroness of New Mexico, the Virgin Mary, to her special throne in the old settlement's church. When he arrived at the central plaza, however, he found that the palace was inhabited by Pueblo Indians. De Vargas approached the palace unarmed and demanded that the Native Americans reaffirm their allegiance to the king.

According to legend, the people occupying the palace asked if De Vargas was staying. When he answered in the negative, the people reaffirmed their allegiance to the king and De Vargas went on to the next pueblo. This event is called the *entrada* (entrance) or "peaceful reconquest of New Mexico."

Oral tradition maintains that De Vargas vowed to celebrate the statue's name every year if she would let him peacefully resettle Santa Fe. The celebration was made official in 1712 and has been celebrated every year since. Events include a queen's procession and a reenactment of the *entrada*. The traditional celebration had a religious component of a Mass of thanksgiving at the cathedral, followed by a half-mile candlelight procession to the Cross of Martyrs, commemorating twenty-one Spanish priests killed during the Pueblo Indian revolt of 1680. An important icon in the religious observances is the Virgin Mary statue known as Nuestra Señora del Rosario (Our Lady of the Rosary)—colloquially called La Conquistadora (Lady of the Conquest)—now housed in St. Francis Cathedral. The twenty-eight-inch crowned statue, according to some accounts, was handmade out of willow by an anonymous Spanish carver in the seventeenth century who used red paint and gold-leaf to decorate the figure. She is the centerpiece of the "De Vargas Procession," parading from the Conquistadora Chapel in the Parroquia to the Rosario Chapel outside the town and back. In the past, young veiled women carried the statue, often surrounded by white-clad girls and members of the Caballeros de Vargas (Vargas's horsemen) wearing colonial-styled shirts with puffy sleeves and bright red sashes.

Artist Will Shuster in the 1920s began a tradition initiating the September Fiestas de Santa Fe celebrations with the creation of a spectacle of burning *Zozobra* or Old Man Gloom, a fifty-foot-high papier-mâché figure, to dispel the anxieties of the past year. In so doing, Shuster managed to secularize the celebration and expand its appeal. The spectacle functioned to augment the historic celebration with a carnivalesque festival marking the end of the summer season and the soberness of labor in the fall. The huge white effigy of a male figure decorated often with black bands, green eyes, and exaggerated red lips waves its arms and growls ominously before the burning, while spectators chant, "Burn him," until he is destroyed. Ethnographer Ronald L. Grimes in a major study of Santa Fe rituals, *Symbol and Conquest* (1976), interprets the event as a ritualized contemplation or enactment of death intended to renew life. Shuster's inspiration for *Zozobra* reportedly came from the Holy Week celebrations of the Yaqui Indians of Mexico; an effigy of Judas, filled with firecrackers, was led around the village on a donkey and later burned. Some residents of Mexican ancestry also make the connection to stories of the bogeyman *el cucui*, a monstrous imaginary figure that in folktales still circulating in Santa Fe are said to abduct or scare misbehaving children. Shuster constructed the figure of *Zozobra* until 1964, when he gave his model of the figure to the Kiwanis Club to continue the tradition.

A highlight of the kickoff event is the appearance of the fire spirit dancer, dressed in a flowing red costume, who appears at the top of the stage to drive away the white-sheeted "glooms" from the base of the giant effigy. In a bow to apprentice tradition, dancer Jacques Cartier, who created and performed the role for thirty-seven years, handed it over to a student, James Lilienthal, in 1970. He, in turn, handed it over to his daughter, Katy Lilienthal, early in the twenty-first century. Modern additions to the performance have included pyrotechnic displays.

Another regular feature in the past has been the costume ball and a fashion show called La Merienda (afternoon snack). Both of these events emphasized through elaborate dress the unifying effect of Spanish colonial heritage in the identity of Santa Fe. Although Native American costume were spotted in the balls, Spanish colonial symbols of lace adornments and mantilla headdresses for women, and sombreros and sashes for men, predominated. Some observers viewed the costumes as unifying Santa Fe residents by their fi-

delity to heritage. Class and ethnic distinctions are also evidenced in the historical pageants, particularly in the homage to the Fiesta Queen and her court, representing the legacy of local aristocracy. Prized family heirlooms are displayed in the fashion show, while Mexican chocolate is served in fine cups with *biscochitos*, Mexican anise-seed cookies associated with affluent leisure.

Frivolity is evident in the carnivalesque aspects of the fiesta, including such regularly scheduled events as the Desfile de los Niños (Children's Parade), Santa Fe Melodrama, and Hysterical Historical Parade, a ritual inversion of municipal authority. In the *desfile*, children march with pets dressed in ridiculous-looking costumes, typically human attire. In the Melodrama, a kind of playful drama, actors poke fun at municipal leaders and political figures. Spoofing of local authorities and their rules continues in the Hysterical Historical Parade, often satirizing the city's obsession with its Spanish past, while marching bands and horses strut down the street.

Architecture

Besides street and building names, the most visible reminder of Native American and Spanish presence in Santa Fe is the architecture. It is often called "adobe architecture," even though the term refers to the building material rather than the design. Adobe is made of mud water, and organic material such as hay or straw. Although Native Americans used a mud-puddle technique for constructing their multifamily houses, which the Spaniards later called *pueblos* (village), it was the Europeans who formed the adobe into sun-dried blocks and stacked them. They had adopted the idea from the Moors of North Africa, who brought it to Spain starting in the eighth century. The adobe refers to massive, round-edged earthen walls supporting flat roofs. They typically feature *vigas* (heavy timbers) extending through the walls, which serve as main roof support beams, and *latillas* (poles) placed above *vigas* in angled patterns to form the ceiling. They may include *bancos* (benches) that protrude from the walls and *nichos* (niches) carved out of the wall for display of religious icons. Spanish influence is further evidenced in the use of porches held up with *zapatas* (posts) and heavy wooden doors.

The Palace of the Governors, considered the oldest public building still in continuous use in the United States, is an example of Spanish colonial architecture—a thick-walled, one-story, flat-roofed structure with a covered porch or portal. Originally constructed in adobe in 1609 as Spain's seat of government for what is today the American Southwest, the building now houses the Museum of New Mexico. Another traditional adobe landmark is the Mission of San Miguel of Santa Fe on the Old Santa Fe Trail. The mission is one of America's oldest churches. Built in 1625 by forced indigenous labor, this Spanish colonial building was nearly destroyed during the Pueblo revolt of 1680 and rebuilt by the Spanish in 1710. Mass is still held in the church every Sunday. The chapel's interior is dominated by a painted altar screen with a *bulto* (devotional statue carved from wood) of St. Michael the Archangel in a center niche.

A modern religious structure built in 1939 with traditional adobe techniques is Cristo Rey Church, acknowledged as the largest Spanish adobe building in the United States. Parishioners made adobe bricks for the church from earth on the site. Local architect John Gaw Meem designed the building in traditional mission style. It holds magnificent stone *reredos* (altar screens) created by the Spaniards during the colonial era. Many dwellings in the city reflect the Spanish colonial past in their styles. Although they are not necessarily made of adobe, a similar look is achieved by using stucco or plaster in earthen colors over a wood frame sheethed with plasterboard, often covering stacks of straw bales, aluminum cans, or old tires. Some of the houses have enclosed patios and elaborate corbels.

The Santa Fe style refers to limitations on buildings created by the Santa Fe Historic Zoning Ordinance of 1957. In that year, Santa Fe became the first U.S. city to enact a mandatory ordinance

for the purpose of preserving traditional styles. The ordinance controls the height of buildings as well as the size and placement of windows and the color of the stucco. It requires certain styles of architecture in the historic district, thereby emphasizing the city's colonial heritage.

Foodways

Santa Fe cuisine refers to foods that reflect a mixture of New Mexican and indigenous influences. The food that lends cultural distinction as well as hot spice to Santa Fe's cuisine is the chile pepper, especially when it is still green. The Spaniards brought this vegetable with them from Mexico, and it became the most important food crop in New Mexico. Green and red chilis come from the same vegetable; green chilis are picked before they turn red. Green chiles are roasted, peeled, and generally made into a tasty sauce or sprinkled fresh on almost everything for spicy effect. The red chiles, after picking, are hung in the sun to dry in *ristras* (strings). With the seeds and veins removed, the dried red pods are crushed into chili powder and made into the tasty red sauce. The red *ristras* are also used as decorations.

Santa Fe chile recipes are distinct from Tex-Mex or Californian Mexican varieties. Santa Fe chile evolved from traditional Native American recipes, based on three basic, earthy ingredients: cornmeal, green chile, and pinto beans. In addition to using chile for salsa, Santa Fe cooks use the spice in enchiladas, jams, jellies, and pastas. The city is host to an annual wine and chile fiesta every September.

From Native American roots came the central role of corn in the cuisine, especially the distinctive New Mexico corn. The corn is ground into meal and flour for use in tortillas, and processed into two unique New Mexican products—posole and chicos (dried roasted corn). Posole is prepared by soaking hard kernels of field corn (traditionally white, although blue is sometimes used now) in powdered lime and water. After several hours, when the corn kernels have swollen, the liquid is allowed to evaporate and the kernels to dry. Posole is often compared to hominy, another kind of processed corn, which tends to be softer and more bland. One folk tradition among Santa Feans is to celebrate life's blessings on Christmas Eve by having a bowl of posole stew with pork and red chili. Various versions of the stew are handed down in families. Some make it with chicken rather than pork; some prefer to use green chili. Another popular dish, *calabacitas*, combines Native America squash with corn, cheese, and chili. Squash is a favorite vegetable in Santa Fe gardens, and one can still encounter ancient varieties being cultivated, such as the blue-fruited Acoma pumpkin, the green-striped Santo Domingo squash, and the Calabaza Mexicana, or long-neck pumpkin.

A dessert dish especially associated with Santa Fe cuisine is a form of fried bread called *sopapillas* (little pillows), thought to have originated in New Mexico in the colonial period. The crisp, puffy, deep-fried pastry (resembling an air-filled pillow) is typically served with honey or honey butter. Many who partake wash it down with New Mexico coffee, roasted with native *piñon* (pine) nuts. The nuts also distinguish a dessert referred to as southwestern bread pudding, traditionally baked with bread soaked in milk and covered with tequila sauce.

Once associated with folk cookery prepared at home, Santa Fe cuisine continues to develop with creative restaurant chefs competing to create memorable dishes based on traditional southwestern tastes by introducing exotic chilis, wild game, and international spices. The Santa Fe School of Cooking, specializing in promoting and developing the local cuisine, sponsors classes and special events featuring traditional foodways.

Art

For a city its size, Santa Fe has a high number of art galleries, and is especially rich in showcases for folk art. It is estimated to be the third-largest art market in the United States. It has approximately 250 galleries, including many devoted to traditional Native American and Hispanic artists. The area has attracted artists and writers since the late nineteenth century because of modernist interest in the folk designs of indigenous cultures, especially in pottery and textiles. For many, however, the greater attraction was the natural beauty of the landscape and the quality of light in the high desert. Once settled, artists became active members of the community, volunteering for the fire department, weighing in on local issues in the city council, and taking a prominent role in the commercial and civic life of the city.

By the mid-twentieth century, many artists had taken up residence on Canyon Road. Although now mostly galleries and restaurants, it remains the "art street" in Santa Fe, housing almost two-thirds of the galleries in the city. The area also features several major art museums, including the Museum of International Folk Art, Museum of Spanish Colonial Art, Institute of American Indian Arts Museum, Museum of Indian Arts and Culture, and Wheelwright Museum of the American Indian, featuring traditional arts.

Every year, Santa Fe hosts several important outdoor markets in the plaza area where artists can sell their works. The two most significant are the Indian Market in August and the Spanish Market in July. Attracting more than one hundred thousand visitors, the Indian Market, established in 1922, features twelve hundred artists from more than one hundred tribes. The Spanish Market, held annually since 1952, boasts more than three hundred traditional Hispanic artists, as well as live music and regional foods, and claims to be the oldest and largest sales venue for Spanish colonial art in the United States. At the Native American markets, folk artists typically exhibit decorated pottery, woven blankets and rugs, and jewelry distinguished by traditional tribal designs. Hispanic craftspeople and artists produce traditional colonial art forms, such as punched- and cut-tin containers, *retablos* (small oil paintings on wood that depict Catholic saints), *santos* (or *bultos*, devotional statues generally carved from wood), *colcha* (embroidery made of a long, coarse stitch in wool yarn), and furniture.

Having built a reputation as a market center for folk art, Santa Fe has been a prominent meeting location for international organizations devoted to the study and preservation of folk culture. Efforts have also been made by local groups and institutions to sustain folk art not only as a historic artifact but as a living tradition into the future by encouraging educational programs for families and youth. The Museum of New Mexico sponsors series of workshops on traditional crafts such as pottery design, willow basket crafts, and tamale making. New Mexico Arts has a program, a division of the state's Department of Cultural Affairs, has initiated a program of fieldwork with a folk arts coordinator seeking apprentices to work with master folk artists to carry their traditions on. Inspired by the cultural surroundings of Santa Fe, the Fund for Folk Culture, a private nonprofit organization established in 1991, was established to support the conservation of folklife throughout the United States. Its mission of viewing folk art as a living tradition that enriches communities is characteristic of much of the driving force in Santa Fe, but as the rise of the above organizations and programs suggest, residents into the twenty-first century recognize that initiative is necessary to take a more active role in conserving this tradition and responding to changes in the city's communities.

Stefanie Beninato and Simon J. Bronner

See also: Folk Art; Folk Festivals; Foodways; Museums and Exhibitions; Southwest; Southwestern Indians.

Sources

Dewitt, Dave, and Sue Gerlach. *The Food of Santa Fe.* London: Periplus, 1998.

Gross, Steven, and Sue Daley. *Santa Fe Houses and Gardens.* New York: Rizzoli, 2002.

Hoerig, Karl A. *Under the Palace Portal: Native American Artists in Santa Fe.* Albuquerque: University of New Mexico Press, 2003.

Lovato, Andrew Leo. *Santa Fe Hispanic Culture: Preserving Identity in a Tourist Town.* Albuquerque: University of New Mexico Press, 2004.

Pierce, Donna. *Vivan Las Fiestas!* Santa Fe: Museum of New Mexico Press, 1985.

Rehberger, Dean. "Visions of the New Mexican in Public Pageants and Dramas of Santa Fe and Taos, 1918–1940." *Journal of the Southwest* 37 (1995): 450–69.

Simmons, Marc. *New Mexico.* Albuquerque: University of New Mexico Press, 1976.

Weigle, Marta, and Peter White. *Folklore of New Mexico.* Albuquerque: University of New Mexico Press, 2003.

Wilson, Chris. *The Myth of Santa Fe: Creating a Modern Regional Tradition.* Albuquerque: University of New Mexico Press, 1997.

SCOTTISH COMMUNITIES

Scottish communities include descendants of Scottish immigrants from Ulster (or "Scots-Irish"), who came to America in the eighteenth century and put their imprint particularly on Appalachia, and later immigrants who came directly from Scotland and headed for cities. While sometimes acknowledged as a major contributor to American folk architecture, speech, and music, the Scottish identity in America has not been as visible as that of German and French settlers who came at the same time, perhaps because it blended into an Appalachian or wider frontier cultural affiliation. Still, social organizations, dance clubs, and festive events such as Highland Games continue to promote a unique Scottish heritage into the twenty-first century. According to the 2000 U.S. census, 9.2 million Americans claimed Scots or Scots-Irish ancestry as their primary ethnic origin—an increase of nearly 50 percent over 1990.

Ulster Scots

The Scots-Irish, also called Ulster Scots and Scotch-Irish, are so named because they migrated in the seventeenth century from Scotland to Ulster in Ireland. They moved to Ulster because lowland Scotland in the seventeenth century had become overpopulated and rents were high for land that was difficult to farm. By 1715 more than one-third of Ulster's six hundred thousand inhabitants were Scottish. Several factors pushed the Ulster Scots to relocate to America. Mostly Presbyterian in faith, the Scots were legally restricted from participating in government by the Anglican Church (the official Church of Ireland) and were forced to pay tithes. Native Irish Catholics, meanwhile, resented the Protestant practices of the Scots as well as being displaced from their land by the immigrants. Preaching that God had appointed a country for the Scots to be freed from bondage in Ireland, comparable to that of the "promised land" of Israel for the Jewish slaves of Egypt in the Old Testament, Presbyterian ministers viewed America as a sacred destination. In addition, a number of Scots were known to have settled in the American colonies during the seventeenth century. Some went to Virginia as traders or tobacco workers; others, such as the two hundred followers of the Earl of Argyll were deported to East Jersey in 1685 for rebellion.

It was not uncommon in the wave of immigration from Ulster between 1715 and 1770 for entire congregations to leave for America, led by their ministers. During that period, around 250,000 Ulster Scots came to America. If not moved by religious reasons, Ulster Scots were pushed to act by rising rent, low wages, and low prices on goods, combined with periods of crop failure. America had a labor shortage and did not have immigration restrictions or a language barrier. The Ulster Scots were familiar with the linen trade and found that a trade route existed between Ulster and Philadelphia. Finding abundant land available inland beyond areas of German settlement, many of the Scots-Irish pushed west into the Appalachians and moved down the Shenandoah Valley into western Maryland and Virginia. South Carolina, settled predominantly by African slaves at that time, offered land, tools, and seeds to white settlers, thus also attracting Ulster Scots to Charleston as an entry port. From there, Scots-Irish also moved west into the Piedmont of the Carolinas, where land was available.

In America, the group became known as Scotch-Irish or Irish Presbyterians to distinguish them from Irish Catholics, who began immigrating in the mid-nineteenth century. In the late twentieth century, however, as people from Scotland referred to themselves as Scots and sometimes considered Scotch an ethnic slur because of its reference to whisky, the term Scots-Irish predominated. Some scholars have surmised that the Scots lost their distinctiveness because of the cul-

tural exchange that occurred among German, Welsh, and English settlers in their movement west and therefore developed more of an American regional identity. Another perspective is that they were aware of their Scots-Irish background but since they did not have Old World loyalties or long to return to Scotland or Ireland, they took on a New World identity. Although many of their customs can be traced to a Scottish heritage, in some of the isolated areas they settled, they did not have the kind of ethnic consciousness of being culturally different that occurred in urban areas or coastal areas.

In American folklife, the Scots-Irish influence is especially prevalent in the highlands southern dialect stretching from East Texas to the south up into Pennsylvania to the north. It tends to be faster and higher-pitched than tidewater southern and more nasal than other forms of English. Various features of the dialect persist, such as use of the possessives "hisn," "hern," "yorn," and "theirn," and "them" often with the addition of "those" used as an adjective in place of "their" as in "them those boys." There is also a propensity to use compound nouns that are characteristically Appalachian, such as "menfolk," "man-child," and "kinfolks." Some phrases traced to Scots-Irish use have entered general American English, such as "can't hold a candle to," "sharp as a tack," "I am fixing to go," "I reckon," and "all tuckered out." Distance words from Scots-Irish such as "this here," "that there," and "that yonder" can also be heard widely in America. More regionalized around Appalachia is use of "sack" for a bag, "pail" for a bucket, "beholden" for being indebted, "mosquito hawk" for a dragonfly, and "snap beans" for green beans. Dropping the ending "g" in "something" (somethin') and "nothing" (nothin') derives from Scots-Irish dialect because Celtic languages had no "ng" sound. An American development attributed often to Scots-Irish influence is the tendency in the highlands dialect to exchange parts of speech, as in "She prettied herself up," "It pleasures me," and "He daddied that child."

In folk architecture, stone masonry and the

A Highland Games athlete participates in the caber toss, a quintessentially Scottish competition, at a heritage festival in West Virginia. The caber, which symbolizes a tree, can weigh more than one hundred pounds. *(Bob Bird/Getty Images Sports)*

double-pen form of the house that became prevalent in much of the American frontier, and still influences the perception of a standard central-door house with two front rooms, probably derives from British influence, including the source areas of the Scots-Irish. In Ireland, farmhouses often had an interior partitioned into a large heated room and a smaller unheated room. Farm buildings arranged in a line on valley slopes are characteristic of patterns established in Ulster, which probably combined with the German influence of log construction in Appalachia. Scholars have observed that the Scots-Irish adapted particularly to

the American frontier because of their familiarity with the lone farm sited on hilly land on which the nuclear family formed the basic social unit, thus encouraging a willingness to farm on isolated areas past the coastal flatlands where earlier settlers made their claims. Some scholars have credited this frontier pattern established by the Scots-Irish to general American attributes of rugged individualism and independence.

A Scots-Irish connection is also often seen in the development of country music, particularly in the fondness for tragic ballads "Barbara Allen" and "Black Jack Davy" and lighter social songs such as "Froggie Went a Courtin' " and "The Cuckoo," and in the fiddle tunes such as "Paddy on the Turnpike" (also known as Jinny or Jenny in the Lowlands) and "Flowers of Edinburgh" (Americanized often by fiddlers as Edinsburg or Ebensburg) that accompany clogging dances. In addition to preserving ballads and songs from the British Isles in mountain life such as "House Carpenter" and "Pretty Polly," the stanza structure from these songs was used to produce songs adapting to the American experience, such as "Tom Dula" (Tom Dooley), which became nationally popularized by the Kingston Trio in 1959. The song, about a Civil War veteran from North Carolina who was convicted of murdering a "poor girl, twenty-one years of age at the time of her death," was known in oral tradition for almost a century in the Blue Ridge Mountains. Some of the legend for this and other songs concerned Dula's flight from justice until he was caught in Tennessee. The song follows in theme and structure traditional Scottish ballads such as "Little Musgrave and Lady Barnard" (identified by ballad scholar Frances James Child in *English and Scottish Popular Ballads*, 1882–1898, as no. 81), about a love triangle that ends in the dastardly murder of a young innocent girl. Known by folksingers in Appalachia as "Little Mattie [or Massie] Grove," "Lord Thomas," and "The Red Rover," in most southern versions the girl is attending church, while in northern versions she is playing ball. Besides continuing the ballad repertoire, themes, and structure drawn from British tradition, singers of Scots-Irish heritage also were known for a performance style sometimes characterized as a "high lonesome sound." Songs tended to be performed with a rigidly pitched voice, high, rubato, and nasal. The lyrics were set to simple melodies and rhythms and rendered in a dispassionate manner.

The Scots-Irish ballad tradition strongly influenced the repertoire of country music as it developed, with performers such as Uncle Dave Macon and the Carter Family adapting folk songs in the early twentieth century for records and radio broadcasts. While these songs often came out of domestic traditions of singing for family and friends around the hearth, a community tradition of dancing to the fiddle deriving from Scots-Irish sources also spread nationally through country music. Appalachian musicians performed joyful jigs, hornpipes, and reels from Celtic tradition and gave them an American inflection by playing them rapidly, often with use of slurred notes played two strings at a time, produced with a rhythmic short-bow saw stroke. The popular folk-dance tune "Turkey in the Straw" (also known as "Sugar in the Gourd"), for example, has been traced to the old Scottish tune "Bonny Black Eagle"; "Billy in the Low Ground" has a strong relation to a Celtic jig from the early eighteenth century called "All the Blue Bonnets Are Over the Border." Sometimes known as southern "breakdowns," the tunes often were renamed for American frontier experiences significant to the Scots-Irish, for example, "Tennessee Wagoners" and "Cumberland Gap," although some airs played in America such as "My Love She's but a Lassie Yet" and "Green Grow the Rushes" (also known as "Over the Hills and Far Away") retained their Scottish titles.

Dancing that accompanied Scots-Irish fiddling in America developed into what came to be known as clogging, or "flatfooting." Sometimes claimed as a unique American dance form associated with Appalachia, and now with country dance, it clearly has roots in Celtic dances featuring a stiff upper body with the feet employing rapid steps and hops. The word "clog" comes from a Gaelic word meaning "time," and applies to percussive dancing in time to music, usually with the heel keeping rhythm. When folk festivals such as the Mountain Dance and Folk Festival held in Asheville, North Carolina, began featuring folk dancers as well as musicians during the 1920s, competitions for clogging were staged to parallel the old-time fiddlers' contests. This movement led to the formation of dance competition teams, such as the pioneering Soco Gap Cloggers from western North Carolina, who continue to showcase the tradition in stage shows and contests, including the USA National Clogging Championship in Nashville, Tennessee, over Labor Day Weekend.

Urban Scots and Highland Games

Waves of immigration directly from Scotland came in the decades before and after 1900 and again after World War I, with immigrants settling mostly in the industrial cities of the Northeast and Midwest. Much of the immigration was propelled by economic depression, and most of it came to the United States and Canada. Between 1852 and 1910, more than 475,000 Scots entered the United States. In the half century after 1870, 53 percent of all Scottish emigrants went to the United States. As unemployment rose in Scottish heavy industry and textile plants after World War I, a dramatic rise in emigration occurred in the 1920s, with 160,000 Scots coming to the United States, more than double the total of the previous decade. Unlike the emigration of the Ulster Scots, most of this population came from industrialized areas of Scotland, and there was more of a return migration when America suffered its own economic depression during the 1930s. Still, by the mid-twentieth century, almost a quarter of a million American residents, most of whom resided in urban areas, claimed Scottish birth.

The cultural impact of the twentieth-century wave of immigrants is often not as pronounced because the Scots were not known for forming ethnic enclaves comparable to southern and eastern European immigrants in cities, or they assimilated quickly into English-speaking society. Yet a lasting cultural connection for many Scottish immigrants was in the "clans"—lodges that adopted the names and tartans of Highland families—that were organized in many cities. An order of Scottish clans was founded in St. Louis in 1878, and many societies such as the Clan Donald Society of America, Clan MacLachlan Association of North America, Clan MacNeil Association of America, and the Clan Campbell Society of North America, had local branches. In 1972, as an ethnic revival occurred in the United States generally, a Council of Scottish Clans and Associations was incorporated to act as an umbrella organization for the many clan associations and according to its mission statement to "preserve and promote the customs, traditions and heritage of the Scottish people." The common program to develop a Scottish identity sponsored by these organizations is the Highland games and festivals staged throughout North America.

The Highland games originated with the ancient Celts in Ireland, thriving and evolving in the competitive environment of the clan structure of Scotland. It is commonly believed that the Scottish king Malcome Canmore (Malcolm III) initiated the games in the eleventh century with a race up a mountain. Contemporary competitions include dancing, bagpiping, tug of war, and the so-called heavy events, such as traditional hammer throwing and tossing the caber. This last event is considered the quintessentially Scottish athletic competition. The caber is a pole representing a tree trunk; throwing it requires great strength and skill. Competitors must choose a caber, then run and toss it so that it lands straight out at a twelve-o'clock position; in other words, the caber is tossed for accuracy rather than distance. The judge must "call it" just as the stick hits the ground; a side judge will sometimes be used to determine whether the caber rotated 90 degrees (if not, it is declared a "fifer" and the throw is disallowed). The caber comes in various sizes; a length more than nineteen feet and a weight more than one hundred pounds are not uncommon.

In addition to hosting athletic contests, many games and festivals feature Scottish fiddling and step-dance competitions and demonstrations. Games and festivals as markers of Scottish folk identity have become so extensive that an organization called the Association of Scottish Games and Festivals, established in 1981, was created to provide coordination and information for the many Scottish events in America. According to the organization, the states with the most Scottish games and festivals are Florida and North Carolina, each with eight, followed by New York and California, with seven and six, respectively.

During clan gatherings and Highland games, many Scottish Americans dress in the namesake tartan of their clans. Some participants also encourage making their own kilts (a wrap-over pleated skirt) out of wool. Scottish historians are quick to point out that specific tartans (also known as "plaids"), such as Mackintosh tartan and MacLachlan tartan, are modern attempts at clan solidarity. In early and medieval Scotland, tartans were highly individualistic, designed and woven by skilled weavers and artisans. When going to a clan gathering or Scottish festival, one might wear the modern Highland dress: a kilt (that famous men's "skirt"), a sporran (bag attached to the belt), knitted hose (kneesocks), possibly garters to hold up the hose, black shoes, a belt, and a bonnet (like a French beret, with a bobble or pompom at the top); a silver "bodkin" may be used to hold the top portion of the dress kilt to the wearer's shirt. As early Scots preferred to carry money in the form of jewelry or decorated weaponry, a ceremonial knife often completes the Highland dress.

Scottish Revivals and Holidays

An important, if often overlooked, legacy of Scottish immigration to America is the spread of Presbyterianism. Presbyterian practice is especially strong in locations of Scottish settlement, such as Pennsylvania, New York, Ohio, Illinois, Virginia, North Carolina, and Texas. Churches often promote observance of St. Andrew's Day on November 30 because of his role as patron saint of Scotland. Many communities have St. Andrew's societies, which hold dinner meetings and Scottish festivals. For St. Andrew's Day, special church services and dinner events with bagpipe performances and dances are common. Some churches also preserve a Scottish theme for New Year's Eve, or Hogmanay, including the traditional singing of Scottish poet Robert Burns's "For Auld Lang Syne," which has become widespread in American culture.

Every year on January 25, Scottish American clans and organizations honor the birthday of Robert Burns with a so-called Burns Dinner. Burns came from humble beginnings in rural southwest Scotland and is known throughout the world for vernacular poems drawing on Scottish folk tradition. The menu for the dinner has gone relatively unchanged since Burns's death in the late 1700s. The five-course menu typically includes haggis (sheep innards baked in a pie), cock-a-leekie soup, tossed salad, beef with neeps and tatties (turnips and potatoes), peas, cinnamon scones with butter, and dunfillan fruit pudding. Attendees come in full Highland dress, and the night is punctuated with singing, dancing, bagpiping, and storytelling.

Two traditional Scottish games that were probably spread by nineteenth-century immigrants and that have made a lasting impact on American culture are the winter sport of curling and golf. Curling is a team sport played on ice with granite stones; players attempt to slide the stones across the ice to a target area in such a way as to maximize points while protecting key stones from being knocked out of play by opponents. In 1832, the Orchard Lake Curling Club near Detroit became the first of its kind in the United States, with a roster dominated by Scottish members. The oldest continuously operating curling club in the United States, founded in 1845, is located in Milwaukee, Wisconsin; the largest, with more than seven hundred members, is in St. Paul, Minnesota. Since the mid-nineteenth century, curling has been most popular in Wisconsin, Minnesota, and other Great Lakes states, as well as North Dakota and New England. The United States Curling Association, based in Wisconsin, estimates that there are fifteen thousand curlers in more than 135 clubs in the nation. Golf, of course, has become even more of a national game than curling. Early golf clubs, including ones in Montreal, Canada (1873), and Yonkers, New York (1888)—the latter named St. Andrew's, after the patron saint of Scotland—were founded by Scotsmen. It is still common for Scottish organizations to sponsor golf tournaments, such as the Kilted Golf Tournament organized by the St. Andrew's Society of St. Louis at the Aberdeen Golf Club.

A modern development to promote Scottish identity is the observance of Tartan Day on April 6. The date was chosen because it is the anniversary of the declaration of Scottish Independence at Abroath Abbey in 1320. Begun as a movement in Canada during the 1980s to recognize Scottish contributions, Tartan Day was officially recognized by the U.S. Senate in 1998, and many states with Scottish populations recognize Tartan Days on their government calendars. Besides holding dinners and dances, Scottish groups also organize parades for the day, usually featuring bagpipers and drummers. The largest, called the Tunes of Glory Parade, with as many as ten thousand bagpipers marching, is in New York.

Amy Waddell and Simon J. Bronner

See also: Appalachia; Houses; Irish Communities; Northern Appalachian Region (Catskills and Adirondacks); Pennsylvania Culture Region; Shenandoah Valley Region.

Sources

Bayard, Samuel P. *Dance to the Fiddle, March to the Fife: Instrumental Folk Tunes in Pennsylvania.* University Park: Pennsylvania State University Press, 1982.

Blethen, H. Tyler, and Curtis W. Wood, Jr., eds. *Ulster and North America: Transatlantic Perspectives on the Scotch-Irish.* Tuscaloosa, AL: University of Alabama Press, 1997.

Brown, Mary Ellen Lewis. "Folk Elements in Scotch-Irish Presbyterian Communities." *Pennsylvania Folklife* 18, no. 1 (1968): 21–25.

Donaldson, Emily Ann. *The Scottish Highland Games in America.* Gretna, LA: Pelican, 1986.

Erickson, Charlotte. *Invisible Immigrants: The Adaptation of English and Scottish Immigrants in 19th-Century America.* Ithaca, NY: Cornell University Press, 1972.

Kennedy, Billy. *Faith and Freedom: The Scots Irish in America.* Greenville, SC: Ambassador-Emerald, 1999.

MacDonell, Margaret. *The Emigrant Experience: Songs of*

Highland Emigrants in North America. Toronto: University of Toronto Press, 1982.

McWhiney, Grady. *Cracker Culture: Celtic Ways in the Old South*. Tuscaloosa: University of Alabama Press, 1989.

SENEGALESE COMMUNITIES

Frequently with the assistance of relief agencies, the United States since the 1980s has been a haven for thousands of Senegalese immigrants from West Africa. From 1990 to 2005 alone, more than seven thousand Senegalese entered the United States. Many were classified by the Immigration and Naturalization Service (INS) as refugees because they had been displaced by a civil war raging since 1982 between the people of the Casamance (southern region of Senegal) and the government in Dakar. The nation's natural resources had also been adversely affected by drought and desertification, forcing many Senegalese to seek economic opportunities outside the country. Once a colony of France, Senegal gained independence in 1960, and still to the present day, most Senegalese are French-speaking Muslims, with a small minority being Roman Catholics. Many Senegalese also speak a tribal language and have an indigenous identity—Wolof (43.3 percent), Serer (14.7 percent), Pulaar (8 percent), Jola (3.7 percent), and Mandinka (1.1 percent).

The most common destinations for Senegalese emigrants are the states of New York and California; sizable communities have formed in cities such as New York, Washington, D.C., Atlanta, Philadelphia, and Los Angeles. New York City's community is the largest, with more than two thousand residents having been born in Senegal. The Senegalese foreign-born population of America is estimated at more than ten thousand, with strong social networks that help them preserve traditions from the West African homeland. Often connected to West African communities as a folk group, the Senegalese have linguistic (commonly speaking French, Wolof, and tribal languages) and religious (Mouride) differences, and cultural expressions of drumming, dance, and food that give them a sense of ethnic identity in America.

Mourides

Many of the Senegalese in America are followers of Cheikh Ahamadou Bamba. In 1886, Bamba founded a community called Murīdiyya, the most powerful Islamic brotherhood in Senegal. The disciples of Bamba are called Mourides (*murīd*), a type of brotherhood well known in the world of Islam, a *Sūfī tarīqa* organized by the descendants of a holy man, where the followers hope to attain paradise through the special holiness and redeeming power of their religious guides. Bamba encouraged his adherents to guarantee their community's success by submitting to a religious leader (*shaikh*) and cultivating the spiritual virtues of hard work.

The *shaikh*'s special role is to transmit spiritual *baraka* (redeeming gifts), a form of blessings, from Bamba, who has mystical powers. In Mouride belief, to eat food the *shaikh* has left or to touch his clothes is to benefit from this form of grace, which not only has benefits for the next life but is thought to bring success in worldly enterprise. The *shaikh* also commands respect and has power over supernatural powers that allow him to extend protection against the evil eye, witches, and various malevolent spirits. This is done through the preparation of amulets or talismans, the use of magic formulas and magical procedures of Islamic origin. The spirits and divinities of Senegalese animism have been adapted to the Islamic *jinn* (supernatural invisible beings, often raising evil, who have a status below angels) and angels.

Mouride expatriates rely on a system of social and economic organization created by Bamba. The system is centered on the Da'ira, a religious school that trains its members in spiritual, administrative, and financial matters. It offers followers a chance to study the texts and chants of the founder, collect funds, organize members for job recruitment, and stay in contact with the central organization of the khalifate. The Da'iras in America fulfill similar functions, especially in New York City, where Mourtada Mbacke, the son of Bamba, visits once a year to bless his disciples and encourage them to continue working.

Many of the Mouride women work in street vending, "summer markets" and small businesses (such as driving cabs, braiding hair, and cooking in restaurants) similar to those of their husbands. These markets are at African street festivals where they sell African-styled clothing, jewelry, wood-carvings, and drums. Many of the men have skills in goldsmithing, leatherworking, and woodcarving. The men wear long cotton sheaths, called *boubous*, in blue or green, while the women wear long peach or purple gowns and a rising head-wrap that accentuates their head, unlike the scarf worn by many Americans. Mouride women also have their own Da'ira, in which they fulfill expectations similar to those of the men. Some of the Mouride artisans compose a subgroup of the Senegalese called *gnegnos* and have formed an organization called the United Gnegnos of America that organizes social gatherings and mutual aid. In Senegal, the *gnegnos* held a low status as an artisan class, but have been attracted to the United States because of opportunities to prosper economically and socially, especially in African American areas where their traditional African hair braiding, headwrap and dressmaking, and wood and metal craft skills are in demand.

Foodways, Customs, and Cultural Conservation

Many Senegalese women besides the Mourides have become business owners, especially of restaurants featuring foods from their African homeland. The restaurants often feature traditional Senagalese food such as *thiebu djeun*, a rich fish stew cooked with rice that is the national dish of Senegal. In Philadelphia, the Senegalese community strengthens its identity through activities such as *tan-ber* or *soirée dansantes*, lavish parties in which music and dance figure prominently. As is the custom in Senegal, dances often do not begin until after midnight. Senegalese Muslims often join other Africans in celebrations of Eid el-Fitr, Eid el-Adha, and Mawlad el-Nabi. Eid el-Fitr occurs at the end of the month of fasting known as Ramadan and often involves a ritual meal of chicken bought from *halal* (ritually pure)

butchers and social occasions with relatives and friends. Two months and ten days after Eid el-Fitr, Eid el-Adha celebrates Abraham's offer to sacrifice his son to God and also involves prayer followed by social visits and meals. Lamb symbolic of a ritual sacrifice is usually offered at meals. Mawlad el-Nabi involves singing of poems known as *qasidas*, including texts linked to venerated poets such as Shaykh Alhaji Malick Sy of Senegal.

Assisting the Senegalese community in America is the Association of Senegalese in America (ASA), based in New York. Founded in 1988, the ASA seeks to protect the rights of Senegalese immigrants and provide assistance on issues such as cultural adjustment, English-language training, and reunification of families. The association maintains an Internet Web site and a radio station. The Senegalese communities in New York City, Washington, D.C., Atlanta, and other American cities have weekly radio shows in which they update their compatriots on immigration laws and news from the homeland. These shows provide listeners with information on food, travel, accessories, and entertainment businesses owned by Senegalese and other immigrants. They report news and information in Senegalese languages such as Pulaar, Wolof, Serer, and French.

With a new generation of American-born children of Senegalese parents, efforts are being made in Senegalese communities to perpetuate folklife, particularly in music and dance. In Washington, D.C., American-born children learn dance and drumming at a school directed by Senegal-born Assane Konte. The most common drum is the *sabar*, which is larger at the top than in the middle and tapers out at the base. A *nder*, longer and higher-pitched than the others, usually takes the lead. *Sabar* players are traditionally male and get a chance in performances to improvise on basic patterns established by the *nder*. Traditional rhythms performed in new American contexts include the *gajarde*, a victory rhythm played for victorious wrestlers, referring to the national sport of Senegal.

The *griot* tradition (called a *jali* in Mandinka) of relating stories of the past through songs is important for linking Senegal folklife in America to African heritage. In Washington, D.C., Senegal-born Djimo Kouyate plays the *kora* (Mandinka harp-lute) and performs songs to remind countrymen of their heritage at baptisms, weddings, and religious holidays. He is touted as the 149th *jali* in his family and a descendant of the first *griot* and diplomat in the court of the thirteenth-century king of the Mali Empire, Kankan Moussa. Kouyate is one of many traditional performers included in the African Immigrant Folklife Study Project by the Smithsonian Institution and featured at the 1997 Festival of American Folklife on the National Mall in Washington, D.C. In Philadelphia, the Senegalese community was one of the African groups featured in 2001 in an ethnographic exhibition called "Extended Lives," which has inspired other African drumming and dance performances sponsored by the Philadelphia Folklore Project.

Babacar M'Baye and Simon J. Bronner

See also: African American Communities; New York City; Religion; West African Communities.

Sources

Association of Senegalese in America. www.asaweb.org.

Babou, Cheikh Anta. "Brotherhood Solidarity, Education and Migration: The Role of the Dahiras Among the Murid Muslim Community of New York." *African Affairs* 101 (2002): 151–70.

O'Brien, Donal B. Cruise. *The Mourides of Senegal: The Political and Economic Organization of an Islamic Brotherhood.* Oxford: Clarendon Press, 1971.

Swigart, Leigh. *Extended Lives: The African Immigrant Experience in Philadelphia.* Philadelphia: Balch Institute for Ethnic Studies, 2001.

SEPTEMBER 11TH

The terrorist attacks of September 11, 2001, have generated a number of cultural responses that have become part of American folklife. Folklorists first took notice of spontaneous shrines and memorials arising quickly after the event that followed patterns of other tragedies such as the Oklahoma City bombing in 1995 and the Texas A&M University bonfire deaths of 1999. A second form of folk response was in home and community assemblages of displays of patriotism, often involving uses of red, white, and blue bows and ribbons for victims and presentations of the American flag, frequently accompanied by sayings of unity such as "God Bless America." A third response that drew folkloristic interest was the circulation of rumors and legends, including narratives with anti-Semitic and anti-Islamic content, and those that expressed unresolved anxieties about the event. Fourth, folk humor, much of it visual in nature and disseminated over the Internet, emerged shortly after the events. The events of September 11, 2001, entered folk speech as "Nine Eleven," rendered in writing as "9/11," with symbolic implications of a national tragedy of mass proportions. Although much of the folklore of September 11 was short-lived and based on topical references, it illustrated several deeply rooted traditions of response to disaster.

On September 11, 2001, terrorists associated with al-Qaeda, an extreme Islamic movement, simultaneously hijacked four American jetliners, crashing two of them into the towers of New York City's World Trade Center. A horrified television audience watched broadcasts of the second plane hitting the center and the devastating collapse of both towers soon afterward. Meanwhile, a third plane crashed into the Pentagon in Washington, D.C., while a fourth plunged into farmland in Pennsylvania, apparently after a group of passengers attempted to regain control of the cockpit. The events, which together cost thousands of lives, were the most successful act of sabotage committed in the United States and created a shock that penetrated American society to all levels. Many observers noted the psychological need to express grief or release anger through folklore. The tragedy had a wide impact, many commentators thought, not only because of the vivid television broadcast of the destruction of the World Trade Center, but also because the towers were American symbols of success in what many people thought of as America's most prominent city.

Memorials and Tributes

The first response to emerge was spontaneous shrines, places near an appropriate wall or fence where visitors left memorabilia such as flowers and angel figurines. Traditionally, such shrines have sprung up at or near the very site of a tragic death. Due to heightened security, such tributes could not be placed at the World Trade Center or the other two crash sites. For this reason, memorials were placed at a variety of surrogate locations within sight of the Pentagon and the Pennsylvania impact site and at various publicly visible places in Manhattan, such as Times Square, and at churches, firehouses, and police stations throughout the city. These impromptu memorials tended to become pilgrimage sites, where passersby came to see the accumulating memorabilia and offer something themselves. In addition, the Internet also served as an internationally accessible location for hundreds of spontaneous "cybershrines." These included montages of photographs of victims as well as opportunities to leave virtual messages of sympathy and encouragement for mourners.

Within a day of the event, impromptu memorial rituals were being organized. On Friday, September 14, nationwide gatherings were held at noon and again at 7 P.M. to honor the dead and display national solidarity. A fast-moving e-mail message encouraged participants in the evening event to "step out your door, stop your car, or step out of your establishment and light a candle." Because such messages gave the date of the tribute simply as "Friday," they continued to circulate after the official celebration on September 14, encouraging others to light a candle spontaneously on subsequent Fridays. Along the way, the message gathered the erroneous motif that if enough Americans lit a candle at once, the light could be photographed from outer space.

As had happened many times previously, tribute songs were written and performed soon after the event, often in the context of concerts given to raise money for the families left bereaved or for other worthy causes. Such songs, while short-

Flowers, flags, and heartfelt messages appeared at makeshift memorials throughout lower Manhattan in the days after September 11, 2001. *(Beth A. Keiser/AFP/Getty Images)*

lived, continued a long-lived tradition of writing "tribute" or "tragedy" ballads commemorating accidents resulting in mass deaths, such as the sinking of the *Titanic* in 1912. Many of the songs that were performed had traditional themes of rescuing heroes (firefighters) and expressions of unity. "A Sacrifice So Dear," written by New York Fire Department lieutenant Jim Coyne soon after the tragedy, for example, circulated widely on the Internet, often without attribution. It included verses such as the following, extolling firefighters as heroic figures:

When firefighters give their lives,
even angels shed a tear.

For as martyrs, saints and patriots
it's a sacrifice so dear.

Among the ethnic compositions devoted to the event were those from the Mexican *corrido* (ballad) tradition popular along the United States/ Mexican border. Songs such as "Tragedia en Manhattan" and "Septiembre Negro" contained formulas familiar from earlier ballads on topical themes. "Tragedia" began:

Era un martes 11 de septiembre	It was a Tuesday, September the Eleventh
cuando los hechos pasaron	When this came to pass;
un martes en la mañana	A Tuesday, in the morning,
dos torres se derrumbaron	[When] the Two Towers collapsed.

Many earlier ballads on disaster begin by stating the date of the event (e.g., "On a Monday morning, just about one o'clock / The great *Titanic* began to reel and rock"). Other songs, such as "El Corrido de Bin Laden," by Rigoberto Cárdenas Chávez, were critical of U.S. government policy, typical of the political commentary often included in this genre:

Por cielo, mar y por tierra	Over sky, sea, and land
Osama te andan buscando	They go looking for Osama
Bin Laden el terrorista	Bin Laden, the terrorist
la CIA te ha preparado	That the CIA trained.
ese fue el error más grande	That was the biggest mistake ever made
del gobierno americano.	By the American government.

Rumors and Legends

The weeks following the attack produced an intense series of rumors implying that the public was not being told the whole truth and that future attacks were imminent. One early claim was that many Jews had been tipped off in advance not to report for work that morning. Such a claim proved the vitality of anti-Semitic conspiracy myths that blame virtually every war or disaster on a mysterious cabal of Jews controlling world politics and economics. According to other rumors, police had apprehended trucks carrying dangerous cargoes driven by suspicious Arabs, but, lacking the power to detain them, let them go on their way.

Rumors such as these inspired a contemporary legend complex about "The Grateful Terrorist." These legends describe an American citizen doing a Middle Easterner a favor; in gratitude, the Middle Easterner gives the American a hint about the time and location of the next attack before disappearing. Such legends continue an older scenario in which a mysterious stranger, often a Vanishing Hitchhiker, repays a kind act by giving a supernatural warning of an imminent calamity. In the most widespread American version, the terrorist warns his girlfriend not to fly on any planes on September 11 or go to any shopping malls on Halloween (the legend emerged after the attacks and before Halloween). In a version that originated in Great Britain but soon appeared in the United States, the benefactor does the Arab a small favor, giving him change when he is short a few cents in a store or returning a dropped wallet. In return, the stranger warns him not to go through the Baltimore Tunnels (or visit some other nearby site) on Thursday (or some other nearby date). This legend became especially popular in the United States as the anniversary of the attacks approached in 2002, often warning the listener not to consume any products made by a certain corporation until after September 11.

A distinctive feature of legends inspired by the attacks is that many of them involved photographs. Soon after the tragedy, two authentic photographs were circulated with instructions on how to find "the face of Satan" in the billowing smoke from one of the damaged Towers. This continued a tradition of "miraculous photographs" in which one could find images of divine (or diabolical) beings in clouds or smoke. More controversial was a photograph that purported to have been developed from film from a camera found in the building's debris. It showed an unaware tourist having his picture taken on one of the World Trade Center towers' observation deck, while the fatal plane is seen zooming in behind and beneath him. The "unlucky tourist" photo was exposed by *Wired News* as a private joke originally perpetrated by a Hungarian tourist and subsequently distributed over the Internet.

Humor

An emergent genre of "cybercartoons," visual images expressing reactions to the event, was one of the most widespread folk responses to the terrorist attacks. Within twenty-four hours of the events, a modified photograph was already being distributed showing a plan for a restored World Trade Center—four towers in the shape of a fist, with the middle finger extended. As Americans got more distance between themselves and the tragedy, a wider range of cybercartoons began to appear. These included an array of "revenge fantasies" with images of Osama bin Laden or other stereotypical Arabs about to be killed, usually by missiles or military aircraft seen through the frame of a mirror or an office window. Paradoxically, such cartoons functioned in much the same way as "gross" jokes about previous disasters, such as the *Challenger* space shuttle explosion in 1986: taking the most horrifying visual image broadcast by media coverage—the fiery crash of the plane into the second tower—and making it palatable.

The humor paralleled the militaristic rhetoric being aired by political leaders, who advocated a swift military attack on Afghanistan in reprisal for the attacks. Thus it was not surprising that a cycle of anti-Arab jokes, first circulated during the Desert Storm conflict of 1991, were revived and recycled at this time. These included one-liners such as "How is Bin Laden like Fred Flintstone? Both may look out their windows and see Rubble." However, the most durable forms of humor proved to be those that implied antimilitarist points of view that poked fun at the extreme security measures imposed after the attacks. One commented, ironically, that a little old lady had been removed from a domestic air flight when knitting needles were found on her: "Apparently officials were afraid she'd knit an Afghan." Another widely circulated joke claims that police had apprehended terrorists nearby with names like "bin Drinkin," "bin Loafin," "bin Fightin," and the like, but were unable to find "bin Workin." This joke had originally appeared in Australia, but it spread to North America within a week of its first appearance on the Internet. Early versions featured local "numskull" stereotypes (such as "hillbillies" from Appalachia or the Ozarks, "Newfies" from Newfoundland, and African Americans), but the joke quickly lost its ethnic-regional edge and became a standard item in workplace photocopy humor. The most common version now warned the reader to be suspicious of anyone in the office who resembles "bin Workin."

Other humorous items parodied the most common rumors and urban legends. The "unlucky tourist" photograph inspired a number of cybercartoons, pasting the image of the same person into photos of the explosion of the Hindenburg in 1937 and other familiar disaster images. Another item claimed that the CIA had received intelligence that alligators controlled by Islamic terrorists were planning to rise out of toilet bowls and bite American citizens on their backsides. These items had a relatively short life, but a parody of "The Grateful Terrorist" persisted. Like the legend, it tells of an act of courtesy done to a person of Middle Eastern appearance, who then cautions his benefactor not to go to a certain restaurant (often the Hard Rock Café). The narrator asks why, expecting that it will be the site of the next terrorist attack, but the mysterious man simply says, "I went there yesterday evening—the food was [awful] and the dessert selection extremely limited."

The folklore produced by this event therefore illustrated a threefold response to cultural stress, involving collective acts of mourning and solidarity, a period of heightened vigilance and suspicion, followed by a renewed ability to distance oneself from shock through humor. The longest-lived traditional items were jokes, particularly those that poked fun at suspicion of cultural outsiders. This suggests that while militarism and scapegoating are predictable in the wake of such disasters, they do not have deep roots that allow them to survive beyond the time of crisis. When another such event does occur, these traditional responses are likely to reappear at about the same times and fulfill the same cultural functions.

Bill Ellis

See also: Arab Communities; Humor; Internet; Muslims; Nationalism; Oral and Folk History.

Sources

Ellis, Bill. "Making a Big Apple Crumble: The Role of Humor in Constructing a Global Response to Disaster." *New Directions in Folklore* 6 (June 2002).

Grider, Sylvia Ann. "Spontaneous Shrines: A Modern Response to Tragedy and Disaster (Preliminary Observations Regarding the Spontaneous Shrines Following the Terrorist Attacks of September 11, 2001)." *New Directions in Folklore* 5 (October 2001).

Hathaway, Rosemary V. " 'Life in the TV': The Visual Nature of 9/11 Lore and Its Impact on Vernacular Response." *Journal of Folklore Research* 42 (2005): 33–56.

Kirshenblatt-Gimblett, Barbara. "Kodak Moments, Flashbulb Memories: Reflections on 9/11." *Drama Review* 47 (2003): 11–48.

Kuipers, Giselinde. "Media Culture and Internet Disaster Jokes: Bin Laden and the Attack on the World Trade Center." *European Journal of Cultural Studies* 5 (2002): 450–70.

SERBIAN, SLOVENIAN, AND MONTENEGRIN COMMUNITIES

The homeland of Serbians in America is located in southeastern Europe between Bosnia-Herzegovina and Albania, although most Serbian Americans draw their immigrant roots not to the Kingdom of Serbia but to Serbian settlements in the Austro-Hungarian Empire to the northwest. Serbians share a language with Croatians to the northwest, and early immigrant organizations in the United States often combined the two groups into a South Slavic union (along with Slovenians). However, political, literary, and religious differences (Croatians are mostly Roman Catholic and use the Latin alphabet, Slovenians are also Catholic but have their own language, while Serbians and Montenegrins align themselves with Eastern Orthodoxy and use the Cyrillic alphabet) into the twentieth century influenced the formation of separate ethnic identities. While neighboring Montenegro, with a coastline on the Adriatic Sea, has its own political identity, Serbia shares a common cultural and religious heritage with the Montenegrins; after the breakup of Yugoslavia in 1991, in fact, Serbia and Montenegro formed a federation linking the two republics. Throughout the nineteenth and twentieth centuries, the region has been beset by war, ethnic violence, and economic crisis, pushing many residents to emigrate. The influx in the United States was especially heavy during the great wave of immigration from 1880 to 1920, when immigrant labor was sought in factories and steel mills of the industrializing Northeast and Midwest. At the start of the twenty-first century, almost half of all Serbs and Montenegrins lived outside Serbia proper, giving them a diasporic ethnic connection.

The immigrants who established ethnic urban enclaves in America were already used to minority status in the Austro-Hungarian Empire, especially Croatia and Vojvodina; an estimated 40 percent of Serbians lived in Austria-Hungary before the outbreak of World War I. Beset by an economic crisis in the late nineteenth century caused by overpopulation, high taxes, and increasing division of peasant land (by 1897, the majority of farms were 5 hectares or less), Serbians were willing to migrate to escape the cycle of poverty. With industrial development in Serbia burdened by land policy maintaining small-scale agriculture, the ready wages of American factories and mills and the support network of Serbian communities were pull factors on immigration. One sign of the diaspora is the prevalence of the *jekavian* Serbian dialect, spoken in many of the older Serbian American communities. (Late-twentieth-century immigrants from Serbia use a dialect called *ekavian*, and many Serbian American radio programs are shifting to the latter to serve the new population.)

Although the number of Serbs coming to the United States was up to four times higher than the number of Montenegrins, emigration by the latter constituted a higher percentage of the homeland population. The twenty thousand Montenegrins in the United States before World War I accounted for about one-tenth of the country's total population; since most were rural males between the ages of nineteen and twenty-four, the émigrés constituted an even higher percentage of the male population, especially in the countryside. Once in the United States, most Montenegrins joined larger Serbian communities and adopted Serbian ethnicity. Serbian ethnic enclaves formed in the coal towns, factory centers, and steel-mill cities such as Steelton, McKeesport, and Pittsburgh, Pennsylvania; Akron, Youngstown, and Cleveland, Ohio; Detroit, Michigan; Chicago, Illinois; East Chicago and Gary, Indiana; Milwaukee, Wisconsin; St. Louis, Missouri; and St. Paul, Minnesota. The profile of Serbian communities compared to that of other immigrant groups is that it is among the smaller, but most concentrated and persistent; churches and fraternal organizations form the center of a close ethnic enclave, promoting a vibrant ethnic folklife evident in religious festivals, music, and dance. Immigrants who came in later waves, such as displaced persons after World War II and refugees during the Serbian-Croatian War of the 1990s, both adapted to and reinvigorated community life. By 2000, more than 140,000 Americans claimed Serbian ancestry, including many that migrated internally after the deindustrialization of the Northeast and Midwest in the late twentieth century to California and Arizona—especially communities in Los Angeles, San Francisco, Sacramento, and Jackson, California, and Phoenix, Lowell, Globe, and Bisbee, Arizona.

Slovenians also coming from the Austro-Hungarian empire (since becoming independent from Yugoslavia in 1991, the Republic of Slovenia is located in an area between Croatia and Austria) were also affected by economic crisis during the late nineteenth century and between 1892 and 1910, some six thousand to nine thousand immigrants came annually to the United States, mostly drawn to industrial cities in the Midwest and Pennsylvania, often alongside Catholic Croatians in joint Slovenian-Croatian parishes, forming concentrations in Cleveland, Ohio; Calumet, Michigan; Chicago, Illinois; Duluth, Minnesota; and Pittsburgh, Pennsylvania. In the 2000 U.S. census, 175,000 Americans claim Slovenian ancestry with more than one third of that number residing in Ohio. Although Slovenians were viewed as assimilating more quickly than Serbians or Croatians, polka and waltz music (Frank Yankovic [1915–1998] from Cleveland, Ohio, often called America's polka king, was of Slovenian heritage) is a prominent ethnic identifier in America. "Slovenian style polka" refers to a fast-paced melodies featuring the button-box accordion. Although Slovenian restaurants are not commonplace, Slovenian foods such as sour turnip soup, *krompir* (russet potatoes sautéed in oil and garlic), and *potica* (nut bread) are frequently featured at ethnic festivals and homes. A notable celebration of Slovenian ethnic identity is Slovenefest held annually in Elon Valley, Pennsylvania (northwest of Pittsburgh), since 1972. It is sponsored by the Slovene National Benefit Society (SNBS), an ethnic fraternal organization founded in 1904 in Pittsburgh, which besides providing insurance to immigrants has been committed to promoting Slovenian language and culture in the United States. It established the Slovenian Heritage Center at the SNBS Elon Valley site to display traditional Slovenian arts and crafts, costumes, and customs as reminders of Slovenian ethnic identity and especially the experience of immigrants who came to America during the early twentieth century.

Religion and Celebration

Central to the maintenance of Serbian language and ethnicity in America is the Serbian Orthodox Church. Serbian churches were established during the great wave of immigration in multiethnic cities such as Jackson, California, in 1893; McKeesport, Pennsylvania, in 1901; and Steelton, Pennsylvania, in 1903. In 1921, the Serbian Orthodox Diocese of the United States and Canada, based in Cleveland, was formed by the Serbian patriarchate in Belgrade. The Serbian Orthodox Church is distinguished from other national orthodox churches by a number of customs and the veneration of St. Sava—celebrated as the founder of the church in the early thirteenth century and as patron saint of education and medicine. St. Sava Day is observed on January 27 on the Gregorian calendar (January 14 on the Julian calendar, still observed by the Serbian Church). A round *slavski kolač* (slava cake, although it is actually a bread), usually decorated with a cross and dove of peace, is blessed, and choirs sing. In keeping with St. Sava's identification as an educator, children typically prepare essays for the event, often about Serbian identity. Thus, the celebration functions to underscore maintenance of Serbian traditions among parents and children alike.

A related observance that Serbs view as unique and important to their religious orthodoxy is the *krsna slava*, or family patron saint's day. Folklorists point out that the observance is pre-Christian in origin, deriving from the pagan custom of honoring protective spirits of hearth and home, adapted to commemorate the conversion to Christianity in the ninth century. Each family celebrates its own saint, thereby strengthening the bond between family and church. A *slavski kolač* is decorated with family symbols. *Koljivo* (also called *žito*), a thick bowl made of boiled wheat, is served, typically with walnuts and honey or sugar. The wheat is said to symbolize the Resurrection of Christ and dead family members; the honey or sugar signifies the sweetness of the event. On the day of a *slava*, the family attends church services and partakes in Holy Communion. Following the service, the parish priest comes to the family's home, blesses the *slavski kolač* and *koljivo*, and lights the *slava* candle. Friends and community members are free to stop by without an invitation. Common saint's days include St. Nicholas on December 19, St.

George on May 6, St. John the Baptist on January 20, and St. Demetrius of Salonica on October 15.

Saints' days and other church events are also occasions for legend telling, often with nationalistic overtones. Jovan Vladimir, also known as King Vladimir (ruler of the first Serbian state of Zeta, from 970 to 1016), is the subject of many of the stories. King Vladimir waged war for several years with Czar Samuel of Macedonia, who finally took him captive. Legend has it that Samuel's daughter, Princess Kosara, saw the prisoner and fell in love with him. She implored her father to spare the imprisoned king, who ultimately became the czar's son-in-law. The story has a tragic ending, however, with a lesson about treachery. After Samuel died, his nephew Vladislav invited Vladimir to Struga to confer with him and had him killed. According to the legend, Princess Kosara had tried to convince Vladimir of Vladislav's evil intent, but Vladimir persisted in his trust, out of a good heart. After Vladimir's death, Zeta was beset by strife over rights to the throne. The graves of Vladimir and Kosara lie in Scutari, their story an inspiration to Serbian literature and folklore for centuries; Vladimir was made a saint by the Orthodox Church. The legend complex also fits a common theme in Serbian epic poetry, revived in the twentieth century, of self-sacrificing heroism, especially for a people who feel they have been politically dominated for much of their history.

The subject of a classic epic and much of Serbian visual culture, Lazar (now a name commonly given to Serbian children), the last monarchical ruler of Serbia in the fourteenth century, purportedly had a vision of St. Elijah on the night before the Battle of Kosovo (1389) with the Ottoman Turks. According to legend, folk poetry, art, and song, Lazar was given the choice of an earthly kingdom for victory or a heavenly crown, and devoutly chose the latter.

The widely celebrated American Christian holidays of Christmas and Easter also are distinguished in the Serbian church by long-held folk customs. Christmas is observed on January 7 in the Gregorian calendar, and includes ethnic customs of lighting the *badnjak* (yule log), baking a honey cake with a coin inside (the recipient is believed to receive luck and fortune), spreading straw on the dining-room floor to recall the manger in which Christ was born, and preparing the traditional Christmas dinner of suckling pig. At Easter, regarded in the community as the most important Christian holiday, Serbians observe a long-held tradition of decorating eggs, in which solid red dye symbolizes the life force and happiness to come in the Resurrection. The first egg to be dyed is set aside and used as a guardian charm called "Protector of the House" (*Cuvarkuca*). It is placed beside the family icon and saved for St. George's Day on April 23; St. George is another martyred hero (his saint's day commemorates his decapitation in 303 C.E.) about whom many legends are told. On Palm Sunday, it is traditional to bless pussy willows rather than palm fronds. At the Easter meal, lamb, signifying the consecrated body of Christ, is central to a menu that traditionally includes lamb soup, *sarma* (a form of stuffed cabbage), and roast lamb.

Serbian orthodoxy is also reflected in family structure. Godparents—the *kum* (godfather) and *kuma* (godmother)—are important members of the family, chosen as sponsors at baptism and as witnesses at weddings. Folklorists have observed that close relationships form between the godparents and the families, enhancing the cohesion of the entire Serbian community by linking families to one another. The godparents also serve ceremonial functions at traditional events, representing especially spiritual guidance at rites of passage. At the wedding, for example, the *kum*, sometimes adorned with a brilliant sash in the colors of the Serbian flag, enjoys the privilege of exchanging rings for the couple to be married. The *kum* and *stari svat* (bridesman) are handed candles, which they hold throughout the betrothal service. The symbolism of the candles is often explained as being connected to the biblical parable of five maidens, who unlike the five foolish maidens, wisely took flasks of oil with their lamps that enabled them to receive the bridegroom (Matthew 25:1–13). Priests may also comment that the candles signify the perpetual light of Christ.

The climactic moment of the wedding ceremony is the crowning of the bride and groom. The couple receives gold crowns, following scriptural allusions to the honor that "crowns" the newly married couple (Ps. 8:5; Heb. 2:7), and references are made to them as king and queen of a new home. The bride and groom share wine from a common cup, and a procession called the dance of Isaiah the Prophet follows. The newlyweds invoke the magic of a protective circle by walking around the altar three times. After the blessing by the priest, attendants congratulate the couple while the choir sings such traditional favorites as "Mnogaja Ljeta" (Many Years).

At the death of a loved one, the family brings *koljivo*, wine, and flowers to a funeral, usually with an open casket. The priest conducts the funeral service at church, after which those in attendance—ending with the family—bid farewell to the departed. The casket is then closed and taken to the grave for the burial service. Those present are then invited to the family home or a restaurant for a meal that will conform to the fasting days in the calendar. A connection to the homeland is sometimes enacted by sending the body to the old country for burial, often less expensive than paying for the funeral and cemetery costs in the United States.

Music and Dance

A central symbol of Serbian cultural heritage in America is its public music and dance. The Serbian Singing Federation, established in 1931 in Chicago (now based in Madison Heights, Michigan), has been instrumental in fostering a choir tradition that is more prevalent in the United States than in Serbia. While it cooperates with the Serbian Orthodox Church, the federation insists that it is a separate organization, allowing secular as well as liturgical performances. Since 1941, it has sponsored an annual choir festival, alternating between cities in the western and eastern United States.

Tamburitza (or *tamburica*, a diminutive form of the Serbian *tambura*) bands are also a signal of Serbian identity, often sponsored by Serbian parishes along with folk dancing troupes decked out in traditional peasant costumes. The tamburitza is a stringed instrument with four to six metal strings, similar to the mandolin or balalaika. Like those instruments, the tamburitza can be struck once or with a tremolo technique to sustain tones. A characteristic design of the instrument is a curled head and a decorated scratchboard on the body. Typically comprising several tamburitza instruments in different sizes and ranges, the bands will include violins, a bass, and sometimes an accordion. Many of the bands travel in a summer circuit to picnics sponsored by local churches. St. Nicholas Serbian Orthodox Church in Steelton, Pennsylvania, for example, owns a park (which it calls "Serb Park") where lively picnics are held. Two or three bands play continuously at each event for Serbian folk dancers. No workshops are held for the dances; young people imitate the steps of experienced dancers in a folk process, often in round formation dances called *kolo*. Attendees can also buy *sarma* and fresh roasted lamb while they socialize. Meanwhile, the Tamburitza Association of America, established in 1974 in Missouri, claims twenty-five hundred members and operates the Tamburitza Hall of Fame. The organization sponsors an annual Tamburitza Extravaganza in different cities, bringing together Serbian and Croatian musicians devoted to the instrument.

One of the legendary Serbian musical groups is the Popovich Brothers Tamburitza Orchestra of Chicago, composed of a family of Serbian immigrants who began playing professionally in 1926. Bandleader Adam Popovich was the recipient of a National Heritage Award in Traditional Arts from the National Endowment for the Arts in 1982 for his role in carrying on the tradition. The band ceased in 2001 but inspired many younger musicians to take up the instrument and maintain a folk musical legacy that has been important to Serbian cultural identity. Often the tamburitza bands are associated with Serbian folk dance ensembles, such as the Sumadija Serbian Folk Dance

Ensemble in Milwaukee, affiliated with the St. Sava Serbian Orthodox Cathedral and frequently linked at festivals with the Sloboda Orchestra. The group dresses in folk costume, performs a variety of dances, and hosts dance events at the St. Sava Serbian Cultural Center for members of the community.

Fraternities and Festivals

Besides the church, several cultural and fraternal organizations are devoted to the maintenance of Serbian language, customs, and identity. During the great wave of immigration, no fewer than eight fraternal organizations were in operation; today there is only one, the Serb National Federation, established in 1901 in Pittsburgh. Like many ethnic fraternal organizations, it offers members life insurance and other social benefits; in addition, it runs a Folklore Federation to preserve and promote Serbian heritage. The organization sponsors an annual festival, encouraging adult folklore groups and children's ensembles to perpetuate music, dance, epic poetry, and clothing traditions in Serbian communities. It also maintains the Serbian Heritage Museum and Library in its home office in Pittsburgh, displaying artifacts and fostering research on Serbian American folklife. With a fresh wave of immigration in the late twentieth century, the fraternal organization has renewed its traditional function of social assistance for new arrivals and mediation between old and new ethnic communities.

One of North America's largest folklore groups, the Serbian Cultural Association (Oplenac), is located in metropolitan Toronto and Mississauga, Canada. The organization maintains a facility for language instruction and culture classes, in addition to music, dance, and dramatic performances. It also hosts the Days of Serbian Culture festival and a homeland celebration of its roots in Vojvodina. With so much attention paid to music and dance, some municipal organizations, such as those in Kansas City and Pittsburgh, organize Serbian food festivals. Many local groups, such as the Serbian Cultural Club in Indianapolis, participate in international or Balkan festivals.

While many Serbian American groups serve political advocacy functions, a new set of cosmopolitan social organizations—comprised largely of recent immigrants in urban centers—are taking the place of the old fraternal societies, which were composed of the peasant stock that arrived during the great wave of immigration. Among the more recent organizations are the Association of Young Serbian Professionals, the L.A. Serbs, and the Organization of Serbian Students. Such groups point to a new chapter in Serbian cultural heritage, connecting the Serbian diaspora via the Internet, for example, but they also show continuity in nationalistic applications of folklife and the symbolic importance placed on ancient legacies of folk music, dance, holidays, and foods for ethnic identity and continuity.

Simon J. Bronner

See also: Bosnian Communities; Bulgarian Communities; Chicago; Cleveland; Croatian Communities; Eastern Orthodox Christians; Pittsburgh.

Sources

Blank, Les. *Ziveli! Medicine for the Heart.* VHS. El Cerrito, CA: Flower Films and Video, 1987.

Kisslinger, Jerome. *The Serbian Americans.* New York: Chelsea House, 1990.

Mijatovic, Elodie Lawton. *Serbian Folk Lore.* 1874. Reprint, Manchester, NH: Ayer, 1968.

Milanovich, Anthony, Stith Thompson, Yvonne J. Milspaw, and Linda Dégh. "Serbian Tales from Blanford." *Indiana Folklore* 4 (1971): 1–60.

Padgett, Deborah. *Settlers and Sojourners: A Study of Serbian Adaptation in Milwaukee, Wisconsin.* Brooklyn, NY: AMS Press, 1990.

The Popovich Brothers of South Chicago. VHS. Directed by Jill Godmilow. Chicago: Facets Multimedia, 2000.

Vrga, Djuro J., and Frank J. Fahey. *Changes and Socio-Religious Conflict in an Ethnic Minority Group: The Serbian Orthodox Church in America.* San Francisco: R and E Research Associates, 1975.

SHAKERS

Shakers are members of the United Society of Believers in Christ's Second Appearing, an American communal society dating to the eighteenth century in England. This society reached its peak in the nineteenth century with six thousand members and eighteen major communities. In the twenty-first century, one community remains, with five members, in Sabbathday Lake, Maine. Observers called the group Shakers because of members' ecstatic body movements during worship services. The group was originally referred to pejoratively as the "Shaking Quakers," because of their roots in the Quaker tradition of seeking a personal experience with God and the possibility of attaining perfect holiness. Besides its ritual worship, the distinctive folklife of the group includes music, basketry, furniture, and architecture in their communal settlements.

Origins and Development

The origin of the Shaker movement can be traced to a small branch of English Quakers who adopted the purificatory worship practices of jumping, trembling, and dancing under the influence of the Holy Spirit to be freed from sin and worldliness. Under the leadership of Jane and James Wardley near Manchester, England, in 1746, the group held meetings encouraging communion with the spirits of the dead and experiencing visions. Ann Lee joined the Wardleys in 1758 and rose to prominence with public preaching about an imminent second coming of Christ and the sinfulness of worldly life.

Ann Lee married Abraham Standerin (or Stanley or Standley) in 1762 at the urging of her parents. Together they had four children, all of whom died at an early age. Ann was not happy in marriage and sought to terminate her relationship with Standerin after the death of their children. Unwilling to release his wife from matrimony, Abraham wanted Anglican parish officials to intercede. In their oral historical narratives, Shakers express the belief that the involvement of the church in her marriage was the turning point in Ann's life. She fasted and deprived herself of sleep during the course of the conflict.

Shakers believe that the hardships she endured led Ann to her conviction of faith. Shakers, like Quakers and other nonconformist religious

The Sabbathday Lake Shaker Community in Maine is the last surviving Shaker group in America. Members practice farming, light manufacturing, and crafts. The eighteen-hundred-acre grounds include the historic meetinghouse building (1794). *(Library of Congress, HABS, ME,3-SAB,1-2)*

groups, were persecuted for their beliefs. Ann and members of the society suffered derision, beatings, and stoning. She was frequently imprisoned for dancing and shouting on the Sabbath, and in one prison stay, she experienced several visions that led her to the revelation that she was the Second Coming of Christ, initiating a new millennium. After this revelation, the group selected her as "Mother in Spiritual Things" and she began calling herself "Ann, the Word" and "Mother Ann" in reference to the belief that she embodied the vital female component of "God the Father-Mother." This belief was considered heretical because it favored a view of God as a gendered duality rather than the traditional Christian trinity. In 1772, she became the official leader of the society. Her preaching of her revelation served to increase the persecution of the group in England, and moved by her vision of a holy sanctuary in the New World, she led eight followers to New York City in 1774.

Two years later, the Shakers moved from the city and established a communal farm in the township of Watervliet, near Albany, in upstate New York. The settlement was designed to represent their beliefs. The village was divided into "families," though they were not related by parentage. To express belief in simplicity, the houses were typically plain-white wood-frame structures. Simplicity was also apparent in the plain cut of their dress and hair. In each dormitory house, men and women were strictly segregated, even using different staircases and doors. Although they worshipped together, no physical contact was allowed during the service, including during the jumping and dancing. Celibacy was central to the group's belief, based on the view that it was a burden believers had to bear as penance for the original sin of Adam and Eve. Mother Ann also preached that it promoted equality between men and women, since women would not be subservient wives and mothers. Women and men thus addressed each other as "sister" and "brother."

Although the Shakers felt freer to proselytize in the United States, their pacifist beliefs in the midst of the Revolutionary War opened them to criticism and imprisonment. As the war drew to a close, millennialist religious revivals sweeping

New York and New England raised interest in the millennialist message and emotional worship of the Shakers. A number of converts in New Lebanon established the New Lebanon Society in 1787, not far from the Watervliet farm, and it became the parent ministry for other later communities. By 1797, eleven communities had been established in New York and New England, including Hancock in West Pittsfield, Massachusetts (lasting from 1790 to 1960), and East Canterbury, New Hampshire (lasting from 1792 to 1992). The Shakers followed this revivalism when it spread into Ohio and Kentucky in the early nineteenth century and established communities such as Pleasant Hill, Kentucky (active from 1806 to 1910), the largest Shaker settlement, and South Union, Kentucky (active from 1807 to 1922), the westernmost village.

Shaker communities were known for producing handmade crafts and agricultural goods that were sold in the worldly market and brought economic success in the nineteenth century. They sold herbs and garden seeds as well as making oval boxes in many communities, wove linen in Alfred, Maine, and made applesauce in Shirley, Massachusetts. The Shakers were known for preaching the purificatory functions of work in mottoes such as "hands to work and hearts to God," and through their labor gained reputations for cleanliness, honesty, and frugality. Every Shaker village, laid out in ordered plans, had standard work buildings, including a cow barn, horse barn, blacksmith shop, sawmill, gristmill, spinning and weaving shop, carpenter shop, and laundry.

Factors frequently mentioned as contributing to the decline of the Shakers include an end to millennialist religious revivalism and utopian social experimentation with the Civil War. Industrialization displaced many of the handmade Shaker crafts and rendered the severe simplicity of the Shakers more extreme. The doctrine of celibacy meant that the society was not passing down its beliefs to a younger generation. By the late twentieth century, a community of five believers, three sisters and two brothers, in Sabbathday Lake Shaker Village, New Gloucester, Maine, was the only active Shaker community.

Cultural Traditions

Common dress among Shakers serves to downplay individuality and connect members to the religious virtues of simplicity and humility. In America, Shakers adopted a plain dress for women of a bonnet cap and black or white cape folded in a triangular shape with the point at the waist and back. Dresses were usually long, dark, and pleated to ensure modesty. Men frequently donned vests along with a long coat, frequently in a subdued color such as brown. The men also are known for wearing smock shirts with puffy sleeves.

The value placed on simplicity is especially apparent in Shaker crafts, distinguished by their ordered, clean lines. The characteristic smoothness of the surfaces in furniture also suggests their religious emphasis on perfection. Shaker songs, for example, referred to Mother Ann as a carpenter who takes the crooked stick and makes it straight and square. The metaphors of furniture as straight, upright, and foursquare were applied to the goal of moral perfection in Shaker belief. Shaker design is likewise evident in built-in cupboards and cases of drawers. Although not originating with the Shakers, built-in cases became a specialty of the Shakers with features such as a central bank of small drawers between cupboard doors. They are also known for building tapered drawers with sides that are thinner at the top and thicker at the bottom. Requiring extra work from the carpenter, tapering eliminated weight without reducing the width of the bottom edge.

The style of Shaker chairs is also seen as a sign of a distinctive folklife, although they fit generally into the category of slat-back seats. Slats are typically narrower at the bottom than at the top, and some observers suggest that the graduated effect is in keeping with the Shaker emphasis on ordered perfection because the narrower bottom slat visually balances the proportions. Shaker chairs are also distinctive because of a pronounced backward slant, providing more comfort for the sitter, but requiring the meticulous attention of the chair maker to the proper angle when drilling for the posts. The rear feet of the chairs frequently had "tilts," or ball-and-socket feet, allowing the sitter to lean back and keep the back legs of the chair flat on the floor.

Colored oval boxes, often made of maple with pine bottoms and lids, and frequently made to hold dried herbs, powdered paint pigments, spices, thread, and buttons, are also associated with Shaker folklife because they express the utility and uniformity valued in Shaker culture. As with other crafts, the Shakers did not originate the design but were known for refining and standardizing it. Shaker boxes have uniformly slender sides, symmetrical joints, and neat, tight-fitting lids. The joints, sometimes known as "swallowtails" because of the tapering of the wood to thin points, are placed on the flat side of the oval. While the swallowtails were seen as decorative, they were a utilitarian feature since the space between the swallowtails reduced buckling by allowing the joints to expand and contract as the climate changed. The joints were applied to other Shaker crafts such as carriers for sewing materials and spittoons.

While emphasizing plainness, the Shakers did not avoid artistic expression. In keeping with the Shaker belief in experiencing visions and communicating with the spirits of departed members, there is a tradition of "inspirational drawing," colorful watercolors depicting messages and designs inspired by the communion with the spirit world. Many of the sheets produced have a spiritual message such as "Build ye on the rock then ye shall have eternal life" illuminated with geometrical designs. They also have stylized trees, fruits, flowers, stars, and even tiny figures. Related to the creation of these sheets are cards in the shape of a heart, olive leaf, or fan presented to faithful members, usually older adults, as a token of esteem. They usually were inscribed with religious messages and decorated with doves, crowns, swords, flowers, and pillars. Stencil patterns often form a border on the outside of the hearts, leaves, and fans.

An important feature of Shaker oral tradition is the music that became a significant part of a number of services and meetings, including "union meetings," small groups of brothers and sisters gathering for singing; "singing meetings" for the practice and learning of songs; and "family meetings" in the dwelling house for worship. Performance of the songs distinctively including "motioning," as the Shakers called it—pantomiming the songs. Singers bowed their heads, stamped their feet, and put their hands up to act out images in the texts. Folklorists have connected many of the religious texts to tunes of eighteenth-century English melodies of secular songs, but note distinctive developments such as "gift songs" describing the heavenly gifts of simplicity and humility. The unusual features of these songs are use of pidgin English perhaps imitating Native American spirits or unknown languages, known as "speaking in tongues" or glossolalia. Texts with English lyrics emphasized the virtue of childlike qualities and the inspiration of Mother Ann's example ("How excellent it is to be little and not know much / Like Mother's little Lambs we will skip and we'll play"), extolled the state of purity ("O Lord make me pure and holy / O Lord do now set me free"), and encouraged steadfast faith ("Come my soul press on press on / To obtain the gospel prize"). Themes of their hymns relate to songs of other millennialist faiths, but in keeping with their theology, they emphasize that the day of Jubilee has arrived rather than being desired, and instead of the kingly Father, they refer to the feminine component of God revealed in and through Mother Ann.

The Living Community of Sabbathday Lake

The Sabbathday Lake Shaker Community, the only Shaker group still active today, was founded as Thompson's Pond Plantation in 1783. Within a year, close to two hundred people came together at the Maine site. Considered among the poorest and smaller eastern Shaker communities, Sabbathday Lake has nonetheless persisted. The Sabbathday Lake Community maintains regular community worship. A typical day begins with the summons to breakfast at 7:30 A.M. Morning prayers begin shortly thereafter: two psalms are read responsively, followed by biblical readings, prayer, and silent prayer, and then the prayers close with a Shaker song. The work of the community continues until 11:30 A.M., when midday prayers are given prior to the noon meal. Following dinner the Shakers resume working, ending with supper at 6 P.M. A Sunday meeting is conducted in the morning hour and a prayer meeting is held in midweek.

The Shakers at Sabbathday Lake still continue the practice of the annual reading of the Shaker Covenant, of around 1830, which is done the first Sunday following New Year's Day. The covenant is a community pact, an agreement between leaders and members to consecrate themselves to God and accept the basic belief that Christ made his second appearance to eradicate sin and establish a kingdom on earth. Other traditional practices include the Practice of Confession, Yearly Sacrifice or Fast Day, held in late November or early December, observed for the purpose of confession and repentance. The yearly fast is part of the Advent season, observed in Christmas preparation for full reconciliation prior to the holy day.

The Shakers also observe Mother Ann's birthday on February 29. Traditional hymns, prayer songs, and spirituals are sung regularly at the religious meeting representing Ann Lee's birthday. These old musical arrangements are also part of Sunday worship throughout the year. A traditional Thanksgiving song, "All at Home," is shared before the noon meal.

> What shall be the theme of the passing hour?
> What shall be the measure of the song, what the strain?
> Once more the circle's made wider and broader,
> The household of faith have all met again.
>
> Come, the feast is ready
> While the table's loaded
> With the choicest fruit from afar and near,
> While leaders and people, parents and children,
> Love and affection, all are here.
> All at home. All at home.

Songs are sung as the spirit moves members, without schedule, and ceremonial compositions continue to be accompanied by traditional movements and gestures. With the numbers of Shakers

dwindling, a special effort has been made in the 1990s to record the group's oral tradition in film documentaries such as *The Shakers* by Ken Burns (1985) and CDs such as *Let Zion Move* with songs sung by members of the Sabbathday Lake and Canterbury communities (1999) and *Early Shaker Spirituals* by Sister Mildred Barker (1996), who received a National Heritage Fellowship from the National Endowment for the Arts in recognition of her preservation of Shaker musical legacy.

Shaker mealtime practices also continue in traditional form. In the dining room, men and women eat at different tables. The meal is served family style in large serving dishes. The table is set in a square configuration, with each group of four diners sharing a set of serving dishes. It is common to hear the mealtime folk expression "Shaker your plate," used to mean eating everything one takes from the serving dishes.

The Shakers at Sabbathday Lake continue to plant and harvest an abundance of produce for home consumption. An important village industry is seed and herb production. Herbs were first grown for sale at Sabbathday Lake in 1799. Today, a thriving herbal business continues, offering tea, culinary herbs, and rose water. Due to the small size of the community, the group has outside help in maintaining the herbal business; the business even has a Web site linked to the Sabbathday Lake Shaker Village.

Handicrafts also continue at Sabbathday Lake. Although members do not make chairs and cupboards, taping, or "listing," a chair seat, a practice dating to the nineteenth century, continues. In this process, Shakers weave colored fabric to cover chair seats. Not only is it stronger and longer lasting than rush or cane, it is simple and quick to weave. A traditional technique among the Shakers is to weave two contrasting colors (maroon and beige, for example) to achieve a checkerboard pattern. Special orders for woven cloaks and other items for the museum store are made using community looms.

A blending of old and new traditions is evident in Sabbathday Lake Shaker Village. A crank-operated telephone provides communication within the village, yet modern telephones connect the community to the world. Wood-burning stoves continue to be the preferred heating method, although oil heat has been installed in some places. Kitchen duties are no longer rotated, as members now share in the daily preparation, but seating is maintained in traditional manner. The future of Shaker folklife is uncertain. With only five members currently following the religion at Sabbathday Lake Shaker Village, the prospect of revival seems bleak. Nonetheless, members in the early twenty-first century with an average age in the forties regularly express commitment to maintaining the Shaker Community into the future. Although membership does not show signs of growing, public interest in Shaker customs and material culture drives the preservation of historic Shaker sites such as Pleasant Hill, Hancock, and Canterbury. At Sabbathday Lake, non-Shakers attend the Shaker meeting on Sundays and participate in internships on Shaker herb gardening. The Shaker message for contemporary society posted on the Sabbathday Lake Shaker Village Web site, and the basis of their folklife, is as it was from its founding: "Above all else that God is Love and that our most solemn duty is to show forth that God who is love in the World."

Jan M. Swinehart and Simon J. Bronner

See also: Communal Societies; Dance, Liturgical; New England; Quakers.

Sources

Andrews, Edward Deming. *The People Called Shakers: A Search for the Perfect Society.* New York: Dover Publications, 1963.

Brewer, Priscilla J. *Shaker Communities, Shaker Lives.* Hanover, NH: University Press of New England, 1986.

Kassay, John. *The Book of Shaker Furniture.* Amherst: University of Massachusetts Press, 1980.

Nicoletta, Julie. *Architecture of the Shakers.* Woodstock, VT: Countryman Press, 2000.

Patterson, Daniel W. *The Shaker Spiritual.* 2nd ed. New York: Dover Publications, 2000.

Sabbathday Lake Shaker Village. www.shaker.lib.me.us.

The Shakers: Hands to Work, Heart to God. DVD. Directed by Ken Burns. Los Angeles: Paramount Home Video, 2004.

Sprigg, June. *Shaker Design.* New York: Whitney Museum of American Art, 1986.

Stein, Stephen J. *The Shaker Experience in America: A History of the United Society of Believers.* New Haven, CT: Yale University Press, 1992.

Swank, Scott T. *Shaker Life, Art, and Architecture: Hands to Work, Hearts to God.* New York: Abbeville Press, 1999.

They Do Not from the Truth Depart, in Word or Work, in Hand or Hearts: Sabbathday Lake in 1800, 1900, and 2000. New Gloucester, ME: United Society of Shakers, 2000.

Wertkin, Gerard C. *The Four Seasons of Shaker Life: An Intimate Portrait of the Community at Sabbathday Lake.* New York: Simon and Schuster, 1986.

SHENANDOAH VALLEY REGION

Lying between the Blue Ridge Mountains to the east and the Allegheny Mountains to the west, the Shenandoah Valley stretches from Augusta County in western Virginia to Jefferson County in West Virginia. From headwaters in these mountains, the north and south forks of the Shenandoah River flow in a northeasterly direction, join at Riverton, and then flow into the Potomac River at Harpers Ferry. Extending from outside Harrisonburg to Strasburg, the Massanutten Mountain range bisects the valley, forming a natural barrier between the two forks of the river. Historically and culturally, the region has been associated with America's early frontier. Its blend of colonial era Old World traditions into a distinctive regional culture is often viewed as an example of the rise of an American folklife in early American history.

Much of the folklife of the region originated in the shared ethnicity of the valley's early settlers: Swiss and Germans from the Rhineland Palatinate region and Pennsylvania. Other ethnic groups—most notably the Scots Irish—also migrated to the valley, and the mix of cultures has contributed to the distinctive composition of Shenandoah folklife. With the combination of English settlers from east of the Blue Ridge, who entered through the northern valley, and Africans and African Americans forcibly brought to the region, the region presented a culture different from that of the rest of Virginia by the early nineteenth century. In the twenty-first century, the

Shenandoah Valley is home to a widening spectrum of ethnic groups, particularly Latinos and refugees from eastern and central Europe.

Musical and Material Traditions

The Shenandoah Valley stakes a claim as one of the most influential contributors to the history of southern gospel music. In 1810, Ananias Davisson, a Presbyterian teacher, published *Kentucky Harmony*, a songbook that introduced shape-note singing to the region. Published in Harrisonburg, a crossroads town on the migration route known as the Great Wagon Road, the publication achieved a success that was not lost on the ethnically German groups who maintained a tradition of choral singing in the valley. By 1816, Joseph Funk, a Mennonite schoolteacher in the Harrisonburg area, had published *Die Allgemain Nutzliche Choral-Music* (The Universally Useful Choral-Music Book). Funk is best known, however, for his 1832 publication, *Genuine Church Music*, later called *The Harmonia Sacra*. Twenty-eight thousand copies of the book had been printed by 1847, and it became the basis for a tradition of group singing that continues in the region today. Funk's grandson, Aldine Kieffer, formed a publishing company with Ephraim Ruebush in 1866, and the two began printing *The Musical Million,* a periodical designed to encourage singing schools in the valley. Kieffer, in fact, is credited with founding the South's first Normal Singing School in the Shenandoah County town of New Market in 1874.

Along with such oral traditions, the material culture of the Shenandoah Valley reflects the heritage of the region's ethnic groups. *Fraktur,* decorated birth and baptismal certificates, by regional artists attest to the Germanic background of the many Lutheran congregations in the area, as does the eighteenth-century architecture that continues to grace the valley landscape. The stone-and-log *flurkuchenhaus*, with its three-room floor plan and central chimney, demonstrates the early adherence to traditional architectural forms. Later structures, displaying symmetrical facades emulating the English I-house that hide the three-room floor plan, illustrate the eventual acculturation of these groups. By the second half of the nineteenth century, construction of ethnic house types dwindled and the I-house became the most common type on the landscape.

Another traditional structure is much more common on the valley landscape—the large forebay barn. Recognizable by its overhanging front and sloping barn bridge in the back, the form creates a significant link with the valley's cultural hearth in south-central Pennsylvania. Originating in Switzerland, where farmers built barns on the sides of hills to facilitate entry into the second level, the form was brought south into the region by migrant Swiss, German, and Scots-Irish farmers who recognized the utility of the structure. In the early twenty-first century this building form is the most common architectural indicator of the Shenandoah Valley's cultural past.

Two other traditions demonstrate the importance of traditional life in the valley: pottery and white-oak basket making. In the nineteenth century, the region was home to perhaps several hundred potters who found the natural resources of the valley to be excellent for both stone- and earthenware. Strasburg, located at the northern end of Shenandoah County, was the center of pottery production for many years. Families such as the Bells and Eberleys established generations of potters who turned artful and functional pieces that were marketed throughout the region. Rockingham County, to the south, also hosted a long family tradition of potters. Artisans such as Andrew Coffman, John D. Heatwole, and Emanuel Suter produced pottery from the 1830s until 1900. As with many traditional crafts, however, the community's adoption of newer technologies brought the well-known pottery tradition to an end.

White-oak basket making in the Shenandoah Valley, on the other hand, demonstrates the perseverance of a craft through numerous family generations, offering an example of how a tradition can be maintained in an era of commercially produced materials and a consumer-oriented society. Originally a necessary craft in the valley, white-oak basketry in the region can be traced to the eighteenth-century English craftsman Thomas Nicholson. His descendants settled in Virginia's Blue Ridge Mountains, where they are known to have made baskets until being displaced from their homes as the federal government claimed land for the Shenandoah National Park. Moving westward into the valley, the family continued to carry the knowledge of choosing appropriate trees, preparing the splits, and fashioning proper forms through the early twenty-first century. The contemporary baskets often serve a more decorative purpose, but the forms and the strength of the pieces attest to the longevity of the tradition in the region.

Cultural Heritage

As the basketry tradition suggests, many older traditions have been maintained up to the present. Depending on their heritage, residents eat pork and sauerkraut (Germanic) or black-eyed peas (Scots-Irish) on New Year's Day, and the promise of a ham potpie dinner frequently lures many to traditional fund-raising events. And, while the region now offers a wide variety of religious opportunities for the spiritually minded, congregations dating to the eighteenth century provide links to the past and the religious faith of the original ethnic groups. For example, communities settled initially by the Mennonites and the Church of the Brethren (once known as German Baptists) continue to practice the traditions of their beliefs in the valley; numerous early Presbyterian congregations still meet in early church buildings, reflecting the initial Scots-Irish settlements.

Traditional music, too, persists in the valley, as communities of musicians pass along tunes and songs in oral tradition. Impromptu sessions as well as community-sanctioned events assure that the bluegrass and old-time music heard in the region for generations will persist. Old-time music is featured, for example, at the Edinburg Ole Time Festival in Edinburg, Virginia, the Rock-

bridge Mountain Music and Dance Festival in Buena Vista, Virginia, and the Frontier Culture Museum in Staunton, Virginia. Still, as the population of the Shenandoah Valley increases, the continued influx of residents from other regions will play a part in determining what traditions will be carried on, contribute to their evolution, and help make them unique symbols of the valley's mixed and ever-changing cultural heritage.

Scott Hamilton Suter

See also: Appalachia; Pennsylvania Culture Region; Pennsylvania German Communities; Scottish Communities.

Sources

Comstock, H.E. *The Pottery of the Shenandoah Valley Region.* Winston-Salem, NC: Museum of Early Southern Decorative Arts, 1994.

Koons, Kenneth E., and Warren R. Hofstra. *After the Backcountry: Rural Life in the Great Valley of Virginia, 1800–1900.* Knoxville: University of Tennessee Press, 2000.

Mitchell, Robert D. *Commercialism and Frontier: Perspectives on the Early Shenandoah Valley.* Charlottesville: University Press of Virginia, 1977.

Smith, Elmer Lewis, John G. Stewart, and M. Ellsworth Kyger. *The Pennsylvania Germans of the Shenandoah Valley.* Allentown, PA: Schlecter's, 1964.

Suter, Scott Hamilton. *Shenandoah Valley Folklife.* Jackson: University Press of Mississippi, 1999.

———. *Tradition and Fashion: Cabinetmaking in the Upper Shenandoah Valley, 1850–1900.* Dayton, VA: Shenandoah Valley Folk Art and Heritage Center, 1996.

Wust, Klaus. *The Virginia Germans.* Charlottesville: University Press of Virginia, 1969.

SHOWERS, WEDDING AND BABY

Although the origin of the shower tradition is uncertain, all the likely explanations point to the same purpose: ensuring that a bride and groom begin their life as a married couple with the necessities to make a home. And when marriage eventually leads to a baby in a carriage, it is likely that the carriage itself may have come from another shower. Wedding showers and baby showers enable family members and friends to convey their joy and best wishes to the bride or mother-

At a traditional American wedding shower, a hat for the bride-to-be is fashioned out of the ribbons saved from gift boxes. Ever an occasion for gift giving, the wedding shower today is generally more casual, fun, and sometimes risqué than in previous generations. *(Simon Bronner)*

to-be by presenting them with gifts. Dinner may be served, or just dessert, games may be played and items made, but presents are always given. It has been an evolving tradition, and particularly since the late twentieth century, a number of changes have crept into the traditions of both wedding and baby showers.

Wedding

Folklorists have interpreted the designation of the shower as a women's event in the extension of social support for the bride-to-be or mother-to-be who symbolically has more risk, and displays more change, than the man in the life passage. The assignment of social roles is also implied, since the gifts given to the honoree in the shower often refer to her role as manager of the household and family. In her feminist examination of weddings, *Here Comes the Bride* (2001), Jaclyn Geller bemoans the fact that showers are one more instance of friends and family of the bride being forced to reward her for having snagged a man and being willing to submit to matrimony. The shower, she contends, has two purposes: "A last night to indulge in the pleasure of friendship before retreating into marital isolation" and to "set the stage for what has been billed as an eve-

ning of female sexual initiation and rapturous bliss: the wedding night." Because of changes in social and sexual mores, however, advice giving in the modern American wedding shower typically pertains to marriage more than to the wedding night.

Among religious groups that still encourage abstinence prior to marriage, the gift of lingerie may elicit teasing, and slightly risqué shower games may be played. One young Mormon bride watched while her shower guests designed lingerie for her out of paper plates and cups and napkins, which she then modeled. The friends of many Mormon brides still hold showers to which no older women—especially the mother of the bride—are invited and where it is understood that the gifts will be lingerie or pampering items such as bubble bath, skin lotion, or candles.

While not usually determined by who is invited, theme showers are gaining popularity in contemporary American society. And the themes go beyond the kitchen or bath. For example, the hostess might assign a letter of the alphabet to each guest, whose gift should start with that letter. In a holiday shower, each guest brings gifts and decorations for different holidays. In another variation, the guest might be asked to bring a favorite recipe along with the nonperishable ingredients.

Because showers are often held by friends, co-workers, and family, some brides may be the object of celebration several times; others may have only one event. In an example of a shower with the extended family as the main guests, a woman and her cousins were given lengths of tulle and balloons and designed wedding dresses—which they modeled while giving karaoke performances, with the mother of the bride and her aunts serving as the judges. It was a fun, inclusive way to celebrate her upcoming wedding. The decorations for the shower were, in her words, "Big, fat Barbies with shaving cream wedding dresses on them. Because in our family whenever anyone asks what a present is we always say 'a big, fat Barbie.' " Thus her shower also reinforces family traditions and jokes.

Not all showers are so casual, fun, or reasonably priced. Another woman writes, "I attended a shower for 120 ladies at the Bridgeport, Connecticut, American Legion Hall—a six-course dinner *avec* fifteen piece orchestra. The engraved invitations just happened to mention the names of the bride's silver and china patterns and the stores where they could be purchased. The evening's jollies consisted of her opening each of the hundred-odd shower gifts that literally engulfed the stage, including two vacuum cleaners, a king-size bed and THREE color TV sets."

In contrast to such opulence, shower games reminiscent of simpler times find their way into current parties. Ribbons are saved from the gifts and, with the aid of a paper plate and a little adhesive tape, become beautiful bridal bouquets and hats. Or as the bride opens her presents, the hostess or assigned guest surreptitiously writes down her utterances and reads them back as what the bride will say to her new husband on their wedding night. The computer age has inspired Web sites devoted to "organizing" traditions. Sites abound with party ideas. Generally these sites are also willing to ensure success as a hostess by selling the very decorations and party favors described on their Web sites.

Other modern variations on the shower include couple parties that might include a casual meal and gifts that reflect the interests of the couple or the all-male tool shower. Since men do not have the traditional framework in place for showers, sometimes even friends with the best intentions fail to follow through. Despite shifting familial patterns, the all-female bridal shower still reigns supreme.

Baby Showers

Baby showers have undergone dramatic changes as more women enter the workforce. With more women working, office showers have gained popularity. One woman describes the surprise shower organized by some of her girlfriends at the office: "They had collected money from everyone. And then when we went to lunch, they would talk to me about the things that I needed and where I was registered. It was a complete surprise. One day my boss came up and said that they were

having sandwiches in the lunchroom as a treat before my maternity leave. She took me in and everyone was there—the entire corporate staff was there. They had used the money to have lunch catered from a local bakery. And there was a cake. With the rest of the money they purchased a car seat and lots of other practical presents. They bought some things from my baby registries."

Registering for babies is now as common as bridal registries once were. It is not unusual for a mother-to-be to register in several different stores with the help of electronic devices. Registries can often be accessed online, and gifts may also be purchased and delivered to the expectant mother from the privacy of the purchaser's home computer. Rather than eliminating tradition, modern technology adds new layers and nuances.

One development of shower gift-decoration available for sale at several Internet sites is the diaper cake. This inedible delicacy is made of rolled diapers tied with ribbons reflecting the sex of the baby or interests (such as Disney or Winnie-the-Pooh) of the soon-to-be-parents. The rolled diapers are arranged in large circles and once again tied with ribbon. The layers are stacked, and baby items such as clothing, baby wash, lotion, powder, and rattles are tied on or tucked into the "cake."

Another practical shower decoration is fashioned by putting up a small clothesline and hanging from it the baby clothes given to the expectant mother. One activity that results in a gift is to give each guest a fabric square, and a fabric or permanent marker. The guest decorates the square and the squares are then put together as a quilt for the new baby.

Shower games also abound through both the Internet and traditional methods. Many test practical child-rearing skills—name that baby food, identify that baby item in the brown paper bag, and name that messy diaper. The messy diaper is created by melting chunks of broken chocolate bars onto the diaper in a microwave. The results are surprisingly realistic. Passed around the group, each guest gets a chance to smell the diaper and identify the original candy. The winner does *not* get to eat the diaper.

Baby showers are generally scheduled at least

a month before the due date to avoid cancellation due to early babies. This also allows the mother time to purchase items she needs and does not receive. Generally baby showers are held only for first-time mothers. Among some groups such as observant Jews, however, holding a baby shower is avoided because it is considered bad luck (or presumptuous before God) to celebrate *before* the birth.

Wedding and baby showers grow stronger despite economic and societal changes that might seem to render them obsolete or socially backward. Showers exist in the liminal space between life as a single person and life as a spouse, childlessness and motherhood. The shower appears to respond to the perception in America that the woman's passage to the status of bride and mother deserves special celebration and extra social support. While some critics grumble over costs and seemingly greedy brides and mothers, most women involved in the events relate that showers help focus honorees on the joy rather than the tribulation of weddings and births, making even minimal participation in the event, giving a gift, rewarding.

Kristi A. Young

See also: Birth; Rituals and Rites; Weddings and Marriage; Women.

Sources

Geller, Jaclyn. *Here Comes the Bride: Women, Weddings and the Marriage Mystique.* New York: Four Walls Eight Windows, 2001.

Grant, Gail Paton. "Getting Started: Outfitting the Bride in Seaside." *Canadian Folklore* 15 (1993): 69–81.

Riches, Suzanne Volmar. "Threads Through a Patchwork Quilt: The Wedding Shower as a Communication Ritual and Rite of Passage for the Mormon Woman." Ph.D. diss., University of Utah, 1987.

Seligson, Marcia. *The Eternal Bliss Machine: America's Way of Wedding.* New York: William Morrow, 1973.

SHRINES AND CROSSES, ROADSIDE

Shrines are ritual sites of prayer or contemplation; they are frequently erected at locations attached to tragedy or its victims. "Memorial" usually implies the commemoration of violent death and typically invites the placement of objects symbolically connected to the tragedy or its victims. However, the two terms are often used interchangeably to describe impromptu material responses to fatal incidents of various kinds, including automobile accidents and homicides. These folk productions, sometimes called "spontaneous shrines" by folklorists, are also known as *cruces* (crosses), *crucitas* (little crosses), *descansos* (places of rest), roadside crosses (one or more crosses as the focal point), memorial assemblages, and memorial markers, and have analogues in traditions around the world.

Antecedents and Patterns

While the earliest large-scale spontaneous memorial in the United States in living memory was perhaps the outpouring of grief in the form of flowers, wreaths, and religious icons left at Dealey Plaza in Dallas following the assassination of President John F. Kennedy on November 22, 1963, people have marked death sites in North America for hundreds of years in accordance with religion-based beliefs and traditional practices. Roadside crosses represent one of the oldest of such traditions, blending the spiritual beliefs of indigenous peoples with Roman Catholicism. The journals of Spanish explorers, dating from the late seventeenth century onward, document the use of crosses—carved into trees, painted on rocks, and fashioned by hand—to mark both death and burial sites. In both Mexico and the southwestern United States, such memorials became shrines at which travelers stopped to pray, both for themselves and for the souls of the departed. Roadside memorials may mark the site of a culturally defined "bad death," an unexpected accident that left the deceased unprepared for the afterlife, in which case the prayers of passersby are crucial.

Roadside crosses are most often constructed of wood but may also be fashioned from metal, cement, or a combination of all three. The surrounding assemblage, which visitors to the site create and re-create over time, usually consists of religious icons in various forms (statues, holy cards, rosaries), real and artificial flowers, and handwritten notes. Memorials for children and young adults often include toys and school-related memorabilia such as spirit ribbons, photographs of friends, T-shirts, and graduation tassels. Favorite foods or beverages of the deceased are also left as remembrances, a direct link to the memorial practices that constitute enduring festivals of death such as the Mexican Day of the Dead.

Roadside memorials do not always center on a cross or other religious symbol. A tree struck in an accident may become the focus of an assemblage. Mourners attach photographs, notes, and other memorabilia to the trunk or hang them from branches. Similarly, the concrete support for a roadway overpass may function as the canvas for a memorial message, as has the side wall of many a building in highly urbanized areas. New York City's tradition of such murals includes memorials to victims of gang violence and police brutality. Newer murals commemorate the terrorist attacks of September 11, 2001. Flowers, candles, and other items were left on the sidewalk at the base of these painted tributes. City residents also constructed memorial assemblages near the entrances of fire stations, on park fences, and on light poles. In each case, the materials used were adapted to the memorial environment: posterboards fastened to poles displayed messages and photographs, and T-shirts and flowers were intertwined in metal fencing.

The form and content of a memorial is related not only to the cultural heritage and spiritual beliefs of its creators, but also to its physical setting. Structures meant to withstand the vagaries of weather and human interference are fashioned from sturdier materials than those intended to be more temporary. For example, memorial crosses that have been vandalized are sometimes reset in concrete. Annual or perennial flowers or shrubs are planted to bring bursts of color and life to these sites so deeply marked by death. Additionally, individuals outside the immediate area may send remembrances to be placed at the site. Virtual memorials on the Internet, often referred to as "cybershrines," although freed from many of the constraints of the material world, continue to incorporate the traditional funerary symbolism of flowers, candles, and religious iconography while often foregrounding textual remembrances in the form of guestbooks and other electronically posted tributes.

Performance

While the memorial practices described above are certainly influenced by long-standing cemetery decoration custom, the public nature of shrine and memorial assemblages suggests a performative aspect of grief and commemoration. Roadside crosses have been used by Mothers Against Drunk Driving (MADD) as silent reminders of the dangers of driving while intoxicated. These crosses are differentiated from those of folk tradition by the use of a small plaque (the color varies by MADD chapter) at the crosspiece, which indicates that the fatal accident was caused by drunken driving. In some areas of the country, official MADD crosses are the only approved roadside memorial markers. Those not formally connected with MADD, however, may actively convey similar messages, such as the one stenciled on a bridge support in Austin, Texas, that reads "Don't Drink & Drive, You Might Kill Someone's Kid." The need to mark sites of death and destruction, to sanctify violent tears in the fabric of the everyday life, is a cornerstone of cultural tradition. Beyond the outlet they provide for grieving mourners, however, these shrines are also material cues to a cautionary narrative about the dangers of a society built on complex machinery and the responsibilities of the humans who operate them. The markers are particularly elaborate for the premature death of youth and the implicated sins of drivers intoxicated with alcohol and drugs.

While graveyards are more removed from public view in modern society than in preindustrial society and therefore may not relate such narratives to passersby, roadside crosses in the automobile age remind viewers of dangers in modern society and mark hallowed ground. Given the modern tendency to quickly cover or build over signs of tragedy, roadside crosses are at once cautionary narratives for the mechanized public speeding on impersonal roads with little thought of their own mortality and an outlet for mourners of untimely, premature death.

Holly Everett

See also: Automobiles; Death and Funerals; Gravemarkers; Shrines and Memorials, Spontaneous and Vernacular.

Sources

Cooper, Martha, and Joseph Sciorra. *R.I.P.: New York Spraycan Memorials.* London: Thames and Hudson, 1994.

Everett, Holly. *Roadside Crosses in Contemporary Memorial Culture.* Denton: University of North Texas Press, 2002.

Foote, Kenneth. *Shadowed Ground: America's Landscapes of Violence and Tragedy.* Austin: University of Texas Press, 2003.

Grider, Sylvia. "Spontaneous Shrines: A Modern Response to Tragedy and Disaster." *New Directions in Folklore* 5 (October 2001).

Griffith, James S. *Beliefs and Holy Places: A Spiritual Geography of the Primería Alta.* Tucson: University of Arizona Press, 1992.

Reid, Jon, and Cynthia Reid. "A Cross Marks the Spot: A Study of Roadside Death Memorials in Texas and Oklahoma." *Death Studies* 25 (2001): 341–56.

Santino, Jack, ed. *Spontaneous Shrines and the Public Memorialization of Death.* New York: Palgrave Macmillan, 2006.

Zeitlin, Steven, and Ilana Beth Harlow. *Giving a Voice to Sorrow: Personal Responses to Death and Mourning.* New York: Perigee, 2001.

SHRINES AND MEMORIALS, SPONTANEOUS AND VERNACULAR

Spontaneous or vernacular shrines are temporary and ephemeral sacred shrines erected to memorialize specific individuals. They are typically placed at the site of a murder or other catastrophic accident, usually involving multiple deaths. Official, permanent memorials are generally architectural or sculptural structures erected by communities, municipalities, and nations to memorialize wars and national heroes. Vernacular memorials have no official sanction and memorialize local, less well-known individuals. Memorials generally are not created at the site of death.

Roadside crosses are temporary assemblages of personal memorabilia, religious items, flowers, and candles that appear near the site of a tragic event. This memorial was a gathering place for the friends and classmates of a seventeen-year-old girl following the car accident that took her life. *(Linda Manning)*

Spontaneous Shrines

Spontaneous shrines are made up almost exclusively of artifacts from the popular culture, such as teddy bears and other stuffed animals, balloons, clothing and hats, posters, photographs, and items identified with the particular site, such as the Israeli flags prominent in the shrine created at the National Aeronautics and Space Administration following the February 1, 2003, crash of the space shuttle *Columbia,* which had one Israeli crewman. Many of the artifacts placed in spontaneous shrines are idiosyncratic; that is, the meaning of the item is so personal that it is not readily apparent to a viewer. Religious items such as crosses, rosaries, angel figurines, and Bibles are also common in most assemblages. Flowers and candles are practically universal in spontaneous shrines.

Although these assemblages of artifacts are not random, neither are they "makeshift," the term popularized by the media. Most shrines begin when an anonymous mourner places an item near the site of the tragedy and then other mourners add their memorabilia close by; thus, the shrines grow by accretion. Mourners are generally careful not to cover up other offerings with their own and attempt to create aesthetic arrangements, such as candles in a semicircle at the base of the assemblage. Security fences at disaster sites are commonly selected as the armature on which artifacts are placed.

Since no official organization is in control of or responsible for the creation of a spontaneous shrine, there is no agreement about when or by whom it is dismantled. If the shrine is in a heavily populated area, local inhabitants will take responsibility for lighting and replacing the candles, straightening up the shrine when it gets windblown, and so forth. In the case of major catastrophes, such as the Oklahoma City bombing or the shootings at Columbine High School, authorities and local people cooperate to remove the shrine respectfully and with dignity. In these latter instances, families of the victims are often invited to take away whatever items they want from the shrines. Furthermore, usable objects, such as stuffed animals or quilts and pillows, are cleaned and distributed to orphanages, hospitals, nursing homes, and the like. Sometimes local governments will arbitrarily sweep up a shrine when it begins to obstruct traffic or becomes an eyesore. Conservation and long-term management of collections of these artifacts are extremely expensive and time-consuming.

Historical Background

The contemporary ritual of marking violent deaths with spontaneous shrines is a modern development. The custom of placing idiosyncratic artifacts at the base of the Vietnam Veterans Memorial in Washington, D.C., which was dedicated in 1982, and the widespread media coverage of the phenomenon are the probable impetuses for the more general creation of idiosyncratic shrines at the sites of violent deaths. Media coverage has helped spread the custom of creating spontaneous shrines. Those created at Oklahoma City following the bombing of the Murrah Federal Building in April 1995 were reported in nationally broadcast television programs, for example, and probably inspired comparable shrines at the sites of other disasters. A section of the security fence was installed as

part of the permanent Oklahoma City National Memorial to provide people with a place to deposit their memorabilia. Close to one million people have participated in this grieving ritual, and thousands of the artifacts are housed in the archives of the memorial. Similarly, the death of Britain's Princess Diana in 1997 was the object of media saturation; flowers, candles, memorial photographs, and other artifacts blanketed the area outside Buckingham Palace and other sites in London. The flowers were ultimately composted; usable stuffed animals, quilts, and other objects were gathered up and distributed to hospitals and orphanages. In 1999, the shrine at Columbine High School in Littleton, Colorado, following the fatal 1999 shooting rampage by two teenage students was a source of controversy because someone erected crosses for the two murderers as well as the victims. The terrorist attacks of September 11, 2001, resulted in the creation of hundreds of elaborate spontaneous shrines in New York City, Washington, D.C., Shanksville, Pennsylvania, and elsewhere.

Public Vernacular Memorials

The World Wide Web provides access to hundreds of thousands of virtual memorials created in memory of the dead. Unlike spontaneous shrines, these Web pages are not necessarily dedicated to victims of violent death. Any loved one, including a pet, can be memorialized in this way. Most cybershrines contain photographs, drawings, and elaborate graphics, and it is often possible to place a "virtual" flower or sign a "virtual" condolence book as part of an interactive Web page. As is the case with any newly emerging tradition, scholarly terminology describing this phenomenon is in flux. Terms currently in use for this phenomenon include: "cybershrine," "cyber memorial," and "virtual memorial."

Deaths from inner-city gang warfare and police violence are being memorialized more frequently with murals painted on the walls of local buildings. In some communities, local artists specialize in this particular art form, and local citizens commission and pay for the creation of a memorial mural. The murals become pilgrimage sites, and mourners frequently create spontaneous shrines at the bases of the walls on which the murals are painted.

To commemorate the lives of people who have died from AIDS and draw attention to the cause of fighting the disease, the NAMES Project organized the creation of the vast AIDS quilt. Mourners create individually designed, idiosyncratic panels to memorialize their loved ones. These standard-size panels are then periodically displayed in a prominent place, such as the National Mall in Washington, D.C. Quilt blocks contain a blank space where visitors can write directly on the panel to express their own feelings about the person who died, the AIDS epidemic in general, or anything else that a visitor thinks is appropriate. Today the quilt has become so large—with more than forty thousand panels—that it is no longer possible to display the entire project at one location.

Spontaneous shrines and other forms of vernacular memorialization express communal grief and bewilderment in the face of violent and disruptive death. By creating shrines, people create order in the midst of chaos and consecrate the spot where both loved ones and strangers have died. The shrines are temporary, liminal, sacred spaces where the living can commune with the dead by leaving notes and other messages addressed directly to the dead. The shrines can also be locations of protest where people express their outrage at senseless death and the violence that caused it. The artifacts that make up these shrines, no matter how mundane, are sacred gifts to the dead and tangible expressions of grief.

Sylvia Grider

See also: Death and Funerals; Gravemarkers; Grottoes; Material Culture; Rituals and Rites; Shrines and Crosses, Roadside.

Sources

Arrelano, Estevan. "Descansos." *New Mexico Magazine* 64 (February 1986): 42–44.
Cooper, Martha, and Joseph Sciorra. *R. I. P.: Memorial Wall Art.* New York: Henry Holt, 1994.
Doss, Erika. "Death, Art, and Memory in the Public Sphere: The Visual and Material Culture of Grief in Contemporary America." *Mortality* 7, no. 1 (2002): 63–82.
Haney, C. Allen, Christina Leimer, and Juliann Lowery. "Spontaneous Memorialization: Violent Death and Emerging Mourning Ritual." *Omega: Journal of Death and Dying* 35, no. 2 (1997): 159–71.
Hass, Kristin Ann. *Carried to the Wall: American Memory and the Vietnam Veterans Memorial.* Los Angeles: University of California Press, 1998.
Jorgensen-Earp, Cheryl, and Lori Lanzilotti. "Public Memory and Private Grief: The Construction of Shrines at the Sites of Public Tragedy." *Quarterly Journal of Speech* 84 (1998): 150–70.
Linenthal, Edward. *The Unfinished Bombing: Oklahoma City in American Memory.* New York: Oxford University Press, 2001.

SICILIAN COMMUNITIES

Sicily is an autonomous region of Italy and the largest island in the Mediterranean Sea. Sicilians have long treasured their own identity, as distinct from that of other Italians. This owes in large part to the geophysical separation of the island from the mainland and to a long-standing resistance to political and economic domination by the northern Italian government. These same conditions also spurred the largest influx of Sicilians to the United States in the years following Italian unification in 1870. Sicilians came primarily from rural villages that had experienced natural disasters, epidemics of cholera and malaria, and heavy taxation from the North.

From *Contadini* to Citizens

The initial purpose of Sicilian *contadini* (peasant) immigrants was to make enough money to return home, purchase land or a business, and become members of the *signori*, or leisured class. Most of the Sicilian immigrants were males between the ages of fifteen and fifty. Once in the United States, some lived in boarding houses run by relations or *paesani* (fellow villagers), and others resided in company towns or camps, where they worked with Poles, Italians, Slovaks, Germans, Irish, and other immigrants as unskilled laborers.

Eventually, however, after seeing that they could make a better living in America than in their homeland and had more opportunity for advancement, many of the Sicilian immigrants decided to stay. They sent for their families, became U.S. citizens, and began adapting their village folk traditions to America. They settled heavily in urban and industrial districts, where they developed vibrant folk communities in Italian neighborhoods and enclaves.

The willingness of Sicilian Americans to work, their frugality, and their entrepreneurial spirit made them prosperous within a generation of arrival. For example, Sicilians became prominent in the fruit and produce markets, construction trades, and garbage-hauling businesses in Chicago, Detroit, Cleveland, New York, Philadelphia, and New Orleans. Sicilians owned coal and silver mines in West Virginia, Pennsylvania, and Colorado. They became successful truck farmers in rural Texas, Louisiana, Arkansas, Mississippi, and Georgia; purchased sheep and cattle ranches in Wyoming and Arizona; and gained influence in the agricultural and fishing industries of northern California.

The sudden Sicilian prosperity unsettled nativist Americans, who viewed the swarthy newcomers with their peculiar customs and clannish behaviors as a threat to American values. Southern Italians had had to face the same kind of racial and cultural discrimination, but the Sicilians, because of their aggressive desire to succeed and their association with extortion networks such as the Black Hand and the Mafia, had to cope with the prevailing belief that they were natural-born criminals. Popular thinking asserted that if Sicilians succeeded, it was not because of their business skills or political prowess; it was because they possessed an innate propensity to conspire among their own using underhanded techniques and then resorting to the gun and the knife in vendettas (Italian for "revenge") to get what they wanted.

Little Palermos and Ethnic Enclaves

Discrimination forced the islanders to bond together into a cohesive group with a distinctive regional identity. The ties of village loyalty that had been traditional back home and that had existed during the early years of immigration began to wane. From about the 1890s through the 1950s, Sicilians clustered in enclaves, or "Little Palermos," in cities such as New Orleans, Detroit, and New York. They stayed in these neighborhoods to raise their families and observe the customs and traditions of their island culture without outside interference.

Few Little Palermos have survived into the twenty-first century, but their spirit is revived when former neighbors meet at baptisms, first Communions, confirmations, weddings, funerals, picnics, and reunions. The colonies often had ironic names, such as Cacalupo (Wolf's Den in the Boondocks) in Detroit, La Montagna (the Mountain) in flat St. Louis, and Mount Allegro (Happiness Mountain) in the industrial section of Rochester, New York. Greenbush was a Sicilian enclave in Madison, Wisconsin, formed in the early twentieth century. During its prime, the "Bush" was a thriving neighborhood of cobblers, barbers, bricklayers, laborers, and painters. This Sicilian community, like others, included village club picnics, street dances, and All Saints Day celebrations. Commercial establishments such as grocery stores, butcher shops, pool halls, and taverns served as places for neighbors to meet and exchange gossip as they went about their daily chores. The "Bush" represented a way of life that lasted until the 1960s, when the city of Madison ordered that every building (including St. Joseph's Church, rectory, convent, and school), home, street, park, and garden be eliminated as part of an urban renewal project. The community scattered to different parts of the city, but former Greenbush residents and their children still gather as part of the Greenbush Reunion Project. In addition to organizing social gatherings, the project hosts Sicilian dances at the Italian Workmen's Club and sponsors a bocce club.

Foodways, Customs, and Cultural Conservation

Among the traditional activities frequently associated with Sicilian communities are gardening; wine making; preparing *strattu* (tomato paste), *caponata* (sweet-sour eggplant salad), and *sfincione* (deep-dish pizza); celebrating pan-Sicilian religious holidays such as St. Joseph's Day with meatless dishes and St. Lucy's Day with *cuccia* (wheat berries and honey); men arguing politics at the local bar after work; women washing every Monday and baking bread every Friday; and "the boys" playing baseball, football, *morra* (a finger game), and bocce (Italian bowling) among themselves or against other ethnic neighborhoods.

Some Sicilian traditions, such as Sunday dinner, are confined to the extended family. In the Sunday dinner, close relatives and godparents congregate at the home of an elder or respected individual for a leisurely meal and convivial talk. The food is prepared by a family member selected for his or her cooking skills; it was often a grandmother or grandfather, but if neither was around, an aunt, uncle, son, or daughter could continue the tradition. In his memoir of Sicilian life in Rochester, New York, *Mount Allegro* (1942), Jerre Mangione describes the role of his father and others in the Sicilian neighborhood as the designated Sunday family cooks. His meal began with soup, salad, and pasta. The main entrée included four meat courses—such as lamb, veal, chicken, and *brusciuluna*, an intricately prepared rolled and stuffed beef specialty—four or five vegetables, celery, fennel, bread, and wine.

Afterward, the cook, who also served as master of ceremonies, would stand up, announce that it was getting dark, and proceed to "light" the room by pouring red wine into the glasses of the guests. The "lightings" might continue for two more hours before the master began toasting each relative in rhyme, pouring vermouth in a special glass that guests passed around the table. The rhymes were complimentary or congratulatory, or poked fun at the foibles of particular individuals. Although variations of the after-dinner recitation, poetry reading, or storytelling performance are held at many family gatherings in many communities, Sicilian Americans especially enjoy the closeness of family, traditional foods, and boisterous good cheer that might not be considered proper in some contexts.

Today, the descendents of the immigrant Si-

cilian generation generally do not speak the village dialect and do not always like the foods their mothers or grandparents prepared for Sunday dinners, holidays, or other ceremonial occasions. However, many are aware that they are different from mainstream Americans and other ethnics, including mainland Italians, and have used this awareness to construct an ethnic identity. Interest in genealogy, for instance, has become an obsession, as Sicilian Americans go to the Ellis Island Web site or participate in Listservs and chat rooms to find out more about their backgrounds. Others focus on Sicilian cooking, collecting vanity press cookbooks and searching for exotic Sicilian recipes to try out.

Active conservation of folklife in Sicilian communities and reclamation of Sicilian identity has been a relatively recent phenomenon compared to that of other ethnic groups. The Sicilian Culture Web site includes a "Folklore, Legends, and Traditions" page and information on Sicilian communities in Boston; Baltimore; Milwaukee; New York City; St. Louis; Wilmington, Delaware; and Montreal. But not all of the folklife efforts have been in urban communities. The Louisiana Folklife Program, for example, provides research on the rural Sicilian community of Independence, Louisiana, which also sponsors the annual Independence Italian Festival.

Although Sicilian folklife is sometimes folded into Italian American programming by public agencies, Sicilian organizations since the late twentieth century have lobbied for recognition of their own identity in cultural event planning. The Michigan Council for the Arts, for example, sponsored a series of exhibits dedicated to Detroit Sicilian family folklife traditions that featured folk music, stories, proverbs, riddles, beliefs, recipes, and domestic crafts. During the 1990s, the Associazone Culturale Siciliana sponsored an annual Festivale Siciliano in San Diego's Little Italy, and in 2003, a Sicilian society in Houston separated from the Italian society to hold its own festival, called La Festa Siciliana, featuring local folk foods, crafts, dance, and music. Like their forebears, modern Sicilian Americans identify with their island and believe that the heart of their folk culture lies in community and family.

John Allan Cicala

See also: Detroit; Foodways; Gangs; Italian Communities; New York City.

Sources

Becnel, Harry P., Jr. "Customs, Traditions, and Folklore of a Rural Southern Italian-American Community." In *Folk-life in the Florida Parishes,* 77–88. Baton Rouge: Louisiana Folklife Program and Center for Regional Studies, Southeastern Louisiana University, 1989.

Cordasco, Francesco, and Eugene Bucchioni. *The Italians: Social Backgrounds of an American Group.* Clifton, NJ: Augustus M. Kelley, 1974.

Gambino, Richard. *Blood of My Blood: The Dilemma of the Italian Americans.* Toronto: Guernica, 1997.

Lopreato, Joseph. *Italian Americans.* New York: Random House, 1970.

Mangione, Jerre. *Mount Allegro: A Memoir of Italian American Life.* 1942. Reprint, Syracuse, NY: Syracuse University Press, 1998.

Mangione, Jerre, and Ben Morreale. *La Storia: Five Centuries of the Italian American Experience.* New York: HarperPerennial, 1992.

Murray, Catherine. *A Taste of Memories from the Old "Bush": Italian Recipes and Fond Memories from the People Who Lived in Madison's Greenbush District.* 2 vols. Madison, WI: Greenbush Remembered, 1988, 1990.

Noyes, Dorothy. *Uses of Tradition: Arts of Italian-Americans in Philadelphia.* Philadelphia: Philadelphia Folklore Project, 1989.

Sicilian Culture. www.sicilianculture.com.

SIKHS

The word "Sikh" is derived from the Sanskrit term *shishya,* which literally means "disciple." Sikhism, the religion of the Sikhs, was born approximately five centuries ago in the Punjab, a region of northern India where Sikhs remain most heavily concentrated. In the twenty-first century, there are approximately twenty-three million Sikhs throughout the world; an estimated 350,000 reside in the United States and another 150,000 in Canada. Concentrated American Sikh communities are located in New York City, Houston, Washington, D.C., Detroit, and northern California. Sikhs are often noticed because of their folk customs of wearing a turban and carry-ing a *kirpan,* a ceremonial dagger considered a sacred symbol of Sikhism.

The spoken and written language of the Sikhs is Punjabi, a variant of Hindi with some Persian influence. Male members of the Sikhs use the name Singh (meaning "lion") as their middle or last name; their female counterparts use the name Kaur (meaning "princess"). Sikh men may be distinguished from other Indian men by their grooming: by tradition they wear beards and do not cut their hair, binding it in turbans to signify commitment to their faith.

Sikhism was founded by Guru Nanak Dev (1469–1539), who sought to combine tenets of Islam and Hinduism in a single creed. Religious leadership was handed down from Guru Nanak through a succession of nine later gurus (spiritual and religious teachers), selected on the basis of their exemplary lives. Before his death in 1708, Guru Gobind Singh, the tenth and last guru, declared that there would be no more successors and that the Sikh community was to seek its inspiration and guidance from the scriptures. From that point on, the *Adi Granth,* the Sikh sacred scripture, became the unchallenged authority on all matters of Sikh belief and life.

Immigration

Sikhs are usually considered the first South Asian group to emigrate to North America in significant numbers. Between 1903 and 1908 about six thousand Punjabis, most of whom were Sikhs, went to Vancouver, recruited as cheap labor, and sometimes strikebreakers, to work in lumber mills and logging camps. As anti-Asian sentiment grew in Canada and erupted into riots and led to lobbying by the Asiatic Exclusion League for immigration restrictions on South Asians, half the Punjabi population of Vancouver crossed into the United States.

With their experience in lumbering, many of the Sikh migrants worked in the logging industry in the American Northwest, but the majority went to northern California, where the Western Pacific Railway was hiring ethnic labor. Sikhs also were involved in public works projects, including

Members of a Sikh community in New York hold a candlelight vigil for the victims of the September 11, 2001 terrorist attacks. Because of their turbans and beards, Sikh men have been mistakenly associated with the Taliban and attacked, sometimes physically, for being terrorists. *(Robert Nickelsberg/Time Life Pictures/Getty Images)*

construction of bridges and tunnels. The projects were typically in the midst of fruit farms, which attracted the Sikhs because of their agricultural background in their homeland and higher wages. Northern California was also luring because of the similarity in weather and geographical conditions to those of the Punjab. The first group of Sikhs arrived in the Sacramento Valley in 1907, working in the fruit orchards of the Folsom, Orangeville, Loomis, and Newcastle areas. Others found Marysville and Yuba City, the rice-growing districts, more desirable. Immigration restrictions by the U.S. government at first prevented chain migration from the Punjab, but, after the restrictions were lifted by the Immigration Act of 1965, a number of Sikhs from the Punjabi homeland joined the Sikh pioneers in northern California and elsewhere. A major push to force Sikhs out of their homeland occurred from 1980 to 1992,

when political instability in the region resulted in the suppression of democratic rights and anti-Sikh riots. Sikhs had a variety of urban destinations in the late twentieth-century immigration to the United States, including New York City, Houston, Washington, D.C., Chicago, and Detroit, often seeking small business opportunities.

Customs and Issues of Adjustment

The Sikh communities in the United States have tried to preserve their folklife but have faced a number of challenges. For example, some Americans have confused Sikh boys, with their long hair knotted atop their heads, with members of the opposite sex—making them frequent objects of ridicule in school. Many Sikhs have also faced discrimination in seeking jobs because of distrust or prejudice against dark-skinned people with beards and turbans. Despite the risk of becoming family outcasts, this has prompted many young Sikhs to cut their hair and shave their beards. Sikhs who migrated to the United States during the period of restrictive immigration laws in the mid-twentieth century faced yet another problem. Most had been married in India and had left their families back home. The immigration laws did not allow them to bring their wives to the United States, and they were barred from visiting their homeland and then returning to the United States. Some Sikh men responded by marrying Mexican women, which led to occasional violent retaliation by Mexican men against the Sikh men and their Mexican wives.

Since the terrorist attacks of September 11, 2001, Sikh men are sometimes mistaken for terrorists because of their turbans and beards. No doubt influenced by media coverage of the war in Afghanistan, some Americans mistakenly associated Sikhs with the Taliban, who also wear turbans and beards.

Sikh folklife is perpetuated through religious, social, and cultural practices. Among the most important religious festivals are the *gurpurabs* (birthdays of the ten Sikh gurus) and *Baisakhi*, on April 13, commemorating the founding of the *Khalsa* (the Sikh brotherhood) by Guru Gobind Singh. *Baisakhi*, an important harvest festival in the Punjab, is the occasion many Sikhs choose for baptism into *Khalsa*. Traditionally, all religious festivals are celebrated in the *gurdwara*, or house of worship. Observances start two days before the festivals themselves with a continuous reading of the *Guru Granth Sahib* for forty-eight hours. Professional Sikh singers and priests sing hymns followed by prayers. Sikh religious festivals are not complete without the free *langar*, food prepared by the members of the Sikh community.

Although Diwali, "The Festival of Lights," is essentially a Hindu festival, the Sikhs also celebrate this day. One reason is that on Diwali day in 1619, the most famous Sikh *gurdwara* in the world, the Golden Temple in Amritsar, was illuminated with many lights to welcome home and celebrate the release of the sixth guru, Guru Hargobind, from imprisonment in Gwalior Fort at Jaipur. Sikhs continue to celebrate Diwali by decorating their homes with multicolored lights and candles. Children look forward to the fireworks and family feasts.

Traditional music and dance are very popular among Sikh men and women. The emotionally expressive folk music of Punjab is popular not only in India but in all the countries where Sikhs have migrated. Sikh songs are varied and colorful, conveying happiness, sadness, pain, and sorrow. Some of the popular forms of male folk dance are *bhangra, jhummer, luddi, julli, dunkara,* and *dhumal. Bhangra* is often the most recognized because of its lively motions and accompanying upbeat music.

Sikh Cultural Conservation

To expose current and future Sikh generations to their religious and cultural heritage, many Sikh communities in the United States have established community centers and cultural organizations in addition to *gurdwaras*. Regular open houses at the *gurdwaras* are part of a continuing effort by Sikhs to educate the American public about their five-hundred-year-old religion and to dispel the notion that they are terrorists. *Gurdwaras* are located in a total of thirty-seven states, with California claiming the largest number. *Gurdwaras* not only offer a space of worship but help the Sikh community interact socially, maintain native culture, and provide language instruction. Since command of Punjabi is vital to reading Sikh religious scriptures, classes are offered on Sundays at various Sikh *gurdwaras* or centers throughout the United States.

The Association of Sikh Professionals, a nonprofit organization dedicated to the welfare, growth, and benefit of the Sikh community, was formed in 1984 by Sikhs in the Midwest. Since then it has expanded its membership throughout the United States.

The Sikh American Heritage Organization (SAHO) promotes and fosters fellowship with the American mainstream and other minority communities while maintaining Sikh heritage, values, and identity. SAHO participates in Asian American events, interfaith programs, community affairs, social affairs, and other American activities. Members of SAHO organize annual sports festivals, Sikh retreats for college students, religious training camps for youth, and recognition dinners and awards to honor high school and college students from the community. Sikh societies and associations sponsor summer camps throughout the United States to promote the perpetuation of Sikh heritage among youth.

Rajinder Garcha

See also: Farmers; Northwest Coast; Religion; South Asian Communities.

Sources

Garcha, Rajinder. "The Sikhs in North America: History and Culture." *Ethnic Forum: Journal of Ethnic Studies and Ethnic Bibliography* 12, no. 2 (1992): 80–93.

Gibson, Margaret A. *Accommodation Without Assimilation: Sikh Immigrants in an American High School.* Ithaca, NY: Cornell University Press, 1988.

Gonzalez, Juan L., Jr. "Asian Indian Immigration Patterns: The Origins of the Sikh Community in California." *International Migration Review* 20, no. 1 (Spring 1986): 40–54.

Hawley, John Stratton, and Gurinder Singh Mann. *Studying the Sikhs: Issues for North America.* Albany: State University of New York Press, 1993.

Leonard, Karen Isaksen. *Making Ethnic Choices: California's Punjabi Mexican Americans.* Philadelphia: Temple University Press, 1992.

Thompson, M.R. *Sikh Belief and Practice.* London: Edward Arnold, 1985.

SKATEBOARDERS

Being a skateboarder, colloquially known as a "skater"—one who rides a narrow platform called a "deck" with wheels in a standing or crouching position—is, for many, more than a recreational pursuit. It has been a source of identity associated since the late twentieth century with adolescent boys who use a distinctive speech, dress in a certain way, and meet in places such as "skate parks" suited to their pastime.

The first skateboards were a folk craft made at home in the 1920s by attaching wheels from roller skates to wooden planks. Surfers in the 1950s began making skateboards as surfboard imitations to practice balancing on a board on land. In 1959, the first commercial adaptation of the homemade skateboard was sold as the "Roller Derby Skate Board Kit" with roller-skate "trucks" (mountings for the wheels) with clay wheels and base plates designed to mount to boards. Advances in technology during the early 1970s, especially the advent of the polyurethane wheel, allowed the boards to achieve greater speed and flexibility. The platforms were widened, and kicktails, a slope of the last three to four inches of the board, were introduced for stability. Later, toward the end of the twentieth century, skateboards narrowed again to less than eight inches, and the front nose was designed to be longer and steeper than the back tail. Wheels became smaller and harder, allowing boards to slide and rotate more easily during flip tricks.

Youth Group Identity

The idea of a youth group identity centering on skateboarding is often traced to the late 1970s in Venice, California, when a group of teenage boys calling themselves Dogtown and the Z Boys introduced an aggressive style of skateboarding based on big-wave surfing maneuvers. The Dogtown gang began skating in nontraditional places, such as drained swimming pools and schoolyard embankments, and pioneered the tradition of performing "airs," or stylistic jumps above the lip of a ramp or pool. The aggressive Dogtown style gained renown in early skateboarding magazines and on national television and inspired the competitive trick-centered riding of the twenty-first century.

A repertoire of tricks is central to a skater's status. The more tricks one can perform, and with greater style, the more prestige one has in skateboard folk groups. Skateboarders value a smooth trick performance executed with little effort. Reflecting the importance of masculinity to skateboarder identification, it is common for skaters to refer to a skilled rider as "the man."

During the late 1970s, Kona Skateboard Park in Jacksonville, Florida, with its series of ramps and half-pipes for performing tricks, inspired the construction of hundreds of similar parks nationwide. In addition, homebuilt ramps became popular, giving skateboarders more opportunities to

A repertoire of tricks, the more smoothly executed the better, is the key to status and prestige among skateboarders. Tony Hawk and other celebrity competitors have transformed skateboarding from counterculture recreation to mass-culture commercial sport. *(Jamie McDonald/Getty Images Sport)*

refine their skills. Both skate parks and homebuilt skateboard ramps are folk environments where skateboarders form social bonds. They are also sites where skateboarders learn how to skate, or improve their skill, by watching others. Skaters frequently mark these territories with graffiti of names of local and famous skateboarders, or the names of skateboarding products.

As an adolescent social group, skateboarders fit into what can be called "alternative" high school cultures. Alternative refers to the oppositional stance they often take to the mainstream high school culture of athletes and academic achievers. Skateboarders identify with street life and its groups, in contrast to institutional hierarchies. Skaters often link with other alternative groups associated with street life and music such as punk, rave, and hip-hop, and often simultaneously hold one of these other identities. Factors that unite skateboarders with such kindred groups are shared tastes in music and fashion, and a self-perception as freethinking individuals. Youth festivals such as the Gravity Games and the Vans Warped Tour, held annually in such locations as Philadelphia, Pennsylvania, and Copper Mountain, Colorado, combine punk rock and hip-hop acts with skateboarding.

Relation to High School Culture and Extreme Sports

While skateboarding requires physical effort equal to that of traditional high school sports, there is often an opposition between skaters and traditional high school athletes, or "jocks." One of the reasons for this opposition is that skaters view traditional sports as putting limits on creativity and individualism. Traditional sports require strict observation of rules and a competitive ethic, an overriding concern with winning, and the wearing of uniforms, all of which are antithetical to a skater's sense of freedom. Whereas jocks usually dominate high school popularity hierarchies, skaters typically achieve status in their own groups for being antipopular. Aware of skater folk attitudes, skateboard companies promote brand names such as Zero and Anti-Hero.

Typically, skateboarders get along well with, or engage in, other kinds of "extreme," or alternative, sports such as surfing, snowboarding, and freestyle BMX riding (bicycles with twenty-inch wheels designed after MX, or motor-cross, bikes). Since skateboarding has roots in surfing culture, it shares a number of cultural traits with surfing, especially the folk speech of "frontside" and "backside" (in surfing, the direction surfers turn if they are traveling up a wave, and in skating the direction of one's rotation). However, there is often animosity between skaters and in-line skaters. Socially, skaters often think of in-line skaters in derogatory terms, typically categorizing the activity as female or juvenile. In creating outsider categories of jocks and in-line skaters, skaters reinforce their own masculine, antipopular identity.

In addition to organizing themselves in relation to other high school groups and alternative sports, skateboarders classify themselves on the basis of riding terrain. Street skaters take advantage of urban environments, seeing park benches, trashcans, stairs, handrails, and other obstacles as sites for trick performances. Ramp skaters, on the other hand, tend to ride ramps called "half-pipes." Some half-pipes have vertical riding surfaces, making them "vert" half-pipes. Pool skateboarders ride in drained swimming pools or in simulated pool spaces in skate parks. Freestyle skateboarders, by contrast, require no obstacles and perform skateboarding tricks on flat, paved surfaces. Although skateboarders often segment themselves into one of these riding styles, there is often an amazing degree of crossover. For example, freestyle and ramp tricks have merged with street skating, and street-skating tricks have become popular on ramps. Moreover, many skaters ride one or more of the aforementioned terrains, making them "all-around skaters." In addition, skate parks often feature a combination of street obstacles, ramps, and pools, giving skaters the opportunity to perfect their skills in a number of riding situations. No single riding terrain is considered superior in skating culture, although street skaters dominate the sport.

Folk Speech and Dress

Riding style is a common subject of skater talk. One who has poor style or barely lands a trick is said to have a "sketchy" style. One who is able to skillfully create variations in tricks or to link a series of complicated tricks is said to be a "technical" skateboarder. Skaters who perform tricks popular in the 1980s or before are often referred to as having an "old-school style." Those who keep current with the latest tricks are referred to as having a "new-school style."

Skateboarders have more names for tricks than tricks themselves. Some of the most common ones are called the "ollie," the "grind," the "air," and the "stall." Many tricks have more than one name. For example, the "ollie nosebone" and "ollie melancholy" are the same trick, in which the rider "ollies" (performs a jump on the board), grabs the board, and tweaks it forward. Another example is the "ollie zit," "one foot," or "ollie north," in which the rider ollies and kicks his or her front foot off the front of the board. Variations in trick terminology vary across geographic boundaries.

Oral traditions exist with respect to talking about tricks as well. A skateboarder who spends a lot of money on equipment or wears skater-style clothing, yet does not ride, is called a "poser." A trick performed on a large staircase or ramp is called "gnarly" because it is difficult and even dangerous. Borrowing slang from hip-hop culture, tricks can be "phat" or "dope," meaning that they are performed with expert skill. If an especially challenging trick is performed, it may be referred to as being "sick," meaning that the trick is amazing and innovative.

Skateboarders often wear baggy clothes, such as oversized cargo shorts and pants, and oversized T-shirts, that contribute to their social identities. In addition to being stylistic indicators, baggy clothes serve a functional purpose in skating, allowing for easy movement. However, it is likely that skateboarders adopted the wearing of baggy clothing from hip-hop culture, since both are associated with street life. Baggy clothing is another means by which skaters differentiate themselves from traditional organized sports. Where baggy clothing conceals body outlines, sports uniforms tend to accentuate muscularity. Skaters also wear T-shirts with skateboard company logos or worker-style shirts complete with nametags.

Hero and Commercial Culture

Skaters also share in a distinctive hero culture. Since skateboarding adopted competitions and teams in the 1970s, skaters have looked up to professional skateboarders as celebrities. Skaters often show deference to their heroes by consuming that skater's brand of videos, skateboard decks, shoes, clothing, and video games. Some go so far as adopting their favorite skateboarder's style. It is not uncommon for skaters to refer to each other's styles in reference to their favorite professional. For example, a street skater adept at combining complicated tricks might be said to skate like Eric Koston, known as a master of street skateboarding (who won the X Games in San Francisco and the Gravity Games in Providence, Rhode Island, in 2000). The hero culture has come to conflict with claims of countercultural individuality, putting skateboarding squarely in the realm of mass-culture sports that promote heroes based on athletic performance. One fundamental distinction, however, is that many professional skateboarders do not compete in contests, but instead perform demonstration shows and make appearances in skateboard videos.

Veteran skateboarders who prided themselves on the vernacular character of the activity complain that the hero worship and commercialism of twenty-first-century skateboarding prevents young skateboarders from developing localized folk groups that are not tied to market conceptions of how a skater should look and act. Indeed, many skateboarders growing up in the era of organized televised competitions such as the X Games and other advertiser-driven "extreme sports competitions," aspire to be professional skateboarders, spending long and grueling hours of practice at the expense of fun. In this respect, critics of commercial culture observe, skateboarding is meeting a fate similar to that of hip-hop, a tradition arising from street life that developed into a popular commercial form. Still, in many high schools, the identity of skater groups persists as an alternative social tradition in which members are recognized by their speech and dress as well as their recreational interest.

Michael McCombs

See also: Adolescents; Children's Groups; Games and Toys; Gangs, Youth; Hip-Hop; Popular Culture; Students.

Sources

Borden, Iain. *Skateboarding, Space and the City: Architecture and the Body.* Oxford: Berg, 2001.
Brooke, Michael. *The Concrete Wave: The History of Skateboarding.* Toronto: Warwick, 1999.
Davis, James. *Skateboarding Is Not a Crime: 50 Years of Street Culture.* Richmond Hill, Ontario: Firefly Books, 2004.
Dogtown and Z Boys. DVD. Directed by Stacy Peralta. Culver City, CA: Sony Pictures, 2002.
Hawk, Tony. *Hawk: Occupation Skateboarder.* New York: ReganBooks, 2001.
Thatcher, Kevin, ed. *How to Build Skateboard Ramps: Halfpipes, Boxes, Bowls, and More.* San Francisco: High Speed, 2001.

SKINHEADS

The term "skinheads" or "skins" is applied generally to teenagers and young adults who shave their heads and associate with an alternative youth subculture. The act of shaving the head in a society that values the style of hair or imitates elite, individualized tastes typically symbolizes social solidarity and the countercultural attitude of most skinheads. The shaved head communicates a working-class or military aesthetic and is often interpreted as being aggressive. In addition to shaving their heads, skins adopt other expressions of a folklife, including dress, speech, and music. Originating in England in the 1960s and spreading to the United States and Canada in the 1970s and 1980s, the skinhead movement comprises several categories, often in opposition to one another. Nazi skinheads, also called White Power, advocate racist beliefs and are highly political, while groups calling themselves SHARP (Skinheads Against Racial Prejudice), ARA (Anti-Racist Action), and RASH (Red and Anarchist Skinheads) work intensively against racism. A third set of skinhead groups identifies with the original movement in music, dress, and working-class pride. They often use the names "traditional," "trad," Trojan (after the Trojan Records label), or "original skins." Even within these broad categories, there are subgroups, such as "redskins" (communists), "hammerskins" (militant racists), and gay skinheads. The Anti-Defamation League estimates that the number of organized skinheads in the United States grew from approximately a thousand members in twelve states during the 1980s to more than three thousand in forty states by the year 2000. Mag-

A group of skinheads congregates outside a London shop in the mid-1980s. The original skin culture was in decline by this time, replaced by groups in Britain and the United States—some neo-Nazi—that popularized the style with which skinheads became associated: jeans, bomber jackets, and steel-tipped boots. *(Sue Adler/Hulton Archives/Getty Images)*

azines and Web sites featuring skinhead music and ideology claim many thousands more. The Southern Poverty Law Center counted forty-eight chapters of twenty-eight named racist skinhead groups in 2004, up from eighteen chapters in 2002. The states with the greatest number of skinheads are New Jersey, Texas, Oregon, California, Florida, Michigan, and Virginia.

British Roots

The first skinheads appeared in England during the 1960s. Skinhead culture had its roots in two English working-class youth cultures of the 1960s: the Mods and the Rude Boys. Mods were working-class white youth whose culture focused on style, specifically expensive clothing and mod-

ified Vespa scooters. Rude Boys were working-class Jamaican or West Indian youth from southeast London who were as style-conscious as the Mods. Rude Boys favored reggae music, although it was a reggae that blended elements of jazz, blues, and soul into two distinctly British sounds: ska and rocksteady.

By 1968, some of the tougher element broke off from Mod culture and formed their own group as skins. The early skins felt that the stylish Mod culture, as it was developing, and the back-to-nature hippie movement, identified by unstyled long hair, clashed with their working-class roots. Concurrently, football (soccer in the United States) was becoming more popular, and the early skins became passionately devoted to their teams, giving them a chance to publicly show solidarity and an opportunity to pick fights with supporters of other teams.

Racism did not become a part of skinhead culture until much later in the 1970s. Many early gangs were actually multiracial, and the Rude Boy culture was much admired. The shared social and cultural connection lay in the working-class backgrounds and a sense of being cut off from the dominant society. By the end of the 1970s, traditional skin culture was in decline, and a new skin movement called Plastic Skin became the dominant skinhead culture. Plastic Skins adopted Nazi regalia on their clothing, Nazi tattoos (as well as "Made in London" tattooed across their foreheads, indicative of their new, ethnocentric perspective), and what is now considered typical skinhead style—jeans and bomber jackets, steel-toed boots (Doc Martens), and shaved heads. Jeans and jackets could not be torn in a fight, steel-toed boots made effective weapons, and shaved heads limited the enemy's ability to grab hold of them. The function of skinhead gangs changed by this time as well; it was no longer about following music and sports teams as much as about drinking and violence.

American Skins

Early American skins were violent street gangs, such as the Romantic Violence in Chicago and the West Side Boot Boys in Detroit, whose members openly were fans of punk rock bands such as Skrewdriver, from England, featuring songs with racist lyrics. By the late 1980s, Tom Metzger of the hate group White Aryan Resistance in Fallbrook, California, began to mobilize skins by financing and promoting what were called "Aryan Woodstocks." These events were outdoor music festivals featuring Skrewdriver and American-bred bands such as Bound for Glory (from Minnesota) and Das Reich (from Wisconsin). A skin backlash began in New York City in 1987 with the founding of SHARP. SHARP began as a nonviolent, antiracist organization and as a reaction to the dominant white-power skin ideology in the United States at the time. Within a few years, however, SHARP splintered, as some members

felt that the best way to combat hate was with physical confrontation. During the 1990s, rock concerts became a frequent setting for racist and antiracist skinhead fighting.

Early American skin style for both men and women generally followed British skin style. Men shaved their heads and eschewed facial hair, with the exception of sideburns, and wore air force flight jackets with tight, turned-up jeans and suspenders. Tattoos were typically of Norse mythology such as the evil god Loki, supremacist organization initials, and Nazi symbols. Doc Marten shoes were also popular with American racist skins, and the color of the laces was symbolic: white laces stood for white pride; red laces indicated a neo-Nazi willing to shed blood; and green laces indicated a gay basher. While Mods and the earliest British skin gangs practiced a form of gender equality, racist American skin women, called "skingirls" and "skinbyrds," adopted a more subservient role, with the function of having many Aryan babies. Female skin style during the 1980s included a punkish haircut dyed green, yellow, or purple, or a "feathercut" haircut (short hair on the crown, sides, and back, with a longer fringe in the front and on the neck). Women's dress often imitated male skin garb, but the short kilt skirt or other miniskirt with fishnet stockings and Doc Martens was also popular for the women.

Into the twenty-first century, racist skins have modified their style, growing out their hair and covering their tattoos. As with other gangs that wish to become successful, racist or neo-Nazi skins have found that a low profile limits police contact and makes for a more effective organization. Contemporary skin music is exemplified by Resistance Records, which produces the current generation of skin (Skrewdriver-style) music. Straight Edge gangs, while similar in appearance to skinheads in that they are made up of white youth and tend toward shaved or very closely cut hair, stand ideologically between SHARP and neo-Nazi skin gangs. The defining characteristic of Straight Edge gangs is their rejection of tobacco, alcohol, drugs, and casual sex.

A number of highly publicized convictions of racist skins for conspiracies and violent acts during the 1990s brought national attention to the problem of American skins. The U.S. Department of Justice established a skinhead task force within its Civil Rights Division in 1989. A prominent case was the arrest of members of the Fourth Reich Skinhead gang in Los Angeles, California, in 1993, for a plan to incite a race war by, among other things, bombing an African American church, sending a letter bomb to a rabbi, and assassinating several well-known African American figures.

In the twenty-first century, organizations that monitor hate groups differ on whether skinhead activity peaked during the 1990s or is entering a new growth phase by changing some of its practices. Some observers report that new skinheads operate independently, socializing in relatively small crews apparently not affiliated with larger organizations. Some racist skinhead groups organize invented traditions to bind the group, such as ceremonies marking Adolf Hitler's birthday on April 20; the Northwest Hammerskins tried to establish "Martyr's Day" as an annual event in Whidbey Island, Washington, in 2004, to honor Robert Matthews of the hate group called the Order who was killed at the island in a 1984 shootout with the FBI. The Southern Poverty Law Center observed in 2004 that New Jersey was a hotbed of racist skinhead activity, with active crews of Eastern Hammerskins, AC Skins, Bergen County Hooligans, and Trenton State Skinheads. The center was also concerned about an increase in the number of skinhead Web sites, reaching twenty-six in 2004, reflecting the growth of electronic communities subscribing to racist skinhead ideology and practices. While skinhead culture continues to attract teenage males in particular, it appears that skins in the twenty-first century have diverged from the working-class tradition of the movement and come from a diversity of socioeconomic backgrounds.

Pamela Preston and Simon J. Bronner

See also: Gangs; Gangs, Youth; Ku Klux Klan; Nationalism.

Sources

Bushart, Howard L., John R. Craig, and Myrna Barnes. *Soldiers of God: White Supremacists and Their Holy War for America.* New York: Kensington, 1998.

Christensen, Loren W. *Skinhead Street Gangs.* Boulder, CO: Paladin, 1994.

Knight, Nick. *Skinhead.* London: Omnibus, 1982.

Landre, Rick, Mike Miller, and Dee Porter. *Gangs: A Handbook for Community Awareness.* New York: Facts on File, 1997.

Moore, Jack B. *Skinheads Shaved for Battle: A Cultural History of American Skinheads.* Bowling Green, OH: Bowling Green State University Popular Press, 1993.

Valdez, Al. *Gangs: A Guide to Understanding Street Gangs.* 3rd ed. San Clemente, CA: Law Tech, 2000.

Wooden, Wayne S., and Randy Blazak. *Renegade Kids, Suburban Outlaws: From Youth Culture to Delinquency.* Belmont, CA: Wadsworth, 2001.

SLANG

See Folk Speech and Language

SLOVAK COMMUNITIES

Slovak American communities typically trace their heritage to eastern European immigrants who came to the United States in the late nineteenth and early twentieth centuries to work in industrial factories and mines from New York, New Jersey, and Pennsylvania in the East to Ohio, Illinois, Michigan, and Wisconsin in the Midwest. Slovakian immigrants came from what is known today as the Slovak Republic in central Europe, distinguished from the Czech Republic and Austria to the west, Poland to the north, Ukraine to the east, and Hungary to the south. Until World War I, Slovakia was a part of the Austro-Hungarian Empire, becoming part of a new, integrated Czecho-Slovak republic in 1918. Since the Austro-Hungarian Empire included the territory of neighboring Poland and Ukraine, many Slovak emigrants shared cultural characteristics with their Slavic neighbors. Aside from a short period of formal independence during World War II, Slovaks lived in a common state with Czechs until January 1, 1993, when a spirit of nationalism based on religious and linguistic differences led to the creation of independent nation-states.

According to the 2000 U.S. census, about eight hundred thousand people in America declared at least partial Slovak ethnic heritage. An additional thirty-one thousand people of Slovak ancestry live in Canada. Slovak communities containing ethnic centers such as fraternal organizations, churches, and cultural centers have been centered since the late nineteenth century in cities of the East and Midwest such as Pittsburgh, Johnstown, and Hazleton, Pennsylvania; Youngstown and Cleveland, Ohio; and Chicago. Notable Slovak communities emerging in the twentieth century include those in New York City and Los Angeles.

Immigration and Politics

Although the first known U.S. immigrant from the territory of Slovakia, Isaac Ferdinand Sarosi (*Sarišský*), settled in Germantown, Pennsylvania, in 1677, the mass influx of Slovaks to the United States did not begin until the 1870s. The primary reason for emigration from the homeland was economic hardship, as well as effort by the ruling Magyars (Hungarians) to eradicate the Slovak language and culture. The number of Slovaks entering the United States is difficult to estimate because most of those who arrived before the census of 1910 were registered as Hungarians, according to their country of origin. In addition, the folk identity of many was more closely tied to a regional (Šariš, Spiš, Orava, or Zemplín) rather than national (Slovak or Austro-Hungarian) heritage. By 1914, about half a million Slovaks—equal to almost one-quarter of the entire Slovak nation—lived in the United States. Most of them came from the poor regions of eastern and northern Slovakia. In 1945, about five thousand sympathizers with the Slovak regime during World War II, compromised by collaboration with Nazi Germany, sought safe haven largely in the United States and Argentina. The next politically motivated wave of immigration followed the events of August 1968, when Soviet tanks crushed the democratic reforms known as "Prague Spring." The most recent influx, after the fall of communism, mainly comprises economic emigrants looking for a better life. While the immigrants of 1945 were still generally willing to connect with the established Slovak American communities (since many newcomers represented the dream of Slovak in-

dependence), the emigrants of 1968 and 1989 settled mostly in major cities such as New York, Chicago, and Los Angeles and showed less enthusiasm for Slovak fraternal activities.

According to unofficial estimates by the Slovak embassy, about a hundred thousand Slovaks have come to the United States in the 1990s. Some are legal workers in the high-tech sector, but a large percentage are illegal workers who have overstayed their tourist visas. Although their goal is often to dissolve into U.S. society, these more recent immigrants participate in ethnic folklife by gathering for dances, cultural and social events, or friendly soccer matches, where they often share in Slovak cuisine.

Religious Traditions

Several factors have determined the character of Slovak American folklife, in ways that both separated it from and connected it with the Slovak homeland. One notable difference is the industrial and urban life for those who arrived at around the turn of the twentieth century. Four out of five Slovak immigrants were poor farmers, and about two-thirds were men. Most found a new livelihood in heavy industry—mainly in coal mines and steel mills. Church services and church-related fraternal activities were the natural center of social life, and clergymen were often the only intellectuals.

At the same time, religion was also a strong dividing factor among Slovak communities. Although Slovakia is predominantly Roman Catholic, the proportion of Roman Catholics to Greek Catholics and Lutherans is more balanced among American Slovaks. Because Lutherans used Old Czech as their liturgical language, they were comfortable with the idea of a common state with predominantly Protestant Czechs. Catholics, however, tended to advocate for Slovak independence. *Za Boha a Národ* (For God and Nation) is still the subtitle of the most influential Slovak American Catholic newspaper *Jednota* (Union) founded in 1891.

The early immigrant community of Hazleton, Pennsylvania, located in the state's anthracite coal-mining region, exemplifies the religious foundation of Slovak communities and the persistence of religious folklife. Worshippers in the town, many of whom are descendants of nineteenth-century immigrants, are served by two Slovak Catholic, two Slovak Lutheran, and one Slovak Greek Catholic churches. St. Joseph Roman Catholic Church, founded in 1882, claims to be the oldest Slovak Catholic church in the Western Hemisphere. The accent of ethnic Slovaks, along with Poles and Lithuanians—all indiscriminately referred to as "Hunkies" (Hungarians)—is still commonly heard. Later generations, however, are sometimes referred to as "*Jak še maš?* [How are you?] Slovaks," referring to the fact that they know little more of the language than the common greeting. Yet, the Easter liturgy in Catholic churches still includes Slovak procession traditions. In the afternoon of Biela—White Saturday, preceding Easter—worshippers are organized into a procession behind a cross carried by an altar boy. Following behind the cross are, in order, small children, school-age children, single women, single men, the remaining altar boys, and the priest carrying a monstrance beneath a canopy. Worshippers sing Easter hymns; at several points in the procession, they pause and face the priest with the monstrance, who gives a blessing for the sick in all four directions.

Although many Slovak Catholic churches have merged with other formerly ethnic churches or limited their use of the Slovak language, some, such as St. Simon the Apostle Church in Chicago, established by Slovak immigrants in 1916, continue to serve the ethnic community. Besides sponsoring Slovak-language classes, it hosts breakfasts for Slovak speakers and is home to the Slovak Society to preserve the national heritage.

The Slovak Zion Synod, comprising 6,010 Lutherans in thirty-two congregations across the Midwest and Northeast, is the last remaining Lutheran synod in the Evangelical Lutheran Church in America organized on ethnic grounds, although many of its pastors are non-Slovak in origin. At Hazleton's St. Peter and Paul Slovak Lutheran Church (founded in 1902), services were held in Slovak until the 1960s, when the switch was made to English. Churches such as St. Peter and Paul Lutheran Church in Lakewood, Ohio, hold Slovak services twice a month, while others, such as the Ascension Lutheran Church in Binghamton, New York, do so periodically.

Food and Festival

Entering a Slovak American house, one may notice painted majolica dishes hanging on the walls and crystal glasses in the living room. Painted eggs are a typical decoration for Easter. A handful of Slovak American artists perpetuate craft traditions of embroidery, glass painting, ceramics, and basket or wheat ornament weaving. Slovak folk artist Sidonka Wadina of Lyons, Wisconsin, is known especially for her handwoven straw designs based on traditional harvest mythology and folk symbols of abundance, good fortune, and health. Making straw ornaments, decorating Easter eggs, and painting wood, she has been featured as a master of Slovak folk art at a variety of folklife festivals and has promoted the tradition by conducting workshops at Slovak cultural centers and societies.

Slovak folklife is perhaps most visible in the kitchen. Slovak Americans enjoy eating pierogi, filled pasta similar to Italian ravioli, and *holupki*, cabbage leaves stuffed with minced meat and rice. Pierogis generally come in four varieties: filled with cottage cheese, stewed prunes, potatoes, or a bacon-cabbage mixture. Many Slovak foods are evident at Easter time. Traditional fare includes hard-boiled eggs, *sunka* (smoked ham), *klobasy* (smoked sausage), *slanina* (smoked bacon), *cvikla schrenom* (a mixture of grated beets, horseradish root, salt, and vinegar), rye bread, *syrek* (a custardlike cheese made of eggs, milk, salt, sugar, and vanilla), and a baked stuffing called *plnka* or *nadievka*, made from white bread rolls, diced ham, eggs, onions, broth, and seasonings. Easter breads called *paska* and *babka*, as well as *vel 'konočy baránok* (a special Easter cake in the shape of a lamb), also are served.

The most colorful tradition still observed among American Slovaks is the celebration of Christmas. According to the central European tradition, it culminates in the Christmas Eve family dinner, called by some *Vilija* (vigil), by others *Štedrá večera* (bountiful dinner). The celebration starts when the first star appears in the sky. "With roots in the Passover supper of the Old Testament, the meal is filled with ritual and meaning," writes Fr. George M. Franko of Youngstown, Ohio. Although there are some common features, each family has its own menu and tradition. The observance starts with readings from the Bible, carol singing, and blessings by the head of the family. Everyone gets *oplátky* (thin wafers), as reminders of Christ's Last Supper. The wafers are dipped in honey (symbolizing the sweetness of life), but some families also use pepper (for the harshness of life) and garlic (for good health) as accompaniments. Hay spread on the floor signifies the lowly birth of the poor Christ child, and money placed on the table symbolizes prosperity. Each family member receives and opens a walnut or apple from a basket on the table; the fruit inside promises good health in the upcoming year. The main dishes—ever plentiful and abundant—follow. The most common, perhaps, is *kapustnica* (sauerkraut soup with mushrooms and dried prunes). *Pupáčky, opekance,* or *bobaľky* (the name varies by region of origin) are small pieces of baked bread dough softened in hot milk, served with ground walnut or poppy seed, and sweetened with honey. The main dish among Catholic families is fish (traditionally *kapor*, or carp); Lutherans may serve pork, beef, or poultry. Tea or coffee follows, served with *koláče* (walnut or poppy-seed rolls).

After dinner, families sing *koledy* (carols). In the old days the children went out to *vinšovať* or to sing carols to their neighbors. The Christmas season ends at *Tri krále* (Feast of the Three Kings, on January 6). Catholic priests bless the houses on that day, marking the "G+M+B" (*Gašpar, Melicher, Baltazár*) sign above the doorway. Although most Slovak American families follow American traditions regarding gift giving, followers of the old tradition open their Christmas gifts immediately after the dinner. In the Slovak tradition, there are no stockings on Christmas Day. Instead, small gifts are given to the children on the morning of December 6, the feast of St. Nicholas. Children put their polished shoes in the window the night before, and find candies, little toys, or books inside. There is always a little bit of coal to remind children of their bad behavior. Greek Orthodox Slovaks follow the old Eastern calendar and celebrate the Christmas season starting on January 6.

Slovak American groups often hold picnics during the summer, many organized around the feast of St. Cyril and St. Methodious, two Greek Slavic brothers from Thessalonica who came to Slovakia in 863 C.E. with the mission of spreading Christianity and literacy. Cyril was the author of the original (and eponymous) Cyrillic Slavic alphabet and is recognized as the author of the first translation of the Bible (the Gospel of St. John) into the Paleo-Slavic language, still the liturgical language among the Greek Catholics. Slovak Catholics observe the annual feast of the Virgin of Seven Sorrows, Slovakia's national patron, on September 15.

Public festivals sponsored by cultural organizations such as the Federated Slovak Societies celebrate folklife to help preserve ethnic heritage. One of the oldest is Slovak American Day in Franklin, Wisconsin, established in 1930, featuring food, dance, and music. It typically features organized bands of musicians and dancers, such as the Lipa Slovak Folk Dancers from Bloomington, Minnesota, who dress in peasant-style costumes and punctuate their circle and couple dances with stomps, whistles, and twirls. Dedicated to the maintenance of Slovak heritage in future generations, such groups offer instruction in folk arts at schools and cultural centers. Slovak Garden, a retirement community in Winter Park, Florida, declares as its mission to perpetuate the "Slovak language, cultural heritage, and music," sponsoring a Slovakfest, Slovak Day, and a Slovak museum featuring crafts and other elements of national folklife. Fraternal organizations such as Czech and Slovak Sokol in Minnesota sponsor "cultural day camps" and reach out to children to involve them in learning Slovak traditions such as songs, dances, and crafts.

Juraj Kittler and Simon J. Bronner

See also: Catholics; Chicago; Czech Communities; Easter; Lutherans; Pittsburgh; Polish Communities; Polka.

Sources

Alexander, June Granatir. *The Immigrant Church and Community: Pittsburgh's Slovak Catholics and Lutherans, 1880–1915.* Pittsburgh: University of Pittsburgh Press, 1987.

Cincura, Andrew. "Slovak and Ruthenian Easter Eggs in America: The Impact of Culture Contact on Immigrant Art and Custom." *Journal of Popular Culture* 4 (1970): 155–93.

Krajsa, Joseph C., ed. *Slovaks in America.* Middletown, PA: Slovak League of America, 1978.

Nettl, Bruno, and Moravcik, Ivo. "Czech and Slovak Songs Collected in Detroit." *Midwest Folklore* 5 (1955): 37–49.

Pirkova-Jakobson, Svatava. "Harvest Festivals Among Czechs and Slovaks in America." *Journal of American Folklore* 69 (1956): 266–80.

Seckar, Alvena V. "Slovak Wedding Customs." *New York Folklore Quarterly* 3 (1947): 189–205.

Stolarik, M. Mark. *Growing Up on the South Side: Three Generations of Slovaks in Bethlehem, Pennsylvania, 1880–1976.* Lewisburg, PA: Bucknell University Press, 1985.

SLOVENIAN COMMUNITIES

See Serbian, Slovenian, and Montenegrin Communities.

SNAKE-HANDLING SECTS

Snake-handling sects derive their name from a literal interpretation of the Gospel according to Mark 16:17–18. In this passage, Jesus says, "And these signs shall follow them that believe; In my name shall they cast out devils; they shall speak with new tongues; they shall take up serpents; and if they drink any deadly thing, it shall not hurt them; they shall lay hands on the sick, and they shall recover." Snake handlers (or serpent handlers, as they prefer to be called) believe they are carrying out the words of Jesus by handling snakes and drinking "any deadly thing." Thus, the climax of a snake-handling service is the release of snakes for worshippers to pick up or poison to drink. Originally part of the Pentecostal movement in America in the early twentieth century,

snake-handling preachers formed independent Pentecostal Holiness churches, generally known as the Church of God with Signs Following, during the 1940s.

Each snake-handling or "sign-following" church is autonomous. Membership typically consists of a number of extended families; indeed, the community itself represents a kind of large extended family. Since many churches do not report or advertise their snake-handling practices, estimates of the number of snake-handling churches vary, but probably are in the range of one hundred. Owing to the autonomy of each snake-handling group, it is difficult to know exactly how many people currently are members of snake-handling sects, but estimates range between one thousand and two thousand church members, of which only five hundred actively practice ceremonial snake handling, mostly centered in east Tennessee and Kentucky, but also found in Florida, Texas, North Carolina, Virginia, West Virginia, North Carolina, and Georgia.

Origins and Development

The Baptist preacher George Went Hensley is generally regarded as the first person in the twentieth century to handle a serpent in obedience to biblical text. Legend has it that in 1910, after reading Mark 16:18 to the congregation, he took a rattlesnake box into the pulpit of the Church of God in Cleveland, Tennessee, and lifted out a viper to demonstrate his faith in God. He then challenged his congregation to do the same. According to other accounts, a group of men attempting to make fun of Hensley put a box of rattlers at his feet while he was preaching Mark 16, but, without missing a step, Hensley reached into the box, picked up a snake, and continued to preach. Whichever version is true, news spread throughout the hills of southeastern Tennessee, and before long others joined in the handling of snakes in the Church of God. The practice continued for ten years, until one of the faithful died of a snakebite.

Ambrose J. Thomlinson, a traveling Bible salesman and founder of the Church of God of

Prophecy (a Pentecostal denomination), ordained Hensley into the gospel ministry, and for the next ten years he preached and demonstrated snake handling throughout Tennessee. Amid marital difficulties in the 1920s, Hensley resigned his ministry and was arrested for assault with a knife and selling liquor (illegal under Prohibition). He was sent to work on a chain gang but escaped to Ohio, where he remarried and resumed preaching and handling snakes. He moved back to Kentucky, and his fame spread.

In 1928, the Church of God in Prophecy revoked Hensley's license to preach and forbade its members from further handling of snakes. Interest in the practice began to ebb. In the 1940s, however, snake handling saw a resurgence led by Raymond Harris and Tom Harden, who started the Dolley Pond Church of God with Signs Following in Grasshopper Valley, in southeastern Tennessee. During this period, reports estimated the number of snake handlers at twenty-five hundred.

The 1945 snakebite-related death of a congregant led to the 1947 banning of snake handling in Tennessee. Hensley, now advanced in years, nonetheless persisted in the practice and in 1948 was arrested in Chattanooga under the new statute. North Carolina followed suit and shut down the Interstate Convention of believers in Durham in 1947. Ensuing court challenges to the laws were left unresolved. After three people died in Tennessee and Georgia in 1971 from either snake bites or strychnine poisoning, snake handling came under attack once more. The ban was challenged, this time on First Amendment grounds, but the Tennessee State Supreme Court reaffirmed it in 1973. Nevertheless, local authorities were reluctant to enforce the statutes, and snake handling persisted. Between 1936 and 1973, a total of thirty-five persons were reported to have died from poisonous bites. Among them was Hensley, who died on June 24, 1955, at age seventy-four.

While snake handlers in North Carolina, Kentucky, Tennessee, and Virginia all trace their heritage to George Hensley, the sign followers in Alabama and Georgia have a different origin. In-

Snake-handling or "sign-following" churches date to the early 1900s in Tennessee and underwent a revival throughout the Southeast in the 1940s. Although it is illegal in many states, snake handling is still practiced in certain fundamentalist Christian churches. *(Francis Miller/Time Life Pictures/Getty Images)*

dependent of Hensley, James Miller brought the practice of serpent handling to Sand Mountain, Alabama, around 1912, and by 1920 he had spread the practice into southern Georgia.

Much about the snake-handling movement—even its origins—is not without controversy. Since the movement has its roots among what were then largely illiterate people, the historical facts of the movement have been passed from one generation to the next orally. As a result, some sources say the movement began in 1909, 1910, or 1913. Much is legend, often conveying the religious fervor and righteousness of the movement's founders.

Religious Beliefs and Traditions

Although conservative Christians generally believe in the inerrancy of the Bible, holding that God inspired its authors to write an error-free text, the concept applies only to the original copies and not to later additions, deletions, or so-called corrections. Among the latter, some believe, are the passages after Mark 16:8. Thus, since the practice of serpent handling is based on Mark 16:17–18, it is possible that the serpent-handling sects base their faith on an "apocryphal addition" to the Bible. In fact, some versions of the Bible do not include the controversial passages, and few fundamentalist churches take the Bible literally on serpent handling. Besides the handling of serpents, some congregations encourage the drinking of poison during the worship service. They base their beliefs on Mark 16:18: "And if they drink any deadly thing, it shall not hurt them." The most common substance is strychnine.

The sign-follower movement has been associated with isolated Appalachian mining communities, but the social profile has expanded in the twenty-first century to include urban areas such as Atlanta. Regardless, the tradition is still of an intensely close-knit group. Worshippers usually come from less than a few miles away and are often interrelated by family bonds. Little more than the Bible has been read. Television is frowned upon; movies are seldom attended; no biblical commentaries are ever read; church history is unknown. The Bible is communicated primarily through oral tradition. There is little awareness of other world religions.

Contrary to what many Christians have accused them of doing, serpent handlers say they are not testing their faith, nor do they feel that they are testing God. Serpent handlers believe that they are protected because they take the Bible literally. A typical snake-handling meeting usually consists of songs of worship and preaching, as in other Pentecostal churches. The designated area for handling snakes is behind the altar at the front of the church. Many participants bring their own boxes containing rattlers, copperheads, and other poisonous species. According to scripture, the snakes symbolize Satan. Thus, by picking up the snake, the handler demonstrates his or her power over Satan. As the service progresses, those who believe they have received a special blessing from God open the box lids and lift the snakes high into the air. Some hold several snakes at a time, allowing them to slither and wrap themselves around their bodies. Usually the snake-handling members slip into altered states of consciousness during such episodes. Their eyes roll back and they twirl or dance in the Spirit and speak in tongues.

Snake-handling churches embrace the Oneness Pentecostal doctrines, including baptism in the name of Jesus (rather than the Holy Trinity), baptism for remission of sins, the giving of the Holy Ghost subsequent to baptism, and speaking in tongues as the evidence of salvation. In addition, they call upon their members to practice holiness in dress and demeanor. Women are forbidden to wear pants or cut their hair. Members of the same sex greet each other with a "holy kiss." They rarely go to doctors or take medicine, believing in faith healing by the laying on of hands, according to Mark 16:18 ("they shall lay hands on the sick, and they shall recover").

Music plays a prominent role in church services, with preachers using it to get worshippers "in the Spirit"—that is, prepared to handle snakes or to receive laying hands on the sick. Folklorists have observed that many of the improvised melodies played on guitars and pianos are based on commercial bluegrass and country music with twelve- and sixteen-bar blues progressions; tambourines are a common accompaniment. The melodies are typically set to religious prose and biblical texts. It is not uncommon for worshippers to dance to the music in the area between the pulpit and pews where the serpent handling and poison drinking occurs. Such use of music and dance, ethnographies suggest, contributes to creation of altered states of consciousness that worshippers describe as the "anointment" or "gift" of the Holy Ghost, or the Spirit of God entering or possessing an individual. Testimonies describing the experience of anointment often refer to a spiritual trancelike power or a physical numbness. Many attribute the feeling to the release of evil or "demon power" from one's body, which at the same time draws out the devilish serpents from the box.

Churches that practice snake handling tend to

be wary of publicity. The desire for privacy stems from negative media coverage that inevitably follows death or injury from snakebites or the drinking of strychnine. With few exceptions, newspapers, magazines, motion pictures, and the electronic media paint snake handlers as exotic, bizarre, and grotesque. At best, snake handlers are condescendingly described as naive, misguided, backward Appalachians; at worst, they are portrayed as psychologically disturbed cultists. Folklorists who have studied them, such as Thomas Burton in *Serpent-Handling Believers* (1993), while recognizing that the practice is dangerous, advocate the view that sign followers be approached respectfully and sensitively as American Christians holding complex traditional religious beliefs. Most states have treated snake handling as a criminal offense because it intentionally exposes people to venomous reptiles, giving priority to the protection of public safety over the religious beliefs of worshippers.

Despite the legal suppression of snake-handling sects, the practice of handling serpents and drinking strychnine as part of a Pentecostal service continues in America today. The legal statutes against snake handling have forced an even tighter social connection among believers than in years past and have influenced a religious folklife revolving around the central practices of serpent handling and strychnine drinking. Although predictions are frequently made that legal measures and deaths of fellow worshippers will convince sign followers to give up the practice, snake handling appears to be a resilient religious tradition, particularly in Appalachia.

Al Henderson

See also: Appalachia; Belief; Pentecostals; Religion; Rituals and Rites; Supernatural; Symbol and Structure.

Sources

Brown, Fred, and Jeanne McDonald. *The Serpent Handlers: Three Families and Their Faith.* Winston-Salem, NC: John F. Blair, 2000.

Burton, Thomas. *Serpent Handling Believers.* Knoxville: University of Tennessee Press, 1993.

Conkin, Paul K. *American Originals: Homemade Varieties of Christianity.* Chapel Hill: University of North Carolina Press, 1997.

Covington, Dennis. *Salvation on Sand Mountain: Snake Handling and Redemption in Southern Appalachia.* New York: Penguin, 1996.

Farley, Yvonne Snyder. "Holiness People Revisited." *Goldenseal: West Virginia Traditional Life,* Summer (1999): 10–19.

Hood, Ralph W. "When the Spirit Maims and Kills: Social Psychological Considerations of the History of Serpent Handling Sects and the Narrative of Handlers." *International Journal for the Psychology of Religion* 8 (1998): 71–96.

Kimbrough, David L. *Taking Up Serpents: Snake Handlers of Eastern Kentucky.* Macon, GA: Mercer University Press, 2002.

Schwartz, Scott. *Faith, Serpents, and Fire: Images of Kentucky Holiness Believers.* Jackson: University Press of Mississippi, 1999.

SOLDIERS

Soldiers are men and women engaged in military activity. Given the deadly serious nature of what soldiers do, it should not be surprising that their folklife often carries didactic messages bearing upon survival, not to mention victory in battle. Because soldiers' work is an endeavor requiring mutual reliance and intense discipline, soldiers' groups develop traditions and identities related to their camaraderie, aggressiveness, hierarchy, and distinctiveness from the general population. Indeed, entering military folklife involves rites of passage to make the transition from the "soft" civilian life to the "hard" life of the soldier. Soldiers are hardened, skilled, and tough and proud of these designations. The ceremonies for becoming a soldier are far more elaborate than for leaving the military, thus suggesting that it is a permanent identity. Even ex-soldiers gather to share experiences, renew identities, and display traditions in reunions, legion organizations, memorials, and parades. At the opening of the National World War II Memorial in Washington, D.C., in May 2004, for example, elderly men and women showed no difficulty in snapping a regulation salute or standing at attention, as they were taught by their sergeants and drill instructors in the 1940s.

Marine Corps drill instructors demand maximum intensity from recruits. In boot camp, initiates are imbued with a culture, tradition, and identity that will last a lifetime—as well as the discipline and training necessary to succeed in combat. *(Photo by Cpl. Jess Levens)*

Especially notable in the folk repertoire of soldiers is the "war story," which has also become a general American term for a narrative about reaching a goal against difficult obstacles or undesirable odds. Another is the frequently caricatured "boot camp," a term and setting entering into American imagination for a kind of conversion experience, filled with imaginative chants, calls, and rituals. The military has its own subcultures; besides the official designations of Army, Navy, Marine Corps, Air Force, and Coast Guard, many occupational groups and military divisions claim their own distinctive traditions. All told, the U.S. military community constitutes a significant social group: According to the 2000 U.S. census, more than one million men and women were on active duty, with another 1.3 million in reserves; about one-quarter of U.S. soldiers on active duty are stationed abroad. Some twenty-five million Americans claim veteran status.

Becoming Military

The scene is classic, yet ever fresh: a bus pulls into a military facility and out come dozens of young recruits, dressed and groomed like a cross-section of American youth. The setting might be Army Ranger School at Fort Benning, Georgia, or Marine Corps boot camp at Parris Island, South Car-

olina. Each service branch has its own specific venues, but the overall mission remains the same everywhere: take a group of individuals in their teens and early twenties, and mold them into a cohesive, competent body with a strong sense of shared identity and an overarching commitment to one another, according to the rules, regulations, and shared traditions of whatever military branch is doing the training. The young initiates come under the close supervision of an expert whose job it is to forge their new common culture and imbue them with the traditions that will make that identity stick over a lifetime.

In the Marines, this trainer is the drill instructor (DI), whose ubiquitous presence permeates every boot camp experience. The DI is often the subject of the chants that marines call out responsively during training exercises: "I wanna be a Drill Instructor / I wanna cut off all my hair / I wanna be a Drill Instructor / I wanna earn that Smokie Bear!" The "Smokie Bear" is the DI's distinctive hat, dating back to the 1850s; the DI's signature headgear thus puts recruits in touch with one of the myriad traditions that set the Marines apart and to which new "jarheads," as marines are called, can be expected to grow attached. Their chants address the physical privations and mental trials they endure in order to become members of an elite corps: "I jump from the rack in the middle of the night! / I make a headcall and I'm ready to fight!" or, "Up in the mornin' by the break of day / I don't like it. [clap] No way!"

It is precisely the hardness of the hard-core experience that makes the military crucible so effective at creating new Marines or soldiers. Young men and women come together, train together, learn together, endure together. This, in fact, is the main point of pride when newly minted marines parade at the end of boot camp. Having passed their trial, they march together in dress blues as members of the corps: "Mama, Mama can't you see? / What the Marines done for me? / I'm walkin' tall and feeling good / I'm doing things I never thought I could!"

And the story is an old one. When Army

Ranger hopefuls show up at Fort Benning, they soon learn the first set of standing orders given by Major Robert Rogers in the 1750s. Included are such bromides as "Don't forget nothing," "See the enemy first," and "Don't sleep beyond dawn." First handed down during the French and Indian Wars, such instructions may be archaic in some particulars, but Rangers learn right away that they are part of a long, proud, elite tradition. Ranger school, they are told, will prepare them for hardships that surpass even the battlefield; to survive it is to be better trained and better equipped than the enemy—not just with pride, but with a better chance at survival and victory. Rangers revere the traditional "toughest two months a soldier ever has to face" claim, and all who have gone through it feel bonded, as well as sharpened, by the experience. Rangers are never vague about their identity, Marines chafe at being referred to as "soldiers," and Air Force pilots remind some that they are not in the Army or Navy. Every successful unit must make its new members feel proud at having achieved membership.

Once past their initiation experience, military folk of all stripes still have traditions to forge and master. Sailors crossing the equator for the first time have been doused, toasted, or hazed for as long as the Navy has sailed; in combat conditions, the distinctions between a frontline veteran and a new arrival or a rear-echelon figure are well understood. Submariners cherish their dolphin pins and see themselves as proudly dissimilar from their Navy mates who sail on, not under, the ocean. Airborne paratroopers keep track of their jumps; World War II bomber crews knew the value in racking up high numbers of successful missions over German-held territory. During particularly harsh frontline fighting in every war, hardened infantry veterans sometimes wait before getting to know their fresh comrades, lest they forge relationships doomed to be short. Added to such divisions are the natural differentiations among ranks, units, and branches—a host of divisive markers that serve to accentuate immediate loyalties and perhaps to counterbalance the image of uniformity in the uniformed services. Indeed, the uniforms themselves often attest to a desire for distinctiveness in the midst of a regulation-revering environment. Shoulder tabs, unit symbols, and other seemingly decorative touches can be of enormous importance to various units taking pride in their collective, yet distinct, identities. When, for example, the Army decided that the black berets specific to elite units should be worn throughout the ranks, they heard screams of anger from veterans for whom wearing those berets was a symbol of specific pride.

Officers and Those Who Follow

As most who wear the colors of their country can attest, one of the first requirements for success in any military enterprise is one of the hardest to quantify: good leadership. Officers can earn their troops' affection through goodwill, but competence is the necessary ingredient for earning soldiers' trust. Numerous American generals have attained legendary and hero status for their leadership, beginning with the first, George Washington. Like any general, Washington faced the task of keeping thousands of often-rowdy soldiers marching in line toward a difficult objective. "Yankee Doodle" reminds listeners with the lines "There was Cap'n Washington / Upon a slappin' stallion / A-givin' orders to his men / I guess there was a million." This identification with the man who was not only the "Father of his Country" but, more immediately, the "Father of the United States Army," shows the degree of intimacy and authority that is necessarily part of the profile for one who would successfully lead dozens, hundreds, or thousands of men in battle.

If the perquisites of rank make close association with enlisted men and women impossible, the reverse relationship shows that the lower ranks are not shy about labeling their superiors, either intimately or irreverently. Confederate general Thomas J. Jackson, whose nickname "Stonewall" became the leading edge of his contemporaneous elevation to folkloric status, was notably austere and eccentric. The severe elements of his character—a religiosity that bordered on the grim, for example—were muted in campfire songs: "Silence men, now all hats off /

Old Blue Light's going to pray / Strangle the fool that dares to scoff / Attention! It's his way!" Idiosyncrasies real or imagined lent the remote Virginian a human touch otherwise absent from his profile; habits such as lemon sucking or avoiding pepper were talked up around the bivouacs as endearing traits.

Dash and braggadocio help some, but not all, officers. George Patton's smacking of a shell-shocked soldier and his penchant for quarreling with his own superiors became part of his legend; soldiers saw the behavior as part of his hard-charging style. Patton's numerous victories against the Wehrmacht afforded him such latitude from soldiers who sought not only to live but to triumph. Soldiers want victory for several reasons, ranging from conviction to the profound desire to go home; for many, Patton was a leader who brought the victory they needed, despite (or because of) his problems with punctilious regulations intrinsic to uniformed life.

Grunts, Gyrenes, and Swabs: The Enlisted Ranks

If officers generate folklore, it is the enlisted men who propagate it. The U.S. military legacy has one dominant narrative stripe—the countervailing, sometimes conflicting image of American soldiers as civilians temporarily in military garb, obeying and coping with officialdom out of necessity but not sacrificing their individuality beyond a certain point. As citizen-soldiers, recruits carry a rough-around-the-edges reputation in folklore. The stories continue down through all wars, like the tradition that Theodore Roosevelt recruited his Rough Riders among Texans drinking in a San Antonio saloon. But citizen soldiering has its serious implications, too. Sergeant Alvin York, himself a country boy who knew how to handle a shootin' iron, gained his fame in capturing 132 Germans during the 1918 Meuse-Argonne campaign to liberate the "Lost Battalion." His saga took on special resonance when Gary Cooper played him on the silver screen, stressing York's roots as a pacifist Christian from Tennessee's Cumberland Mountains who wrestled with religious compunctions about military service before agreeing to fight. York was the perfect symbol for a country that needed to move from being too proud to fight to making the world safe for democracy—the conflicting formulations of President Woodrow Wilson.

When it comes to independence and back-country skills, Native Americans have long held a special purchase in the cultural imagination. Their role in military folklore is fittingly ambiguous. Native Americans have been used as a national symbol by the dominant culture, which placed them on its currency, and seen as enemies who needed to be extirpated or assimilated by onrushing settlement. Their riding and fighting skills were incontestable, yet their fierceness in defending their own cultures struck many as savage and alien—not dissimilar to the blend of respect and repudiation Americans assigned to the Japanese in World War II. Time living with and learning from Native Americans became part of white leaders' legends, supporting the frontier-as-character-builder myth. In such a fashion was Texas frontier hero Sam Houston imbued with special qualities learned from his wilderness sojourns with Native Americans. But Native American leaders themselves gave rise to their own legends, and not for nothing were their warriors called "braves." Crazy Horse, Geronimo, Sitting Bull, Cochise, Tecumseh: the famous warriors of various tribes were often admired at the same time that they were pursued and killed. Their foes, for example, General George Armstrong Custer, could similarly be criticized and lionized for losing or winning. Once the frontier was "tamed," it became easier for America to lay aside the "savage" and resurrect the "noble" Native American.

Set at variance with the citizen-soldier motif is the professionalism of the military caste, exemplified by the service academies. National requirements made West Point, Annapolis, Colorado Springs, and New London the crucibles within which future officers are trained for military leadership. Each academy has its own specific traditions, some harmless and for show, such as the Air Force flyover at Falcon football games, others quite serious and meant to instill in military professionals the differences between their chosen path and the civilian way of life. The Long Gray Line and the Midshipmen always salute each other at the annual Army-Navy football showdowns, yet they root against each other during the games. Such traditions are intentionally implemented in formalistic ways, functional in organizations that are proudly rule bound. Many are held in common; perhaps the easiest to understand is the ubiquity of each academy's honor code, which holds all cadets and midshipmen responsible not only for their own conduct, but for that of their peers as well. This is a custom meant to provide training for an environment predicated on teamwork and interdependence.

Service branches create and cultivate their tales of the tribe—none more successfully than the Marine Corps, which proudly points to its distinct traditions when building the "Semper Fi" spirit ("Once a Marine, always a Marine.") The navy, originally less high-profile than its Army counterpart, takes from its antecedents stories such as John Paul Jones's defiant "I have not yet begun to fight" in building its traditions. These have real power, necessary for a nation that has always needed a strong maritime presence. As James Fenimore Cooper noted in 1828, "The spirit of the seamen was often exhibited in a manner to show that the nation possessed an extraordinary aptitude to that particular species of service." This held true 150 years later, even in highly secret conditions, when the Navy dueled with its Cold War Soviet foes above and below the seas. Whispered tales of secret submarine missions percolated through the military culture, assuring all who told and listened that American sailors were as daring and able as ever. Indeed, the classified nature of the tales gave them an appropriate cold war tone. American airmen, meanwhile, had a reputation for charisma long before the jet-age image made famous by legendary test pilots such as Steve Yeager. World War I's Lafayette Escadrille kept two pet lions as mascots, Whisky and Soda. The hotshot persona today is that of the top gun, and women, too, can be part of aviator lore now that the cockpit is a mixed-gender work site.

Food takes on totemic qualities in the military environment. In southern ranks during the Civil War, soldiers bemoaned the irregularity of their supply trains and frequently had to bolster their skimpy rations with peanuts harvested from roadside patches. "Just before the battle, the general hears a round / He says, 'The Yanks are coming, I can hear their rifles sound!' / He looks around in wonder / And what do you think he sees? / The Georgia Militia, eating Goober Peas." Some men in gray swore years later that it was unripe Pennsylvania peaches and cherries that lost the Battle of Gettysburg for Robert E. Lee, with so many rebels forced to do "the soldiers' trot" to a nearby latrine or tree. The men in blue, for their part, grew wearily intimate with "hard crackers," the staple of their diet, too tough to chew without a thorough dunking in hot campfire-brewed coffee. But when complaints led to the biscuits' replacement by softer stuff, they recanted: "Now to groans and to murmurs / There has come a sudden hush / Our frail forms are fainting at the door. / We are starving now on horsefeed / That the cooks call mush. / Oh, hard crackers come again once more." Their adaptation of Stephen Foster's song "Hard Times" was true to their era, yet not far removed from a marine chant popular 150 years later: "I eat my breakfast [clap] too soon, / Hungry as a Drill Instructor by noon. / I went to the mess hall on my knees, / 'Mess sergeant, mess sergeant feed me please.' / Mess sergeant said with a big ol' grin, / 'If you wanna be hard-core you gotta be thin!' "

If complaining about rations is an old soldier and sailor tradition, Americans and their allies are still unlikely to appreciate other nations' culinary traditions. The British thought the American K and C rations disgusting, loaded with strange confections such as spearmint gum. "It's got nothing on British treacle," claimed one Tommy, while an American was likely to take the inevitable British tea and simply blend it with coffee to make a stiffer drink. American soldiers in Vietnam continued their military tradition of wanting to eat and drink items from, or evoking, home. Some soldiers, linking food and survival in ritual ways, carried around a lucky oatmeal cookie or hoarded canned peaches, not only for their tastiness, but because these items became treasured reminders of what they were missing. Other nationalities fighting in the theater ate their own favorites. Australians wondered at American pizza, while Americans marveled at the South Koreans' kimchi, which, according to American soldier legend, could dissolve the solder in a tin can. Tastes of home remind one of going home, which is the most universal and heartfelt wish at the core of most military stories.

Ultimately, a soldier's or sailor's greatest challenge is to endure and survive. There is always an element of chance involved, which may help to explain the traditional fondness for gambling during the interminable waiting phases that mark military life. Sometimes, such games of chance are linked to subsequent fortune on the battlefield, and every war carries the tale of a soldier who unloads his belongings in a card game because of a premonition of battlefield death. Generally, however, the folklore and habits that soldiers purvey have hopeful, helpful, and pragmatic messages designed to decipher a specific and different lifestyle to which all military members must grow accustomed. In its American context, military folklife blends fatalism with a strong degree of individual assertion.

As long as Americans continue to serve their country, the variegated threads of military folklife will continually be woven into a tapestry designed to teach and support the uniformed service members. These tales will help to explain the military world for those in civilian life. Therefore, the increasing appearance of initiatives such as veterans' oral history projects, including the largest, at the American Folklife Center, show promise not just for capturing the memories of those in uniform but for providing scholars of folklife and culture the chance to learn why military experience was, is, and will always be so profound for those who go through it. The regimented style of military life scares off some scholars who prize folklife's organic nature. But especially in a society that still prizes the citizen-soldier, it is worth remembering that those wearing the uniform do so in a lore-rich atmosphere. In his World War I novel *A Soldier of the Great War* (1991), American novelist Mark Helprin, himself a veteran of the Israeli

Army, set a scene in which passing farmers gaze at two soldiers on an overlook. One soldier asks the other why they, two silent sentries, should be objects of such interest to the civilians. "To enrich their folklore," the older soldier replies.

Charles Kupfer

See also: Dress and Costume; Men and Masculinity; Rituals and Rites; Sailors.

Sources

Barton, Michael, and Larry Logue, eds. *The Civil War Soldier: A Historical Reader.* New York: New York University Press, 2002.
Boatner, Mark Mayo. *Military Customs and Traditions.* Westport, CT: Greenwood, 1976.
Burke, Carol. *Camp All-American, Hanoi Jane, and the High-and-Tight: Gender, Folklore, and Changing Military Culture.* Boston: Beacon, 2004.
Carey, George. "A Collection of Airborne Cadence Chants." *Journal of American Folklore* 78 (1965): 52–61.
Cleveland, Les. *Dark Laughter: War in Song and Popular Culture.* Westport, CT: Praeger, 1994.
———. "Military Folklore and the Underwood Collection." *New York Folklore* 13 (1987): 87–103.
Ferris, William R., Jr. "The Enlisted Man: Army Folklore." *New York Folklore Quarterly* 2 (1976): 229–34.
Fish, Lydia M. "General Edward G. Lansdale and the Folksongs of Americans in the Vietnam War." *Journal of American Folklore* 102 (1989): 390–411.
Motely, Mary Penick. *The Invisible Soldier: The Experience of the Black Soldier, World War II.* Detroit, MI: Wayne State University Press, 1975.
Veterans History Project. A Project of the American Folklife Center at the Library of Congress. www.loc.gov/folklife/vets/.

SOUTH, THE

The American South is an extensive geographical region usually defined broadly as the landmass south of Pennsylvania's Mason-Dixon Line surveyed between 1763 and 1767. As a historical reference, the term designates the eleven states of the former Confederacy (Alabama, Arkansas, Florida, Georgia, Louisiana, Mississippi, North Carolina, South Carolina, Tennessee, Texas, and Virginia), or "Dixie" (also "Dixieland") in folk speech.

Culturally, the western extent of the South is often disputed, since non-Confederate areas of Kentucky, Missouri, Oklahoma, and Texas were

The Confederate flag, to some a symbol of southern pride and to others a reminder of slavery and racism, remains a source of controversy. When the South Carolina Senate voted to remove the flag from atop the state capitol in 2000, protestors turned out by the thousands. *(Erik Perel/AFP/Getty Images)*

settled by self-identifying Southerners who left a deep Southern imprint on the landscape and everyday life. Indeed, an area of northeast Missouri is often identified as "Little Dixie" and characterized as "the essence of the Old South" or "more Dixie than Dixie." Missouri is not included in the U.S. census's count of the South, but Texas, Oklahoma, Kentucky, West Virginia, Maryland, Delaware, and the District of Columbia are.

The South is environmentally and socially varied, with diverse topographical and cultural landscapes—from the tidewater plain along the Atlantic coast and the rolling Piedmont of central Virginia and the Carolinas, to the Appalachian Mountains down into Alabama, the Mississippi River Delta, and the piney woods of East Texas. Still, a regional identity is expressed, with references to the historical connection of Dixie in the Civil War and the Jim Crow era; the agrarian and mining economic base in coal, cotton, rice, sugar, indigo, and tobacco; and cultural features of old-time music, religion, foodways, and architecture.

As a cultural term, the South refers to a region associated with plantation and slavery heritage, mountain song and story, fundamentalist religion, and a distinctive dialect that covers a broad area on both sides of the Mississippi River. Tracing the movement of folk traditions such as hominy grits and double-pen houses, cultural geographers often view areas of the "northern" states of Indiana, Illinois, and Ohio as culturally southern. The South's social complexion has been an often tense racial mix of black and white. The South is also defined by a contrast with the "other" of the North, although northerners do not claim the kind of cultural identity that southerners do. Indeed, someone is more likely to claim the folk identity of a "southerner" than a "northerner" and to claim that tradition is more important in the South than in the North.

Folk beliefs about the distinguishing traits of southerners and southern life suggest the South as a perceptual region as well as an objectively charted geographic, historical, and cultural region. The South, as Charles Regan Wilson and William Ferris present it in the *Encyclopedia of Southern Culture* (1989), exists as a psychological state of mind, referring to the perception that there is something behaviorally distinctive about being southern. Some cultural geographers use the term "vernacular region" to talk about the place in which residents cognitively map themselves. In border states such as West Virginia, residents may align themselves variously with the South, East, and North. In the popular American imagination, the South is often perceived and depicted as America's most identifiable and romanticized folk region.

Historical and Social Background

The historical roots of the folk region lie in the coastal colonial settlements by the English Protestants of Virginia, the Carolinas, and Georgia, especially in the formation of a plantation economy and landscape. The French and Spanish, meanwhile, came into the Gulf Coast and influenced a distinctive ethnic mix in the Mississippi River valley. When the later colony of Pennsylvania in the Middle Atlantic was formed, German and Scots-Irish settlers moved inland and down the Shenandoah Valley, joining descendants of English settlers moving west from the coast. An especially significant migration affecting the social character of the South was that of enslaved Africans, beginning as early as 1619. By 1750, slaves constituted as much as one-third of the population in some southern colonies. One distinctive folklife pattern that emerged from racial segregation was the rise of all-black towns (often without political jurisdiction) and sections of cities, such as Mound Bayou, Mississippi; Greenwood, Alabama; North Shreveport, Louisiana; and Bennetsville, South Carolina.

In 1820, the Missouri Compromise used the Mason-Dixon Line as the basis for dividing free soil to the north and slave states to the south, thereby fixing the regional division of the United States on the basis of the slave issue. In the first decade of the nineteenth century, the Louisiana Purchase brought a large tract of land around the Mississippi River, and its French and Spanish influences, into the slave economy of the Deep South. A Native American presence by Choctaw, Chickasaw, Muskogee, Cherokee, and Seminole tribes affected cultural development, but they were forcibly removed to Oklahoma during the 1830s. Although often associated with rural life, the South developed important urban centers in the antebellum period, among them Atlanta, Charleston, and New Orleans. In the rural mountains, meanwhile, largely homogeneous white settlements predominated.

Influenced by social migrations during the colonial period from ports of entry on the Atlantic and Gulf coasts and the natural boundaries of the mountains, several cultural-geographic regions formed below the Mason-Dixon Line. These include the Lowland or Deep South, extending from the Atlantic Coast into the Gulf Coast states; the Upland South, roughly following the Appalachian Mountains; and the Ozark Mountains of Arkansas, Missouri, and Illinois. Some geographers view French Louisiana, or Acadiana, as a distinctive subregion of the South, and in parts of east Texas, business enterprises often identify themselves as southern or Dixie, and residents express a strong southern identity.

Architecture and Speech

Folklife researchers have made efforts to map the traditions of the South as well as interview residents about their subjective views of what it means to be southern. In architecture, one finds a historical development from the English cottage or "hall and parlor" house in the coastal South to the enlarged Tidewater house and I house, consisting of a two-story, one-room-deep structure that spread throughout the Lowland South. Adapting to the moist ground and hot climate, builders often elevated the structure and put chimneys on the exterior ends. A somewhat different pattern emerged in the Upland South, where German, Scots-Irish, and English traditions tended to mix. Together with log construction, probably brought by German settlers, settlers merged the double-pen house with Celtic influences in the hall and parlor plan to create the Appalachian design. Variations such as the saddlebag (with a central chimney) and dog-trot house (chimneys at the ends and a breezeway in the middle) arose from this pattern. A more African-influenced form spread through French Louisiana, often called the "shotgun house." Instead of following the European pattern of two rooms across the front, the shotgun house has one room behind the other. Southern barns are often distinguished from northern examples by the presence of storage cribs separated by an open aisle instead of a planked, closed threshing floor. This has often been explained by the southern reliance on corn, which requires no threshing, rather than northern wheat. The double-crib pattern could be expanded by adding another double-crib beside the older one, sometimes creating a four-crib barn with cross-passages and a sizable storage loft.

Beyond the historical floor plans is the influence of the front porch, which many folklife researchers believe owes to African influence. Providing shade from the hot sun, the porch faced the road or community and was also a location for hospitality and social exchange. A frequent furnishing for the porch was the rocking chair, an icon of southern ease, typically made by local craftsmen. Houses in the Charleston area often included doors that led to a side porch area or piazza, which served as a visiting area. The advent of air conditioning and suburban development changed the social orientation of many public "front-porch" communities to private backyards. Still, "southern hospitality" and visiting customs are widely observed in the interest of preserving community.

Folk speech often expresses names for foods that follow the outline of the South. An example from linguistic surveys in the twentieth century is the name for sides of pork preserved in salt or pickled in brine. Below the Mason-Dixon Line, residents tend to call this "middlin" or "middlin meat"; north of it one hears it referred to as "sidemeat" or "side of pork." In Arkansas and Texas, the term "sowbelly" is used. Similarly, a burlap bag is consistently called a "tow sack" across the Lowland South, while in Appalachia one hears it referred to as a "gunnysack." The southern "drawl" extends through both lowland and upland areas, and traditional southern greeting phrases, such as "howdy" and "y'all," have entered into popular culture.

Religion and Music

A dominant pattern of Baptist affiliation marks the South from Virginia across to Kentucky and Missouri and east Texas. The outline of Appalachia from western Virginia into Pennsylvania, however, is predominantly Methodist and Presbyterian. French Louisiana, southeastern Florida, and southern Texas are distinguished from the rest of the South by being primarily Catholic. While the panhandle of Florida shares with the rest of the South a Baptist orientation, southern Florida is more religiously diverse, reflecting a late-twentieth-century population boom of retirees from across the nation. The essence of the Old South is sometimes referred to as the "Bible Belt," indicating those religious bodies that believe in the literal interpretation of the Bible. Tennessee is often referred to as the heart, or "buckle" of the Bible Belt, with a concentration of Baptist conventions and publishing houses.

A major tradition associated with southern identity is country music, with roots often declared in nineteenth-century old-time music and dance from Appalachia and the Deep South. As the music has become commercialized, its content has become more nationalized, but many songs still extol the virtues of the Southland. The fiddle, banjo, and dulcimer are often associated with the southern old-time band, playing tunes for square dances, and southern recreation. Although British-inspired fiddle tunes and ballads were found throughout the country, a distinctive country sound was promoted as part of southern heritage at institutions such as the Grand Ol' Opry in Nashville, at fiddlers conventions, and later on the radio. There was emerging evidence of a uniquely southern style in fiddling, characterized by slurred notes and double-bowing, in contrast to the northern style of distinct notes. Yet country music is also a cultural hybrid, drawing on African American blues and Louisiana Cajun influences as well as British fiddle tunes. Blues and black gospel music, many observers have noted, derive from African sources and were shaped into distinctive styles within the predominantly black areas of the Mississippi Delta and Piedmont regions of the South.

Cultural Icons and Foodways

Other cultural icons of the South have gone national besides blues and country music. The core fan base of stock-car racing remains in the South, especially in its roots in the Carolinas. While the breeding and use of quarter horses are widespread in the grazing country of the West, the Tennessee Walker is common in Kentucky, Virginia, North Carolina, Alabama, Georgia, and Mississippi, as well as Tennessee. Other traditions, while not as diffused, are also regarded as emblematic of the South. Traditions of glazed pottery and split-oak basketry thrive today as markers of southern identity in North Carolina and Georgia. Jack tales, British-derived narratives about a young man who outwits imposing foes, have been celebrated by the storytellers of the Beech Mountain area of North Carolina. African

American folk narratives of animal trickster figures are also frequently connected to the South. Indeed, storytelling in the American popular imagination often has a southern accent. Not to compromise that image, the National Storytelling Festival is held in Jonesborough, Tennessee.

Many foods are common to the South and have general southern associations. Corn bread, for example, can take many forms, including hoecake, hushpuppies, and cracklin' bread. A by-product of corn kernels widely known in the South, especially as a breakfast food, is hominy grits. Traditional grits are commonly produced from hard corn kernels that are coarsely ground and sifted to remove the hulls. The grits are then cooked into a thick porridge and flavored with butter or gravy, served with sausage or ham, baked with cheese, or sliced cold and fried in bacon grease. Another breakfast food associated with the South is biscuits and gravy. Turnips, cowpeas, and sweet potatoes are sometimes referred to as "the great triumvirate of southern vegetables." Black-eyed peas and crowder peas, variations of cowpeas, are often cooked on New Year's Day to ensure good luck. Across the Mason-Dixon Line in Pennsylvania, German-influenced pork and sauerkraut are preferred for New Year's. Beyond the inventory of southern foods are the food events traditionally associated with southern life, such as the picnic or dinner "on the grounds," fish fries, and box suppers.

Old and New South

The South extends beyond its geographic borders because of various migrations in the twentieth century. The South was regionally separated for many years because of its traditions of segregation and Jim Crow laws and the spread of the Ku Klux Klan. Through the twentieth century, economic opportunities and industrialization in the North, the escape from violence, and the search for civil rights caused a mass migration of blacks out of the South. With them went a number of southern black traditions, giving rise to the blues scenes in Chicago and Detroit, for example, and the rise of "soul food" and barbecue restaurants.

Migration out of Appalachia into such cities as Detroit, Michigan and Toledo and Columbus, Ohio, for economic opportunities gave rise to large migrant communities.

The "New South" of the post–civil rights era has often been noted for its increasing diversity—the globalization of places such as Atlanta, the Vietnamese and Chinese communities in the Gulf Coast, the spread of Native American-run casinos, new immigration from Europe and Latin America, the growing leisure industry of Florida and Louisiana, and a return migration of blacks after northern deindustrialization. Although traditions are changing as a result, southern regional identity continues to be invoked by some residents. Several organizations document and promote southern identity with special attention to the folklife of changing communities. The Southern Folklife Collection at the University of North Carolina is a major archival resource for folk cultural research in the South. The Southern Arts Federation supports an organization called Folklorists in the South, devoted to sharing information on a region-wide basis. The Center for the Study of Southern Culture at the University of Mississippi, the Center for the Study of the American South at the University of North Carolina, and the Southern Council for Folk Culture in Waynesboro, Virginia, help folklorists monitor southern culture, past and present, and ask the perennial question of what southernness means.

Simon J. Bronner

See also: Appalachia; Atlanta; Blue Ridge Region; Cajun Communities; Carolina, Down East; Charleston and Low-country South Carolina; Coastal Carolina Plain Region; Creoles, Louisiana; Delta, Mississippi River; Gullah or Geechee Communities; Memphis; Nashville; New Orleans; Southeastern Indians; Wiregrass Region.

Sources

Glassie, Henry. *Pattern in the Material Folk Culture of the Eastern United States.* Philadelphia: University of Pennsylvania Press, 1968.

Jordan-Bychkov, Terry G. *The Upland South: The Making of an American Folk Region and Landscape.* Sante Fe, NM: Center for American Places, 2003.

Joyner, Charles W. *Shared Traditions: Southern History*

and Folk Culture. Urbana: University of Illinois Press, 1999.

Marshall, Howard W. *Folk Architecture in Little Dixie: A Regional Culture in Missouri.* Columbia: University of Missouri Press, 1981.

McNeil, W.K., ed. *Appalachian Images in Folk and Popular Culture.* 2nd ed. Knoxville: University of Tennessee Press, 1995.

———, ed. *Southern Folk Ballads.* 2 vols. Little Rock, AR: August House, 1987.

Tullos, Allen, ed. *Long Journey Home: Folklife in the South.* Chapel Hill, NC: Southern Exposure, 1977.

Vlach, John Michael. *The Afro-American Tradition in the Decorative Arts.* Athens: University of Georgia Press, 1990.

Wilson, Charles Reagan, and William Ferris, eds. *Encyclopedia of Southern Culture.* Chapel Hill: University of North Carolina Press, 1989.

SOUTH ASIAN COMMUNITIES

South Asians—representing the seven countries of Bangladesh, Bhutan, India, Nepal, the Maldives, Pakistan, and Sri Lanka—have significant commonalities in their colonial pasts, migration patterns, and traditions in America, although they also display often sharp religious and political differences. Various social and cultural organizations use the phrase "South Asian" to identify the common experiences of these groups in America, such as the South Asian Student Association, active on many college campuses, or organizations such as the South Asian Heritage Foundation, National South Asian Bar Association, and the South Asian Gay and Lesbian Association. In addition, academic centers such as the Center for South Asian Studies at the University of Virginia and the Center for South Asian Studies at the University of California, Berkeley, accept the premise that the homelands are culturally and politically integrated. While maintaining ethnic distinctions, Americans of South Asian heritage often come together for social functions and cultural displays such as folk festivals. Particularly large and active South Asian communities, supported by these social and cultural centers, have been established in the late twentieth century in New York City, Washington, D.C., Houston, San Francisco, Los Angeles, and Boston.

Migration History

People from the Indian subcontinent have been migrating for centuries to areas throughout the world. The first major wave of emigration did not occur until the 1830s, however, when systematic migration arose in the form of indentured labor in the Caribbean on British sugar plantations in Trinidad, Jamaica, and Guyana. The second major wave of South Asian emigration began with the demise of the indenture system and the rise of industrialization in America and elsewhere in the early twentieth century. A significant migration from South Asia to the United States occurred in the early part of the twentieth century as agriculturalists from Punjab, many of whom were religiously Sikh, attracted by the need for labor in the lumberyards of the Pacific Northwest, began relocating to the American West. By 1914, there were approximately ten thousand migrants from South Asia working in California, many of whom resumed their agricultural activities as landowning farmers. Restrictive immigration laws based on a system of national origin quotas passed during the 1920s severely cut the rate of South Asian immigration to the United States until the Immigration and Nationality Act of 1984 eliminated the quota system in favor of family reunification and of allowing desirable professionals to enter the country.

In addition to Sikhs, the new immigration included more Hindus and Muslims from throughout the Indian subcontinent. According to the 2000 U.S. census, the number of people identifying themselves of Asian Indian ancestry reached 1.7 million, nearly double the figure in 1990. Pakistanis, mostly of Muslim background, constitute the next-largest group from the subcontinent, with more than 150,000 residents. The largest concentrations of South Asian communities are in California, followed by New York, New Jersey, Texas, and Illinois.

Religion

The most pervasive demonstration of South Asian folklife is through the expression of religion.

Maintaining timeworn religious practices in the United States is perhaps the most meaningful manifestation of ethnicity, reflected in the increasing number of Sikh *gurdwaras*, Hindu temples, and Muslim mosques around the country. The importance of religion is also seen in the visibility of religious attire, such as the *hijab* (head covering for Muslim women) and turban (wound cloth headdress worn by Sikhs).

Temples and mosques often serve multiple purposes for the community, acting not only as places of worship, but also as venues to interact with others from the homeland, give religious instruction, participate in traditional arts, and organize youth groups. If a religious center is based on a community from a particular region in South Asia, the center may also offer instruction in language, an important aspect of religious folklife. The same centers form the basis for community activities such as citywide festivals and religious parades. Events such as the United Muslim Day parade in September, the Sikh Day parade in May, and the celebration of Hindu festivals such as Diwali (in which candles and lamps are lit to greet Laksmi, the goddess of wealth), Ganesh Chathurti (a ten-day festival dedicated to the elephant-headed son of Shiva and Parvati, regarded as the embodiment of success and wisdom), and Holi (a colorful spring festival symbolizing the destruction of the wicked mythological figure Holika), are central markers of religious folklife as well as ethnic identity for South Asians in America.

While the practice of religion in South Asia varies widely across regions, the religious folklife of South Asians in the United States shares common themes whether one is Hindu, Jain, or Buddhist. For example, building a Hindu temple is regarded as building a whole community. Thus, a temple in America may bridge regional differences and be the center for *pujas* or prayer services, as well as the singing of *bhajans* (religious folksongs). Likewise, a mosque may bring together Pakistanis and Bangladeshis during the religious fasting month of Ramadan to hold the performance of distinctive prayers in South Asian Muslim culture, or *taraweeh* (derived from the

Arabic root word *raaha*, which means to rest, signifying the rest after cycles of prayer until the *taraweeh* is complete).

Customs, Sports, and Foodways

Weddings in South Asian communities often become elaborate festivals of ethnic display as well as marriage ceremonies. The night before a wedding, for example, henna is applied to the hands of the bride and groom, often accompanied by traditional songs and dances. The bride wears a traditional yellow dress to represent her initiatory status. In Pakistani Muslim weddings, a ceremony is held for the *nikah*, or the official signing of paperwork in the presence of the *imam* (Islamic religious leader). The bride wears a heavily embroidered outfit with an abundance of jewelry, and other women are dressed in bright-colored silk dresses. After the *nikah*, the bride's family accompanies her to a stage where she sits with the groom. Symbolic of the departure of the woman from her family into a new life, the bride goes to a *shadi* (marriage) with her own family and goes home with the groom's family. The event is hosted by the bride's family and is usually held at a large hall. Participants in the *shadi* wear ornate traditional clothing. The *dulha* (groom) wears a white or gold-flecked *sherwani* (long formal coat) with an elaborate headdress and slippers, and the *dulhan* (bride) usually wears red, the traditional wedding color. The ceremony often includes the ritual of *joota chupi*, in which one of the sisters of the *dulhan* steals the slippers from her new brother-in-law and refuses to return them until he pays a large sum of money. A large, boisterous negotiation ensues, with cousins from both sides throwing out figures at each other and cracking jokes at the frugality of the *dulha*. There may also be an additional reception hosted by the groom's family, called the *valima* in Muslim tradition, to announce the wedding to the community.

Another prominent ethnic marker among South Asians in America is the sport of cricket. Many cities with South Asian communities have cricket clubs dominated by Indian and Pakistani membership. In Washington, D.C., the cricket league established during the 1970s has grown to twenty-six teams, bringing together Pakistani and Indian immigrants on the same rosters despite political tensions between their nations of origin. The northern California league has a total of twenty-five teams; the Santa Clara cricket club boasts a varied mix of nationalities, including members from Bangladesh, India, Pakistan, and Sri Lanka. A league in Houston also boasts about two dozen teams, although separate clubs represent India, Pakistan, and West Indian communities. A few prominent cricket players have achieved legendary status among South Asians in the United States, among them Nazim Sirazi, from Bangladesh, who moved to Los Angeles in the 1980s, and Kapil Dev, from India, who makes appearances at American clubs.

Preparing ethnic foods at home and gathering at restaurants are other common markers for many South Asians. Although the Indian restaurant has become part of the popular restaurant landscape in many American cities, many South Asians identify with a subregional cuisine. The commonality among most of them is the varied use of vegetables and the use of aromatic spices, curd, and lentils. South Indian food centers on rice, usually served with *sambhar* (a thick gravy made of lentils, chili, coriander seeds, and other spices), *rasam* (a thin soup), and curried vegetables. Coconut is prevalent in South Indian food, used in chutneys, *avail* (curry), and desserts. North Indian cuisine features unleavened breads such as *chappatis* and *pooris* (unleavened flat breads). The cooking uses curries that are mild and made in *ghee* (clarified butter), vegetables seasoned with yogurt or pomegranate powder, and greens such as spinach and mustard greens cooked with *paneer* (a form of cottage cheese). *Nimbu pani* (lemon drink) and *lassi* (iced buttermilk) are traditional drinks in northern Indian cuisine that have been transplanted to America. Tandoori cooking is actually a North Indian specialty that has become associated with South Asian cooking in the American mind. The term "tandoor" refers to the cylindrical clay pot-oven in which the food is cooked over charcoal. In the process, the tandoor becomes hot and cooks the meat—usually lamb and chicken—quickly from all sides at once. In addition to these broad differences, regional folk cookeries are maintained in many communities, such as the Punjabi (in northwest India, where many Sikhs come from) use of *parathas* and *rotis* (types of unleavened flatbreads) made of corn flour, the Bengali (in northeast India) sweets made from burned milk and curd, and the use of spices by immigrants from Andhra Pradesh (in southeast India), reputedly the hottest in South Asian cuisine.

The folklife of later-generation South Asian Americans has found new expression in the combination of traditional Indian folk and religious music with popular culture. The remixing of Indian movie ballads or traditional folk songs with hip-hop or techno beats is the latest illustration of hybridized youth culture. The growing number of second-generation South Asians dancing at New York City's clubs to the redesigned *bhangra* beat combines aspects of cultural heritage with life in the United States. In addition, traditional dances, music, cuisine, and crafts are frequently featured at a number of urban folk festivals devoted to South Asian culture, such as the month-long South Asian Heritage Festival in Toronto, established in 2003, coinciding with Asian Heritage Month in Canada (through a governmental declaration passed in 2001) and Asian/Pacific American Heritage Month in the United States (established by presidential decree in 2001). Other notable public festivals celebrating South Asian folk arts have been held in San Francisco (South Asian Arts Festival), Jackson, New Jersey (South Asian Festival), and Radford, Virginia (South Asian Cultures Festival). South Asian American folklife emphasizes the diversity of cultures and generations while at the same time connecting traditional and modern influences.

Fariha I. Khan and Simon J. Bronner

See also: Hare Krishna; Hindus; Holidays; Muslims; New York City; Sikhs.

Sources

Bacon, Jean. *Life Lines: Community, Family, and Assimilation Among Asian Indian Immigrants.* New York: Oxford University Press, 1996.

Brown, Richard Harvey, and George Coelho, eds. *Tradition*

and Transformation: Asian Indians in America. Williamsburg, VA: Department of Anthropology, College of William and Mary, 1986.

Fenton, John Y. *Transplanting Religious Traditions: Asian Indians in America.* New York: Praeger, 1988.

Jensen, Joan M. *Passage from India: Asian Indians in North America.* New Haven, CT: Yale University Press, 1988.

Leonard, Karen Isaksen. *The South Asian Americans.* Westport, CT: Greenwood, 1997.

Lessinger, Johanna. *From the Ganges to the Hudson: Indian Immigrants in New York City.* Boston: Allyn and Bacon, 1995.

Maira, Sunaina Marr. *Desis in the House: Indian American Youth Culture in New York City.* Philadelphia: Temple University Press, 2002.

Saran, Parmatma, and Edwin Eames, eds. *The New Ethnics: Asian Indians in the United States.* New York: Praeger, 1980.

Shankar, Lavina D., and Rajini Srikanth, eds. *A Part, Yet Apart: South Asians in Asian America.* Philadelphia: Temple University Press, 1998.

Tinker, Hugh. *The Banyan Tree: Overseas Emigrants from India, Pakistan and Bangladesh.* New York: Oxford University Press, 1977.

SOUTHEASTERN INDIANS

The Southeastern Culture Area extends westward from the Atlantic coast to East Texas and southeastern Oklahoma and includes Arkansas, Louisiana, Tennessee, Mississippi, Alabama, Florida, Georgia, and the Carolinas. Peripheral to this core area are parts of Missouri, Virginia, Kentucky, Maryland, and the Ohio River Valley. Although the area includes a number of tribes with linguistic and cultural differences, there is evidence of cultural exchange, particularly along the Carolina Piedmont into Georgia. Another cultural concentration lies in a band through the Gulf Coast states from Louisiana to Florida. The categorization of the area as a distinct cultural region for Native Americans owes to a number of seminal anthropological and folklife studies in the early twentieth century, such as Frank Speck's "Some Outlines of Aboriginal Culture of the Southeast" (1907) and John Swanton's "Aboriginal Culture of the Southeast" (1924–1925).

Among the largest tribal communities is the Eastern Band of the Cherokee, based in Cherokee, North Carolina, which claims twelve thousand members and a population more than six thousand on the reservation in the western part

A woman of the Caddo Nation in Oklahoma displays the traditional Turkey Dance attire—two-piece cotton dress with apron, fringed shawl, and long ribbons with silverwork and mirrors. The Turkey Dance is made up of more than fifty separate songs that document significant events in tribal history. *(Courtesy of Dayna Bowker Lee)*

of the state. The Eastern Band of Cherokee Indians traces its roots to about a thousand Cherokees who managed to elude the U.S. government's forced removal of the tribe to Oklahoma. In 1925, the Cherokee tribal homelands were placed in federal trust to ensure that they will forever remain in Cherokee possession. These lands include fifty-two tracts, totaling 56,688 acres, scattered across five North Carolina counties (Cherokee, Graham, Jackson, Macon, and Swain). Most of this land is known as the Qualla Boundary. Towns within the boundary include Big Cove, Birdtown, Paintown, Snowbird, Wolftown, and Yellowhill. The tribe is keenly aware of maintaining its folklife, establishing a recreation of a traditional village, collections for a cultural museum, and an association for promoting native artists pursuing traditional crafts.

A member of the Choctaw Nation of Oklahoma visits the National Museum of the American Indian in Washington, D.C. Southeastern Indians in the twenty-first century continue to confront the challenges of cultural retention. *(Alex Wong/ Getty Images News)*

Another substantial group in the region is the Choctaw, who number around five thousand living on about fifteen thousand acres in eastern Mississippi. The Choctaw Reservation in Mississippi is a chain of eight communities: Bogue Chitto, Bogue Homa, Conehatta, Crystal Ridge, Pearl River, Red Water, Tucker, and Standing Pine. Although the reservation has established casinos and attracted industrial firms, it maintains its commitment to preserving traditional culture in programs for teaching new generations the tribe's folk music, mythology, dance, cooking, and basketry. For more than fifty years, the Choctaw Nation has sponsored the midsummer Choctaw Indian Fair, with roots in the Green Corn festival celebrating the ripening of corn. The event attracts nonnatives with popular entertainment, while promoting Native crafts and giving homage to tribal traditions.

Other recognized tribes in the region include the Piscataway Conoy and Pocomoke in Maryland; Seminole and Miccosukee in Florida; Lumbee in North Carolina; Catawba in South Carolina; Nansemond, Chickahominy, Rappahannock, Mattiponi, and Monacan in Virginia; Natchez in Georgia; Echota Cherokee in Alabama; and Tunica-Biloxi, Coushatta, and Chiti-

macha in Louisiana. Many of these groups hold powwows and festivals that attract participants from various tribes throughout the region, sponsor language and culture programs, and host publications and Web sites that document their traditions.

Prehistoric Period

The biodiversity and mild climate of the region attracted small, nomadic bands of aboriginal Native Americans to the area during the last glacial period. From about 13000 to 8000 B.C.E., Paleoindians pursued a seasonal economy based on gathering plants and hunting small game and large mammals. Archaeological sites bearing lanceolate, fluted stone points, scrapers, bone needles, and awls give evidence of steady population growth in the Paleoindian Southeast.

Dramatic climate changes at the end of the Pleistocene contributed to the disappearance of the megafauna and significantly altered the regional environment. Archaic Native Americans (ca. 8000–1000 B.C.E.) maintained a hunting-gathering economy made more efficient by the use of tools such as the *atlatl*, or spear thrower. Seasonal occupation of some sites and the formation of semipermanent settlements in major river valleys fostered the simple domestication of plants. The late Archaic period was notable in folklife for artistic traditions such as ground and polished stone ornaments and tools, simple twined basketry, woven cloth, and fired clay ceramics. Ceremonial treatment of the dead, the inclusion of burial goods, and the beginnings of earth architecture, primarily domed mounds and simple earthworks, suggest that Archaic societies shared Native belief systems in which an afterlife was conceptualized.

Southeastern societies continued to grow in size and social complexity during the Woodland period (ca. 1000 B.C.E.–900 C.E.). Woodland Indians lived in extended matrifocal settlements and engaged in a mixed economy of corn, beans, and squash agriculture supplemented by hunting, fishing, and gathering. They maintained artistic traditions established in the late Archaic and continued to construct labor-intensive earthworks. Precontact Southeastern Indian cultural expression culminated in the Mississippian tradition, around 900–1600 C.E. The Mississippian Southeast was made up of numerous highly stratified complex chiefdoms connected through the Southeastern Ceremonial Complex (SECC), a regional belief system that combined aspects of ancestor worship, fertility, and warfare into a sophisticated symbolic language. Clay and shell engravings found in the Southeast carry such motifs as the winged serpent and eagle warrior. Eye-in-hand and wide-jawed-skull symbols have been found on objects recovered from Moundville, Alabama. Sacral chiefs used SECC symbolism to help ensure their control of trade and commerce, receive tribute, and practice redistribution of goods. Along important waterways, large ceremonial centers defined a sacred landscape in which tall platform mounds were placed around a central plaza used for games of chunkey (in which polished stones are used as targets for spear throwing) and other ritual activities. Commoners in outlying communities participated in earthwork construction and other communal activities designed to create solidarity. Highly skilled specialists incorporated SECC symbolism into design elements on fine ceramics, cane basketry, and regalia made from local and exotic materials. Elaborate mortuary traditions and sumptuous grave goods marked the passing of elite individuals from this world to the next.

Historic Period

Spanish explorers were the first Europeans to encounter late Mississippian societies, some of which persisted well into the eighteenth century. Motivated by the quest for mineral riches, the Spaniards entered North America through southern Florida early in the sixteenth century. Early attempts to lay claim to the new land were met with ambivalence or violent opposition by the Native inhabitants, but these brief forays provided eyewitness accounts of Native lifeways, as well as testimony from Native Americans who were captured and enslaved. Even before the *entrada* of Hernando De Soto reached Florida in 1539, information about Native weaponry, houses, dress, and agriculture was available to Spanish explorers. Spain eventually secured a foothold in the Southeast, with missions and settlements placed among the tribes of coastal Florida by the mid-sixteenth century. From this point forward, European colonization in the Southeast proceeded at a steady rate. The English extended settlement down the Eastern Seaboard to establish Charleston in 1670, followed within a few years by the French arrival in lower Louisiana.

In Mexico, the Caribbean, and Florida, indigenous Americans were assaulted by repeated waves of European pathogens for which they had no immunities. Pandemics of influenza, measles, smallpox, and other diseases of European origin spread from the coast to the interior tribes, causing devastating population loss. Large interior nations such as the Creek, Choctaw, Cherokee, and Caddo fared better than small coastal groups such as the Mougulasha, Chouasha, Bayougoula, and countless others who vanished as individual entities within a few years of encountering Europeans. Small, remnant bands sought the protection of larger, more powerful nations or coalesced along linguistic lines to form new, pan-tribal identities.

Colonial European economic strategies exacerbated Native population decline and cultural stress. European traders upset seasonal subsistence strategies by persuading Native American allies to devote more time to hunting to supply hides and furs, and incited Native American wars designed to extend colonial boundaries and to acquire slaves from French and Spanish allies. English traders freely supplied alcohol and encouraged their allies to incur heavy debts, seizing tribal territory when debts could not be repaid. Nations wedged between Spanish Florida and English Charleston were forced to compete for available territory, while incidents of violence and abuse by English traders resulted in Native American uprisings against the colonists.

French colonists more readily adapted to Native lifestyles to advance their interests. Many traders were ritually tattooed and given fictive kinship, a Native strategy that kept commercial benefits within the "family." They adopted native dress and language, married Native American women, and brought up their ethnically mixed children in tribal villages. Still, conflict was not absent from French and Native American interaction. Raids on Chitimacha villages to enslave young women and children resulted in at least one extended war, and powerful chiefdoms such as the Natchez, which resisted French interference and expansion, were eliminated. Entrepreneurial nations such as the Choctaw, Creek, Tunica, and Caddo became highly adept at manipulating European competition to acquire better weapons and trade items, but the availability and attraction of European goods hindered production and innovation in native crafts and increased economic dependency.

Throughout the colonial period, Southeastern Indians had for the most part maintained Native lifestyles. Observers documented the rich variety of dances, songs, stickball games, religious rituals, and artistic traditions that sustained tribal communities through times of severe stress. Administrators in the Louisiana colony, French and later Spanish, maintained reciprocal relations with their Native American allies, treating them as sovereign nations with clear title to communal lands.

The American Period

A primary issue faced by the new American Republic was how to separate Native American populations from their agriculturally rich provinces east of the Mississippi River. President Thomas Jefferson settled on a strategy to eliminate tribal identities through assimilation and education, a tactic that would inform government policy well into the twentieth century. Families and communities were at first encouraged to voluntarily exchange lands east of the Mississippi for property in Indian Territory (now Oklahoma), but under President Andrew Jackson, Native American relocation became an imperative instead of an option. Forced removal displaced thousands of Creek, Choctaw, Chickasaw, and Cherokee, many of whom had so successfully adapted to Eu-

ropean ways that they were collectively called the "civilized" tribes. Regardless of their willingness to adapt, Southeastern Indians were forced to abandon ancestral homelands, possessions, and relatives. The Seminole, an amalgamated group made up of remnants of southeastern tribes and escaped black slaves, were eventually rounded up and relocated, but not without long and expensive wars that cost the Americans in dollars and in personnel. Robbed of support and the services of their U.S. agency, the Louisiana Caddo were left with no alternative but to cede their lands and migrate into Spanish Texas. Native American people who chose to remain in the American Southeast existed on the margins of white settlements, pushed onto less desirable lands, where they practiced subsistence agriculture, worked occasionally as wage laborers, and made baskets and tanned deer hides to sell to their white neighbors. Some small groups eventually blended into the general population, while others, often in isolated areas, managed to preserve Native languages and cultural identity.

Despite government efforts to sever tribal bonds and to subvert traditional forms of religion and government, southeastern people in the Indian Territory quietly maintained native traditions. Tribal towns and dance grounds were reestablished, and sacred fires were rekindled from embers carefully transported from ancestral villages. Those who accepted Christianity syncretized Western religion with Native belief systems, sometimes practicing both. Even forced attendance at Native American schools, designed to eliminate tribal languages and separate children from Native traditions, failed to rob Southeastern Indians of their social identities. Continued existence required negotiation, compromise, and subtle resistance, but Southeastern Indians continued to employ traditional cultural strategies to adapt to changing circumstances.

Contemporary Folklife and Cultural Conservation

Southeastern Indians in the new millennium continue to confront problems of cultural retention.

Marriage to non-tribal members, jobs that take members away from tribal communities, factionalism, language loss, and outside influences remain serious issues for which there are no easy answers. Still, Native American people find sustenance in the oral and material traditions and communal activities that connect them to their ancestral beginnings. The Choctaw Nation in Mississippi, for example, established its Cultural Affairs Program in 1995 to more formally promote and preserve the cultural traditions. The Cultural Affairs Program holds community workshops on a regular basis. Workshop topics are determined by community interest and have included cultural skills such as food preparation and outdoor cooking, traditional Choctaw clothing, chant and dance, and handicrafts. Identifying and documenting endangered traditions is another part of the community-based work of the Cultural Affairs Program. Staff members conduct research and interview tribal elders to obtain first-hand knowledge of Choctaw history and culture.

Among the Cherokee, the Qualla Arts and Crafts Mutual, established in 1946, acts on behalf of more than three hundred traditional crafts workers. Especially prevalent is the making of river-cane baskets, woven from a hollow reed that grows in the bottomlands of southeastern rivers. Other common materials include buckrush, honeysuckle vine, and split oak, which are usually colored with natural dyes made from plants such as yellowroot for yellow, butternut for black, walnut for brown, and bloodroot for shades of red. The oak or cane is woven into geometrical patterns for baskets used as storage boxes, flat cylindrical shapes, concave vessels, and large "burden" baskets that were traditionally worn on the back.

The Monacan Indian Nation of Virginia, comprising about a thousand members remaining on their ancestral homeland around Bear Mountain in Amherst County, has hosted an annual powwow at various sites that attracts many visitors from outside the tribe. Similar events are organized by the Cherokee in Guntersville, Alabama; Lumbee in Pembroke, North Carolina; Tunica-Biloxi in Marksville, Louisiana; and Mattaponi in King William, Virginia. Such events

are occasions for educational programs on traditional storytelling, dancing, clothing, crafts, and drumming.

Some tribes have sponsored Green Corn festivals—also known as Green Corn dances and Green Corn ceremonies—in conjunction with powwows or as separate events, such as the Five Nations Powwow and Green Corn Festival in Rockmart, Georgia. The dates vary from June through September. Although the tradition of a harvest festival has taken various forms, the modern pan–Native American version includes a thanksgiving dance and ceremony for the corn, rain, sun, and harvest. It is also common to have a bonfire (also called a busk) as a symbol of renewal. Tribal members bring items representing "filth" and damaged goods into a common heap and burn them. As a thanksgiving festival, the event invariably includes a food feast. Such examples of Native American food traditions as corn soup, corn bread, beans, and squash are served.

For the Choctaw, dances exemplify a spirit of cooperation because of the way the chanters, dance leaders, and dancers work together. They are generally divided into three kinds: war dances, social dances, and animal dances. War dancing is typically led by a chanter, who keeps time by striking a pair of sticks. Social dances mark life events such as initiation, courtship, and marriage and may include the ritual stealing of friends, and animal dances often mimic the behavior of their namesakes, with dancers darting in and out of the dance circle like playful raccoons or forming a line that coils and uncoils like a snake. The House Dance is a legacy of the cultural exchange during the Historic and American periods. Dancers use steps and movements from the American square dance and French quadrille, as instructed by a caller and often accompanied by traditional southern fiddle tunes.

The Choctaw and Cherokee also promote the traditional male sport of stickball, often organized in tournaments and sometimes held in conjunction with festivals and powwows. Stickball is a rough game resembling lacrosse. Goal posts are erected on both ends of a long field, and players use hickory sticks shaped like miniature tennis rackets to knock a small ball, made of deer hair and hide, through the goal.

Tribal leaders use contemporary folklife as a form of both economic development and cultural education. Increasingly, Native events become public stages for non-Natives to witness and appreciate the meaning of cultural continuity for Native identity. However, many important social and ritual activities remain exclusively within the tribal domain, reinforcing the bonds of identity and traditional culture.

Dayna Bowker Lee and Simon J. Bronner

See also: Appalachia; Baskets and Basketry; South, The.

Sources

Bense, Judith. *Archaeology of the Southeastern United States: Paleoindian to World War I.* New York: Academic Press, 1993.

Debo, Angie. *A History of the Indians of the United States.* Norman: University of Oklahoma Press, 1970.

Griffin, James B. "Comments on the Late Prehistoric Societies in the Southeast." In *Towns and Temples Along the Mississippi,* ed. David H. Dye and Cheryl Anne Cox, 5–15. Tuscaloosa: University of Alabama Press, 1990.

Haas, Mary R. "Southeastern Indian Folklore." *Journal of American Folklore* 60 (1947): 403–6.

Hudson, Charles. *The Southeastern Indians.* Knoxville: University of Tennessee Press, 1976.

Speck, Frank G. "Some Outlines of Aboriginal Culture in the Southeastern States." *American Anthropologist* 9 (1907): 287–95.

Swanton, John R. "Aboriginal Culture of the Southeast." *Annual Report of the Bureau of American Ethnology* 42 (1924–1925): 673–726.

———. *The Indians of the Southeastern United States.* Washington, DC: Smithsonian Institution Press, 1946.

Thornton, Russell. *American Indian Holocaust and Survival: A Population History Since 1492.* Norman: University of Oklahoma Press, 1987.

SOUTHWEST

The southwest region of the United States is usually distinguished by its arid climate, scenic desert landscapes, and strong native and Mexican cultural presence. For more than fifteen thousand years, the area has been occupied by many cultures, including the prehistoric Anasazi and Mollogon cultures, whose ruins are central to modern images of the Southwest. Arizona and New Mexico make up most of the Southwest, but parts of Texas, Colorado, Utah, and Nevada also figure into perceptions of the region's boundaries. Because of its prehistoric residents and Arizona and New Mexico's statehood in 1912, the Southwest is sometime characterized as both the oldest and youngest part of the country. Although unique in cultural identity, the Pueblo, Navajo, and Apache Indians have contributed significantly to the region's artistic traditions, including pottery, weaving, and architecture. The influences of Spanish, Mexican, Anglo, and modern Latino cultures have also contributed to an overlapping of cultural traditions shared by many Southwest occupants.

Historic and Social Background

Before the Spanish arrival at the end of the sixteenth century, Arizona and New Mexico were the center of Native American settlement because no other cultures existed there. At the beginning of the twenty-first century, the largest number of Native Americans still reside in the Southwest, yet the migration of Spanish, Mexican, and Anglo (referring to whites of European ancestry) people into the region has created a heavy intercultural mix. The Navajo and Pueblo Indians are the largest Native American groups in the country. Within the boundaries of the Southwest, Native American tribes maintain a strong ethnic identity and a prominent cultural tradition. As early as the sixteenth century, Spanish and Mexican explorers documented the cross-fertilization of Southwestern Indian culture with the Spanish and Mexican traditions. In 1598, Juan de Oñate led large groups of Spanish and Mexican people into the region, claiming it as Spanish territory and naming it New Mexico. Known as "El Camino Real" (the Royal Road) for its location on the route from Mexico City, Santa Fe became the capital of New Mexico; thus, today it is the oldest capital city in the United States.

Nowhere in the United States is there more

Mexican mariachi music has been a staple of the American Southwest for centuries. The *vihuela*, a small, round-backed guitar, gives the music its rhythmic energy. Hand-woven shawls and bright, sequined skirts highlight the women's costumes. *(Denver Public Library, Western History Collection, X-21636)*

of an influence of Spanish and Mexican tradition than in the Southwest. Most towns and cities in the Southwest, including Santa Fe, continue to use Spanish in the naming of streets, businesses, schools, and parks. As a result of Mexico's defeat in the Mexican-American War, Mexico ceded all lands between Texas and California to the United States. Following the Treaty of Guadalupe Hidalgo between the United States and Mexico in 1848, many Anglos settled in Arizona and New Mexico, establishing the Santa Fe Trail on their westward migration. In 1853, the Gadsden Purchase gave Arizona and New Mexico an additional thirty thousand square miles of land. The completion of transcontinental rail lines the following decade brought an overflow of people to the West, with subsequent lines through Santa Fe and Albuquerque. By 1869, a great many pio-

neers had settled in those towns, laying the foundations of the modern Southwest.

A surge of Mexican immigration in the 1930s changed the regional identity forever, and the Chicano movement of the 1960s brought an increased Mexican American presence to the political arena, along with a resurgence of ethnic art, popular music, literature, and social awareness. Residents self-identify variously as Latino or Latina, Hispanic, Mexican American, Spanish Mexican, Mexican Indian, Spanish Indian, Chicano or Chicana, and Tejano or Tejana.

Traditions and Celebrations

No other tradition is more celebrated by people in the Southwest than the holiday of Cinco de Mayo (the Fifth of May), which commemorates the victory of the Mexicans over the French army at the Battle of Puebla in 1862. While it is primarily a regional holiday, Cinco de Mayo has gained popularity throughout the country, spreading cultural awareness of Southwestern folklife. In the Southwest, it is celebrated as a reminder of Mexican heritage and culture. At the heart of the festivities is a community spirit that brings together people with foods, music, beverages, dance, and customs unique to the Mexican tradition.

A common feature in Cinco de Mayo celebrations is the enchanting musical ensembles of the mariachi. A complete mariachi group typically features six to eight violins, two trumpets, and a guitar; some include a round-backed *guitarró* called the *vihuela*, which when strummed gives the mariachi its unique rhythmic energy. Included in almost every mariachi ensemble are the vocal stylings of male and female singers. Also special in the mariachi ensemble are the *Jalisco* or *charro* outfits worn by the men and the handwoven shawls and bright, sequined skirts worn by the women, with intricate leather designs, silver buttons, and detailed embroidery.

Mariachi music has been celebrated for hundreds of years in the Southwest. Incorporated into almost every Spanish, Mexican, and Southwest tradition, the mariachi ensemble is employed in family baptisms, weddings, holidays, funerals, and parties, no matter how big or small. The roots of Tejano and *conjunto* music come from mariachi influence. Highly stylized mariachis with a contemporary flavor entertain audiences from all backgrounds. In the 1940s, the Pachuco movement that originated in El Paso, Texas, also contributed to the Tejano and *conjunto* style. Mariachi orchestras have inspired Mexican, Cuban, and Anglo musicians to incorporate swing and jump music into the repertoires of popular folk dances of the region. Polkas, waltzes, *redovas*, *rancheras*, *danzones*, mambos, boleros, and *corridos* are celebrated in most rural areas of the Southwest, but their popularity has spread into urban settings, forever changing dance and music to meet the needs of contemporary audiences. At the same time, religious festivals perpetuate the mariachi tradition throughout the Southwest.

Catholicism has remained a strong presence in the Southwest. Celebrations honoring *La Virgen de Guadalupe* (the Virgin of Guadalupe) range from extended-family traditions to seasonal feasts. In most Catholic families of the Southwest, *quinceañeras* are celebrated on a girl's fifteenth birthday, marking the transition from childhood to womanhood. The *Quinceañera* tradition includes a convocation of female family before the official celebration to make full-length pastel-color decorative gowns adorned with frills and lace. Accompanied by her *damas* (maids of honor) and their *chambelanes* (chamberlains), the girl places a bouquet of flowers on an altar honoring the Virgin Mary or *La Virgen de Guadalupe*. At the end of the Mass, family and friends celebrate the girl into adulthood with dance, music, and abundant food.

Southwest folklife often revolves around celebrations and feasts among family members, including the Nuestra Senora de Guadalupe Feast on December 12, the beginning of the Christmas season. Throughout the Southwest at this time, one can see the *rios de luces* (rivers of lights), also known as *luminarias*. Our Lady of Guadalupe is the patroness of saints in the Americas, and the Fiesta de Nuestra Senora de Guadalupe honors her loyalty in protecting homes and children during the course of the year. Dating to 1531 in Mexico, Nuestra Senora de Guadalupe has been celebrated in the Southwest ever since the Spanish arrival. The most famous local observance is held in a small village south of Las Cruces, New Mexico, called Tortugas. Dances are performed by local residents including a small group of Tiwa Pueblo Indians; crowds of people eat, dance, and pray at specially erected booths and altars.

Dia de los Muertos (Day of the Dead) is also a widely and exuberantly celebrated tradition in the Southwest. Contributing to the region's art, craft, and food economy, Dia de los Muertos is a fixture in Southwest culture. On November 1 (All Saints Day) and November 2 (All Souls Day), *La Muerte* (death) is honored with offerings laid out on commemorative altars and at religious sites. The altars are designated for the remembrance of deceased infants and children, referred to as *angelitos* (little angels), and loved ones of all ages. Offerings, including edible treats made of sugar such as *pan de muerto* (sweet rolls), as well as gifts of *flores de la muertos* (flowers for the dead) and votive candles, are meant to protect the dead in the afterlife. The holiday has been important to the craft economy of the Southwest, as young and old participate in the making of candles, intricate tissue-paper cutouts, ornate wreaths, decorative crosses, and elaborate sugar toys. As modern society has capitalized on Mexican tradition, long-held customs have fallen to the wayside and *ofrenda de muertos* (offerings to the dead) are sold to visiting tourists.

Tourism and Cultural Conservation

Tourism contributed to the Southwest's economic boom of recent decades. Phoenix and Tucson have experienced especially rapid growth in high-tech industries, while New Mexico cities such as Ruidoso and Taos have become popular ski resorts and tourist centers. Pecos National Monument, Chaco Canyon, Mesa Verde, Casa Grande, Montezuma Castle, Grand Canyon National Park, White Sands National Park, Hoover Dam, and other sites have contributed immensely to the regional tourism industry, which has replaced much of the farming and mining economy. At the same time, the rise of tourism and spread of development—including sprawling retirement communities—have raised fears among preservationists of destructive changes in the geophysical and cultural landscape.

Several prominent folklife centers in the region conduct fieldwork, run public programs, and inform preservation policies that link the region's complex constellation of distinctive groups and landscapes. The Southwest Folklore Center at the University of Arizona, for example, has been especially active in creating exhibitions, Web sites, and publications on traditional arts and architecture of the Southwest Borderlands. The New Mexico Heritage Center at New Mexico State University in Las Cruces has as its mission the conservation of traditional cultures whose history and heritage are bound to the land. It offers an extensive program of research and educational activities and sponsors the popular New Mexico Folklife Festival.

Christopher J. Pérez

See also: Chicano and Mexican Communities; Consumerism; El Paso; Jews, Crypto- and Protestant Millennialism; Metal and Metalworkers; Pottery; Rugs and Rug Making; San Diego; Santa Fe; Southwestern Indians.

Sources

Campa, Arthur L. *Hispanic Culture in the Southwest*. Norman: University of Oklahoma Press, 1993.
Griffith, James S. *A Shared Space: Folklife in the Arizona-Sonora Borderlands*. Logan: Utah State University Press, 1995.
———. *Southern Arizona Folk Arts*. Tucson: University of Arizona Press, 1988.
Heyck, Denis L., ed. *Barrios and Borderlands: Cultures of Latinos and Latinas in the United States*. New York: Routledge, 1994.
Peña, Manuel. *The Texas-Mexican Conjunto: History of a Working Class Music*. Austin: University of Texas Press, 1985.
Rothman, Hal, ed. *The Culture of Tourism, the Tourism of Culture: Selling the Past to the Present in the American Southwest*. Albuquerque: University of New Mexico Press, 2003.
Teague, David W. *The Southwest in American Literature and Art: The Rise of a Desert Aesthetic*. Tucson: University of Arizona Press, 1997.
Udall, Sharyn Rohlfsen. *Contested Terrain: Myth and Meanings in Southwest Art*. Albuquerque: University of New Mexico Press, 1996.
Weber, David J. *Myth and the History of the Hispanic Southwest*. Albuquerque: University of New Mexico Press, 2002.
Weigle, Marta, and Peter White. *The Lore of New Mexico*. Albuquerque: University of New Mexico Press, 1988.

SOUTHWESTERN INDIANS

Nowhere in the United States are there more Native Americans than in the Desert Southwest. Including Arizona, New Mexico, and parts of Texas, Colorado, Oklahoma, Nevada, and Utah,

For the Hopi and other Pueblo Indians of the Southwest, kachina dolls represent ancestral spirits that bring rain for crops. The dolls are used ceremonially by Hopi dancers and are given to women and children as effigies of nature spirits. *(Robert F. Sisson/National Geographic/Getty Images)*

the Southwest is home to more than one hundred indigenous tribes; despite centuries of conflict over land rights and sovereignty, more land is held by Native Americans here than in any other region of the United States. The region has attracted many anthropologists and folklorists since the nineteenth century, noting adaptation to desert conditions, a persistent oral tradition of myths and tales, and a wide array of decorative folk arts such as blankets, rugs, and pottery.

The Southwest contains remnants of prehistoric cultures that existed more than twelve thousand years ago, including the Anasazi, Mogollon, and Hohokam. These cultures engineered elaborate and sophisticated habitat structures and produced highly refined crafts such as pottery, textiles, basketry, and jewelry. They are still evi-

dent in modern Native American traditions unique to the cultural foundation of the Southwest. While little is known of the prehistoric cultures other than their physical remains, the mythologies of many present-day Southwestern Indians reflect millennia-old ways of life. As reflected in their creation stories, however, the Southwestern Indians did not belong to a single culture. Nor are the regional Native Americans of today mere artifacts of the past; they constitute a living presence in the desert Southwest.

As for many Native Americans, land is culturally significant to the tribes living in the Southwest. While the climate is arid in most areas, with rugged mountains of sand and stone, the Southwestern Indians have developed exceptional ways of working and living in such difficult environments. Almost all ancient Native Americans were primarily hunters and gatherers, but modern Native Americans have come to rely on agriculture and horticulture.

Passage of the Indian Reorganization Act (IRA) in 1934 marked a dramatic change in federal policy toward Native American tribes by promoting Native American sovereignty to conduct autonomous affairs, including the operation of businesses. The IRA allowed Native American nations to organize as corporate bodies in order to borrow money and rebuild reservations. Since the 1970s, Native American sovereignty has increased significantly due to efforts to preserve Indian identity and cultural traditions. The Indian Child Welfare Act of 1978, for example, gave tribes the authority to determine tribal membership of children. Courts during the 1970s also upheld hunting and fishing rights guaranteed in treaties. Tribes can levy taxes, establish environmental restrictions, land-use regulations, and building codes, and enforce criminal statutes.

Pueblos and Apaches

There are more than thirty villages of Pueblo Indians on the Colorado Plateau in northern Arizona and New Mexico. The Pueblo tribes are divided into two main groups based on location. Eastern Pueblo tribes live near the Rio Grande and have a permanent water supply that enables irrigation of food crops. Corn, or maize, is a principal crop of the Pueblo Indians. Western Pueblo tribes lack a steady supply of water and depend on dry farming of crops such as corn for subsistence. Water supply affects various aspects of Pueblo tribal life, from specific cultural traditions to food production to religion. Almost all Pueblo Indians are agriculturalists, but some also raise small herds of cattle and sheep. Specific tribes of Pueblo Indians include the Hopi, Zuni, Pima, and Papago. The Pueblo ("village" in Spanish) Indians were named by Spanish explorers, in recognition of their distinctive architecture, made of sand, stone, and adobe, which distinguishes them from other Southwestern Indians. Most Pueblo towns have existed since the sixteenth century; the

Pueblo Indians are thought to be descendants of the Anasazi and Mogollon cultures. While the Pueblo Indians suffered centuries of suppression by Europeans, many Pueblo tribes have remained on their land, adapting to new circumstances while sustaining distinct material traditions. These traditions are reflected, for example, in their kachina (or katchina) religion, marked by dancing, singing, and giving gifts to children. There are more than three hundred distinct kachina spirits, revered by the Pueblos for their power to bring rain for growing crops.

Except for the Southwest's various Pueblo groups, almost all of the remaining Native Americans of the region are made up of some branch of the Apache peoples. Like the Pueblo, the Apache Indians are divided geographically into eastern and western groups. There are more than fifty thousand members in all, living on reservations that cover three million acres. Eastern Apache Indians include the Jicarilla, Mescalero, and Chiricahua; western Apache Indians include the Carrizo, Pinal, Mazatzal, and Cibecue. Apache ancestors entered the Southwest region around 1100 B.C.E., and modern Apache Indians have remained faithful to traditional ways of life introduced by their ancestors. The men live with and work for their wives' families in a matrilineal social order. Wild game, seed and fruit gathering, livestock, and horticulture remain the subsistence base, with cattle, timber, and tourism providing additional income. The Apaches were once known as fierce warriors, epitomized by the revered folk hero Geronimo. The Apache speak a variety of languages, of which the Na-Dene is the most common.

Considered close cultural cousins of the Apache, the Navajo have achieved remarkable retention and relative indigenous purity, making them exceptionally distinct in the Southwest region. The Navajo, or *Diné*, as they call themselves, are the largest and most concentrated group of Native Americans in the United States, with fourteen million acres of land in parts of Arizona, New Mexico, Colorado, and Utah and more than two hundred thousand members. Among their various cultural traditions, the Navajo produce finely crafted weavings and silverwork that have become highly cherished, especially by tourists. Sheep are a vital part of Navajo cultural life and economy because they provide wool for weaving rugs, blankets, and clothes. Navajo were among the first to make items to trade in neighboring towns. Trading posts were later built on Navajo reservations to sell handmade crafts, which are still produced today. In religious rituals, the Navajo emphasize individual goals rather than community, but they still live in matrilineal societies. Navajo Indians live in roundhouses called hogans that are made from wooden poles, bark, grass brush, and mud. During World War II, Navajo recruits became renowned for their language abilities, which were used for communicating vital military information. The Navajo "code talkers" are recognized in annual celebrations today.

Language and Art

While English is the most widespread language among Southwestern Indians today, linguists estimate that there have been more than two thousand different Native American languages, of which more than one hundred are still spoken today. A third of all Native Americans remain fluent in their native language, but the highest frequency of native speakers is found among the Apache, Navajo, Papagos, and Pima Indians. As disease and other devastations reduced entire nations, several languages became extinct in the Southwest. Pressure to assimilate also caused many Native Americans to stop speaking their native languages. Boarding schools founded by the federal government since the late 1800s to "civilize" Native Americans separated children from their families, and many generations felt disconnected from traditional culture. Recently, the American Indian Movement (AIM) has sought to establish model schools for Native Americans. Before 1968, there were no Native schools that provided traditional education to Native peoples. In the late twentieth century, the Navajo Community College in Tsaile, Arizona, offered a range of courses on Navajo culture, including language ac-

quisition and curing traditions. It was the first college to be founded and run by Native Americans, and others soon followed, helping conserve the cultural traditions of Southwestern Indians.

Encouraged by a tourist and collector economy in the Southwest, art is maintained as a cultural tradition among Southwestern Indians. There is an artisan in almost every home of every Southwestern Indian tribe. Many Native Americans sell their art to supplement their income. Southwestern Indian art has maintained high standards, techniques, and aesthetic visions important to conservation efforts. Until the twentieth century, the finest objects were made for ceremonial purposes to ensure the continuation of Native American life. While finely made objects such as weavings, pottery, basketry, jewelry, and sculpture are intended to be enjoyed by each tribe or individual who makes them, tourism and art-world interest in the twenty-first century have created a market for Southwestern Indian crafts. Although tourism has had a negative effect on some Native American arts and crafts traditions, it has ensured that other Native skills and styles have survived into the present. The tourist demand for souvenirs has led to the sale of millions of cheap wooden and plastic pseudo–Native American replicas, but the Indian Arts and Crafts Act (1990) prohibited non–Native American people from marketing imitation work as original. The legislation helped Native American economy and sovereignty, since art is inextricably linked to cultural identity: the symbols and patterns of Native American art reflect religious and secular significance. Despite the popularity of Native American art, the most successful Native-owned businesses in the United States are casinos. Wealth produced by casinos tends to be redistributed among various Native communities on the reservation that owns the casino. These funds help to improve the tribal infrastructure by building schools, roads, and museums.

Although many Southwestern Indian tribes remain autonomous within reservation communities, there continues to be pressure to adapt and assimilate to mainstream society. While many Southwestern Indians have made the transition from hunting-and-gathering societies to farming, then herding, then wage-earning societies, most tribes remain devoted to ancient traditions such as religion, folk art, and family-oriented social organization.

Christopher J. Pérez

See also: Metal and Metalworkers; Pottery; Rugs and Rug Making; San Diego; Santa Fe.

Sources

Courlander, Harold. *The Fourth World of the Hopis: The Epic Story of the Hopi Indians as Preserved in Their Legends and Traditions.* Albuquerque: University of New Mexico Press, 1987.

Davies, Wade. *Healing Ways: Navajo Health Care in the Twentieth Century.* Albuquerque: University of New Mexico Press, 2001.

Duff, Andrew I. *Western Pueblo Identities: Regional Interaction, Migration, and Transformation.* Tucson: University of Arizona Press, 2002.

Haley, James L. *Apaches: A History and Culture Portrait.* Norman: University of Oklahoma Press, 1997.

Harlow, Francis H. *Two Hundred Years of Historic Pueblo Pottery.* Albuquerque: University of New Mexico Press, 1991.

Iverson, Peter. *Diné: A History of the Navajos.* Albuquerque: University of New Mexico Press, 2002.

Levy, Jerrold E. *In the Beginning: The Navajo Genesis.* Berkeley: University of California Press, 1998.

Lyons, Patrick D. *Ancestral Hopi Migrations.* Tucson: University of Arizona Press, 2003.

Powers, Willow Roberts. *Navajo Trading: The End of an Era.* Albuquerque: University of New Mexico Press, 2001.

Wyaco, Virgil, Carroll L. Riley, and J.A. Jones, eds. *A Zuni Life: A Pueblo Indian in Two Worlds.* Albuquerque: University of New Mexico Press, 1998.

SPIRITUALISTS

Spiritualism is a form of Christianity that emerged in the United States during the mid-nineteenth century based on the belief that the spirits of the dead live on and are available to communicate with the living through mediums, or intermediaries. Spiritualism shares with Christianity a belief in the fatherhood of God, an afterlife similar to heaven, and the practices of holding Sunday services and singing hymns. Spiritualists hold that God is a divine energy (Infinite Intelligence) present in everything that exists. In their view, humans are a representation of God's creation, God is within them, and they seek teachings regarding compassion and love.

Spiritualists believe that divine activity can be perceived by the five senses; if science deals with that which is tangible, they hold, religion should be no different. The folklife of Spiritualists is particularly evident in the practice of the séance, a sitting in which the spirit is said to become visible. Nonbelievers, therefore, are not asked to believe on the basis of faith alone; instead, they are asked to investigate and observe scientific demonstrations in which the spirit can be observed. Another folk aspect of Spiritualism is the use of spiritual healers, who, either through their innate power or through mediumship, are able to transmit curative energies to ailing individuals. Spiritualists today practice their religion in churches by various names, including the Church of the Living Spirit in Phoenix, the First Church of Divine Science in Houston, and the Church of Two Worlds in Washington, D.C. Many belong to the National Spiritualist Association of Churches (NSAC) of the United States, established in 1893 and based in Lily Dale, New York, which ordains ministers, certifies mediums, commissions Spiritualist healers, and confers National Spiritualist Teacher Degrees. Many Spiritualist churches actively sponsor camps and camp meetings involving meditation, services, and classes.

The NSAC describes Spiritualism as a science and philosophy characterized by the following principles (representing "the consensus of a very large majority of Spiritualists" rather than a formal, unified creed):

1. We believe that the phenomena of Nature, both physical and spiritual, are the expression of Infinite Intelligence.
2. We affirm that a correct understanding of such expression and living in accordance therewith, constitute true religion.
3. We affirm that the existence and personal identity of the individual continue after the change called death.
4. We affirm that communication with the so-

The origin of modern Spiritualism is traced to events on March 11, 1898, at Fox cottage in Hydesville, New York. Two young girls purportedly made contact with the spirit of a murdered man, whose ghost answered their questions with rapping and clicking noises. *(Library of Congress, LC-USZ62-79458)*

called dead is a fact, scientifically proven by the phenomena of Spiritualism.

5. We believe that the highest morality is contained in the Golden Rule: "Whatsoever ye would that others should do unto you, do ye also unto them."

6. We affirm the moral responsibility of individuals, and that we make our own happiness or unhappiness as we obey or disobey Nature's physical and spiritual laws.

7. We affirm that the doorway to reformation is never closed against any human soul here or hereafter.

8. We affirm that the precepts of Prophecy and Healing are Divine attributes proven through Mediumship.

In 1890, the U.S. census reported forty-five thousand members of Spiritualist churches. In the early twenty-first century, estimates of the number of Spiritualists vary from a few hundred thousand (those who participate in Spiritualist events or churches) to several million (the number of people who claim to have talked to or seen the spirits of the dead). The state with the most churches in the NSAC directory is California (ten), followed by Illinois (eight), New York (seven), and Maine (six).

Historical Background

Spiritualism in the modern sense can be traced to 1848 at a farmhouse in Hydesville near Rochester in western New York State. It was there that sisters Kate and Margaret Fox, ages twelve and fourteen, claimed that they had made contact with the ghost of a murdered man who had lived in the house. The girls reported that they heard mysterious raps and clicking noises coming from the walls and furniture, which formed patterned answers to their questions about such things as the age or number of children a family had. Curious visitors crowded the house to witness the mysterious messages. As time passed, the raps were said to become more sophisticated, answering not only yes or no and giving numbers, but spelling out letters of the alphabet. Forty years after the first reported contacts with the dead in their home, the Fox sisters confessed that they had concocted the noises by cracking their toe and knee joints. Nevertheless, the belief that certain people have the power to channel the spirits of the dead and the practice of holding séances became widely popular.

While contact with the dead by the Foxes is often cited as the origin narrative of Spiritualism, the medium Andrew Jackson Davis is usually credited with establishing the church and given the moniker "John the Baptist of Modern Spiritualism." Born in Blooming Grove, New York, in 1826, Davis is said to have shown signs of clairvoyance as a boy and, on the advice of a spirit, convinced his father to move to Poughkeepsie in 1838. He was influenced there by lectures on mesmerism, named after its originator, Franz Anton Mesmer, a physician from Vienna who claimed to cure ailments by use of magnets and hypnosis. In a hypnotic trance, Davis appeared to be able to diagnose medical disorders, claiming that the power came from the "spirit eyes" at the center of his forehead. In 1844, he claimed to have contact with the ghost of the deceased Swedish theosophist Emanuel Swedenborg, who revealed to Davis ideas of the essential nature of matter and its relation to the spirit world. His connection to the Fox sisters occurred when he said he heard voices calling him to "a living demonstration" at the moment the girls made contact with the dead. Spreading his message on the lecture circuit, Davis influenced the establishment of early Spiritualist churches such as the Working Union of Progressive Spiritualists (later changed to the First Spiritual Temple) near Boston in 1883 and the Plymouth Spiritualist Church in Rochester, New York, in 1906. The latter is often called the "Mother Church of Modern Spiritualism" because of its location where the Fox sisters acted as mediums.

Throughout the history of Spiritualism, most mediums have been women. The tendency has been explained as a reflection of the affinity between the feminine sphere and the morally sacred spaces of home and family. The concept of heaven, where spirits reside, has a similar connotation and is likewise thought of as an extension of women's space. Since women were seen to be more passive, more pious, and more domestic than men, they were more likely to be candidates for channeling spiritual messages. Spiritualist women, therefore, were pioneers in the religious sphere in that they were able to speak in public, often on tour, and to write books and articles when other religions forbade women access to theological power. It is not surprising, therefore, that many Spiritualists were active in the women's rights movement and reform movements in the nineteenth century.

Beliefs and Practices

A typical early Spiritualist performance would include a medium, who would enter a cabinet or enclosure, often curtained off with a black fabric from the rest of the room. She (or he) would then go into a trance and emerge as the materialized spirit. In this state, the medium would speak with the spirit's voice, perform automatic writing (in which the spirit is said to guide the hand), or paint pictures while blindfolded. Sometimes music could be heard. Other mediums would produce flowers or doves that were attributed as gifts from a specific spirit.

Spiritualists claimed that a viscous substance called ectoplasm could emanate from the body of a medium through the mouth or other orifice and then produce living forms. By 1911, Spiritualists reported ectoplasm taking the shape of hands, limbs, and feet. As more extraordinary acts were reported, critics such as the magician Harry Houdini claimed during the 1920s that so-called mediums used trickery to create the effects reported as spirits of the dead. Houdini's great nemesis was the Boston medium Mina Crandon, known as Margery, who in 1923 claimed to communicate with the spirit of her brother Walter, who had died in a train crash twelve years before. Margery submitted to scientific tests that appeared to vindicate her, but Houdini publicly denounced her as a fraud after attending a séance in which spirits supposedly tipped the table and spoke through her. Spiritualists point to the perpetrators of such frauds as charlatans who exploit common belief in the spirit world, but they insist that genuine mediums can communicate with the dead.

Spiritualists have traditionally had centers or camps where devotees congregate. They are most often located near water, because of the belief that spirits are attracted to it and that it is a source of "magnetic" energy. The oldest and probably best-known camp, the Cassadaga Free Lake Association, was founded in 1879 by the Spiritualist church in Laona, New York. In 1906 it was renamed Lily Dale, inspired by the lilies that grew around the Cassadaga Lakes. A sprawling eighty-acre site with several hundred cottages, a healing temple, stores, meeting places, and a hotel, Lily Dale gained notoriety for having the Fox family's cottage moved from its original location at Hydesville to the camp, thereby creating a shrine for "the birthplace of Spiritualism." The renowned medium Flo Cottrel used the cottage for readings after 1911, and participants claimed to hear the raps produced by the spirit of Walter. The cottage burned down in 1956, but the camp established a Fox Cottage Museum and meditation garden. Lily Dale became a mecca for Spiritualists, eventually becoming the largest Spiritualist community in America. One of its best-known features is the Inspiration Stump, where "message services" for mediums to communicate with the dead are held. A number of legends are associated with the tree stump—that its strong vibrations have caused people to have heart attacks, that those who stand behind it will feel their hair rise, and the like.

Another notable camp is Temple Heights, Maine, founded in 1882 by Dr. Benjamin Colson, who used herbs to heal the daughter of Frederick Robie, then the governor of the state. In gratitude, Robie granted Colson four thousand dollars and one hundred acres of land to get the camp

started. In 1894 a group of Spiritualists, mostly from Lily Dale, formed another camp, the Cassadaga Spiritualist Camp in central Florida. Originally intended to be winter retreat for Spiritualists from New York, it continues to flourish as a tourist destination. Visitors come from all over the United States and other countries for a Spiritualist reading or healing. Like Lily Dale, it also offers numerous workshops and classes. Cassadaga is the oldest active religious community in the southeastern United States. Approximately seventy-five people, mostly mediums, live in the camp.

Healing, according to modern Spiritualists, can occur with and without spiritual intervention. With intervention, Spiritualists refer to an "unseen healing force" that cleanses the healer's mind and body and allows him or her to heal others. In "absent healing" a curative power is sent by a person or group to someone at a distance. Spiritualists believe that this power, based on energy from the spirit realms, comes through mediums or "spirit doctors." In "contact healing," or the "laying on of hands," physical contact helps the healer transfer curative energy to the recipient. The healer's hand or hands are placed on the recipient's head, shoulders, or both, bringing spiritual energy to the ailing person. Many contact healers place one hand on the recipient's forehead and another on the back of the neck. A common prayer used in spiritual healing is as follows:

> I ask the great unseen healing force to remove all obstructions from my mind and body and to restore me to perfect health.
>
> I ask this in all sincerity and honesty, and I will do my part. I ask this great unseen healing force to help both present and absent ones who are in need of help and to restore them to perfect health. I put my trust in the love and power of God.

For most Spiritualists, spiritual healing does not exclude biomedical help. Spirit doctors, the NSAC acknowledges, work with in cooperation with the medical community, also regarded as an instrument of the "Infinite."

Churches such as the First Spiritual Temple in Boston regularly include spiritual healing and laying on of hands as part of the Sunday worship, often with the help of an identified spirit (at First Spiritual Temple, it is called John). Churches often claim that the sermon is delivered by the spirit (at the First Spiritual Temple, it is called Syrsha) through the "trance mediumship" of the minister. There is a communion service, but Spiritualists point out that it is not Eucharistic in nature; they do not perceive the bread and wine as representing the body and blood of Christ. For Spiritualists, the bread represents the flesh and body of the individual; the wine represents the individual's God-given spirit, which resides in the flesh. The ritual of communion is therefore a symbolic representation of these two elements of earthly life coming together in harmony and communion. Like other Christian churches, Spiritualists celebrate Christmas and Easter.

Following the roots of Spiritualism in Mesmerism, some healers use "magnetic healing" as a form of nonspiritual healing. Spiritualists believe that an abundance of magnetic energy within the physical being of some persons helps facilitate the transference of extra healing energy to others. "Suggestive healing" is another nonspiritual intervention utilizing positive thoughts implanted in the mind to promote healing. Affirmations such as "Every day in every way, I am getting better and better" work like sympathetic magic in the Spiritualist belief that "like thoughts in turn create like conditions."

Many Spiritualists believe that acceptance of the religion's basic ideas in mediumship is increasing in the twenty-first century, as people look for spiritual experiences and alternative healing in the postmodern world. Meanwhile, related traditions with beliefs in mediumship, such as Espiritismo (Caribbean Spiritism) and neo-Shamanism (based on the role of shamans in traditional societies of healing and connecting to the spirit world), are gaining recognition in the United States as a result of new immigration for the former and the new age movements for the latter. Adherents also believe that Spiritualism has an appeal to agnostics and atheists, as it helps

with bereavement and comforts in times of war and global distress.

In the third century of the movement, Spiritualists are working to cultivate their heritage by promoting figures such as the Fox sisters, Davis, and Crandon whom the NSAC labels as "pioneers." The organization sponsors conventions and pilgrimages to the Rochester birthplace and "mother church" of its movement. Looking to the future, the NSAC contemplates the establishment of an Internet church and the spread of Spiritualism from the United States to Europe and Canada.

Kristin G. Congdon and Simon J. Bronner

See also: Belief; Religion; Supernatural.

Sources

Brandon, Ruth. *The Spiritualists: The Passion for the Occult in the Nineteenth and Twentieth Centuries.* New York: Knopf, 1983.

Braude, Ann. *Radical Spirits: Spiritualism and Women's Rights in Nineteenth-Century America.* Boston: Beacon, 1989.

Lewis, I.M. *Ecstatic Religion: A Study of Shamanism and Spirit Possession.* 2nd ed. New York: Routledge, 1989.

Lucas, Phillip C., John J. Guthrie, Jr., and Gary Monroe, eds. *Cassadaga: The South's Oldest Spiritualist Community.* Gainesville: University Press of Florida, 2000.

Moore, R. Laurence. *In Search of White Crow.* New York: Oxford University Press, 1977.

"Spiritualism: Pathway of Light." National Association of Spiritualist Churches. www.nsac.org/spiritualism/index.htm.

Weisberg, Barbara. *Talking to the Dead: Kate and Maggie Fox and the Rise of Spiritualism.* San Francisco: HarperSanFrancisco, 2004.

Wicker, Christine. *Lily Dale: The True Story of the Town That Talks to the Dead.* San Francisco: HarperSanFrancisco, 2003.

Sports Teams

Sports teams, often relying on close cooperation among members and pressure to perform in high-stakes competition, commonly possess a set of traditions that is distinctive to the particular team and another that is associated with the sport. On many occasions, athletes individually adapt beliefs and customs as their own. While these pat-

The mascot, colors, and lore of a professional or amateur sports team help bind its followers in a highly passionate hometown folk group. Players and coaches represent an even narrower subset, in which ritual and belief play no small role. *(Dave Sandford/Getty Images)*

terns constitute the folklife known by the athletes, the lore surrounding sports teams has entered more widely into American culture. From the professional to the amateur level, America's major sports—baseball, football, basketball, and others—inspire rich and ever-evolving folk expressions.

Beliefs and Taboos

Underscoring the significance of these traditions are instances when they are broken. For example, New York Yankees pitcher Allie Reynolds on July 12, 1951, caused a stir when he defied one of baseball's oldest traditions: when a pitcher has a no-hitter in the making, no one on the team must mention it. In the dugout at the end of the sev-

enth inning, Reynolds turned to teammate Eddie Lopat and wondered loudly enough for all to hear, "Well, Ed, what do you think? Can I pitch a no-hitter?" Lopat was thunderstruck, speechless. When Reynolds blithely continued the conversation with his catcher, Yogi Berra, he scurried away in shock. So strong is the taboo that some broadcast announcers remain reluctant to discuss a no-hitter, looking for an acceptable way to let the audience know without jinxing the pitcher.

As it happened, Allie Reynolds pitched not one, but two no-hitters for the Yankees in 1951, the second in a high-pressure, late-season game against the rival Boston Red Sox with the pennant at stake. After the latter game, sportswriters surrounded Reynolds, peppering him with questions. "I didn't kid around today," he told the scribes. "You fellows wrote your stories about what I said last time—how I kept talking about my no-hitter before I wrapped it up. And I got a sackful of letters from fans all over the country, bawling me out for breaking a baseball tradition." Reynolds explained his return to tradition, "You'd be surprised at how many people were sore about it. So this time I didn't mention it to *anybody*!"

In challenging one of his game's oldest folk beliefs, Reynolds shed light on the ever-endangered state of the athlete. Why do some players never step on the white lines when returning to the bench? Why would a tough-as-nails hockey player refuse to touch, or even to look at, the Stanley Cup before a playoff game? When a basketball player reaches down and fiddles with her socks before shooting a free throw, is she superstitious or just uncomfortable? The sports world is ever parlous. Columnist George Will insightfully observed that "successful athletes compress into such a short span most of life's inevitable trajectory and decline." Being injured, demoted, cut from the roster; slumping, playing poorly, or losing a game: these are the Damocles swords hanging over every member of every team. And so, over time, in a high-tension, rules-based environment where any edge might make the difference between success and failure and where demonstrable solidarity is a requirement, a large number and variety of beliefs, habits, and folk behaviors have emerged that many players and onlookers take very seriously. Some swear by talismans—medallions, tattoos, or other good-luck charms. Others perform rituals, from slight tics to elaborate displays. So recognizable is the tendency that movie audiences intuitively understood the gag in the film *Major League* (1989) in which a Caribbean-born outfielder includes his bats in a locker-room Santería ritual, chasing away juju that might chase away hits.

Narratives and Customs

In his seminal article "Locker Rumors," folklorist William H. Beezley set out categories within which the sporting world breeds folk legends and customs, identifying the Coach, Team Jokers, and Players' Codes as deserving special attention. Although normative formalism is essential to the structure and conduct of a game, athletes on the court, field, or diamond create and perpetuate an enormous amount of habitual, ritual, and ceremonial behaviors as part of their play and preparation regimens. Beezley's categories remain useful in examining these traditions.

As designated group leaders, coaches have long been the source of much sports lore. The focus of coach tales relates to a winning, discipline, and leadership style, often with a humorous nod to requisite ego. In many cases, the identity of a long-term coach conflates with that of his team. Vince Lombardi, the legendary coach of the Green Bay Packers, spawned innumerable stories, spread by adoring players, fans, and writers, that combined to form the hagiography of one of football's saints. The usual narrative engine in these stories is Lombardi's boundless authority. The tale was told, for example, that Lombardi was run over by a boat—while walking on water. Beezley recalled another illustrative joke, in which a dead football player mounts to heaven, only to find a team of angels running football drills while a short figure on the sideline shouts instructions. Asking St. Peter who the shouter is, the deceased player is told: "Oh, that's God. He thinks he's Vince Lombardi." Other legendary coaches who became the objects of such

lore and humor include college basketball's Bob Knight (Texas Tech and Indiana University) and college football's Woody Hayes (Ohio State).

The pep talk, reflecting the belief that athletes can be inspired to perform beyond their capabilities, is the forum for the most popular coach-as-motivator stories. From psychologist to father-confessor to Svengali, most successful college coaches have their preferred roles and methods for coaxing the maximum performance from their players. (In the National Football League [NFL], the professional status and relative age of players generally render them less susceptible to varsity-level rhetoric.) The most famous college pep talks supersede the world of ball games, speaking to larger issues. Such was the case when Pop Warner, the coach of Carlisle Indian School in Pennsylvania, where Jim Thorpe played before World War I, prepared to play Army. Prior to kickoff, Warner took his Native American players aside and lectured them on the game's implications. "From the shores of Little Big Horn to the banks of Wounded Knee Creek, the spirits of your people call you," intoned Warner, proceeding to recapitulate Chief Joseph's retreat and the Cherokee Trail of Tears. "These men are soldiers," he reminded his squad. "These are the Long Knives. You are Indians. Today we will know if you are warriors." The fact that his impressionable young men rolled to an upset victory over the U.S. Military Academy made the lesson of this talk one that all football fans—and coaches—could appreciate. But just the right balance must be struck if the coach is not to overreach. A famous rib on the pep talk theme came when a Yale coach devised an acrostic, using the letters Y, A, L, and E to spell out the values he expected his players to defend on the field. "It's a good thing we don't attend the Massachusetts Institute of Technology," one bored player cracked.

During the early 1980s, when the Baltimore Orioles pitching staff was hard to beat, pitching coach Ray "Rabbit" Miller made an observation that no doubt struck outsiders as peculiar. Asked by an onlooker why the team's left-handed pitchers ran their warm-up sprints on a hillside, Miller replied, "There ain't a left-hander in the world that can run a straight line. It's the gravitational pull of earth's axis that gets 'em." The assumption that left-handed pitchers are somehow "different" fit neatly into baseball's dossier of conventional wisdom. So it was that Miller's tale reinforced an in-baseball prejudice—that southpaws are oddballs—even as it played up his own reputation as a sort of wizard whose bizarre insights help decipher the goings-on at the pitcher's mound.

Another belief prevalent among teams is that some players account for supernatural intervention or good luck, even if their talents are not up to the level of other players. The iron-fisted, hot-tempered manager John McGraw, who would sooner punch a player than argue with him, revealed a strongly superstitious streak in 1911, when he signed an eccentric drifter who showed up with the message that a fortune-teller told him to pitch for the Giants. The new player, improbably named Charles Victor Faust, was hardly of major-league caliber, but something in McGraw told him that the fates were at work. Faust held a spot on the roster for the entire season, more for his purported good-luck powers than for his hurling ability. When the Giants won the pennant, McGraw proudly claimed, "I give Charlie Faust full credit." Even more tellingly, the story is rarely told in baseball circles with any hint of mockery against McGraw for relying on superstition to help run his team. Indeed, there is invariably an implicit acceptance of Faust's magical destiny and admiration for McGraw's willingness to set aside skepticism, spot the mojo at work, and keep Faust on the team.

Winning is the essential ingredient for any coach to be deemed worthy of spawning folklore. Otherwise, discipline can seem capricious and idiosyncrasies look more like neuroses. The same holds true for players. It is doubtful that John F. Kennedy would have remembered Johnny Blood with any fondness if football's "Magnificent Screwball" had not been a star. As it was, when they were introduced, the president shook hands delightedly with the man whose name was a household word in the Kennedy home. A Minnesotan, Blood played at little St. John's and went on to fame in the NFL during the 1930s. His irrepressible behavior off the field—such as hanging out of a high-rise window, and doing handstands on the railing of a train's observation car—marked Blood as a fitting example of what Beezley called a "team joker." But as with Blood, team jokers, whose function is to alleviate the sometimes daunting pressure that builds up in the hypercompetitive team environment, are tolerated best if they also play well. Almost no one would talk back to Lombardi, but the Packers did have a designated pair of kidders, Max McGee and Paul Hornung, whose specialty was teasing their coach and amusing their teammates. When a sarcastic Lombardi held up a ball, explaining, "This is a football," McGee asked him, "Could ya go a little slower, coach?" The team joker thus flummoxed the disciplinarian, but in a harmless way that did not contest authority.

Players' Codes

As for Players' Codes, these are behavioral modifiers—dos and don'ts that assert and reify the time-honored social arrangements on a roster which, by its very definition, is always changing and never fixed. They provide structure and promote unity. Some of them revolve around specific roles or players. In football, for example, the quarterback has a special status and must not be harmed during practice; kickers are considered weird. In baseball, a batter who hits a home run and admires the flight of the ball while jogging slowly around the bases runs the risk of being beaned (hit by a pitch) in his next at-bat, or of having his teammates beaned as punishment for his showboating. Players must stick up for one another, but dirty play complicates the loyalty factor.

The delicate matter of race must always be bound up with American sports traditions, since both evolved during the twentieth century and because racial issues, and styles, are still part of the discourse on sports in the twenty-first century. Until Jackie Robinson's arrival with the Brooklyn Dodgers in 1947, segregation kept the black and white baseball worlds apart. Remembrances of former Negro League greats such as Buck Leonard reveal that the African American players had a similar set of codes, which would not have been unfamiliar to their major league counterparts. Showing off at an opponent's expense was discouraged, even if the Negro Leagues had more space for individual flourishes during play. Today, with officially segregated leagues part of the past, race underpins one of the more important player codes: solidarity—the idea that all members of a roster are in it together and that there should be no divisions off the field that might cause the team's performance to suffer.

One of the persistent tensions on any team roster is the arrival of the rookies, the newcomers who must try and win away jobs from the veterans. In most sports, a host of hazing rituals ensures that rookies will not feel too comfortable, too soon. Sometimes these behaviors collide with modern adult sensibilities. In baseball, where tradition holds it amusing for veterans to hide a rookie's clothes before a road trip and replace them with outlandish garb, reactions are monitored with care. A rookie who protests too much runs the risk of being labeled a malcontent. In football, where the hazing might require a rookie to do the laundry, carry the equipment of a veteran, or stand on a training table and sing a college fight song, the same pressures are applied.

Nor is the code of rookie conduct restricted by gender, despite comforting notions of womanly solidarity in the otherwise competitive athletic field. While the WNBA, a professional basketball league for women launched in the 1990s, markets itself in part on the basis of women's solidarity, other female sports figures recall that their environments were just as competitive as that of their male counterparts. Sis Waddell, a rookie for the Rockford Peaches of the wartime All-American Girls' Professional Baseball League—itself a dimly remembered piece of baseball folklore until the hit film *A League of Their Own* (1992)—remembered how veterans waited for fans to buy them postgame Cokes. Rookies were not welcomed until they had proven themselves. There was a hierarchy, but good play

might gain a player entry into the Coke klatch. "Finally this one little girl, she saw I wasn't gettin' a Coke, so she started buyin' me one," recalled Waddell. "Then every night, she was out there with my Coke." No longer an anonymous player, Waddell had earned her own following and entered the veterans' circle.

Player and Spectator Practices

The last and largest area of sports folklife is the hardest to quantify. This is the list of beliefs and practices maintained by each player. Some are easy to understand and decode, such as the Catholic batter who crosses himself before every pitch or the hoopster who tapes his dead friend's name to his sneakers. Some stem from a mysterious interstice where factors such as nutrition, physical and mental preparation, and training preparations collide with the murkier world of faith. Wade Boggs, a Hall of Fame baseball player, was notorious for eating chicken, and only chicken, before every game. In a landmark June 1964 article for the *New York Folklore Quarterly*, Lee Allen compiled and elucidated a list, "The Superstitions of Baseball Players." Reaching back to the game's nineteenth-century roots, he identified a host of "fixed beliefs, related to luck," many of which remain in force today. Some—such as Sam Wise's habit of carrying a small potato in his pocket as a guard against aches and pains—were idiosyncratic but understandable. Others have modern counterparts aplenty. The player who ate lima beans at every meal or the batboy whose arrival made him a good-luck charm to the players still fit into that athlete's world, where failure, ignominy, and oblivion are never far away. In particular, beliefs and charms abound for improving hitting, since the failure rate is high. (There are fewer extraneous practices associated with fielding, probably because the risk of failure is far lower.)

Some of the customs start in early childhood. Fielders, for example, cosset and jealously guard their baseball gloves, molding and tending the leather during the off-season, using proprietary combinations of balm, spit, heat, and rubber bands to "break it in," sleeping on or with the mitt to ensure its proper shape and safety. All Little Leaguers know the magic of the "rally cap" (turning the cap inside out for good luck when trailing late in the game). They learn such behaviors from watching major league role models, who themselves learned the behaviors as children. Whether the magic of the rally cap inheres in some unknowable mystery, or whether it simply demonstrates the team solidarity and optimism that can lead to hits and runs, is for the believers to decide. The practice is the important thing, and it begets its own belief.

From the stands, spectators participate in sports folklife by showing solidarity with their favorite team and engaging in rituals designed to spur the team to victory. Forms of identity building include the wearing of team colors and insignias and the use of animal mascots. Cheerleaders urge spectators to root for their team performing gymnastic feats to generate excitement. The familiar "rah, rah, rah" of college cheers derives from the "hip, hip, hurrah" of British yells and has become elaborated into creative rhymes and routines.

College football enthusiasts set off cannons, ring bells, and perform any number of rituals in support of their team. At the University of Texas, for example, it is traditional to illuminate a thirty-eight-story light tower in the color orange when the team wins a game. Texas is also home to the best-known gesture in college football—the "Hook 'Em Horns," introduced by Longhorn fans in 1955. Made by extending the index and little fingers and tucking the middle and ring fingers beneath the thumb, the signal is jokingly turned upside down by rival Oklahoma fans, creating the sign of the horns hitting someone in the rear end.

Fans at Texas A&M University, meanwhile, are known for their Twelfth Man tradition. According to legend, after the Aggie football players were put of commission by numerous injuries, the coach called a student-athlete out of the stands to suit up. Since 1922, the Aggie student body stands to indicate their readiness to serve as the twelfth man for the team. Aggies may also give the "Gig 'em" sign by clenching their right hand as if calling someone out in baseball. Kansas University Jayhawk fans "wave the wheat" by stretching their hands over their heads and moving them back and forth. They have also been well known for their haunting "Rock Chalk, Jayhawk, KU!" chant since the late nineteenth century. The Jayhawk rhyme refers to the chalk rock on Mt. Oread, the university's campus. As player rituals provide control over uncertain situations, the collective antics of spectators generate vibrancy intended to energize the players and raise the game to the level of spectacle.

Charles Kupfer

See also: Belief; Bodybuilders and Weightlifters; Detroit; Little League Baseball and Youth Sports Organizations; Martial Artists; Men and Masculinity; Organization, Corporate and Work; Rituals and Rites; Wrestling, Professional.

Sources

Allen, Lee. "The Superstitions of Baseball Players." *New York Folklore Quarterly* 20 (1964): 98–109.

Beezley, William H. "Locker Rumors: Folklore and Football." *Journal of the Folklore Institute* 17 (1980): 213–21.

Bronner, Simon J. *Piled Higher and Deeper: The Folklore of Student Life.* Little Rock, AR: August House, 1995.

Coffin, Tristram P. *The Old Ball Game: Baseball in Folklore and Fiction.* New York: Herder and Herder, 1971.

Graham, Frank, Jr. *Baseball Wit and Wisdom: The Folklore of a National Pastime.* New York: Scholastic Books, 1965.

Peterson, Elizabeth. "American Sports and Folklore." In *Handbook of American Folklore,* ed. Richard M. Dorson, 257–64. Bloomington: Indiana University Press, 1983.

Rogosin, Donn. *Invisible Men: Life in Baseball's Negro Leagues.* New York: Atheneum, 1983.

STEELWORKERS

Just as cotton shaped the culture and landscape of the South in the antebellum period, so steel changed the way of life and physical appearance of many northern industrial cities, particularly in Pennsylvania, Ohio, and Illinois, during the nineteenth and early twentieth centuries. Although the industry in America has declined in the late twentieth century, steel was responsible for bringing a large variety of ethnic groups to U.S. shores

By the early twentieth century, the burgeoning American steel industry had altered the nation's physical, social, and cultural landscape. Less than a century later, the occupational folklife of steelworkers had become the object of several major preservation efforts. *(Library of Congress, LC-USZ62-107112)*

and for changing the face of American society. Along with a willingness to work hard, these groups brought customs and beliefs that became a permanent part of American folklife. The steelworkers of yesterday are also folk heroes in stories concerning unfair labor practices and disputes.

A wealth of mineral resources, technological advances, and organizational innovation all contributed to the rise of steel production in the United States. In the latter part of the nineteenth century, America produced half as much pig iron (a cruder form of steel) as the United Kingdom. By 1900, it surpassed Britain by 150 percent and led all other countries in steel manufacturing.

Not only did steel dominate the world market, it also controlled the U.S. manufacturing sector. By the late 1950s, more than 40 percent of all manufacturing jobs in the nation depended on steel. A halt in steel making would soon put a stop to automotive and railroad production, as well as curtail the construction of large buildings and bridges.

In addition to mills, steel companies own iron mines, coal mines, and limestone quarries. Some operate railroad lines and boats that carry raw materials. Scrap metal plants and coke ovens are run by steel companies as well, though they are large enough to be classified as separate industries. Of course, warehouses, research laboratories, machine shops, and repair departments are satellite businesses and must be counted as part of the overall industry.

Social Characteristics

Steel centers in the United States arose near the supplies of coal used in steel production. Thus, about 75 percent of the mills were located in Pennsylvania, Ohio, Indiana, Illinois, and New York. In some cases, the mill owner built houses and opened company stores for workers, which created neighborhoods dependent on the steel industry. The children and grandchildren of steel laborers grew up thinking that their destiny was to work in the mills, just as their ancestors had.

Early working conditions were hard in steel mills. Irish and Scottish immigrants in the early days were skilled laborers with specific job responsibilities. They organized labor groups and fought for higher wages, which they enjoyed until companies began union-busting practices in the 1890s. The Homestead Strike of 1892 near Pittsburgh was a major defeat for workers that resulted in the demise of the local union as well as the deaths of four strikers. Workers were forced to take drastic pay cuts. Another union was not organized and became effective until the 1930s.

To maintain cheap labor, steel companies hired new immigrants for unskilled jobs. After the Irish workers, the next wave of new immigrants came from eastern Europe and Italy. They began arriving in the late nineteenth century and usually lived in neighborhoods with people of the same ethnicity. African Americans from the South also migrated to mill towns around the same time. Every new group that came into an area was looked upon with animosity by the workers who were already there, who feared displacement or cuts in pay. Although the economic climate and labor relations in the steel industry are radically different today, prejudices between new immigrant groups and established workers still exist. Mexican and Asian laborers arriving from the 1970s to the 1990s were often looked on with suspicion by older steelworkers.

Despite the obstacles, each ethnic group managed to leave its mark in the steel-producing areas they settled. In Detroit, Youngstown, Chicago, Gary, Pittsburgh, and other rust-belt manufacturing centers, the old neighborhoods are scattered with ethnic bakeries, churches, and grocery stores. Streets and neighborhood parks often carry names of Poles, Germans, or other ethnic figures. Many neighborhood parks still have war monuments with the names of local boys who lost their lives in conflict. Cultural organizations sponsor ethnic music and dance groups, sell traditional crafts, and offer foreign-language instruction. Ethnic diversity has become a symbol of pride for many of these cities, and ethnic festivals are held throughout the year to celebrate each group's contribution.

Lore and Life of the Mills

Working conditions in steel mills have also improved, though steelworkers still recount stories about dangerous conditions. In field surveys conducted for his book *Land of the Millrats* (1981), Richard Dorson recorded stories about steelworkers who lost their lives as a result of work accidents. The lore at most mills includes stories of people who died in a vat of molten steel. In Donora, Pennsylvania, the molten steel in which one man was killed was said to have formed a slab and been buried in a local cemetery. A lost finger is considered an emblem of experience among older steelworkers.

Anger toward the steel company because of unfair practices is still prominent in the lore of today's mills. Workers often tell tales about people stealing from companies or destroying property. A favorite story is about mill workers who destroy a soda machine and nearly cause the workers to strike; they are convinced that the company canteen is taking advantage of them by charging high prices for poor food and refusing to repair the vending machines. Much like the

songs and stories of the old labor movement, such tales make heroes of vandals and rule breakers.

Workers also react to the boredom of repetitive work by pulling pranks and shirking on the job. Some workers use cranes or other machinery to launch paper airplanes; others take naps while on duty. Sometimes the pranks fall into the realm of vandalism, like spilling grease on carpeted floors or jamming expensive equipment.

New mill workers are often subjected to an initiation process, in which, for example, they are sent to fetch equipment that does not exist or to perform a nearly impossible task. Examples might include a "left-handed wrench" or a "bucket of steam." Many of these pranks have an ancient lineage in tradition as "fool's errands." As in the old days, workers have a sense of camaraderie toward their coworkers and often give them nicknames that reflect their behavior or appearance.

Another prevalent figure in steel-mill folklore is the rat. Owing to the size and age of some mills, rat populations are said to be enormous—exaggeratedly so. Workers tell tall tales of rats moving large equipment and opening metal lunch pails.

By the 1980s the steel industry in America was no longer a world leader. The city known for steel production in the past, Pittsburgh, produced less steel than the Chicago area. Today dark clouds of pollution no longer hang over Gary, Youngstown, or Pittsburgh, and people who live there are proud of their green cities. Jokes are made about never needing a lawn mower when the mills were active. By the early twenty-first century, residents joked that one needs two lawn mowers because the grass grows so fast.

Documenting Steelworkers' Heritage

Efforts to document the heritage of steelworkers and analyze the identities of steel regions and communities emerged in the late twentieth century. The United Steelworkers of America oral history project, featuring extensive narrative and folklife material, is housed at Pennsylvania State University at University Park. The Smithsonian Institution developed plans in 1998 for a new National Museum of Industrial History at the former Bethlehem Steel Plant in Bethlehem, Pennsylvania. The Rivers of Steel National Heritage Area, based in Homestead, Pennsylvania, features folklife programming of the region's steel heritage and assistance to folk artists and ethnic communities. Among its public folklife offerings has been a series of half-hour radio programs entitled *Tradition Bearers*, featuring shows such as "Mill Worker Memories," with former steelworkers recounting lore about life in the mills.

Cindy Kerchmar

See also: Allegheny Region; Occupational Folklife; Pittsburgh.

Sources

Brody, David. *Steelworkers in America: The Nonunion Era.* Urbana: University of Illinois Press, 1998.

Dickerson, Dennis C. *Out of the Crucible: Black Steelworkers in Western Pennsylvania, 1875–1980.* Albany: State University of New York Press, 1986.

Dorson, Richard M. *Land of the Millrats: Urban Folklore in Indiana's Calumet Region.* Cambridge, MA: Harvard University Press, 1981.

Hinshaw, John H. *Steel and Steelworkers: Race and Class Struggle in Twentieth-Century Pittsburgh.* Albany: State University of New York Press, 2002.

National Museum of Industrial History. www.nmih.org.

Serrin, William. *Homestead: The Glory and Tragedy of an American Steel Town.* New York: Random House, 1992.

"Tradition Bearers." Rivers of Steel National Heritage Area. www.riversofsteel.com.

Warren, Kennedy. *Big Steel: The First Century of the United States Steel Corporation, 1901–2001.* Pittsburgh: University of Pittsburgh Press, 2001.

STONE

Stone, quarried and shaped into various forms, is a pervasive and enduring element of the American cultural landscape. American crafts workers have used limestone, granite, slate, marble, and sandstone in the construction of nearly every kind of building, from vernacular to popular to elite, in public, commercial, and religious contexts alike. Vernacular styles of stone construction are widespread, especially in rural areas, based in part on the historic settlement patterns of various immigrant groups. Yet even where architectural or artistic styles are not of folk origin, the folk traditions of building and carving are still a part of American stone craft. The organization of work according to the apprenticeship system and the passing of skills and tools from father to son have their origins in the medieval guilds of Europe, refreshed and modified by new waves of immigrants. Where stone has been quarried, even the land itself has been permanently modified.

The decision to use stone over other available materials may be complex, depending on economic, functional, and symbolic factors, as well as the presence of skilled craftspersons to do the work. Economic considerations include the cost of materials, transportation, and labor, and the availability of raw materials. The advantages of stone include its durability and insulating and fire-resistant qualities, but the symbolic and aesthetic attributes are often what consumers and later generations value most. The permanence and strength of stone, its weightiness and bulk compared with other materials, its sculptural possibilities, its cost, and even its classical and biblical associations (in temples, altars, and monuments) have all led to its widespread use in government buildings, historic landmarks, churches, statuary, gravestones, and other structures meant to endure. The most common types of stone used in America include sandstone and limestone (sedimentary), granite (igneous), and marble and slate (metamorphic).

Quarrying Stone

Workers have obtained stone from a number of sources, depending on its intended use. Glacial deposits ranging from pebbles to boulders in the northern part of the continent have supplied stone for walls and foundations, although these sources are not suitable for large-scale building. Ledges and outcrops exposed by wind or water action have provided access to varieties of stone, usually for local and small-scale purposes. Commercial supplies usually require subsurface quarrying. Several different methods for splitting stone developed in early New England, including channeling with picks or axes, firing the stone along a line and splitting it with a hammer or cold water, and blasting with gunpowder. The most commonly referred-to method from the late eighteenth to the twentieth century is variously called the "plug and feather" or "wedge and feather" technique: The quarrier drills a line of holes along the desired split line, places two shims, or feathers, in each hole, and drives a wedge between them, systematically applying even force along the line with a hammer. This creates a clean line of cleavage from the parent rock. The loose block can then be pried out and hauled by stone boat (a sled) or hoisted by derrick to a stone shed, where it can be further split, or squared and dressed (surface prepared) by stonecutters for its intended use. Dressing is done with a variety of tools including points, chisels, straight edges, and hammers to achieve a rough finish. Smooth finishes are achieved with the use of abrasive stones and sand. Softer stone such as sandstone might also be sawed to size with a toothless saw, sand, and water. While all of these methods have been subject to change with the introduction of steam and electrically driven tools, the principles remain the same; older methods continue to be used for noncommercial quarrying.

Quarrying and stonecutting are dangerous work and were especially so before the introduction of health and safety regulations in the twentieth century. Injuries and fatalities were a regular occurrence in the quarries, but the most insidious danger was silicosis, a lung disease caused by breathing in the dust from stonecutting in cramped sheds. Unionization efforts came early to the industry, beginning with the masons and extending to stonecutters and quarriers through the later nineteenth and early twentieth centuries. Wages, hours, and health conditions were the chief concerns, and strikes were often met with violence and replacement by nonunion, or "scab," workers.

Occupational Life

Craftspersons within the stone trades make distinctions among workers by specialization, with an implicit hierarchy based on training and skill level. Quarriers appropriate the raw materials to the specifications requested; stonemasons specialize in laying stone for walls and other structures; stonecutters finish rough-cut stone for use and provide ornamentation in two dimensions; and carvers create three-dimensional works, including statues. While all these crafts require special training, carvers must also be educated in formal art techniques and have a working knowledge of solid geometry. Master cutters and carvers are responsible for translating the drawings of architects and the models of artists into the stone medium. Master carvers at the National Cathedral in Washington, D.C., for example, often began their exposure to the craft as children, through family businesses in Italy or elsewhere, slowly developing the skills and knowledge of all aspects of the stone trade. Stonecutters in the limestone belt of southern Indiana typically have a lifelong immersion in the craft, with the best carvers demonstrating their creativity in the nonbuilding arts as well—including sculptured lawn furniture and garden ornaments from benches to birdbaths. The National Cathedral carvers have the opportunity to demonstrate this creativity on the job in freehand carvings of gargoyles and other ornamentation whose details are not specified by the architect or sculptor.

In the ranching environment of Paradise Valley, Nevada, stone construction shares the landscape with buildings of wood and adobe. Italian stonemasons and their families settled in the valley beginning in the 1860s. All had been trained in the artisan shops of northern Italy and brought with them construction traditions that they modified to the needs of cattle ranches and small towns. Some buildings feature the hipped roof common to the Italian Piedmont, while others are more nondescript. Working as architects and contractors, masons there quarried granite and sandstone themselves and built ranch houses, bunkhouses, stables, churches, commercial buildings, and walls throughout the region. Most of the men retired by the 1940s, and few of their children continued in the trade.

Cobblestone Architecture

A path stretching from eastern New York to the Wisconsin-Illinois border, but concentrated in western New York, contains hundreds of cobblestone buildings built in the middle third of the nineteenth century. Associated with the late- and postcanal building period, they were erected by stonemasons who introduced the style from England. In this portion of the Great Lakes region, river valleys and lakeshores contain abundant rounded cobbles, which were sorted by size and color for a variety of surface effects, such as hexagon and herringbone patterns. Masons applied this folk style to the houses of prosperous farmers and some commercial buildings. Construction techniques included the use of mortared coursed lines of cobbles, some in integrated walls, others in double walls with rubble fill, tied together at several points with "through rocks" (rocks long enough to reach across the double wall). Some later buildings have a cobblestone veneer only, with cobbles of smaller size. Texture was the most important feature of cobblestone construction, with masons developing individual styles of patterning and mortar joint treatments, such as beading or a projecting V.

Stone Walls

Whether referred to as stone walls (New England, Ontario, and eastern New York), stone fences (Pennsylvania and western New York), or rock fences (Virginia and Kentucky), the many thousands of miles of this stone construction are an important element of the cultural landscape and an enduring part of the folk tradition in many regions. Nevertheless, function, style, and quality of construction all vary within and between regions and over time. Construction may be coursed or uncoursed (layered or not), mortared or laid dry, single- or double-walled, fieldstone or cut stone, and the work of a master craftsman or an untrained farmer. The walls have several functions—protecting crops and gardens or penning livestock, accumulating stones cleared from agricultural fields (especially in glaciated areas or uplands), and marking boundaries between properties, between property and road, or around cemeteries.

Many of the better dry walls are of double-wall construction, with the interior filled with smaller stones and the walls connected at many points with larger stones that extend the full width, variously called through stones, tie stones, or through puts. The wall rests on a foundation laid in a trench dug below the frost line. There should be no vertical joints. Courses of rock should be laid "two over one, one over two" to prevent vertical weaknesses. The structure is often "battered" or tapered, so that a wall thirty inches at the base may be eighteen inches at the top. Finally, the wall may be capped (or coped) with large, flat stones extending across the width or beyond, laid either horizontally (as in New England) or near vertically (as in Kentucky). Commonly, walls range from three to five feet in height, with shorter walls often incorporating other types of construction materials, such as rail or wire. Mortared walls became more popular after 1900, when walls were often built for aesthetic qualities rather than for function.

Nineteenth-century rock fences in the Kentucky bluegrass region were built largely by Irish masons. Slaves and, later, freedmen were often the labor force the masons used, and these "apprenticeships" led to a nearly complete replacement of Irish masons by African Americans in the craft by 1900.

With automation in the stone industry and the decline in demand for building stone and carving, the number of workers in the stone trades has fallen considerably from its height in the early twentieth century. Preference for steel and concrete in building has reduced the need for large numbers of highly trained crafts workers and endangered the traditional system of training new ones. The apprenticeship system does survive, albeit with some interesting modifications. At St. John the Divine Cathedral in New York City, a work in progress for more than a century, the continuing need for stone carvers prompted master crafts workers in 1979 to organize the Cathedral Stoneyard Institute for the training of at-risk youth in traditional stone crafts. A new generation of carvers continues work on the cathedral.

Jeff Wanser

See also: Barns; Farmers; Folk Art; Gravemarkers; Grottoes; Houses.

Sources

Gage, Mary, and James Gage. *The Art of Splitting Stone: Early Rock Quarrying Methods in Pre-Industrial New England, 1630–1825.* Amesbury, MA: Powwow River Books, 2002.

Hunt, Marjorie. *The Stone Carvers: Master Craftsmen of Washington National Cathedral.* Washington, DC: Smithsonian Institution Press, 1999.

Marshall, Howard W. *Paradise Valley, Nevada: The People and the Buildings of an American Place.* Tucson: University of Arizona Press, 1995.

Mastick, Patricia. "Dry Stone Walling." *Indiana Folklore* 9 (1976): 113–33.

McKee, Harley J. *Introduction to Early American Masonry: Stone, Brick, Mortar and Plaster.* Washington, DC: Preservation, 1973.

Murray-Wooley, Caroline, and Karl Raitz. *Rock Fences of the Bluegrass.* Lexington: University of Kentucky Press, 1992.

Noble, Allen G., and Brian Coffey. "The Use of Cobblestones as a Folk Building Material." *P.A.S.T.: Pioneer America Society Transactions* 9 (1986): 45–51.

Ola, Per, and Emily d'Aulaire. "Now What Are They Doing at That Crazy St. John the Divine?" *Smithsonian* 23, no. 9 (December 1992): 32–44.

STORYTELLING

Traditional storytelling takes place wherever small groups gather to work or socialize. In rural and small-town America, such settings traditionally have included general stores (with the inevitable "liars bench" out front), fishing boats, hunting camps, barbershops, and home porches or firesides. In modern America, jokes are shared around the office water cooler and after work at bars; scary stories are told at spend-the-night parties and around the campfire on scouting trips and at summer camp; and urban legends circulate in beauty parlors, shopping malls, school cafeterias, and college fraternity and sorority suites.

As oral literature, folk stories differ from their

Master storyteller Ray Hicks (1922–2003) of Beech Mountain, North Carolina, was especially fond of recounting the group of Appalachian *märchen* known as Jack tales. He is seen here in 1959, dancing to music by family members. *(Photo by Frank Warner, from the Anne and Frank Warner Collection, American Folklife Center)*

printed short-fiction counterparts in their variation (resulting from mouth-to-ear transmission and creative retelling) and their performance to and interaction with a live audience. While the folk narrator may share certain word skills with the writer, storytelling techniques are more akin to those of acting and public speaking. Varying with community preference and the narrator's personal style, these can involve such nonverbal and quasi-verbal support of the verbal message as gestures, facial expressions, and imitation of sounds and characters' voices. An archaic feature of some storytelling traditions is formulaic "runs," such as the ending sometimes tagged onto African American trickster tales: "I stepped on a piece of tin, the tin bent, and that's the way my story went."

The Storyteller's Repertoire

Folklorists divide traditional narratives into two main categories based on the attitudes of the storytelling community. Folktales are understood as fictitious and function mainly as entertainment, but they also convey values. Myths and legends, on the other hand, are regarded as true accounts; they can be entertaining but serve primarily as folk history and to support the belief system. Major groups of American folk stories also include fairy tales, trickster tales, tall tales, and jests.

Myths

Myths, as defined by folklorists, are the sacred stories of a religion; they often explain the present order as the creation of divinities, who are the chief characters. In the United States, oral or folk myths (as opposed to the written mythology of the Bible) are found mainly among Native Americans, with those of the Southwest surviving best. In practice, myth can be combined with such diverse genres as song, medicine, visual art, and architecture. Appropriate sections of Navajo mythology, such as the creation of First Man and First Woman by the gods from ears of corn, are used in "chantway" healing prayers, with further power channeled from the spirit world when the "singer" or shaman "paints" the corresponding scene on the floor of the patient's hogan (earth-covered Navajo dwelling) with colored sand from the Holy Mountains.

A few pre-Christian myths are still told by Native Americans of the eastern United States. North Carolina Cherokees, for example, explain the mountainous terrain of their Appalachian homeland as resulting from the flapping of a primordial buzzard's wings in the mud as he searched for dry ground after various animals brought up land from the bottom of the watery world. This "earth diver" motif (a recurring narrative element) is common in Native American flood myths.

Legends

American folklore is often associated with such real or imagined backwoods superheroes as Davy Crockett, Mike Fink, and Paul Bunyan. Today, however, the public's impression of these larger-than-life figures derives from print and film, not oral tradition. Genuine personal legends about strong men and yarn spinners such as

Maine's Barney Beal, Texas's Gib Morgan, New York State's John Darling, Indiana's Abraham "Oregon" Smith, and Idaho's Len Henry tend to be limited to their home areas.

Although seldom reliable as factual history, legends offer invaluable insights into the core attitudes of America's diverse regional, ethnic, occupational, and religious groups. For example, the Utah counterparts to European saint legends are accounts of miraculous appearances by the three Nephites, or prophets, to assist Mormons in time of need; while residents of coastal Maine echo New England Puritanism when telling of a becalmed sea captain whose boat is wrecked by a gale after he blasphemously tries to "buy" wind from God by tossing money overboard.

Some supernatural creatures of Old World folk belief, such as fairies, werewolves, and vampires, have not survived well in legendry of the United States, but ghosts, in which Americans seem willing at least to suspend their disbelief, are an exception. In the Hispanic Southwest, for example, encounters with *La Llorona* (the Weeping Woman), a spirit condemned to wander the earth for infanticide, are still reported.

By far the most active and widespread tradition of belief tales in America today is that of urban legends. Often inspired by current events and validated by the claim that they happened to a "friend of a friend," they reflect the anxieties blighting modern society, such as tainted consumer goods and deranged criminals—the horrors lurking in fast-food establishments, lovers' lanes, and, worst of all, the presumed security of our own homes. Such classics as "The Hook Man," "AIDS Mary," and "The Kentucky Fried Rat" are aided in their rapid spread by the mass media.

Märchen

The term "folktale" brings to mind the kind of stories made famous by German folklorists Jacob and Wilhelm Grimm: lengthy tales of adventure and magic that end happily for the clever and helpful young hero. Although they embody the rags-to-riches theme of the American dream, an oral tradition of these märchen (often translated as a wonder or fairy tale), as the Grimm brothers called them, is weak in the United States. They certainly were brought by early European immigrants, for they are represented in Pennsylvania German and Louisiana French collections and were borrowed by Native Americans (as the Zuni adaptation of "Cinderella" illustrates).

English-language fairytales, most likely of Scots-Irish origin, are concentrated in the southern Appalachian and Ozark mountains, as exemplified by the Jack tales (such as "Jack and the Beanstalk") of North Carolina's Ward-Harmon-Hicks family. Traces of Old World fantasy remain in the Jack tales: fire-breathing dragons, unicorns, giants, and magical gifts. But they also reflect American democracy, with Jack "hollering out" the king from his house, and incorporate such features of mountain folklife as log cabins and baskets of woven splits.

Trickster Tales

Folktales featuring an amoral trickster are emphasized in the Native American and African American traditions. In the former, animals such as Coyote (Southwest and Plains) or shape-shifters such as Wadjunkaga and Manabozho (Upper Midwest) behave as cruel and bawdy rule breakers in some episodes and as mythic culture heroes in others. In black storytelling, Brother Rabbit or his enslaved human counterpart, John, outwit more powerful animals and Old Master. The most famous trickster tale, popularized by Joel Chandler Harris in his first Uncle Remus book (1880) as "The Wonderful Tar-Baby Story," is first reported thirty-five years earlier among the Oklahoma Cherokees, although it likely was borrowed from African Americans and, like many other Brother Rabbit tales, originated in West Africa.

Tall Tales

Folktales whose humor relies on absurd exaggeration, best told in the first person with a straight face, are thought by some to be uniquely American, but in fact have European precedents such as *The Surprising Adventures of Baron Munchausen*

(1785). The very real hardships of the American frontier and the extreme physical conditions of each region echoed in such "lies," though, do help to explain their favored place both in oral tradition and print in the United States. For example, New Englanders experience winters so cold that they speak in ice cubes which must be melted to be understood; the Ozark Mountains are so steep that livestock are born with shorter legs on one side than on the other so they can stand upright. Georgia's most famous storyteller, Lem Griffis, set his yarns in the Okefenokee Swamp, where he was a fishing and hunting guide. One features his uncle Paul, whose walking stick is struck by a venomous swamp snake and swells into a giant log. He has a sawmill cut the log into ten miles of railroad crossties, but when a rainstorm washes the poison out of the ties and they shrink, the enterprising old man gathers them up and sells them for toothpicks.

Jests

Jests or jokes (not to be confused with joking riddles, which have a question-and-answer form) are stories meant to provoke laughter; their humor is derived from character, situation, or an unexpected ending ("punch line"). The most prevalent type of folktale today, jokes are so much a part of American life that they are not always recognized as folktales.

One older type of jest is the numskull or noodle tale, sometimes applied as a type of ethnic joke by attributing absurd ignorance to minority groups such as Swabians among the Pennsylvania Germans, Molbos (from the peninsula of Mols) among Danish Americans, and the "fool Irishmen" Pat and Mike among the general English-speaking population. In an example from Nebraska, Molbos sink their precious church bell in the ocean to hide it from invaders; in order to find it later, their "smart" leader marks the side of the boat exactly where they drop it. When such stories are told about an individual, such as Jean Sot (Foolish John) among the Louisiana French, the numskull seems to represent the formative stage of child development with which everyone can identify.

Modern jests—often inspired, like urban legends, by current events—include so-called dirty jokes that derive shock value from the otherwise taboo subjects of sex, bodily waste, or profanity. But such humor is not always as modern as it first appears, for old tales can be recycled to keep them current. A number of examples circulated about President Richard Nixon's White House after the 1973 Watergate break-in hearings.

Storytelling in Modern Society

To what extent is storytelling still a viable form of expression in today's television- and movie-dominated society? While the impact of mass media on such face-to-face entertainment is undeniable, it may be more a matter of kind than degree. Older, longer types of narrative, which require a commitment of time and attention on the part of both teller and audience, have given way to briefer, more conversational legends and jests.

Partly as a romantic reaction to passive mass-media entertainment, a storytelling revival took off in the 1970s. This movement is appropriately based in the South—a region known for its longstanding love affair with the spoken word—at Jonesborough, Tennessee, headquarters of the National Association for the Preservation and Perpetuation of Storytelling. At its annual festival and at numerous smaller gatherings around the country, professionals conduct workshops and perform stories they mainly invent or learn from print. But traditional narrators such as Jack tale-teller Ray Hicks of Beech Mountain, North Carolina, were involved, and these theatrical, large-audience venues could be the training grounds for a new generation of American folk storytellers.

John A. Burrison

See also: Dialect Stories; Folklore; Humor; Legends; *Märchen*; Names; Narrative, Personal; Taxi Drivers.

Sources

Baughman, Ernest W. *Type and Motif Index of the Folktales of England and North America.* The Hague: Mouton, 1966.

Brunvand, Jan Harold. *Encyclopedia of Urban Legends.* Santa Barbara, CA: ABC-CLIO, 2001.

Burrison, John A., ed. *Storytellers: Folktales and Legends from the South.* Athens: University of Georgia Press, 1989.

Dorson, Richard M., ed. *Buying the Wind: Regional Folklore in the United States.* Chicago: University of Chicago Press, 1964.

Hand, Wayland D., ed. *American Folk Legend: A Symposium.* Berkeley: University of California Press, 1971.

Sobol, Joseph Daniel. *The Storytellers' Journey: An American Revival.* Urbana: University of Illinois Press, 1999.

Thompson, Stith, ed. *Tales of the North American Indians.* Bloomington: Indiana University Press, 1966.

STRAIGHT EDGE

Straight Edge is a fringe youth movement originating and spreading in the United States that emphasizes abstinence from drugs, tobacco, alcohol, and casual sex, developing into a kind of gang folklife. Many participants have also adopted veganism or other vegetarian diets, and a concern for animal rights and radical environmentalism. Estimated to have several thousand adherents nationwide, Straight Edge emerged out of the hardcore music movement of the early 1980s, which eschewed the nihilism of punk rock in favor of championing political causes. Ian MacKaye, leader of the band Minor Threat, coined the term "Straight Edge" in a 1980 song of the same name. Early Straight Edge groups took stands against racism, sexism, and fascism, especially against neo-Nazi skinhead gangs that began to gain notoriety during the 1980s. Promoting Straight Edge as a force for positive change, many participants belong to grassroots political organizations such as Amnesty International, People for the Ethical Treatment of Animals, and Green Peace. Straight Edgers are often distinctive in high school youth culture, and out of their shared beliefs has emerged a folk group bound by self-conscious traditions, including body modification, music, religious associations, and identifying clothing.

Social Characteristics and Beliefs

Straight Edgers are mainly adolescent, white, middle class, male, and heterosexual. The goal of being Straight Edger is to gain total self-control over one's body and mind. Straight Edgers believe that intoxication of any kind is akin to slavery and that promiscuous sex is evidence of a lack of emotional self-control. The assertion of self-control is often in response to their perception of a society out of control because of moral decay and governmental intrusion. Straight Edge can be compared to "citizens groups" that view the government and corporate America as evil entities intent on the subordination of the populace. While not associated with any religion in itself, the asceticism in Straight Edge has been combined with various fundamentalist strains of Christianity as well as new religious movements such as Hare Krishna, known as Christiancore and Krishnacore, respectively. Some of the Christian and antigovernment beliefs of Straight Edge members have brought them into alliance with skinhead and ultranationalist groups, who find the militant and sometimes antihomosexual beliefs of Straight Edgers complementary to their pursuits of white, heterosexual purity and strength.

Many Straight Edge youth form gangs, often called brotherhoods or crews. The gangs act as a support network for staying sober and avoiding peer pressure. Not unlike other adolescent gangs, some Straight Edge gangs tend toward violence. Salt Lake City, Utah, is notorious for its violent Straight Edge gangs, who have perpetrated violence against bar patrons, smokers on city streets, and corporations such as McDonald's because of its use of animal products. Straight Edge bands such as Earth Crisis support a radical form of Straight Edge that combines the movement's fundamentalism with ecoterrorist activism.

Cultural Expressions

Body piercings and tattoos are also common among Straight Edgers, many of whom also have adopted the baggy clothing style of skateboarders to mark themselves as a countercultural group. Straight Edgers generally also wear oversized hooded Champion brand sweatshirts and football or hockey jerseys. The jerseys and sweatshirts act as uniforms, strengthening bonds of team unity. The symbolism of football and hockey refer to their aggressive, masculine ethic.

The most common way that Straight Edgers identify themselves physically is to color bold "X's" on the backs of their hands with black markers. Seriously devoted Straight Edgers sometimes get the "X" tattooed on a hand or other part of their body. The practice started in the early 1980s as a way for bartenders to distinguish minors from those of drinking age at open concerts held in bars. Variations on the "X" symbol include "sXe," (pronounced "sexy") and "sXe" with an "h" at the top of the "X" and a "c" at the bottom, standing for "Straight Edge Hardcore." The "X" announces that one is Straight Edger and committed to sobriety.

Authorities in many cities have developed task forces to educate the public and high school faculties about the symbols and beliefs associated with Straight Edge. Many schools prohibit Straight Edgers from wearing "X's" on their hands during school hours as a means of curbing violence at school. In Salt Lake City, Straight Edge gangs are classified in the same rank as more organized gangs, such as the Crips and Bloods. Police keep a file on youth associated with the Straight Edge movement as a way of monitoring gang membership and activities. Straight Edgers resist the gang label, maintaining that they are dedicated to positive messages rather than drugs and prostitution.

Michael McCombs

See also: Adolescents; Gangs, Youth; Punk; Skateboarders; Skinheads; Students.

Sources

Blush, Steven, ed. *American Hardcore: A Tribal History.* Los Angeles: Feral House, 2001.

Flory, Richard, and Donald Miller, eds. *Gen X Religion.* New York: Routledge, 2000.

Lahickey, Beth, ed. *All Ages: Reflections on Straight Edge.* Huntington Beach, CA: Revelation Books, 1997.

Valentine, Bill. *Gangs and Their Tattoos: Identifying Gangbangers on the Street and in Prison.* Boulder, CO: Paladin Press, 2000.

STUDENTS

Because students formally pursue academic learning, they as a group are often overlooked in folklife studies, which emphasize cultural traditions in informal settings of home and work. In various institutional and occupational settings, however, students participate in longstanding cultural traditions and form distinctive social identities. The central features of the student experience are an association with a school and the social bonds formed within the institutional setting. Some of these traditions are administratively organized, and others are formed or performed by students themselves, sometimes as activities that subvert the administration. Much of student lore relates to the power relationship between student and teacher, and the formation of a cohesive group or groups of students who are relative strangers to one another.

As an occupational activity, student life includes the special tasks and milestones of study—reading, essay writing, test taking, first-year initiation, and graduation. As an institutional activity often with a social connection to youth, student folklife also deals with extracurricular activities and residence on campuses. A strong theme of this folklife is the implication that the student experience involves maturation from a novice to an accomplished stage in preparation for life, as well as from one age to another. Therefore, student life is by its definition transitional, and many of its rituals and traditions involve references to tensions caused by various transitional passages—between home and work, individual and family, youth and adulthood, campus and town, apprentice and professional.

K–12 Grades

In elementary school, student traditions are typically relegated to a generalized children's folklore, although some lore may be grade specific. Often overlooked are the types of student traditions that arise in response to the institutional setting. For example, since it is common for students in grade school to be more regulated than in high school or college, they learn to communicate with one another by passing "secret" notes, typically folded in neat squares. Paper folding may also be applied to create playthings for use at institutional lunches, such as tabletop football, paper airplanes, and fortune-tellers (sometimes called "cootie catchers"). Younger students may inherit "secret" languages, such as pig Latin or "G-talk," involving the manipulation of syllables in English, to bond small groups, or cliques. The tendency to assert friendship groups at this age in the impersonal context of the school inspires various traditions. Through the late twentieth century, home-crafted friendship bracelets made of yarn, safety pins with decorative beads, and the wearing of specific colors were common signs of social connection in the elementary grades. Students at this level also exhibit beliefs about color, such as dressing in green on Thursday represents "queerness" or sitting in a chair the same color as that of a student of the opposite sex indicates a love relationship. Signifying the imbalance of the power relationship between student and teacher is a host of jokes concerning a trickster figure, the unruly "Little Johnny," who typically embarrasses the teacher in the punch line. It is psychologically significant that the figure is male, since a tension often exists between the maturing boy separating from female authority in the elementary grades (creating a symbolic equivalence of mother and teacher) as a sign of his developing masculinity. For girls, student lore and behavior often emphasize status assigned to popularity, courtship, and appearance—as in the use of "slam books," in which girls write opinions about one another.

Perhaps the most widespread tradition in elementary grades is that of song parodies fantasizing the burning and closing of the school. Familiar to almost all students are the lines to the tune of the "Battle Hymn of the Republic": "Mine eyes have seen the glory of the burning of the school / We have tortured every teacher and we've broken every rule." The theme continues in various other forms, such as the parody of "Joy to the World": "Joy to the world, the school burned down / And all the teachers died / We're looking for the principal / He's hanging on the flagpole / With a rope around his neck." While these verses indicate violent fantasies about the school experience or bonding by the sharing of an enemy, the tradition of exchanging autograph rhymes in a book upon graduation at sixth or eighth grade shows a theme of fond remembrance, even if expressed in humor and parody. A number of inscriptions refer, for example, to social memory as the significant experience of school:

> Remember Grant
> Remember Lee
> The heck with them
> Remember me.

> Remember the tests
> Remember the fun
> Remember the homework
> That never got done.

> Remember the fork
> Remember the spoon
> Remember the fun
> In Andrea's room.

The importance of social status and identity is heightened in high school with the recognition of numerous folktypes, narratives, and rituals. In the late twentieth century, for example, identities such as "jocks," "nerds," "goths," and "geeks" were associated with high-school culture and expressed in distinctive dress and language as well as shared interests. Compared to other national educational systems, American high schools feature sports and social clubs to a high degree. Schools in Pennsylvania and Texas have reputations for treating Friday night football games as grand festive events, while basketball in Indiana and Iowa have sacred status. These events often showcase participatory rituals sometimes led by cheerleaders, whose routines and cheers are often passed down from a preceding group, and sometimes initiated by groups in the crowd, such as

standing and turning one's back to the floor as the opposing team enters. Even more than graduation, the senior prom in many locations has attained the status of the grand culminating experience of high school. It celebrates the maturation of the students and the development of intimate relationships, even as it deals with the anxieties of imminent separation. While autograph books are considered juvenile by the high school level, students may sign each other's yearbooks with formulaic inscriptions as a sign of social remembrance.

College Life

The college experience is especially associated with student folklife because of the frequent separation from home of youth on college campuses. As a result, the identity of the student appears to be total, socially communitarian in dormitory complexes, and confined to a distinct landscape. The cultural challenge in this environment is often to create social bonds among students arriving from diverse backgrounds. On many campuses, the process begins with rituals that strip first-year students of their "home" identities and integrate them into campus culture. At small colleges, there may be events that pit one class against another in competition. At Hope College in Holland, Michigan, for example, the "Pull" is a tug-of-war between freshman and sophomore men, tugging a six-hundred-foot, twelve-hundred-pound hawser rope. Both have student coaches who work their teams across opposite sides of the muddy Black River. A modern addition to the tradition, which began in 1897, is to have "morale girls" cheer and comfort the contestants. No longer a contest over the right to remove "beanies" formerly worn by freshmen, the Pull is now a matter of pride and spirit at the small liberal arts college.

Military schools have some of the most active initiation ceremonies, which at times have become controversial because of the addition of women to the cadet body and the questions raised about abusive hazing in the initiations. At Virginia Military Institute (VMI), initiation lasts a year. Called a "rat line," the initiation calls for upperclassmen to order freshmen to perform rigorous physical exercises. Classmates thus refer to one another as "Brother Rats" and work toward incorporation at "Breakout," the proud day when upperclassmen recognize the rats as a class worthy of the VMI name. On this day, referred to as the class birthday, the younger cadets are symbolically reborn. Many even engrave the date on their class rings. Such initiations symbolize evolution or maturation within the four years of college, with lowly rats or "green" babies rising from the first stage to become men and women.

Women in colleges often develop separate initiation rituals that instill artistry and creativity, rather than brawn, as core values. At Hope College, first-year and sophomore women compete in song, oration, and drama for the coveted Nykerk Cup, established in 1936. "Song women," as the competitors are called, sit properly, backs straight, with gloved hands on their laps; "morale guys" offer support with booming cheers and thoughtful gifts. Several hundred women present a play and an oration, and participate in the chorus. Although the judges determine a winner, the women—in the spirit of cooperation—have a ritual "meeting in the middle," a chaotic conglomeration of all the happy participants in which losers cannot be separated from winners. Many women's colleges have "lantern nights" early in the first semester. At Bryn Mawr College, near Philadelphia, representatives of the three upper classes present wrought-iron lanterns to new students at a solemn ceremony in October. Dressed in black academic gowns, participants assemble at dusk in a cloistered garden at the heart of the campus. Upperclasswomen sing a Greek hymn as they present the lanterns, and new students respond with one of their own after they receive the gifts.

College is also a time for students to develop a number of subidentities. On many campuses, one way to gain a sense of belonging is to pledge to a fraternity or sorority. For weeks before Pledge Week, or "Hell Week," as it is colloquially known, pledges learn songs, follow rules of address and etiquette, and fashion special clothing or emblems. Pledges are assigned big brothers or sisters and take part as a group in sports, drink-offs, barbecues, "walk-outs," and sing-a-thons. In the name of building brotherhood, fraternities are known for ritual "dousings" and "reversals." Some houses use dousing in a nearby pond or in the showers to mark the passage from a pledge to an active fraternity member. In reversal weekends, pledges act like actives; they are relieved of work details and pledge tests, and they get the run of the house. Today, hazing as part of fraternity pledging has come under public scrutiny, as examples of abandonment in remote locations, forced excessive alcohol consumption, and ritual beatings by paddles have been reported. While sharing in the process of pledging, sororities frequently emphasize themes of family and expressiveness. In comparison with the grim ceremonies of male fraternities, sorority initiations involve more requirements of benevolent gift giving and less physical demands.

Distinguishing pledging in historically black fraternities is the use of "lines," "step shows," "signals," and occasionally "branding." Based on African American musical forms, stepping is a study in coordination and unity. Pledges in lines break into a series of precisely synchronized steps that create a syncopated beat. The pledges accompany the steps with chanting and singing proclaiming loyalty to the fraternity or sorority. Different black fraternities and sororities have distinctive hand signals and yells they sound at parties and picnics. Members of Omega Psi Phi, for example, bark "Woofa, woofa" and form an inverted Omega with their hands over their heads. Deltas make a triangle with their fingers and holler "Oo-ooo-oop!" A controversial folk practice as part of initiation rituals is branding. Members voluntarily take twelve-inch heated irons and shape omega or sigma symbols on their arms or backs. Although the national organizations discourage the practice, it persists as a distinctive sign at the grassroots of black fraternity brotherhood.

A historical change in identity on many campuses is the transition from loyalty to a class or fraternity in the old-time college to identification with a major or academic department in the massive university or "multiversity" of today. A sign of the increasing bureaucratization of the multiversity, narratives related by students often underscore the rivalries among majors or the attributes of a certain major. At Pennsylvania State University, for example, an engineering hall with severe straight lines and unfriendly glass and steel is said to be emblematic of the major. According to the account of architectural students, engineers designed the building to be nine stories tall and, recognizing the miscalculation of the ground's ability to hold the structure, architects divided the building into three side-by-side sections. Variations of the tale exist at many campuses. At the University of Pennsylvania, for instance, students swear that the Irvine Auditorium was designed by a student who flunked out of the school of architecture.

Tests and Other Anxieties

The demands of tests and papers on students, and the anxieties they produce, distinguish the student's occupation and are expressed through folk narratives and customs. The custom of the "primal scream" or "door slams" on campuses indicates the kind of tension that finals produce among students. At the University of California, Berkeley, a cry that reverberates around the campus late in the evening around finals week has taken the name "Pedro," usually drawn out to "Peeeeedrooooh." The explanatory narrative is that the college president, dean, or professor lost his pet dog and announced that finals will be canceled if someone finds the dog. From that time on, generations of students during finals call out for Pedro.

A host of legends and jests circulate among students regarding tests. A common motif is of the nonconformist student who gives clever, earthy retorts to lofty-sounding final-exam questions. Probably the most familiar is about the philosophy exam with the single question "Why?" While most of the students write lengthy essays, one student answers "Why not?" (or "Because") and gets an A. Variations are told about student fears of "blanking out" on a test. One student

who blanked out supposedly wrote on the final fall exam in religion, "God only knows the answer to this question. Merry Christmas." The good professor returned the exam with the note "God gets an A; you get an F. Happy New Year." A student commentary on exams in a large lecture hall also implies the impersonal nature of the multiversity. A professor calls out a student in a large class for cheating. The student brings his test to the front of the room and shoves it into the middle of a stack on the table. He asks the professor, "Do you know who I am?" Then he turns to face the remaining students still taking the exam to ask them, "Do you know who I am?" No one responds and he runs out of the room. The teller's explanation is that since no one could identify him, he got away with cheating and, in fact, got a good grade.

Once told exclusively in college dorms and cafeterias, campus legends and jests have become global through communication technology. The computer, which has made possible broad waves of folkloric transmission and the creation of Internet folk communities, is also the subject of folklore. There are numskull tales of naive computer users, wonder stories of love and hate by and for the machine, and rumors about a modem tax and exploding components. Stories abound, especially among dissertation writers, about the need for backups and not putting too much faith in the computer, just as a precomputer generation was regaled with sad tales of students who failed to make copies and their professors who lost them. Student "hackers" and "technoterrorists" have become new folktypes, with legends about their motives for creating computer viruses that infect college networks or their abilities to hack records to change grades.

After students enter the "real world," as they say, they still may engage their cultural experience as students in alumni and fraternity reunions. These occasions may evoke storytelling about student life. Another location for expressing college identities is the ritual tailgating (picnicking in stadium parking lots) and social gatherings that occur during the fall football season at major sports schools. For many people, the student experience forms an institutional identity that continues long past their years in school.

Simon J. Bronner

See also: Children's Groups; Education; Fraternal Organizations; Gangs, Youth; Legends; Martial Artists; Occupational Folklife; Rituals and Rites; Skateboarders; Skinheads; Sports Teams; Straight Edge.

Sources

Baker, Ronald L. "The Folklore of Students." In *Handbook of American Folklore*, ed. Richard M. Dorson, 106–14. Bloomington: Indiana University Press, 1983.

Bronner, Simon J. *American Children's Folklore*. Little Rock, AR: August House, 1988.

———. *Piled Higher and Deeper: The Folklore of Student Life*. Little Rock, AR: August House, 1995.

Dundes, Alan, and Lauren Dundes. "The Elephant Walk and Other Amazing Hazing: Male Fraternity Initiation Through Infantilization and Feminization." In *Bloody Mary in the Mirror: Essays in Psychoanalytic Folkloristics*, ed. Alan Dundes, 95–121. Jackson: University Press of Mississippi, 2002.

Mechling, Jay. "Mediating Structures and the Significance of University Folk." In *Folk Groups and Folklore Genres: A Reader*, ed. Elliott Oring, 287–95. Logan: Utah State University Press, 1989.

Moffat, Michael. *Coming of Age in New Jersey: College and American Culture*. New Brunswick, NJ: Rutgers University Press, 1989.

Nathan, Rebekah. *My Freshman Year: What a Professor Learned by Becoming a Student*. Ithaca, NY: Cornell University Press, 2005.

Toelken, Barre. "The Folklore of Academe." In *The Study of American Folklore: An Introduction*, ed. Jan Harold Brunvand, 502–28. 3rd ed. New York: W.W. Norton, 1986.

SUBURBS

The American suburb began in the mid-nineteenth century as a cultural and spatial unit separate and distinct from the city while still within its political boundaries. The suburbs were defined both by their populations, middle- and upper-class white families, and by their location on the periphery of an urban center, thereby combining the best of city and country life. With single-family detached houses being the primary residential unit, early suburbs were also characterized by a domestic ideology that emphasized family life and separate spheres for men and women. These benefits stood in sharp contrast to the perceived ills of the urban environment, including disease, crime, and lack of private space that imperiled family life. At the same time, however, the early suburbs relied on the central city for jobs, goods, and services. Examples of nineteenth-century suburbs included Frederick Law Olmstead's Riverside in Illinois and Llewellyn Park, New Jersey, designed by Llewellyn S. Haskell and Andrew Jackson Davis. Often viewed in American folklife as a sterile cultural zone between the pioneer earthiness of rural America and the immigrant grittiness of cities, the suburbs nonetheless can claim evolving cultural traditions of their own from legendry about automobile-driven society to customs of lawn and backyard activity.

Building and Community Traditions

Between the Progressive Era and World War II, advances in homebuilding (such as balloon-frame construction, in which light, precut wood studs are held together by factory-produced nails) and in transportation technology (including the commuter rail and automobile) made suburban home ownership affordable and accessible to more people. Still, it was not until the boom times of the postwar period that the modern American suburb came into its own. As Kenneth Jackson describes it in *Crabgrass Frontier* (1985), the postwar suburb was defined by five characteristics: peripheral location, low density, architectural similarity, easy availability, and economic and racial homogeneity. A number of factors accounted for the phenomenon, not least of which were changes in finance and construction. Government agencies such as the Veteran's Administration and Federal Housing Authority subsidized construction by insuring private mortgages and by protecting consumers through formal manufacturing standards. While such innovations expanded the opportunities for home ownership, they did not do so for *all* Americans. Practices such as redlining and racial covenants contributed to the segregation of suburban areas by restricting the access to African Americans.

The advent of affordable single-family housing developments in the decades after World War II introduced new elements in the physical and cultural landscape of America: the streets, yards, and sidewalks of suburbia. *(Robert W. Kelley/Time Life Pictures/Getty Images)*

Most prominent among the early builders of suburbia was Brooklyn-born William J. Levitt, who introduced mass-production methods in single-family housing construction. By developing large tracts of land and building sprawling developments of uniform stand-alone houses, he was able to reduce construction labor costs and lower the price of private homes; the result was affordable home ownership for a growing middle class. Families moved out of the city and thrived in their economic independence, the green spaces of the suburbs, and the emerging mass-consumer culture. In synergy with the latter, Levitt equipped his homes with new kitchen appliances and washing machines. Commentators noted that Levitt tied the house to the car not only as transportation to get to a larger home than one could have in the city, but also as a model of mass consumption with styles, brands, and fashions that could nonetheless be customized for social needs.

The chief result of these changes was an unprecedented expansion of the suburban population and concurrent decline in the urban population. By 1960, a plurality of Americans, nearly 34 percent, lived in the suburbs. Included in this growth were more traditional, planned developments known as "new towns," such as Columbia, Maryland, that sought to be more community oriented and ethnically inclusive. The more predominant trend throughout the 1960s and 1970s, however, was a decentralization of industry and employment: business enterprises and jobs followed the movement of the population out of downtown areas and into the suburbs. The character of the suburbs itself began to change. What once had been quiet havens of family life and privacy were now increasingly encompassed by corporate parks, malls and shopping centers, and commuter traffic. Gone were the separate spheres of home life and work life. These new formations, born largely in the last decades of the twentieth century, have come to be called "exurbs" or "edge cities." Among their defining characteristics are economic, social, and cultural disconnection from the central city, housing subdivisions of varying size and affordability, and a full range of goods and services—formally available only in the city—within easy access.

Levittown and other postwar suburbs created the foundation of community through both formal and informal voluntary associations. Formal associations such as the Veterans of Foreign Wars were defined by common experience often outside the suburban environment or preceding life there. Others, such as the local Parent-Teacher Association and chamber of commerce, were formed around common interests that often centered on neighborhood, civic, and family issues. Indeed, these organizations were taken to be the essence of the community. Still, less formal associations among suburbanites were also important to the folklife of the community. Coffee klatches, backyard barbecues, pool parties, or casual get-togethers among friendly neighbors disseminated information and allowed people to share in both middle-class consumer culture and the lives of their children. Regardless of the content or quality of the relationships, it was this neighboring that perhaps most characterized suburban life.

Holidays and Celebrations

American suburbs are also identified with their celebration of traditional holidays, such as Independence Day and Memorial Day, as well as more localized events such as the opening day of the Little League season or founder's day (honoring the founders of a community-service organization or other local group). All are typically accompanied by parades, carnivals, fairs, and private parties. Participation in national holidays is partly attributable to a shared allegiance to country, culture, and tradition, but most suburban celebrations of these parties typically include a small network of family and friends at the backyard pool and barbecue. As such, they are as much a celebration of the privilege of home ownership and the focus on family life as of the national commemoration. Epitomizing the tension between public and private celebration is the traditional fireworks display on the Fourth of July. Many towns sponsor public fireworks shows, but suburban residents are often more inclined to set off their own firecrackers, sparklers, and rockets—sometimes illegally—in the backyard.

Many suburban communities sponsor local festivals to promote a hometown feel to what many view as a temporary or artificial location. By emphasizing the use of the streets and sidewalks for pedestrians rather than taking the highway to work, the festivals define a center for dispersed suburban towns. Such street festivals typically include rides, finger foods, and concerts, often underscoring the Americanness of the place. They are also opportunities to bring people from outside the suburbs into the center and recognize the location as a community. A prominent example is the Mechanicsburg, Pennsylvania, Jubilee Day, established in 1923, originally sponsored by the automobile and merchants association. Mechanicsburg's population is less than ten thousand, but on Jubilee day in June some sixty thousand people pack into the town, making it one of the largest one-day street fairs in the country.

Legendry

One way in which the cultural distinction of the suburbs is made is through legend telling—particularly what has become popularly known as "urban legends." Folklorists often refer to them as "contemporary legends" or "belief legends" because they are not solely an urban phenomenon. These legends are defined as apocryphal stories, told as true but incorporating traditional motifs and usually attributed to a friend or a friend of a friend. They are usually cautionary tales that reflect the fears of suburban parents regarding children and crime.

The ethnic identity of most suburbs as white enclaves is similarly broached in urban legends, such as the story of the famous person seen clipping hedges or mowing the lawn who is mistaken for the ethnic gardener by suburbanites. Such stories have been circulated about the likes of Thurgood Marshall, Bill Cosby, Flip Wilson, and Carl Rowan.

The intersection of consumer culture with the safety of the family is integral to understanding urban legends and the folklife of suburbia. The ubiquity of products and the pervasiveness of the consumer mentality shape much of the folklore of the suburbs. Such legends express fears about the threats posed to home and family that exist at sites of consumption and in mass-produced goods themselves. Some, for example, have to do with toxins in popular brand products such as laundry detergent, shampoo, and soft drinks. Stories like these reinforce the domestic ideology of the suburbs, where women and children are safest at home. Their influence is further enhanced by the informal associations that quickly spread the information. E-mail, instant messaging, and forums on the World Wide Web—all highly prevalent in the suburbs—help to perpetuate these cautionary tales even when they try to debunk them.

Yard Customs

Often defining the suburban life is the orientation of activity for the nuclear family in the backyard. This orientation stands in contrast to the cultural expectation of front-porch socializing in the country and the living room or terrace social space in the city apartment. Within the backyard space, a material culture may exist with a field for family play, a surrounding garden, and a wooden deck with the important feature of the grill. The tradition of grilling has traditionally been a male domain, featuring meats such as chicken, hot dogs, ribs, hamburgers—and a suburban mythology of higher-priced "steaks on the grill." Folklorists are not alone in having observed the connection between this suburban American tradition and preindustrial society, where men assumed the role of hunter-provider.

The front yard in suburban folklife is signified by the lawn, which, according to some cultural critics, is another allusion to preindustrial life. The devotion of time, money, and work to achieve the clean, uniform look of a manicured suburban lawn can be interpreted as an attempt to re-create the image of a pasture, once granting high status in rural society. Although livestock do not graze on it, the front lawn provides a setting through which visitors pass to reach the house, in imitation of an old country estate. As a culture based on access to automobiles, including the family minivan, suburbia also gives a prominent place to the multicar garage and paved driveway,

often with the characteristic basketball hoop as part of the material culture.

Suburban yards and homes provide a frontier for folklife research still in development. Often overlooked as a cultural destination because the sense of community does not seem natural or spontaneous, suburbia is, in the twenty-first century, a prime cultural symbol of America and significant aspect of its cultural tradition. In the legends told about them, the customs emerging in them, and the landscape they create, the suburbs are a distinctive element of the modern American folk imagination.

Kyle Riismandel and Simon J. Bronner

See also: Film and Video; Folk Festivals; Landscape; Legends; Urban Folklife.

Sources

Baxandall, Rosalyn, and Elizabeth Ewen. *Picture Windows: How the Suburbs Happened.* New York: Basic Books, 2000.

Bronner, Simon J. *Grasping Things: Folk Material Culture and Mass Society in America.* Lexington: University Press of Kentucky, 1986.

———. "Suburban Houses and Manner Books: The Structure of Tradition and Aesthetics." *Winterthur Portfolio* 18 (1983): 61–68.

Brunvand, Jan Harold. *The Truth Never Stands in the Way of a Good Story.* Urbana: University of Illinois Press, 2000.

Donovan, Pamela. *No Way of Knowing: Crime, Urban Legends, and the Internet.* New York: Routledge, 2004.

Dorst, John. *The Written Suburb: An American Site, An Ethnographic Dilemma.* Philadelphia: University of Pennsylvania Press, 1989.

Fishman, Robert. *Bourgeois Utopias: The Rise and Fall of Suburbia.* New York: Basic Books, 1987.

Gans, Herbert J. *The Levittowners: Ways of Life and Politics in a New Suburban Community.* New York: Pantheon, 1967.

Hayden, Dolores. *Building Suburbia: Green Fields and Urban Growth, 1820–2000.* New York: Vintage Books, 2003.

Jackson, Kenneth T. *Crabgrass Frontier: The Suburbanization of the United States.* New York: Oxford University Press, 1985.

Thomas, G. Scott. *The United States of Suburbia: How the Suburbs Took Control of America and What They Plan to Do with It.* Amherst, NY: Prometheus Books, 1998.

SUPERNATURAL

Supernatural beliefs attempt to explain events in the perceived gap between consensus reality and events that seem to defy the normal laws of experience. Because consensus reality is culturally defined, what is regarded as "supernatural" may vary over time and place. Folklorists therefore understand the term in the context of how a community provides convenient language for individuals to describe experiences outside the norm.

Stories and Beliefs

Various folklorists and philosophers of religion have defined experiences with the supernatural as "numens," or personal experiences that challenge definitions of reality. A person who encounters a numinous phenomenon must, however, rely on existing cultural models of the supernatural in order to interpret it. Most cultures provide a "belief language" that allows individuals to talk to others about their supernatural experiences in terms that are controversial but shared by enough persons so that they do not seem simply bizarre. That is, most Americans would take a story beginning "I saw a ghost in the cemetery last night," as an acceptable *type* of story. Even though they might respond with skepticism to the particular story being told and suggest rational explanations for the events described, they would not assume that its teller was automatically irrational.

If the story falls outside of culturally accepted categories, however, tellers risk being labeled "crazy," even if the phenomenon they describe is in fact relatively common. In a famous case combining medical with folkloristic investigation, David Hufford in 1982 found that a form of sleep paralysis in which victims feel they are in the presence of an evil entity that is suffocating them was well known in Newfoundland witchcraft lore. In the United States, where witch beliefs are not so widespread, persons who experienced such paralysis preferred not to talk about it with others, fearing that they might be regarded as mentally ill. Convenient language for such a frightening experience provides a measure of comfort because it allows people to give a name and shape to the experience, and also reassures them that others have had similar ones. When a culture does not provide such language, the experience may remain unshared even though keeping it to oneself may be extremely stressful.

Supernatural beliefs continue to arise in many areas of contemporary American folklore because numinous experiences continue to be reported regularly. Recent surveys show that between one-half and two-thirds of Americans say that they have had at least one experience that they believed was supernatural in nature, ranging from extrasensory perception to contact with the dead. The latter phenomenon is common enough that "ghost stories" of various kinds remain one of the most common types of belief legend, especially told as a personal experience. Belief in ghosts remains a vital part of ordinary personal experience and continues to inspire narratives of hauntings and messages from the other, or unearthly, world. In a more practical vein, an active tradition of parapsychological "ghostbusters" helps explain and terminate unwanted hauntings.

Belief in diabolical agencies remains strong in many subcultures. The 1970s saw a strong revival in exorcism as a religious experience. Such beliefs held that many health problems, mental and physical, resulted from the invisible influence of demons who could, however, be ritually identified and banished. Such beliefs also motivated, in a paradoxical way, adolescents' interest in séances and Ouija board rituals, in which evil spirits were often invited to manifest themselves in exciting ways. Both belief complexes gave rise to influential mythologies to the effect that satanic cults were responsible for such social problems as teen suicide and child abuse.

Contemporary Supernatural Mythologies

Many similar mythologies have emerged among investigators of unidentified flying objects (UFOs). So-called flying saucers, like "mystery lights," are natural anomalies that may have a rational explanation. But UFO investigators have often formed active subcultures, driven by a desire to explore and understand where they come from and who controls them. Active discussion networks, for example, have been devoted to the UFO abduction experience, in which individuals feel they are being drawn into another space by strange, nonhuman entities. Such an experience has much in common with fairy kidnap narratives, and in any case abduction narratives have generated many religious and apocalyptic beliefs. This is not unusual, for supernatural experience underlies folk religious beliefs in all world cultures.

The supernatural marks the active border between belief and fantasy. Too real to dismiss as make-believe but too transitory to document as fact, supernatural phenomena inspires the generation and perpetuation of folklore.

Bill Ellis

See also: Belief; Fetishes; Healing, Faith; *Märchen*; Religion; Spiritualists; Voodoo and Santería.

Sources

Bullard, Thomas E. "Abduction Reports: The Supernatural Kidnap Narrative Returns in Technological Guise." *Journal of American Folklore* 102 (1989): 147–70.

Dégh, Linda. *Legend and Belief: Dialectics of a Folklore Genre.* Bloomington: Indiana University Press, 2001.

Denzler, Brenda. *The Lure of the Edge: Scientific Passions, Religious Beliefs, and the Pursuit of UFOs.* Berkeley: University of California Press, 2001.

Ellis, Bill. *Raising the Devil: Satanism, New Religions, and the Media.* Lexington: University Press of Kentucky, 2000.

Goodman, Felicitas D. *How About Demons? Possession and Exorcism in the Modern World.* Bloomington: Indiana University Press, 1988.

Hufford, David J. *The Terror That Comes in the Night: An Experience-Centered Study of Supernatural Assault Traditions.* Philadelphia: University of Pennsylvania Press, 1982.

McClenon, James. *Wondrous Events: Foundations of Religious Belief.* Philadelphia: University of Pennsylvania Press, 1994.

SUPERSTITION

See Belief

SWEDISH COMMUNITIES

Sweden is one of the five Scandinavian countries in northwest Europe, and, with Norway, saw a significant portion of its population emigrate to America during the nineteenth century. It has been estimated that America in the late nineteenth century gained a quarter of Sweden's population. Pushed by overpopulation, famine during the 1860s, compulsory military service, and religious persecution of groups outside the Church of Sweden (including Baptists, Mormons, and Janssonists) and pulled by the promise of fertile farmlands, more than 100,000 Swedes came to America between 1868 and 1873 and another 475,000 arrived between 1880 and 1893. It has been estimated that one in four Swedish immigrants was engaged in agriculture in the Upper Midwest; among those who headed to cities such as Chicago and Minneapolis, women were known for working as domestics, while men were sought for industrial labor. Mostly rural laborers and artisans in the homeland, the bulk of immigrants came from the poorer agrarian provinces of Halland and Värmland in southwest Sweden; thus, Swedish American folklife reflects the background of this regional culture.

Historical and Social Background

Swedes on American soil did not just transplant their culture, but in new communities formed traditions distinct from those of Sweden. Generations into the twentieth century, after the settlers of this mass immigration had died and assimilation was apparent, many communities promoted folk revivals, reconnection with Sweden and their Swedishness, and in some cases building transnational tourism around Swedish American festivities.

Prior to the period of mass migration to the United States between 1865 and 1900, Sweden had a minor role in the European colonization in America, establishing in 1638 a small settlement of no more than five hundred persons called New Sweden on the Delaware River near what is now Philadelphia. The colony lasted only seventeen years before being taken over by the Dutch and a decade later by the English. New Sweden figures significantly, however, in speculation among folklife researchers that Swedes and Finns in the settlement may have introduced dovetail notching techniques that influenced the development of American log construction.

Communities to this day known for their Swedishness are small towns such as Kingsburg, California; Brevort, Michigan; Bishop Hill, Illinois; Lindstrom, Minnesota; New Sweden, Maine; and Lindsborg, Kansas. In urban centers, significant centers have formed in Chicago (including an area called Swede Town on the Near North Side), Minneapolis (Swedish immigrants constituted 31 percent of the foreign-born population in 1930), New York City (where the Swedish Cottage is a landmark in Central Park), and Seattle (home to a Swedish Cultural Center). All these communities sponsor festivals and feature hallmarks of Swedish American folklife in foodways, art and craft, and holiday celebrations. According to the 2000 U.S. census, almost four million Americans claim Swedish ancestry (second to Norwegian, at 4.5 million, as a Scandinavian identity), most of whom affiliate with the Lutheran Church and relate to pioneer "homelands" in the Midwest or Northwest. The total number of Swedish Americans includes fifty-eight thousand Swedish-born residents and one hundred thousand who speak the Swedish language. In addition, Swedish ethnic identity is evident in Swedish summer schools, church services with sermons and hymns in Swedish, and celebration of Christmas with *lutefisk* (boiled ling, a form of cod, soaked in lye), *potatiskorv* (potato sausage), and *julotta* (Christmas matins).

Unlike the descendants of nineteenth-century immigrants who relate to the pioneer experience in the American Midwest and Northwest, Swedish-born immigrants, who mostly arrived in the late twentieth century as students, businesspeople, and professionals, maintain connections to their hometown or city or the country in general through regular visits and business trips. The relationship among recent immigrants, Swedish Americans of several generations, and those who identify themselves as Swedish Americans by choice is dynamic. There are many ways of being Swedish in America.

There is a vital difference in meaning between the word *svenskamerikan*, used in Sweden, and the term "Swedish American," used in the United States. In Sweden, *svenskamerikan* refers to a person of Swedish ancestry. In the United States, however, the identity of "Swedish American" and the related concept of "Swedishness," a feeling of being Swedish, are more flexible. "Swedish Americans" means more than a group defined only by shared lineage or living in a particular community.

Swedish Finns

Among the groups who identify themselves as Swedish Americans are the descendants of emigrants from Swedish-speaking regions of Finland during the late nineteenth and early twentieth centuries. Approximately seventy thousand Swedish-speaking Finns came to the United States from 1870 to 1930 and formed communities in Massachusetts, the Upper Peninsula of Michigan, Wisconsin, Colorado, Utah, and Washington. Members of this ethnic group formed a separate Baptist denomination in Chicago in 1901 called the Finska Baptist Missionforinigen (later the Baptist Mission Union), with services in Swedish. About twenty churches were formed around the country in the early twentieth century until the Baptist Mission Union joined the Baptist General Conference in 1961.

Like many ethnic groups, the Swedish-speaking Finns had their own fraternal organizations, such as the Swede-Finnish Benevolent and Aid Association of America, organized in Bessemer, Michigan, in 1900 (merging in 1920 with the Swede-Finnish Temperance Society to form the Order of Runeberg, named after Johan Ludvig Runeberg, a renowned Swedish-speaking Finnish poet who wrote the lyrics to the Finnish national anthem), to provide insurance and social aid. Lodges of the Order of Runeberg still function in the United States, but the order has suffered a decline in membership from its heyday in the 1920s. At that time, the lodges promoted Swede-Finnish ethnic folklife by sponsoring *kulturfests* (cultural festivals) with singing and food on the Fourth of July, midsummer festivals and picnics, monthly dances and whist parties, and choir concerts often culminating in *singerfests* (song festivals) around Labor Day.

Swedish-speaking Finns, who have language in common with one group and nationality in common with another, have had a tendency to vanish in the American context. Many Swedish Finns who came to America in the late nineteenth and early twentieth centuries stressed, for political reasons, their Swedish ties rather than the Swedish Finn relations. Although many descendants identify themselves as Americans and regard their Swedish Finn background as a special ethnic affiliation, especially when coupled with Baptist Mission Union religious heritage, there are also many descendants of Swedish Finn immigrants who have grown up with a Swedish American community identification, and they are therefore more inclined to articulate their heritage as Swedish.

Ethnic Celebration

Descendants of the nineteenth-century Swedish "pioneers" and more recent Swedish-born immigrants have joined together to emphasize Swedish American distinctiveness in public festivals. In some rural communities in the Midwest, the public celebration of *julotta* is an unbroken tradition observed since the arrival of the pioneers. Many Swedish descendants use the Christmas smorgasbord with *potatiskorv* and lutefisk to convey to younger generations where their relatives came from. In comparison with Christmas celebrations, St. Lucia (held the second Saturday of December) and midsummer celebrations are comparatively recent. These celebrations are not synchronized with the holidays in Sweden.

St. Lucia is also known as St. Lucy of Syracuse and is the only saint celebrated by the Lutheran Swedes. Observed on December 13 in Sweden, the celebrations often have pre-Christian elements of a midwinter light festival ("lucia" means light). Traditionally, the celebration includes a procession of women holding candles, led by a young woman portraying Lucia who wears a crown to which lit candles are attached. The candles symbolize the fire that refused to take Lucia's

life in a legend of her martyrdom in Syracuse (Italy) during the persecution of Christians of 303 B.C.E. The women sing a song honoring Lucia while entering the room, either *Natten går tunga fjät* (The Night Walks in Heavy Footsteps) or *Sankta Lucia, ljusklara hägring* (Saint Lucy, Bright Illusion). The songs describe and cherish the light with which Lucia overcame the darkness. After finishing this song, the women usually sing Christmas carols or more songs about Lucia. Boys have been added to the procession in recent years, often dressed in white robes and a cone-shaped hat decorated with golden stars, or dressed up like Santa Claus and carrying lanterns.

Official public celebrations of St. Lucia date from the 1960s, when Swedish communities such as Lindsborg, Kansas, organized St. Lucia processions as part of Christmas events on Main Street. Beginning as a performance by a woman dressed as St. Lucia in a white robe, red sash, and a head wreath of evergreen and lit candles in a brass crown accompanied by female and male attendants dressed in Swedish peasant costumes, the celebration grew into a pageant featuring the construction of a large *julbock*, a gift-giving goat figure fashioned out of straw and displayed during the Christmas season in Sweden and decoration with *julkärver*, traditional sheaves of grain customarily left during the Swedish Christmas season for birds. The demonstration of Swedish folk dances, the crowning of a Lucia Queen, and the serving of coffee and ginger cookies to Main Street shoppers completed the festivities.

Midsummer (Swedish *midsommar*) festivals celebrate the summer solstice, usually around June 24. The main celebrations include raising and dancing around a huge *majstång* (maypole). Before the maypole is raised, greens and flowers are collected and used to cover—to "may"—the entire pole. Raising and dancing around a maypole is primarily an activity that attracts families, even though it traditionally was a fertility ritual. Dancing around the pole is often accompanied by traditional music and the wearing of traditional folk costumes. Meals accompanying the maypole activity include the year's first potatoes, pickled herring, sour cream, and possibly the first strawberries of the season. After the midsummer ceremonies, the poles are often left standing, typically until August, although in some regions they are left standing all year round as a sign of community spirit.

Folk revivals of midsummer occurred in many Swedish American communities during the 1970s. The celebration in Brevort, Michigan (in the Upper Peninsula), for example, began at that time after a hiatus of almost twenty years. The revival was instigated by a Swedish American couple who visited Sweden and were inspired to restart the tradition by the *midsommarstång* (midsummer poles) that dotted the Swedish countryside. A smaller version (thirty-five feet tall; some in Sweden extend over one hundred feet) of the maypole was constructed, with carvings of ships at the top representing the four seasons. The ships also connect the Michigan celebration to its regional heritage in the Swedish homeland of the Åland Islands, since the carving of ships for the maypole distinguishes the Swedish region. A reminder of American identity is the placement of American flags at the ends of three crossbars of the pole. Below them are six decorative wreaths familiar in Swedish maypoles that Brevort's residents call "crowns" and believe to symbolize the six days that it took the creator to finish the earth. A whirligig with spinning arms on a male figure sits at the top; some say this figure ties the tradition to the religious observance of St. John's Day on June 24 in Sweden, by representing humanity, God's greatest creation, or St. John himself, although the feature of the carved man smoking a pipe has been puzzling to contemporary observers. The carver of the figure on the new maypole explains it as a copy of the design begun by his Swedish grandfather. In the original tradition, the gathering of poplar leaves to decorate the pole was restricted to men, but in the revival women freely participated. The celebration was taken over by the Trinity Lutheran Church, who sponsors it as a community event with a potluck dinner drawing Swedish Americans from throughout the region. The tradition drew the attention of Michigan folklorists and in 1996 was featured for public appreciation at the Michigan Folklife Festival downstate in East Lansing.

Often called the largest midsummer celebration in the United States, the public "Swedish Midsummer" in Battery Park, New York City, began in 1996 with the sponsorship of the Battery Park City Parks Conservancy and the Consulate General of Sweden in New York. To accommodate people who work, the celebration begins on June 24 at 5:00 P.M., when the public helps decorate the pole with leaves and flowers. The completed pole is carried in procession, preceded by fiddlers and accordionists, to a lawn where it is raised. Officials of the city and of Sweden typically make welcoming remarks, followed by a folk dance demonstration by children and adults from area folk dance teams, after which the public is invited to join in traditional ring dances and games. Accordionists and fiddlers provide music throughout, and children's activities such as sack races and tug-of-war are held.

Among the thousands of festivals with ethnic themes in the United States, those labeled Swedish are particularly numerous in the Midwest, from Michigan and Minnesota to Kansas and Nebraska. Some of the oldest have expanded in size and practice, such as Svenskarnas Dag, established in 1934 and celebrated annually in Minnehaha Park, Minneapolis, and Svensk Hyllningsfest, in Lindsborg, Kansas, which was initiated in 1941 and is celebrated biennially in honor of the Swedish settlers and their descendants. Others are more recent creations, such as the Swedish Heritage Days in Holdredge and the Swedish Festival in Oakland, both in Nebraska. There are also examples of festivals established in the 1990s. One example is the Skandi-Fest, established in 1991 in Turlock, California, and held annually to celebrate the community's Scandinavian heritage with food, dance, music, and art displays. The idea of expressing ethnic belonging through dress is common at these festivals. While the various authenticities expressed in dress during these festivals may include Viking helmets and T-shirts emblazoned with *svensk flicka* (Swedish girl) or *svensk pojke* (Swedish boy), folk costumes tend to dominate. The ways in which folk costumes are made and worn can be tied not only to the Swedish parish or parishes from which one's ancestors came, but to the length of time a person's family has lived in an American community settled by Swedes.

People who identify themselves as Swedish Americans commonly express and reflect upon their heritage through jokes. When Swedish Americans (and Norwegian Americans) are crafting jokes about lutefisk, the characters Ole, Sven, and Lars and their female counterpart Lena express experiences on both collective and individual levels. While lutefisk jokes elicit wild laughter in reference to the acquired taste of the food (which only Swedish Americans seem to be able to acquire), such messages are unknown in Sweden. In the Svensk Hyllningsfest Parade in Lindsborg, Kansas, for example, humorous representations of lutefisk in floats are common. When the parade is over, lutefisk jokes from the parade resound in verbal form. The ongoing delight in lutefisk floats has been complemented by the production of jocular paraphernalia often seen in the Upper Midwest, such as bumperstickers and refrigerator magnets that claim, "Legalize lutefisk," and coffee cups with "Gone lutefisking" printed on them. Lutefisk, portrayed in Swedish America as foul smelling and weird in consistency throughout the years, has been used by Swedish Americans as a source of ethnic pride and a way to define themselves.

Expressive Traditions

Ole and Lena appear in American jokes about Swedes in the United States and in performances of "Ol' Swedes," where the protagonists often are named Sven and Lars. This comic stereotype was nurtured in early-twentieth-century Swedish American sketches such as *Olle i Skratthult*, enacted by Hjalmar Petersson from Munkfors in Värmland, Sweden. Traveling the Midwest, *Olle i Skratthult* drew large audiences in Minneapolis and Chicago, as well as Lindsborg, Kansas. As in Sweden, many people of Swedish background in the United States have ancestors who were farmers and who often scratched out a meager existence. From the perspective of the now integrated

and financially secure Swedish American, these "greenhorn" Swedes and poor Swedes become funny.

Folk art, such as Dala horse painting and wood carving, is another example of how Swedish Americans express their ethnic affiliation. Although the Dala horse (first developed as a toy in the province of Dalarna, it became popular among Swedish Americans following its display at the 1939 World's Fair in New York City) is used to communicate Swedish affiliation in numerous places across America, its presence is exceptionally prevalent in Lindsborg, Kansas, where people have carved and painted Dala horses in their homes since the 1940s. Selected as the town emblem in the 1960s, the Dala horse has been instrumental in the shaping of this town into "Little Sweden, USA."

Organizational Life and the Making of Cultural Heritage

The Swedish Council of America, based in Minneapolis, was founded in 1972 to preserve and promote Swedish heritage, and according to the council's Web site in 2005, the umbrella organization has more than three hundred affiliates: organizations, schools, interest groups, and museums of various sizes. Among the many prominent affiliates are the American Swedish Institute in Minneapolis, established in 1929, and the Swedish American Museum Center in Chicago, started in 1976. One of the largest member organizations is SWEA (Swedish Women's Educational Organization), founded in Los Angeles in 1979. Serving post-1945 emigrants and their descendants, SWEA aims to maintain the Swedish language and Swedish traditions, and to serve as a network for Swedish women living in the United States and abroad. The Folklife Institute of Central Kansas, located in Lindsborg, features educational programs on Swedish traditions such as folk art and craft workshops, traveling exhibitions, elderhostels, and weeklong seminars on Swedish American folklife. Colleges with Swedish heritage, such as Augustana in Rock Island, Illinois, Gustavus Adolphus in St. Peter, Minnesota, and Bethany College in Lindsborg, Kansas, support Swedish folklife with sponsorship of Swedish folk choirs and coursework.

The making of Swedish heritage in Sweden and Swedish America refers to a desire for culturally authentic traditions. The process of negotiation with commercial culture shows which phenomena lend themselves to heritage making in an American context. This process reveals that certain phenomena belong to a transnational or even international repertoire, while others, such as the never-ending lutefisk and Ole and Lena jokes, are bound to the Swedish American (and Norwegian American) folk context. Among the transnational symbols that are selected and reselected and therefore gain value over time, the Dala horse, folk costume, and Viking stand out as important. It is not in the objects themselves, but in their symbolism and the act of altering them, that a shared Swedish and Swedish American heritage is created.

Lizette Gradén and Simon J. Bronner

See also: Danish Communities; Finnish Communities; Foodways; Little Sweden; Norwegian Communities.

Sources

Danielson, Larry. "The Dialect Trickster Among the Kansas Swedes." *Indiana Folklore* 8 (1975): 39–59.

———. "St. Lucia in Lindsborg, Kansas." In *Creative Ethnicity: Symbols and Strategies of Contemporary Ethnic Life*, ed. Stephen Stern and John Allan Cicala, 187–203. Logan: Utah State University Press, 1991.

———. "Swedish-American Mothers: Conservators of the Tradition." In *Folklore on Two Continents: Essays in Honor of Linda Dégh*, ed. Nikolai Burlakoff and Carl Lindahl, 338–47. Bloomington, IN: Trickster, 1980.

Klein, Barbro Sklute. *Legends and Folk Beliefs in a Swedish American Community*. 2 vols. New York: Arno, 1980.

Leary, James P., ed. *So Ole Says to Lena: Folk Humor of the Upper Midwest*. 2nd ed. Madison: University of Wisconsin Press, 2001.

Swanson, Lynne. "Celebrating Midsummer in Brevort." In *1996 Michigan Folklife Annual*, ed. Ruth D. Fitzgerald and Yvonne R. Lockwood, 22–28. East Lansing: Michigan State University Museum, 1996.

SYMBOL AND STRUCTURE

Symbolism is vital to the development of folklife and its study because social values and messages are condensed and embedded in expressive culture, and hence symbolized, in the rituals, narratives, and arts of a community. Implied in the use of symbols is a structural or systemic meaning: a symbol is understood as a structured form within a cultural system—sometimes as broad as national (the system of flags as structures of colors on cloth) and as particular as a relationship between two people (dining annually, for instance, at the location of their first date). A question often faced by folklorists observing such activities is whether the meanings of these symbols are in or outside the awareness of participants. Is the participant's explanation of the meaning of an event sufficient? Further, the question arises whether the symbols are universalized or particular to the community, or even event, and whether different participants view the meanings of the symbols differently.

The wedding, for example, is replete with symbolism, perhaps because it is considered a major life changing event involving risk and uncertainty about the future. To ask the bride and groom about the purpose of the wedding is likely to elicit a response akin to "a celebration of getting married." Others may see in the event not only the joining of two individuals in matrimony but also the union of two families. Evaluating the components of the event may lead observers to see the stabilizing force of weddings for a society, and the ethnic and social values that are conveyed through the many rituals of the event. Thus, the controversy in the early twenty-first century over legalization of gay marriage became an emotional issue because of a fundamental split in opinion over weddings as symbols of expressing love and commitment, on one hand, and of enacting a definition of a family unit as the basis of society and culture, on the other.

Symbols in Texts as Enactments of Social Structure

Important to the understanding of symbols in folklife is the discernment of events as "texts" to be read and interpreted for figurative meanings, much like written documents. One common way to interpret a text is to view it as an enactment of social structure. The works of anthropologists Clifford Geertz and Victor Turner in Bali and Africa, respectively, are influential in pointing out that folk events serve not only to reflect, but also to support, social hierarchies and to convey the values and beliefs of the group. Applied to communities in America, the approach of treating events as texts of social structure has been employed for interpretation of musical performances, religious services, festive gatherings and rites of passage, hunting and military rituals, and storytelling events for age groups ranging from children to older adults, ethnicities from the Amish to Zen Buddhists, and occupational groups from actors to wrestlers. In one folklife study, for example, Thomas A. Burns and J. Stephen Smith looked at Sunday morning services of an urban black Holiness church and concluded that such regular events constituted rituals with symbolic components beyond the spiritual intention. According to Burns and Smith, the service revealed the social hierarchy of the sect, or what they identified as a confirmative symbol of one's position. The service, they said, also encouraged movement into a more advanced status within the sect—in other words, it was a transformative symbol.

Symbols of social structure are frequently observed in material as well as behavioral texts, and can be traced historically or geographically. Brightly colored hex signs painted conspicuously on Pennsylvania barns, for example, may have referred to witchcraft in Europe at an earlier time, but in the United States they became symbols of ethnic awareness among Pennsylvania Germans in the 1840s, as growing English and state control threatened maintenance of Pennsylvania German communities. In the twentieth century, the signs underwent a revival as tourists sought nostalgic reminders of their travel to a rustic landscape. Where and how the material gets displayed can therefore have symbolic value. Folklorist Gerald Pocius found that symmetrical, geometrically repetitious hooked rugs in Newfoundland tend to be used almost exclusively in the kitchen. Such "egalitarian" designs, recognized widely by the community, are displayed in contexts where equals meet, say, among fishing families. On the other hand, rugs with individualized designs are used in the front room, where hierarchical interaction takes place, such as between residents and

merchants and clergymen. As this example bears out, folklorists applying a symbolic reading find social meanings particularized to a cultural scene or community.

Symbols of Mind and Behavior

A broader reading, and one that involves even more meanings *outside* the awareness of participants in a culture scene, is taken from psychological interpretation, forming what could be called "depth folkloristics" (after depth psychology). Returning to weddings, for instance, one may view binary oppositions in the structure of bride and groom, and the sequence of moving from unmarried to married. Thus, symbols such as flowers may be more than decorative. Folklorist Alan Dundes suggests a psychological interpretation of the ritual act of the bride throwing away her floral bouquet—that it signifies her willingness to be, or intention of being, deflowered.

Other texts are not so literal; they require connections to the culture. Dead-baby jokes, for example, popular among schoolchildren in the late twentieth century and unusual to many because of their "gross" humor, were symbolically explained as a connection to the abortion issue. By redirecting the disturbing issue to symbolic humor, the jokes unconsciously relieved anxiety. If the joke tellers were aware of the reference to abortion, Dundes argues, they would not need to tell the jokes. Among its functions, according to this interpretation, folklore provides a socially sanctioned outlet for the expression of what cannot be articulated in the usual, direct way.

This is not to say that the uncovered symbols are necessarily universal; folklorists point out that it is important to ground the symbolic interpretation in the traditional symbolic repertoire of a group or a cultural context. Often, symbolic beliefs in one cultural context are compared and contrasted with those prevalent outside the context for similarities that can be summarized as the group's culturally shared outlook, or worldview. One example is American individualism as a "folk idea" expressed in key proverbs and sayings (e.g., "looking out for number one," "do your own thing," "it's a free country"), which becomes especially evident in comparison to Japanese symbols of group orientation (proverbs such as "a nail that sticks up gets nailed down" and social customs of building group harmony).

Designs of houses and crafts, often viewed as creative behaviors, are read for clues to the mental processes that are the basis of personal and culturally shared aesthetics. In his seminal work, *Folk Housing in Middle Virginia* (1975), Henry Glassie ties the evolution of house designs toward symmetry and enclosure as reflecting a shared cognitive need for order during a time of disorder—the period of impending chaos before the American Revolution. Drawn to the structure of an individual's craftwork, Michael Owen Jones, in his important behavioral study *The Hand Made Object and Its Maker* (1975), discerns an imposing sense of enclosure when the maker was near crowded spaces. The traditional Appalachian chair maker he studied created rockers with low armrests and easy spaces in the back to facilitate social gathering on a porch. When he moved to the city to seek work, the adjustment from his countryside background was difficult, and he expressed this anxiety in the construction of chairs with tall sides and closed backs. This symbolic response was also tested in other studies, such as Simon Bronner's study in *Grasping Things* (1986) of a working-class urban craftsman who was used to gathering in front of his folk-decorated house with friends. In response to gentrification in his neighborhood, the craftsman began to build enclosures around his social space of the front stoop. As with Jones's chair maker, the craftsman did not articulate his reasons for the design change, but the folklorist inferred motivations for his actions and objects. From a symbolist viewpoint, this observation showed that traditional designs can be connected not just to historic precedents but also to psychological responses, expressed culturally, to personal and social anxieties.

Structuralism

Invoking the concept of structure in folklife studies implies a search for base concepts or a cognitive grammar guiding the apparent fluidity of cultural expression. Most ideas of structuralism in folklife scholarship usually follow from the methods used by the "structuralists" Vladimir Propp and Claude Lévi-Strauss. Propp complained that the arrangement of tales according to theme was misleadingly narrow and had a bearing on their symbolic interpretation. Tales about animals were separated from tales of magic, for example, but a tale could have elements of both, he argued. Themes and actors change in the tales, but the actions tend to be constant. Symbols are assigned to the actions, and the actions are arranged in sequence to offer a linear representation of structure. Propp devised representations for typical actions (which he called functions) in the tale such as villainy (A) or marriage (W), and analyzed folktales according to this system so as to be able to compare their structures. He found the sequence of "functions"—the act of a character to advance the plot—to be identical, and suggested that the sequences reveal the process by which tales are composed and told. Though the structure was described, explanation still had to come from the comparison with cultural reality, especially when different kinds of sequences are familiar to various cultural groups. Propp's model is sometimes referred to as a "syntagmatic" or "linear-structure" model, in contrast to Lévi-Strauss's "paradigmatic" model.

Lévi-Strauss's approach is designed to delve deeper into the cognitive process through the composition of narrative. Rather than identify a sequence, the analyst takes key concepts out of order and regroups them to reveal basic relations, usually expressed in binary oppositions. These binary oppositions represent the basic dramas that individuals in a culture must work through in their everyday lives, such as good and evil, male and female, light and darkness. Lévi-Strauss described the procedure as a simultaneous "orchestra score." All the written notes vertically constitute "one gross constituent unit, i.e., one bundle of relations." Where Propp found structural continuities, Lévi-Strauss stressed structural discontinuities and sought to describe the overall "paradigm" of the tradition. If high-low, night-day, male-female, and other oppositions occur anywhere in a narrative, Lévi-Strauss felt free to extrapolate them and reorder them in his delineations of the paradigm.

Lévi-Strauss emphasized myths as the most effective means of explaining the world. Other folklorists have applied paradigmatic analysis to a range of cultural expressions, revealing basic binary oppositions in the composition of houses, dress, and art. When examined free of their contexts, houses as utilitarian and aesthetic constructions on a natural landscape offer a mediation between nature and culture; they reveal, as myths do, concepts of order. They can be tied to ideas of the structure of language by suggesting that unconscious rules can be discerned by comparing the structures of houses. Thus, a cognitive, culturally inherited, generative "grammar" can be uncovered that guides the construction of form. For instance, American buildings tend to work in pairs in traditional construction; one tends not to find houses with three rooms across. They may expand in pairs, then, with rooms extending to the back or on top of one another. Comparison with "reality" suggests the possibility that this design arises out of the house's symbolic representation of the marriage, or union, of two individuals into a family unit, reflected in the saying "making a home."

Another structural connection to language is the meaning of symbols from the standpoints of participants and analysts. In folklife research, the difference is expressed in the distinction between an "emic" (from "phonemic") and "etic" (from "phonetic") approach. Emic approaches are usually construed to be actor oriented. Emics describes patterns of culture with reference to close observation of the culture itself. Etics approaches are analytical, imposed on a culture. Emic units are structural in that they relate to a cultural system; etic units are nonstructural in that they are comparative and culture free. Etic units are more communicative; emic units are perceptual. Both units, however, can be subjective, despite claims to the contrary, because views of participants typically represent a diversity of opinion that the analyst must interpret. Etic units, although based on observable characteristics, are open to individual perceptions.

Structuralism, in summary, takes apart and then builds up. It dismantles heard (or seen) expressions to describe their wholeness. Dundes, for example, has pointed out the importance of tripartite structure in American culture, from the division of the flag's symbols into "red, white, and blue" to the racing signal "ready, set, go." The sense given is that three represents completeness; if that is the case, then four units signify abundance, or "more than enough." Thus, American sizes divide into the three units of "small, medium, and large." More than enough is expressed as a fourth unit—an extension of the third size, or "extra large." It has been argued that American colleges require four years for completion, not because anyone has proven that education is completed in that time, but because of the belief that proceeding through four stages (freshman, sophomore, junior, senior) is abundant. Following the guideline that structure is itself a symbol, one needs to explore further meanings that lie outside of awareness. One idea is that in a culture stressing human dominion, three is a projection of human form—the head and body flanked by two arms and two legs. By contrast, many Native American systems are based on four as the symbol of completeness, for it represents "everywhere" in the sense of signifying the four cardinal points. Following this line of thought, Chinese narratives that tend to project five as a magic number of wholeness add a cardinal position for the self. This opens for analysis other kinds of divisions that become taken for granted as culturally based customs: two as a marital unit, seven as a lucky number, thirteen as unlucky.

Structure and symbol are also related in the task of defining genres that compose folklife, from the perspectives of both participants (emic) and analysts (etic). People may recognize a saying as a proverb because of its metaphorical structure; symbolically, the form of the expression invokes conventional wisdom. It may be further identified as American because of its reference to a social value. Some analysts suggest that many American proverbs tend to express optimism or a future orientation. The content of proverbs may appear similar to riddles, rhymes, and beliefs, but may be distinguished by the underlying linguistic structure. An American children's rhyme such as "Mary Mack, All Dressed in Black," for example, could be expressed as a riddle if it contained a query about the references.

Composition and Performance

The implication of discerning cognitive structures that guide performance is that people are able to relate stories, or interpret their experiences as story, not because they have memorized the text but because they understand through cultural inheritance the structure of a narrative and are able to adapt and improvise within that structure. Interpretations of American narrative performances ranging from preachers' sermons to hip-hop performances have utilized this perspective, sometimes called "oral-formulaic" theory. Efforts have been made to identify the "grammar" or laws governing narrative genres such as European American ballads and epics, including their linearity, two characters to a scene, and usual reliance on three episodes. An underlying universal structure has also been suggested for rituals, which are often understood as having three stages to symbolically mark passage: separation of the initiate from the group, a transition with a task to be completed, and incorporation back into the group, often with a celebration. In folk art, too, aesthetics are often described structurally, by the form and content that are appropriate to the culture. The African American aesthetic of syncopation and asymmetry provides a structural contrast in music and quilts, for example, to the British American emphasis on regularity and unity. In blues music, for example, the *aab* structure of many songs perceived as being in the genre allows for improvisation and borrowing from a number of verses. The structure sets up an anticipation of the final line, which usually is emphasized or carries an ironic twist.

Once such structures have been identified, questions arise about their meaning and sources. African American reliance on syncopation and asymmetry for some can be traced to the his-

torical source area of West African cultures. But in the American context, it has also been interpreted as a sign of ethnic identity, particularly in the action of giving the asymmetrical design of quilts to other African Americans but making more symmetrical designs for whites. Some scholars have gone even further, interpreting these aesthetic features as a sign of resistance or adaptation. Contrasting suburban white and inner-city black schoolyard games of basketball, for example, folklorists have observed that the latter often involve one player challenging all the others in a limited space; white games, by contrast, typically allow for fairer odds. According to a social interpretation this structural difference, black games emphasize improvisation and determination against longer odds in tight urban spaces. As with other symbolic readings, the interpretation depends on an identification of the structure underlying the composition of an expressive tradition. The symbols used in the expression are correlated to the values and beliefs in the culture, and often compared with other traditions to determine whether the meaning attributed to the expression is unique to the culture or broader based.

Simon J. Bronner

See also: Communication; Folklore; Function and Functionalism; Humor; *Märchen*; Performance Approach and Dramatic Arts; Psychology; Rituals and Rites; Text.

Sources

Ben-Amos, Dan, ed. *Folklore Genres.* Austin: University of Texas Press, 1976.

Bronner, Simon J. *Grasping Things: Folk Material Culture and Mass Society in America.* Lexington: University Press of Kentucky, 1986.

Dundes, Alan. *Analytic Essays in Folklore.* The Hague: Mouton, 1975.

———. *Interpreting Folklore.* Bloomington: Indiana University Press, 1980.

Foley, John Miles, ed. *Oral-Formulaic Theory: A Folklore Casebook.* New York: Garland, 1990.

Geertz, Clifford. *The Interpretation of Cultures.* New York: Basic Books, 1973.

Glassie, Henry. *Folk Housing in Middle Virginia: A Structural Analysis of Historic Artifacts.* Knoxville: University of Tennessee Press, 1975.

Jones, Michael Owen. *The Hand Made Object and Its Maker.* Berkeley: University of California Press, 1975.

Lévi-Strauss, Claude. *Structural Anthropology.* Translated by Claire Jacobson and Brooke Grundfest Schoepf. Garden City, NY: Doubleday, 1967.

Maranda, Pierre, and Elli-Kaija Köngäs Maranda, eds. *Structural Analysis of Oral Tradition.* Philadelphia: University of Pennsylvania Press, 1971.

Propp, Vladimir. *Morphology of the Folk Tale.* 2nd ed. Translated by Laurence Scott and revised by Louis A. Wagner. Austin: University of Texas Press, 1968.

TATTOO

See Body Modification and Tattooing

TAXI DRIVERS

Taxi drivers are operators of vehicles hired for one trip at a time, paid by meter or by predetermined rate. They constitute an occupational group who share a number of distinguishing traditions. The word "taxi" is itself a form of folk speech, short for "taximeter," the machine used to determine fares based on distance traveled and wait time. Drivers are also known as "cabbies" (a derivative of "cab," a shortened form of the word "cabriolet," for a one-horse carriage or coupe). They are occasionally called "hacks," a short form of "hackney horse," which originally pulled carriages for hire in England. The special driver's license they must obtain is called a "hack license." According to the *Oxford English Dictionary*, the first use of the term "hack" in America was recorded in Boston in 1795, while "cab" (1827) and "taxi" (1907) are newer terms reflecting newer technologies.

In America, taxis usually belong to a fleet of cars in a particular town or city; drivers are paid either by salary in smaller towns or by a percentage of total fares plus all-important tips in larger cities. The occupation is one of the last in the country to be overwhelmingly male; women may make up as little as 1 percent of the taxi drivers in New York City. It is also one of the most dangerous occupations in the United States, particularly in cities.

Several writers have observed that taxi drivers occupy a unique status and social class in world culture. The contemporary Greek author Vassilis Vassilikos has called them "a class unto themselves" and notes that "they form . . . public opinion as if they constituted a newspaper, which . . . is not printed and yet is heard." While many drivers in America have made driving their career, a significant number have used the occupation to support themselves while studying or pursuing careers in other fields, notably performing arts or literature.

In American popular culture, taxi drivers have famously been depicted as alienated loners (as in the Martin Scorsese film *Taxi Driver*, 1976) or as dreamers, misfits, immigrants, or persons simply trying to get back on their feet (as in the comedy series *Taxi*, 1978–1983). Some of these images may come from a suspicion of those who work in a semi-itinerant environment wrongly perceived as asocial.

Immigrants and Migrants

The profession has been disproportionately filled by immigrants, because of the limited English needed to perform the tasks and because the essentially unsupervised workplace offers a freedom not found in factories, kitchens, and the other kinds of jobs where most immigrants find themselves. It has also long been known as a profession that can provide some upward mobility for immigrants, especially when drivers own their cars. The corps of drivers in different cities represent the different mix of immigrants in each city. In New York, South Asians have dominated since the late twentieth century, with Bangladeshis the largest single group, in addition to Pakistanis and Indians (mostly Sikhs); there are also sizable numbers of West Africans, Egyptians, and Russians. Across the Hudson River in Jersey City, Egyptians and Haitians predominate. Somali refugees make up the largest group in Minneapolis, while Somalis and Ethiopians both drive taxis in large numbers in Washington, D.C.

Southern-born African Americans filled the ranks of drivers in the northern cities to which they migrated during the mid-twentieth century; in many cities, they were replaced by foreign-born drivers as they retired. The last U.S.-born African American driver in Newark, New Jersey, retired as the new millennium approached; the fleet is now mostly made up of drivers from Haiti and West Africa. Small towns and cities have also seen start-up fleets owned by Latin American immigrants, with company names that reflect the origins of the owners; Acapulco Taxi and Tucan Taxi are two such companies established in central New Jersey during the 1990s.

Vehicle Classes and Designs

In large cities there are also sometimes hierarchies of taxis, or social subclasses within the profession. In New York, for example, medallion cabs, which are yellow and strictly regulated in number, are the industry standard. Livery cabs, which do not have a meter, operate outside of Manhattan or above One Hundredth Street, and the price of a ride is negotiated with the driver beforehand. Livery cabs are prohibited from picking up fares in prime locations. A third class of unmarked cabs, without official status, operates informally (if not illegally), negotiating prices and picking up passengers seen hailing other cabs; because they are unmarked, unregulated, and rootless, these cars are known as "Gypsy cabs."

American taxis have long been defined by their color (yellow) and by the graphic logo as-sociated with the Checker automobile company, which manufactured the industry standard for more than sixty years. Both can be traced to early-twentieth-century entrepreneurs in Chicago: John Hertz, who founded the Yellow Cab Company and was the first to paint his taxis yellow because of its visibility; and Russian immigrant Morris Markin, a tailor who purchased a small autobody-manufacturing company and renamed it Checker, after a cabdrivers' association in Chicago that invested in the business. The Checker Marathon model became the most widely used taxi in America until production ceased in 1982. The Checker Marathon was a large sedan with a slightly rounded roof that did not change its style or appearance for years. The last surviving Checker cab, number 1N11, was retired from duty in New York in 1999. The logo of the Checker car company, however, has become part of the logo of taxis more generally; almost all taxi merchandise now available in souvenir shops in New York either references the Checker, or includes white and black checkered patterns in combination with the trademark yellow.

Verbal Traditions

The world of taxi drivers has generated various forms of expressive culture. As with much occupational folklife, it is defined by the nature and spatial-temporal context of the work itself. Taxis are unique settings for human interaction because they almost always involve brief meetings between two or more people who, except in small towns, do not know each other and have not had any advance interaction. Contact takes place in a small, enclosed space, a moving vehicle, with participants facing the same direction, and with the passenger(s) in most cases sitting behind the driver. Eye contact, when it is made, is through the rearview mirror (not all passengers realize that this is possible). There is a barrier (seat back) between the participants, which sometimes includes a plastic partition that extends to the ceiling. The space and nature of the meeting in itself is a unique staging of actors in a human drama.

The taxi driver is commonly depicted in American popular culture as a loner, dreamer, or social misfit. The limited English necessary to do the job, unsupervised workplace, and opportunities for success through hard work have made the profession especially attractive to immigrants. *(Library of Congress, LC-USF344-000829-ZB)*

Thus, a great deal of the occupational folklife of taxi drivers takes place in the form of brief dialogues with perfect strangers. Equally important in the culture of drivers are gatherings after shifts, when drivers relax at a common space, usually a garage or a restaurant, and share stories and experiences. The first American folklorist to observe taxi driver narratives as folklore was B.A. Botkin, who published their orally collected stories in 1946. The post-shift gatherings often break out along linguistic lines, since restaurants and some garages, at least in large cities, tend to cater to specific ethnicities and drivers prefer to mingle with people who speak their language.

Because the nature of the job consists of a series of relatively short human interactions, each driver has a body of potential short narratives to work with every day, if any of the fares become notable enough to shape into a narrative form. The memory of these stories is long, and when prompted, drivers will relate oft-told stories of passengers from years past. As one West Indian female driver in New York observed, "Every driver's got a hundred stories." Though the practice is uncommon, drivers may also carry mementos for years of famous passengers or memorable rides, good or bad, such as receipts of large unpaid fares. (Of course, many passengers have their own "taxi stories," reflecting the perspective from the back of the cab.)

The restaurants and garages, most of which are open twenty-four hours in major cities, are important recreational sites as well as places that provide rapid and essential services, such as repairs, meals, and toilets. Since time spent on break is money lost, the emphasis is on speed, though restaurants are also known for their low prices. New York has many excellent taxi restaurants that cater to Bangladeshi, Pakistani, and Sikh or Punjabi drivers. Usually these offer informal, cafeteria-style service where platters are reheated in microwave ovens and patrons dine while standing at counters.

Another major genre of taxi driver folklife is the written memoir. A number of books have been published, especially in recent years, by drivers recounting the best stories of their work lives. These tend to be either self-published or published in small, or even subsidized (vanity) presses. The foreign-language press in America has also been an outlet for some drivers; in New York there have been regular columns by taxi drivers in Russian- and Bengali-language newspapers within the last twenty years, and probably others whose work has not been made known to English speakers. There are also newspapers and newsletters that cater to taxi drivers, such as *Taxi Talk* in New York City. Since the advent of the Internet, a number of taxi drivers, particularly in small towns, have developed Web sites and chat rooms not to promote their companies, as one might think, but to provide a forum for telling and trading taxi driver stories.

Social and Material Traditions

Drivers in some cities have formed their own associations. The New York Taxi Workers Alliance, while not a union, is a labor advocacy organization on behalf of taxi drivers. And there are also social clubs. Fraternal associations and clubs of drivers established social events and recreational activities as far back as the 1940s. In New York's community of Bangladeshi drivers, there are at least three organizations that sponsor summer picnics. The first and largest of these is the Bangladesh Yellow Society New York, a registered not-for-profit organization founded in 1994. At these picnics, which typically include prepared meals and the performance of folk music on traditional instruments, sports matches in soccer and volleyball are usually divided between teams representing day-shift and night-shift drivers.

One feature common to taxis worldwide is the decoration of cabs inside and out. Although passengers sometimes observe a stuffed animal mounted on the front grille or a driver dressed as the Easter Bunny, such displays are generally rare in America. Inside the vehicle, however, American drivers frequently apply ethnic, religious, and personal decorations to the rearview mirror and dashboard as personal creative expressions. One item widely associated with the occupational folklife of the taxi driver is the "cabbie's hat." Once referring to a chauffeur's hat, which might feature the design of a Checker cab, today it more commonly refers to a flat cap. While no longer the standard garb that it once was, the cabbie's hat—often decorated with buttons declaring a union affiliation or other group affiliation—remains an item of material culture associated with the taxi driver's life.

William Westerman

See also: Automobiles; Dress and Costume; New York City; Occupational Folklife; Storytelling.

Sources

Botkin, B.A. "Living Lore on the New York City Writers' Project." *New York Folklore Quarterly* 2 (1946): 252–63.

———, ed. *New York City Folklore.* New York: Random House, 1956.

Burns, Jane. " 'Everyone Has Good': A Study of the Occupational Folklife of a St. John's Cab Driver." *Culture and Tradition* 4 (1979): 79–87.

Mathew, Biju. *Taxi! Cabs and Capitalism in New York City.* New York: New Press, 2005.

Nusbaum, Philip. "The Importance of Storytelling Style Among New York City Taxi Drivers." *New York Folklore Quarterly* 6 (1980): 67–88.

Vassilikos, Vassilis. *And Dreams Are Dreams.* Translated by Mary Kitroëff. New York: Seven Stories, 1996.

Winston, Mary Ellen, and Holly Garrison. *The New York Cabbie Cookbook: More Than 120 Authentic Homestyle Recipes from Around the Globe.* Philadelphia: Running Press, 2003.

TEENAGERS

See Adolescents

TEXAS

Texas is in the southcentral part of the United States, lying between New Mexico to the west and Louisiana and Arkansas to the east. The Rio Grande River forms a natural and political border with Mexico to the south. Sometimes associated regionally by geographers with the Great Plains, South, or Southwest, for many Texas residents the state forms its own cultural unit. One of its characteristics is its large scale. Geographically it is the largest state of the forty-eight contiguous states and second only to California in population. The public perception of Texas as a land of unlimited opportunity inhabited by larger-than-life characters began almost as soon as the first Americans were allowed to immigrate into what was, in the 1820s, the northern province of Mexico. By the end of the nineteenth century, the modern stereotype was already fixed in the public consciousness. For example, in Bram Stoker's Gothic masterpiece *Dracula* (1897), the tall and taciturn Texan—Quincey Morris—not only shoots a marauding vampire bat with his six-shooter, but he kills Dracula by driving his Bowie knife through the villain's heart.

Metaphorical Nationalism: "The Texas Mystique"

A constellation of macho images revolves around the Lone Star State—cowboys, stampeding longhorns, oil wells, Cadillacs, unimaginable wealth, recklessness, gun battles, and so on. All of these images are intertwined to form what is known as the "Texas mystique."

The root of that mystique lies in the unique

The longhorn cattle, cowboy hat, and lone star, icons of the "Texas mystique," are all pictured in this 1930s poster for a stage comedy sponsored by the Works Progress Administration. *(Library of Congress, LC-USZC2-5162)*

history of the territory, under six flags: those of Spain, France, Mexico, the Republic of Texas, the Confederacy, and the United States. The Spanish crown claimed Tejas in the sixteenth century, and in 1540 Francisco Vázquez de Coronado led his ill-fated expedition across part of it in search of the fabled Seven Cities of Gold. French explorers under the command of René Robert Cavelier Sieur de La Salle made a brief incursion along the Gulf of Mexico in 1685–1686. After their ship sank, however, disgruntled troops murdered La Salle, effectively ending French interests in Texas. (One of his ships, *La Belle*, was discovered by archaeologists in 1996.)

It was Mexico, however, that placed an indelible stamp on modern Texas. The war for Texas independence in 1835–1836 was the pivotal event in regional history, giving Texas the unique distinction of relinquishing nationhood to

become a state. The independent Republic of Texas lives on in the Texas mystique, infused as it is with a metaphorical—now stereotypical—spirit of nationalism. The Lone Star symbol of the Republic of Texas was adopted for the state flag and is a constant reminder of Texas pride. History, fiction, and folklore converge in the iconic cry "Remember the Alamo!"; the Alamo mission in San Antonio is one of the most frequently visited sites in America, and countless novels and movies have assigned mythic status to the battle of February–March 1836, sometimes with little historical veracity.

Transcending even the heroes of the Alamo—Davy Crockett, Jim Bowie, and William B. Travis—is the quintessential Texan: the cowboy. The trail-driving period of the cattle industry was born in Texas following the economic collapse after the Civil War. The romantic cavalier on horseback may be more myth than reality, but the cowboy remains the most famous of all American folk heroes.

Anglos learned the basics of rounding up and herding wild longhorns from the Mexican cowboys, or *vaqueros*. From these intercultural beginnings, Anglos adapted techniques and tools of livestock management on horseback, including the distinctive broad-brimmed hat and boots we know today. Cowboy "lingo," much of it derived from Spanish, enriched the English vocabulary with such words as "lariat," "rodeo," "remuda," "ranch," and "buckaroo." The image of young men on horseback wrangling thousands of longhorn cattle from south Texas to the railroad heads in Kansas and Missouri captured the imagination of the nation and ultimately the world. The great trail-driving period in American history in fact was short, lasting only about fifteen years—from 1865 to 1880—but in that brief time the cowboy emerged as a true folk hero.

The economy created yet another cast of distinctive and no less macho Texas characters, the oilmen—wildcatters, roughnecks, and roustabouts. The most dramatic oil strike in American history was the gusher at Spindletop in coastal Texas on January 10, 1901, which ushered in the

The Battle of the Alamo in 1836 has attained mythic status in the annals of Texas. History, fiction, and folklore converge in the cry "Remember the Alamo!" and the mission in San Antonio is enshrined as "the cradle of Texas liberty." *(Library of Congress, LC-USZ62-87798)*

modern petroleum industry. Fortunes were made overnight as landmen bought and traded mineral rights to previously worthless land. The stereotype of the fabulously wealthy "Texas oil millionaire" is indeed based in historical reality, kept alive by the media, especially in movies such as *Giant* (1956), and a seemingly endless cycle of Texas oil millionaire numskull jokes.

Football is widely regarded as the secular religion of Texas. Before the Houston franchise was sold in 1996, the state's two professional football teams were the Dallas Cowboys (known to some as "America's Team") and the rival Houston Oilers, whose stadium, the Astrodome, was "the first fully air-conditioned, enclosed, domed, multipurpose sports stadium" in the world; the professional team in Houston today is the Texans. Boys learn football in Texas with the same macho zeal that boys learn basketball in Indiana or baseball in Florida.

History in Texas folklore is reflected no less in regional culture than in folk heroes such as the Alamo defenders, cowboys, oilmen, and football players. One of the great paradoxes in Texas folklife is whether the state should be classified—culturally and geographically—as western or southern. The answer is both. The state's enor-

mous size—Texas is larger than France—encompasses practically every climate on the continent, from the tropical Gulf to the western deserts. Furthermore, immigration helped create the human geography of Texas with a massive influx of settlers from the Deep South after the Civil War. The landscape of Texas was unscathed by the battles that devastated other southern states, and the transplanted Confederates brought their culture with them as they transformed parts of east Texas into southern enclaves. Later, as the historian Walter P. Webb explains in his trenchant study *The Great Plains* (1931), the physical landscape dictated that the West began at the 100th meridian, where the rainfall level would no longer sustain cotton.

Although grounded in historical reality, the Texas mystique is highly selective. Omitted, for example, is the great multicultural saga of the blending of Anglo and Mexican culture that is the bedrock of modern Texas. African Americans and other ethnic groups—including Germans, Czechs, and other Europeans—are invisible in the mystique's version of Texas. Although cotton was the backbone of the Texas agricultural economy for decades, the mystique ignores King Cotton, which lacked the romantic appeal of swashbuckling cowboys and oilfield roughnecks. Most surprising of all, the mystique barely acknowledges women, except as dutiful pioneer housewives or prostitutes. One exception is the enduring tale of the Yellow Rose of Texas, allegedly a mulatto slave woman captured by the Mexican general Santa Anna. She is credited with "distracting" Santa Anna during his siesta so that he was unprepared for the assault of the Texas forces at the Battle of San Jacinto on April 21, 1836. The battle marked the end of the Texas Revolution and gave birth to the independent Republic of Texas.

Culture and Folklife

In addition to cowboys and oilfield characters, a number of other images are often identified as distinctly Texan. According to oral tradition, for example, everything is bigger in Texas. Underlying this image is the sheer physical size of the state, of course, but the perception is extended to a generalized hyperbole that everything in Texas is meaner, wilder, prettier, richer, or bigger than anyplace else. Texans have embraced the hyperbole and turned it into outrageous bragging and self-confidence, along with self-deprecating humor. The mythical Texas landscape is inhabited by imaginary "critters" such as the jackalope (a cross between an antelope and a jackrabbit), which in reality seem no more unbelievable to newcomers or gullible "greenhorns" than such real creatures as the horned toad, rattlesnake, or longhorn cattle.

Texas folk speech is characterized by a regional variation of the "southern drawl," or twang, and a distinctive vocabulary and syntax that includes such terms as "fixin' to" (getting ready to) and "y'all" (a full declension second-person pronoun). Texans generally speak slowly, even when they slur words together. Reflecting the settlement history of the state, the Texas accent or dialect is softer in east Texas, with its southern influence, and "twangier" to the west, which was settled primarily by Appalachian pioneers, especially Tennesseans.

In spite of the ethnic exclusions characterized by the Texas mystique, a multicultural musical tradition has developed in Texas. Scott Joplin, known as the "Father of Ragtime," grew up in and around Texarkana. Later, African American blues was infused with a Texas flavor by such bluesmen as Huddie "Leadbelly" Ledbetter, Blind Lemon Jefferson, T-Bone Walker, Mance Lipscomb, Lightnin' Hopkins, and Robert Shaw. "Deep Ellum," a ghetto section of Elm Street in Dallas, became the mecca for Texas blues. Anglo Bob Wills and his Texas Playboys perfected an early country-and-western musical dance style known as "Texas swing" by combining the "heat of blues and swing of jazz." Another style of dance music developed out of the Tejano tradition. Known generally as *conjunto* (musical group), this music features accordions, guitars, bass, and fiddles playing polkalike rhythms. Lubbock's Buddy Holly and the Crickets (all Anglo) galvanized rock 'n' roll with their distinctive instrumentation and vocals, which led many early

radio listeners to assume the group was African American. Through radio and live performance, all of these musical styles have crossed ethnic lines and are widely appreciated today. Austin, the state capital, has emerged as a national musical center, publicized in part by PBS's popular and award-winning *Austin City Limits*, with its concert performances of distinctly American music.

Texas foodways enjoy national and even international popularity. Barbecue is a Texas staple, almost as popular as chicken-fried steak. The enchiladas, tacos, and fajitas of Tex-Mex cuisine are derived from the Hispanic heritage of the state but are enjoyed by all ethnic groups. In part because of early German immigration, beer is part of nearly all Texas gatherings, whether football tailgate parties or family reunions. The Lone Star brewery upholds the metaphorical nationalism of Texas by proclaiming its beer "the national beer of Texas." Oral tradition maintains that the margarita, a popular summer drink of tequila, sweet liqueur, and lime juice mixed with ice in a blender and served in a chilled glass with salt on the rim was created in San Antonio.

Texas is a unique blend of history and tradition that seems to grow stronger as the decades and centuries pass. Although contemporary social realities are not always consistent with the Texas mystique, Texans nevertheless take pride in their state and honor their heritage of independence, hyperbole, determination, and good humor.

Sylvia Grider

See also: Chicano and Mexican Communities; El Paso; Migrant Workers and Hoboes; Nationalism; Rio Grande Border Region; Shrines and Memorials, Spontaneous and Vernacular; South, The.

Sources

Abernethy, Francis Edward, ed. *The Folklore of Texan Cultures.* Austin: Encino Press, 1974.

Abernathy, Francis Edward, Patrick B. Mullen, and Alan B. Govenar, eds. *Juneteenth Texas: Essays in African-American Folklore.* Denton: University of North Texas Press, 1996.

———, ed. *Observations and Reflections on Texas Folklore.* Austin: Encino, 1972.

Bauman, Richard, and Roger D. Abrahams, eds. *"And Other Neighborly Names": Social Process and Cultural Image in Texas Folklore.* Austin: University of Texas Press, 1981.

Boatright, Mody. *Folklore of the Oil Industry.* Dallas: Southern Methodist University Press, 1963.

Grider, Sylvia Ann. "The Function of Texas Historical Legends." *Artes Populares* 16–17 (1995): 314–28.

Harmon, Jack. *Texas Missions and Landmarks.* San Antonio: University of Texas Institute of Texan Cultures at San Antonio, 1977.

Leach, Joseph. *The Typical Texan: Biography of an American Myth.* Dallas: Southern Methodist University Press, 1952.

Owens, William A. *Texas Folk Songs.* Dallas: Southern Methodist University Press, 1976.

Sewell, Ernestine P., and Joyce Gibson Roach. *Eats: A Folk History of Texas Food.* Fort Worth: Texas Christian University Press, 1989.

Tyler, Ron, ed. *Handbook of Texas.* 6 vols. Austin: Texas State Historical Association, 1966.

Text

Central to folklife studies—as well as to linguistics, anthropology, literary criticism, and other related disciplines—the concept of "text" has expanded since the twentieth century to encompass written depictions of a wide range of human behavior that attempt to represent the behavior as comprehensively and accurately as possible. The recording of texts is important because it helps establish material as folklore by drawing attention to its multiple existence and variation, especially when links of learning and customary practice from one person to another are difficult to ascertain. For linguists and anthropologists of the nineteenth century and much of the twentieth century, "text" referred to written documentation of the verbal component of discourse. Researchers scrupulously reproduced exactly what they heard, sometimes using phonetic symbols to represent sounds in languages they did not understand. Such texts provided linguists with their primary resources for analyzing vocabulary, pronunciation, and grammar, while anthropologists used them as sources of information about the cultures of the individuals whose spoken language they had documented.

In early folklife studies, "texts" came to mean the words spoken by a storyteller or sung by a traditional singer. One role of the folklore collector, following the lead of linguists and anthropologists, was to capture these words verbatim, using dictation or mechanical recorders. Despite slight variations in the requirements of what constitutes a verbatim text, folklorists have generally agreed that texts should preserve the tradition bearer's exact words—no matter if they are ungrammatical, obscene, or nonsensical—to document the creative performance. Even if a storyteller confuses the ordering of the plot, for example, the text must not correct what the person has said, since the alteration, or mistake, may in fact be cultural evidence of the composition and performance process. An ethical basis of the rendering of texts that separates many humanists from folklorists is the insistence of folklorists that texts should not be improved or rewritten for re-telling. For the purpose of analysis, folklorists avoid combining elements from different renditions of a story, even by the same teller, to create a more satisfying printed product.

Verbal and Ethnographic Texts

Focusing exclusively on the text can result in analysis similar to the literary criticism that dominated much of the twentieth century. Such an approach often ignores the tradition bearer, the cultural background, the particulars of the situation that generated the verbalization, and aspects of it that complement the spoken word, such as gestures, facial expressions, and changes in vocal tone, tempo, and volume—all of which may be defined as "context." Thus, many folklorists have placed broader emphasis on "context," "behavior," "event," or "performance"—a view of the communication that embraces more than the purely verbal—than on the text.

Along with this broadening of interest has come a wider view of what constitutes a text itself. Folklife scholars and anthropologists working with the methods of ethnography—analyzing bounded cultural scenes for symbolic communication—realized that their efforts typically involve the conversion of human behavior into written documents. Ethnographically oriented scholars were encouraged to capture fully and faithfully in writing what they encountered as participant observers. They began to recognize their texts as translations that transformed experience into primary materials for anthropological analysis and vicarious experiences for readers. Following this anthropological concern with a process called "textualization," the folklore text might be a record of not just what was said by a verbal artist but the entirety of the artistic performance, including a verbatim transcript of the words, a thorough and detailed presentation of paralinguistic devices and body language, a description of the physical and cultural milieu (the entire ambience of when and where the performance occurred), an account of the reactions of the audience, and the personal background of the tradition bearer. The text becomes an attempt to reproduce the event, a methodology called the "ethnography of performance."

Another dimension in the reevaluation of the concept of "text" in folklife studies has recognized that even the most scrupulous attempt to reproduce a tradition bearer's words will be affected by the attitudes and perceptions of the folklorist, whose identity (particularly in terms of gender, age, and ethnicity) affects what has been said by the tradition bearer and how the folklorist hears and interprets it. For example, the pioneering British scholar Cecil Sharp, who is often given credit for drawing public as well as scholarly appreciation to Old World ballads in the southern Appalachian Mountains, is often criticized for missing opportunities to collect new song adaptations and compositions because as a British scholar he was primarily interested in comparing British ballads sung by Americans with medieval ballad texts in the British Isles. Feminist scholars have also pointed out that many male collectors concentrate on public performances of narrative and craft by men and frequently overlook the rendering of more privately shared texts by women in the domestic sphere.

Material Texts

Folklorists influenced by the culture theory of the last half of the twentieth century, which placed emphasis on the symbolic patterns linking cultural expression, may also refer to nonverbal products of human behavior—vernacular arts, crafts, and architecture, for example—as "texts." This stance allows them to analyze material forms with tools adapted from art as well as literary criticism. The objects and images are "read" in the sense that symbols are discerned to convey the ideas and values of their makers and users. Moreover, the intentions of the makers and the settings of the objects over time and space also figure into the discernment of meaning. Some folklife scholars have argued that this reading is more multidimensional and multisensory than the reading of words and involves recognizing the impact of shape, image, and texture (and sometimes even smell and taste) in layers of communication.

Objects in relation to one another may be also analyzed as narratives of cultural experience, sometimes arranged historically or regionally. An example is the tracing of hex signs on barns in the Pennsylvania German region, where talismans once used as protection from evil spirits became ethnic symbols to mark Pennsylvania German identity in the face of Anglicization. Later in the twentieth century, the symbols became commodified in cultural tourism of the central Pennsylvania region, which produced non-German images such as shamrock hex signs for St. Patrick's Day and patriotic symbols for Independence Day. Although the hex signs do not contain words, they nonetheless convey themes and traditions that may vary by the background or purposes of the maker and viewer.

The Folklorist's Identity

Folklorists still commonly include texts as transcriptions of the words that a storyteller or singer uses, as a record for public appreciation and a tool of analysis. Texts are often approached as a way to render and organize performances for structural and comparative analysis. Folklorists use terminology such as "motif" for a character, action, or object in a story, "type" for a narrative that is recognizable as a plot (with a predictable sequence of motifs), "version" for any text as a performance, and "variant" for a version of a basic type. Some structurally oriented folklorists also use texts to define the rules of composition (sometimes called a cultural "grammar") and the very boundaries of the genre, which are difficult for traditional performers to articulate because they are part of their cultural experience. A number of pivotal reference projects use texts as tools of analysis to show the diffusion of cultural expression across time and space around the globe and in individual countries and regions, or as guides to concentrations of theme, function, and structure in expressive traditions: motif and type indexes; codified catalogues of beliefs, proverbs, riddles, rhymes, and games; and taxonomies of houses, crafts, foods, settlement patterns, and furnishings.

Yet many contemporary folklorists realize that texts can be more ethnographic than strictly literary and, once they have considered how the folklorist's identity has contributed to producing the text, turn to matters beyond the verbal to examine the texts for what they reveal about the dynamic interrelationships among such performance variables as audience, situation, performer psychology, and general cultural background. The collection, identification, and interpretation of texts within cultural contexts are skills that define the folklorist's enterprise of discerning tradition.

William M. Clements

See also: Archives and Libraries; Communication; Context; Ethnography and Fieldwork; Function and Functionalism; Legends; *Märchen*; Names; Narrative, Personal; Performance Approach and Dramatic Arts; Proverbs and Sayings; Riddles and Riddling; Symbol and Structure; Toasts and Dozens.

Sources

Barrick, Mac E. "Folklore and the Verbal Text." In *100 Years of American Folklore Studies,* ed. William M. Clements, 16–17. Washington, DC: American Folklore Society, 1988.

Clements, William M. *Native American Verbal Art: Texts and Contexts.* Tucson: University of Arizona Press, 1996.

Fine, Elizabeth C. *The Folklore Text from Performance to Print.* Bloomington: Indiana University Press, 1984.

Jones, Steven Swann. "Slouching Toward Ethnography: The Text/Context Controversy Reconsidered." *Western Folklore* 38 (1979): 42–47.

Titon, Jeff Todd. "Text." *Journal of American Folklore* 108 (1995): 432–48.

Vlach, John Michael. "Folklife and the Tangible Text." In *100 Years of American Folklore Studies,* ed. William M. Clements, 18–20. Washington, DC: American Folklore Society, 1988.

Wilgus, D.K. "The Text Is the Thing." *Journal of American Folklore* 86 (1973): 241–52.

THEATER

See Drama

THANKSGIVING

Thanksgiving is a fall holiday devoted to a festive meal intended to show gratitude for the bounty of the land; in its evolving customs since the nineteenth century, the holiday has also taken on strong associations with American patriotism, family bonding, and prosperity. In the United States, Congress fixed the holiday in 1941 as the fourth Thursday in November. In Canada, the government in 1957 proclaimed the second Monday in October as Thanksgiving. Although both national traditions probably have roots in traditional harvest observances in Europe, they derive from different historical inspirations in the New World. Canadians trace the holiday to a feast held by Sir Martin Frobisher (a British seafarer looking for a Northwest Passage to the Pacific and who explored much of Canada in the process) in Newfoundland in 1578. The first Canadian Thanksgiving after confederation was held in April 1872 to celebrate the recovery of the Prince of Wales from illness; after 1879, it was regularly observed as a harvest festival.

In the United States, the holiday has been associated since the late nineteenth century with the story of a shared meal after the first harvest in 1621 by the Wampanoag and the Pilgrims who settled in Plymouth, Massachusetts. It was a founding narrative promoted during the mid-nineteenth century to reaffirm the ancestry and ideals of the New England Puritans, particularly at a time when the nation was divided. Although the iconography of the holiday in contemporary America reflects the Pilgrim mythology, for many people Thanksgiving is a secular occasion for homecoming, family, and social connection. It is distinctive among American holidays in that for many celebrants it extends over a four-day rather

Volunteers at a church in San Francisco prepare Thanksgiving meals for the less fortunate. In many communities, efforts to feed the poor and homeless have become as much a part of the holiday tradition as feasting and football. *(Justin Sullivan/ Getty Images News)*

than a three-day weekend. For many students in the Northeast, the holiday may be even longer in school districts that close for the beginning of hunting season, usually beginning the Monday after Thanksgiving. Unlike most holidays that include a festive meal as a component, for Thanksgiving the meal itself defines the observance. With the growing emphasis in the twentieth century on shopping for Christmas, Thanksgiving has also emerged as a seasonal marker of the beginning of the Christmas season; the day after, the busiest single shopping day of the year, has come to be known as "Black Friday."

History and Politics

The story of the Pilgrim harvest celebration was chronicled in journals by Pilgrim leaders William Bradford and Edward Winslow, published in *Mourt's Relation* by George Morton in London in 1622. Their accounts described a feast with Native Americans lasting several days after a successful harvest; the fare included fish (cod and bass), venison, waterfowl, and "Indian corn." Bradford mentions "a great store of wild turkeys" and recounts that the celebrants "took many" of them. Scholars have speculated that the feast of 1621 drew on English church-based harvest festivals often held in September (called "harvest home" in many areas), and perhaps the events surrounding Michaelmas, held around the same time, but the separatist Pilgrims are known to have eschewed the celebration of saints' days and church feasts. Since they lived for eleven years in Leiden in the Netherlands before embarking for the New World, they may have been influenced by Leidens Ontzet (the relief of Leiden), a public thanksgiving celebration featuring local foodways (herring and white bread). The Pilgrims' desire to preserve at least some measure of Dutch tradition in their collective memory is evidenced by the presence of a Leyden Street in the early Plymouth Colony, the first street laid out by the Pilgrims.

Puritan Thanksgiving became a regional commemoration in the Massachusetts Bay Colony in 1630 and frequently thereafter until about 1680, when it became an annual festival in that colony; it was also observed in Connecticut as early as 1639 and annually after 1647. The Pilgrims were not alone in holding a Thanksgiving celebration after the harvest—earlier feasts with Native Americans were recorded in Virginia and St. Augustine (in present-day Florida), and the Dutch in New Netherland appointed a day for giving thanks in 1644—but these celebrations were remembered regionally in oral tradition and from Bradford's chronicle. Thanksgivings were proclaimed by Presidents George Washington, John Adams, and James Madison during the early years of the New Republic, and by 1858 the governors of twenty-five states and two territories had declared Thanksgivings (although most were not connected to the Pilgrim story). Reflecting the sectional rivalries of the period, some southern states objected to a New England connection; Pennsylvania Germans called for a model based on their harvest home observance in September, involving redistribution of harvest foods to the poor. During the Civil War, President Abraham Lincoln proclaimed a national Thanksgiving Day as a sign of unity to be observed on the final Thursday of November—on which it continues to be observed to the present day. During the late nineteenth century, in the face of mass immigration, many nativists promoted the Pilgrim story as a founding narrative for the "birth of America." Thanksgiving was made an integral part of Americanization programs for newcomers, and the New England feast became a national icon of the Puritan work ethic and commitment to an English-based society.

During the twentieth century, with the growth of the consumer culture, the day after Thanksgiving came to be identified as the first day of the Christmas shopping season. During the Great Depression, to encourage purchasing and boost the economy, President Franklin Roosevelt proposed pushing Thanksgiving back to the third Thursday in November. The public reacted negatively to altering the holiday tradition, and in 1941 Congress officially established the fourth Thursday in November as Thanksgiving.

Another Thanksgiving controversy erupted during the late twentieth century concerning the representation of Native Americans in the Pilgrim mythology. In 1970, at the 350th anniversary of the landing of the Pilgrims, Native Americans staged a protest on Thanksgiving Day that featured a ceremonial burial of Plymouth Rock. Since then, Thanksgiving has been an occasion for Native American activists to declare a "National Day of Mourning" for the tragedy that befell their ancestors with the arrival of white settlers. Protestors often call for a march to counter the Pilgrims Progress Parade in Plymouth, held annually on Thanksgiving to commemorate Pilgrim experience in the "founding" of the nation. In 1998, after disruptions and violence the two previous years, the Plymouth Historical Alliance agreed to erect a plaque that revised the Pilgrim story to include a narrative of suffering by Native Americans. The society continued to sanction its annual procession, however, which features muskets and halberds (interpreted by the Native American activists as symbols of violence and oppression).

At the national political level, Thanksgiving has been an occasion for presidential proclamations of the principles of freedom that form the foundation of American democracy. Prior to the proclamation, in a ritual of mercy begun in 1947, the president spares the life of a turkey and declares it free to live the rest of its days peacefully on a farm. In addition, the National Turkey Federation presents the president with two large dressed turkeys as a sign of American abundance. And in another public gesture associated with the holiday during the late twentieth century, civic leaders and other prominent figures help serve Thanksgiving dinners to the homeless at soup kitchens and missions for the inner-city poor.

Customs and Traditions

The stuffed turkey is the centerpiece of the holiday meal, and compliments are generally extended to the cook for its crisp, brown skin, juiciness, and plump breasts. Indeed, American slang for Thanksgiving is "Turkey Day." Usually the bird is roasted in the oven for hours, although deep-frying is an alternative technique that has some favor in the South. Southerners generally make their stuffing from cornbread, while in other parts of the country white bread is the base, to which oysters, apples, chestnuts, sausage, or the turkey's giblets may be added. The growth of the animal rights movement and vegetarianism in the late twentieth century has prompted some to use meat substitutes such as "tofurky," made from the soy product tofu; others maintain that this merely perpetuates the symbol of the killed bird. Some vegans (who abstain from eating any food derived from animals) use homemade bread or butternut squash instead. Groups who use the occasion to reflect on the Native American experience feature foods such as the "three sisters" (squash, corn, and beans) and Pueblo corn pie.

Also popular at the Thanksgiving dinner table are candied sweet potatoes (also called yams) and cranberry jellies. The former dish most likely represents a southern contribution, while the latter derives from New England. Regional blending into national tradition is also evident at dessert, when pumpkin pie, associated with New England, is served together with pecan pie, connected with the South. Other regional dishes include sweet potato pie (South), shoofly pie (Pennsylvania), sauerkraut (Maryland), Dungeness crab (West Coast), turducken (Louisiana), and corn pudding (South). Mashed potatoes, creamed cauliflower, turnips, and radishes are passed around in large serving dishes, appropriate to the communal character of the meal.

Rituals and activities other than sitting down to the meal mark the social significance of Thanksgiving, particularly in defining family and gender roles. It is common practice for the woman of the house to cook the turkey and for the man to carve it ceremoniously at the table. The normative seating pattern has the elders of the family at the head and foot of the table. Family bonding is emphasized by the saying of grace (or a secular expression of gratitude) and eating from communal dishes. Christian gatherings may include the singing of "We Gather Together," derived from a Dutch folk thanksgiving hymn from the late sixteenth or early seventeenth century and thought to have been introduced in America by Dutch settlers in New Netherland. Translated into English by Theodore Baker in 1894, the song opens with an expression of gratitude to God:

> We gather together to ask the Lord's blessing,
> He chastens and hastens His will to make known.
> The wicked oppressing now cease from distressing,
> Sing praises to His name, He forgets not His own.

After the meal, usually held in the late afternoon, a common tradition is to watch professional football games on television; since 1934, the Detroit Lions have been perennial Thanksgiving participants. Before football became the dominant sporting holiday event in the mid-twentieth century, it was common in local communities to hold Thanksgiving shooting contests testing manly target skills, such as pigeon shoots and turkey shoots. The shoots were also warm-ups for the big-game hunting season, which opened in Pennsylvania and other states on the Monday after Thanksgiving. Many hunters trekked to hunting camp on the weekend and engaged in another seasonal tradition: a venison or steak dinner as a wilderness hunting parallel to the farm harvest theme of Thanksgiving. For Christmas shoppers, the hunt is for bargains at stores that open early in the morning on the Friday after Thanksgiving.

Signaling the transition to Christmas is the Macy's Thanksgiving Day Parade in New York City, which traditionally ends with Santa Claus on a reindeer-led float bedecked with elves, gumdrops, candy canes, wreaths, ribbons, ornaments, and gifts. The parade is traced to street performances by immigrant employees of Gimbel's in Philadelphia and Macy's in New York City during the early 1920s. Following eastern European harvest festival traditions, they created a carnival atmosphere with a holiday costume procession. The parade evolved over the years into a high-profile marketing and public relations event that celebrates consumer culture and is aimed at children. The main attractions are huge floating balloons of popular animated characters and comic superheroes and appearances by celebrities from the world of popular entertainment. Similar formats are followed in rival Thanksgiving parades in Houston, Philadelphia, and Detroit.

Although many Americans attend a parade or football game on Thanksgiving, many people come home—their parents' house or the town they grew up in—for the holiday. Indeed, Thanksgiving is often referred to as America's "homecoming" and family celebration. Transportation providers often tout it as the busiest travel time of the year as a result. Thus, it seems clear, an important function of the holiday is to provide communal identity for an increasingly mobile, dispersed society. Since the twentieth century, young people are more often expected to leave home and seek opportunities outside the communities where they were raised. And even if they are not able to come home for the holiday, many Americans create a sense of family and community by sharing the holiday with "second families" of friends, neighbors, and coworkers. The customs and traditions associated with Thanksgiving refer to social connections at both the local and national levels—reflecting the immediacy of family and community, while invoking narratives of the nation's founding and ideals.

Simon J. Bronner

See also: Animals; Cape Cod; Christmas; Detroit; Foodways; History and Heritage; Holidays; Nationalism; New England; New York City.

Sources

Adamczyk, Amy. "On Thanksgiving and Collective Memory: Constructing the American Tradition." *Journal of Historical Sociology* 15, no. 3 (2002): 343–65.

Appelbaum, Diana. *Thanksgiving: An American Holiday, an American History.* New York: Facts on File, 1984.

Greninger, Edwin T. "Thanksgiving: An American Holiday." *Social Science* 54 (1979): 3–15.

Linton, Ralph, and Adelin Linton. *We Gather Together: The Story of Thanksgiving.* New York: Schuman, 1949.

Santino, Jack. *All Around the Year: Holidays and Celebrations in American Life.* Urbana: University of Illinois Press, 1994.

Siskind, Janet. "The Invention of Thanksgiving: A Ritual of American Nationality." *Critique of Anthropology* 12 (1992): 167–91.

TIBETANS

Although only a few thousand Tibetans reside as of 2006 in the United States, the Tibetan community established in the late twentieth century has been remarkably successful at maintaining and presenting many aspects of its traditional folklife, even as it adapts to new and unfamiliar settings. Since the invasion of Tibet by Communist Chinese forces in the 1950s and the flight of the Dalai Lama into exile, approximately 140,000 Tibetans have left their homeland and resettled in India, Nepal, and smaller settlements throughout the world. Tibetans in these exile communities have expressed a strong commitment to preserving their culture in the hope of one day reestablishing a Tibetan nation. Most Tibetans in the United States today have lived for years (in some cases, all of their lives) in other countries of exile. In 1990, the U.S. Congress granted visas for a thousand Tibetans to resettle in twenty-two widely dispersed "cluster sites." The first groups arrived in 1992, and within a few years most of the visa recipients were able to bring their immediate families to join them.

Years of living in exile taught Tibetans that traditions can be kept alive only through sustained, creative effort. From the beginning, each Tibetan community in the United States made plans to develop cultural education programs, establish performing arts groups, and encourage celebrations of traditional Tibetan holidays. In addition to helping pass on traditional knowledge to a new generation, such undertakings were intended to make outsiders more aware of the unique aspects of Tibetan culture and to become involved in the movement for Tibetan self-determination. While the idea of preserving culture places an emphasis on older forms that are seen as more authentic, in practice Tibetan folklife in the United States actively incorporates elements from many places and cultures the group has encountered during the period of exile. Contact with Han Chinese in Tibet as well as the folk cultures and mass media of India, Nepal, and the United States all have influenced the dress, eating habits, language, play, performance, home décor, and religious practice of Tibetan Americans.

Folk Arts

Music and dance troupes, the most visible elements of Tibetan folklife, have been formed in most of the larger Tibetan settlements in the United States. These groups typically perform pieces from many regions and segments of traditional Tibetan society. Musical performances often include mountain songs that require powerful voices, short romantic songs, stylized pieces from Tibetan opera and the court settings of Lhasa, and work songs meant to pass the time and coordinate effort as groups of people tamped dirt rooftops or harvested crops. The troupes sometimes include adaptations of black-hat and skeleton dances, normally enacted by monks as part of religious ceremonies. The performances, often featuring ornate homemade or imported costumes, typically take place at Tibetan community celebrations, street festivals, schools, and other local venues. Other Tibetan American performers have played with the boundaries of traditional forms, inventing styles that incorporate elements of hip-hop, rock, blues, New Age, and Indian film music. A few Tibetan American performers, such as Nawang Khechog and Yungchen Lhamo, have achieved widespread recognition, but most concentrate on local performances while circulating their CDs and tapes through friends and relatives.

Among those Tibetans who have resettled in the United States are a good number of trained traditional visual artists. Some learned their art forms from older relatives or as apprentices in Tibet or exile communities. Others were trained in special schools, such as the Norbulingka Institute, set up by exiled Tibetans to preserve traditional arts suppressed by Chinese authorities in Tibet. Sadly, many skilled Tibetan artists found that continuing this work in the United States was too difficult. Skilled weavers cannot afford to ship their looms or have found that they do not have sufficient space or a viable source of materials. Painters of *thangkas* (religious scroll paintings)

are unable to obtain the right pigments. Metalworkers lack forges and other large-scale equipment. Moreover, the cost of living in the United States is so high for most Tibetan Americans that even artists who are able to find the proper supplies cannot make a living devoting many hours to creating pieces that could be imported from settlements in South Asia for much lower prices.

On the other hand, some Tibetans have managed to find a balance with established American occupations. Palden Namgyal, a metalworker who resettled in Minnesota, for example, found work with a local jewelry firm. He creates both American-style pieces and Tibetan-inspired designs, and his work earned him an award as Minnesota Goldsmith of the Year. Sonam Lama, who trained as a stoneworker during his youth in Tibet, set up a successful business in Massachusetts that specializes in New England–style stone walls. He also builds *chortens*, Tibetan Buddhist structures that traditionally house relics and are focal points for devotional activities. Other artists continue to work in their spare time and give presentations of their respective traditions at schools and cultural fairs.

On a day-to-day basis, most Tibetans dress in fairly typical American clothing, sometimes adding pieces of traditional jewelry or Tibet-themed T-shirts as more visible symbols of their culture. Tibetan Buddhist monks and nuns, in keeping with their monastic code, wear simple saffron and maroon-colored robes, although sweatshirts, coats, and other garments are sometimes added to cope with the extremes of American weather. For special occasions, many Tibetan laypeople wear traditional styles of clothing, such as *chubas*, long-sleeved coats that wrap across the body for extra warmth, or women's brightly colored, strip-woven aprons. Fur hats, embroidered leather or felt boots, and fancy hair ornaments are also commonly seen at these events. *Gzi* stones, many of which are passed down as treasured heirlooms, are often worn on necklaces or rings. These banded stones are widely believed to have special powers and benefits; imitation stones have become quite popular. The black and white stripes of the stone are also evoked by *rangzen* bracelets, braided wristbands of black and white cord that are often worn as a symbol of the movement for Tibetan independence.

While Tibetans are generally as fond of television and movies as other Americans, traditional storytelling is still popular at their gatherings. Adults use animal stories and *jatakas* (tales of the past lives of the Buddha) to entertain and teach children about morality. Certain *jatakas*—such as the one about four different animals who cooperate for a greater purpose, or the one about a man who gives his own body to keep a hungry tigress from eating her cubs—are so popular that they are often depicted on decorative objects. Legends about historical figures from Tibet's past, such as the poet-saint Milarepa, King Songtsen Gampo, and the epic hero Gesar of Ling, are well known. Humorous monologues are often performed at parties, and stories of the wild, bawdy adventures of the trickster Uncle Tompa are especially well loved.

Religious and Festive Traditions

In their homes, many Tibetan Americans display antiques, crafts, or photos as reminders of their homeland. Perhaps the most widespread and distinctive features of Tibetan households are home altars. As a part of daily religious practice, nearly all Tibetans keep an assortment of sacred images and objects, along with incense and offerings, in a special part of their homes. In the United States, home altars may be as simple as a few items arranged on the top of a television set, or as elaborate as an intricate hand-carved and painted case filled with precious statues and ritual items, surrounded by a wall-sized gathering of *thangkas*. Ideally, an altar should house symbols of the body, speech, and mind of the Buddha. Nearly all Tibetan home altars also include sets of seven water bowls. Even the poorest household can afford to make an offering of water, but water is also precious, as life depends on it. Most Tibetans start and end each day with prayers and offerings at their home altars. An altar provides a site for religious activities, a place to gather consecrated images and special possessions, and a striking visual reminder of Tibetan identity.

For many Tibetans, religious commitment is a crucial part of everyday life. Most Tibetan communities in the United States regularly host groups of monks and nuns from India and Nepal, as well as traveling religious teachers. Several larger communities support local monasteries that operate year-round to serve the ritual needs of families in the area. Tibetan monks conduct public services and offer special ceremonies for healing, protection, and long life, and for dead or dying individuals. They consecrate statues and *thangkas* for religious practice and give teachings and empowerments to laypeople. As a part of their duties, many Tibetan monastics learn specialized arts such as the creation of temporary sacred images from tinted butter or colored sand, the manufacture of amulets, and the playing of drums, long metal horns, and other ritual instruments. In a gesture of outreach to the broader public, the monks sometimes create intricate sand mandalas in spaces such as museums, schools, and shopping malls.

Festive occasions such as Losar (Tibetan New Year), the Dalai Lama's birthday, and Democracy Day are an especially important part of Tibetan American folklife. Taking time from busy work schedules, families gather to make offerings, recite prayers, watch performances, share potluck meals, play, gossip, and relax with friends. The food at these gatherings typically includes Tibetan specialties such as *momos* (steamed dumplings), noodle soups, and butter tea, Indian and Nepalese curries, and American snacks and sodas. In Tibet, picnic meals have been popular for many generations, and in the United States, even indoor, wintertime gatherings are a time for Tibetan families to spread carpets and blankets on the floor, share food, gamble, and chat. Soccer games and traditional circle dances add to the excitement. Formal performances by dance and music groups, chanting by monks, announcements of community news, readings of proclamations by Tibetans and U.S. officials, and open-mike sessions often run throughout these celebrations.

As these communities have grown and settled into their new surroundings, some have been working to create more permanent centers in which to hold classes, rehearse performing arts, and house monks and nuns. Tibetan parents worry about their children, who are heavily influenced by school, friends, and the media. By building community centers, they hope to give younger generations more exposure to their cultural heritage and to ensure the continuation of a distinctive Tibetan folklife in America.

Peter Harle

See also: Aesthetics; Folk Art; Religion; South Asian Communities.

Sources

Beyond the Land of Snows: Tibetans at the Smithsonian Folklife Festival. VHS. Washington, DC: Conservancy for Tibetan Art and Culture and the Smithsonian Center for Folklife and Cultural Heritage, 2001.

Diehl, Keila. *Echoes from Dharamsala: Music in the Life of a Tibetan Refugee Community.* Berkeley: University of California Press, 2002.

Dorje, Rinjing. *Food in Tibetan Life.* London: Prospect Books, 1985.

Jackson, David Paul, and Janice A. Jackson. *Tibetan Thangka Painting: Methods and Materials.* Boulder, CO: Shambhala, 1984.

Jones, Schuyler. *Tibetan Nomads: Environment, Pastoral Economy, and Material Culture.* Edited by Ida Nicolaisen. Carlsberg Foundation's Nomad Research Project. New York: Thames and Hudson, 1996.

TOASTS AND DOZENS

Folklorists often link toasts and dozens together as African American folk poetry, although their performance contexts are distinguished from each other. African Americans use the term "toasts" to identify a specific narrative oral form with rhymed couplets. The name suggests short drinking testimonials, but the content of toasts is closely tied to long, rhymed barroom recitations in the early twentieth century such as "The Shooting of Dan McGrew," "Lady Lil," and "The Face on the Barroom Floor." There may be a connection to drinking verses, however, since the form of declarative rhyming appears structurally similar to that of many traditional drinking verses with misogynist themes. Most often told by young men, African American toasts recount the

hypermasculine exploits of trickster figures, badmen, or tragic heroes—as in "Signifying Monkey," "Stagolee," "Joe the Grinder," "Shine and the Titanic," "Dolomite," and "Flicted Arm (or Piss Pot) Pete." Toasts, collected vigorously during the 1960s and 1970s, are often cited as the roots of rap and hip-hop street rhyming in the twenty-first century. Among other features, folklorists are interested in the common themes and connected narrative strategies of different toasts, as in the openings of "Stackolee" and "Shine and the Titanic":

> Back in forty-nine when times was hard
> I carried a sawed-off shotgun and a marked deck of cards
> I stumbled through rain and crawled through mud
> On this bad town called "Bucket of Blood."

> Back on the day of the eighth of May
> The year of Nineteen and Twelve, was a hell of a day
> Up popped from the deck below,
> Saying, "Captain, Captain, you don't know, about forty feet of water on this boiler-room floor."

"Dozens" (also referred to as "capping," "jiving," "joning," "sounding," "snapping," "signifying," and "woofing") is the most common term used by African Americans for rhymes used in ritualized insult contests. As such, they are directed at other persons. For example, an insult exchange that relies on traditional rhymes goes as follows: "Bullfrog, bullfrog, bank to bank, your momma built like an Army tank," followed by the reply, "I hate to talk about your momma, she's a good old soul, she got a humpback boodle like a G.I. Joe." The dozens is more of a "game" played between two participants in the street, while the toast is an individual oral performance for one's buddies in a bar, pool hall, military barrack, or prison. The dozens is popular among preadolescents; toasts are more common among older groups. The most prominent common feature in the performance of dozens and the recitation of toasts is the poetic rhythm.

Performance and Meaning of Dozens

Dozens are often expressed in rhymed couplets, especially using the formula "I (saw, screwed) your mama (on, in, by, or between) ——. / She ——." While the teller may rely on colorful examples he may have heard, he also may try to create new insults based on the structure of the formulas. The subcategory of snaps or rank-outs often follows the formula of "Your mother's like ——; she ——," or "Your mother's so ——, she ——." Examples are "Your mother's like a doorknob; everyone gets a turn" and "Your mother's so low, she could play handball on the curb." "Playing" or "doing" the dozens, therefore, involves quick referential thinking and linguistic creativity, skills that audiences reinforce with their approval. So that the aggression in insult contests does not escalate into violence, the playfulness of dozens is often cued by the formulas and mock gestures of confrontation.

The origin of "dozens" is obscure. Blues songs about the "dirty dozens" circulated in African American communities early in the twentieth century. They often had twelve verses, with each one referring to a different sex act. The content of dozens in insult contests often includes descriptions of sex. Noting the competitive basis of dozens in performance, folklorist Roger Abrahams conjectures in *Deep Down in the Jungle* (1970) that the dozens may refer to the throw of 12 in craps, which is hard to match and is considered unlucky. According to musician Quincy Jones, "dirty dozens" was understood in the oral tradition that he inherited as a slavery term; auctioneers were said to have grouped undesirable slaves in lots of twelve to move their sale. Jones remembered that "insulting your mama was meant to make you feel as low as one of the dirty dozens." The form of ritualized insult contests among young American blacks has been traced to African antecedents by several folklorists who have pointed out initiation ceremonies involving same-age boys referring to one another's mothers pornographically. Some folklorists have documented a separate insult contest tradition among white preadolescent boys called "ranking" or "rank-out

contests," although it employs less of the rhyming insults against the opponent's mother.

The language of the dozens is rough and the themes are risqué, but the composition is creative. The boys challenge each other to top every retort, and the responses of listeners are the measure of the insulter's success. As social entertainment usually performed by preadolescent, lower-class African American boys, the dozens have sparked considerable sociopsychological commentary. According to one such interpretation, the dozens represent a striving for masculine identity by black boys in a matrifocal society. They represent a symbolic rejection of the woman's world—or indeed the black world they see as run by the mother—in favor of the male gang life. In dozens playing, black boys hone the verbal and social skills they will need as adult males. The structure of insulting one's mother is significant because it puts the boy in the position of simultaneously separating from the mother figure by aggressively dominating her and defending her honor from outsiders' attack. White insult contests tend to focus more on appearance and intelligence as features of adult success than on separation from the mother.

Identity and Expression in Toasts

While the dozens is often reported among preadolescents, toasts are most often heard among teenagers and young adults. Toasts use many of the rhyming and rhythmic schemes and the rough imagery of the dozens, but are performed by young men as extended poetic recitations rather than ritualized insults. The performance of toasts is intended to be dramatic. The settings are typically barrooms and jungles; the characters are badmen, pimps, and street people; the props are often drugs, strong drink, and guns. Here, for example, is an excerpt from a frequently collected toast, "The Signifying Monkey":

> Down in the jungle near a dried-up creek,
> The signifying monkey hadn't slept for a week
> Remembering the ass-kicking he had got in the
>   past

He had to find somebody to kick the lion's ass.
Said the signifying monkey to the lion that very
   same day,
"There's a bad mother heading your way.
The way he talks about you it can't be right,
And I know when you two meet there going to
   be a fight.
He said he screwed your cousin, your brother,
   and your niece,
And he had the nerve enough to ask your
   grandmom for a piece."
The lion said, "Mr. Monkey, if what you say
   isn't true about me,
I'll run your ass up the highest tree."
The monkey said, "Now look, if you don't
   believe what I say,
Go ask the elephant. He's resting down the
   way."

These poems provide a form of street entertainment, especially validating the high status accorded in black culture to the man of words in the pulpit as well as on the street. Many of the themes—such as misogyny, hypermasculine self-assertion, sexual bravado, and gunplay in relation to a fast but dangerous life—find similar expression in rap. But rappers emphasize the originality rather than traditionality of their recitations, and emphatically use rhythms in performance.

Black and White Recitations

One toast common to black and white adolescent repertoires is that of "Lady Lil," sometimes called "Piss-Pot Pete" or "Flicted Arm Pete" in black tradition. The poem concerns a fornication contest in the Wild West between an unappealing "half-breed" named Pete and the sophisticated Lil, often identified as a "schoolmarm" from back East. Folklorists have commented on the recitation's function in adolescent development, as it combines the authority figures of the schoolteacher and mother in a single character. In the fantasy of the toast, the authority figure is dominated to announce separation and triumph by the short, underdeveloped, unsightly male. The young male performer relates to the underdeveloped character and establishes his independence and maturity

by defeating the mature mother-schoolteacher in a contest to the death. The character of Pete is not taken seriously because of his appearance, but he demonstrates his worthiness and earns respect by sexual exploits and violent actions. In white versions, Pete emerges triumphant, while in black versions he dies, leading to speculation about the fatalism expressed by African American male performers.

In the North, most texts of toasts and dozens come from cities. Although southern examples are reported in cities including New Orleans and Austin, southern texts are more often documented in rural and small-town communities. Themes and heroes of the toasts have a connection to southern black folk songs, including "Stackolee" and "The Titanic." The blues also are influenced by the erotic and violent verses of the toasts, and sanitized versions of Stackolee became rock 'n' roll hits in the mid-twentieth century. Other connections are found between toasts and southern black animal folktales featuring the monkey and the toast "Signifiying Monkey."

While toasts and dozens have their roots in African American folklife, they also have entered into American popular culture. The black stage comedian Rudy Ray Moore entertains audiences with renditions of "Signifying Monkey," "Shine and the Great Titanic," "Dolemite," and "Pimping Sam." Movies also feature dozens and toasts, often to convey the distinctiveness of African American ghetto life, as in *White Men Can't Jump* (1992).

Dozens and toasts stand out because they are framed as play or performance, and they contain strong themes and sounds that signify folklife marked by race, gender, region, and age. They creatively manipulate imagery and metaphor to bring drama to words. The boy telling dozens may eventually tackle the more sophisticated toasts. Indeed, adolescents often dismiss dozens as juvenile by proclaiming, "I don't play" or "I don't go for signifying." Mastering the techniques in these traditional performances gives the reciter a sense of prestige and power among his peers, while expressing fantasies and hyperbole that draw attention to themselves. Dozens and toasts entertain friends and pass the time. The content often relates to the settings of their performance—prisons, pool halls, and street corners. The performers of dozens and toasts, still evident in the twenty-first century, are narrators of imagined scenes and cultural critics for the audiences they entertain. The tellers also draw attention because they vicariously recount their experiences through the traditional structures of the verses and their colorful characters. In the twenty-first century, rap forms have displaced many of the set toasts and the insulting play of dozens in ghetto street performances, but the structural and thematic influence of dozens and toasts are still evident in the verbal arts of African American folklife.

Simon J. Bronner

See also: Adolescents; African American Communities; Children's Groups; Hip-Hop; Men and Masculinity; Performance Approach and Dramatic Arts; Prisoners; Psychology; Rituals and Rites; Storytelling; Text.

Sources

Abrahams, Roger D. *Deep Down in the Jungle . . . Negro Narrative Folklore from the Streets of Philadelphia.* Chicago: Aldine, 1970.

Baker, Ronald L., and Simon J. Bronner. " 'Letting Out Jack': Sex and Aggression in Manly Recitations." In *Manly Traditions: The Folk Roots of American Masculinities*, ed. Simon J. Bronner, 315–50. Bloomington: Indiana University Press, 2005.

Bronner, Simon J. "A Re-Examination of Dozens Among White American Adolescents." *Western Folklore* 37 (1978): 118–28.

———. " 'Who Says?' A Further Investigation of Ritual Insults Among White American Adolescents." *Midwestern Journal of Language and Folklore* 4 (1978): 53–69.

Jackson, Bruce. *Get Your Ass in the Water and Swim Like Me: Narrative Poetry from Black Oral Tradition.* Cambridge, MA: Harvard University Press, 1974.

———. *Get Your Ass in the Water and Swim Like Me! Narrative Poetry from the Black Oral Tradition.* Rounder Records, CD 2014. 1998.

Jemie, Onwuchekwa. *Yo' Mama! New Raps, Toasts, Dozens, Jokes and Children's Rhymes from Urban Black America.* Philadelphia: Temple University Press, 2003.

Labov, William. "Rules for Ritual Insult." In *Rappin' and Stylin' Out: Communication in Urban Black America*, ed. Thomas Kochman, 265–314. Urbana: University of Illinois Press, 1972.

Moore, Rudy Ray. *Rudy Ray Moore—Greatest Hits.* Capitol, CD 35735. 1995.

Wepman, Dennis, Ronald B. Newman, and Murray B. Binderman. *The Life: The Lore and Folk Poetry of the Black Hustler.* Philadelphia: University of Pennsylvania Press, 1976.

TOURISM

See Consumerism

TRADITION AND CULTURE

A key term in the study of folklife, "tradition" refers to the collective customs and knowledge of a group or society. Tradition, it is assumed, is a source of basic learning, occurring even before formal education begins and continuing throughout life. Its usual connotation is a process of "handing down" knowledge from generation to generation, especially by oral and customary means. The term has other meanings as well, referring to the substantive results of this process, such as a story or ritual; a precedent given importance through repeated practice; knowledge whose official source cannot be verified but is held widely; or a concept (i.e., a mode of thought or behavior) characteristic of people generally.

The reverence commonly afforded to tradition indicates that people follow it, willingly or not, and—significantly for the study of folklife—may define themselves through its presence. Whether following tradition means unconsciously adhering to a severe form of cultural authority or choosing from tradition that one finds appropriate can be a cause for dispute among folklife scholars. Implied in this difference is a questioning of whether tradition forces stability and conformity or fosters change and progress. Inherent in the concept is a duality that is constantly negotiated in society: tradition's reference on the one hand to the past (as the source of knowledge and action) and on the other hand to the present (as living practice, often adapted and adjusted for particular needs and conditions).

Tradition Invoked for Identity

The significance of tradition in cultural inquiry is the way it is invoked by people to form identities, shape values, and guide behavior. Most evident in folklife scholarship from the nineteenth century into the twenty-first century are understandings of tradition as (1) an everyday past, often ancient, represented as stable and immutable; (2) learning as a kind of custom or process, usually described as being outside formal institutions and involving older generations passing on "lore" to younger ones; (3) a shared body of knowledge and belief, that is, conventional wisdom existing outside of formal records; (4) a repeated, variable expression or performance emerging from social interaction; and (5) a symbol or mode of thought characteristic of a group's identity.

Associated with precedent, continuity, and convention, tradition is often referred to as a basis for directing future action. Whether one wants the future to break with or continue the pattern of tradition dictates judgments of tradition as negative or positive. Especially common in the modernist literature of culture are statements emphasizing tradition as a guide or choice. Many contemporary writers suggest that in the modern push toward novelty and fashion, choosing tradition, a social connection hearkening back to a past, preserves individual freedom and diversity in a homogenizing mass culture. Hence, folk musicians, folk artists, and folk tradition bearers are often touted as exemplars of free will in a mass society that exerts pressure to conform. There is noticeable irony in the invocation of tradition as a sign of individualism, for it can also be used for social conformity and stability through continuity, as in such tradition-bound groups as the Amish.

Although people often relate their identities to a tradition or culture, there are shades of difference in the meanings of "tradition" and "culture." In the case of tradition, there is a sense that the individual can grasp it, participate in it, and invoke it more easily than the abstraction of culture. Tradition connotes a social connection and

historical precedent that underlie a cultural presence. Tradition suggests continuity of practice through time—a familiar a way of doing things—while culture suggests an unconsciously experienced existence, or a way of thinking about things. Culture in the past was a reference to place, often to a language group bounded in space, whereas traditions were more variably social, possibly referring to family, age, and gender. In academic circles, tradition is more broadly defined than is culture, as in the use of such terms as "Western tradition" and "Eastern tradition"; here "tradition" is used as a synonym for "pattern." Culture, by contrast, is applied to all types of associations as well as bounded groups. The view persists that traditions define a culture, rather than the reverse, and the "science of tradition" in European American intellectual history—whose purpose is to objectify and organize tradition—has been associated with folklore and folklife study.

Tradition as Reference for Minority and Majority Groups

Rather than use tradition to describe national or hemispheric patterns, many folklorists apply it to minority cultures and small groups. Arguably, national traditions have been categorized as histories while marginal groups have often been described in terms of culture or tradition. The frequent characterization of tradition as a collective memory links historical and folk tradition, but distinctions often arise. In keeping with a concern for past events and figures causing change, historical tradition often implies the inherited narrative of what happened previously, what acted as a cause toward a present effect. The term "folk tradition," when it is used, commonly refers to the process or result of oral transmission or imitation characteristic of the persistence of legends, tales, songs, and so on. The passage of time is implied, but more in the foreground is the factor of social participation.

In American public or political discourse, tradition may be invoked in proposals for maintaining national or majority "traditional values," or preserving the sanctity provided by tradition for institutions of the nuclear family and religion in daily life. Debates arose through the late twentieth century and into the twenty-first century over virtues that constituted the basis of American culture. Associations such as the Coalition for Traditional Values, Toward Tradition, and Concerned Citizens for Traditional Values took on the label of "tradition" to represent conservative religious groups in lobbying for prayer and religious programming in the schools, prohibiting gay marriage, public support for parochial institutions, and school voucher programs. Although sounding secular and broad-based, "traditional" in the organizational titles came to stand for an orthodox morality upholding the centrality of religion in public life. It invoked the merit of "traditional" to describe national "values" proven worthy by time and by popular usage. The implication by advocates of traditional values is that rapid social change has undermined "mainstream" or national values, while opponents argue for establishment of new or multiple traditions that are culturally relative and legitimate even if they are different from the mainstream. Sometimes the culturally relative keyword of "multiculturalism," implying that traditions are created anew in contemporary life, may be set against the concept of "culturalism," connoting the stability of values passed from generation to generation. Both views, sometimes stated as sides in an American "culture war," invoke tradition for social legitimacy.

Tradition as a Living Practice

Noticeable among folklorists is the special concern for tradition as a living practice in the present, evident in the emergence of new traditions as well as the adaptation of long-standing traditions. Instead of viewing tradition as the blind repetition of a precedent, folklorists are likely to draw attention to communal and individual creativity in the shaping of tradition. Public discourse, and folkloristic discourse in many instances, tends to question the continuity of tradition as a category for community, locality, and

religion. At issue in America, a nation associated historically with rapid progress and orientation toward the future, is the effect of change. Various forms of change lay in the background of the discourse of tradition—physical displacement, social fragmentation, historical modernization. Change in various rhetorical guises—progress, modernity, movement, fashion, invention—appears as the assumed constant of a normal life. Tradition in America is often understood as a means of balancing the push for novelty and change; it is a source of cultural stability and diversity amid rapid change and homogenization.

In the United States, "tradition" has been a publicly contested term for viewing different priorities of building national unity and multicultural community. "Tradition" rarely stands alone. Modifiers to tradition such as "national," "ethnic," "religious," "folk," "cultural," "family," and "local" have implied a need to place a feeling of social connectedness, a collective memory, in an identified niche within mass society. The association of tradition with folklife especially brings out the perception of tradition's strength in small groups, in everyday life. The social conflicts between ideas of a technological mass culture of convenience and uniformity exist against the idea of a spiritual folk society with its bonds of intimacy and identity.

Folklife as a study of tradition has contributed to making the cultural challenges before societies and individuals more explicit. It has especially examined the social landscape growing out of the past and the need for social expression of the ways that people relate to one another. Set against the background of change, tradition's role in the way that people live and view the world commands renewed attention as new forms of communication arise. As industrialization and urbanization of the late nineteenth century in America brought folklife prominently into view as the new century approached, trends of computerization and reorganization in the late twentieth century raised thorny questions about the future of tradition. Seen as a process fundamental to social existence, tradition is guaranteed a future, but viewed as a formulation of the past, as a type of knowledge or authority, tradition and its future are beset by doubt, and the door is thus opened to calls for preservation, memorialization, manipulation, and invention.

Simon J. Bronner

See also: Community and Group; Context; Ethnography and Fieldwork; Folklife and Folk Culture; Folklore; Function and Functionalism.

Sources

Ben-Amos, Dan. "The Seven Strands of *Tradition:* Varieties in Its Meaning in American Folklore Studies." *Journal of Folklore Research* 21 (1984): 97–132.

Bronner, Simon J., ed. *Creativity and Tradition in Folklore: New Directions.* Logan: Utah State University Press, 1992.

———. *Folk Nation: Folklore in the Creation of American Tradition.* Wilmington, DE: SR Books, 2002.

———. *Following Tradition: Folklore in the Discourse of American Culture.* Logan: Utah State University Press, 1998.

Cothran, Kay L. "Participation in Tradition." In *Readings in American Folklore*, ed. Jan Harold Brunvand, 444–48. New York: W.W. Norton, 1979.

Finnegan, Ruth. "Tradition, but What Tradition and for Whom?" *Oral Tradition* 6 (1991): 104–24.

Gailey, Alan. "The Nature of Tradition." *Folklore* 100 (1989): 143–61.

Glassie, Henry. "Tradition." In *Eight Words for the Study of Expressive Culture*, ed. Burt Feintuch, 176–97. Urbana: University of Illinois Press, 2003.

Shils, Edward. *Tradition.* Chicago: University of Chicago Press, 1981.

TRIAL LAWYERS

In addition to being highly trained professionals who play a vital role in the American system of justice, trial lawyers constitute a distinctive folk group that relies on telling stories. From the moment they meet prospective jurors until the verdict is finally in, they engage in artful performance: a storytelling contest whose purpose is to make their version of events more believable than their opponent's. Their chances of winning a favorable outcome depend on their mastery of narrative, stylistic, and legal skills that belong to a complex craft tradition.

Only a small proportion of all legal disputes ever go to trial—probably less than 1 percent of the civil cases and 5 percent of the felony cases filed in state court. A trial is a last resort. It occurs when the contending parties cannot reach agreement but a decision about the truth must be made. To resolve the impasse, some societies depend on oracles, others on judges. The United States, with its democratic preference for juries composed of ordinary citizens, relies on an adversarial system requiring zealous advocacy of each side's version of the truth. Since the truth of disputed events cannot be known directly, lawyers rely on performance to create the *appearance* of truth.

Courtroom Performance

Good courtroom performances require the orchestration of myriad elements. First, lawyers need to fashion a version of events that has mythic resonance: a story that, while offering a plausible rendering of the evidence, speaks to the jurors' fears and aspirations, their beliefs about how the world works, and their sense of what is right. Second, lawyers need to stage witness testimonies and their own arguments in ways that take advantage of the trial's dramatic potential. Third, lawyers need to project a convincing courtroom persona, exploiting aspects of cultural identity (ethnicity, race, gender, class, region, age, and the like) to validate themselves and authenticate their story. Their opponents, meanwhile, dealing with the same necessities, attempt to trip them up and undermine their stories. From the start of the trial to the final verdict, each lawyer tries to outmaneuver the other while building layers of mutually reinforcing appearances, so that wherever jurors direct their attention they find confirmations of truth.

This art of advocacy is learned mainly through on-the-job experience, observation, and advice from other practitioners. As in other crafts, trial lawyers develop a repertoire of skills, consisting of materials and patterns for action, encoded in memory, that are instantly available to meet the demands of unfolding situations. Examples range from words and gestures that are used formulaically, to larger set pieces designed to fit specific needs, to characteristic ways of framing and refuting whole stories. The repertoire enables economy of effort. Armed with reliable means of handling recurrent circumstances, lawyers are freed from having to figure out too much in the heat of performance and are able to focus on specific issues as well as a larger strategy. The breadth and quality of lawyers' repertoires vary greatly. Mediocre attorneys get stuck in inflexible patterns, whereas skilled attorneys are attuned to the subtle dynamics of shifting trial contexts. Aware of what they need to learn, they are more able to correct their mistakes.

Trial Craft

Trial lawyers themselves see their work as a craft. Most believe that the more skilled you are, the more likely it is that you will win. While an outright victory in a tough case is impressive, winning is not understood simply in all-or-nothing terms. It means doing better than could be expected given the evidence you have to work with, especially when the evidence is so unfavorable that it points to defeat. Certain lawyers who enjoy great success with juries develop formidable reputations among their peers. Over time, a small number achieve legendary status within local or even national legal circles.

Consider two examples of stories performed by outstanding attorneys in uphill battles in notorious criminal trials of the 1990s. In the O.J. Simpson case in 1995, lead defense counsel Johnnie L. Cochran, Jr., called on the jury to acquit Simpson of murder as a repudiation of racism and slipshod conduct by the Los Angeles Police Department. Cochran had had decades of prior experience defending African American clients and suing the City of Los Angeles on grounds of racial mistreatment by the police department. He was thus well prepared to stage a story exploiting the prosecution's vulnerabilities to such charges. Like telling a cante fable (a traditional narrative form in which a story is told partly in verse or song), Cochran repeated, "If it doesn't fit, you must acquit," through his closing argument, the refrain invoking both the glove Simpson allegedly wore

and other inconsistencies the defense claimed to have uncovered in the prosecution's case.

In the first trial of Terry Nichols as coconspirator in the Oklahoma City federal building bombing in 1997, defense attorney Michael J. Tigar repeated the phrase "he was building a life, not a bomb," at the time of the horrific event, to weave a narrative of Nichols as a stable family man in contrast to the devious wanderer and coconspirator Timothy McVeigh. Prosecutor Beth Wilkinson improvised a narrative in her rebuttal: "He wasn't building a life, he was building a bomb and he was building an alibi." Tigar also used the narrative ploy of casting doubt on a witness's credibility with the opprobrium of being "bought and paid for." Tigar modeled his successful plea to spare his client's life on the approach of Clarence Darrow, a master of anti–death penalty rhetoric, whose style and modes of argument were at once elevated and colloquial. Both Cochran and Tigar perfected folk personas and performance strategies that put them at the top of their profession.

The inherent tension between skill and evidence accounts for the shadowy status of trial craft within the legal system. Naturally, the public wants jury verdicts to be based on an objective weighing of what actually happened, not on the attorneys' respective abilities. To give the craft official prominence would undercut the judicial view of trials as rational searches for justice. Public skepticism about trial lawyers arguably has grown in recent years, fueled by media exposure of lawyers' stratagems. Experts' commentaries on real trials and dramatized portrayals of fictional trials have become staples of media coverage, while trial proceedings broadcast on television have become an armchair spectator sport.

Trial lawyers shift seamlessly between official and unofficial discourse about their work. When speaking as officers of the court, they stress the pursuit of justice. But when they talk shop, they talk craft. In the (mostly) humorous "war stories" they tell about memorable courtroom exploits, they convey their ambivalence about their role in the justice system. Many of these narratives are of personal experience; others are well-traveled legal folktales. They contain such stock characters and themes as the innocent client who is pure of heart, the smart jurors who ferret out the truth, the biased judge who abuses authority, the cocky expert who fumbles on the witness stand, and the egocentric lawyer who asks one too many questions. War stories show lawyers to be keenly aware of the moral ambiguity of their actions as they navigate along a slippery slope from shading to distortion to deceit.

Ethics of Fabulists

Trial law, like every profession, is dogged by endemic moral challenges. Attorneys, for example, must deal with matters of personal conscience in deciding the lengths to which they will go in attempting to win. Beyond individual conduct, the occupation faces deep-seated ethical challenges regarding equal treatment within the legal system. These challenges follow from a corollary of the craft axiom that the more skilled a lawyer is, the better his or her chances of winning: namely, that *the more evenly matched the lawyers, the better the chances for justice.* When the opposing attorneys are of roughly similar caliber and each has adequate resources to put into trial preparation, they tend to neutralize each other, leaving jurors better able to judge a case on its merits. Such parity, however, is often lacking, because access to skilled advocacy is as stratified as other valuable benefits in American society. Barriers to effective representation encountered by persons who are poor, not white, or otherwise disadvantaged are well documented—nowhere more starkly than in continuing revelations of erroneous or dubious convictions in death penalty cases.

The craft of trial lawyers bears resemblances to persuasion in the realms of politics, advertising, entertainment, and personal relations. It is closely allied with the work of novelists, playwrights, directors, and actors, all fabulists who create elaborate representations of the human circus. The lawyer's art is unruly compared to theirs, but what it lacks in polish it makes up for by its character as storytelling about real events whose recounting to an audience has fateful conse-

quences for people's lives. Lawyers take the stage for days, weeks, even months. Then the jury alone decides. In the prolonged intensity of the encounter and the high stakes of the outcome, the jury trial is unparalleled as an American occasion for oral performance.

Sam Schrager

See also: Narrative, Personal; Occupational Folklife; Storytelling.

Sources

Montell, William Lynwood. *Tales from Tennessee Lawyers.* Lexington: University Press of Kentucky, 2005.

Neufeld, Peter, Jim Dwyer, and Barry Scheck. *Actual Innocence: Five Days to Execution, and Other Dispatches from the Wrongly Accused.* New York: Doubleday, 2000.

Schrager, Sam. *The Trial Lawyer's Art.* Philadelphia: Temple University Press, 1999.

St. Johns, Adela Rogers. *Final Verdict.* Garden City, NY: Doubleday, 1962.

TRUCK DRIVERS (LONG-HAUL TRUCKERS)

The folklife of truck drivers is centered in the workaday world of "long-haul truckers," mostly men, who drive "big-rig" eighteen-wheel tractor-trailers for long distances, days at a time. Their image as rugged individualists filled with youthful vigor leading a nomadic life on the open highway, expressed in their speech and song, has led to comparisons with the romanticized cowboy of the nineteenth century. Like them, truckers are recognized by signature dress—steel-capped boots or cowboy boots, shiny, large belt buckles brandishing images of their rigs, and their own genre of hats—and meet up in their own "watering holes" (trucker slang for truck stops). Driving rigs filled with freight over long expanses of interstate highway further raises comparisons with the open plains across which cowboys drove cattle to be packaged for ordinary citizens, who underappreciated their skills and grit. Now their cargoes are not so much driven animals as hauled goods, but—as occasional job actions by truckers remind the nation—they have a central function in the modern consumer culture, delivering the

A trucker in Texas uses a GPS navigation system and wireless computer system to chart his route and get pickup information. High-tech communications equipment and appliances such as microwave ovens, TVs, and refrigerators have transformed the life and culture of truckers. *(Joe Raedle/Getty Images News)*

American way of life. And like the cowboys, truckers, despite a public perception of crudeness, have produced an artistic and folk legacy; legends abound about truckers who come through in a crisis and lend a kind hand to children and adults in need. Truckers, too, stage their own rodeos, and trucks have their own resonant calls (a blow on the air horn rather than a "yippee-ay-yay").

If not the cowboy, then the trucker engaged in "shipping" is occasionally thought of romantically as a skipper-sailor of the concrete sea, taking pride in his rig-ship as home and workplace with decoration and polish. Often part of a "fleet," truckers pull into "docks" for their cargo and are referred to as "over-the-road" drivers, linguistically connected to a phrase associated with sailors, "over the sea." They dwarf in power and size the lesser boats, or cars ("roller skates" in trucker slang), and demand priority on the sea, or highway lanes. Like sailors, they are also viewed as rough talking and seductive toward women of ill repute ("lot lizards" in trucker lingo) when in port, or truck stop.

Yet the trucker folklife also diverges in significant ways from that of preindustrial forebears, as truckers are part of industrial associations of craft unionism and at the same time represent modern corporate interests. They have a blue-collar con-

sciousness, in many cases having been born to owner-operators from deindustrialized areas and displaced farms who were attracted to the independence of trucking so as to maintain their multigenerational residences. More than drawing on a connection to cowboys, truckers inherit historic ties to "teamsters"—drivers of teams of horses, mules, or oxen for heavy hauling. Their unionism began in 1903, before many motorized trucks were on the road, with the formation of the International Brotherhood of Teamsters in Niagara Falls, New York. Bolstered by a successful strike in Minneapolis in 1934, the Teamsters grew quickly with the organization of interstate truckers in the following decade.

The links in the American imagination between trucking and southern speech and country music owe to the relocation of many carriers to the South to avoid unionization during the 1940s. Another common association with truckers—aggressive independence and a rough-around-the-edges working-class persona—is also based in part on violent and illicit union tactics and on the rejection of big-union authority. The solidarity and long-standing frustration of American truckers have been manifested on several occasions: the milestone blockade of highways during the fuel crisis of 1973; a protracted strike against the nation's largest carrier, United Parcel Service, in 1997; and the pugnacious leadership of legendary James "Jimmy" Hoffa, a former dockworker who during the 1960s became the most powerful labor leader in America.

As an organized group, truckers often express a rebellious spirit—against government regulation of their work (limits on the hours they can continually drive) and loads (restrictions on weights hauled), rising taxes and tolls, and highway speed limits. Their rigs are juggernaut machines that require an extensive support network of depot workers, mechanics, bookkeepers, and agents. They operate sophisticated communication devices and keep detailed records. The darker side of their romanticized reputations includes problems with drug abuse (amphetamines, used to stay awake for long trips) and supporting prostitution. Additionally, despite their image of independence, only 10 percent of the estimated 3.3 million truck drivers in the United States are owner-operators. An even smaller minority, estimated at barely more than 150,000, are women. The U.S. trucking industry today is dominated by 360,000 companies, and the largest American employers of truckers at the beginning of the twenty-first century are the package delivery services United Parcel Service and Federal Express. Of the 15.5 million trucks on American roads, just under two million are tractor-trailers.

Still, since the late twentieth century, neither the number of individuals taking up long-haul truck driving nor the distinctive culture associated with it shows any sign of declining. The number of people in the U.S. industry has increased steadily since the late twentieth century, and the cultural landscape of depots, truck stops, truck shows, and weighing stations is a material reminder of the occupational legacy.

Speech

Trucker folk speech received popular attention when CB (citizens band) radio spread from truckers to nontruckers during the 1980s, and homes and cars began deciphering the slang truckers used to communicate. Even before CBs came into use, however, a trucker lingo was being reported as a modern occupational folk speech. In 1942, linguist Bernard Porter recorded a number of specialized terms, especially for particular types of drivers and equipment. Many of the terms are still in use, such as "rig" for truck, "box" for trailer, and "hand" for driver. Antecedents in teamster heritage can be discerned in references to the tractors as "horses" and to driving a tractor without a trailer as riding "bareback." Another term in the motorized age that probably owes to teamster days is "pushing" for "driving" (being able to move the truck without horses, or pushing it manually).

Much trucker slang arose with the advent of the interstate highway system in the 1940s and 1950s—the highway was the "big road" or "super slab," the passing lane was the "bumper lane." The antiauthoritarian ethos is evident in

the number of terms for police—"Smokey Bear" (from the cartoon character) for highway patrol officers; "county mounty" for sheriff; "Evel Knievel" (after the daredevil performer) for motorcycle police; "plain white wrapper" or "brown paper bag" for an unmarked police car; "sneaky snake" for hidden patrol car; "Kojak with a Kodak" or "bear taking pictures" for an officer with a radar gun; and "local yokel" or "city kitty" for municipal police. Getting arrested is likely to be referred to as being "in the pokey with Smokey." The weigh stations where loads are checked may be scorned as "chicken coops" or "pigpens"; they "roll you across" if they are open but are "all locked up" or "clean" if they are closed. The driver's logbook, which must reflect activities that conform to regulations, is disdainfully referred to as the "comic book."

When the CB radio became part of popular culture, many terms passed into general American usage, such as "roger" for okay and "over and out" for signing off. Although the CB radio faded from popular use, the equipment remains in many trucks alongside cell phones, satellite radios connected to trucker stations, and global positioning systems. One can still hear numerical codes being recited by truckers over CB channels—such as 10-4 for general approval, 10-9 for "repeat message," and 10-100 to refer to a restroom break. Some of the older slang has evolved or faded from use, such as "good buddy," once thought to refer to a trucker friend but now carrying the implication (typically negative in this group) of homosexuality. An extensive repertoire of nicknames differentiates types of trucks and truckers, with the implication that independent "big rigs" (eighteen-wheel tractor-trailers) are the top of the driving hierarchy. United Parcel Service drivers are called "Buster Browns" (for the color of their trucks and uniforms), moving companies are "bedbuggers," tanker-trailers are "thermos bottles," cement trucks are "muck trucks," and a "mobile" is a logging truck. Brands of trucks are lent an air of familiarity with such nicknames as "Petercar" or "heavenly body" for a Peterbilt, "Freightshaker" for a Freightliner, "Jimmy" for a GMC, "Big Mac" (from the hamburger) for a Mack, and "KW" or "Kenny Whopper" for a Kenworth. CB equipment has gained its own slang lexicon. The "tin can" or "set of dials" is the CB rig, the "container" or "beast" is the CB shell, and a "blessed event" is a new CB. Social connections within the folk group, as well as divisions in it, are apparent in folk terms for drivers: a "hand" (or "old hand") is a complimentary term for a fellow driver; a "Gypsy" is an independent owner-operator; a "legal beagle" is a driver who follows regulations; and a "grating Jane" is a new female truck driver.

Song and Story

One aspect of trucker culture that raises comparisons with that of cowboys is a legacy of song, often adapting traditional blues and ballad forms to country music. An early popular hit was "Truck Driver's Blues," recorded in 1939 by Cliff Bruner (composition by Ted Daffan), which improvised on a blues stanza structure (aab) and conveyed the mythos of the weary, lonely, and harried truck driver.

> Keep them wheels a-rollin', I ain't got no time
> to lose
> Keep them wheels a-rollin', I ain't got no time
> to lose
> Just a low down feelin'
> Truck driver's blues.

Working in the industrialized Texas Gulf Coast, Bruner and Daffan linked the rising oil truck-transport trade with a general appeal in Depression-era uprooting and migration, especially in the dust-ridden plains.

More lyrical bravado is evident in the boom times of trucking during the 1960s, when trucker classics, many of which entered oral tradition, dominated the airwaves. One of the best known is Dave Dudley's "Six Days on the Road" (1963; composition by Earl Green and Carl Montgomery). The writers were furniture movers, and Dudley went on to be identified in the public mind with truckers and their music, leading the Teamsters Union to give him an honorary membership card in solid gold. Besides building on the

image of the defiant, self-confident, masculine trucker, the song includes trucker folk speech and references to truckers' independent occupational life:

> I got me ten forward gears and a Georgia
> overdrive,
> I'm taking little white pills and my eyes are open
> wide,
> I just passed a Jimmy and a White,
> I've been passing everything in sight,
> Six days on the road, now I'm gonna make it
> home tonight.

Trucker folk speech, derived from CB talk, was also central to the C.W. McCall hit "Convoy" (1975; words and music by Bill Fries and Chip Davis, respectively). Opening with the sound of a CB transmission, the song introduced the idea of "handles" (radio nicknames, such as "Rubber Duck" and "Pig Pen") to popular audiences:

> Ah, breaker one-nine, this here's the Rubber Duck. You gotta copy on me, Pig Pen, c'mon? Ah, yeah, 10-4, Pig Pen, fer shure, fer shure. By golly, it's clean clear to Flag Town [Flagstaff, Arizona], c'mon. Yeah, that's a big 10-4 there, Pig Pen, yeah, we definitely got the front door [lead truck], good buddy. Mercy sakes alive, looks like we got us a convoy.

The militaristic image of a truck convoy, a demonstration of strength against state patrols, was in the classic trucker tradition of defying authority. Fries was inspired, he said, by the idea of truckers as "modern cowboys of the road."

Commercial song also drew attention to oral tradition in the form of modern adaptations of trucker ghost legends. In 1967, Red Sovine recorded "Phantom 309," relating the story of a vanishing truck driver who, despite the stereotype of gruffness, sacrifices his life for a child. Unlike popular American versions of the "Vanishing Hitchhiker," about an automobile passenger who mysteriously disappears, the trucker-lore version recounts the tale of a driver and his rig, which, like a ghost ship, vanishes. The driver acts like a guardian spirit, akin to water spirits who rescue ships and sailors at sea. In "Phantom 309," a rescued rider tells truckers gathered at a stop that "Big Joe" picked him up and sends them greetings. Years before, he is told, the trucker plunged down a cliff to avoid a stalled school bus, and his ghost now comes to the aid of drivers in distress. In an oral variant, the ghost teaches a fledgling driver the "ropes" before vanishing and leaves the rookie his truck.

Cycles of folk humor are also evident in contemporary trucker lore, especially about large carriers that are viewed as heartless (a commentary on the incorporation of modern trucking). One example of the cycle is the narrative of a corporate driver who is reprimanded for ignoring a crashed colleague. The driver replies, "Ha, we don't have wheels on top of our trucks." Truck-stop graffiti may also mock the big carrier companies and glorify the independent driver of lore, as in messages scribbled beside toilet-paper rolls of company job applications.

Material and Visual Culture

Some truck drivers play up their cowboy image by dressing in western-style hats and cowboy boots. But the "trucker hat" in occupational tradition is a baseball cap, identified by its open mesh in the back. The front panel is emblazoned with some identifying message or logo, a phrase such as "Rocking Rig Trucker" or the emblem of a truck brand. The outlaw image of truckers might be expressed by a pirate skull and crossbones or military camouflage pattern. A signature image that has become associated with trucker folklife is the "mud-flap lady," the silhouette of an alluring woman that appears on hats, truck mud flaps, belt buckles, and key chains. The mud-flap lady expresses the hypermasculine image of "redneck" truckers and for many observers reflects their misogynist bent. Countering this image is a subculture of truckers called "Christian truckers," who may wear caps emblazoned with the words "Listen to Jesus" and mount a cross in lights on the front of their rigs (called "jewelry" in trucker folk speech). They are also apt to attend truck-stop chapels, which have spread since

the first permanent one catering specifically to truckers was established by Transport for Christ in Harrisburg, Pennsylvania, in 1986. More commonly, "mobile chapels" are set up in truck trailers, parked in locations such as Nashville, Tennessee (1996), Toledo, Ohio (1997), Cordele, Georgia (1998), Denver, Colorado (1999), and Sacramento, California (2000).

Although trucking often is perceived as the domain of the lone-wolf driver, the expansion of sleeping quarters in truck cabs and a string of truck stops along interstates have encouraged a subset of male-female couples to take to the road. Sometimes the spouses are institutionalized into the life with a militaristic nickname such as "first sergeant" (who "rides shotgun" in the passenger seat) or the indication of commitment in the nickname "other half." At truck stops, one can count on a "rain locker" (shower room) and a cup of "mud" (coffee). Truck-stop etiquette generally reserves prime seating for long-haul drivers; breakfast is served round the clock, underscoring the constant need among truckers for a "wake-up" meal.

Truck shows, rodeos, and championships are occasions for socializing and for sharing truck decoration and customizing techniques. In rodeos, "beauty shows" for the prettiest trucks, and other expositions and competitions, drivers are evaluated on their ability to safely negotiate their rigs around a course that tests their parking, backing, and turning skills. Among the biggest events are the National Truck Driving Championship in Orlando, Florida; the Mid-American Truck Show in Louisville, Kentucky (claiming to be the largest in the world, with eighty thousand attendees); Truckerfest in Reno, Nevada; and the North American Trucker Show in Boston. Ethnic gatherings have also arisen to provide social support for minority truckers, such as the Truck Show Latino in Pomona, California.

Conversation and narrative often refer to the costs, financial and physical, of long-haul trucking. Some may wax nostalgic about the hardy "old days" before electronic equipment made life on the road easier and may fret about the effects of incorporation on the independence of owner-operators. Even amid competition for the best drivers and the most powerful and prettiest rigs, a strong social camaraderie is evident among truckers. Coming to the assistance of drivers in trouble is fabled in occupational folklife. Truckers are aware of the risk of accident and take pride in their status as professional drivers. With all their independence of spirit, truckers evoke the bonds of the folk group in wishing one another a safe trip in traditional ways as they part company: "Keep your eyes open and your black stack smoking," "Keep the shiny side up and the greasy side down," "Keep them between the ditches," "Keep your rubber down and your metal up," and perhaps most of all, "Keep the wheels spinning."

Simon J. Bronner

See also: Automobiles; Cowboys; Folk Music and Song; Folk Speech and Language; Legends; Occupational Folklife.

Sources

Belman, Dale. *Sailors of the Concrete Sea: A Portrait of Truck Drivers' Work and Lives.* East Lansing: Michigan State University Press, 2005.

Blake, Joseph A. "Occupational Thrill, Mystique and the Truck Driver." *Urban Life and Culture* 3 (1974): 205–20.

Danker, Frederick E. "Trucking Songs: A Comparison with Traditional Occupational Song." *Journal of Country Music* 6 (1978): 78–89.

Jacobs, Michael. *Complete CB Dictionary.* North Miami, FL: Success, 1978.

Kalčik, Susan J. "Women's Handles and the Performance of Identity in the CB Community." In *Women's Folklore, Women's Culture,* ed. Rosan A. Jordan and Susan J. Kalčik, 99–108. Philadelphia: University of Pennsylvania Press, 1985.

Porter, Bernard H. "Truck Driver Lingo." *American Speech* 17 (1942): 102–5.

Runcie, John F. "Truck Drivers' Jargon." *American Speech* 44 (1973): 200–209.

Wise, Marc F. *Truck Stop.* Jackson: University Press of Mississippi, 1995.

Wyckoff, Daryl D. *Truck Drivers in America.* Lexington, MA: Lexington Books, 1979.

TULSA

Tulsa, Oklahoma, known in folk speech as "T-Town" and "Tullsee," is located in the northeast corner of the state in an area called Green Coun-

try. Lying at the intersection of the South, the Southwest, and the Midwest, Tulsa is a varied city, not easily fitting into any clear regional or cultural category. Ethnically, it boasts a significant Native American population estimated at 5 percent and an African American community amounting to 14 percent of the city's total. The racial experience of the city is marked by one of the worst race riots in the American experience. In 1921, violence and arson lasting three days virtually destroyed the Greenwood section of Tulsa. The area was restored to prosperity in the 1930s and 1940s, and came to be called the "Black Wall Street" because of African American entrepreneurship. The riot is still an important part of Tulsa's collective memory, and now marked on the landscape with a memorial, community center, and museum in the Greenwood section.

The discovery of oil in 1901 established the economic foundation of the city, but Tulsa's

Tulsa's annual Bluegrass and Chili Festival—which also features country-and-western and gospel music—is one of several regular events that sustain the city's lively and culturally diverse music scene. *(Doug Henderson Photography & Design)*

greatest building boom did not occur until the 1920s and 1930s. Not surprisingly, therefore, it features one of the highest concentrations of art deco-style structures in the United States—a prime example of which is the Boston Avenue Methodist Church. For a time, Tulsa was known as the "Oil Capital of the World"; other nicknames promoted by the chamber of commerce have included "America's Most Beautiful City" and "America's Most Livable City." In January 1992, *American Demographics* designated Tulsa the "Most Typical Town in America." And as the home of the evangelists Oral Roberts and Kenneth Hagen, it vies with Nashville for the title of "Buckle of the Bible Belt."

Tulsans tend to see themselves as different from other Oklahomans. They tend to be more Republican and contrarian in their politics, and perceive themselves as more cosmopolitan, with institutions such as art museums, a ballet, and an opera. Among the city's featured annual events are the Arkansas River Sand Castle Building Contest and the Gatesway International Balloon Festival.

Music, Art, and Festivals

Tulsa is the home of widely varied styles of music, and the homegrown music often is a mixture of country-and-western, rock 'n' roll, jazz, and blues. Bob Wills and the Texas Playboys, known as the "Kings of Western Swing," used Tulsa as a home base from 1934 to 1943, broadcasting a weekly radio show from Cain's Ballroom, whose dance floor was built on truck springs to move as people danced. Wills's music, western swing, is a style that mixes country-and-western music with the swing jazz popular in the 1930s and 1940s. Wills featured the city in one of his signature songs, "Take Me Back to Tulsa (I'm Too Young to Marry)." Other notable songs about the city, such as "Livin' on Tulsa Time" (written by Danny Flowers in 1978 and referring to the theme of Tulsa as a relaxed place) have become common in country music repertoires. Distinct from the pop Nashville Sound, the so-called Tulsa Sound is a grittier combination of blues shuffles, country-and-western, and early rock 'n' roll that

developed in the 1970s, often accompanying line dances called "Tulsa shuffles" (exemplified by the song "Tulsa Shuffle" written by Tulsan Steve Ripley in 1993 and recorded by the Tractors in 1994).

Several festivals sustain the vibrancy and diversity of the Tulsa music scene. The annual Bluegrass and Chili Festival, featuring bluegrass, country-and-western, and gospel music alike, is held on the second weekend of September. Others include Mayfest (a family-oriented arts festival); Oktoberfest (growing out of the substantial German American presence in Tulsa); the Tulsa State Fair, including a popular fiddling contest; Tulsafest, including performances of jazz and big band music; Reggaefest; Festival Hispano; and the Greek Holiday festival. The significant African American heritage of Tulsa, particularly in its musical culture, is recognized in the Greenwood Heritage Festival and the Juneteenth Blues and Jazz Festival (celebrating the African American commemoration on June 19 when many slaves in Texas learned they had been freed by the Emancipation Proclamation). The Tulsa Indian Art Festival encompasses arts, traditional foods, historical exhibits, and more. Additionally, there is the Pow Wow of Champions, where more than thirty-five tribes gather for dance contests and other cultural activities. The world-famous Lyon's Indian Store in downtown Tulsa features American Indian artifacts, old and new.

Popular public art in Tulsa includes the work of renowned chainsaw sculptor Clayton Coss, who crafts statues of notable figures and animals from logs and tree stumps. His statue of folk hero Johnny Appleseed from a twenty-foot tree stands in Appleseed's birthplace of Leominster, Massachusetts. In Tulsa, Coss's works can be seen in two parks, a main boulevard, and a downtown shopping center.

Crossroads

Folklife scholars often view the area surrounding Tulsa as geographically enigmatic because it reflects various regional cultural influences. A strong "western mystique," however, can be discerned in the city's culture. The fabled Route 66 runs through the city, making it a kind of gateway to the West. Although Tulsans take pride in their cosmopolitanism, it is not unusual to see people wearing cowboy hats and boots. Many of the city's prominent oilmen, such as the legendary Waite Phillips, a founder of the Phillips Petroleum Company and municipal developer, were seen in western garb—whether a business suit with cowboy hat and boots, as is common in the West, or the more garish cowboy style associated with Gene Autry and Roy Rogers.

Tulsa's Thomas Gilcrease Institute of American History and Art, also known as the Gilcrease Museum of Art, boasts the world's largest collection of art pertaining to the American West. The collection includes works by Frederic Remington, Charles Russell, and George Catlin, along with numerous Native American artifacts and other Americana dating back to the time of Columbus. Thomas Gilcrease was one-eighth Creek Indian and made his fortune in the oil boom. He sold his collection of more than two hundred thousand items to the city, and supported the museum in its efforts to become a major center for traditional as well as modern arts.

Western and southern influences come together in the traditional food that Tulsans take particular pride in as their own: barbecue. Located south of Kansas City, north of Texas and west of Memphis, where distinctive styles of barbecue reign, Tulsa claims a regional hybrid that Tulsans like to call Oklahoma-style barbecue. In Oklahoma, barbecue refers to meat that has been slowly cooked over wood smoke at a low temperature. The woods most commonly used for smoking meat include hickory, oak, and pecan. Tulsans like the beef brisket favored by their neighbors in Texas, the sweet spicy sauce typical of Kansas City, and the wet pork ribs with a vinegar-based sauce that are found in Memphis. However, Tulsa barbecue also includes pork, chicken, sausage, and bologna. Barbecue cook-offs are regularly featured at festivals to honor the best barbecue, and many restaurants advertise slow-cooked, or "hot-smoked" "Oklahoma-style" barbecue, especially to distinguish it from the similar, but rival, Texas barbecue, which tends to have a red-tinged meat when fully cooked and a pink smoke ring around the edges.

Although oil and aircraft industrial folklife of the twentieth century in Tulsa is still recounted in historical accounts, the city in the twenty-first century is emphasizing the continuity between past and present deep-seated values of family, community, and religion that have marked the social traditions of its residents. Folklife events such as powwows, ethnic festivals, cowboy poetry gatherings, rodeos, gospel sings, food festivals, and blues jams are viewed as important to building the public heritage of Tulsa as a crossroads city bringing together the East, West, and South.

Robert M. Lindsey and Simon J. Bronner

See also: African American Communities; Cowboys; Folk Music and Song; Great Plains Region; Texas.

Sources

Arnett, David. *In the Trees of Tulsa: A Guide to the Chainsaw Art of Clayton Coss.* Tulsa: Crow Creek Publishing, 1995.

Franks, Clyda. *Tulsa: Where the Streets Were Paved with Gold.* Charleston, SC: Arcadia, 2000.

Goble, Danney. *Tulsa: Biography of the American City.* Tulsa: Council Oak Books, 1997.

Hamill, John. *Tulsa: The Great American City.* Montgomery, AL: Community Communications, 2000.

Johnson, Hannibal B. *Black Wall Street: From Riot to Renaissance in Tulsa's Historic Greenwood District.* Burnet, TX: Eakin, 1998.

Vaughn-Roberson, Courtney Ann. *City in the Osage Hills: The History of Tulsa, Oklahoma.* Boulder, CO: Pruett, 1984.

TWELVE-STEP GROUPS

Beginning with the formation of Alcoholics Anonymous (AA) in 1935 in Akron, Ohio, a proliferation of "fellowship" groups arose during the course of the twentieth century to support people in recovery from addictions, among them Narcotics Anonymous (NA), Gamblers Anonymous (GA), and Overeaters Anonymous (OA). Such groups have features of social organizational folklife by virtue of their guiding principles or "traditions," spiritual beliefs, narrative and meeting customs, and bonds of fellowship. Allied groups for families and friends of addicts—such as Al-Anon, Alateen, and Families Anonymous—constitute offshoots of the organizations. One of the principles of AA is that each group needs the least possible organization; the emphasis is on social support. In fact, individuals who hold offices at the meetings are called "trusted servants"; participants, in keeping with the tradition of personal anonymity, are identified familiarly by their first names. Connecting all the groups, however, is a reliance on the delineation of twelve steps toward recovery from the admission of a problem to having a spiritual awakening and spreading the message of the steps.

Founding Narratives and Beliefs

AA's founding narrative is recounted in "Bill's story." Bill W. (Wilson), as he is known in AA, was a New York stockbroker trying to recover from alcoholism. He helped maintain his recovery by working with other alcoholics, and from this experience he came up with the saying, "You've got to give it away to keep it"—in other words, by helping others in a similar predicament, you help yourself. A meeting with Dr. Bob (Smith), a surgeon from Akron, Ohio, and also an alcoholic, resulted in the establishment of support groups for alcoholics in Akron's City Hospital. A central premise of their work was that alcoholism is a "disease," which they characterized as "a malady of mind, emotions, and body." The concept of being sick went against the popular notion that alcoholics are simply bad or degenerate individuals. Spiritual recovery from the disease, they insisted, was as important as physical recovery. In the fall of 1935, a second group of alcoholics formed in New York, and a third emerged in Cleveland in 1939. Also in 1939, the fellowship published *Alcoholics Anonymous*, known to twelve-step groups as "The Big Book." The text, written by Bill, offered lessons in the form of "stories," or personal accounts of suffering from alcoholism and subsequent recovery. It also outlined the "Twelve Steps" that lead to recovery.

By 1940, membership in AA had jumped to six thousand, with the number of meetings mul-

tiplying in proportion. Spreading across the United States, Canada, and then overseas, the fellowship mushroomed worldwide to one hundred thousand by 1950. Concerned about how this growth would affect the intimate feeling of the original meetings, Bill W. codified the foundational social principles for groups and their meetings in a document called "Twelve Traditions of Alcoholics Anonymous." Although membership grew to an estimated two million in one hundred thousand groups before the end of the century, the traditions held that AA should remain forever "non-professional" and that each group constitutes a "spiritual entity" with one primary purpose: "carrying its message to the alcoholic who still suffers." Other fellowships that rely on these traditions include Narcotics Anonymous, Gamblers Anonymous, Debtors Anonymous, Emotions Anonymous, Clutterers Anonymous, Workaholics Anonymous, Sex Addicts Anonymous, Incest Survivors Anonymous, Parents Anonymous, Shoplifters Anonymous, Child Abusers Anonymous, Nicotine Anonymous, and Overeaters Anonymous. Each fellowship uses the disease model and "The Big Book" as its foundation. They all advocate admitting powerlessness and asking for the help of God or a "higher power"—the first of the twelve steps.

Social Structure and Spiritual Elements

The social structure requires that members acquire a "sponsor," who advises and encourages them in recovery. In many groups, members are encouraged to "lose" previous associations (in AA terms, "people, places, and things") that contributed to their disease and to regularly attend and participate in meetings. Meetings of twelve-step groups follow customs such as a ritual introduction: "Hello, I'm [first name] and I'm an [alcoholic or other label]." The group answers, "Hello," in an affirmation of support. Opening narratives are usually told by members who have been sober (or abstinent, or "clean") for ninety days or more, and recount the suffering caused by compulsion (described in the group's folk speech as "hitting bottom"). Members identify where they are in the program, from the first step (admitting that one is powerless and that life has become "unmanageable") to the last ("spiritual awakening," carrying the message to other alcoholics, and practicing principles of the program in all of one's affairs).

Spiritual elements pervade the process, such as making a decision in step three to "turn our will and our lives over to the care of God as we understood Him," and in step eleven to seek "through prayer and meditation to improve our conscious contact with God as we understood Him, praying only for knowledge of His will for us and the power to carry that out." The group recites the "serenity prayer" in the oral tradition of twelve-step groups:

> God grant me the serenity
> to accept the things I cannot change;
> courage to change the things I can;
> and wisdom to know the difference.

The remaining part of the prayer is not typically recited but may appear on inspirational posters. It contains the key metaphor for all twelve-step groups: "one day at a time."

> Living one day at a time;
> Enjoying one moment at a time;
> Accepting hardships as the pathway to peace;
> Taking, as He did, this sinful world
>   as it is, not as I would have it;
> Trusting that He will make all things right
>   if I surrender to His Will;
> That I may be reasonably happy in this life
>   and supremely happy with Him
> Forever in the next.
> Amen.

The group may stand and hold hands during the prayer's recital, reinforcing the principle that sufferers are not alone. In addition to recalling the message "one day at a time" (ODAT), members are also reminded to take "one step at a time" (other variations are one minute or meal at a time), much as a newborn learning to cope with the world. The idea of rebirth, embracing a "fresh start" and new beginning, or having a second chance through the program pervades personal narratives shared at meetings.

Members are warned about "picking up" or returning to their addiction with the acronym HALT ("Hungry, Angry, Lonely, Tired"), representing conditions that can lead to relapse. The phrases "Easy Does It" and "Keep It Simple" (a folk variation is KISS for "Keep It Simple, Stupid") are often hung on the walls of twelve-step meeting halls and emblazoned on jewelry, bumper stickers, key chains, mugs, and plaques. These objects serve to guide the owner in maintaining his or her recovery and to identify members of the program as kindred spirits. Slogans and phrases can also have functions in ritualized performance. For example, meetings often end with participants cheering each other on: "It works if you work it, so work it, you're worth it!"

GreySheeters Anonymous as Folk Group

Some groups foster their own cultural identity that may be at odds with the official "Anonymous" groups. One example is GreySheeters Anonymous (GSA), an offshoot (or renegade body, as some claim) of Overeaters Anonymous (OA). Like members of OA, GSA members define abstinence as "the action of refraining from compulsive eating," but they take a more forceful approach, requiring a specific plan for eating, delineated on a grey sheet of paper and explained by a sponsor. The color has come to symbolize the subculture's worldview of learning to "live in the grey" of life. Members become versed in "weighing and measuring" life, as well as food, so as not to "pick up" or indulge in compulsive behavior. Social connections among members are frequently intense. Members often eat together, go on vacation together, and attend an annual "round up." For the ritual introduction, the GSA member recites "Hi, my name is [first name]. I'm a compulsive overeater. I'm abstinent according to the Grey Sheet, which means that I weigh and measure three meals a day with nothing in between but black coffee, tea, or diet soda, which I call in to my sponsor."

Many GSA members are not aware that their ritual repetitions—following the archetypal numbers of three for completeness and four for abundance—pervade the oral tradition. They are ingrained as part of the GSA culture. For example, new members are called upon to make three phone calls every day to another abstinent person. (The related tradition in AA is attending ninety meetings in ninety days, compounding the magical effect of three multiplied by thirty). If one needs to change a food item, it must be called in (or in GSA folk speech, "turned over") to a member with more than ninety days of GSA abstinence. GSA calls for four ounces of protein and eight ounces (doubling four) of fruit at breakfast, and eight ounces of cooked vegetables and eight ounces of salad at lunch and dinner. Like other twelve-step groups, GSA identifies the fourth step—taking a moral inventory—as the most difficult and therefore the most important.

Composed mostly of women, GSA groups are concentrated in New York and Los Angeles. Special meetings are arranged for "double-winners" (AA and GSA or NA and GSA) and for intensive twelve-step study (called "Step Study"). Unlike other twelve-step groups, GSA does not provide any food or beverage at its meetings, and deals with the anxiety that the substance that is a compulsion for members is also necessary for sustenance. The movement has its own slogans, including DENMW ("Don't Eat No Matter What"). A variation of GSA is found in another acronymic group, HOW, which stands for "Honesty, Openness, and Willingness," emphasizing an equally rigorous observance of its food plan. It underscores commitment by invoking the motto that since the disease is absolute, following the program must be a total way of life.

Tradition and Change

A significant development for twelve-step groups since the late twentieth century is the use of the Internet to create support networks. Through various "online meetings," message boards, chat rooms, and discussion groups, the communities for compulsions have greatly diversified. The ODAT Web site for overeaters alone lists more than thirty discussion groups, including ones for the homebound, Latter Day Saints, Pagans, teens, Jews, diabetics, pregnant women, mothers, and the grieving.

Although not a traditional communal society or ethnic community, twelve-step groups have attracted folklife interest because of their transmission of traditions, storytelling events, and rituals. Twelve-step groups and traditional communities notably share the common feature of mutual aid. In social organizational folklife, mutual aid may be interpreted as compensation for a growing culture of selfish individualism and a mobile population. Yet twelve-step groups are distinctively modern by not being bound to place; they allow any individual in recovery to join, *wherever* he or she is. Fellowship is accessible at almost any time in almost any place in the world. Cultural connection is gained through familiarity with the group's rituals, customs, and slogans. The spiritual element of such organizations evokes a traditional community of faith and believers. Twelve-step groups are often considered part of modern "therapeutic culture," in which people seek alternatives to inherited institutions such as religion, family, and neighborhood for social support. The groups they turn to embrace traditions that help them to deal with life one day at a time.

Sally Jo Bronner and Simon J. Bronner

See also: Foodways; Organizations, Voluntary and Special Interest; Religion; Rituals and Rites; Supernatural.

Sources

Alcoholics Anonymous. 4th ed. New York: Alcoholics Anonymous World Services, 2000.

Alcoholics Anonymous. *Twelve Steps and Twelve Traditions.* Center City, MN: Hazelden, 1989.

Browne, Basil R. "Really Not God: Secularization and Pragmatism in Gamblers Anonymous." *Journal of Gambling Studies* 10 (1994): 247–60.

Eastland, Lynette S., Sandra L. Herndon, and Jeanine R. Barr. *Communication in Recovery: Perspectives on Twelve-Step Groups.* Cresskill, NJ: Hampton, 1988.

Irvine, Leslie, and Brian Klocke. "Redefining Men: Alternative Masculinities in a Twelve-Step Program." *Men and Masculinities* 4 (2001): 27–48.

Jensen, George H. *Storytelling in Alcoholics Anonymous: A*

Rhetorical Analysis. Carbondale: Southern Illinois University Press, 2000.

Monahan, Molly. *Seeds of Grace: Reflections on the Spirituality of Alcoholics Anonymous.* New York: Riverhead Books, 2002.

Rapping, Elayne. *The Culture of Recovery: Making Sense of the Self-Help Movement in Women's Lives.* Boston: Beacon, 1996.

Swora, Maria Gabrielle. "Narrating Community: The Creation of Social Structure in Alcoholics Anonymous Through the Performance of Autobiography." *Narrative Inquiry* 11 (2001): 363–84.

UKRAINIAN COMMUNITIES

While most Old World Ukrainians now live in the independent republic of Ukraine, established after the breakup of the Soviet Union in 1991, for historical purposes Ukraine is best understood as a cultural-linguistic rather than a political entity. In other words, it is the territory in east Europe where people speak Ukrainian. Because of shifting political borders through the course of history, many Ukrainians who came to America have been misidentified as Poles, Austrians, or Russians. According to the 2000 U.S. census, almost nine hundred thousand Americans claim Ukrainian ancestry, representing a 20 percent increase over 1990. Many of the people claiming Ukrainian ancestry are descendants of those who came to the United States during the great wave of immigration from 1880 to 1914 seeking industrial jobs in cities (and a small number taking up farming in places such as North Dakota). They often maintained their folk traditions by settling in ethnic enclaves close to their churches. As a result, the majority of Ukrainian communities lie in the industrial belt from New York and Pennsylvania in the east to Michigan and Illinois to the west. With a new wave of arrivals and changing migration patterns, California, which was not even on the list of top ten states with Ukrainian populations in 1930, ranked third in 2000. New York, with almost 17 percent of Americans claiming Ukrainian ancestry, leads the nation in the total number of Ukrainians, followed by Pennsylvania. Pennsylvania, however, holds the distinction of being the state with the highest percentage of Ukrainians as a portion of state population. Major urban centers for Ukrainians include New York City; Buffalo, New York; Newark, New Jersey; Philadelphia; Pittsburgh; Cleveland, Ohio; Chicago; and Detroit.

Historical and Social Background

A scattering of Ukrainians arrived in the United States before the Civil War, most notably among Russian settlers in Alaska and California, but no Ukrainian communities as such were established until immigrants began arriving en masse around 1876. The vast majority of these were from the westernmost reaches of Ukraine, the Carpathian mountain region controlled at the time by Austria-Hungary. These settlers identified themselves not as Ukrainians but by regional group designations such as Lemko, Hutsul, or Boyko. Referred to in older sources as Ruthenians, Carpatho-Russians, and other terms, today they generally refer to themselves as Carpatho-Rus, Carpatho-Rusyns, or simply Rusyns.

Most nineteenth-century Ukrainian immigrants to the United States were recruited as low-cost laborers by agents of Pennsylvania's coal and steel industries. In some cases, because they spoke no English, they were unknowingly used as strike breakers, resulting in some violent clashes with earlier immigrant groups whom they were supplanting.

The outbreak of World War I prevented further large-scale immigration from Ukraine, which found itself a battleground between the Central Powers and Russia. After the fall of the czarist

Embroidery remains prominent among the folk arts of Ukrainian Americans. Elaborately embroidered fabrics are used in everything from altar cloths, church vestments, and ritual coverings to wedding clothes, ethnic costumes, towels, and tablecloths. *(Simon Bronner)*

empire in 1917, Ukrainians within the borders of the newly formed Soviet Union found their movements severely restricted and emigration nearly impossible. A few thousand Ukrainians, again from the Carpathian region, migrated to America from the interwar Polish state in the 1920s and 1930s. When this region was absorbed into Soviet Ukraine after World War II, Ukrainian immigration virtually ceased.

While some Ukrainians in America melded in with earlier Russian or Polish groups, most formed their own tightly knit communities revolving around a church. A few Eastern Orthodox churches were established, but the majority were Ukrainian Catholic, a branch of the Eastern Rite of the Catholic Church, which allows pa-

rishioners to hear the mass in their own language and to emphasize their own national saints, such as Olga and Volodymyr.

Religion

The church plays a crucial role in fostering cultural consciousness among America's Ukrainians. In the years before a credit economy, the establishment of a parish meant that church construction fell to the members and their personal resources, a project requiring a great deal of community organization and cohesiveness. As parishioners strove to duplicate the ornate churches of their homeland and to preserve their culture, the building of a church and the need to generate income to ensure its survival encouraged the continuation of artistic traditions.

Icons play a prominent role in both the Ukrainian Catholic and Orthodox churches, not only as artwork but as venerated objects. Painted on wood, they allow the faithful to view divine beings, saints, and biblical events not as part of a distant past but as relevant to modern life. Particularly in the Orthodox Church, icons function as doors into the spiritual world. Icon painters generally strive to use techniques that date to antiquity, so that their style has not changed significantly over time. The icon tradition is ordinarily passed down by master artists to apprentices. The same may be said of the ornate wood carving seen in many of the churches, particularly in the iconostasis wall, the screen separating the altar from the congregation.

Fraternal organizations have linked religious and social purposes in Ukrainian American life since the late nineteenth century, and they continue to play an important role in maintaining Ukrainian traditions today. The Providence Association of Ukrainian Catholics, established in 1912 in Philadelphia, for example, offers support for Ukrainian American youth groups in addition to providing insurance services. The Ukrainian Fraternal Association, established in 1912, in Scranton, Pennsylvania, sponsors the annual Ukrainian Youth Festival featuring folk dancing and traditional foodways.

Folk Art

Embroidery has been maintained as a prominent folk art among Ukrainian Americans. Although few of the classical embroideries found in museums, typically featuring a central figure attended by animals and symbols going back to pre-Christian times, are made in America, embroidery in the Ukrainian American community today is seen in church vestments, altar cloths, tablecloths, and traditional wedding costumes. *Rushnyks* are decorative towels used in a number of rituals, as well as for framing icons or wedding photographs. *Pascha* covers wrap the baskets of bread brought to church for blessing on Holy Saturday or Easter Sunday. Their design may include a cross, the *pascha* bread, or flowers along with the Ukrainian words for "Christ has risen." Wedding costumes commonly display ancient symbols, especially pertaining to fertility, even if the embroiderers and the persons wearing the costumes are not always aware of their meanings.

The folk art tradition for which Ukrainians are best known throughout the world is no doubt the *pysanka* (plural, *pysanky*), or decorated Easter egg. Among the Slavic peoples of eastern Europe, the egg has had important ritual and symbolic significance since pre-Christian times. The hatching egg was a conspicuous model to primitive peoples of the creation of life, and the egg itself came to play a prominent role in fertility rituals—such as burial in the ground to ensure bountiful harvests—and as charms by expectant mothers. As Ukraine became Christianized, beginning in the tenth century, the popular mind easily made a connection between the central doctrine of the new religion—the promise of rebirth, as personified by Christ—and the miraculous process of life emerging from nonlife, as embodied in the hatching egg.

Like Ukrainian embroidery, the decorated eggs contain a mixture of pagan and Christian symbols whose original meanings may or may not be familiar to the artist. The eggs, left raw by traditionalists but boiled or blown out by others, are decorated by a reverse dye process. Using a stylus dipped in melted beeswax, the artist covers those parts of the egg that are to remain white. The egg is then dipped in yellow dye, and the artist covers the parts that are to remain yellow. The process continues through a succession of different dye baths, with black ordinarily the last color. The wax is then melted off the egg, either over a candle or in an oven, revealing the complete design.

Pysanky have always been exchanged as gifts among Ukrainians. Historically, the design symbols had something of a ritual significance: a *pysanka* containing the depiction of a reindeer or horse, for example, might be given to a young bride as an expression of hope for fertility. In modern America, the continuation of the *pysanka* tradition has been largely a function of fundraising for Ukrainian churches, particularly at spring bazaars, for which parishioners fashion and provide eggs for sale.

Foodways and Customs

Ukrainian Americans have retained many of their old-country foodways, preparing traditional recipes both for home consumption and for church fund-raisers. *Pyrohy* dinners, featuring dough pockets filled with potato or sauerkraut, are commonly organized by Ukrainian churches, especially during the Lenten season, but in some cases on a monthly or even weekly basis. Ukrainians are also known for their cabbage rolls (*holubtsi*); smoked ham sausage (*kovbasa*); crepes (*nalysnyky*); and beetroot, tomato, and cabbage soup (*borshch*).

Nearly every large American city has a Ukrainian population that organizes some kind of annual celebration. Among the largest are the Ukrainian-American Cultural Foundation's Festival at Verkhovyna (begun in 1975 and held every year since in July), a resort in New York's Delaware Valley; the Ukrainian festival at the University of Pittsburgh's Cathedral of Learning, held every September since 1981; St. George's Catholic Church annual festival in New York's East Village, taking place on a May weekend; and a spring festival in North Port, Florida, paying homage to the Ukrainian poet Taras Shevchenko.

In the twenty-first century, the Ukrainian Cemetery in South Bound Brook, New Jersey, has become a mecca for Ukrainian Americans, particularly on the first Sunday following Orthodox Easter, a traditional day for commemorating the dead. The cemetery is also home to the Memorial Church of Saint Andrew, dedicated to the Ukrainians killed and churches destroyed by the Soviet Union.

Ukrainian American Identity

Viewing the Ukrainian Catholic Church as a focal point for Ukrainian nationalist and separatist sentiments, the Soviet government outlawed it, forcing it to go underground while much of its property was transferred to the Orthodox Church. This led to a certain tension between the Catholic and Orthodox communities in America which was exacerbated after the Soviet demise when a resurrected Catholic Church sought restoration of its property. Even so, relations between the two communities have been characterized more by cooperation than by conflict, as for the most part they have had similar goals in regard to the homeland. During the Soviet period, both the Catholic and Orthodox communities built churches, community and cultural centers, and monuments; they published works forbidden in the Soviet Union and wrote political tracts urging independence for Ukraine. Since Ukrainian independence was established in 1991, they have concentrated on more mundane matters such as sending money, food, medical supplies, and books to Ukraine and supporting Ukrainian students studying in America. Successful business advisers travel to Ukraine to help its nascent capitalist economy, offering expertise and investing in new enterprises.

Ukrainian Americans have self-consciously retained their cultural traditions, stimulated in part by a perception that the survival of their national culture was in danger of eradication by policies of the Soviet Union. With the establishment of an independent Ukraine in 1991, a new phase of cultural relations with the homeland began. "Roots" tours, for example, to visit the towns their immigrant parents and grandparents came from, are common for Ukrainian Americans. The American connection to the Ukraine was further highlighted with the visit of Ukrainian president Viktor Yushchenko in 2005. His "first lady," Katya Chumachenko Yushchenko, was born in Chicago and called it her "hometown." Shops in the Ukrainian quarter of Chicago were filled with pictures of the couple, and yellow-and-blue flags decorated the streets during their visit. Events such as the Ukrainian Heritage Festival in Yonkers, New York, and the Baltimore Ukrainian Festival feature acts and artists from the home country, facilitating exchange between Ukrainian and American communities that was often unavailable during the Soviet period.

Peter Voorheis

See also: Easter; Eastern Orthodox Christians; Folk Art; Russian Communities.

Sources

Dyen, Doris J. "Pysanky: Craftsmanship, Ritual Meaning, and Ethnic Identity." In *Craft and Community: Traditional Arts in Contemporary Society*, ed. Shalom Staub, 99–106. Philadelphia: Balch Institute for Ethnic Studies and Pennsylvania Heritage Affairs Commission, 1988.

Geist, Troyd A. *From the Wellspring: Faith, Soil, Tradition; Folk Arts from Ukrainian Culture in North Dakota.* Bismarck: North Dakota Council on the Arts, 1997.

Grobman, Neil R. *Wycinanki and Pysanky: Forms of Religious and Ethnic Folk Art in the Delaware Valley.* Occasional paper. Pittsburgh: Pennsylvania Ethnic Heritage Studies Center, University of Pittsburgh, 1981.

Isajiw, Wsevolod W., ed. *Ukrainians in American and Canadian Society: Contributions to the Sociology of Ethnic Groups.* Jersey City, NJ: M.P. Kots, 1976.

Joyce, Rosemary. "Pysanky: The Ukrainian Easter Egg in Ohio." *Journal of the Ohio Folklore Society*, n.s., 5 (1978): 3–9.

Klymasz, Robert B. *Ukrainian Folklore in Canada.* New York: Arno, 1980.

Satzewich, Vic. *The Ukrainian Diaspora.* London: UCL Press, 2000.

Zabytko, Irene. *When Luba Leaves Home.* Chapel Hill, NC: Algonquin, 2003.

UNIONS

Unions are labor organizations that perform the functions of collective bargaining and conflict resolution on behalf of workers. They are most often associated with blue-collar and industrial workers, and their heritage includes a distinctive body of folk music and narrative. The Bureau of Labor Statistics estimated at the beginning of the twenty-first century that more than sixteen million Americans, or 13.5 percent of all workers, belonged to unions—a significant population, but a far smaller percentage than in the heyday of unions during the mid-twentieth century. Union membership among wage and salary workers shows a distinct geographic pattern, with membership highest in the Northeast, Midwest, and Pacific regions, and lowest in the South. Some areas have what could be termed "union cultures," where membership rates are higher than 15 percent and there is a tradition of union social and cultural activity: New York, Michigan, New Jersey, Pennsylvania, Ohio, and Illinois. California, however, boasts the largest number of union members, with 2.4 million; New York ranks second with 2.0 million.

Union coal miners pose for a group photo during a 1922 strike in West Virginia. Bound by shared ordeal and common purpose, members of mine, railroad, trade, and other unions created a rich folklife that has endured in song, lore, and organizing events. *(Library of Congress, LC-USZ62-42068)*

Collecting Union Folklife

The earliest labor unions in America were organized to protect the interests of workers in a particular trade. Group cohesion in preindustrial unions was hampered by ethnic and religious differences between workers, which company owners sought to foment to discourage organization efforts and undermine labor solidarity. By the beginning of the twentieth century, however, labor unions had begun to make serious inroads in organizing workers by promising to protect them from exploitation at the hands of company owners. To unify workers of diverse backgrounds, the unions had to embrace new immigrants as well as more established groups—which they had not always done. In the latter half of the nineteenth century, unions tended to view recent immigrants with ambivalence: on one hand they saw the newcomers as a way to increase union membership; on their other hand, they were concerned about offending the core constituencies, who resented the willingness of immigrants to work for lower wages.

By the time workers began to coalesce under union banners, many occupations had already accumulated rich folk traditions, much of them captured in song-poems and stories that were adapted from those workers had sung and told in their homelands. As tensions increased between labor and capital, organizing drives and strikes became increasingly contentious, and work songs were transformed to serve the purposes of the labor unions. By the 1930s, American folklorists began to show interest in worker folklore and issues of class and agency, following the lead of their European and British counterparts. Collection efforts in America, however, were hampered by the reluctance of labor leaders to cooperate with folklorists, whom they perceived as academic outsiders.

Among the early collectors of folklife to overcome this barrier was George Korson, a journalist working in the anthracite region of northeastern Pennsylvania. He was able to develop an unusually close relationship with the United Mine Workers of America, which provided him direct access to the miners who were the tradition bearers of mining and union lore. So amicable was Korson's relationship with the union that much of the material that would later be compiled in his books on the folklife of the bituminous and anthracite industries was first published in the pages of the *United Mine Workers' Journal.*

Perhaps the most extensive tradition of union song is that of the International Workers of the World (IWW), or Wobblies. In 1910, just five years after its formation, the IWW published the pocket-sized *Little Red Song Book*, provocatively subtitled *IWW Songs to Fan the Flames of Discontent.* Group singing was a common feature at IWW gatherings, whether picnics, picket lines, marches, parades, or rallies. The Wobblies, seeking to change the foundation of American capitalist society, also brought an increased militancy to union song.

The legitimacy of American unions as a distinct folk group has long been debated in academic circles. Some scholars argue that as labor groups achieved economic gains, workers were integrated into mainstream culture and began assimilating middle-class values. While few argue that the stability, isolation, and continuity of the company-town and work-camp environments (common in the early extractive industries of mining and logging) provided an ideal milieu for the development of a folk culture, some have questioned whether American industrial and factory workers in the 1930s and 1940s were sufficiently connected to constitute a social movement, let alone a folk group. Archie Green, who followed Korson as a prominent collector of worker and union song, has worked tirelessly to defend what he calls "laborlore" as a worthy area of scholarly inquiry. His efforts were instrumental in helping to establish the first formal collaboration between labor (the American Federation of Labor and Congress of Industrial Organizations [AFL-CIO]) and academics at the Smithsonian Institution's 1976 Festival of American Folklife. That event, now known as the Smithsonian Folkife Festival, continues to highlight the folklife of working men and women in America.

Social and Cultural Unionism

While industrialization led to changes in the workplace and worker living arrangements that in turn hindered the formation of group bonds, some labor unions made a concerted effort to create social networks to help workers feel a part of, and embrace, a "union way of life." In this cultural reorientation, these unions believed that values of cooperation, solidarity, and activism needed to become part of the social fabric of workers' lives to counteract the hierarchy and individual alienation characteristic of industrial work. This "social unionism," as it has been called, was an outgrowth of the labor unions' commitment to extend themselves beyond the usual concerns of organizing workers and securing better wages and benefits. It sought to develop an infrastructure that involved its members in social and community activities, provided assistance for workers in times of personal difficulty, exposed workers to cultural and educational programs, and encouraged their activism in social causes.

Women played a particularly active role in strike relief efforts, extending the union community from an organization of card-carrying tradesmen to a wider network of union families that shared a kinship based on their distrust of company owners and their faith in the union and one another. In a sense, the union wrested from the company owners the paternalistic role it had once occupied by demonstrating genuine concern for the well-being of workers and their families.

The approach of social unionism was especially prevalent in the highly charged political and cultural climate of the 1930s, when labor leaders and educators, as well as their occasional allies in socialist and communist party movements, saw recreational activities—sports, picnics, musical and theatrical performances, and public education forums—as a means to develop and sustain solidarity among workers. The International Ladies Garment Workers Union (ILGWU) exemplified this effort to build camaraderie among members. The ILGWU owned and operated the Labor Stage Theatre in midtown Manhattan, assembling a troupe of performers from the rank and file who performed plays focusing on labor issues. The ILGWU also established Unity House, a vacation resort and education center in Pennsylvania's Pocono Mountains, the largest union-owned facility of its size and one of only a few of its type in the United States. It was a place where workers could commune with other members, learn about the history and aims of the union, and form associations in a relaxed environment. Entertainment was often provided by the ILGWU's chorus, whose programs drew on the history of American labor and the garment industry specifically, providing yet another vehicle for espousing the cause of working people and the union movement.

Choruses became a fixture in many unions. In some cases, the choruses were affiliated with union locals composed of members of like ethnic or racial background, and the songs they performed reflected dual identities. Workers often saw points of convergence between their religious and cultural beliefs and the quest for social justice at the core of the labor movement.

Members of the Jewish community in New York, for example, founded Yiddish-speaking locals whose choruses provided both a means of ethnic expression and a tool for recruiting Jewish workers. The activism was influenced by the cultural experiences of workers, including forms of communal organization, communication styles, and other expressive behavior offering ethnic variations on the theme of class solidarity.

The experience of black steelworkers in Alabama during the New Deal suggests a similar confluence of cultural and union values. Many in the black workforce of Birmingham at this time were active as singers with the jubilee gospel quartets—an interweaving of the social contexts in which they expressed themselves: the workplace, union hall, company town, and church. It was common in this community for religious songs to be transformed into union songs that glorified the labor movement and its leaders. The result was a merging of the ideologies of evangelical Protestantism and democratic unionism; the prolabor songs provided an active mode in which black industrial workers could articulate an emerging consciousness and a new collective identity. The union, it has been suggested, came to be viewed by many workers as a kind of secular church.

Decline and Maintenance of Union Culture

Since the twentieth century, many observers of the decline of the social and cultural role of unions have blamed mass culture. While on one hand the tools of mass communication certainly aided the AFL-CIO in its national organizing drives, over time the close social contact necessary to maintain a traditional culture became a less prevalent aspect of union membership. Gone today are the close associations of unions specific to particular trades; in their place are larger, conglomerate-style unions that represent workers in unrelated occupations. Although such organizations may work to defend the common aims of all workers, they have had difficulty maintaining the close identification found in unions composed of workers with their own well-defined occupational traditions and customs.

Union membership in America has been declining steadily since the 1970s, as the globalization of the economy has brought increased foreign competition, the export of jobs to low-wage foreign markets, and the deregulation of key domestic industries. Labor groups still make regular use of traditional songs and other folklife forms at annual conventions, organizing rallies, parades, and regional arts and culture festivals to promote group and occupational identity. An important gathering for activists involved in "creative organizing" since the 1980s is the Great Labor Arts Exchange, held in the Washington, D.C., area. Some localities also build on their union legacy with cultural events, such as the Mother Jones Festival in Mount Olive, Illinois, featuring a parade with union locals and concerts of union songs. But such events, and the efforts of organizations like the Labor Heritage Foundation, established in 1984 in Washington, D.C., seem to focus more on celebrating labor's collective heritage than on social and cultural unionism of the future.

Gregg M. Scully

See also: Detroit; Occupational Folklife; Organization, Corporate and Work.

Sources

Bird, Stewart, Dan Georgakas, and Deborah Shaffer. *Solidarity Forever: An Oral History of the IWW.* Chicago: Lakeview, 1985.

Green, Archie. *Wobblies, Pile Butts and Other Heroes: Laborlore Explorations.* Urbana: University of Illinois Press, 1993.

Greenway, John. *American Folksongs of Protest.* Philadelphia: University of Pennsylvania Press, 1953.

Hyman, Colette. *Staging Strikes: Workers' Theatre and the American Labor Movement.* Philadelphia: Temple University Press, 1997.

Kornbluh, Joyce L. *Rebel Voices: An IWW Anthology.* Chicago: Charles H. Kerr, 1998.

McCallum, Brenda. "Songs of Work and Songs of Worship: Sanctifying Black Unionism in the Southern State of Steel." *New York Folklore* 14 (1988): 9–33.

Romalis, Shelly. *Pistol Packin' Mama: Aunt Molly Jackson and the Politics of Folksong.* Urbana: University of Illinois Press, 1998.

Shuldiner, David. *Of Moses and Marx: Folk Ideology and Folk History in the Jewish Labor Movement.* Westport, CT: Bergin and Garvey, 1999.

Wolensky, Kenneth, Nicole Wolensky, and Robert P. Wolensky. *Fighting for the Union Label: The Women's Garment Industry and the ILGWU in Pennsylvania.* University Park: Pennsylvania State University Press, 2002.

Working Americans Program, Smithsonian Bicentennial Festival of American Folkife. *Ring Like Silver, Shine Like Gold: Folklore in the Labor Press.* Washington, DC: Smithsonian Institution Press, 1976.

URBAN FOLKLIFE

Urban folklife is the study of traditions, historical and contemporary, pertaining to a particular city or of the traditions of contemporary urban life in general. With the emphasis in folklife scholarship during the nineteenth century on documenting rural life that folklorists thought was vanishing in the wake of industrialization, urban folklife often was overlooked or thought not to exist. But as the concept of folklife expanded to include the living traditions of modern industrial and urban settings in the twentieth century, the city, as a place where folk groups such as immigrants and religious groups maintain their traditions, or where residents have traditions connected to urban living, became more of a cultural field to explore, collect, and interpret.

Urban Environments and Traditions

The urban environment of any city results from a complex combination of factors, including geography, economics, and political boundaries, as well as the settlement patterns of new arrivals. Groups with a shared ethnic, cultural, or religious identity often concentrate in neighborhoods that provide them with goods and services to support traditional ways, such as kosher butchers, bodegas, *salumerias*, religious relic stores, and ethnic heritage day schools, but might appear to outsiders as fostering segregation. When diverse peoples arrive in urban areas, whether for economic opportunity or political asylum, they typically bring customs, traditions, and values that flourish, adapt, or disappear in the new environment. Some urban traditions become a polyglot, or "mixture," of traditions—such as a Chinese Cuban restaurant or a Korean American grocery store. In the public or street culture of the city, opportunities often exist for cultural exchange. Festivals in which patron saints are paraded throughout city streets, traditional foods are available, and ethnic costumes are on display are ways in which members of the community as well as outsiders can mingle.

Other traditions related to cities are their folk names, occupations, and arts. Chicagoans refer to their home as the "Windy City"; Boston is the self-proclaimed "Hub of the Universe"; New Orleans residents live in the "Big Easy." New Yorkers employed in the garment district refer to it as the "Rag Trade," and cab drivers are often called "Mac." In cities such as New York and Los Angeles, community gardens have sprouted up out of a desire to beautify a particular neighborhood. Colorful murals and graffiti on walls and subways cars might carry a political or social message, or identify a street gang.

Children respond to the limited open space by playing games specifically designed for, or adapted to, sidewalks, buildings, and streets. Manhole covers become bases for street stickball; sidewalk boxes become courts for "box baseball," "Chinese handball," and "hit the coin"; front stoops are places for telling stories or playing games; and adults use old trolley rails for *bocce* courts. Double Dutch, a variant of jump rope in African American communities, is still played on the street, even if other traditional sidewalk games, such as marbles, have been replaced by indoor electronic games. A common sight on city streets is skateboarders, groups of adolescents who jump, race, and twirl off sidewalks, walls, staircases, and railings—sometimes in specially designed city parks.

City living is often associated with a fear of crime, a distrust of strangers, and the stress of living in a densely populated area. To relieve tension, urbanites complain about city life—a pervasive urban tradition itself—by forming these experiences into narratives. Crime victims, for example, tell of the day they got mugged, where and when it happened, and the result of the confrontation. While such narratives often reinforce prejudices and stereotypes, they also serve as a way to share the informal culture of the city or to reinforce one's mental map as to safe and unsafe areas, and to learn about the city streets, unsavory characters, and ways to protect oneself from future crime events. Others may brag about how they got from one area of the city to another in an unusually short amount of time by taking shortcuts using their "mental maps" of neighborhoods and cross streets. Others may spread urban legends—stories believed to be true—that circulate throughout the country, such as the white albino alligators that roam the sewers of New York or *La Llorona*, a Mexican woman crying for her lost children in Mexican American urban neighborhoods.

The city is often symbolically connected in the popular imagination to modernization and the rise of technology. As a result, some folk genres labeled "urban," such as "urban legends" or "photocopy folklore," are not restricted to cities but draw attention to their association with a modern urban society. Alan Dundes and Carl Pagter's groundbreaking *Urban Folklore from the Paperwork Empire* (1975), for example, documents folk humor circulated with the aid of photocopying and facsimile machines. Based on the assumption that the corporate office environment is a function of city living, they claimed that the photocopied folk humor "represents part of the human response to some of the ills of urban life." As the folklore of office workers and technology became apparent in suburban and rural environments, the label changed to "photocopier folklore" or "Xeroxlore." While "urban legend" has been popularized by the broadcast media, folklorists increasingly refer to it as "contemporary legend" or "belief legend."

Cultural Conservation

Into the twenty-first century, urban folklife organizations collect cultural traditions of city life and organize programs for their appreciation and preservation. The Lowell Folklife Festival, the largest free urban festival, held every July in Lowell, Massachusetts, brings thousands to the postindustrial urban center to celebrate the city's many different ethnic groups and the region's diverse traditions through music, craft demonstrations, and ethnic cuisines. City Lore brings together New Yorkers to "discover, interpret, celebrate and protect places that hold memories, anchor traditions and help tell the history of our communities and city" and sponsors exhibits, poetry gatherings, and in-school programs. In addition to featuring the many ethnic groups that give the city its international flavor, the organization also documents and presents material from occupations and traditions that mark life in New York, such as cab driving, graffiti, sidewalk games, and foodways. The Philadelphia Folklore Project, meanwhile, is devoted to improving the quality of urban life by working for "the persistence, diversity, and vitality of our vernacular folk cultures" through cultural partnerships with neighborhood groups to devise programming. These kinds of projects demonstrate the varied ways that the city, once thought to epitomize the destruction of tradition, is home to a wide and distinctive array of folklife.

Eleanor Wachs

See also: Atlanta; Boston; Charleston and Lowcountry South Carolina; Chicago; Cleveland; Detroit; Harlem; Hasidim and Misnagidim (Haredim); Los Angeles; Memphis; Milwaukee; Minneapolis-St. Paul Metropolitan Area; New York City; Philadelphia; San Francisco Bay Area; Taxi Drivers; Washington, D.C.; West African Communities.

Sources

Botkin, B.A. "Living Lore of the New York City Writers' Project." *New York Folklore Quarterly* 2 (1946): 252–63.

———. *New York City Folklore.* New York: Random House, 1956.

Brunvand, Jan Harold. *The Vanishing Hitchhiker: American Urban Legends and Their Meanings.* New York: W.W. Norton, 1981.

Dorson, Richard M. *Land of the Millrats.* Cambridge, MA: Harvard University Press, 1981.

Dundes, Alan, and Carl R. Pagter. *Urban Folklore from the Paperwork Empire.* Austin: University of Texas Press, 1975.

Kirshenblatt-Gimblett, Barbara. "The Future of Folklore Studies in America: The Urban Frontier." *Folklore Forum* 16 (1983): 175–234.

Laba, Martin. "Urban Folklore: A Behavioral Approach." *Western Folklore* 38 (1979): 158–69.

Paredes, Américo, and Ellen J. Stekert, eds. *The Urban Experience and Folk Tradition.* Austin: University of Texas Press, 1971.

Wachs, Eleanor. *Crime Victim Stories: New York City's Urban Folklore.* Bloomington: Indiana University Press, 1988.

Warshaver, Gerald. "Urban Folklore." In *Handbook of American Folklore,* ed. Richard M. Dorson, 162–71. Bloomington: Indiana University Press, 1983.

VIETNAMESE COMMUNITIES

After the fall of South Vietnam to the Communist North in 1975 and the end of the war in Southeast Asia, many South Vietnamese refugees relocated to the United States and formed ethnic enclaves in such cities as Houston; Seattle; Oklahoma City; and San Francisco, Sacramento, and Westminster, California. To many Americans, the Vietnamese American presence today is seen most prominently in restaurants with the distinctive traditional dish of *pho* (noodle soups), but cultural continuity between the homeland and the new setting is also apparent in storytelling, music, festivals, crafts, and dress.

Often sponsored by congregations and businesses, the Vietnamese refugees settled in towns as well as large cities throughout the United States. Two states—California (43 percent) and Texas (11 percent) accounted for half of all the new Vietnamese residents. According to the 2000 U.S. census, more than 988,000 Vietnamese-born immigrants live in the United States, constituting the fifth-largest immigrant group in the country and 3 percent of all foreign-born residents. Nevertheless, California is the only state in which Vietnamese immigrants constitute more than 1 percent (1.2) of the total state population. Other states with more than 30,000 foreign-born Vietnamese are Washington, Virginia, and Massachusetts. The largest local concentration of Vietnamese anywhere outside of Vietnam iself is found in Orange County, California, where more than 130,000 residents claim Vietnamese ancestry. Vietnamese American businesses are ubiqui-

tous in what has come to be called Little Saigon, located in Westminster and Garden Grove, California, where Vietnamese immigrants constitute 30.7 percent and 21.4 percent of the population, respectively. In addition, many Vietnamese Americans have established businesses in Chinatowns throughout North America. Many first- and second-generation Vietnamese immigrants became owners of small businesses such as restaurants, groceries, beauty salons, barbershops, and auto repair shops. In Louisiana, many Vietnamese Americans work in the fish and shrimp industries, some as business owners.

After living for a time with their sponsors and adjusting to a new way of life, many Vietnamese Americans in the 1980s and 1990s began to relocate throughout the United States to be with friends and relatives. Areas with climates similar to that of their homeland were especially attractive. In addition to the Little Saigons of California and Texas, Vietnamese residents headed for Georgia, Tennessee, and North Carolina, which saw their Vietnamese populations increase by 309, 269, and 230 percent, respectively, during the 1990s. A new wave of immigration rose in the early twenty-first century as established Vietnamese Americans sponsored their family members and friends back in Vietnam. Concentrations of Vietnamese grew in major cities throughout the United States, particularly in Los Angeles, San Francisco, Philadelphia, Washington, D.C., and New York, although significant increases were also noted in the states of Vermont (630 percent), Nebraska (494 percent), and New Hampshire (456 percent).

Members of the Vietnamese community of Westminster, California, observe the thirtieth anniversary of the 1975 fall of South Vietnam, which forced the greatest exodus of asylum seekers in modern history. Westminster's Little Saigon is the largest Vietnamese business district in the United States. *(David McNew/Getty Images News)*

Religious Traditions and Festivals

Vietnamese Americans practice a variety of religions, including Catholicism, Buddhism, Taoism, and Confucianism. Although each religious group practices specific holidays according to its members' beliefs, there are also shared beliefs and celebrations that bring together all Vietnamese. An example of this occurs during the Tet Nguyen Dan (New Year) celebration, when participants enact a visit by the chief guardian spirit of the kitchen, who reports on activities of the family. This holiday known as *Le Tao Quan*, or "feast of the household gods," falls on the twenty-third of the twelfth month of the lunar year. A new spirit is then assigned to the household for the coming year to replace the previous one. On the day of *Le Tao Quan*, customs to honor the kitchen god may include burning sacrificial gold paper and offering a fish such as carp for the god to ride on the journey to heaven. Cross-cultural religious connections are also demonstrated through the communal patriarchal family structure, a strong emphasis on fate, and a belief that correct behavior will bring good fortune through the rewards of ancestral spirits.

Tet Nguyen Dan, the lunar new year festival, is a time for family reunions, gift giving, and celebrations. Painstaking care is taken to start the year right, as it is believed that the first week will determine one's fortunes for the rest of the year. Houses are cleaned, new clothes are purchased, old debts are repaid, and arguments are settled. The first visitor to one's house on the morning of Tet is very important; it should be someone who is prosperous and prestigious.

In Vietnam, the celebration of Tet lasts from ten to twenty-one days. In America, however, secular customs and working conditions often force Vietnamese Americans to limit their celebrations to the weekends. Community members typically rent a hall, serve food and drink, and host a talent show and pageant. A particular highlight of the Tet celebration is the Dragon Dance, in which a team of trained dancers don a dragon costume and performs acrobatic tricks. Handing money to the dragon or receiving money from the dragon is a sign of good luck and prosperity for the year.

The food is cooked by community members and contains special dishes for the holiday. The most traditional dish is *banh chung* (New Year's cake), which consists mostly of marinated rice steamed in banana leaves. The banana leaves tint the rice green; green food coloring is used in areas of the United States where banana leaves are not available.

Other important elements of the Tet celebration include the giving of good-luck money (*li xi*) and the exchange of New Year's wishes (*mung tuoi*). Children receive good-luck money in small red envelopes designed especially for the occasion; the envelope is given after the children have wished the giver good health and prosperity for the coming year.

After family members and friends exchange ritual holiday wishes, the entertainment begins. Gambling and card games are popular, along with song and dance presentations. Traditional Vietnamese folk songs are often romantic in subject matter, telling tales of young, unrequited love. Traditional instrumental music is typically played on stringed zithers, bamboo xylophones, and wooden drums. If the more traditional instruments are not available, guitars are used.

Many Tet celebrations include beauty pageants in which young women wear the national dress, called *Ao Dai*. The *Ao Dai* is a full-length contoured dress worn over loose-fitting trousers with a split in the front and back; the material is usually of a bright color and embroidered. This dress is an important feature of Vietnamese national identity, reflecting both Asian and French influences in an elegant and distinctive design. Silk hand embroidery is not restricted to Tet celebrations and are traditionally applied to many household items by many older Vietnamese in the United States.

Food and Culture

Rice and noodles are the most common foods among the Vietnamese, and their abundance are viewed as symbols of prosperity and long life. Although in America many Vietnamese restaurants also serve Chinese fare, Vietnamese cooking tends to avoid frying in oil or using soy sauce; it is characterized instead by simmering and the use of peppers and mint for spice. Fish and small amounts of meat are served with most dishes. The Vietnamese are especially known for their noodle soup (*pho*), eaten at every meal. Homemade egg rolls—smaller than Chinese egg rolls and stuffed mostly with meat—are often served to guests and on special occasions. Another common element in Vietnamese cuisine is fish sauce, or *nuoc mam*, the condiment used to season every dish. At home, children ask their parents to eat first, expressing the social value placed on filial piety and respect for ancestors; the preferred food, moreover, is served to elders.

With the second and third generations of Vietnam Americans coming of age in the twenty-first century, more effort has been made in many communities to preserve folk traditions representing Vietnamese culture. Vietnamese Culture and Heritage Camps have been organized for children in Minnesota, Colorado, Maryland, and elsewhere. Children in these programs learn the language, as well as traditional dances, tales, songs, games, and crafts. In San Jose, California, the community organized a Viet Heritage Society, and in Washington, D.C., the Vietnamese Cultural Society. Both organize festivals and classes to preserve and present Vietnamese folklife for American-born generations. In San Jose, a major project is the development of a Vietnamese cultural garden and museum, where the culture and history of Vietnam are represented in various plants, trees, and flowers, as in art and architecture. In Washington, D.C., the society organized an Autumn Moon Children's Festival (*Tet Trung Thu*), a harvest festival based on the lunar calendar formerly used in Vietnam. Children parade with colorful lanterns and perform traditional dragon and flower dances. Moon cakes made with lotus seeds, ground beans, and orange peels, with a yolk in the center representing the moon, are made and consumed. At many festivals in the United States, Vietnamese Americans express gratitude for their freedom. During Tet and other celebrations, many sing the American national anthem along with that of the fallen South Vietnamese government.

Cindy Kerchmar and Simon J. Bronner

See also: Hmong Communities; Holidays; Lao Communities; Montagnard-Dega Communities; South, The.

Sources

Balaban, John, ed. *Ca dao Viet Nam: A Bilingual Anthology of Vietnamese Folk Poetry*. Greensboro, NC: Unicorn Press, 1980.

Cam, Nguyet Nguyen, and Dana Sachs, eds. *Two Cakes Fit for a King: Folktales from Vietnam*. Honolulu: University of Hawaii Press, 2003.

Do, Hien Duc. *The Vietnamese Americans*. Westport, CT: Greenwood, 1999.

Freeman, James A. *Hearts of Sorrow: Vietnamese-American Lives*. Stanford, CA: Stanford University Press, 1989.

Gold, Steven. *Refugee Communities: A Comparative Field Study*. Newbury, CA: Sage, 1992.

Nash, Jesse W. *Vietnamese Catholicism*. Harvey, LA: Art Review Press, 1992.

Ngo, Bach, and Gloria Zimmerman. *The Classic Cuisine of Vietnam*. Woodbury, NY: Barron's, 1978.

Pham, Mai. *Pleasures of the Vietnamese Table*. New York: HarperCollins, 2001.

Rutledge, Paul J. *The Vietnamese Experience in America*. Bloomington: Indiana University Press, 1992.

VISUAL CULTURE

The term "visual culture" came into scholarly use during the late twentieth century as a counterpart to "material culture." Whereas material culture referred to the patterns and production of three-dimensional objects and environments that could be touched, visual culture drew attention to pictorial images, designs, and symbolic representations, usually two-dimensional, that were meant to be *seen*. A primary question in folklife studies is how images, signs, and designs become cultural or traditional by being incorporated into the visual repertoire expressed in various media. Thus, the "meaning" and uses of visual culture are in the minds of the users and viewers and are open to interpretation. Although folklorists often apply ethnographic fieldwork, cross-cultural comparison, and archival documentation to uncover the "views" of cultural participants, interpretations outside their awareness but ascribed to them as motivations and mental processes through psychological, historical, and structural analysis are also part of the approach of visual culture.

Visual culture is related to earlier studies of "iconography" or "iconology," which interpreted the use of images and symbols to represent ideas, but also raised more cultural questions about the ways that perceptions of images and symbols are affected by social, political, and historical contexts, and in particular are produced and consumed variously across cultures. One of those contexts is the discipline of art history and institutions of galleries and museums that arbitrate highbrow tastes and define art and beauty. The emerging concept of "visual culture" suggested a broadening, even a democratization, of the arts to include the uses of images in everyday life and various culturally constructed ways of "seeing" the world (as both belief and aesthetic in folk cultures) through written and handcrafted forms as well as by the electronic media of television, film, photography, and computer. If "seeing is believing," as the saying goes in American folk speech, then folklorists pose the questions, What is believed, and Why is it seen the way it is? The visual culture perspective also suggests an inquiry into why sight verifies belief—an orientation manipulated in narrative (as in the pictorial tale and rebus), magic (in the creation of optical illusion and the use of symbols viewed as magical), craft (in the creation of apparent three-dimensionality in quilt designs such as "tumbling blocks" and the identification of ordinary objects as "ethnic" or cultural by an applied symbol or decoration), and food (in the idea that plate "presentation" improves taste).

Substantial work on interpreting the cultural sources (or "folk roots") of images and designs preceded the visual culture movement and especially drew attention to drawing and various graphic representations as expressive traditions. Joined to the concept of visual culture, this legacy contributes to new interdisciplinary inquiries of pictorial and iconographic tradition expressed in various media, worldview as an aesthetic system, and the traditionalization of symbolic representations.

Pictorial Tales and Magical Formulas

One of the ways that folk tradition teaches children how to obtain knowledge visually is through a genre that folklorists call "the pictorial tale." This is a narrative form in which the storyteller draws details of a picture representing narrative descriptions that lead to a surprising ending, depicted in the final drawing. The pictorial tale is a means of conveying narrative graphically and a reminder that telling a story is a visual as well as an oral exercise. In one traditional pictorial tale found commonly in Great Britain and America, the figure of a bird is formed from the narrative description of an oval pond (forming the center of the bird's body), cattails at one end of the pond (the bird's tail), a house with one window (the bird's head), a path from the house to the pond (the bird's neck), and two Native Americans living in tents who come up two paths for water (the bird's feet). A variant commonly collected in the southern United States describes two men working in a briar patch (forming the feet) who go for water and return (forming the tail), while a father and a son live in a house with a lookout. When the son investigates the noise made by the men, he returns to his father and says, "Ain't nothing but a crane, pop." The final drawing reveals the figure of a crane. Visually, the stories suggest the representational appeal of birds as graceful figures that cannot be easily held by humans. They enter the imagination as signs of flight and story.

Pictures may also be presented as a form of riddle called the "droodle" (combination of "doodle" and "riddle"), encouraging referential (nonliteral) thinking in children. The droodle shows a single boxed drawing with a clue as to its representation. A common example is two parallel vertical lines with semicircles on them. When the drawer asks, "What is this?" the answer is a bear climbing a tree or a giraffe's neck. Another form of graphically rendered puzzle is the rebus, a series of words or syllables represented by pictures of objects or by symbols whose names resemble the intended words or syllables in sound. Rebuses often challenge the convention of linear reading (culturally defined in English as left to right, although in Hebrew the visual culture is from right to left and in Chinese from top to bottom) by emphasizing visual literacy, or ways of knowing through sight:

B	Mary	REST
R	+Mary	YOUR
BREED		_____
E		_____
D		

The answers are "Crossbreed," "Summary," and "You're under arrest."

American children also learn visual literacy through play in traditional graphical games such as connect the dots. The dots are arranged in rows and columns, and the players take turns drawing lines from one dot to an adjacent one; the object is to complete more squares than the other players. From a visual culture perspective, the game emphasizes the importance of the square as a structural concept in American culture, representing expansive linear thinking (expressed verbally in such expressions as "going straight" and "being square") rather than a cyclical worldview (adherents of which are often portrayed as strange, evil, or crazy, as depicted by using one's forefinger to make circles around one's ear). Chinese American children may be

shown how to make a *pi* disc, formed by drawing a hexagram and connecting the outside points to form a circle, and then drawing another circle inside the hexagram. The child can then draw another hexagram within that circle, thereby encouraging him or her to work inwardly (or introspectively) to appreciate inner designs as well as the cycle of life. In American culture, the *pi* disc can be seen in the layout of "Chinese checkers," in contrast (like so many other forms of play labeled "Chinese") to the square shape of American checkers.

Many Native American groups employ a special form of the pictorial tale in which figures are drawn to represent symbols used in episodes of a story. The symbols are brought together at the conclusion in one encompassing picture, conveying the lesson that apparently disconnected material in the universe is naturally linked. Among the Oglala Dakota, for example, the story of the hero Wic'o'Wic'aga was collected as a pictorial tale. In this story, the hero travels westward and sees seven fireplaces; then he comes to a valley in which he sees seven camps. He continues on and sees a large camp with seven teepees, on six of which are drawn different pictures. The teepee on the end has no picture, and Wic'o'Wic'aga is instructed to go to that one to find out about the rest of his journey. Inside he receives presents, such as a pipe, a bow and arrow, and a medicine bag. The final picture includes the figures that have previously been drawn and the concluding moral: "Just as he went through trials and tribulations and got gifts for his reward, so people say that those who endure hardship in a manly way will enjoy the privileges of a good man." The story also reinforces a visual cultural worldview in which the patterns one recognizes on the journey of life have spiritual significance as guiding signs.

Closely related to pictorial tales are magical shapes, because their origins are thought to come from legends. The ancient Chinese legend of *Lo Shu*, for example, is about a turtle that walks around a ritual sacrifice; a visual puzzle on the turtle reveals the number of sacrifices that must be made. Boxes, circles, stars, and triangles with anagrams and palindromes (in letters or numbers) all are thought to have magical properties in many cultures. Perhaps best known is the magical charm "abracadabra," represented visually as a triangle worn around the neck or hung on a wall as a protective amulet.

ABRACADABRA
BRACADABR
RACADAB
ACADA
CAD
A

The charm in the top line takes in the evil spirit and diminishes it visually to the bottom. In some symbolic analyses, *A* is said to stand for "alpha," representing a new beginning or purity; in some historic analyses, a connection is drawn between the Greek symbol of the letter and the magical moon. Magic is attributed to the arrangement of letters allowing one to read abracadabra diagonally up and down the outside of the triangle.

Symbols, Signs, and Graffiti

One conspicuous way in which images form, intrude, or express a visual culture is by use of public space. After the terrorist attack on the World Trade Center on September 11, 2001 (represented as "9/11" in visual culture), an expression of American unity was to wear a folded red, white, and blue ribbon. The three-dimensional object was a reference to the traditional wearing of mourning ribbons and a symbolic representation of the American flag. Sometimes taking the shape of a bow, it also evoked the gesture of tying a yellow ribbon around trees, used to express hopes for safe return of hostages from Iran in 1980 and soldiers in the Gulf War of 1990. In two-dimensional form, the ribbons were widely displayed on cars, clothes, buttons, flyers, and refrigerators. Variations proliferated, often interpreted differently by viewers; yellow had a pacifist or antiwar implication, expressing a desire to bring the troops home, while blue or green

camouflage was seen as support for the wars. Other symbols of American patriotism used in folk art have developed since the founding of the nation, including the populist figure of Uncle Sam, with a red, white, and blue top hat (also associated with small-town America, especially at fairs); the aggressive, confident American eagle (which in a different form has become an icon for the pan–Native American movement); and the Statue of Liberty, representing America's role as a pluralist haven for immigrants and minorities.

American religious identity is displayed as a sign of the wearer's loyalty as well as an exhortation of faith. The abstract image of a fish on bumper stickers, decals, jewelry, and magnets is a public statement for many of Christian devotion. The origins and interpretations of the *icthus* (Greek for "fish") are varied. One is the legend that early Christians, during their persecution at the hands of ancient Rome, scratched the secret symbol of a fish on the ground to identify themselves to one another. Others cite it as an allusion to scripture: "Come after me, and I will make you become fishers of men" (Mark 1:17). Those who display the image assert different reasons as well. Some think of it as an expression of faith, with the implication that it transcends differences among Christian denominations; others display it for the purpose of "spreading the message" of Jesus Christ. Other prominent images in Christian visual culture include the cross, of course, as well as lamps and lanterns (visualizing Ps. 119:105— "Thy word is a lamp unto my feet"), doves (representing Jesus as a "dove of peace"), and the sun (as a source of light and warmth, or as a homonym for "son" of God). Some symbols have different meanings, depending on the cultural context. The rainbow, for example, is used as a background for such devotional inscriptions as "Jesus is Lord" (light blue for the heavenly sky is also used), but it is also associated in contemporary American society as a sign of identification with, or tolerance of, homosexuals; in the 1980s it was a politically charged symbol of support of multiculturalism and racial equality.

By placing or drawing signs and pictures in public spaces, people intentionally engage visual culture, often with a "viewpoint" and often with the effect of being intrusive or defiant. Folklorists, for instance, have sought to explain the functions and sources of graphical representations called graffiti (Italian for "scratched") as a primary example in American culture. Graffiti take a variety of forms and serve a variety of purposes: "I was here" declarations in the form of a name or symbol painted on a wall or etched on a tree (such as "Kilroy was here," the identifier of U.S. GIs during World War II; the names or initials of lovers, typically inside a heart; "tags," stylized gang names spray painted on walls in the inner city); "latrinalia," or phrases written on bathroom walls with the expectation that others may add remarks in an anonymous interactive chain; and complex systems of murals, often created illicitly, on subways and building exteriors. In folklife, such expressions draw attention to ethnic, community, youth, and occupational visual cultures. Mexican American youth in the West are known for using Aztec symbols, street gang signs, and Gothic lettering in elaborate pictorial murals, often signed "cs" or "c/s" (abbreviation of con safos, with the idiomatic meaning of "don't mess with me [or it]"). While the Aztec symbols evoke an ancient (or warrior) identity, the Gothic lettering (called colloquially "cholo style," "West Coast style," or "old style") has been reported as representing the same honor and formality associated with the letterforms used on diplomas and other official documents. Folklorists have also observed that graffiti artists form folk groups of their own based on their artistic work, identified as "crews" (working groups) for self-protection and collaboration.

Graphical Folklife

Modern technology has created new opportunities to manipulate and reproduce visual traditions. In the nineteenth century, printing made widely available birth and baptismal certificates, family registers, bookplates, house blessings, and mourning pictures, continuing patterns of handmade forms, particularly in Pennsylvania German folklife, and allowing for users to color in designs or add decorative details. Particularly persistent in Pennsylvania German areas is the *himmelsbrief*, or "heaven letter," often a text illuminated with images of heaven (such as seven lightning bolts and a guardian angel) telling the story of a letter sent from St. Peter in a golden box carried by a raven or guardian angel. Typically hung on a wall, it is intended to ward off evil. Religious broadsides (defined as one-page prints), often with depictions of Christ, the Virgin Mary, or Our Lady of Guadalupe, are also hung as protective blessings in Mexican American homes in the Southwest. And broadsides are used for traditional purposes among other groups as well, for example, the Jewish practice of using them for illuminated marriage contracts called *ketubbot*, and sailors' use of them for certificates acknowledging initiation into "the order of the deep" upon crossing the equator.

The advent of the photocopier and facsimile ("fax") machines in the late twentieth century increased access to reproduction of broadsidelike material for easy circulation. The material, sometimes called "xeroxlore" or "photocopied folklore," has been identified as traditional in cases where the images relate to ancient visual depictions and imagery that gains currency by repetitive transmission, much like oral lore. A great deal of the photocopied and faxed material, however, is graphical humor, showing cartoons, puzzles, applications, memos, and rebuses, often contrasting the graphical image with the written caption—as if to say, "Don't believe what you hear; seeing is believing." In cartoons variously depicting an outhouse or a baby on a chamber pot, a roll of toilet paper was prominently displayed; the caption read, "No job is over until the paperwork is done." Similarly, the proverb expressing the American ethic of "Work hard and you will be rewarded" is depicted in a cartoon of a portly, aging man with a screw through his belly. Like these examples, much photocopied folklore consists in office humor pertaining to the modern service and information economy, providing an outlet for the view of workers as small cogs in the big corporate wheel. Often the depictions are particularized for corporate occupations such as secretaries, insurance workers, and students.

Computers and cameras have also given rise to their own productions of visual culture. For example, home photography has created its own traditions regarding occasions for picture taking and expected poses—hunters holding up the antlers of a "bagged" buck, brides and grooms feeding each other wedding cake, and mischievous children holding up "rabbit ears" (index and middle fingers forming a v) behind a sibling's head. Even the display of photographs takes traditional forms. They may be placed in family albums or scrapbooks, to be viewed recurrently at holidays, reunions, and anniversaries; placed in frames to be displayed on mantels and furniture; or hung in a place of honor in the home, called "the family wall" in folk speech. As a sign of family identity or friendship, wallet-size portraits are carried for private reminders or proud display; teenagers keep self-adhesive pictures of best friends on their bulletin boards or school books; and baby photographs may be posted in the workplace for name-that-employee contests. At special occasions, such as retirements and family reunions, it is common to have "memory boards," display panels created with assemblages or montages of family snapshots taken over the years. Computers have created "virtual" memory boards, albums, and scrapbooks where families and groups can post pictures. The humorous tradition of altering photographs (going back to the drawing of an outrageous mustache or beard to mock a figure) has taken on new life with the ability to cut and paste images digitally on the computer.

The computer has appropriated the rhetoric of home visual culture—such terms as "wallpaper," "windows," and "tiles"—and provides users with the ability to present themselves and their interests in creative displays of imagery. From the perspective of modern folklife, this creative activity has raised the question of how people "traditionalize" display in new visual media, taking ideas inherited from their culture (such as the meanings of colors and symbols) and adapting them to the creation of a personal or group identity (especially when media are shared in a family

or among a group of friends). Cell phone callers can be observed using their devices to capture or create images that—in keeping with the idea of tradition—promote social bonding through the sharing of images. Whether drawn or printed as a homemade "card" or mediated by digital tools, expressions of social connection can be structured and symbolized according to traditions as graphical folklife.

Simon J. Bronner

See also: Aesthetics; Film and Video; Folk Art; Internet; Material Culture; Nationalism.

Sources

Bronner, Simon J. "Pictorial Jokes: A Traditional Combination of Verbal and Graphic Processes." *Tennessee Folklore Society Bulletin* 44 (1978): 189–96.

Castleman, Craig. *Getting Up: Subway Graffiti in New York.* Cambridge, MA: MIT Press, 1982.

Dundes, Alan, and Carl R. Pagter. *Work Hard and You Shall Be Rewarded: Urban Folklore from the Paperwork Empire.* 1975. Reprint, Bloomington: Indiana University Press, 1978.

Mirzoeff, Nicholas, ed. *The Visual Culture Reader.* London: Routledge, 2002.

Morgan, David, and Sally M. Promey, eds. *The Visual Culture of American Religions.* Berkeley: University of California Press, 2001.

Ohrn, Steven, and Michael E. Bell, eds. "Saying Cheese: Studies in Folklore and Visual Communication." Special issue, *Folklore Forum* 13 (1975).

Smith, Shawn Michelle. *American Archives: Gender, Race, and Class in Visual Culture.* Princeton, NJ: Princeton University Press, 1999.

Sturken, Marita, and Lisa Cartwright. *Practices of Looking: An Introduction to Visual Culture.* New York: Oxford University Press, 2001.

VOODOO AND SANTERÍA

Major folk religions of African diasporic communities in the Caribbean, voodoo and Santería are generally considered syncretistic or "creolized" religions—born from the meeting of two cultures—since, in their traditional forms, they combine African spiritual practices and deities with those of French and Spanish Catholicism. In the twenty-first century, many large cities with Latino populations such as New York, Miami, and Los Angeles have Santería communities, and New Orleans is a haven for traditional and popular revival forms of voodoo and hoodoo (an American term usually referring to magical practices of African Americans influenced by Native Americans in the South). Many Catholics from the Caribbean practice Santería alongside traditional Catholicism. Brazilians practice versions of Santería under the names Candomble, Umbanda, and Quimbanda. The sacrifice of animals in Santería and voodoo rituals has sparked controversy in some communities and led to highly publicized court cases testing the rights of Santería adherents to maintain their religious folklife in America.

Haitian Voodoo and North American Hoodoo

Voodoo (variously spelled vodou, voodoon, vaudou, and vaudoux) originated in the native practices of Gold Coast Africans who were brought to the Americas through the slave trade. The term derives from the Fon word for "spirit" (*vodu*). Driven underground by the French Catholic Code Noir, which outlawed the assembly of slaves for non-Catholic religious worship and proscribed the baptism of all slaves, voodoo practitioners continued to carry out their native traditions in private, though publicly their rites took on increasingly Catholic forms, including the adoption of Catholic iconography and elements of Catholic cosmology. When Haiti was liberated from French rule in 1804, the majority of whites inhabiting the island were either assassinated or banished, leaving African Haitians in control of public life. Following Haitian independence, through the influence of voodoo priests and priestesses (*houngans* and *manbos*), voodoo became Haiti's dominant public religion.

Voodoo is a monotheistic religion, though its rites and iconography reflect a pantheistic worldview. One God, Bondyè, is manifested in the physical world and communes with practitioners through the spirits of ancestors and a pantheon of deities (*loa, lwa*) responsible for overseeing various natural phenomena. The spirit world and the physical world are permeable, and their meeting point is at a "crossroads" between heaven and earth, life and death. Voodoo practices take place

Santería (way of the saints), a Caribbean variation of voodoo introduced by West African slaves, has up to one million adherents in America today. Rites are conducted by a priest—such as this man in Little Havana, Miami—or priestess. (*State Library and Archives of Florida*)

either at a literal crossroads or, more formally, beneath a peristyle, a covered area arranged to form an *axis mundi* ("center of the world" or "cosmic pillar"). Practitioners refer to the center post upholding the peristyle as the *poteau-mitan*, or solar support.

The *poteau-mitan* represents the deity Legba, who controls the passage between worlds. Personified as an elderly man, Legba has his counterpart in Kalfu, a younger, more dangerous deity who also resides at the crossroads and who controls evil spirits. A third important crossroads deity, Ghede, watches over the crossroads between life and death. His symbol is a crossed tombstone, though he is responsible for both death and resurrection. A trickster figure, Ghede is also the deity of eroticism and play. Since, collectively, these deities are both benevolent and potentially malevolent, voodoo services are accompanied by animal sacrifice, usually of a chicken, to placate them. The practice itself involves dancing, chanting accompanied by drums, and the manifestation through spirit possession of one of the *loa*, often an ancestor, who offers guidance and advice to the community. Voodoo practitioners refer to themselves as "followers of the *loa*."

While a number of African deities are important in voodoo cosmology, the three guardians of the crossroads are the most common in popular North American representations, though they are often manifested in different forms, such as that of the bluesman who sells his soul to the devil at a crossroads in exchange for astonishing talent. Arguably, the archetype of the bluesman himself represents a synthesis of these three African archetypes: the crossroads bluesman is often imaged as a wizened man (Legba) with youthful musical exuberance (Kalfu) and a preternatural mastery over the mysteries of life, death, and sex (Ghede).

African slaves in North America practiced forms of folk religion resembling voodoo rooted in Congo and Angolan cosmologies, though, due to Protestant suppression, these practices were never formalized to the degree that African practices were in the Catholic colonies. African traditions managed to persist in Haiti as a relatively formal and organized religion transmitted generationally among slaves on large plantations, but North American slavery dispersed and fragmented these traditions, as it did slave communities. For this reason, African folk magic in North America appeared in regional beliefs and herbal healing practices, while formal African ceremonies were gradually reorganized around Protestant practices such as Baptist water magic and Pentecostal spirit possession.

A syncretistic form of voodoo was introduced into North America in the 1830s by Marie Laveau, a New Orleans hairdresser who began practicing voodoo after meeting Haitian *houngans*. Known for leading dances in New Orleans' Congo Square, Laveau also popularized folk prac-

tices and objects not found in the Haitian voodoo peristyle, such as palmistry, spell casting, luck charms (*mojo*), and the voodoo doll. Collectively, these popular innovations, combined with other folk customs, became known as hoodoo. New Orleans hoodoo rituals, though practiced in "secret," were known to draw white and black audiences seeking magical solutions to practical problems of love, health, and money. By the late nineteenth century, hoodoo dancers in Congo Square were integrating their identification with Native American struggle into their practices, adopting a Native American spirit, Black Hawk, into the *loa* pantheon and integrating elements of the ghost dance, including Native American headdress, into their rituals, which were fast becoming popular public performances.

Hoodoo terms and beliefs entered mainstream American culture in the first half of the twentieth century primarily through representations in film and novels and through the language of popular music. Horror films and novels about zombies derive from the myth that Haitian medicine men (*nganga*) can raise the dead and from the central figure of Marie Laveau's voodoo, Li Grand Zombi, a snake deity. Late in the twentieth century, movies such as *Night of the Living Dead* (1968 and 1990) and television shows such as *Buffy the Vampire Slayer* (1997–2003) would cull from the zombie myth with varying degrees of complexity. A sensationalized version of voodoo zombies appeared in the 1993 film *The Serpent and the Rainbow*. In addition to contributing to blues (and later rock) the image of the musician as satanically inspired, hoodoo introduced the term "mojo," which, derived from the West African word *mojuba* (magic), referred to hoodoo amulets and later began to suggest sexual energy and personal magnetism.

Santería and Lukumí

Santería, a Spanish Caribbean variant of voodoo, was also introduced into the Americas by African slaves, and it, too, involves ancestor veneration, spiritualism, possession, and crossroads religious practice. The supreme deity of Santería is Olorun, or Olódùmarè (literally, "the owner of heaven"). The ancestors and spirit guardians of Santería are called orisha. The term "Santería" means "way of the saints" and was used derisively by Catholics in the Spanish Caribbean. Many practitioners of Santería rituals prefer the Yoruba term Lukumí. Although the term Lukumí is used as shorthand for Yoruba spiritual practices influenced by Spanish Catholicism, especially in Cuba, a distinction can be made between organized Santería practices and the individual spirit work (*espiritismo*) practiced in the home by initiates and noninitiates alike. While Lukumí practice is highly secretive and basically African, folk practices of Santería are highly public and syncretistic.

When exploring the relationship between "religions of the folk" and the established religions of priests, scholars of religion often use the terms "right-handed" and "left-handed." Right-handed religions are those that theologically dominate a culture, setting the basic cosmological terms that practitioners of left-handed religions, or cults, follow. These terms are often applied to practices such as Santería and voodoo, which are referred to as left-handed, syncretistic, or creolized religions. Such designations are inherently complicated (left-handedness retains premodern associations with "weirdness," and the designation "right-handed" is always biased toward literacy), and, together, Santería and voodoo complicate the matter even further. If Santería is a left-handed folk religion, then its right hand can only be the Catholic Church, making it, essentially, a kind of folk Catholicism. Further, if voodoo practices are characterized as "syncretistic," by implication they depend on Catholic cosmologies for their coherence.

Though it is often noted that Santería was a syncretistic evasion of Spanish Catholic law, it is equally probable that Spanish Catholics were content with Santería's outward forms of Catholic worship and pressed the matter no further, leaving Lukumí practices brought from Africa to continue, though secretly, without the adoption of Catholic forms. Three elements of Santería's history and practice suggest this. First, "Santería" was a derogatory term, implying that Catholic au-

thorities were aware that "illegal" African spiritual practices, barely concealed by a veneer of Catholic iconography, persisted among the slaves. Second, Lukumí rituals remained secret in the Spanish Caribbean, suggesting that the Santería "assimilation" of Yoruba practices into Catholic cosmology was neither total nor convincing to Catholic authorities. Finally, Lukumí rituals do not make use of Catholic saints or Catholic cosmologies.

Santería, in other words, is a folk form of Lukumí, associated with home altars, herbal healing, divination, and personal meditation. Its most visible outward sign is *Las Siete Potencias Africanas* (the Seven African Saints) candles, which depict Catholic saints labeled with the names of Lukumí orisha. While Santería is usually associated with Cuban Lukumí culture, practices similar to Lukumí occur in the South American Candomble and Umbanda traditions and in the Shango tradition of Trinidad. Botanicas—stores that sell Santería herbal remedies and supplies—are found in Florida, New Jersey, New York, California, and other locations with large Hispanic populations. Santería remedies, votives, altars, and prayers are used in Catholic households as well as by practitioners.

Santería practices of animal sacrifice have been the subject of two important American court cases. In the first, *First Church of Chango v. American Society for the Prevention of Cruelty to Animals* (1983), a New York court found that Lukumí animal sacrifice was illegal in the state because it violated several statutes related to animal slaughter. In the *Church of Lukumí Babalu Aye v. City of Hialeah, Florida* (1993), the U.S. Supreme Court found that the city of Hialeah could not enforce statutes specifically designed to ban Lukumí services. While this ruling did not legalize animal sacrifice, it was a landmark decision for Santería practitioners since, on First Amendment grounds, it recognized Santería as a legitimate, organized, and legally protected religion. In contrast, French authorities in Haiti and President Fidel Castro in Cuba have launched campaigns to suppress Santería and voodoo.

Antivoodoo campaigns constitute a folk tradition in themselves, spawning a literary sub-genre (the antiwitchcraft and anti–rock 'n' roll sermon), a film genre (*Night of the Living Dead*), and political rhetoric (Presidents John F. Kennedy and Jimmy Carter both blamed voodoo for popular uprisings in Haiti, and Ronald Reagan was accused of practicing "voodoo economics"). For the most part, voodoo in the United States is practiced by small, unorganized groups and by individuals living in New York, New Orleans, and parts of Florida. An estimated sixty million people worldwide practice some form of voodoo, and few of these in the United States do so in association with an organized and recognized congregation. Influenced by liberation theology, however, Catholic churches in Haiti and those in the United States with Haitian and Cuban congregations have integrated animistic language and Catholicized animistic rituals into seasonal "low Mass" liturgies celebrated around such holidays as Easter.

James Patrick Brown

See also: Altars; Haitian Communities; Miami; New Orleans; Supernatural.

Sources

Brown, Karen McCarthy. *Mama Lola: A Voodoo Priestess in Brooklyn.* Berkeley: University of California Press, 2001.

Cosentino, Donald J. *Voudou Things: The Art of Pierrot Barra and Marie Cassaise.* Jackson: University Press of Mississippi, 1998.

Hurston, Zora Neale. *Mules and Men.* Philadelphia: J.B. Lippincott, 1935.

Jacobs, Claude, and Andrew Kaslow. *The Spiritual Churches of New Orleans: Origins, Beliefs, and Rituals of an African-American Religion.* Knoxville: University of Tennessee Press, 2001.

Mason, Michael Atwood. *Living Santería: Rituals and Experiences in an Afro-Cuban Religion.* Washington, DC: Smithsonian Institution Press, 2002.

Murphy, Joseph. *Santería: African Spirits in America.* Boston: Beacon, 1993.

Olmos, Margarite Fernandez, and Lizabeth Paravisini-Gebert. *Creole Religions of the Caribbean: An Introduction from Voodoo and Santería, to Obeah and Espiritismo.* New York: New York University Press, 2003.

Tallant, Robert. *Voodoo in New Orleans.* New York: Pelican, 1983.

Ward, Martha. *Voodoo Queen: The Spirited Lives of Marie Laveau.* Jackson: University Press of Mississippi, 2004.

WALLOON

See Netherlands Dutch and Belgian Communities

WASHINGTON, D.C.

Washington, D.C., a sixty-eight square mile area along the Potomac River tucked between Virginia and Maryland, is more than a city but less than a state. It is the seat of the U.S. federal government, officially identified as the District of Columbia but more commonly known as Washington, "the District," or simply D.C. It attracts many temporary residents who come and go on the basis of who occupies the White House and which party holds a majority in Congress, but it is also a city where roughly 40 percent of the population (572,000 according to the 2000 U.S. census) is native born. It is famous for its monuments, memorials, and federal buildings, but it is also home to 127 recognizable residential neighborhoods. It is a city that President John F. Kennedy described ironically as mixing northern charm and southern efficiency (reversing the stereotypical characteristics of the two regions). For many cultural geographers, D.C. is an urban aberration that does not fit into any of the distinctive cultural regions of North America.

Historical and Social Background

The U.S. Constitution authorized a federal city in 1787, but it was not until 1790 that the slave states of Maryland and Virginia agreed to cede land along the Potomac River to establish the District of Columbia (Virginia's portion was returned in 1846). The new city was designed in 1791 by Pierre-Charles L'Enfant, a French-born engineer and architect, combining a grid pattern with diagonally intersecting broad avenues. When the federal government officially moved from Philadelphia to "the Territory of Columbia" in 1800, Washington, D.C., was born. It was not only the first national capital to be created by legal statute, but also the first to be comprehensively planned and designed.

Although L'Enfant's original plan was never completely realized, its essential grandeur—combined with the splendor of imposing national buildings and impressive monuments—has made Washington visually distinct from other cities in the United States. Thanks in part to congressional restrictions on the height of buildings, Washington (more like Paris, and less like Boston, New York, or Chicago), has remained a low-rise city with wide vistas and high-rise suburbs (located in Virginia and Maryland).

The people who came to live in Washington were also different. Without a major industrial base, the city never attracted the large numbers of European immigrants who flocked to other major urban centers, toiling in factories and steel mills. Instead, Washington's role as the nation's capital lured those who saw themselves as "the best and the brightest," aspiring to reach the West Wing of the White House, the corridors of the Pentagon, or congressional cloakrooms where deals are brokered. Other aspirants, also hoping

The museums, archives, and programs of the Smithsonian Institution have helped make Washington, D.C., a major center of folklife research and preservation. The First Americans Festival marked the opening of its National Museum of the American Indian in 2004. *(Brendan Smialowski/AFP/Getty Images)*

to influence policy and legislation, were attracted by the professional associations, communications companies, law firms, and political action committees headquartered in Washington. Known as lobbyists—because they once congregated in the lobby of the Willard Hotel (on Pennsylvania Avenue between the White House and the Capitol)—they now populate the long lines of office buildings along and adjacent to K Street N.W.

As a result, the occupational culture of Washington has long been based largely on power and influence: where "What do you do?" is the requisite question when making someone's acquaintance; where congressional staffers, Supreme Court clerks, and White House workers may be accorded more respect than investment bankers or corporate executives; where senators, not movie stars, are the reigning celebrities; and where even interns can sway the bastions of power. Anyone working within this extended world of government and politics is said to be "inside the Beltway," so called for the interstate highway that circumnavigates Washington; those who are not part of this world—meaning the rest of the United States—are said to be "outside the Beltway."

In matters of fashion and style, however, Washington has generally lagged behind many other urban centers, particularly New York and Los Angeles. Even the best-dressed government workers and lobbyists (both male and female) tend to dress conservatively, favoring suits, leather briefcases, and (as a fashion accessory) the omnipresent photo identification badge hanging from a metal chain or cloth lanyard.

African American Community

What may not be known to many first-time visitors or newly arrived government workers is that African Americans constitute a majority (60 percent, according to the 2000 census) of the population of Washington, D.C. Free blacks began migrating to the city early in the nineteenth century, and arrived in much larger numbers during and after the Civil War. An estimated thirty thousand former slaves sought refuge in Washington during the war, and tens of thousands more moved from the South afterward, seeking not only the protection of the federal government but also the opportunities of Reconstruction employment. By the end of the nineteenth century, Washington boasted the largest urban community of African Americans anywhere in the United States.

As was the case in many American cities, Washington was racially segregated—but with one peculiar twist. Hidden within many predominantly white neighborhoods were sizable enclaves of African Americans. The homes of whites faced outward onto main thoroughfares, while in back the homes of African Americans faced inward onto narrow alleys. Although only a few of these alley dwellings can still be found in Washington today, there were at least nineteen thousand alley residents in 1897, more than 90 percent of whom were African American.

African Americans in the nation's capital have long had a significant impact on the overall culture of Washington, D.C. One reason is that the black residents of Washington—as is generally the case for all Washingtonians—have higher levels of education and income than those found in other urban areas. Moreover, prestigious educational institutions such as Howard University (established in 1867) and Dunbar High School, as well as civil-service employment opportunities in the federal government, have enabled the local black population to share some of the power and influence for which Washington is known.

In every election since the first Home Rule Charter was approved by Congress in 1973, the District of Columbia has elected a black mayor and a majority of black city council members. Nevertheless, there has long been suspicion among African Americans that influential whites (although a minority of the population) are conspiring to take back control of city government. "The Plan," as this conspiracy is known, might qualify as urban legend, but the sting operation that caught longtime mayor Marion Barry smoking crack cocaine in 1990 came as confirmation to some residents that "The Plan" did exist.

Oral and Musical Traditions

Other urban legends that can be found in circulation today include the notion that Washington, D.C., was built on a miasmal swamp; that the Georgetown neighborhood lacks a Metrorail station because prosperous whites feared that the subway would bring an influx of poorer (mostly black) residents; that Washington has no J Street (in between I and K streets) because Pierre-Charles L'Enfant strongly disliked John Jay, the first chief justice of the Supreme Court; and that John Dillinger's penis has been preserved in the recesses of the Smithsonian Institution.

Whatever the validity of these legends, the District of Columbia has made several unchallenged contributions to larger American culture. One is the distinctive musical sound known as "go-go," which started in Washington, D.C., in the early 1970s but has since spread across the nation, with its slow tempo, syncopated beat, and call-and-response interaction between performer and audience. Another is "stepping," a rhythmic dance originally performed by members of African American fraternities and sororities at Howard University.

In the twenty-first century, Washington remains a vibrant metropolitan area. The influx of immigrants from Latin America (especially El Salvador during the 1980s) has dramatically trans-

formed neighborhoods such as Adam's Morgan and Mount Pleasant. Hispanics now make up 8 percent of the city's population, and immigrants from Southeast Asia (primarily Vietnam, Cambodia, and Laos) have added new cultural dimensions to the old Washington.

Even the slogan on the city's newest license plates, "Taxation Without Representation," confirms the District of Columbia's unusual status and its preoccupation with power and influence. Whereas other state license plates may celebrate their historic characters (such as "Land of Lincoln" and "First in Flight") or their agricultural virtues ("Famous Potatoes" and "America's Dairyland"), only Washington would think to call attention to the political fact that its citizens pay federal taxes but do not elect representatives to the U.S. Congress.

James I. Deutsch

See also: African American Communities; Nationalism; Organization, Corporate and Work.

Sources
Borchert, James. *Alley Life in Washington: Family, Community, Religion, and Folklife in the City, 1850–1970.* Urbana: University of Illinois Press, 1980.
Cary, Francine Curro. *Urban Odyssey: A Multicultural History of Washington, D.C.* Washington, DC: Smithsonian Institution Press, 1996.
Garreau, Joel. *The Nine Nations of North America.* Boston: Houghton Mifflin, 1981.
Lornell, Kip, and Charles C. Stephenson, Jr. *The Beat: Go-Go's Fusion of Funk and Hip-Hop.* New York: Billboard, 2001.
Smith, Kathryn Schneider, ed. *Washington at Home: An Illustrated History of Neighborhoods in the Nation's Capital.* Northridge, CA: Windsor, 1988.
"Washington, D.C.: It's Our Home." In *2000 Smithsonian Folklife Festival Program Book,* ed. Carla M. Borden, 12–37. Washington, DC: Smithsonian Center for Folklife and Cultural Heritage, 2000.

WEDDINGS AND MARRIAGE

In the United States, the celebration of marriage has engendered a rich diversity of customs and rituals, often varying by ethnicity, religion, and, increasingly in recent times, by the special interests of the bride and groom. The sheer elaborate-

The conventional American wedding—white gown for the bride, white tiered cake, and rituals including the tossing of the bouquet—remains pervasive, but many couples seek ways to make their special day unique and personal. *(Florida Folklife Archive)*

ness of weddings—in many communities the most elaborate of all rites of passage—signals the importance of the transition of two individuals into a new social union and the creation of a new family identity. During the period of history when couples were born, married, and died within a radius of a few miles, marriage marked a significant community event. While still a cause for celebration, weddings that now bring together dispersed families and multiethnic families often require negotiation among communities and the adaptation of traditions. In addition, commercial culture and the rise of an extensive wedding industry may create expectations of a "standard" American wedding—a white wedding gown for the bride, a white tiered cake that the bride and groom feed each other, the first dance between the bride and groom to mark their union, the bride throwing her bouquet to women guests (the one who catches it destined to be the next to marry), and guests who shower the bride and groom in rice (or, in some adaptations, birdseed or bubbles) as they exit the church.

Persistent beliefs also surround the event: the bride must wear "something old, something new, something borrowed, something blue"; the groom must not see the bride in her wedding dress before the ceremony, risking bad luck if he does. Relatively new traditions such as the bachelor party, the bachelorette party, the wedding shower, and the honeymoon became ingrained in American culture during the twentieth century. In the wedding shower, typically attended only by women, the bride may wear a hat or carry a bouquet fashioned from the ribbons and bows that decorated the gift packages. The bridal shower replaced the more ancient custom of sending household presents to the bride-to-be upon the official announcement of her betrothal.

Ethnic Weddings

Since weddings mark the perpetuation of community as well as family, they are steeped in ethnic symbolism, even as they increasingly adapt to American standards. In a Jewish wedding, for example, the bride and groom stand under a traditional *huppah* (canopy), the couple drinks a ritual cup of wine during the ceremony, the groom places a ring on the index finger of the bride, and the bride circles around the groom seven times. At the end of the ceremony, the groom steps on a glass—for which various explanations are given. Some authorities understand it as a reminder of the destruction of the Second Temple in Jerusalem; others suggest that it marks a transition from the solemn ceremony to the joyous celebration that follows. In the festivities, the common dance is the hora, a circle folk dance that invites participation by all guests. It is traditional during the dance that a group of men lifts the bride and groom on separate chairs and parades them around the room while other guests clap and cheer.

In South Asian tradition, women gather the day before the marriage for the *mehndi* ritual—applying henna in intricate designs to the palms and feet as an omen of good luck. On the day of the wedding, the bride's skin is cleansed with herbs and wholemeal flour. After a Hindu purification ritual, she is anointed with sweet-smelling oils and clothed in a colorful sari. The groom may give the bride a *mangel sutra*, a golden neck chain with small black beads, which symbolizes the union. The bride and groom greet each other with flowers while children toss petals at them and elders tuck money into their garments. In Hindu ceremonies, hymns are chanted while the couple performs *parikrama*, seven symbolic walks around a holy fire.

Japanese traditions encourage the showing of gratitude to and by the parents of the bride and groom. Fathers provide thank-you gifts to the guests as a memento of the occasion and as an expression of thanks for the contributions guests have made to the lives of the bride and groom. The mothers of the bride and groom are presented with bouquets by their new daughter-in-law or son-in-law; the flowers express the appreciation of the bride and groom for the years that their mothers-in-law spent raising and loving their children so that they would be good spouses.

Family is also central in Maori weddings. It is not uncommon for a young Maori couple to go through several weddings in varying locales, allowing even distant relatives to participate in the ceremony. A lavish dinner is served after the vows, and it is important to eat well because the reception may last from three to five hours. The families of both the groom and bride are involved in what some call "speechifying." The tributes generally begin with the fathers, but each immediate family member—and some members of the extended family—are given an opportunity to speak. With each person addressing the guests for fifteen to twenty minutes, Maori weddings can go on for hours. When the speechifying is finally over, groups composed of family and friends entertain the guests with traditional songs and dances. Despite its origins as a war dance, the *haka* is performed regularly. All of the wedding events work together to honor the family and Maori tradition.

Event Weddings

While the expectations of the community and family traditions are especially important elements in the planning of an ethnic marriage cer-

emony, the wishes and interests of the couple are having an increasingly prominent effect on the conduct of contemporary weddings. As the average age at marriage rises, many couples are established in their careers and are willing to foot the bill for their own weddings rather than rely on the generosity and guidance of parents.

A growing tradition in the United States is to make the wedding a personal "event," individualizing the ceremony and celebration rather than conforming to an ethnic or historic standard. One such event is a "destination wedding," held on a Caribbean island or other location of special importance to the couple. The event might entail several days of exotic activities for the wedding party and close friends and family. The time spent in a special place with the people closest to them provides the bride and groom with a liminal space that clearly defines the end of one part of their life and the beginning of their new life as a married couple. Individualized theme or personalized weddings are increasingly common in contemporary American culture, and locations are no longer restricted to churches, wedding halls, and backyard tents. Couples now find their way to sites as diverse as theme parks and cruise ships, mountaintops and remote beaches.

For those unable to afford the Caribbean or other exotic destinations, there are always local exotic wedding sites to choose from. In Salt Lake City, it is possible to "tie the knot on our yacht." This company charters weddings on the Great Salt Lake, where "the setting is spectacular. Distant islands reflecting in the Great Salt Lake's famous placid waters. Sunsets that are truly world-class . . . [making] your wedding day truly special."

It is also possible to carve individual space out of a place as ordinary as the local swimming pool, as indicated in collections of folklore archives such as this one from Utah: "I was a lifeguard at the Scera swimming pool [in Orem, Utah] at the time. I always wanted a pool party for my reception. So that's what we planned. I bought a swimsuit just for the occasion and the invitations said to bring your swimsuit and a towel. If the guests wanted to congratulate the bride and groom they could jump in the pool. We had a barbecue planned. It was going to be my dream reception. Unfortunately it rained that day. We moved the wedding into the church gym. I didn't get to wear my new suit."

With the legalization of same-sex unions in Massachusetts in 2003, the way is paved for the development of wedding customs to meet the needs of gay couples. Currently, heterosexual wedding practices are adapted with both women wearing white wedding dresses or men dressed in black tuxedos. Personalizing gay ceremonies can be seen as a variant of the creative or event weddings gaining popularity in the United States.

Making Memories

The trend toward making marriage ceremonies and celebrations unique, memorable, and personal is also a by-product of American culture at large. Television specials documenting celebrity weddings and receptions with narratives by the bride and groom abound. What network television has done for the rich and famous, the Learning Channel's popular program *A Wedding Story* has done for everyday couples. Each episode of the show follows a couple from courtship and engagement through the wedding day. On typically middle-class budgets, the couples plan and execute weddings that reflect their shared tastes and preferences—emphasizing the romantic nature of every union.

Tangible wedding reminders—from photo albums and elaborately produced videotapes to favors and souvenirs from theme weddings—all help to create memories of the beginning of the couple's married life. The couple also helps to shape memories that foster a sense of intimacy between the couple and their guests. In this process of personal narrative, memories of the beginning of a marriage may be imbued with mythological themes and a fairy-tale quality.

Enchanted Weddings

A common trend in modern American weddings is the theme and spirit of fairy-tale enchantment.

One couple, for example, chose to incorporate the fairy-tale theme explicity into their wedding announcement. On the front of the invitation was a colorful drawing of a castle; inside, the wording described the journey of a beautiful princess, the daughter of a queen and king, to a distant land where she met her Prince Charming. The guests were invited to attend a royal ball to be held in their honor. The enchantment theme (if less explicitly invoked by other couples) universalizes the striving for happiness and connects the community to shared values and dreams. While all wedding receptions are intrinsically performance events involving the presentation of self in a momentary role, the couple that sent out the fairy-tale invitation played double roles the day they married. Not only were they cast as bride and groom—they were also royalty. By creating the scenario, they invited their guests to participate in the performance of a "fairy-tale wedding" and made a strong personal statement of their romantic view.

Sharing the Story

Many American weddings become opportunities for sharing dramatic personal narratives with the community. One couple, for example, chose to take advantage of the groom's training in graphic design in creating their wedding invitation. The groom used the invitation to convey personal information about the beginning of his courtship. The front of the invitation contained the words "wedding announcement" only, but the letters were actually formed by words giving an account of the couple's first date, as follows:

> On January eighth of the year 1999, Chuck and Karisa went on a date that would change both of their lives forever. They started by going to a place where they could skate around on some frozen ice and keep each other warm. Then they went to a place where they could sit down and put napkins on and eat food and laugh at each other. Then they went to a place where they could sit by each other and watch a classic video and hold hands with each other. Then it was time for Chuck to

take Karisa back to her house and thank Karisa for the best date ever.

Perhaps the most important aspect of the customs surrounding marriage is the inclusion of family, friends, and community. Wedding ceremonies and celebrations typically involve the people most important to, and closest to, the couple at a landmark moment in their lives. The community is the social milieu out of which one or both of the participants developed as well as a witnessing or sanctioning body for the marriage itself. And whether it is the taking of vows or the tossing of the bouquet, wedding rituals and customs reaffirm the importance of community in married life—and married couples as a building block of community.

Kristi A. Young

Sources

Baker, Margaret. *Wedding Customs and Folklore*. Lanham, MD: Rowman and Littlefield, 1977.

Bal, Mieke, Jonathon Crewe, and Leo Spitzer, eds. *Acts of Memory: Cultural Recall in the Present*. Hanover, NH: University Press of New England, 1999.

Bulcroft, Kris, Linda Smeins, and Richard Bulcroft. *Romancing the Honeymoon: Consummating Marriage in Modern Society*. Thousand Oaks, CA: Sage, 1999.

Geller, Jaclyn. *Here Comes the Bride: Women, Weddings, and the Marriage Mystique*. New York: Four Walls Eight Windows, 2001.

Gillis, John R. *A World of Their Own Making: Myth, Ritual, and the Quest for Family Values*. New York: Basic Books, 1996.

Wallace, Carol. *All Dressed in White: The Irresistible Rise of the American Wedding*. New York: Penguin, 2004.

WEST AFRICAN COMMUNITIES

Culturally distinct from African American communities, who have a legacy of enslavement before the Civil War, are enclaves of West African immigrants and their children, who arrived in the United States during the late twentieth century, sometimes as professionals and students, and occasionally as refugees of war, economic and political upheaval, and ethnic strife in Africa.

According to the 2000 U.S. census, the population of African immigrants in the United States totaled about one million, most of whom came from West Africa. A notable spike in immigration occurred during the mid-1990s, a time of political conflict and armed conflicts in Liberia, Sierra Leone, and Nigeria. Immigration figures for 1996 were indicative of the distribution of national backgrounds among the West African arrivals. The greatest number of arrivals came from Nigeria (more than 10,000), followed by Ghana (6,606), Liberia (2,206), Sierra Leone (1,918), Cameroon (803), and Senegal (641). Many settled in notable West African communities in New York City, Washington, D.C., Atlanta, Houston, Philadelphia, and Los Angeles, where they found reminders of their folklife in food, music, dance, hairstyle, and dress. The largest populations of West Africans reside in California, Texas, and Maryland; their percentage of the total population is highest in the District of Columbia, Maryland, and Rhode Island. Although a number of languages, ethnic associations, and religions are represented in the national backgrounds of West African immigrants, they frequently come together in America under a regional identity for cultural celebrations and social assistance.

Community Profiles

At the start of the twenty-first century, an estimated forty thousand to fifty-five thousand African immigrants lived in the Greater Philadelphia area. These immigrants own food, clothing, and music stores as well as hair salons and restaurants that reflect distinctive African patterns. West African kente cloth (mud-colored fabric), sculpture, jewelry, koras (harp-lutes), *balafons* (xylophones), and drums abound in art stores located in different parts of the city. In Philadelphia, women from Gambia, Senegal, Mali, and Liberia own braiding salons where they offer a variety of hairstyles—corn rows, screws, the Senegalese twist, interlocks, goddess braids, box braids, and Casamance braids. Such establishments are often located near restaurants where authentic West African *mafé* (rice and peanut-butter sauce cooked with succulent meat-and-potato stew), *thiep-bou-djen* (rice-and-fish), and hot plaintains are served.

Like Philadelphia, Washington, D.C., is a haven for West African folklife. By some estimates, Washington has the largest concentration of African immigrants in the United States. As in other communities, a large proportion of the Africans come from Nigeria, and a substantial number come from Ghana, Sierra Leone, and Senegal. The African Immigrant Folklife Study Project, sponsored by the Smithsonian Institution during the late 1990s, documented Senegalese organizing celebrations and traditional wrestling matches at local parks and lamb barbecues on the Muslim holiday of Tabaski. Ghanaians of the Ashanti ethnic group appoint local leaders—an *asantehene* and queen mother of Washington, D.C.—with the ceremony and regalia of the Akan tradition in Ghana. Nigerian Catholics, representing close to 40 percent of Nigerian immigrants, flock to St. Bernard's Church in Riverdale Park, Maryland, where hymns are sung in various Nigerian languages. A number of mosques have been established by Nigerian Muslims, and D.C. is home to the Nigerian Muslim Council in the United States.

In Washington, D.C., public celebration of West African folklife includes festivals of Ghanaian drumming, Zairian *soukous* music, traditional ceremonies for eating Nigerian Jollof rice, and Senegalese hair braiding. In field research for the 1997 Festival of American Folklife, Tonye Victor Erekosima and Molly Egondo Uzo described a masquerade called *Ofirima* that was performed in D.C. by members of a Nigerian association of immigrants called the Rivers State Forum: "The distinctive style of this dance is a leisurly cadence with broad sweeps of the arms and slow pacing of the feet; this shows opulence, casualness, and a dignified bearing. . . . Some say it reflects the slow ebb and flow of water in their geographical setting; others, their history as traders who have trafficked with the outside world for centuries with relative ease." The performance of the Nigerian artists resembles that of Senegalese wrestlers, whose attire and dance before a match signify opulence, courage, expressiveness, and sophistication.

On the West Coast, Los Angeles is a center of West African settlement and culture. Nigerians are especially prevalent in Los Angeles, and have actively organized social and cultural events, including parties with traditional food, dance, and music on October 1, Nigerian Independence Day, to maintain a sense of community and folklife. In South Central Los Angeles, a noontime mass at St. Cecilia's Catholic Church every other Sunday attracts Nigerians with services in their native Ibo language. On Palm Sunday, Easter, and Mother's Day, the church is packed with more than a thousand Nigerians from all corners of greater Los Angeles. The service features such folklife elements as conga drums and African music, with women wearing brightly colored headwraps and traditional dress. Water is central to the ethnic Catholic celebration. Each member of the community comes before the altar to be blessed with this symbol of life, healing, and fertility from a land that has known no end to drought and famine.

In many cities, immigrants from Gambia, Mali, Guinea, Nigeria, and Ghana form social associations that organize concerts featuring renowned African musicians in America; interest in these concerts often crosses cultural boundaries. Immigrants from Mali, smaller in number than other nationalities, are renowned for their musical traditions in drums, strings (such as the kora of twenty-one strings and the *ngoni*, a type of lute), and *balafons*. Representing a fusion of West African and American styles, Mali Music is a band from Berkeley, California, made up of Malian immigrants playing the calabash (gourd used for percussion), *djembe* (goblet-shaped drum), *balafon*, guitars, and flute who proclaim that they combine traditional native music with American rhythm and blues. The Mandingo word *badenya*, which means "big family," was used to describe a festival organized by the Center for Traditional Music and Dance in 1997 and 1998 to allow Malian musicians and dancers to perform in New York City. Malian culture was also featured at the 2003 Smithsonian Folklife Festival on the National Mall in Washington, D.C. The growing public awareness of Malian music in particular is evidenced on the radio airwaves and concert circuit of America.

Festivals and Cultural Conservation

Recognizing the pressure on American-born generations to assimilate, West African immigrant groups have organized programs to teach native languages and promote cultural traditions. The Isokan Yoruba Language Institute in Washington, D.C., for example, was established in the late 1990s by native speakers to teach the Nigerian language of Yoruba. The Museum of African Culture in Portland, Maine, recognizing the needs of a substantial local immigrant population, organized the Discover Africa Day Camp for children. In Chicago organizations such as the Ghana National Council of Metropolitan Chicago sponsor festivals of West African folklife.

In Chicago and other cities with Ghanian communities, the traditional Homowo ("hooting at hunger") harvest celebration is symbolically important as a narrative of Ghanian cultural perserverance and frequently described as an African version of American Thanksgiving. The origin story of Homowo is that the Ga people traveled for many years before reaching the west coast of Africa. Along the way they experienced famine, but because they helped each other, they survived. Later, when their harvests were bountiful, they held a feast featuring plenty of yams at which they jeered at the hunger and hard times that had plagued them. In Portland, the two-day community Homowo Festival commenced with a traditional Ghanaian processional in which volunteers from local African communities assumed the roles of kings, queens, and followers of the royal family of each of Ghana's ethnic groups. A yam feast is featured. As a magnet for various West African groups, and African Americans interested in their African heritage, the festival went beyond the borders of Ghana to present music, dance, crafts, and storytelling from the West African region.

Although African immigrants form bonds along national, religious, and language lines, there are signs of an emerging West African regional identity in America. Many festivals and other events gather a number of groups together under the African or West African label. Many dance and music groups use the title "West African" to describe themselves. Some examples are Diamano Coura West African Dance Company (based on Senegalese Wolof traditions) out of Oakland, California, and the West African Music and Dance Ensemble in Talahassee, Florida (based on Ashanti drumming and vocal traditions from Ghana). Notable festivals that educate the general public and affirm the cultural identity of West Africans are Northern California's African Cultural Festival in Oakland (advertised as the largest seasonal African festival in the United States) and the West African Dance and Drum Festival in New York City.

Babacar M'Baye

Sources

Arnoldi, Mary Jo, and John W. Franklin. "Mali from Timbuktu to Washington." In *37th Annual Smithsonian Folklife Festival,* ed. Carla Borden, 40–67. Washington, DC: Center for Folklife and Cultural Heritage, Smithsonian Institution Press, 2003.

Arthur, John A. *Invisible Sojourners: African Immigrant Diaspora in the United States.* Westport, CT: Praeger, 2000.

N'Diaye, Diana Baird, and Betty Belanus. "The African Immigrant Folklife Study Project." Center for Folklife and Cultural Heritage, Smithsonian Institution, 2005. www.folklife.si.edu/africa/about.htm.

Ndubuike, Darlington Iheonunekwu Iheanacho. *The Struggles, Challenges, and Triumphs of the African Immigrants in America.* New York: Edwin Mellen Press, 2002.

Selassie, Bereket H. "Washington's New African Immigrants." In *Urban Odyssey: A Multicultural History of Washington D.C.,* ed. Francine Curro Cary, 264–75. Washington, DC: Smithsonian Institution Press, 1996.

Stoller, Paul. *Money Has No Smell: The Africanization of New York City.* Chicago: University of Chicago Press, 2002.

Swigart, Leigh, and Vera Viditz-Ward. *Extended Lives: The African Immigrant Experience in Philadelphia.* Philadelphia: Balch Institute for Ethnic Studies, 2001.

WICCANS

Wiccans, or modern witches, practice a revival religion variously called Wicca, Witchcraft, the Craft, or the Old Religion. Part of the larger neo-

The *Witches' Almanac* is one of a number of periodicals, along with a plethora of books, that support, instruct, and inspire the Wiccan community. *(Stan Honda/AFP/Getty Images)*

pagan movement (religions that re-create pre-Christian belief systems of Europe and the Middle East), Wicca consists of magical and spiritual practices revolving around eight major holidays, or sabbats. It draws inspiration from the indigenous pre-Christian religions of Europe and is often called an "earth-based spirituality." There are several different sects of Wicca, not all of which agree on basic beliefs or practices. Some practitioners maintain that only forms inherited from Gerald Gardner—the author of *Witchcraft Today* (1954) and regarded as the founder of the modern movement—are properly called Wicca, but the term has been widely adopted among witchcraft groups, especially those sensitive to the negative connotations of "witch" and "witchcraft" in society at large. The origin of the term "Wicca" is subject to debate, with folk etymolo-

gies suggesting that it comes from the Old English *wicce*, meaning "to shape or bend"—reflecting a witch's ability to shape the world around her or him through magic. Wicca is a religion without a formal creed or sacred scripture; it is a religion of orthopraxy ("right practice") rather than orthodoxy ("right belief"), which posits the primacy of the individual's spiritual experience. Orthopraxy further implies an aversion to dogma and a tolerance or encouragement of varied interpretation of doctrine.

Beliefs and Practices

Emphasizing individuality, personal connections with the divine, and small-group dynamics, Wicca features variation in practice and belief among different sects, among the members of any specific sect, and even within a coven (the basic small working group). All that said, certain common beliefs and features can be identified. Most witches are duotheistic, yet see all deities as aspects of the Goddess and God; some witches are adamant polytheists. The Goddess is generally regarded as the primary deity, with the God serving as her consort, son, or lover, or some combination thereof. Nature is held sacred, humans are said to contain the divine within them, and witches draw on ancient mystery religions for beliefs and rituals to develop the godhead within. The Goddess (commonly referred to as the "Triple Goddess") includes aspects of Maiden, Mother, and Crone, and is identified with both the moon and the earth. The God may be perceived as Lord of the Beasts; the wild or Green Man of the forest; Pan; the dying and reborn grain god; or a solar god of the waxing and waning year. Witches are not Satanists, believing Satan to be a Christian concept. Most Wiccan groups initiate members through rituals to recognize that status as a Wiccan is a new social identity. Initiation implies special knowledge, and Wiccan groups typically reveal many aspects of their practice only to initiates.

Witches practice magic through spellwork, either individual or communal, that is directed toward personal development or changes in the outer world. The main ethical guides for most modern witches are called *The Wiccan Rede* ("An it harm none, do as thou wilt") and the *Rule of Threefold Return* (whatever intention one "sends" out will return to the sender three times as strongly), both of which limit practitioners' use of negative spells or magic. Since the 1970s, most Wiccans have strongly identified with the environmental movement as the political expression of their beliefs in the sacredness of the earth. Some groups work within a specific ethnic tradition, such as Italian witchcraft, Celtic witchcraft, Saxon witchcraft, Slavic witchcraft, or Norse "Vana Troth." The members of these groups may also belong to non-Wiccan neo-pagan ethnic religious groups that emphasize the worship of deities from their specific cultures, such as Asatru (a Norse pagan religion), An Driocht Fein (a modern Druid organization), and revivals of Canaanite, Egyptian, Greek, Roman, and Celtic religions. Such neo-pagan religious groups, however, do not practice magic or specifically Wiccan forms of ritual. Some Wiccans hold initiations in several different sects of Wicca, and others practice an eclectic blend of their own making, drawing from various traditions to form a version of the Craft that suits their particular taste or needs.

Although there are many solitary practitioners, most Wiccans operate in covens of thirteen or fewer that meet regularly. Covens may be part of a larger tradition, such as Gardnerian or Alexandrian Witchcraft; part of a legally established Wiccan Church, such as the Covenant of the Goddess; or entirely independent. There are also more loosely organized circles, which may meet regularly but have no formal commitment or training requirements, and groves, which hold large public rituals and offer training classes in their specific tradition. Wiccans by and large do not have temples or churches, meeting and conducting their rites in private homes, public spaces such as community centers, or wilderness areas.

Neo-pagan festivals held annually throughout the country attract Wiccans and neo-pagans of all stripes, offering seminars, rituals, and the chance to gather with others of like mind. The community is served by several Wiccan journals, and a plethora of books have been published to inspire and instruct witches and would-be witches in a variety of traditions. Witches are found in all social strata and economic levels, and across the political spectrum, although many in the United States tend to be libertarian, liberal, or progressive in their outlook. Wicca is a religion that promotes tolerance, individuality, and free expression; although the many sects may disagree openly and loudly, they acknowledge the right of all Wiccans (and, indeed, all people) to their own spiritual paths.

Rituals

Wiccan rituals are held at the eight main sabbats, or holidays, of the year, and often on the full moons as well. The year is viewed as a wheel and marked by the eight holidays, known by slightly variouis names in different traditions. They correspond to the equinoxes, solstices, and cross-quarter days: Yule (December 21), Imbolc (February 1), Eostara (March 21), Beltane (May 1), Midsummer (June 21), Lammas/Lughnasa (August 1), Mabon (September 21), and Samhain (October 31). The cross-quarter days, marking the start of spring, summer, autumn, and winter, fall halfway between one of the main solar events (two solstices and two equinoxes). They originated as pagan holidays in northern Europe and the British Isles, and have been revived in modern times as neo-pagan holidays. They are often celebrated on the evening before.

Each sect of Wicca has its own mythology of the calendar to explain the meanings of the holidays, although certain features are commonly recognized. Yule is the feast of light in darkness, variously the conception or birth of the sun; Imbolc is the quickening, the beginning of spring; Eostara is the spring holiday; Beltane is the feast of sexuality; Midsummer honors the fertility of the fields, the strength of the sun, and often the marriage of Goddess and God; Lammas is the feast of first fruits; Mabon is the harvest holiday; and Samhain is the feast of the dead, the time when the other world is open, as well as the start of the new year. Rituals include some form of the following practices: casting a circle; calling in the four elements of air, fire, water, and earth; invoking the deities; raising magical energy and sending it off for a specific purpose; releasing the deities and elemental energies; and opening the circle. In ritual, witches may also enact or tell myths, symbolically represent the union of the Goddess and God, drum, dance, chant, and bless and share ceremonial food and drink. Feasting after a ritual is usually believed to be a magical necessity. Songs and chants are an important part of ritual practice; indeed it has been suggested that they constitute the only "canon" of sacred texts on which Wiccans agree.

Folklife common to Wiccans includes rituals, festival customs, prayers, songs, chants, material culture such as pentagrams and other ceremonial objects, herb lore, folk beliefs, folk magic, myths, legends (especially about the origins of the Craft), jokes, and folk speech that includes ritual phrases such as "blessed be" and "so mote it be" (equivalent to "amen") as well as sayings such as "out of the broom closet," for a witch who has made his or her religious allegiance public.

Sects

Wiccan sects, already numerous, are constantly being formed. They may be grouped in several main branches. Gardnerian Witchcraft traces its lineage from Gerald Gardner, the father of the Wiccan revival, who claimed to be initiated into a traditional English coven in the 1930s and went public after the repeal of the antiwitchcraft laws in England in the 1950s. His claims of origin have been disputed by some, but virtually all branches of the Craft have been heavily influenced by his ideas and rituals. Doreen Valiente, a Gardnerian from England, composed a number of the prayers used by most witches today. Alexandrian Witchcraft, an offshoot of Gardnerian Wicca founded by Alex and Maxine Sanders, has been popularized though books by Stewart and Janet Farrar and Vivienne Crowley. Traditional Witchcraft consists of covens that claim to have endured since at least the witch trials of the fifteenth to eighteenth centuries; according to some scholars,

however, these covens can be traced to no earlier than the late nineteenth and early twentieth centuries.

Family Tradition Witchcraft claims an unbroken tradition of magical practices such as various psychic abilities, folk beliefs, folk healing practices (including herbal remedies and charms), and folk magic in practitioners' families. Such practices usually were not considered a separate religion, however, until the revival period in the twentieth century. There are two branches of Feminist Witchcraft, one for women only (Dianic Witchcraft) and one for men and women (Starhawk's tradition); the two branches share a belief in the necessity of connection with the Goddess for women and men, a nonhierarchical structure, an emphasis on improvisation and creativity in ritual, and a political aspect to their faith that includes working magically as well as mundanely for social justice, peace, and environmental causes. The tradition created by Starhawk is the most influential, since her book *The Spiral Dance* (1979) was for many years typically the first one read by an aspiring witch.

Dianic Witchcraft, created in 1971 by Z Budapest in Los Angeles, concentrates on the Goddess in all her forms and is a separatist religion, for women only. Some Dianics may also participate in mixed-gender rituals, and some women from other Wiccan sects may attend all-female Dianic rituals from time to time.

In addition, ethnic forms of Wicca have also begun to appear, usually adapting existing Wiccan formats by including specific cultural practices and deities. Many Wiccans have been active in gaining public acceptance for their religion, forming antidefamation groups, arguing for equal treatment under the law, and promoting the facts about their religion to counteract the popular misconception that it entails devil worship.

Kerry Noonan

Sources

Adler, Margot. *Drawing Down the Moon: Witches, Druids, Goddess Worshipers, and Other Pagans in America Today.* Revised and expanded edition. New York: Penguin Putnam, 1997.

Crowley, Vivienne. *Wicca: The Old Religion for the New Age.* Wellingsborough: Aquarian Press, 1989.

Farrar, Stewart, and Janet Farrar. *A Witches' Bible.* 2 vols. New York: Magickal Childe, 1985.

Hutton, Ronald. *The Triumph of the Moon: A History of Modern Pagan Witchcraft.* Oxford: Oxford University Press, 1999.

Luhrman, Tanya. *Persuasions of the Witch's Craft: Ritual Magic in Contemporary England.* Cambridge, MA: Harvard University Press, 1989.

Magliocco, Sabina. *Neo-Pagan Sacred Art and Altars: Making Things Whole.* Jackson: University Press of Mississippi, 2001.

Magliocco, Sabina, and Holly Tannen. "The Real Old-Time Religion: Towards an Aesthetics of Neo-Pagan Song." *Ethnologies* 20 (1998): 175–201.

Noonan, Kerry. "May You Never Hunger: Religious Foodways in Dianic Witchcraft." *Ethnologies* 20 (1998): 151–73.

Pike, Sarah. *Earthly Bodies, Magical Selves: Contemporary Pagans and the Search for Community.* Berkeley: University of California Press, 2001.

WIREGRASS REGION

The Wiregrass Region, also known as Wiregrass Country, is a cultural region of the American South that stretches from the area north of Savannah, southwest into the Georgia coastal plain, fanning into the southeastern corner of Alabama, and dipping down into the northwestern panhandle of Florida. The Wiregrass Region owes much to its ecosystem, which produces an inordinate incidence of low-intensity forest fires. Of all the pines, only the longleaf can easily endure the sweltering heat of these wildfires. Indeed the survival of this "fire climax" species depends on recurrent blazes; it thrives on such conflagrations because they serve to obstruct the growth of competitive trees and shrubs. Wiregrass (*Aristida stricta*), a prominent feature of the longleaf pine forest, plays a vital role in the ecosystem as an igniter. Wiregrass residents came to regard the forest fire as a tool for controlling the environment; it also helped foster a distinctive folklife in the region.

The Wiregrass Region is historically underpopulated, economically poor, and predominantly white. A reputation for poor soil and the threat of malaria kept farmers from settling in large numbers. King Cotton played a less pronounced role in the region's early economic development than in other areas of the Deep South because soil contents could not support its production. The frontier rather than the plantation typified the Wiregrass lifestyle. As a matter of pride, Wiregrass landowners described themselves as farmers instead of planters. In areas with more of an aristocratic bent, one needed only five hundred acres of land and ten slaves to be considered a planter. African Americans primarily entered the region after their emancipation from slavery elsewhere. They largely migrated into the region because of the prospects of becoming landowners themselves. The legacy of African American settlement is still apparent in Emancipation Day celebrations on May 20, the date when those enslaved in the region received notification in 1865 of the Emancipation Proclamation.

Festivals and Traditions

Festivals celebrating community identities and bonds are especially important in a region such as the Wiregrass Country, which is not known for national attractions. Most Wiregrass towns choose a local theme for their festivals. Several towns (Claxton, Fitzgerald, and Whigham, in Georgia, and Opp, Alabama) host annual Rattlesnake Roundups. These festivals shift public attention to the prevalence of this dangerous species, especially since local laws prohibit burning the woods without a special permit. Organizers justify the roundups as community-oriented events that serve to control the incidence of snakebites, but they also function to declare the special toughness or uniqueness of communities in the region by identifying themselves with the feared snakes. Every year, for example, as many as twenty thousand people attend the parade and festival in Whigham, Georgia (population 605). Claxton promotes its roundup as "the beauty with the beasts" competition: the judging of the snake competition occurs at the same time as the crowning of the Roundup Queen.

Some Wiregrass cities celebrate crops and animals that are significant to their commerce and sense of folk occupational identity. In Georgia, Colquitt sponsors a Mayhaw Festival; the mayhaw fruit grows almost exclusively in Wiregrass Country and is ripe for three weeks in the spring. Festivals that celebrate some more-recognized crops include Morven's Peach Festival; Glennville's Sweet Onion Festival, which competes with its well-established neighbor, Vidalia; and Sylvester's annual Peanut Festival at Possum Poke, the permanent festival grounds. In Alabama, Dothan, too, hosts a gigantic National Peanut Festival. Other festivals celebrate animals important to the region's past and present development, such as Mule Day in Calvary and Swine Time in Climax, Georgia. Florida towns such as Wausau built a Possum Palace to honor the animal central to local survival during the Great Depression, and Blountstown citizens celebrate Goat's Day.

Another significant Wiregrass Country tradition embraces a form of religious music known as "sacred harp." To combat illiteracy, participants attended singing schools and learned to sight-read notes originally based on four shapes (a triangle, oval, square, and diamond). This "fasola" singing tradition still thrives, especially in Ozark, Alabama. Forming a square seating arrangement, participants sing in four-part harmony (soprano, alto, tenor, and bass). In Alabama, an enclave of African Americans continues to perpetuate this tradition with numerous annual events. For most in the region, the tradition evolved with singers switching to a seven shapenote system known colloquially as "do-ray-me." Songbook publishers soon began to sponsor professional duets and quartets to attend these "all-day sings." Waycross, Georgia, and Bonifay, Florida, are renowned for maintaining the tradition of all-night gospel sings. Such events, along with the popularity of singing conventions, highlight the role sacred music plays regionally as a form of entertainment and an evangelical tool.

Both special church services and singing conventions still hold what is known as dinner-on-the-grounds. Owing to the protracted all-day nature of these events, a midday break results in a feast, featuring some of the region's most popular food dishes, often involving pork, chicken, and gray mullet fish. It is traditional to comment at the events on the lemonade (usually prepared by the men in large barrels), which quenches one's thirst after a long morning of singing or preaching. Churches and other community organizations serve chicken pilaf. Fish fries through the region frequently emphasize the saltwater fish mullet. At the Boggy Bayou Mullet Festival in Niceville, Florida, the town of around twelve thousand residents claims that during festival time in October one hundred thousand visitors consume ten tons of the smoked and fried fish.

Narratives and Customs

Stories about wiregrass offer a prominent motif in legends and narratives of the region. Storytellers often incorporate it as part of the plot structure for their personal experience narratives. Wherever it grew, wiregrass became an integral part of the terrain and served as cover for wildlife, a place where quails might nest or predators such as rattlesnakes might lurk. Encounters with rattlesnakes constitute another popular motif, especially when told as warnings about what to do, or not to do, when coming across one.

Wiregrass residents also pepper their personal experience narratives with remembrances of playing fireball. Fireball was a widespread activity among Native Americans, who introduced it to inhabitants within Wiregrass Country. Around sundown, neighbors would gather in an open field with kerosene in washtubs to light burlap sacks tied with ropes, form teams, and propel the missiles at one another for fun and excitement. The rules seemed to conform to today's paintball games. Locals adjudged the sport to be risk-free, playing along with their children, since the balls would harmlessly bounce off on contact. People who grew up playing the game speak of it nostalgically, recalling how the fireballs lit up the night sky.

With the region's many creeks, streams, and pristine forests, Wiregrass residents continue to enjoy fishing and hunting. Fishing in particular is upheld as a so-called poor man's sport, since it can be pursued without much expense. Those who like to fish refer to it as "drowning worms" and developed several ingenious ways of procuring bait. The practice of grunting worms, or worm fiddling, was one prominent means; driving a stick into the ground and rubbing a stone back and forth to make the stick vibrate lured worms out of the ground. Some recall using the stems of wiregrass itself to "tickle" earthworms out of moist soil. On the other end of the spectrum, the Thomasville area gained renown for its elite woodland hunting plantations. Owned by northern industrialists after the Civil War, the large estates recognized quail as the quintessential game bird in Wiregrass Georgia. These properties were frequently self-contained, with their own roads, schools, and churches. Quail season in the region attracted many celebrities, including presidents and royalty. The hunting season abounded with rituals, with the best saved for last. On the closing day, workers "put the fire" to their grounds, inducing a controlled burn of the woodlands. Ironically, it was the near depletion of the quail population that first alerted conservationists to the role of fire in the evolution and regeneration of the pine forest.

Because of the restrictions imposed on burning, wiregrass no longer flourishes as it did in the past. An estimated ninety-three million acres of longleaf pines and wiregrass originally graced the South; today, only one million acres remain. Environmental conservationists are struggling to restore the land by respecting its vegetation, and along with it folk traditions. A folk regional consciousness is apparent in institutions such as the Archives of Wiregrass History and Culture at Troy State University at Dothan, Alabama, and Landmark Park in Dothan, set aside to preserve the cultural heritage of the Wiregrass region and location for the Wiregrass Heritage Festival.

Jerrilyn McGregory

See also: Foodways; South, The.

Sources

Brown, Titus, and James "Jack" Hadley, eds. *African American Life on the Southern Hunting Plantation*. Charleston, SC: Arcadia, 2000.

Cobb, Buell E. *The Sacred Harp: A Tradition and Its Music*. Athens: University of Georgia Press, 1978.

Crowley, John. *Primitive Baptists of the Wiregrass South: 1815 to the Present*. Gainesville: University Press of Florida, 1998.

Flynt, J. Wayne. *Poor but Proud: Alabama's Poor Whites*. Tuscaloosa: University of Alabama Press, 1989.

Hartsfield, Mariella. *Tall Betsy and Dunce Baby: South Georgia Folktales*. Athens: University of Georgia Press, 1987.

Herring, J.L. *Saturday Night Sketches: Stories of Old Wiregrass Georgia*. Boston: Gorham, 1918.

McGregory, Jerrilyn. *Wiregrass Country*. Jackson: University Press of Mississippi, 1997.

Wetherington, Mark. *The New South Comes to Wiregrass Georgia: 1860–1910*. Knoxville: University of Tennessee Press, 1994.

WOMEN

Women's folklife is often associated with activities considered feminine and typically rooted in the home, family, and women's groups. Rituals and beliefs associated with pregnancy, birthing, and menopause are linked to the female domain because of the biological characteristics of women. But other practices such as quilting, needlework, baking, child rearing, and hairstyling are distinguished by their historical, social, and cultural association with women; although men do these activities, they tend to be dominated by women and symbolized in narrative and image as women's traditional practices. Changes in economic and social structures such as more women in the industrial and corporate workforce, the establishment of legal rights of women to equal opportunity and protection, and the rise of feminism have, however, altered the previously mandated roles of women in American society. Thus, the realm of real and perceived genres and practices composing women's folklife has also changed.

Many forms of expressive communication (e.g., personal narrative, gossip, anecdote) are popularly thought of as women's practices because of their cultural connection to the home and family (e.g., foodways, family folklore, home-based holiday traditions, arranged marriages, child-rearing practices, domestic shrines and altars, all forms of needlework), body decoration and adornment (e.g, hairstyling, costuming, south Asian *mehndi*), or pastimes or occupations dominated by women (e.g., midwifery, elementary education, book groups, laundries, textile millwork,

Quilt making, a form of material culture and expressive art traditionally associated with women, has been seen as a symbol of home, community building, the pioneer spirit, and handicraft itself. It is also an apt metaphor for tracing the historiography of women and folklife. *(Minnesota Historical Society)*

nursing and care of the elderly, mourning practices). Observers often try to discern a social and aesthetic pattern in such practices, including the tendency of women to work repetitively and co-operatively (in contrast to men's supposed competitiveness) in restricted spaces, emphasize nurturing of family and community, and use soft materials (fabric and food).

In light of women's expressions increasingly becoming public outside the domestic sphere in the twentieth century, women's values or traits once traditionally considered feminine, such as meekness, nurturing, passivity, moodiness, and flightiness, are now subject to reevaluation and analysis of why these appellations developed and what now sustains them. Scholars may look developmentally, for example, at the texts and patterns of girls' play, categorized in mid-twentieth-century collections as consisting pri-

marily of repetitive, cooperative hand clapping, ball bouncing, and jump-rope games, often with rhyming texts emphasizing courtship and beauty, as a basis of adult feminine traits, and contrast them with the late-twentieth-century popularity of competitive, aggressive sports among girls.

Study of Women's Folklife

Folklorists have drawn attention to traditional women's practices since the professionalization of folklife studies in the nineteenth century and have established concepts of a distinctive women's culture, often revolving around family roles in the home. Many of the early studies examined the role of women in a variety of ethnic and regional settings in transmitting and maintaining singing and storytelling traditions in the domestic sphere. With the rise of feminism in the 1960s and early

1970s, a new generation of folklorists, particularly women, expanded the approach to women's folklife by asking questions about the kinds of empowerment, or lack thereof, that women's traditions provided, set against the background of patriarchal societies and practices. The range of material that was considered expanded beyond storytelling and singing not only to other genres of expression but also to realms of experience outside the home and family.

In addition to widening the scope of appropriate topics worth investigating, scholars have also reevaluated the roles women have played in the performance and maintenance of customs, beliefs, rituals, and activities previously considered the domain of men. Scholars are now attuned to the inescapable impact on any study of the gender of both researcher and subject. Recognition that gender informs and affects any study, from choosing a topic and selecting informants to gathering and analyzing data, is now a routine acknowledgment of folklife scholars' work.

An examination of topics discussed at annual meetings of the American Folklore Society since the mid-1970s reveals the breadth of American folklife studies by and about women: issues of identity among Finnish American rag-rug makers in Michigan's Upper Peninsula; Hmong refugee women embroiderers and cultural transmission; strategies of power among female rappers in the rap music tradition; female gospel announcers and the maintenance of urban religious trations; women's songs from the Appalachian coalfields; birthing chairs and midwives; girls' coming-of-age narratives; honoring quilts among Lakota Sioux; Martha Stewart and the folklore of housework; narratives among women survivors of domestic abuse; women as vectors of creolization; the myth of motherhood; CB handles of female truckers; positive women's roles and women's power in ballads; knitting circles and storytelling; differences in male and female joke telling; personal narratives about divorce; the African American woman's head wrap; female homiletics; and Presbyterian women and the articulation of belief, to name a few.

Traditions of the Life Cycle

Undeniably, women's folklife is associated with conceiving, bearing, and rearing children, as well as with the rites of passage from prepuberty through the onset of menopause. A multitude of stories, beliefs, and customs surround these activities and cycles of life. In America, "sweet sixteen" parties are often held for girls to announce their maturity and "coming out." The sweet sixteen party as a "coming out" is sometimes thought of as a popular version of the debutante ball, and African American variations are staged as "cotillions," often sponsored by black sororities. Many ethnic groups have coming-of-age ceremonies specifically for girls. Among Jews it is the bat mitzvah (at age twelve), among Apaches the na'ii'ees (at as young as age twelve), among the Navajo the kinaalda (usually at age thirteen and when the young woman is experiencing her first menstrual period), and among Mexican Americans the quinceanara (at age fifteen).

To convey the importance of childbirth, it is common for mothers to give elaborate narratives of their own excursions (and the obstacles along the way) to the hospital to deliver babies and the extended labor they endured. Women pass along these stories and beliefs from one generation to another and share them within networks of families, friends, neighbors, and coworkers. It is perceived as both their role and their responsibility to share this information, "nurturing" others in doing so.

Even women who do not have children are quick to share information that might assist another woman in carrying or caring for a child. Stories and beliefs are especially evident in the custom of gathering American women for wedding and baby showers. Pregnant women often remark on the advice they receive, even from total strangers, about everything from predictions on what sex their baby would be based on how high or low the baby was being "carried" to folk wisdom on how to get an infant to sleep through the night (e.g., lullabies, rocking, holding positions). Breast-feeding women have their own array of traditions, from the type of clothing best suited to feeding to what kinds of foods do not pass well through milk and how to breast-feed discreetly in public situations. Internet technology has enabled this sharing on a worldwide scale and has fostered the growth of cyberspace networks of women. As children grow up, mothers often engage in the exchange of personal experience narratives about good or bad parenting behavior and childhood events that draw attention to themselves. Common motifs in these narratives include how children exhibit "cute" or "cool" postures, say embarrassing things, or appear precocious.

Menopause is another female experience of the life cycle that is rife with folklore, from traditional knowledge and stories shared among women about their experiences and how to cope with menopausal symptoms, to ceremonies such as "croning" (from the word "crone," for a withered woman) that mark the passage, to the creation of new social groups of older women such as the Red Hat Societies, to the jokes, tales, and stories told about postmenopausal women.

Contemporary croning ceremonies vary, often drawing on ancient customs and symbols, turning what may be seen popularly as negative and sublimated (aging and menopause) into a festive, celebratory event. In the revived tradition, becoming a crone is considered the third phase of a woman's life after maiden and mother, associated in the ceremony with wisdom and power. Often celebrated at age fifty as a type of initiation conducted by women already identified as crones (sometimes with one dressed as a priestess or "ancestress"), the ceremonies are held in women's circles, birthday parties, social gatherings, and conferences. Many women use the occasion to rename themselves or take a special name. Symbols designating the initiate may include a flower or star garland crown, a crone staff, a cloak or shawl, or a ribbon or flower lei; in the ceremony, she may be anointed with oil, rose petal water, or lavender. The passage into a new stage of life is often represented by crossing a threshold, passing through a curtain, or moving under a woman's legs propped on a chair. The

ceremony might be accompanied by chants, songs, drumming, rattling, and dancing, and followed by a festive meal.

Inspired by references to an old woman wearing a red hat in the poem "Warning" (1961), by Jenny Joseph ("When I am an old woman I shall wear purple / With a red hat that doesn't go and doesn't suit me"), Sue Ellen Cooper of Fullerton, California, created the Red Hat Society in 1998. It spread rapidly with small chapters of twenty or so women over fifty years old, sporting colorful names such as Red Hat Mamas and Red Hat Tamales, encouraged to create their own festive traditions. The informality of the groups is maintained by antihierarchical positions such as the chapter "hysterian" (who records special events), "antiparliamentarian" (who disdains rules), and "e-mail female" (who handles online communication). Led by a chapter leader called the "Queen Mother" or "Queen Mum," members wear red hats and purple attire (junior "postulants" under fifty are allowed to attend if they wear pink hats and lavender dresses) to social gatherings such as tea parties and celebrations of Red Hat Society Day on April 25.

Women's Genres and Groups

A number of American folk traditions have been dominated by women and can be examined for their reflection of changing feminine values. Home food preparation, for example, has traditionally been the provenance of women. It is usually men in American popular imagination who bring home the cultivated crops, the foraged foodstuffs, and the fish and game. It is women, however, who typically preserve and prepare the food; plan, create, serve, and clean up after meals; share recipes and techniques; maintain and decorate the kitchen; select and care for food preparation and serving equipment; and teach others to cook. When men do the cooking, they tend to do so in public, ceremonial situations—the holiday barbecue (reinforcing images of the man as provider of meat from the wild) or the Sunday pancake-and-sausage breakfast. Studies of foodways have highlighted how women as purveyors of nutrition have been critical in the perpetuation of the ethnic, family, community, and religious traditions in which a particular food is a central or supportive feature. A woman may carry a reputation in the family or community for being a good cook or even for a particular dish—"Grandma Johnson's shortcake" or "Vivian's ginger cookies."

Beyond the domestic sphere, women involved in historically or predominantly male occupations such as soldiering, rapping, and truck driving often develop traditions distinguished from those of men in the trade. In all-male military battalions, for example, a tradition of marching cadences called "jodies" had been common throughout the twentieth century. "Jody" represents the civilian man trying to court a soldier's wife or girlfriend. With more women in the ranks, "Jody" could be heard in rhymes representing the woman trying to seduce a husband or boyfriend. A number of improvised cadences about the trials and tribulations of military life, enemies of the United States, and the special qualities of the marchers are led by female drill sergeants.

Differences of women's roles and customs among ethnic and regional groups also demand attention in the examination of American women's folklife. For example, Laotian-Hmong women who immigrated with their families to the United States after the Vietnam War in the 1970s brought with them the skill of making *paj ntaub*, or "flower cloth." Used customarily for the making of clothes, the skills were adapted to American society, where the Hmong donned Western dress. The designs and patterns they employ have symbolic significance in Hmong culture and often are derived from forms in nature, such as triangles for mountains (a symbol of safety and keeping good spirits in) and long spirals for snail shells (symbolizing the family and driving bad spirits away). Applying Hmong symbols to cloth squares, women created material reminders of their heritage for new generations with embroidered representations of folk tales and the Vietnam War. Studies of these immigrant experiences have revealed the central role of women artists in maintaining rituals, ceremonies, belief systems, language, and other traditional cultural practices of their groups from one cultural setting to another.

Traditions of women's groups—including organizations of Catholic rosary societies, synagogue sisterhoods, the National Organization of Women (NOW), cheerleaders, and sororities—often express the values of volunteerism and service. Many women's groups traditionally engage in charitable work, whether in their religious communities, their hometowns, or across the globe. In societies and historical periods in which women had few legal rights or little economic power, participation in charitable activities has been empowering—in addition to redressing the plights of others. As but one example, quilt making by Mennonite women is central to the success of Mennonite relief auctions, which raise funds for the needy worldwide.

Women's groups also provide a pretext and context for sharing female-centered knowledge and stories that might not be told in mixed company. Historically, quilting bees, canning bees, and beauty parlors were places where women freely conversed and shared stories. Today's equivalent might be the Stitch 'n' Bitch clubs (knitting groups that meet in coffee shops and other locations for conversations), book reading groups, or even sideline soccer-mom gatherings.

Quilt making, a quintessentially female pursuit, serves as a useful metaphor for tracing the historiography of women and folklife studies, for describing the scope of those studies, and for reflecting on the impact of feminist scholarship in the study of folklife in general. The history of folklife study has been formed by piecing together bits and fragments. Moreover, its substance, like the fabrics, techniques, and patterns used to construct a quilt, present seemingly unending possibilities for the study of traditions by and about individual women, groups of women, and their individual and collective interactions.

Marsha MacDowell

See also: Baskets and Basketry; Birth; Feminism; Men and Masculinity; Quilting; Rugs and Rug Making; Wiccans.

Sources

Burke, Carol. *Camp All-American, Hanoi Jane, and the High-and-Tight: Gender, Folklore, and Changing Military Culture.* Boston: Beacon, 2004.

Cantú, Norma E., and Olga Nájera-Ramírez, eds. *Chicana Traditions: Continuity and Change.* Urbana: University of Illinois Press, 2002.

Collins, Camilla A., ed. "Folklore Fieldwork: Sex, Sexuality, and Gender." Special issue, *Southern Folklore* 47, no. 1 (1990): 1–83.

———, ed. *Women and Folklore.* Austin: University of Texas Press, 1975.

Farrer, Claire R. ed. "Women in Folklore." Special issue, *Journal of American Folklore* 88, no. 347 (1975): 1–109.

Hollis, Susan Tower, Linda Pershing, and M. Jane Young, eds. *Feminist Theory and the Study of Folklore.* Urbana: University of Illinois Press, 1993.

Jordan, Rosan A., and Frank A. de Caro. "Women and the Study of Folklore." *Signs* 11, no. 3 (1986): 500–518.

Jordan, Rosan A., and Susan J. Kalčik, eds. *Women's Folklore, Women's Culture.* Philadelphia: University of Pennsylvania Press, 1985.

Marling, Karal Ann. *Debutante: Rites and Regalia of American Debdom.* Lawrence: University Press of Kansas, 2004.

Radner, Joan Newlon, ed. *Feminist Messages: Coding in Women's Folk Culture.* Urbana: University of Illinois Press, 1993.

Thiselton-Dyer, T.F. *Folk-Lore of Women.* Chicago: A.C. McClurg, 1906.

WOOD

On land and at sea, wood figures prominently in American folklife because of its adaptability and abundance. Historically, European settlers marveled at the forested environment of the New World and harvested trees for house construction, craft, and food. Woodcrafts such as the preparation of medicines and dyes from bark, the construction of dugout canoes, and building shelters in bark were learned from Native Americans, while Europeans made intensive use of timbers for traditional houses. Wood was, in fact, the chief resource of agricultural settlement and commerce into the twentieth century. Its significance endures: Wood still provides the material for houses, barns, farmstead structures, and their furnishings; commerce in timber provides a livelihood to loggers, carpenters, builders of ships and boats, and makers of furniture and musical instruments; and the use of wood generates a market for a wide variety of metal tools to cut and shape it. Wood and forests also hold symbolic meaning, reflected in American folk speech: "hicks" (rustics, derived from the image of the hickory shirts worn by loggers), "knock on wood" (indicating wood as a luck-inducing substance), and "not seeing the wood for the trees" (conveying the lesson of understanding the general point).

Traditional Uses

North America is home to an enormous variety of native and imported trees. In the Appalachian region alone, more than 125 different species can be found, each with its own characteristics. Craftsworkers and carpenters make a basic distinction between softwoods (such as pine, spruce, hemlock, cypress, and cedar) and hardwoods (such as oak, ash, hickory, maple, black locust, and fruitwoods), based on the strength of the wood and whether it can be easily worked with tools. A further distinction is made between green, or fresh-cut, wood and seasoned, or dry, wood. And makers of musical instruments choose wood for its ability to transmit vibration. Oils and resins derived from root bark, leaves, and berries are essential ingredients of American folk remedies. Botanicals such as birch bark (containing salicylates, used for pain) and hawthorn (containing flavonoids, used for heart disease) found their way into popular and professional pharmacopoeia and were used in the manufacture and sale of patent medicines. As well, wood is still used in a number of traditional divination rituals, such as dowsing or water witching: These techniques involve the use of crossed wooden rods or forked sticks, chiefly used to locate underground water, oil, buried treasure, and lost persons or items.

The most elementary uses of wood are for heat and cooking. For these purposes, wood may be selected for its ability to produce a good fire, or for the aroma and taste added to food or drink during brewing or aging in casks. Hickory and apple wood are among many used for smoking and preserving meats, while tobacco is fire cured with low-burning wood fires on the floors of closed curing barns. Charcoal, made from the controlled burning of wood, acts to remove impurities from liquids, and wood ash is soaked in water to produce lye for soaps. Additionally, the syrups yielded by the sugar maple and other trees have become staples in American regional cuisine, particularly in the Northeast.

Wood and Environments

The forest as natural environment has particular symbolic and practical uses in American culture. A wilderness marking the edge of the lived-in world, the forest is the mythic home of the uncontrollable, of wild things, outlaws, savages, and spirits. It is often viewed in American folklife as a testing ground for manhood or a place to achieve self-reliance. The forest was a resource for trapping, fur trade, and hunting. Decoys used in bird hunting were made from the forest's wood, the body typically carved from softwood and the more detailed head from hardwood. Decoys work when they fool the game, and perceptions of what worked informed the traditions and variations of hunter-carvers. Hunters pursuing their own livelihood were joined at the end of the nineteenth century by those hunting for the upper-class market in game. Since 1900, the forest has been seen as a place of personal renewal, standing in opposition to urban civilization, and hosting resorts, camping, and other forms of ecotourism.

Americans have generally preferred to clear the forests for farming rather than live more intimately with them. Using trees to fence the property and to fashion homes, barns, corn cribs, and animal pens has enabled people to lay cultural claim to the land. Variations in building traditions reveal the cultural borders of different ethnic groups and their paths of settlement. The log house, especially associated with mid-Atlantic settlement, was constructed from the surrounding forest and encouraged mobility into the frontier. Construction of houses, barns, and outbuildings made use of the same techniques: Hardwood logs, typically hewn flat with an adze inside and out, were cut or "notched" at the ends so as to interlock at the cabin's corners. Specific notching systems reflect the origins of the settlers and include the saddle notch (the Upland South, also common in the West), diamond notch (North Carolina, perhaps of Cherokee origin), square or flat notch (the northern Midwest via Pennsylvania), and half-dovetail (the central Midwest via the Upland South) and full-dovetail notches (Pennsylvania German).

Wooden Objects

Carpenters and wheelwrights, among others whose occupations are devoted to woodcraft, select wood based on knowledge of the precise properties required by the object they are making. Lightweight panels and flat-sided pieces used in carpentry, cabinetmaking, and casket making are made of softwoods, while hardwoods are used when special strength or resiliency is required of the wood, or when the design requires the carving or cutting of joints. Tool handles, pegs for joints, spring-pole lathes, musical instruments, chair legs, baskets, bentwood furniture, wooden gears, canes, decorative figures, and structures are all typically made of hardwood. Coopering, the manufacture of storage casks, distinguishes between containers to hold and transport dry materials, made of softwood, and those to store liquids, made of hardwood that resists decay when wet. In shipbuilding, oak was especially sought for the frame, upper planking, pegs, pulleys, heavy-duty equipment, and carved figureheads, while spruce was desired for the masts, and other softwoods were used for lower planking and interior walls. Unlike most other craftsworkers, shipbuilders sought naturally curved wood or created curves by steaming pieces and bolting them together. By-products of wood— wood tar and varnishes from wood resins—were used as sealants and waterproofing agents.

The wood used for instruments must provide resonance and tone, the result of its ability to transmit vibration. Craftsworkers select heartwood, the dead-center section of the tree, which contains metabolic wastes, resins, and oils that add to the tone. The wood must also be very dry; the use of wood seasoned for over a century is not uncommon. Wind instruments tend to be made wholly of softwood; Native American flutes were fashioned from ash, box elder, cane, pipewood, and especially cedar, either hollowed out with a bowed borer or a heated iron rod, or made from two halves glued together with tree pitch and wrapped with hide or sinew. Pieces of hardwood carved in the shape of a bird or other creature were often fitted. Instruments requiring soundboards tend to mix softwood and hardwood. Softwoods are used for the soundboards of fiddles and mountain dulcimers, while hardwoods such as cherry or black walnut are used for the sides, bridge, neck, frets, and tuning pegs. The way the different woods work together is also an important consideration. To achieve a better sound, the frames of modern banjos are often laminates combining softwood and hardwood.

Detail in design goes hand in hand with knowledge of the precise properties of woods, and even an item as simple as a chair can be surprisingly complex. Shaker chairs use maple for the legs, and hickory or birch for the stretchers between them. The stretchers are fitted into precisely cut sockets so that the chairs slant slightly backward for comfort. The rear legs were often hollowed out at the bottom to hold a round maple-wood ball, held in place by a leather thong, that took the sitter's weight when the chair tipped backward. This technique allowed sitters to lean back with the back legs remaining flat on the floor. Chairs made in southern Indiana use fresh red oak for the legs, with stretchers of seasoned hickory. The legs are tapered, and the green wood easily curves back and out, a shape partly maintained by the back slats. The ends of the stretchers interlock within the legs; set into the sockets in the green wood, the dry hickory swells to make a tight joint.

Wood and Community

The process of creating in wood can serve as a basis of community identity. The Amish view barn raisings, for example, as essential to their sense of community. Conducted out of an ethic of mutual assistance, they are also occasions for socialization through cooking and eating food and playing games, and demonstrations of craftsmanship and teamwork. In the early days of logging, teams of day laborers learned the skills for working in dangerous conditions, mastered the specialized language of the trade, and developed a work ethic based on self-reliance and reliance on others in the team. As logging changed to include families in towns, these communities held civic festivals to promote their values through the symbolic display of logs, trucks, images of the woods, the heroic figure of Paul Bunyan, and contests of skill. Logger folk art in wood includes decorated tool handles, carved cedar fans, miniaturized logging tools carved out of wood kept in glass bottles, and boxes shaped like books.

In the religious communities of the Shakers, work was an expression of faith and of duty to God. The craftsworker as an instrument of God's care, enabled wood to respond to the call of God, to become a holy thing, whether a chair or a house of worship. The forms taken by Shaker furniture embody the ideals of simplicity and utility. Shaker design calls for diminishing size and increasing spacing of repeated elements, such as drawers or chair slats. Shaker carpenters studied the properties of different woods and combined different varieties accordingly—pine for frames and panels; maple or chestnut for carved or turned posts and for small wheels and gears; hickory for pins and pegs; birch for planes, wooden tools, and bentwood boxes; and ash for baskets. The wooden objects for which they are known include bentwood boxes, spinning wheels and yarn reels, cabinets and chests, sewing desks and work stands, wheelbarrows, and chairs.

Not dissimilarly, the wooden masks of the Native Americans of the Northwest Coast are means by which the supernatural world is made visible. Carved from local wood and painted, balancing geometric and organic line and shape, these masks depict a variety of human and animal figures, and engage the participants in rituals and symbolic communication. In the late eighteenth century, trade with Europeans brought superior cutting tools, which facilitated the construction of masks with moving parts. The single mask is carved from a solid piece of wood, while the mechanical mask uses strings or hinges to animate its eyes, mouth, or other features. The transformation mask consists of an outer mask that is opened dramatically during ritual to reveal an inner mask.

Wood and the woods also play a vital role in the realm of play and the imagination. Trees in children's play often become transformed into woods where wild beasts roam and chasing games occur. In hide-and-seek, a wooden pole often serves as a place where children are "safe"—a metaphor for home, away from the chasing "it." Specific types of wood are used in making the equipment for many sports (such as ash for baseball bats). Groups such as the Boy Scouts use woodcraft to foster cohesion and instill values, and members carve plaques and neckerchief "woggles" as tokens of ability and identity, while college fraternities display the paddles formerly prominent in initiation rites. Play with wood also involves replication or reiteration of the world. Wooden shoes, intended as practical work footwear, become instruments of creativity when used in clog dancing. Objects associated with working life reproduced in miniature, such as model ships in bottles, serve the maker as an opportunity for leisure as well as for gaining mastery over tough work experiences. Carving wooden chains and caged balls, often associated with older men from rural areas, may be used to demonstrate the skill of their makers and given to friends, children, and grandchildren as tokens connecting generations.

Perhaps in connection with their primeval symbolism, trees found representation on gravestones during the nineteenth and early twentieth centuries. Featured motifs on stone markers included the weeping willow and the tree of life. Tree stumps carved from stone often included renderings of hunting gear, tools, and representative household artifacts. Tree-stump gravestones appealed to fraternal groups such as the Foresters and Modern Woodmen of America, who, as a death benefit for members, provided stones carved in the shape of a tree stump or a stack of cut wood, featuring axes, beetles, and wedges, symbolizing workmanship and the progress of culture.

Modern Adaptations

As the availability of wood changed with advancing settlement and modernization, traditional craft processes changed as well. For example, many traditional basket makers and chair caners in the twenty-first century get their reeds from importers. Others adapt their skills to new wood products. Amish craftsworkers, for instance, have built workshops on their farms for making modern utility sheds, rustic chairs, and garden furniture as a major source of income.

Some woodcrafts, such as decoy carving, continue to be practiced, but the objects are more frequently made for display or collection than for actual hunting. Nevertheless, many wooden artifacts are not easily replaced. Wood is still used to make railroad ties and telephone poles, some of which are being recycled into alternative uses, such as railroad-tie houses in the American West. Power tools introduced during the twentieth century such as chainsaws are used by a new breed of craftsworkers to create massive sculptures (often featuring forest animals such as bears and eagles) out of tree trunks, a craft widely demonstrated at local fairs and festivals.

Woodcraft persists in the twenty-first century because what is made in wood endures, and often evokes folklife. It becomes collectible, restorable, and presentable. Woodcraft is often featured at art and folk festivals as reminders of regional heritage that appeal to tourists in places such as Appalachia, New England, the Ozarks, and the Upper Midwest that are associated with America's frontier or "wooden age" or its logging and shipbuilding heritage. The power of wood as a creative medium lies in its reminder of the transformation of nature through human intervention, the image of clearing the forest for settlement, and the appeal of versatility for those who would link to or revive complex craft traditions.

John Cash

See also: Barn Raising; Barns; Baskets and Basketry; Craft; Folk Art; Houses; Paper Arts.

Sources

Andrews, Edward Deming, and Faith Andrews. *Religion in Wood! A Book of Shaker Furniture.* Bloomington: Indiana University Press, 1966.

Bronner, Simon J. *The Carver's Art: Crafting Meaning from Wood.* Lexington: University Press of Kentucky, 1996.

Dodds, Richard J.S., and Pete Lesher, eds. *A Heritage in Wood: The Chesapeake Bay Maritime Museum's Small Craft Collection.* St. Michael's, MD: Chesapeake Bay Maritime Museum, 1992.

Earnest, Adele. *The Art of the Decoy: American Bird Carvings.* New York: Bramhall House, 1965.

James-Duguid, Charlene. *Work as Art: Idaho Logging as an Aesthetic Moment.* Moscow: University of Idaho Press, 1996.

Jones, Michael Owen. *Craftsman of the Cumberlands: Tradition and Creativity.* Lexington: University Press of Kentucky, 1989.

Norris, Karen, and Ralph Norris. *Northwest Carving Traditions.* Atglen, PA: Schiffer, 1999.

Roberts, Warren E. *Log Buildings of Southern Indiana.* Bloomington, IN: Trickster Press, 1996.

Sherman, Sharon R. *Chain-Saw Sculptor: The Art of J. Chester "Skip" Armstrong.* Jackson: University Press of Mississippi, 1995.

WRESTLING, PROFESSIONAL

Professional wrestlers share with one another a theatrical performance that includes a stage, or ring, on which narratives are acted out and characters are presented. As such, the folklife of professional wrestlers embodies traditions of theater as well as sport. Fans and wrestlers participate in a cultural scene with expectations of seeing performances and hearing narratives in and out of the ring that may be unrelated to the outcome of a match. While characterized along with boxing as a manly combat tradition, the cultural scene of wrestling is distinct from that of professional boxing, which has been described as irreducibly concise—primarily about the declaration of a winner. Whereas boxing proceeds with an inevitable gravity toward certain resolution, professional wrestling defers resolution for as long as possible. Wrestling claims a vast and ever-changing array of motifs, props, paraphernalia, and symbols that distract attention from the contest at hand and, in particularly manic moments, seemingly threaten to overwhelm its coherence altogether.

Even women take part in the dramatic performance—with its own heroes, villains, props, paraphernalia, and motifs—that is professional wrestling. A few scholars have pointed out the similarities between the structure of wrestling matches and that of folk tales. *(Regis Martin/Getty Images Entertainment)*

Folk Narratives

Boxing matches—no matter how hedged about they might be by the compelling biographies of their participants or the prefight hype to which these biographies contribute—ultimately are sporting events that produce winners and losers. Professional wrestling, on the other hand—no matter how legitimately and even hyperbolically athletic its participants might be—ultimately is a dramatic spectacle that produces not winners and losers but heroes and villains. Like all sport, boxing only secondarily can be described as tragic or comic in its outcomes; professional wrestling, however, is tragicomic in the most overt and immediate manner possible. Finally, while both boxing and wrestling share an omnivorous profit-making motive, boxing matches could conceivably be carried out in the complete absence of an audience, while professional wrestling exists for no reason other than to entertain.

The popularity of professional wrestling derives from the tried and true nature of its plot. It can be claimed with plausibility that to have seen one professional wrestling match is to have seen them all. In this regard, professional wrestling matches are quintessentially "popular": not simply by virtue of the fact that they draw on contemporary cultural referents in order to establish the identity of their contestants but, more profoundly, in the manner in which each match, no matter how apparently spontaneous, is based on a formula of deeply proven appeal.

The formula of wrestling matches bears a striking resemblance to the structure of traditional folktales. Indeed, a structural analysis of the repeatable sequences of events and characters of folktales (as suggested by folklorist Vladimir Propp for a "morphology" of Russian folktales, whose identified themes or functions are outlined below) is readily applicable to the predictable pattern of wrestling matches. On the broadest level, a match begins with initial Villainy or Supremacy; through intermediate maneuvers, Villainy receives Retribution or Supremacy encounters further Villainy. Sequences of Supremacy-Villainy-Retribution are repeated and recombined until the formulaic ending resolves the final structure: Villainy Victorious or Supremacy Supreme. Similarly, the heroes and villains of wrestling matches who carry out these acts, along with their allies and antagonists, bear many of the same characteristics as their folktale counterparts.

One major difference, of course, is that whereas the characters of folktales are merely depicted in the spoken word or on the written page, the characters of professional wrestling actually come to life in a ring that is tantamount to a stage. Part of wrestling's considerable folk appeal derives from the fact that its contestants, in the very visible flesh, actually enact the plots of folktales and display the stock traits of their characters that are otherwise accessible only through the imagination. Professional wrestling, in other words, makes the fantastic quality of the spoken or printed tale palpable. Furthermore, while professional wrestling "exhibitions" were commonplace as long ago as the beginning of the last century, the advent of television (the early acceptance of which was considerably facilitated by the broadcasting of professional wrestling matches) helped wrestling begin to achieve what is now its contemporary status as a common cultural denominator. It has thus traveled from folk origins to local arenas to large stadiums on the way to becoming part of the everyday vernacular of American life.

Social Traditions

The broad appeal of wrestling is consistent with its perpetuation of an elemental plot of enduring power. At its simplest level, professional wrestling boils down to a contest between good and evil. That contest has proven to be gripping regardless of whether the competitors of the moment are real or unreal, Robin Hood and his band of merry men versus the oppressive lords of property and privilege, working-class heroes in wrestling garb against high-class sophisticates entering the ring, or American patriots against the invisible enemies of freedom and justice. If the scenario has resonated with varied peoples across time and space, it certainly has been integral to the American worldview, perhaps especially among America's less affluent and more politically conservative and fiercely patriotic citizens. Despite broad appeal, it is from among this group of citizens that professional wrestling has tended to draw its primary audience. While attitudes certainly vary among them, it is fair to say that these are people who generally respect and defer to authority but who see manifested in the person of the referee an embodiment of the imperfection and limitations of justice. They are sufficiently conversant with contemporary events to have strong opinions about how justice is meted out in the prominent national and international conflicts that provide a frequent backdrop for professional wrestling.

The identities of the wrestlers, so crucial to the meaning of the action they engage in, are constructed in such a way as to be immediately comprehensible to this audience: while they might be more or less strong and more or less artful, the combatants are either emphatically villainous or emphatically heroic. They achieve these identities by aligning themselves with readily apparent cultural stereotypes augmented by the display of topical symbols and a rhetoric, employed during the interview and prefight routines, that is either decent (grounded in values embraced by the fans) or despicable (disparaging of values embraced by the fans) both in content and style of delivery. To some extent, wrestlers also may be distinguished on the basis of whether they employ "clean" or "dirty" tactics, but at some point most matches deteriorate into physical brawls in which anything goes for hero and villain alike. The distinction between hero and villain remains clear nevertheless, given the clarity and force of the symbolic contest.

Masculinity and Sexuality

This is not to say, however, that the world of professional wrestling is without ambiguity, especially in regard to exhibited masculinity. Professional wrestling engages its audience precisely by putting on display the overly developed bodies of underdressed men. Moreover, to the extent that these men are dressed, it is with a deliberateness that reveals not only their moral alignment (as hero or villain) but also a heightened level of narcissistic preoccupation at odds with the common conception of masculinity. Indeed, when the wrestlers embrace one another in the inevitable intimacy required for either one to achieve dominance, it is under the intense gaze of an audience whose own presumably traditional sexual orientation must be called into question by virtue of the pleasure it takes in watching what is at least covertly a homoerotic spectacle.

Nor is this aspect of wrestling always merely implied. At least since the time of Gorgeous George, certain wrestlers have based their personae on a flirtation with effeminacy. Performers such as "Pretty Boy" Rick Flair, Golddust, and the Valiant Brothers have established themselves as "heels" by inducing what Marjorie Garber in *Vested Interests* (1997) refers to as a "category crisis" resulting from the blurring of their genders. The Valiant Brothers, for instance, a tag team prominent in the Philadelphia area during the 1970s, sported heart-shaped pink sunglasses, long platinum hair, earrings, feminine capes, and wrestling tights with provocative slogans written across their buttocks. At the same time, they were muscular men with highly developed physiques and a "take no prisoners" style inside the ring.

The contradictory relationship between the Valiant Brothers' soft appearance and their hard manner produced a destabilizing effect on the audience, who at one and the same time delighted in ridiculing these wrestlers for their overtly homoerotic orientation and were forced to acknowledge their equally visible and enviable strength.

One way in which fans are reminded of the sexual power of the wrestlers, however, is the display of attractive "trophy" girlfriends or wives at ringside, typically dressed in sexually suggestive feminine attire. One of the well-known narratives in wrestling, for example, was the relationship of Randy "Macho Man" Savage during the 1990s with the sultry and sophisticatedly dressed "Miss Elizabeth," who stood in his corner of the ring. Performed narratives included Savage turning against his friend Hulk Hogan after accusing him of lusting after Elizabeth, and patriarchally "defending her honor" after Jake "The Snake" Roberts slapped her. The narrative has also been altered to convey the empowerment of women, such as the linkage of male wrestlers to "tough" female wrestling partners—for example, Hunter Hearst Helmsley and the muscular, aggressive Chyna (Joanie Laurer).

Surveys of wrestling fans indicate that professional wrestling audiences are alert to and appreciative of the strategies of manipulation to which they are subjected (and for which they pay) and that they are quite capable of discerning the difference between open-ended sporting events and predetermined dramatic ones. That discriminatory ability does not negate the fact that, as with other instances of effective drama, there are moments at which many fans become sufficiently engaged as to suspend their skepticism and invest themselves in the outcome of a match. Indeed, one of the realities of professional wrestling is that serious and sustained injury does occur among wrestlers.

Wrestling and Culture

Wrestling works on several levels in American culture. On a structural level, it is a textual phenomenon that derives from a long tradition of formulaic expression; on a socioeconomic level, it plays out in the ring as a social tradition of working-class struggle against elites and appeals to the antiauthoritarianism, masculinity, and patriotism associated with "middle America"; on a psychological level, it draws from and comments on the complex universe of its audience in matters such as violence, gender roles, and ethnicity.

Unlike collegiate or Olympic wrestling, whose terms are not in tension with each other, professional wrestling is oxymoronic. Between the two terms of its compound name unfolds an utterly conventional but highly imaginative and dynamic activity that manages to simulate and adorn violence in a manner sufficiently compelling to guarantee the continued affection of all those who unabashedly find pleasure in being professional wrestling fans and to withstand the scorn of all those who would demean or derogate it as a silly charade. Fans, wrestlers, and accompanying characters create a community that understands the folklife it has created and revels in the invented traditions of the ring.

Mark E. Workman

See also: Bodybuilders and Weightlifters; Drama; Dress and Costume; Popular Culture.

Sources

Gutowski, John A. "The Art of Professional Wrestling: Folk Expression in Mass Culture." *Keystone Folklore Quarterly* 17 (1972): 41–50.

Leverette, Marc. *Professional Wrestling: The Myth, the Mat, and American Popular Culture.* Ceredigion, UK: Edwin Mellen Press, 2003.

Mazer, Sharon. *Professional Wrestling: Sport and Spectacle.* Jackson: University Press of Mississippi, 1998.

Workman, Mark E. "The Differential Perception of Popular Dramatic Events." *Keystone Folklore* 23 (1979): 1–10.

———. "Dramaturgical Aspects of Professional Wrestling Matches." *Folklore Forum* 10 (1977): 14–20.

ZYDECO

The term "zydeco" refers to a musical tradition started by French-speaking black Creoles in the bayou region of southwest Louisiana and is strongly associated with dance and social events. It features the accordion and rubboard (or *froittoir*, corrugated steel worn as a vest and scraped for rhythmic effect) as principal instruments and is traditionally sung in French. In American folklife, the music is significant as a central marker of Louisiana Creole identity and is frequently associated with joyful exuberance.

"Creole" was a term used to identify French-speaking blacks and differentiate them from the French-speaking whites of Acadian (later Cajun) descent. Creoles included blacks of various ancestries, including African, Native American, French, and Caribbean. Each group had musical and cultural traditions that contributed to the emergence of Creole culture, which included a French Creole dialect.

Pioneers

The word "zydeco" and the music it referred to did not emerge until the 1940s. Before that time, Cajun music and what would develop into zydeco were more closely linked, especially by the use of the fiddle, which would be phased out by zydeco. The introduction of the accordion had a dynamic effect on Cajun music. The black Creole accordionist Amédé Ardoin was an early pioneer of zydeco, and his songs remain Cajun standards to this day. From the beginning, dance was closely linked to the music, and the accordion provided the accompaniment for waltzes and two-steps at house parties. When French-speaking blacks first began to adopt the accordion, the dance music they created became known as *la-la* (sometimes *juré* and *pic-nic*), an early precursor to zydeco.

Modern zydeco was developed and popularized by the accordion player Clifton Chenier. Inspired by the urban blues he heard in cities such as Houston, Chenier incorporated the instrumentation of the urban blues ensemble, including electric guitar, bass, and drums, into a high-energy style that also inspired a new, fevered style of dancing. As the modern incarnation of zydeco took shape, the location of the performance also changed. In the beginning, house parties—informal social gatherings that included both young and old—were the norm for *la-la* dances. As zydeco spread and became popular, however, house parties were replaced by dance halls, which attracted a rougher, less family-oriented crowd and included alcohol consumption.

The word "zydeco" was widely used to describe Chenier's music by the 1950s, though the origin of the term is still debated today. According to one popular explanation, it derived from the French phrase *zydeco sont pas sale* (roughly translated as "the snap beans aren't salty"), referring to the time when Creoles could not afford the salty meat used to season their beans. As folklorists sought to chronicle the traditional folk music of southwestern Louisiana and the southeastern edge of Texas, the term became more widely employed.

If Clifton Chenier is regarded as the "King of

The Creole accordionist and pianist Buckwheat Zydeco (Stanley Dural), a protégé of the great Clifton Chenier, has been instrumental in taking zydeco music from the bayous of Louisiana to the world stage. *(Tim Mosenfelder/Getty Images Entertainment)*

Zydeco also has a "queen"—Queen Ida and her Bon Ton Zydeco Band. Born in Lake Charles, Louisiana, as Ida Lewis, to a family of rice farmers, she learned to play the accordion from her mother and musicians performing at Saturday night *fai do dos*, or community parties. She recalled lively social events involving cooking Creole dishes for gatherings of thirty to forty people, and this connection of music and food continues in her stage persona today. During the mid-1940s, she moved with her family to San Francisco, where a community of French-speaking Louisianans formed around music and food. It was not until the mid-1970s, however, that she began playing with her brother Al Rapone's band at French dances in San Francisco's Creole community. She became the first female accordionist to lead a zydeco band and in 1983 won a Grammy Award for her *On Tour* album, adding to her international renown. Like the male zydeco stars, she, too, has made the music a family affair, bringing her accordion-playing son, Myrick "Freeze" Guillory, into the group, and frequently featuring her brothers Al Rapone and Willie Lewis along with another son, Ronald, on rubboard.

New Generations

Zydeco has persevered in part because of the strong commitment passed down from generation to generation. Second-generation zydeco musicians include Rockin Dopsie, Jr., C.J. Chenier, Geno Delafose (son of John), and Keith Frank (son of Preston). Chris Ardoin (his great-uncle was Amédé) and his band, Double Clutchin', are vibrant modern performers, as are his brother Sean and band ZydeKool. Children often perform in zydeco bands beginning at a tender age, which results in both the music and the tradition being ingrained into their lives.

Zydeco traditions remain firmly entrenched in a club circuit that runs from Lafayette, Louisiana, through Port Arthur and Beaumont, Texas, and into Houston. Hamilton's Place and El Sid-O's in Lafayette, Richard's and the Offshore Lounge in Latwell, the Dauphine Club in Sparks, and Slim's Y-Ki-Ki in Opelousas are just a few

Zydeco," other important figures helped the music style emerge as a unified force. Boozoo Chavis is credited with the first hit zydeco song, "Paper in My Shoe" (1954), portraying the hardships of poverty-stricken Creoles. His primitive accordion style harkened back to zydeco's rural roots. Rockin' Dopsie (Alton Rubin) was an early friend of Chenier who also advanced zydeco music during its infancy. After Chenier's death, Dopsie would be crowned the new king of zydeco, a tradition of designating ethnic royalty that would continue after his passing. Buckwheat Zydeco (Stanley Dural) was a former Chenier protégé who left Chenier's Red Hot Louisiana Band in 1978 to venture out on his own. He became one of the most recognizable figures in contemporary zydeco and was instrumental in taking zydeco from its Louisiana confines to the worldwide stage.

examples of clubs where zydeco music still flourishes today. The annual Southwest Louisiana Zydeco Festival is held in Plaisance on Labor Day weekend, and a number of zydeco bands have performed at the popular New Orleans Jazz and Heritage Festival. A cultural awareness association known as CREOLE (Cultural Resource Education of Linguistic Enrichment) has been instrumental in preserving zydeco traditions, as well as the Creole dialect and foods, which are inextricably linked to the music. Today in southwest Louisiana it is common to hear zydeco accompanying trail rides and rodeos, gumbo cook-offs, and dance parties.

While Clifton Chenier is credited with forming zydeco music by fusing the traditional sounds of *la-la* with urban blues, twenty-first-century performers are no less adventurous. Nouveau zydeco incorporates many elements of modern popular music, including those of rock, funk, contemporary rhythm and blues, and even rap and hip-hop. Despite bringing in these outside influences, nouveau zydeco keeps the sound and style of traditional zydeco by retaining the signature instruments of accordion and rubboard.

Even with its concessions to modern styles, nouveau zydeco still has far more in common with its folk roots than with mainstream pop.

Troy Peechatka

See also: Blues; Cajun Communities; Creoles, Louisiana; Folk Music and Song; New Orleans.

Sources

Ancelet, Barry Jean. "Zydeco/Zarico: The Term and the Tradition." In *Creoles of Color of the Gulf South*, ed. James H. Dorman, 126–43. Knoxville: University of Tennessee Press, 1996.

Del Sesto, Steven L. "Cajun Music and Zydeco: Notes on the Music of Southern Louisiana." *Louisiana Folklore Miscellany* 4 (1976–1980): 88–101.

Kuhlken, Robert, and Rocky Sexton. "The Geography of Zydeco Music." In *The Sounds of People and Places: A Geography of American Folk and Popular Music*, ed. George O. Carney, 63–76. Lanham, MD: Rowman and Littlefield, 1994.

Minton, John. "Creole Community and Mass Communication: Houston Zydeco as a Mediated Tradition." *Journal of Folklore Research* 32 (1995): 1–19.

Sandmel, Ben. *Zydeco!* Jackson: University Press of Mississippi, 1999.

Savoy, Ann Allen. "Cajun and Zydeco: The Musics of French Southwest Louisiana." In *American Roots Music*, ed. Robert Santelli, Holly George-Warren, and Jim Brown, 104–25. New York: Harry N. Abrams, 2001.

Bibliography

Published Sources

Aarne, Antti. *The Types of the Folktale: A Classification and Bibliography*, translated and enlarged by Stith Thompson. 1961. Reprint, Helsinki: Suomalainen Tiedeakatemia, 1987.

Abernethy, Francis Edward, ed. *The Folklore of Texan Cultures*. Austin: Encino Press, 1974.

———, ed. *Observations and Reflections on Texas Folklore*. Austin: Encino, 1972.

———. *The Texas Folklore Society*. Vol. 1, *1909–1943*; vol. 2, *1943–1971*; vol. 3, *1971–2000*. Denton: University of North Texas Press, 1992, 1994, 2000.

———, ed. *Texas Toys and Games*. Dallas, TX: Southern Methodist University Press, 1989.

Abernethy, Francis Edward, Jerry Bryan Lincecum, and Frances B. Vick, eds. *The Family Saga: A Collection of Texas Family Legends*. Denton: University of North Texas Press, 2003.

Abernethy, Francis Edward, Patrick B. Mullen, and Alan B. Govenar, eds. *Juneteenth Texas: Essays in African-American Folklore*. Denton: University of North Texas Press, 1996.

Abraham, Nabeel, and Andrew Shryock, eds. *Arab Detroit: From Margin to Mainstream*. Detroit, MI: Wayne State University Press, 2000.

Abraham, Sameer Y., and Nabeel Abraham, eds. *Arabs in the New World: Studies on Arab-American Communities*. Detroit, MI: Center for Urban Studies, Wayne State University, 1981.

Abrahams, Roger D. *Deep Down in the Jungle . . . Negro Narrative Folklore from the Streets of Philadelphia*. Chicago: Aldine, 1970.

———. "Interpreting Folklore Ethnographically and Sociologically." In *Handbook of American Folklore*, ed. Richard M. Dorson, 345–50. Bloomington: Indiana University Press, 1983.

———. "Introductory Remarks to a Rhetorical Theory of Folklore." *Journal of American Folklore* 81 (1968): 143–58.

———. "Phantoms of Romantic Nationalism in Folkloristics." *Journal of American Folklore* 106, no. 419 (1993): 3–37.

———. *Positively Black*. Englewood Cliffs, NJ: Prentice-Hall, 1970.

———. *Singing the Master: The Emergence of African American Culture in the Plantation South*. New York: Pantheon, 1992.

Abrahams, Roger D., and Alan Dundes. "Riddles." In *Folklore and Folklife*, ed. Richard Dorson, 129–43. Chicago: University of Chicago Press, 1972.

Abrahams, Roger D., and George Foss. *Anglo-American Folksong Style*. Englewood Cliffs, NJ: Prentice-Hall, 1968.

Abramovitch, Ilana, and Seán Galvin, eds. *Jews of Brooklyn*. Hanover, NH: University Press of New England for Brandeis University Press, 2002.

Achey, Jeff, Dudley Chelton, and Bob Godfrey. *Climb! The History of Rock Climbing in Colorado*. Seattle, WA: Mountaineers Book, 2002.

Adamczyk, Amy. "On Thanksgiving and Collective Memory: Constructing the American Tradition." *Journal of Historical Sociology* 15, no. 3 (2002): 343–65.

Adams, Brooks, and David Revere McFadden. *Hair*. New York: Cooper-Hewitt Museum, 1980.

Adams, Doug. *Changing Biblical Imagery and Artistic Identity in Twentieth Century Liturgical Dance*. Richmond, VA: Sharing Company, 1982.

Adams, Michael Henry. *Harlem: Lost and Found*. New York: Monacelli, 2002.

Adler, Margot. *Drawing Down the Moon: Witches, Druids, Goddess Worshipers, and Other Pagans in America Today*. Revised and expanded edition. New York: Penguin Putnam, 1997.

Adler, Shelley R. "Sudden Unexpected Nocturnal Death Syndrome Among Hmong Immigrants: Examining the Role of the 'Nightmare.'" *Journal of American Folklore* 104 (1991): 54–71.

Adorno, Theodor W. *The Culture Industry: Selected Essays on Mass Culture.* London: Routledge, 1991.

Agar, Michael. *The Professional Stranger: An Informal Introduction to Ethnography.* 2nd ed. New York: Academic Press, 1996.

Albers, Marjorie K. *The Amana People and Their Furniture.* Ames: Iowa State University Press, 1990.

Albertsen, Karsten-Gerhard. *The History and Life of the Reidenbach Mennonites (Thirty-Fivers).* Morgantown, PA: Mastoff Press, 1996.

Alcoholics Anonymous. 4th ed. New York: Alcoholics Anonymous World Services, 2000.

Alcoholics Anonymous. *Twelve Steps and Twelve Traditions.* Center City, MN: Hazelden, 1989.

Alexander, Alex Edward. "The Russian Chastushka Abroad." *Journal of American Folklore* 89 (1976): 335–41.

Alexander, John, and James Lazell. *Ribbon of Sand: The Amazing Convergence of the Ocean and the Outer Banks.* Chapel Hill, NC: Algonquin, 1992.

Alexander, June Granatir. *The Immigrant Church and Community: Pittsburgh's Slovak Catholics and Lutherans, 1880–1915.* Pittsburgh: University of Pittsburgh Press, 1987.

Allen, Barbara. "Personal Experience Narratives: Use and Meaning in Interaction." *Folklore and Mythology Studies* 2 (1978): 5–7.

Allen, Barbara, and Thomas J. Schlereth, eds. *Sense of Place: American Regional Cultures.* Lexington: University Press of Kentucky, 1990.

Allen, Irving Lewis. *The City in Slang: New York Life and Popular Speech.* New York: Oxford University Press, 1993.

Allen, John W. *It Happened in Southern Illinois.* Carbondale: Central Publication, Southern Illinois University, 1968.

———. *Legends and Lore of Southern Illinois.* Carbondale: Central Publications, Southern Illinois University, 1963.

Allen, Lee. "The Superstitions of Baseball Players." *New York Folklore Quarterly* 20 (1964): 98–109.

Allen, Ray. "J'Ouvert in Brooklyn Carnival." *Western Folklore* 58 (1999): 255–77.

Allen, Ray, and Les Slater. "Steel Pan Grows in Brooklyn: Trinidadian Music and Cultural Identity." In *Island Sounds in the Global City: Caribbean Popular Music and Identity in New York,* ed. Ray Allen and Lois Wilcken, 114–37. Urbana: University of Illinois Press, 1998.

Almeida, Raymond A. "*Nos Ku Nos:* A Transnational Cape Verdean Connection." In *1995 Festival of American Folklife,* ed. Carla M. Borden, 18–26. Washington, DC: Smithsonian Institution Press, 1995.

Alotta, Robert I. *Signposts and Settlers: The History of Place Names in the Middle Atlantic States.* Chicago: Bonus Books, 1992.

Altankov, Nikolay G. *The Bulgarian-Americans.* Palo Alto, CA: Ragusan, 1979.

———. "Bulgarians." In *Harvard Encyclopedia of American Ethnic Groups,* ed. Stephan Thernstrom, 186–89. Cambridge, MA: Belknap Press of Harvard University Press, 1980.

Altman, Irwin, and Joseph Ginat. *Polygamous Families in Contemporary Society.* Cambridge: Cambridge University Press, 1996.

Alvarez, Julia. *How the Garcia Girls Lost Their Accents.* New York: Plume, 1992.

American Folklore Society. "American Folklore Society Recommendations to the WIPO Intergovernmental Committee on Intellectual Property and Genetic Resources, Traditional Knowledge, and Folklore." *Journal of American Folklore* 117 (2004): 296–99.

Amira, John, and Steven Cornelius. *The Music of Santeria: Traditional Rhythms of the Bata Drums.* Crown Press, 1991.

Ancelet, Barry Jean. "Zydeco/Zarico: The Term and the Tradition." In *Creoles of Color of the Gulf South,* ed. James H. Dorman, 126–43. Knoxville: University of Tennessee Press, 1996.

Ancelet, Barry Jean, and Elemore Morgan. *Cajun and Creole Music Makers.* Jackson: University Press of Mississippi, 1999.

Ancelet, Barry Jean, Jay D. Edwards, and Glen Pitre. *Cajun Country.* Jackson: University Press of Mississippi, 1991.

Andelson, Jonathan G. "Routinization of Behavior in a Charismatic Leader." *American Ethnologist* 7 (1980): 716–33.

Anderson, E.N., Jr. "On the Folk Art of Landscaping." *Western Folklore* 31 (1972): 179–88.

Anderson, Harry, and Fred Olson. *Milwaukee: At the Gathering of the Waters.* Tulsa, OK: Continental Heritage Press, 1981.

Anderson, Jay, ed. *A Living History Reader.* Nashville, TN: American Association for State and Local History, 1991.

———. "Scholarship on Contemporary American Folk Foodways." *Ethnologia Europaea* 5 (1971): 56–63.

———. *Time Machines: The World of Living History*. Nashville, TN: American Association for State and Local History, 1984.

Andrews, Edward Deming. *The People Called Shakers: A Search for the Perfect Society*. New York: Dover Publications, 1963.

Andrews, Edward Deming, and Faith Andrews. *Religion in Wood: A Book of Shaker Furniture*. Bloomington: Indiana University Press, 1966.

Ansberry, Clare. *The Women of Troy Hill: The Backfence Virtues of Faith and Friendship*. New York: Harcourt, 2000.

Appelbaum, Diana. *The Glorious Fourth: An American Holiday, an American History*. New York: Facts on File, 1989.

———. *Thanksgiving: An American Holiday, an American History*. New York: Facts on File, 1984.

Apter, Emily, and William Pietz, eds. *Fetishism as Cultural Discourse*. Ithaca, NY: Cornell University Press, 1993.

Aquila, Richard, ed. *Wanted Dead or Alive: The American West in Popular Culture*. Urbana: University of Illinois Press, 1996.

Arends, Shirly Fisher. *The Central Dakota Germans: Their History, Language, and Culture*. Washington, DC: Georgetown University Press, 1989.

Armistead, Samuel G., and Joseph H. Silverman. *Judeo-Spanish Ballads from Bosnia*. Philadelphia: University of Pennsylvania Press, 1971.

Armstrong, Elizabeth A. *Forging Gay Identities: Organizing Sexuality in San Francisco, 1950–1994*. Chicago: University of Chicago Press, 2002.

Arnett, David. *In the Trees of Tulsa: A Guide to the Chainsaw Art of Clayton Coss*. Tulsa: Crow Creek Publishing, 1995.

Arnett, Jeffrey Jensen. *Metalheads: Heavy Metal Music and Adolescent Alienation*. Boulder, CO: Westview, 1996.

Arnoldi, Mary Jo, and John W. Franklin. "Mali from Timbuktu to Washington." In *37th Annual Smithsonian Folklife Festival,* ed. Carla Borden, 40–67. Washington, DC: Center for Folklife and Cultural Heritage, Smithsonian Institution Press, 2003.

Arora, Shirley L. *Proverbial Comparisons and Related Expressions in Spanish Recorded in Los Angeles, California*. Berkeley: University of California Press, 1977.

Arrelano, Estevan. "Descansos." *New Mexico Magazine* 64 (February 1986): 42–44.

Arthur, Charles, and Michael Dash, eds. *Libète: A Haiti Anthology*. Princeton, NJ: Marcus Wiener, 1999.

Arthur, Eric, and Dudley Witney. *The Barn: A Vanishing Landmark in North America*. Toronto: M.F. Feheley Arts, 1972.

Arthur, John A. *Invisible Sojourners: African Immigrant Diaspora in the United States*. Westport, CT: Praeger, 2000.

Asada, Joanne, ed. *Finnish-American Folklore. The Legend of St. Urho*. Iowa City, IA: Penfield, 2001.

Levine, Robert M., and Asis Moises. *Cuban Miami*. New Brunswick, NJ: Rutgers University Press, 2000.

Asquith, Lindsay, and Marcel Vellinga, eds. *Vernacular Architecture in the 21st Century: Theory, Education, Practice*. London: Routledge/Spon, 2005.

Assael, Shaun. *Wide Open: Days and Nights on the NASCAR Tour*. New York: Ballantine Books, 1998.

Aswad, Barbara C. *Arabic Speaking Communities in American Cities*. Staten Island, NY: Center for Migration Studies of New York, 1974.

Atencio, Tomás. "Crypto-Jewish Remnants in Manito Society and Culture." *Jewish Folklore and Ethnology Review* 18 (1996): 59–67.

Atkins, Jacqueline Marx. *Shared Threads: Quilting Together Past and Present*. New York: Viking, 1994.

Attebery, Louie W., ed. *Idaho Folklife: Homesteads to Headstones*. Salt Lake City: University of Utah Press, 1985.

Attie, Alice. *Harlem: On the Verge*. New York: Quantuck Lane, 2003.

Au, Dennis M., and Joanna Brode. "The Lingering Shadow of New France: The French-Canadian Community of Monroe County, Michigan." In *Michigan Folklife Reader*, ed. C. Kurt Dewhurst and Yvonne Lockwood, 321–45. East Lansing: Michigan State University Press, 1987.

Augustyn, Frederick J., Jr. *Dictionary of Toys and Games in American Popular Culture*. Binghamton, NY: Haworth Reference Press, 2004.

Austerlitz, Paul. *Merengue: Dominican Music and Dominican Identity*. Philadelphia: Temple University Press, 1997.

Austin, Joe, and Michael Nevin Willard, eds. *Generations of Youth: Youth Cultures and History in*

Twentieth Century America. New York: New York University Press, 1998.

Axtell, Roger E. *Gestures: The Do's and Taboos of Body Language Around the World*. New York: John Wiley and Sons, 1991.

Babou, Cheikh Anta. "Brotherhood Solidarity, Education and Migration: The Role of the Dahiras Among the Murid Muslim Community of New York." *African Affairs* 101 (2002): 151–70.

Babson, Steve. *Working Detroit: The Making of a Union Town*. Detroit, MI: Wayne State University Press, 1986.

Bacon, Jean. *Life Lines: Community, Family, and Assimilation Among Asian Indian Immigrants*. New York: Oxford University Press, 1996.

Bacthi, Siang, InNgeun Baccam Soulinthavong, and Jack Lufkin. "'So We Stayed Together': The Tai Dam Immigrate to Iowa." *Palimpsest* 69, no. 4 (1988): 163–72.

Baddeley, Gavin. *Goth Chic: A Connoisseur's Guide to Dark Culture*. Medford, NJ: Plexus, 2002.

Bainbridge, William Sims. *Satan's Power*. Berkeley: University of California Press, 1978.

Baisly, Clair. *Cape Cod Architecture*. Orleans, MA: Parnassus, 1989.

Bakalian, Anny P. *Armenian-Americans: From Being to Feeling Armenian*. New Brunswick, NJ: Transaction, 1993.

Baker, Frank. *Methodism and the Love-Feast*. London: Epworth, 1957.

Baker, Margaret. *Wedding Customs and Folklore*. Lanham, MD: Rowman and Littlefield, 1977.

Baker, Ronald L. *Folklore in the Writings of Rowland E. Robinson*. Bowling Green, OH: Bowling Green University Popular Press, 1973.

———. "The Folklore of Students." In *Handbook of American Folklore*, ed. Richard M. Dorson, 106–14. Bloomington: Indiana University Press, 1983.

———. *Hoosier Folk Legends*. Bloomington: Indiana University Press, 1982.

———. *From Needmore to Prosperity: Hoosier Place Names in Folklore and History*. Bloomington: Indiana University Press, 1995.

———. *Jokelore: Humorous Folktales from Indiana*. Bloomington: Indiana University Press, 1986.

———. "Sense of Place in Place Name Studies: Some Needed Work in Onomastics." *Names* 49 (2001): 268–72.

Baker, Ronald L., and Simon J. Bronner. "'Letting Out Jack': Sex and Aggression in Manly Recitations." In *Manly Traditions: The Folk Roots of American Masculinities*, ed. Simon J. Bronner, 315–50. Bloomington: Indiana University Press, 2005.

Bal, Mieke, Jonathon Crewe, and Leo Spitzer, eds. *Acts of Memory: Cultural Recall in the Present*. Hanover, NH: University Press of New England, 1999.

Balaban, John, ed. *Ca dao Viet Nam: A Bilingual Anthology of Vietnamese Folk Poetry*. Greensboro, NC: Unicorn Press, 1980.

Baly, Monica E. *Nursing and Social Change*. New York: Routledge, 1995.

Balys, Jonas. "Lithuanian Folk Songs in the United States." *Journal of the International Folk Music Council* 3 (1951): 67–70.

Banks, Amanda Carson. *Birth Chairs, Midwives, and Medicine*. Jackson: University Press of Mississippi, 1999.

Bannatyne, Leslie Pratt. *Halloween: An American Holiday, An American History*. Gretna, LA: Pelican, 1998.

Banta, Melissa, and Curtis M. Hinsley. *From Site to Sight: Anthropology, Photography, and the Power of Imagery*. Cambridge, MA: Peabody Museum Press, 1986.

Barbour, Hugh, and J. William Frost. *The Quakers*. Westport, CT: Greenwood, 1988.

Barden, Thomas E., and John Ahern. *Hungarian American Toledo: Life and Times in Toledo's Birmingham Neighborhood*. Toledo, OH: University of Toledo Urban Affairs Center, 2002.

Barger, Ralph "Sonny," with Keith Zimmerman and Kent Zimmerman. *Hell's Angel: The Life and Times of Sonny Barger and the Hell's Angels Motorcycle Club*. New York: William Morrow, 2000.

Barich, Bill. "Trout and Salvation: A Week in the Rangeley Lakes." *New England Monthly* 1, no. 6 (1984): 42–49.

Barkun, Michael. *Disaster and the Millennium*. New Haven, CT: Yale University Press, 1974.

Barlow, William. *Looking Up at Down: The Emergence of Blues Culture*. Philadelphia: Temple University Press, 1989.

Barnes, H. Lee. *Dummy Up and Deal: Inside the Culture of Casino Dealing*. Reno: University of Nevada Press, 2002.

Barnett, H.G. "The Nature of the Potlatch." *American Anthropologist* 40 (1938): 349–58.

Baron, Robert, and Nicholas R. Spitzer, eds. *Public

Folklore. Washington, DC: Smithsonian Institution Press, 1992.

Barrick, Mac E. "Folklore and the Verbal Text." In *100 Years of American Folklore Studies*, ed. William M. Clements, 16–17. Washington, DC: American Folklore Society, 1988.

———. *German-American Folklore*. Little Rock, AR: August House, 1990.

Barsam, Richard. *The Vision of Robert Flaherty: The Artist as Myth and Filmmaker*. Bloomington: Indiana University Press, 1988.

Barthell, Diane L. *Amana: From Pietist Sect to American Community*. Lincoln: University of Nebraska Press, 1984.

Bartoletti, Susan Campbell. *Growing Up in Coal Country*. Boston: Houghton Mifflin, 1996.

Barton, H. Arnold. *A Folk Divided: Homeland Swedes and Swedish Americans, 1840–1940*. Studia multiethnica Upsaliensia 10. Uppsala: Acta Universitatis Upsaliensis, 1994.

Barton, Michael, and Larry Logue, eds. *The Civil War Soldier: A Historical Reader*. New York: New York University Press, 2002.

Bascom, William. "Four Functions of Folklore." In *The Study of Folklore*, ed. Alan Dundes, 279–98. Englewood Cliffs, NJ: Prentice-Hall, 1965.

Bashe, Philip. *Heavy Metal Thunder: The Music, Its History, Its Heroes*. Garden City, NY: Doubleday, 1985.

Bassett, Fletcher S. *Legends and Superstitions of the Sea and of Sailors in All Lands and at All Times*. 1885. Detroit: Singing Tree Press, 1971.

Batchelor, Dean. *The American Hot Rod*. Osceola, WI: MBI, 1995.

Batchelor, Mary, Marianne Watson, and Anne Wilde. *Voices in Harmony: Contemporary Women Celebrate Plural Marriage*. Springville, UT: Cedar Fort, 2000.

Batteau, Allen. *The Invention of Appalachia*. Tucson: University of Arizona Press, 1990.

Baughman, Ernest W. *Type and Motif Index of the Folktales of England and North America*. The Hague: Mouton, 1966.

Bauman, Richard, ed. *Folklore, Cultural Performances, and Entertainments: A Communications-Centered Handbook*. Oxford: Oxford University Press, 1992.

———. *Let Your Words Be Few: Symbolism of Speaking and Silence Among Seventeenth-Century Quakers*. Cambridge: Cambridge University Press, 1983.

———, ed. *Story, Performance and Event*. Cambridge: Cambridge University Press, 1986.

———. *Verbal Art as Performance*. Rowley, MA: Newbury House, 1977.

Bauman, Richard, and Roger D. Abrahams, eds. *"And Other Neighborly Names": Social Process and Cultural Image in Texas Folklore*. Austin: University of Texas Press, 1981.

Bauman, Richard, and Américo Paredes, eds. *Toward New Perspectives in Folklore*. Austin: University of Texas Press, 1972.

Bautista, Veltisezar. *Filipino Americans (1763–Present): Their History, Culture, and Traditions*. Warren, MI: Bookhaus, 2002.

Baxandall, Rosalyn, and Elizabeth Ewen. *Picture Windows: How the Suburbs Happened*. New York: Basic Books, 2000.

Bayard, Samuel P. *Dance to the Fiddle, March to the Fife: Instrumental Folk Tunes in Pennsylvania*. University Park: Pennsylvania State University Press, 1982.

Bayor, Ronald H., and Timothy J. Meagher, eds. *The New York Irish*. Baltimore: Johns Hopkins University Press, 1996.

Beal, Candy, and Carmine Prioli, eds. *Life at the Edge of the Sea: Essays on North Carolina's Coast and Coastal Culture*. Wilmington, NC: Coastal Carolina Press, 2002.

Bealle, John. *Public Worship, Private Faith: Sacred Harp and American Folksong*. Athens: University of Georgia Press, 1997.

Beardsley, John. *Gardens of Revelation: Environments by Visionary Artists*. New York: Abbeville Press, 1995.

Beatie, Russel H. *Saddles*. Norman: University of Oklahoma Press, 1981.

Beck, Ervin. *MennoFolk: Mennonite and Amish Folk Traditions*. Scottdale, PA: Herald, 2004.

Beck, Horace P. *Folklore and the Sea*. 1973. Reprint, Mystic, CT: Mystic Seaport Museum, 1996.

———. *The Folklore of Maine*. Philadelphia: J.B. Lippincott, 1957.

Becker, Jane S. *Selling Tradition: Appalachia and the Construction of an American Folk, 1930–1940*. Chapel Hill: University of North Carolina Press, 1998.

Becker, Jane S., and Barbara Franco, eds. *Folk Roots, New Roots: Folklore in American Life*. Lexington, MA: Museum of Our National Heritage, 1988.

Beckwith, Martha. *Hawaiian Mythology*. Honolulu: University of Hawaii Press, 1970.

Becnel, Harry P., Jr. "Customs, Traditions, and Folklore of a Rural Southern Italian-American Community." In *Folklife in the Florida Parishes*, 77–88. Baton Rouge: Louisiana Folklife Program and Center for Regional Studies, Southeastern Louisiana University, 1989.

Beemyn, Brett, ed. *Creating a Place for Ourselves: Lesbian, Gay, and Bisexual Community Histories*. New York: Routledge, 1997.

Beezley, William H. "Locker Rumors: Folklore and Football." *Journal of the Folklore Institute* 17 (1980): 213–21.

Behar, Ruth, and Deborah A. Gordon, eds. *Women Writing Culture*. Berkeley: University of California Press, 1995.

Beissel, James D. *Powwow Power*. Willow Street, PA: Crystal Education Counselors, 1998.

Belcove-Shalin, Janet S., ed. *New World Hasidism: Ethnographic Studies of Hasidic Jews in America*. Albany: State University of New York Press, 1995.

Bell, Catherine M. *Ritual: Perspectives and Dimensions*. New York: Oxford University Press, 1997.

Bell, Michael E. *Food for the Dead: On the Trail of New England's Vampires*. New York: Carroll and Graf, 2001.

Bell, Michael J. *The World from Brown's Lounge: An Ethnography of Black Middle-Class Play*. Urbana: University of Illinois Press, 1983.

Bellin, Andy. *Poker Nation: A High-Stakes, Low-Life Adventure into the Heart of a Gambling Country*. New York: HarperCollins, 2002.

Belman, Dale. *Sailors of the Concrete Sea: A Portrait of Truck Drivers' Work and Lives*. East Lansing: Michigan State University Press, 2005.

Belsito, Peter, and Bob Davis. *Hardcore California*. Berkeley, CA: Last Gasp, 1983.

Ben-Amos, Dan. "The 'Context' of Context." *Western Folklore* 52 (1993): 209–26.

———. "The Context of Folklore: Implications and Prospects." In *Frontiers of Folklore*, ed. William R. Bascom, 36–53. Boulder, CO: Westview, 1977.

———, ed. *Folklore Genres*. Austin: University of Texas Press, 1976.

———. "The Seven Strands of *Tradition*: Varieties in Its Meaning in American Folklore Studies." *Journal of Folklore Research* 21 (1984): 97–132.

———. "Toward a Definition of Folklore in Context." In *Toward New Perspectives in Folklore*, ed.

Américo Paredes and Richard Bauman, 3–15. Austin: University of Texas Press, 1972.

Ben-Amos, Dan, and Kenneth S. Goldstein, eds. *Folklore: Performance and Communication*. The Hague: Mouton, 1975.

Benberry, Cuesta. *Always There: The African American Presence in American Quilts*. Louisville: Kentucky Quilt Project, 1992.

Benderly, Beryl Lieff. *Dancing Without Music: Deafness in America*. Garden City, NY: Anchor Press/Doubleday, 1980.

Benes, Peter. *The Masks of Orthodoxy: Folk Gravestone Carving in Plymouth County, Massachusetts, 1689–1805*. Amherst: University of Massachusetts Press, 1977.

Bennion, Janet. *Women of Principle: Female Networking in Contemporary Mormon Polygyny*. New York: Oxford University Press, 1998.

Bennion, Lowell C. "Meinig's 'Mormon Culture Region' Revisited." *Historical Geography* 24, nos. 1–2 (1995): 22–33.

———. "Saints of the Western States (1990)." In *Historical Atlas of Mormonism*, ed. S. Kent Brown, Donald Q. Cannon, and Richard H. Jackson, 128–29. New York: Simon and Schuster, 1994.

Benowitz, Jeán-Paul. "The Old Order Mennonite Division of 1893: An Interpretation." *Pennsylvania Mennonite Heritage* 16, no. 4 (October 1993): 14–17.

Bense, Judith. *Archaeology of the Southeastern United States: Paleoindian to World War I*. New York: Academic Press, 1993.

Benson, Erica J. "Folk Linguistic Perceptions and the Mapping of Dialect Boundaries." *American Speech* 78 (2003): 307–30.

Benson, Kathleen, and Philip M. Kayal, eds. *A Community of Many Worlds: Arab Americans in New York City*. New York: Museum of the City of New York and Syracuse University Press, 2002.

Berger, Josef. *Cape Cod Pilot*. 1937. Reprint, Boston: Northeastern University Press, 1985.

Berger, Peter L., and Thomas Luckmann. *The Social Construction of Reality: A Treatise in the Sociology of Knowledge*. Garden City, NY: Doubleday Anchor Books, 1966.

Berg-Sobré, Judith. *San Antonio on Parade: Six Historic Festivals*. College Station: Texas A&M University Press, 2003.

Berkman, Susan C.J. "'She's Writing Antidotes': An Examination of Hospital Employees' Use of Stories About Personal Experiences." *Folklore Forum* 11, no. 1 (1978): 48–54.

Bernard, Shane K. *The Cajuns: Americanization of a People.* Jackson: University Press of Mississippi, 2003.

Berry, Jason, Jonathan Foose, and Tad Jones. *Up from the Cradle of Jazz: New Orleans Music Since World War II.* Athens: University of Georgia Press, 1986.

Berryman, Jack W. "From the Cradle to the Playing Field: America's Emphasis on Highly Organized Competitive Sports for Preadolescent Boys." *Journal of Sport History* 2 (1975): 112–31.

Best, Amy L. *Prom Night: Youth, Schools, and Popular Culture.* New York: Routledge, 2000.

Bestor, Arthur E. *Backwoods Utopias: The Sectarian and Owenite Phases of Communitarian Socialism in America, 1663–1828.* 2nd enlarged ed. Philadelphia: University of Pennsylvania Press, 1970.

Bethke, Robert D. *Adirondack Voices: Woodsmen and Woods Lore.* Urbana: University of Illinois Press, 1981.

Betsinger, Signe T. Nielsen. "Danes in Iowa and Minnesota." In *To Build in a New Land: Ethnic Landscapes in North America,* ed. Allen G. Noble, 211–25. Baltimore: Johns Hopkins University Press, 1992.

Bettelheim, Bruno. *Symbolic Wounds: Puberty Rites and the Envious Male.* New York: Collier, 1962.

Beyond the Land of Snows: Tibetans at the Smithsonian Folklife Festival. VHS. Washington, DC: Conservancy for Tibetan Art and Culture and the Smithsonian Center for Folklife and Cultural Heritage, 2001.

Bianco, Carla. *The Two Rosetos.* Bloomington: Indiana University Press, 1974.

Biber, Douglas, and Edward Finegan, eds. *Sociolinguistic Perspectives on Register.* New York: Oxford University Press, 1994.

Biederman, Patricia, and Warren Bennis. *Organizing Genius: The Secrets of Creative Collaboration.* New York: Perseus, 1998.

Bielski, Ursula. *Chicago Haunts: Ghostly Lore of the Windy City.* Chicago: Lake Claremont, 1997.

Bieter, John, and Mark Bieter. *An Enduring Legacy: The Story of Basques in Idaho.* Reno: University of Nevada Press, 2000.

Billings, Dwight B., Gurney Norman, and Katherine Ledford, eds. *Back Talk from Appalachia: Confronting Stereotypes.* Lexington: University Press of Kentucky, 1999.

Bird, Donald Allport. "A Theory for Folklore in Mass Media: Traditional Patterns in Mass Media." *Southern Folklore Quarterly* 40 (1976): 285–305.

Bird, S. Elizabeth. *For Enquiring Minds: A Cultural Study of Supermarket Tabloids.* Knoxville: University of Tennessee Press, 1992.

———. "Playing with Fear: Interpreting the Adolescent Legend Trip." *Western Folklore* 53 (1994): 191–209.

Bird, Stewart, Dan Georgakas, and Deborah Shaffer. *Solidarity Forever: An Oral History of the IWW.* Chicago: Lakeview, 1985.

Blackwell, James. *The Black Community: Diversity and Unity.* New York: HarperCollins, 1991.

Blackwell, Lois S. *The Wings of the Dove: The Story of Gospel Music in America.* Norfolk, VA: Donning, 1978.

Blake, Joseph A. "Occupational Thrill, Mystique and the Truck Driver." *Urban Life and Culture* 3 (1974): 205–20.

Blank, Harrod. *Art Cars: The Cars, the Artists, the Obsession, the Craft.* New York: Lark Books, 2002.

Blank, Les. *In Heaven There Is No Beer?* VHS. El Cerrito, CA: Flower Films, 1984.

———. *Ziveli! Medicine for the Heart.* VHS. El Cerrito, CA: Flower Films and Video, 1987.

Blasdel, Gregg N. "The Grass-Roots Artist." *Art in America* 56 (September/October 1968): 24–41.

Blassingame, James. *The Slave Community: Plantation Life in the Ante-Bellum South.* New York: Oxford University Press, 1972.

Blegen, Theodore, and Martin Ruud. *Norwegian Immigrant Ballads and Songs.* Minneapolis: University of Minnesota Press, 1936.

Blethen, H. Tyler, and Curtis W. Wood, Jr., eds. *Ulster and North America: Transatlantic Perspectives on the Scotch-Irish.* Tuscaloosa, AL: University of Alabama Press, 1997.

Bloom, Stephen G. *Postville: A Clash of Cultures in Heartland America.* New York: Harvest Books, 2001.

Bluestein, Howard B. *Tornado Alley: Monster Storms of the Great Plains.* New York: Oxford University Press, 1999.

Blumenreich, Beth, and Bari Lynn Polansky. "Re-Evaluating the Concept of Group: ICEN as an Alternative." In *Conceptual Problems in Contemporary Folklore Study,* ed. Gerald Cashion, 12–17. Bloomington, IN: Folklore Forum Bibliographic and Special Series No. 12, 1975.

Blumer, Thomas. *Catawba Indian Pottery: The Survival of a Folk Tradition.* Tuscaloosa: University of Alabama Press, 2003.

Blush, Steven, ed. *American Hardcore: A Tribal History.* Los Angeles: Feral House, 2001.

Boas, Franz. *Kwakiutl Ethnography.* Edited by Helen Codere. Chicago: University of Chicago Press, 1943.

———. "Mythology and Folklore." In *General Anthropology*, ed. Franz Boas, 609–26. Boston: D.C. Heath, 1938.

Boatner, Mark Mayo. *Military Customs and Traditions.* Westport, CT: Greenwood, 1976.

Boatright, Mody. *Folklore of the Oil Industry.* Dallas: Southern Methodist University Press, 1963.

Boatright, Mody, Robert B. Downs, and John T. Flanagan. *The Family Saga and Other Phases of American Folklore.* Urbana: University of Illinois Press, 1958.

Bodian, Miriam. *Hebrews of the Portuguese Nation: Conversos and Community in Early Modern Amsterdam.* Bloomington: Indiana University Press, 1997.

Bodnar, John. *Anthracite People: Families, Unions and Work, 1900–1940.* Harrisburg: Pennsylvania Historical and Museum Commission, 1983.

Bogolepov, Aleksandr A. *Toward an American Orthodox Church: The Establishment of an Autocephalous Church.* New York: St. Vladimir's Seminary, 2001.

Boje, David. "The Storytelling Organization: A Study of Story Performance in an Office-Supply Firm." *Administrative Science Quarterly* 36 (1991): 106–25.

Boles, Jacqueline, and Lyn Myers. "Chain Letters: Players and Their Accounts." *Deviant Behavior* 9 (1988): 241–57.

Bolkosky, Sidney M. *Harmony and Dissonance: Voices of Jewish Identity in Detroit, 1914–1967.* Detroit, MI: Wayne State University Press, 1991.

Bond, Hallie E. *Boats and Boating in the Adirondacks.* Syracuse, NY: Syracuse University Press, 1995.

Bonkalo, Alexander. *The Rusyns.* New York: Columbia University Press, 1990.

Boorstin, Daniel. *The Americans: The Democratic Experience.* New York: Random House, 1973.

Boosahda, Elizabeth. *Arab-American Faces and Voices: The Origins of an Immigrant Community.* Austin: University of Texas Press, 2003.

Borchert, James. *Alley Life in Washington: Family, Community, Religion, and Folklife in the City, 1850–1970.* Urbana: University of Illinois Press, 1980.

Bord, Richard J., and Joseph E. Faulkner. *The Catholic Charismatics: The Anatomy of a Modern Religious Movement.* University Park, PA: Pennsylvania State University Press, 1983.

Borden, Iain. *Skateboarding, Space and the City: Architecture and the Body.* Oxford: Berg, 2001.

Borun, Thadeus. *We, the Milwaukee Poles.* Milwaukee: Nowiny Publishing, 1946.

Botkin, B.A. "Living Lore of the New York City Writers' Project." *New York Folklore Quarterly* 2 (1946): 252–63.

———. *New York City Folklore.* New York: Random House, 1956.

———. *Sidewalks of New York.* Indianapolis, IN: Bobbs-Merrill, 1954.

Botkin, B.A., and Alvin F. Harlow, eds. *A Treasury of Railroad Folklore.* New York: Crown, 1953.

Bowden, Martyn J. "The New England Yankee Homeland." In *Homelands: A Geography of Culture and Place Across America*, ed. Richard L. Nostrand and Lawrence E. Estaville, 1–23. Baltimore: Johns Hopkins University Press, 2001.

Bowman Carl. *Brethren Society: The Cultural Transformation of a "Peculiar People."* Baltimore: Johns Hopkins University Press, 1995.

Bowman, Robert M.J. *Soulsville, U.S.A.: The Story of Stax Records.* New York: Schirmer, 1997.

Boyd, Nan Alamilla. *Wide-Open Town: A History of Queer San Francisco to 1965.* Berkeley: University of California Press, 2003.

Boyer, Horace Clarence. *How Sweet the Sound: The Golden Age of Gospel.* Washington, DC: Elliott and Clark, 1995.

Boyer, L. Bryce. *Childhood and Folklore: A Psychoanalytic Study of Apache Personality.* New York: Library of Psychological Anthropology, 1979.

Boyer, Paul. *When Time Shall Be No More: Prophecy Belief in Modern American Culture.* Cambridge, MA: Harvard University Press, 1992.

Boynton, Mia. "A Gift of Native Knowledge: The History of Russell's Motor Camps in Rangeley, Maine." *Northeast Folklore* 28 (1989): 1–68.

———, ed. "Folklore in the Industrial Workplace." Special issue, *New York Folklore* 14, nos. 1–2 (1988): 1–106.

Bracken, Christopher. *The Potlatch Papers: A Colonial Case History.* Chicago: University of Chicago Press, 1997.

Brackman, Barbara, and Cathy Dwigans, eds. *Backyard Visionaries: Grassroots Art in the Midwest*. Lawrence: University Press of Kansas, 1999.

Bradley, Martha Sonntag. *Kidnapped from that Land: The Government Raids on the Short Creek Polygamists*. Salt Lake City: University of Utah Press, 1993.

Bradunas, Elena. "If You Kill a Snake, the Sun Will Cry—Folktale Type 425-M: A Study in Oicotype and Folk Belief." *Lituanus* 21 (1975): 5–39.

Brady, Erika, ed. *Healing Logics: Culture and Medicine in Modern Health Belief Systems*. Logan: Utah State University Press, 2001.

———. "Mankind's Thumb on Nature's Scale: Trapping and Regional Identity in the Missouri Ozarks." In *Sense of Place: American Regional Cultures*, ed. Barbara Allen and Thomas J. Schlereth, 58–73. Lexington: University Press of Kentucky, 1990.

Brady, Margaret K. "Transformations of Power: Mormon Women's Visionary Narratives." *Journal of American Folklore* 100 (1987): 461–68.

Brandes, Stanley. "Jewish-American Dialect Jokes and Jewish-American Identity." *Jewish Social Studies* 45 (1983): 233–40.

Brandon, Reiko Mochinaga, Barbara B. Stephan, Enbutsu Sumiko, and Ian Reader. *Spirit and Symbol: The Japanese New Year*. Honolulu: University of Hawaii Press, 1994.

Brandon, Ruth. *The Spiritualists: The Passion for the Occult in the Nineteenth and Twentieth Centuries*. New York: Knopf, 1983.

Brassard, Francois. "French-Canadian Folk Music Studies: A Survey." *Ethnomusicology* 16 (1972): 351–59.

Brasseaux, Carl A. *From Acadian to Cajun*. Jackson: University Press of Mississippi, 1992.

Braude, Ann. *Radical Spirits: Spiritualism and Women's Rights in Nineteenth-Century America*. Boston: Beacon, 1989.

Braun, Mark. *Social Change and the Empowerment of the Poor: Poverty Representation in Milwaukee's Community Action Programs*. Lanham, MD: Lexington Books, 2001.

Braunstein, Susan J., and Jenna Weissman Joselit, eds. *Getting Comfortable in New York: The American Jewish Home, 1880–1950*. New York: Jewish Museum, 1990.

Breault, Gerard G. *The French-Canadian Heritage in New England*. Hanover: University Press of New England; Montreal: McGill-Queen's University Press, 1986.

Brechbill, Laban T. *History of the Old Order River Brethren*, ed. Myron S. Dietz. N.p.: Brechbill and Strickler, 1972.

Brendle, Thomas R. *The Thomas R. Brendle Collection of Pennsylvania German Folklore*. Vol. 1. Edited by C. Richard Beam. Schaefferstown, PA: Historic Schaefferstown, 1995.

Brenneman, Richard J. *Deadly Blessings: Faith Healing on Trial*. Buffalo, NY: Prometheus Books, 1990.

Brestensky, Dennis F., Evelyn A. Hovanec, and Albert N. Skomra. *Patch/Work Voices: The Culture and Lore of a Mining People*. Pittsburgh: University of Pittsburgh Press, 1991.

Brewer, J. Mason. *Dog Ghosts, and Other Texas Negro Folk Tales; The Word on the Brazos: Negro Preacher Tales from the Brazos Bottoms of Texas*. Austin: University of Texas Press, 1976.

———. "Juneteenth" In *Tone the Bell Easy*, ed. J. Frank Dobie, 9–54. 1932. Reprint. Dallas: Southern University Methodist Press, 1965.

Brewer, Priscilla J. *Shaker Communities, Shaker Lives*. Hanover, NH: University Press of New England, 1986.

Brewster, Paul G. *American Nonsinging Games*. Norman: University of Oklahoma Press, 1953.

Briggs, Harold E. "Folklore of Southern Illinois." *Southern Folklore Quarterly* 54 (1941): 57–58.

Brody, David. *Steelworkers in America: The Nonunion Era*. Urbana: University of Illinois Press, 1998.

Bronner, Simon J. *American Children's Folklore*. Little Rock, AR: August House, 1988.

———. *American Folklore Studies: An Intellectual History*. Lawrence: University Press of Kansas, 1986.

———, ed. *American Material Culture and Folklife: A Prologue and Dialogue*. Rev. ed. Logan: Utah State University Press, 1992.

———. *The Carver's Art: Crafting Meaning from Wood*. Lexington: University Press of Kentucky, 1996.

———. *Chain Carvers: Old Men Crafting Meaning*. Lexington: University Press of Kentucky, 1986.

———, ed. *Consuming Visions: Accumulation and Display of Goods in America, 1880–1920*. New York: W.W. Norton, 1989.

———. "Contesting Tradition: The Deep Play and Protest of Pigeon Shoots." *Journal of American Folklore* 118 (2005): 409–52.

————, ed. *Creativity and Tradition in Folklore: New Directions*. Logan: Utah State University Press, 1992.

————. "Elaborating Tradition: A Pennsylvania German Folk Artist Ministers to His Community." In *Creativity and Tradition in Folklore: New Directions*, ed. Simon J. Bronner, 277–325. Logan: Utah State University Press, 1992.

————. "Expressing and Creating Ourselves in Childhood: A Commentary." *Children's Folklore Review* 15 (1992): 47–59.

————. *Folk Nation: Folklore in the Creation of American Tradition*. Wilmington, DE: SR Books, 2002.

————, ed. *Folklife Studies from the Gilded Age: Object, Rite, and Custom in Victorian America*. Ann Arbor, MI: UMI Research Press, 1987.

————. *Following Tradition: Folklore in the Discourse of American Culture*. Logan: Utah State University Press, 1998.

————. "From *Landsmanshaften* to *Vinkln*: Mediating Community Among Yiddish Speakers in America." *Jewish History* 15 (2001): 131–48.

————. *Grasping Things: Folk Material Culture and Mass Society in America*. Lexington: University Press of Kentucky, 1986.

————. "History and Organization of Children's Folklore in the American Folklore Society." *Children's Folklore Review* 20 (1997–1998): 57–65.

————. *Lafcadio Hearn's America: Ethnographic Sketches and Editorials*. Lexington: University Press of Kentucky, 2002.

————. "'Left to Their Own Devices': Interpreting American Children's Folklore as an Adaptation to Aging." *Southern Folklore* 47 (1990): 101–15.

————, ed. *Manly Traditions: The Folk Roots of American Masculinities*. Bloomington: Indiana University Press, 2005.

————. "Material Culture and Region: Lessons from Folk Studies." *Kentucky Folklore Record* 32 (1986): 1–16.

————. "Material Folk Culture of Children." In *Children's Folklore: A Source Book*, ed. Brian Sutton-Smith, Jay Mechling, Thomas W. Johnson, and Felicia R. McMahon, 251–72. New York: Garland, 1995.

————. *Old-Time Music Makers of New York State*. Syracuse, NY: Syracuse University Press, 1987.

————. "Pictorial Jokes: A Traditional Combination of Verbal and Graphic Processes." *Tennessee Folklore Society Bulletin* 44 (1978): 189–96.

————. *Piled Higher and Deeper: The Folklore of Student Life*. Little Rock, AR: August House, 1995.

————. *Popularizing Pennsylvania: Henry W. Shoemaker and the Progressive Uses of Folklore and History*. University Park: Pennsylvania State University Press, 1996.

————. "A Re-Examination of Dozens Among White American Adolescents." *Western Folklore* 37 (1978): 118–28.

————. "Researching Material Folk Culture in the Modern American City." In *American Material Culture and Folklife: A Prologue and Dialogue*, ed. Simon J. Bronner, 221–35. Logan: Utah State University Press, 1992.

————, ed. "Special Section: Historical Methodology in Folkloristics." *Western Folklore* 41 (1982): 28–61.

————. "Suburban Houses and Manner Books: The Structure of Tradition and Aesthetics." *Winterthur Portfolio* 18 (1983): 61–68.

————. "'This Is Why We Hunt': Social-Psychological Meanings of the Traditions and Rituals of Deer Camp." *Western Folklore* 63 (2004): 11–50.

————. "What's Grosser Than Gross?: New Sick Joke Cycles." *Midwestern Journal of Language and Folklore* 11 (1985): 39–49.

————. "'Who Says?' A Further Investigation of Ritual Insults Among White American Adolescents." *Midwestern Journal of Language and Folklore* 4 (1978): 53–69.

Bronson, Bertrand Harris. *Traditional Tunes of the Child Ballads*. 4 vols. Princeton, NJ: Princeton University Press, 1959–1972.

Brooke, Michael. *The Concrete Wave: The History of Skateboarding*. Toronto: Warwick, 1999.

Brown, Cecil. *Stagolee Shot Billy*. Cambridge, MA: Harvard University Press, 2003.

Brown, Fred, and Jeanne McDonald. *The Serpent Handlers: Three Families and Their Faith*. Winston-Salem, NC: John F. Blair, 2000.

Brown, Karen McCarthy. *Mama Lola: A Vodou Priestess in Brooklyn*. Berkeley: University of California Press, 1991.

Brown, Mary Ellen Lewis. "Folk Elements in Scotch-Irish Presbyterian Communities." *Pennsylvania Folklife* 18, no. 1 (1968): 21–25.

Brown, Richard Harvey, and George Coelho, eds. *Tradition and Transformation: Asian Indians in*

America. Williamsburg, VA: Department of Anthropology, College of William and Mary, 1986.

Brown, Titus, and James "Jack" Hadley, eds. *African American Life on the Southern Hunting Plantation*. Charleston, SC: Arcadia, 2000.

Browne, Basil R. "Really Not God: Secularization and Pragmatism in Gamblers Anonymous." *Journal of Gambling Studies* 10 (1994): 247–60.

Browne, Ray B., ed. *Objects of Special Devotion: Fetishism in Popular Culture*. Bowling Green, OH: Bowling Green University Popular Press, 1982.

Brownell, Baker. *The Other Illinois*. New York: Duell, Sloan and Pearce, 1958.

Brubaker, Ken, and Tom Morr. *Monster Truck Mania*. St. Paul, MN: Motorbooks International, 2003.

Bruce, Steve. *Religion in the Modern World: From Cathedrals to Cults*. Oxford: Oxford University Press, 1996.

Brunvand, Jan Harold, ed. 1996. *American Folklore: An Encyclopedia*. New York: Garland.

———. *The Baby Train and Other Lusty Urban Legends*. New York: W.W. Norton, 1993.

———. *Encyclopedia of Urban Legends*. Santa Barbara, CA: ABC-CLIO, 2001.

———. "Folklore in the News (and Incidentally, on the Net)." *Western Folklore* 60 (2001): 47–66.

———. *The Study of American Folklore: An Introduction*. 4th ed. New York: W.W. Norton, 1998.

———. *The Truth Never Stands in the Way of a Good Story*. Urbana: University of Illinois Press, 2001.

———. *The Vanishing Hitchhiker: American Urban Legends and Their Meanings*. New York: W.W. Norton, 1981.

Buckland, Gail. *Reality Recorded: Early Documentary Photography*. Greenwich, CT: New York Graphic Society, 1974.

Bucuvalas, Tina. "Little Havana: The Cubanization of Miami's Cultural Heritage." *CRM: Cultural Resource Management* 20, no. 11 (1997): 54–56.

Bucuvalas, Tina, Peggy A. Bulger, and Stetson Kennedy. *South Florida Folklife*. Jackson: University Press of Mississippi, 1994.

Bucuvalas, Tina, and Steve Frangos. *Techne: Greek Traditional Arts in the Calumet Region*. Merrillville, IN: SS. Constantine and Helen Greek Orthodox Cathedral, 1985.

Buisseret, David, and Steven G. Reinhardt, eds. *Creolization in the Americas*. College Station: Texas A&M University Press, 2000.

Bulbulian, Berge. *The Fresno Armenians: History of a Diaspora Community*. Fresno, CA: Press at California State University, 2000.

Bulcroft, Kris, Linda Smeins, and Richard Bulcroft. *Romancing the Honeymoon: Consummating Marriage in Modern Society*. Thousand Oaks, CA: Sage, 1999.

Bullard, Robert D. *Invisible Houston: The Black Experience in Boom and Bust*. College Station: Texas A&M University Press, 1987.

Bullard, Thomas E. "Abduction Reports: The Supernatural Kidnap Narrative Returns in Technological Guise." *Journal of American Folklore* 102 (1989): 147–70.

Bunch-Lyons, Beverly A. *Contested Terrain: African-American Women Migrate from the South to Cincinnati, Ohio, 1900–1950*. New York: Routledge, 2002.

Burke, Carol. *Camp All-American, Hanoi Jane, and the High-and-Tight: Gender, Folklore, and Changing Military Culture*. Boston: Beacon, 2004.

———. *Vision Narratives of Women in Prison*. Knoxville: University of Tennessee Press, 1992.

Burns, Jane. "'Everyone Has Good': A Study of the Occupational Folklife of a St. John's Cab Driver." *Culture and Tradition* 4 (1979): 79–87.

Burns, Richard Allen. "Folklore and Control at an Arkansas Prison Farm." *Mid-America Folklore* 23 (1995): 1–12.

Burrison, John A. *Brothers in Clay: The Story of Georgia Folk Pottery*. Athens: University of Georgia Press, 1983.

———, ed. *Storytellers: Folktales and Legends from the South*. Athens: University of Georgia Press, 1989.

Burrows, Edwin G., and Mike Wallace. *Gotham: A History of New York City to 1898*. New York: Oxford University Press, 1999.

Burson, Anne C. "Model and Text in Folk Drama." *Journal of American Folklore* 93, no. 369 (July–September 1980): 305–16.

———. "Pomp and Circumcision: A Parodic Skit in a Medical Community." *Keystone Folklore* 1, no. 1 (1982): 28–40.

Burson-Tolpin, Anne. "Fracturing the Language of Biomedicine: The Speech Play of U.S. Physicians." *Medical Anthropology Quarterly* 3 (September 1989): 285–93.

Burton, Thomas. *Serpent Handling Believers*. Knoxville: University of Tennessee Press, 1993.

Bushart, Howard L., John R. Craig, and Myrna Barnes. *Soldiers of God: White Supremacists and Their Holy War for America*. New York: Kensington, 1998.

Byington, Robert H., ed. *Working Americans: Contemporary Approaches to Occupational Folklife*. Smithsonian Folklife Studies, no. 3. Washington, DC: Smithsonian Institution Press, 1978.

Cabral, Stephen Leonard. *Tradition and Transformation: Portuguese Feasting in New Bedford*. New York: AMS Press, 1992.

Caldwell, Benjamin Hubbard, Jr. *Tennessee Silversmiths*. Winston-Salem, NC: Museum of Early Southern Decorative Arts, 1988.

Cam, Nguyet Nguyen, and Dana Sachs, eds. *Two Cakes Fit for a King: Folktales from Vietnam*. Honolulu: University of Hawaii Press, 2003.

Cameron, Richard Morgan. *Methodism and Society in Historical Perspective*. New York: Abingdon, 1961.

Camp, Charles. *American Foodways: What, When, Why and How We Eat in America*. Little Rock, AR: August House, 1989.

———, ed. *Time and Temperature*. Washington, DC: American Folklore Society, 1989.

———, ed. *Traditional Craftsmanship in America: A Diagnostic Report*. Washington, DC: National Council for the Traditional Arts, 1983.

Campa, Arthur L. *Hispanic Culture in the Southwest*. Norman: University of Oklahoma Press, 1993.

Campbell, Marie. "Survivals of Old Folk Drama in the Kentucky Mountains." *Journal of American Folklore* 51, no. 199 (January–March 1938): 10–24.

Cannon, Anthon S. 1984. *Popular Beliefs and Superstitions form Utah*, ed. Wayland D. Hand and Jeannine E. Talley. Salt Lake City: University of Utah Press.

Cantú, Norma E., and Olga Nájera-Ramírez, eds. *Chicana Traditions: Continuity and Change*. Urbana: University of Illinois Press, 2002.

Cantwell, Robert. *Bluegrass Breakdown: The Making of the Old Southern Sound*. Urbana: University of Illinois Press, 1984.

———. *Ethnomimeses: Folklife and the Representation of Culture*. Chapel Hill: University of North Carolina Press, 1993.

———. *When We Were Good: The Folk Revival*. Cambridge, MA: Harvard University Press, 1996.

Caponi, Gena Dagel, ed. *Signifyin(g), Sanctifyin' and Slam Dunking: A Reader in African American Expressive Culture*. Amherst: University of Massachusetts Press, 1999.

Capture, Joseph D. Horse, and George P. Horse Capture. *Beauty, Honor, and Tradition: The Legacy of Plains Indian Shirts*. Washington, DC: National Museum of the American Indian, Smithsonian Institution Press, 2001.

Cardinal, Roger. *Outsider Art*. New York: Praeger, 1972.

Cardoza-Freeman, Inez. *The Joint: Language and Culture in a Maximum Security Prison*. Springfield, IL: Thomas Books, 1984.

Carey, George. "A Collection of Airborne Cadence Chants." *Journal of American Folklore* 78 (1965): 52–61.

———. *A Faraway Time and Place: The Lore of the Eastern Shore*. Washington, DC: Robert B. Luce, 1971.

Carlson, Patricia Ann, ed. *The Literature and Lore of the Sea*. Amsterdam: Rodopi, 1986.

Carmel, Simon J., and Leila F. Monaghan. "Studying Deaf Culture: An Introduction to Ethnographic Work in Deaf Communities." *Sign Language Studies* 73 (1991): 410–20.

Carney, George O. "Urban Blues: The Sound of the Windy City." In *The Sounds of People and Places: A Geography of American Music from Country to Classical and Blues to Bop*, ed. George O. Carney, 241–54. Lanham, MD: Rowman and Littlefield, 2003.

Carpenter, Inta Gale. "Baltic Peoples: Lithuanians, Latvians and Estonians." In *Peopling Indiana: The Ethnic Experience*, ed. Robert M. Taylor, Jr., and Connie A. McBirney, 54–75. Indianapolis: Indiana Historical Society, 1996.

———. "The Christopher Legend in Latvian Folklore." In *Folklorica: Festschrift for Felix J. Oinas*, ed. Egle Victoria Zygas and Peter Voorheis, 71–80. Bloomington, IN: Research Institute for Inner Asian Studies, 1982.

———. "From Lecture to Debate: Generational Contestation in Exile." In *Contemporary Folklore: Changing World View and Tradition*, ed. Mare Koiva, Kai Vassiljeva, and Luule Krikmann, 61–76. Tartu: Institute of Estonian Language and Estonian Museum of Literature, 1996.

Carreira, Antonio. *The People of the Cape Verde Islands: Exploitation and Emigration*. Trans. and ed. Christopher Fyfe. Hamden, CT: Archon Books, 1982.

Carrington, Christopher. *No Place Like Home: Relationships and Family Life Among Lesbians and Gay Men in San Francisco.* Chicago: University of Chicago Press, 1999.

Carter, Isabel Gordon. "Mountain White Folk-Lore: Tales from the Southern Blue Ridge." *Journal of American Folklore* 38 (1925): 340–74.

Carter, Thomas, and Elizabeth Collins Cromley. *Invitation to Vernacular Architecture: A Guide to the Study of Ordinary Buildings and Landscapes.* Knoxville: University of Tennessee Press, 2005.

Cary, Francine Curro. *Urban Odyssey: A Multicultural History of Washington, D.C.* Washington, DC: Smithsonian Institution Press, 1996.

Casey, Edward S. *The Fate of Place: A Philosophical History.* Berkeley: University of California Press, 1997.

Cassens, David E. "The Bulgarian Colony of Southwestern Illinois." *Illinois Historical Journal* 84, no. 1 (Spring 1991): 15–24.

Cassidy, Frederic G., ed. *Dictionary of American Regional English.* 4 vols. Cambridge, MA: Belknap Press of Harvard University Press, 1985.

Castleman, Craig. *Getting Up: Subway Graffiti in New York.* Cambridge, MA: MIT Press, 1982.

Castro, Rafaela G. *Chicano Folklore: A Guide to the Folktales, Traditions, Rituals, and Religious Practices of Mexican Americans.* Oxford: Oxford University Press, 2001.

Catalano, Joseph T. *Contemporary Professional Nursing.* Philadelphia: F.A. Davis, 1996.

Catlin, Amy. *Music of the Hmong: Singing Voices and Talking Reeds.* Providence, RI: Center for Hmong Lore, 1981.

Cauthen, Joyce H. *With Fiddle and Well-Rosined Bow: Old-Time Fiddling in Alabama.* Tuscaloosa: University of Alabama Press, 1989.

Cavender, Anthony. *Folk Medicine in Southern Appalachia.* Chapel Hill: University of North Carolina Press, 2003.

Cayton, Andrew R.L., and Susan E. Gray, eds. *The American Midwest: Essays on Regional History.* Bloomington: Indiana University Press, 2001.

Cazden, Norman, Herbert Haufrecht, and Norman Studer. *Folk Songs of the Catskills.* Albany: State University of New York Press, 1982.

Cecelski, David S. *The Waterman's Song: Slavery and Freedom in Maritime North Carolina.* Chapel Hill: University of North Carolina Press, 2001.

Chada, Joseph. *The Czechs in the United States.* Washington, DC: SVU Press, 1981.

Chase, Hal, and Bill Silag, eds. *Outside In: African-American History in Iowa, 1838–2000.* Des Moines: State Historical Society of Iowa, 2001.

Chase, Richard, ed. *The Jack Tales.* Boston: Houghton Mifflin, 1943.

Chasteen, John Charles. *National Rhythms, African Roots: The Deep History of Latin American Popular Dance.* Albuquerque: University of New Mexico Press, 2004.

Chauncey, George. *Gay New York: Gender, Urban Culture, and the Making of the Gay Male World 1890–1940.* New York: HarperCollins, 1994.

Chavez, Leo R. *Shadowed Lives: Undocumented Immigrants in American Society.* 2nd ed. Belmont, CA: Wadsworth, 1998.

Chen, Yong. *Chinese San Francisco, 1850–1943.* Stanford, CA: Stanford University Press, 2000.

Child, Francis James. *The English and Scottish Popular Ballads.* 5 vols. 1882–1898. Reprint, New York: Dover, 1965.

Chin, Ko-Lin. *Chinatown Gangs: Extortion, Enterprise, and Ethnicity.* New York: Oxford University Press, 1996.

Chodorow, Nancy. *Feminism and Psychoanalytic Theory.* New Haven, CT: Yale University Press, 1989.

Choy, Bong-Youn. *Koreans in America.* Chicago: Nelson Hall, 1979.

Chricton, Jennifer. *Family Reunion.* New York: Workman, 1998.

Chrislock, C. Winston. "The Czechs." In *They Chose Minnesota: A Survey of the State's Ethnic Groups,* ed. June Drenning Holmquist, 335–51. St. Paul: Minnesota Historical Society Press, 1981.

Christe, Ian. *Sound of the Beast: The Complete Headbanging History of Heavy Metal.* New York: HarperEntertainment, 2003.

Christensen, Loren W. *Skinhead Street Gangs.* Boulder, CO: Paladin, 1994.

The Chronicle of the Hutterian Brethren. Vol. 1. Rifton, NY: Plough Press, 1987. Vol. 2. St. Agathe, Manitoba, Canada: Hutterian Brethren, Crystal Spring Colony, 1998.

Chu, Doris. *Chinese in Massachusetts.* Boston: Chinese Culture Institute, 1987.

Cicala, John Allan. "Health, Respect, and the Family: Detroit's Italian Immigrant Food Culture." In *1988 Festival of Michigan Folklife,* ed. Ruth D. Fitzgerald and Yvonne R. Lockwood, 44–48. East Lansing: Michigan State University Museum, 1988.

Cimino, Richard P., ed. *Lutherans Today: American Lutheran Identity in the Twenty-First Century.* Grand Rapids, MI: W. B. Eerdmans, 2003.

Cincura, Andrew. "Slovak and Ruthenian Easter Eggs in America: The Impact of Culture Contact on Immigrant Art and Custom." *Journal of Popular Culture* 4 (1970): 155–93.

Clark, Dennis J. "Irish Folk Life in an Urban Setting." *Keystone Folklore* 23 (1979): 28–40.

Clayton, Lawrence, Jim Hoy, and Jerald Underwood. *Vaqueros, Cowboys, and Buckaroos: The Genesis and Life of the Mounted North American Herders.* Austin: University of Texas Press, 2001.

Clements, William M. "The Folk Church: Institution, Event, Performance." In *Handbook of American Folklore*, edited by Richard M. Dorson. 136–44. Bloomington: Indiana University Press, 1983.

———, ed. *100 Years of American Folklore Studies: A Conceptual History.* Washington, DC: American Folklore Society, 1988.

———. *Native American Verbal Art: Texts and Contexts.* Tucson: University of Arizona Press, 1996.

———. "Ritual Expectation in Pentecostal Healing Experience." *Western Folklore* 40 (1981): 139–48.

Cleveland, Les. *Dark Laughter: War in Song and Popular Culture.* Westport, CT: Praeger, 1994.

———. "Military Folklore and the Underwood Collection." *New York Folklore* 13 (1987): 87–103.

Cleveland Museum of Art. *The Art of William Edmondson.* Jackson: University Press of Mississippi, 1999.

Clifford, James, and George E. Marcus, eds. *Writing Culture: The Poetics and Politics of Ethnography.* Berkeley: University of California Press, 1986.

Cobb, Buell E. *The Sacred Harp: A Tradition and Its Music.* 1978. Reprint, Athens: University of Georgia Press, 2001.

Cobb, James C. *The Most Southern Place on Earth: The Mississippi Delta and the Roots of Regional Identity.* New York: Oxford University Press, 1992.

Codere, Helen. *Fighting with Property: A Study of Kwakiutl Potlaching and Warfare, 1792–1930.* Seattle: University of Washington Press, 1972.

Coe, Brian, and Paul Gates. *The Snapshot Photograph: The Rise of Popular Photography, 1888–1939.* London: Ash and Grant, 1977.

Coffin, Tristram P. *The Book of Christmas Folklore.* New York: Seabury Press, 1973.

———. *The Old Ball Game: Baseball in Folklore and Fiction.* New York: Herder and Herder, 1971.

Coggeshall, John M., and Jo Anner Nast. *Vernacular Architecture in Southern Illinois: The Ethnic Heritage.* Carbondale: Southern Illinois University Press, 1988.

Cohen, David Steven. *The Dutch-American Farm.* New York: New York University Press, 1992.

———. *Folk Legacies Revisited.* New Brunswick, NJ: Rutgers University Press, 1995.

Cohen, Hennig, and Tristram Potter Coffin, eds. *The Folklore of American Holidays.* Detroit, MI: Gale, 1999.

Cohen, Lee M. *Art of Clay: Timeless Pottery of the Southwest.* Santa Fe, NM: Clear Light Publishers, 1993.

Cohen, Norm. *Folk Song America: A 20th Century Revival.* Washington, DC: Smithsonian Collection of Recordings, a division of Smithsonian Institution Press, 1991.

———. *Long Steel Rail: The Railroad in American Folksong.* 2nd ed. Urbana: University of Illinois Press, 2000.

Cohen, Paul. "The Contested Past: The Boxers as History and Myth." *Journal of Asian Studies* 51 (1992): 82–113.

Cohn, Lawrence, ed. *Nothing but the Blues: The Music and the Musicians.* New York: Abbeville, 1993.

Cohn, William H. "A National Celebration: The Fourth of July in American History." *Cultures* 3 (1976): 141–56.

Cole, Douglas, and Ira Chaikin. *An Iron Hand upon the People: The Law Against the Potlatch on the Northwest Coast.* Seattle: University of Washington Press, 1990.

Cole, R. Lee. *Love-Feasts: A History of the Christian Agape.* London: Charles H. Kelly, 1916.

Colegrave, Stephen, and Chris Sullivan. *Punk: The Definite Record of a Revolution.* New York: Thunder's Mouth Press, 2001.

Coleman, Gregory D. *We're Heaven Bound! Portrait of a Black Sacred Drama.* Athens: University of Georgia Press, 1994.

Collier, John, Jr., and Malcolm Collier. *Visual Anthropology: Photography as a Research Method.* Revised and expanded edition. Albuquerque: University of New Mexico Press, 1986.

Collins, Camilla A., ed. "Folklore Fieldwork: Sex, Sexuality, and Gender." Special issue, *Southern Folklore* 47, no. 1 (1990): 1–83.

Collins, Randall. *Interaction Ritual Chains*. Princeton, NJ: Princeton University Press, 2005.

Communities Directory. A Guide to Intentional Communities and Cooperative Living. Rutledge, MO: Fellowship for Intentional Communities, 2000.

Comstock, H.E. *The Pottery of the Shenandoah Valley Region*. Winston-Salem, NC: Museum of Early Southern Decorative Arts, 1994.

Conforti, Joseph A. *Imagining New England: Explorations in Regional Identity from the Pilgrims to the Mid-Twentieth Century*. Chapel Hill: University of North Carolina Press, 2001.

Conkin, Paul K. *American Originals: Homemade Varieties of Christianity*. Chapel Hill: University of North Carolina Press, 1997.

Connell, Janice T. *Angel Power*. San Francisco: HarperCollins, 1995.

Conner, Randy, David Hatfield, and Mariya Sparks. *Cassell's Encyclopedia of Queer Myth, Symbol and Spirit*. London: Cassell, 1998.

Connors, Mary F. *Lao Textiles and Traditions*. Oxford: Oxford University Press, 1996.

Conquergood, Dwight. "Performance Studies: Interventions and Radical Research." *Drama Review* 46, no. 2 (2002): 145–56.

Conway, Cecelia. *African Banjo Echoes in Appalachia: A Study of Folk Traditions*. Knoxville: University of Tennessee Press, 1995.

Conway, Cecelia, and Scott Odell. *Black Banjo Songsters of North Carolina and Virginia*. CD and notes. Washington, DC: Smithsonian Folkways, 1998.

Cooke, John, ed. *New Orleans Ethnic Cultures*. New Orleans, LA: Committee on Ethnicity in New Orleans, 1978.

———, ed. *Perspectives on Ethnicity in New Orleans*. New Orleans, LA: Committee on Ethnicity in New Orleans, 1979.

Coolen, Michael Theodore. "Senegambia Archetypes for the American Folk Banjo." *Western Folklore* 43 (1984): 146–61.

Cooper, Douglas. *Steel Shadows: Drawings of Pittsburgh*. Pittsburgh: University of Pittsburgh Press, 2000.

Cooper, Martha, and Herny Chalfant. *Subway Art*. New York: Henry Holt, 1984.

Cooper, Martha, and Joseph Sciorra. *R. I. P.: Memorial Wall Art*. New York: Henry Holt, 1994.

———. *R.I.P.: New York Spraycan Memorials*. London: Thames and Hudson, 1994.

Cooper, Robert. *The Hmong: A Guide to Traditional Lifestyles*. Singapore: Times Editions, 1998.

Cordasco, Francesco, and Eugene Bucchioni. *The Italians: Social Backgrounds of an American Group*. Clifton, NJ: Augustus M. Kelley, 1974.

Corsaro, James, and Karen Taussig-Lux. *Folklore in Archives: A Guide to Describing Folklore and Folklife Materials*. Schenectady: New York Folklore Society, 1998.

Cosentino, Donald, ed. *Sacred Arts of Haitian Vodou*. Los Angeles: UCLA Fowler Museum of Cultural History, 1995.

———, ed. *Vodou Things: The Art of Pierrot Barra and Marie Cassaise*. Jackson: University Press of Mississippi, 1998.

Cothran, Kay L. "Participation in Tradition." In *Readings in American Folklore*, ed. Jan Harold Brunvand, 444–48. New York: W.W. Norton, 1979.

Coulter, Lane, and Maurice Dixon, Jr. *New Mexican Tinwork, 1840–1940*. Albuquerque: University of New Mexico Press, 1990.

Counts, Dorothy Ayers, and David R. Counts. *Over the Next Hill: An Ethnography of RVing Seniors in North America*. Peterborough, Ontario: Broadview, 1996.

Courlander, Harold. *The Fourth World of the Hopis: The Epic Story of the Hopi Indians as Preserved in Their Legends and Traditions*. Albuquerque: University of New Mexico Press, 1987.

Covington, Dennis. *Salvation on Sand Mountain: Snake Handling and Redemption in Southern Appalachia*. New York: Penguin, 1996.

Cowley, John. *Carnival, Canboulay, and Calypso: Traditions in the Making*. New York: Cambridge University Press, 1998.

Cox, Harvey. *Fire from Heaven: The Rise of Pentecostal Spirituality and the Reshaping of Religion in the 21st Century*. New York: Da Capo, 2001.

Craigie, Carter. "The Picnic Experience." *Tennessee Folklore Society Bulletin* 45 (1979): 161–65.

———. "Vocabulary of the Picnic." *Midwestern Journal of Language and Folklore* 1–2 (1978–1979): 2–6.

Crease, Robert P. "In Praise of the Polka." *Atlantic Monthly* 266 (August 1989): 78–83.

Creel, Margaret Washington. *A Peculiar People: Slave Religion and Community-Culture Among the Gullahs*. New York: New York University Press, 1988.

Crellin, John, and Jane Philpott. *Herbal Medicine: Past and Present.* Durham, NC: Duke University Press, 1990.

Cresswell, Tim. *Place: A Short Introduction.* Malden, MA: Blackwell, 2004.

Crook, Roy, Cornelia Bailey, Norma Harris, and Karen Smith. *Sapelo Voices: Historical Anthropology and the Oral Traditions of Gullah-Geechee Communities on Sapelo Island, Georgia.* Carrollton: State University of West Georgia, 2003.

Cross, Gary S. *An All-Consuming Century: Why Commercialism Won in Modern America.* New York: Columbia University Press, 2000.

Crowder, Linda Sun. "Chinese Funerals in San Francisco Chinatown: American Chinese Expression of Mortuary Ritual Performance." *Journal of American Folklore* 113 (2000): 451–63.

Crowley, John. *Primitive Baptists of the Wiregrass South: 1815 to the Present.* Gainesville: University Press of Florida, 1998.

Crowley, Vivienne. *Wicca: The Old Religion for the New Age.* Wellingsborough: Aquarian Press, 1989.

Crumrine, N. Ross. "Paying and Feasting: Modern Guamanian Fiestas." *Anthropos* 71, nos. 1–2 (1982): 89–112.

Csordas, Thomas. *Language, Charisma, and Creativity: The Ritual Life of a Religious Movement.* Berkeley: University of California Press, 1997.

Cubbs, Joanne, ed. *Hmong Art: Tradition and Change.* Sheboygan, WI: Kohler Arts Center, 1986.

Cuff, David J., William J. Young, Edward K. Muller, Wilbur Zelinsky, and Ronald F. Abler, eds. *The Atlas of Pennsylvania.* Philadelphia: Temple University Press, 1989.

Culin, Stewart. "The Gambling Games of the Chinese Americans." *Series in Philology, Literature, and Archeology.* Vol. 1, no. 4. Philadelphia: Publications of the University of Pennsylvania, 1891.

Cunningham, Keith. *American Indians' Kitchen-Table Stories.* Little Rock, AR: August House, 1992.

Cunningham, Lawrence J., Janice J. Beaty, and Remedios L.G. Perez. *A History of Guam.* Honolulu: Bess Press, 1988.

Cunningham, Patricia, and Susan Voso Lab, eds. *Dress in American Culture.* Bowling Green, OH: Bowling Green State University Popular Press, 1993.

Cunnison, Ian, and Wendy James, eds. *Essays in Sudan Ethnography.* New York: Humanities Press, 1972.

Cussler, Margaret, and Mary Louise de Give. *Twixt the Cup and the Lip: Psychological and Socio-Cultural Factors Affecting Food Habits.* New York: Twayne, 1952.

Cutler, Irving. *The Jews of Chicago: From Shtetl to Suburb.* Urbana: University of Illinois Press, 1996.

Dale, William. "Lore from Harkers Island." *North Carolina Folklore Journal* 20 (1972): 139–44.

Daly, Catherine M. "Anna Mizens, Latvian Mitten Knitter." In *Circles of Tradition: Folk Arts in Minnesota*, ed. Willard B. Moore, 80–87. St. Paul: Minnesota Historical Society for University of Minnesota Art Museum, 1989.

Dance for a Chicken: The Cajun Mardi Gras. VHS. Produced by Pat Mire. Eunice, LA: Attakapas Productions, 1993.

Dance, Daryl Cumber. *Shuckin' and Jivin': Folklore from Contemporary Black Americans.* Bloomington: Indiana University Press, 1978.

Danforth, Loring M. *The Macedonian Conflict: Ethnic Nationalism in a Transnational World.* Princeton, NJ: Princeton University Press, 1995.

Daniels, Roger, Sandra D. Taylor, and Harry H.L. Kitano, eds. *Japanese Americans: From Relocation to Redress.* Seattle: University of Washington Press, 1991.

Daniels, Ted, ed. *A Doomsday Reader: Prophets, Predictors, and Hucksters of Salvation.* New York: New York University Press, 1999.

Danielson, Larry. "The Dialect Trickster Among the Kansas Swedes." *Indiana Folklore* 8 (1975): 39–59.

———. *The Ethnic Festival and Cultural Revivalism in a Small Midwestern Town.* Bloomington: Indiana University Press, 1972.

———, ed. "Family Folklore Studies." Special issue, *Southern Folklore* 51, no. 1 (1994).

———. "Religious Folklore." In *Folk Groups and Folklore Genres: An Introduction*, ed. Elliott Oring, 45–69. Logan: Utah State University Press, 1986.

———. "St. Lucia in Lindsborg, Kansas." In *Creative Ethnicity: Symbols and Strategies of Contemporary Ethnic Life*, ed. Stephen Stern and John Allan Cicala, 187–203. Logan: Utah State University Press, 1991.

———. "Swedish-American Mothers: Conservators of the Tradition." In *Folklore on Two Continents: Essays in Honor of Linda Dégh*, ed. Nikolai Burlakoff and Carl Lindahl, 338–47. Bloomington, IN: Trickster, 1980.

———. "Tornado Stories in the Breadbasket: Weather and Regional Identity." In *Sense of Place: American Regional Cultures,* ed. Barbara Allen and Thomas J. Schlereth, 28–39. Lexington: University Press of Kentucky, 1990.

Danker, Frederick E. "Trucking Songs: A Comparison with Traditional Occupational Song." *Journal of Country Music* 6 (1978): 78–89.

Dargan, Amanda, and Steven Zeitlin. *City Play.* New Brunswick, NJ: Rutgers University Press, 1990.

Dary, David. *Cowboy Culture: A Saga of Five Centuries.* New York: Knopf, 1981.

Dasa, Mahatma. *Krishna Consciousness at Home: A Practical Guide.* Los Angeles: Bhaktivedanta Book Trust, n.d.

Daugherty, George: "A Good People Doing a Good Thing." *Goldenseal: West Virginia Tradition Life* (Summer 2001), 44–51.

Davidson, R. Theodore. *Chicano Prisoners: The Key to San Quentin.* New York: Holt, Rinehart and Winston, 1974.

Davies, Christie. *Ethnic Humor Around the World: A Comparative Analysis.* Bloomington: Indiana University Press, 1990.

Davies, Wade. *Healing Ways: Navajo Health Care in the Twentieth Century.* Albuquerque: University of New Mexico Press, 2001.

Davis, Gerald L. "Afro-American Coil Basketry in Charleston County, South Carolina: Affective Characteristics of an Artistic Craft in Social Context." In *American Folklife,* ed. Don Yoder, 151–84. Austin: University of Texas Press, 1976.

Davis, James. *Skateboarding Is Not a Crime: 50 Years of Street Culture.* Richmond Hill, Ontario: Firefly Books, 2004.

Davis, Martha Ellen. "Dominican Folk Dance and the Shaping of National Identity." In *Caribbean Dance from Abakuá to Zouk: How Movement Shapes Identity,* ed. Susanna Sloat, 127–51. Gainesville: University Press of Florida, 2002.

Davis, Shelton H., and Katrinka Ebbe, eds. *Traditional Knowledge and Sustainable Development.* Washington, DC: World Bank, 1995.

Davis, Susan G. *Parades and Power: Street Theatre in Nineteenth Century Philadelphia.* Philadelphia: Temple University Press, 1985.

Davis-Floyd, Robbie. *Birth as an American Rite of Passage.* Berkeley: University of California Press, 1992.

De Baca, Vincent C., ed. *Hispano History and Life in Colorado.* Denver: Colorado Historical Society, 1998.

de Caro, Frank. *Folklife in Louisiana Photography: Images of Tradition.* Baton Rouge: Louisiana State University Press, 1991.

———. "New Orleans, Folk Ideas, and the Lore of Place." *Louisiana Folklore Miscellany* 7 (1992): 68–80.

De Los Reyes, Guillermo. "Freemasonry and Folklore in Mexican Presidentialism." *Journal of American Culture* 20 (1997): 61–73.

Debo, Angie. *A History of the Indians of the United States.* Norman: University of Oklahoma Press, 1970.

DeChenne, David. "Hungry Hollow: Bulgarian Immigrant Life in Granite City, Illinois, 1904–1921." *Gateway Heritage* 11, no. 1 (Summer 1990): 52–61.

The Decline of Western Civilization. VHS. Directed by Penelope Spheeris. Los Angeles: Nu-Image Films, 1980.

Deetz, James. *In Small Things Forgotten: The Archaeology of Early American Life.* Garden City, NY: Anchor Press/Doubleday, 1977.

Dégh, Linda. *American Folklore and the Mass Media.* Bloomington: Indiana University Press, 1994.

———. *Legend and Belief: Dialectics of a Folklore Genre.* Bloomington: Indiana University Press, 2001.

———. "'When I Was Six We Moved West . . .': The Theory of Personal Experience Narrative." *New York Folklore* 11 (1985): 99–108.

Dégh, Linda, and Andrew Vázsonyi. "Legend and Belief." *Genre* 4 (1971): 281–304.

Deitering, Carolyn. *The Liturgy of Dance and the Liturgical Dancer.* New York: Crossroad, 1984.

del Fierro, Norrie. *Popular Recipes of the Philippines.* Manila, Philippines: National Bookstore, 1986.

Del Giudice, Luisa, and Gerald Porter, eds. *Imagined States: Nationalism, Utopia, and Longing in Oral Cultures.* Logan: Utah State University Press, 2001.

Del Sesto, Steven L. "Cajun Music and Zydeco: Notes on the Music of Southern Louisiana." *Louisiana Folklore Miscellany* 4 (1976–1980): 88–101.

Delanty, Gerard. *Community.* New York: Routledge, 2003.

Delgado, Celeste Fraser, and José Esteban Muñoz, eds. *Everynight Life: Culture and Dance in Latin/o America.* Durham, NC: Duke University Press, 1997.

Deloria, Philip J. *Playing Indian*. New Haven, CT: Yale University Press, 1998.

Delsohn, Steve. *The Fire Inside: Firefighters Talk About Their Lives*. New York: HarperCollins, 1996.

Denby, Priscilla. "Folklore in the Mass Media." *Folklore Forum* 4 (1971): 113–21.

Dennis, Matthew. *Red, White, and Blue Letter Days: An American Calendar*. Ithaca, NY: Cornell University Press, 2002.

Denny, Frederick M. "Islam and the Muslim Community." In *Religious Traditions of the World,* ed. H. Byron Earhart, 603–712. New York: HarperSanFrancisco, 1993.

Densmore, Frances. *How the Indians Use Wild Plants for Food, Medicine and Crafts*. 1928. Reprint, New York: Dover Publications, 1974.

Denton, Sally, and Roger Morris. *The Money and the Power: The Making of Las Vegas and Its Hold on America*. New York: Knopf, 2002.

Denzin, Norman K. *Performance Ethnography: Critical Pedagogy and the Politics of Culture*. Thousand Oaks, CA: Sage, 2003.

Denzler, Brenda. *The Lure of the Edge: Scientific Passions, Religious Beliefs, and the Pursuit of UFOs*. Berkeley: University of California Press, 2001.

Dewhurst, C. Kurt. "The Role of Exhibitions, Fairs, and Expositions in the Study of Folk Art Study." *Kentucky Folklore Record* 29 (1983): 83–88.

Dewhurst, C. Kurt, and Marsha MacDowell. *Michigan Hmong Arts*. East Lansing: Michigan State University Museum, 1983.

———. *"Your Wellwisher, J. B. Walker": A Midwestern Paper Cut-Out Artist*. East Lansing: Michigan State University, 1979.

Dewitt, Dave, and Sue Gerlach. *The Food of Santa Fe*. London: Periplus, 1998.

Dezell, Maureen. *Irish America: Coming into Clover*. New York: Anchor Books, 2002.

Di Leonardo, Micaela. "Oral History as Ethnographic Encounter." *Oral History Review* 15 (Spring 1987): 1–20.

Díaz, Junot. *Drown*. New York: Riverhead, 1996.

Diaz, Vicente M. "Deliberating 'Liberation Day': Identity, History, Memory, and War in Guam." In *Perilous Memories: The Asia-Pacific War(s),* ed. T. Fujitani, Geoffrey M. White, and Lisa Yoneyama, 155–80. Durham, NC: Duke University Press, 2001.

Dickerson, Dennis C. *Out of the Crucible: Black Steelworkers in Western Pennsylvania, 1875–1980*. Albany: State University of New York Press, 1986.

Didion, Joan. *Miami*. New York: Simon and Schuster, 1987.

Dieffenbach, Victor C. "Powwowing Among the Pennsylvania Germans." *Pennsylvania Folklife* 25, no. 2 (1975–1976): 29–46.

Diehl, Keila. *Echoes from Dharamsala: Music in the Life of a Tibetan Refugee Community*. Berkeley: University of California Press, 2002.

Dietz, Myron S. "The Old Order River Brethren." *Brethren in Christ History and Life* 6 (1983): 4–34.

———. "Old Order River Brethren Worship." *Brethren in Christ History and Life* 12 (1989): 125–47.

Discourse of American Culture. Logan: Utah State University Press, 1998.

Dizard, Jan E. *Going Wild: Hunting, Animal Rights, and the Contested Meaning of Nature*. Amherst: University of Massachusetts Press, 1999.

———. *Mortal Stakes: Hunters and Hunting in Contemporary America*. Amherst: University of Massachusetts Press, 2003.

Do, Hien Duc. *The Vietnamese Americans*. Westport, CT: Greenwood, 1999.

Dodds, Richard J.S., and Pete Lesher, eds. *A Heritage in Wood: The Chesapeake Bay Maritime Museum's Small Craft Collection*. St. Michael's, MD: Chesapeake Bay Maritime Museum, 1992.

Dodge, Robert K. *Early American Almanac Humor*. Bowling Green, OH: Bowling Green University Popular Press, 1987.

Dogtown and Z Boys. DVD. Directed by Stacy Peralta. Culver City, CA: Sony Pictures, 2002.

Dolak, George. *A History of the Slovak Evangelical Lutheran Church in the United States of America, 1902–1927*. Saint Louis, MO: Concordia, 1955.

Dominguez, Virginia. *White by Definition: Social Definition in Creole Louisiana*. New Brunswick, NJ: Rutgers University Press, 1986.

Donahue, John J. "The Ritual Dimension of *Karate-do* [empty hand way]." *Journal of Ritual Studies* 7 (1993): 105–24.

Donaldson, Emily Ann. *The Scottish Highland Games in America*. Gretna, LA: Pelican, 1986.

Donovan, Pamela. *No Way of Knowing: Crime, Urban Legends, and the Internet*. New York: Routledge, 2004.

Doogan, Mike. *How to Speak Alaskan*. Seattle: Epicenter, 1993.

Dorgan, Howard. *In the Hands of a Happy God: The "No-Hellers" of Central Appalachia.* Knoxville: University of Tennessee Press, 1997.

———. *The Old Regular Baptists of Central Appalachia.* Knoxville: University of Tennessee Press, 1989.

Dorje, Rinjing. *Food in Tibetan Life.* London: Prospect Books, 1985.

Dormon, James H., ed. *Creoles of Color of the Gulf South.* Knoxville: University of Tennessee Press, 1996.

Dorsett, Lyle W. *The Queen City: A History of Denver.* Boulder, CO: Pruett, 1977.

Dorson, Richard M. *America in Legend: Folklore from the Colonial Period to the Present.* New York: Pantheon, 1973.

———. *American Folklore.* Chicago: University of Chicago Press, 1959.

———. *American Folklore and the Historian.* Chicago: University of Chicago Press, 1971.

———. *Bloodstoppers and Bearwalkers: Folk Traditions of the Upper Peninsula.* Cambridge, MA: Harvard University Press, 1952.

———, *Buying the Wind: Regional Folklore in the United States.* Chicago: University of Chicago Press, 1964.

———. "Collecting Folklore in Jonesport, Maine." *Proceedings of the American Philosophical Society* 101 (1957): 270–89.

———. "Dialect Stories of the Upper Peninsula: A New Form of American Folklore." *Journal of American Folklore* 61 (1948): 113–50.

———, ed. *Folklore and Folklife: An Introduction.* Chicago: University of Chicago Press, 1972.

———, ed. *Handbook of American Folklore.* Bloomington: Indiana University Press, 1983.

———. "Jewish-American Dialect Stories on Tape." In *Studies in Biblical and Jewish Folklore,* ed. Dov Noy, Raphael Patai, and Francis Lee Utley, 111–74. Bloomington: Indiana University Press, 1960.

———. *Land of the Millrats.* Cambridge, MA: Harvard University Press, 1981.

Dorst, John. "Tags and Burners, Cycles and Networks: Folklore in the Telectronic Age." *Journal of Folklore Research* 27 (1990): 179–90.

———. *The Written Suburb: An American Site, An Ethnographic Dilemma.* Philadelphia: University of Pennsylvania Press, 1989.

Doss, Erika. "Death, Art, and Memory in the Public Sphere: The Visual and Material Culture of Grief in Contemporary America." *Mortality* 7, no. 1 (2002): 63–82.

Douglas, Paul. "Bizz-Buzz, Turtles, Quarters, and One Horse Club." *Alcohol Health & Research World* 11, no. 4 (Summer 1987): 54–57, 92.

Douglass, William A. *Beltran: Basque Sheepman of the American West.* Reno: University of Nevada Press, 1979.

Douglass, William A., and Jon Bilbao. *Americanuak: Basques in the New World.* Reno: University of Nevada Press, 1975.

Dow, James R., and Madeline Roemig. "Amana Folk Art and Craftsmanship." *Palimpsest* 58, no. 2 (1977): 54–63.

Doyle, Don H. *Nashville Since the 1920s.* Knoxville: University of Tennessee Press, 1985.

Drake, St. Clair. "The Social and Economic Status of the Negro in the United States." In *The Negro American,* ed. Talcott Parsons and Kenneth B. Clark, 5–36. Boston: Beacon, 1966.

Drake, St. Clair, and Horace R. Cayton. *Black Metropolis: A Study of Negro Life in a Northern City.* Revised and enlarged edition. Chicago: University of Chicago Press, 1993.

Dubois, Abbe. *Hindu Manners, Customs, and Ceremonies.* New Delhi, India: Rupa, 1999.

Dubuffet, Jean. *Asphyxiating Culture.* New York: Four Walls Eight Windows, 1988.

Duchaine, Dan. *The Underground Steroid Handbook II.* Venice, CA: HLR Technical Books, 1989.

Duckert, Audrey R. "Place Nicknames." *Names* 21 (1973): 153–60.

Duff, Andrew I. *Western Pueblo Identities: Regional Interaction, Migration, and Transformation.* Tucson: University of Arizona Press, 2002.

Duggin, Betty J., and Brett H. Riggs. *Studies in Cherokee Basketry.* Knoxville, TN: Frank H. McClung Museum, 1991.

Dunaway, David K., and Willa K. Baum, eds. *Oral History: An Interdisciplinary Anthology.* Nashville, TN: American Association for State and Local History, 1984.

Duncan, Barbara. *Living Stories of the Cherokee.* Chapel Hill: University of North Carolina Press, 1998.

Duncan, Robert J. "Chain Letters: A Twentieth Century Folk Practice." In *What's Going On? (In Modern Texas Folklore),* ed. Francis E. Abernethy, 47–58. Publications of the Texas Folklore Society No. 40. Austin, TX: Encino Press, 1976.

Dundes, Alan. *Analytic Essays in Folklore*. The Hague: Mouton, 1975.

———. *Bloody Mary in the Mirror: Essays in Psychoanalytic Folkloristics*. Jackson: University Press of Mississippi, 2002.

———. "Brown County Superstitions." *Midwest Folklore* 11 (1961): 25–56.

———. "Chain Letter: A Folk Geometric Progression." *Northwest Folklore* 1 (1966): 14–19.

———, ed. *The Cockfight: A Casebook*. Madison: University of Wisconsin Press, 1994.

———. *Cracking Jokes: Studies of Sick Humor Cycles and Stereotypes*. Berkeley, CA: Ten Speed Press, 1987.

———. *Fables of the Ancients? Folklore in the Qur'an*. Lanham, MD: Rowman and Littlefield, 2003.

———. *From Game to War and Other Psychoanalytic Essays on Folklore*. Lexington: University Press of Kentucky, 1997.

———. *Interpreting Folklore*. Bloomington: Indiana University Press, 1980.

———, ed. *Mother Wit from the Laughing Barrel: Readings in the Interpretation of Afro-American Folklore*. Jackson: University Press of Mississippi, 1990.

———. *Parsing Through Customs: Essays by a Freudian Folklorist*. Madison: University of Wisconsin Press, 1987.

———, ed. *The Study of Folklore*. Englewood Cliffs, NJ: Prentice-Hall, 1965.

———. "Texture, Text, and Context." In *Interpreting Folklore*, ed. Alan Dundes, 20–32. Bloomington: Indiana University Press, 1980.

———. "What Is Folklore?" In *The Study of Folklore*, ed. Alan Dundes, 1–3. Englewood Cliffs, NJ: Prentice Hall, 1965.

Dundes, Alan, and Lauren Dundes. "The Elephant Walk and Other Amazing Hazing: Male Fraternity Initiation Through Infantilization and Feminization." In *Bloody Mary in the Mirror: Essays in Psychoanalytic Folkloristics,* ed. Alan Dundes, 95–121. Jackson: University Press of Mississippi, 2002.

Dundes, Alan, and Carl R. Pagter. *Sometimes the Dragon Wins: Yet More Urban Folklore from the Paperwork Empire*. Syracuse, NY: Syracuse University Press, 1996.

———. *Urban Folklore from the Paperwork Empire*. Austin: University of Texas Press, 1975.

———. *Work Hard and You Shall Be Rewarded: Urban Folklore from the Paperwork Empire*. 1975. Reprint, Bloomington: Indiana University Press, 1978.

Dundes, Alan, Lauren Dundes, and Michael B. Streiff. "'When You Hear Hoofbeats, Think Horses, Not Zebras.'" *Proverbium: Yearbook of International Proverb Scholarship* 16 (1999): 95–103.

Dunn, Stephen P., and Ethel Dunn. "Molokans in America." *Dialectical Anthropology* 3 (1978): 349–60.

Durand, Jorge, and Douglas S. Massey. *Miracles on the Border: Retablos of Mexican Migrants to the United States*. Tucson: University of Arizona Press, 1995.

Durnbaugh, Donald F., ed. *The Brethren Encyclopedia*. 3 vols. Philadelphia: Brethren Encyclopedia, 1983–1984.

———, ed. *Church of the Brethren: Yesterday and Today*. Elgin, IL: Brethren Press, 1986.

———, *Fruit of the Vine: A History of the Brethren, 1708–1995*. Elgin, IL: Brethren Press, 1997.

———. "The German Journalist and the Dunker Love-Feast." *Pennsylvania Folklife* 18, no. 2 (Winter 1968–1969): 40–48.

Dyck, Cornelius J. *An Introduction to Mennonite History*. Scottdale, PA: Mennonite Publishing House, 1993.

Dyen, Doris J. "Pysanky: Craftsmanship, Ritual Meaning, and Ethnic Identity." In *Craft and Community: Traditional Arts in Contemporary Society,* ed. Shalom Staub, 99–106. Philadelphia: Balch Institute for Ethnic Studies and Pennsylvania Heritage Affairs Commission, 1988.

Dyrud, Keith P. *The Quest for the Rusyn Soul: The Politics of Religion and Culture in Eastern Europe and in America, 1890–World War I*. Philadelphia: Balch Institute Press, 1992.

Earnest, Adele. *The Art of the Decoy: American Bird Carvings*. New York: Bramhall House, 1965.

Eastland, Lynette S., Sandra L. Herndon, and Jeanine R. Barr. *Communication in Recovery: Perspectives on Twelve-Step Groups*. Cresskill, NJ: Hampton, 1988.

Eaton, Allen H. *Beauty Behind Barbed Wire: The Arts of Japanese in Our War Relocation Camps*. New York: Harper, 1952.

Eberly, Don E., and Ryan Streeter. *The Soul of Civil Society: Voluntary Associations and the Public Value of Moral Habits*. Lanham, MD: Lexington Books, 2002.

Echeverria, Jeronima. *Home Away from Home: A History of Basque Boarding Houses*. Reno: University of Nevada Press, 1999.

Eck, Diana, ed. *On Common Ground: World Religions in America*. CD-ROM. New York: Columbia University Press, 1997.

Eggers, Ulrich. *Community for Life*. Scottdale, PA: Herald, 1988.

Ehrlich, Walter. *Zion in the Valley: The Jewish Community of St. Louis*. Vol. 2, *The Twentieth Century*. Columbia: University of Missouri Press, 2002.

Eicher, Joanne, and Mary Ellen Roach-Higgins. "Definition and Classification of Dress: Implications for Analysis of Gender Roles." In *Dress and Gender: Making and Meaning*, ed. Ruth Barnes and Joanne Eicher, 8–22. Oxford: Berg, 1992.

Eichler, Ernst, Gerold Hilty, Heinrich Löffler, Hugo Steger, and Ladislav Zgusta, eds. *Name Studies: An International Handbook of Onomastics*. 3 vols. Berlin: Walter de Gruyter, 1995–1996.

Eiler, Lyntha Scott, Terry Eiler, and Carl Fleischhauer, eds. *Blue Ridge Harvest: A Region's Folklife in Photographs*. Washington, DC: Library of Congress, 1981.

Eliade, Mircea. *Rites and Symbols of Initiation: The Mystery of Birth and Rebirth*. Putnam, CT: Spring Publications, 1994.

Eliason, Eric A. *Celebrating Zion: Pioneers in Mormon Popular Historical Expression*. Provo, UT: Brigham Young University Press, 2004.

———. "Toward the Folkloristic Study of Latter-Day Saint Conversion Narratives." *Brigham Young University Studies* 38 (1999): 137–50.

Eller, David B. "Church of the Brethren." In *Meet the Brethren*, ed. D.F. Durnbaugh, 69–91. Philadelphia: Brethren Press for the Brethren Encyclopedia, 1984.

Ellis, Bill. *Aliens, Ghosts, and Cults: Legends We Live*. Jackson: University Press of Mississippi, 2001.

———. "The Camp Mock-Ordeal: Theater as Life." *Journal of American Folklore* 94 (1981): 486–505.

———. "Hitler's Birthday: Rumor-Panics in the Wake of the Columbine Shootings." *Children's Folklore Review* 24, nos. 1–2 (2002): 21–32.

———. "Making a Big Apple Crumble: The Role of Humor in Constructing a Global Response to Disaster." *New Directions in Folklore* 6 (June 2002). www.temple.edu/isllc/newfolk/bigapple/bigapple1.html. Accessed July 4, 2005.

———. *Raising the Devil: Satanism, New Religions, and the Media*. Lexington: University Press of Kentucky, 2000.

———. "Speak to the Devil: Ouija Board Rituals Among American Adolescents." *Contemporary Legend* 4 (1994): 61–90.

———. "Why Is a Lucky Rabbit's Foot Lucky? Body Parts as Fetishes." *Journal of Folklore Research* 39 (2002): 51–84.

Ellis, Clyde. *A Dancing People: Powwow Culture on the Southern Plains*. Lawrence: University Press of Kansas, 2003.

Ellis, Edward. *A Chronological History of the Rangeley Lakes Region*. 1983, Reprint, Rangeley, ME: Rangeley Lakes Region Historical Society, 1992.

Ellwood, Robert S. *Religious and Spiritual Groups in Modern America*. Englewood Cliffs, NJ: Prentice-Hall, 1973.

Eng, David L. *Racial Castration: Managing Masculinity in Asian America*. Durham, NC: Duke University Press, 2001.

Englekirk, John E. "The Passion Play in New Mexico." *Western Folklore* 25 (1966): 17–33, 105–21.

Engs, Ruth C., and David J. Hanson. "Drinking Games and Problems Related to Drinking Among Moderate and Heavy Drinkers." *Psychological Reports* 73 (1993): 115–20.

Ensminger, Robert F. *The Pennsylvania Barn: Its Origins, Evolution and Distribution in North America*. Baltimore: Johns Hopkins University Press, 1992.

Erdmans, Marie Patrice. *Opposite Poles: Immigrants and Ethnics in Polish Chicago, 1976–1990*. University Park: Pennsylvania State University Press, 1998.

Erickson, Charlotte. *Invisible Immigrants: The Adaptation of English and Scottish Immigrants in 19th-Century America*. Ithaca, NY: Cornell University Press, 1972.

Erickson, John H. *Orthodox Christians in America*. New York: Oxford University Press, 1999.

Erikson, Patricia Pierce, Kirk Wachendorf, and Helma Ward. *Voices of a Thousand People: The Makah Cultural and Research Center*. Lincoln: University of Nebraska Press, 2002.

Erixon, Sigurd. "International Maps of Folk Culture." *Laos* 3 (1955): 48–98.

Eshleman, Wilmer. "A History of the Reformed Mennonite Church." *Papers Read Before the Lancaster*

County Historical Society 49, no. 4 (1945): 86–117.

Esman, Marjorie R. *Henderson, Louisiana: Cultural Adaptation in a Cajun Community.* New York: Holt, Rinehart and Winston, 1985.

Espiritu, Yen Le. *Filipino American Lives.* Philadelphia: Temple University Press, 1995.

Ethnic Recordings in America: A Neglected Heritage. Washington, DC: American Folklife Center, 1982.

Etter, Don. *Auraria: Where Denver Began.* Boulder: Colorado Associated University Press, 1972.

Evans, David. *Big Road Blues: Tradition and Creativity in the Folk Blues.* Berkeley: University of California Press, 1982.

Evans, Timothy H. *King of the Western Saddle: The Sheridan Saddle and the Art of Don King.* Jackson: University Press of Mississippi, 1998.

Evans-Pritchard, Edward E. *Kinship and Marriage Among the Nuer.* Oxford: Clarendon Press, 1951.

———. *The Nuer: A Description of the Modes of Livelihood and Political Institutions of a Nilotic People.* Oxford: Oxford University Press, 1940.

Everett, Holly. *Roadside Crosses in Contemporary Memorial Culture.* Denton: University of North Texas Press, 2002.

Ewers, John C. *Plains Indian History and Culture: Essays on Continuity and Change.* Norman: University of Oklahoma Press, 1997.

Ezekiel, Raphael S. *The Racist Mind: Portraits of American Neo-Nazis and Klansmen.* New York: Viking, 1995.

Fadiman, Anne. *The Spirit Catches You and You Fall Down.* New York: Farrar, Straus, and Giroux, 1997.

Faherty, William Barnaby. *The Irish in St. Louis: An Unmatched Celtic Community.* Columbia: University of Missouri Press, 2001.

Fainhauz, David. *Lithuanians in the USA: Aspects of Ethnic Identity.* Chicago: Lithuanian Library Press, 1991.

Fair, John D. *Muscletown USA: Bob Hoffman and the Manly Culture of York Barbell.* University Park: Pennsylvania State University Press, 1999.

Farley, Yvonne Snyder. "Holiness People Revisited." *Goldenseal: West Virginia Traditional Life* (Summer 1999): 10–19.

Farr, Francine. Vive *Haiti! Contemporary Art of the Haitian Diaspora.* Washington, DC: Inter-American Development Bank, 2004.

Farr, Marcia, ed. *Ethnolinguistic Chicago: Language and Literacy in the City's Neighborhoods.* Mahwah, NJ: Lawrence Erlbaum, 2004.

Farrar, Charles A.J. *Farrar's Illustrated Guide Book to Rangeley, Richardson, Kennebago, Umbagog, and Parmachenee Lakes, Dixville Notch, and Andover, ME, and Vicinity.* 1876, Reprint: North Waterboro, ME: Humpback Trout Workshops, 2003.

Farrar, Stewart, and Janet Farrar. *A Witches' Bible.* 2 vols. New York: Magickal Childe, 1985.

Farrell, James J. *One Nation Under Goods: Malls and the Seduction of American Shopping.* Washington, DC: Smithsonian Books, 2003.

Farrer, Claire R., ed. *Women and Folklore.* Austin: University of Texas Press, 1975.

———, ed. "Women in Folklore." Special issue, *Journal of American Folklore* 88, no. 347 (1975): 1–109.

Fass, Paula S., and Mary Ann Mason, eds. *Childhood in America.* New York: New York University Press, 2000.

Feather, Laura L. "The Looneaters: Foodways and Change on Harkers Island." *North Carolina Folklore Journal* 37 (1990): 5–12.

Featherstone, Mike, ed. *Body Modification.* London: Sage, 2000.

Federal Writers' Project (Massachusetts). *The Armenians in Massachusetts.* Boston: Federal Writers' Project, 1937.

Feintuch, Burt, ed. *Conservation of Culture: Folklorists and the Public Sector.* Lexington: University Press of Kentucky, 1988.

Feintuch, Burt, and David Watters, eds. *Encyclopedia of New England.* New Haven, CT: Yale University Press, 2005.

Feirstein, Sanna. *Naming New York: Manhattan Places and How They Got Their Names.* New York: New York University Press, 2001.

Feltault, Kelly. *It's How You Pick the Crab: An Oral Portrait of Eastern Shore Crab Picking.* St. Michael's, MD: Chesapeake Bay Maritime Museum, 2001.

Fenton, John Y. *Transplanting Religious Traditions: Asian Indians in America.* New York: Praeger, 1988.

Fernald, Theodore, and Paul R. Platero, eds. *The Athabaskan Languages: Perspectives on a Native American Language Family.* New York: Oxford University Press, 2000.

Fernandez, Ronald, Serafin Méndez Méndez, and

Gail Cueto. *Puerto Rico Past and Present: An Encyclopedia*. Westport, CT: Greenwood Press, 1998.

Ferraro, Pat, Elaine Hedges, and Julie Silber. *Hearts and Hands: The Influence of Women and Quilts on American Society*. San Francisco: Quilt Digest Press, 1987.

Ferris, William, ed. *Afro-American Folk Art and Crafts*. Jackson: University Press of Mississippi, 1983.

———. *Blues from the Delta*. New York: Da Capo, 1984.

———. "The Enlisted Man: Army Folklore." *New York Folklore Quarterly* 2 (1976): 229–34.

———. *Local Color: A Sense of Place in Folk Art*. New York: Anchor Books, 1992.

Fett, Sharla M. *Working Cures: Healing, Health, and Power on Southern Slave Plantations*. Chapel Hill: University of North Carolina Press, 2002.

Fife, Austin E. "Dashboard Amulets." *Western Folklore* 17 (1958): 207–8.

———. *Exploring Western Americana*. Ann Arbor, MI: UMI Research Press, 1988.

Fife, Austin, and Alta Fife. *Saints of Sage and Saddle*. Bloomington: Indiana University Press, 1956.

Fife, Austin, Alta Fife, and Henry Glassie, eds. *Forms upon the Frontier: Folklife and Folk Arts in the United States*. Logan: Utah State University Press, 1969.

Fifield, Barringer. *Seeing Pittsburgh*. Pittsburgh: University of Pittsburgh Press, 1996.

Finckenauer, James O., and Elin J. Waring. *Russian Mafia in America: Immigration, Culture, and Crime*. Boston: Northeastern University Press, 1998.

Fine, Elizabeth C. *The Folklore Text: From Performance to Print*. Bloomington: Indiana University Press, 1984.

———. *Soulstepping: African American Step Shows*. Urbana: University of Illinois Press, 2003.

Fine, Gary Alan. *Manufacturing Tales: Sex and Money in Contemporary Legends*. Knoxville: University of Tennessee Press, 1992.

———. *Shared Fantasy: Role-Playing Games as Social Worlds*. Chicago: University of Chicago Press, 1983.

———. *With the Boys: Little League Baseball and Preadolescent Culture*. Chicago: University of Chicago Press, 1987.

Finnegan, Ruth. "Tradition, but What Tradition and for Whom?" *Oral Tradition* 6 (1991): 104–24.

Finsterbusch, C.A. *Cockfighting All Over the World*. Rev. ed. Surrey, UK: Saiga, 1980.

Fischer, David Hackett. *Albion's Seed: Four British Folkways in America*. New York: Oxford Universty Press, 1989.

Fish, Lydia M. "General Edward G. Lansdale and the Folksongs of Americans in the Vietnam War." *Journal of American Folklore* 102 (1989): 390–411.

Fishkoff, Sue. *The Rebbe's Army: Inside the World of Chabad-Lubavitcher*. New York: Schocken, 2003.

Fishman, Robert. *Bourgeois Utopias: The Rise and Fall of Suburbia*. New York: Basic Books, 1987.

Fitchen, John. *The New World Dutch Barn*. 2nd ed. Ed. Gregory Huber. Syracuse, NY: Syracuse University Press, 2001.

Fitzgerald, Frances. *Cities on a Hill: A Journey Through Contemporary American Cultures*. New York: Simon and Schuster, 1986.

Fleischhauer, Carl, and Beverly Brannan, eds. *Documenting America, 1935–1943*. Berkeley: University of California Press, 1992.

Fleischhauer, Carl, and Charles K. Wolfe. *The Process of Field Research: Final Report on the Blue Ridge Parkway Folklife Project*. Washington, DC: American Folklife Center, Library of Congress, 1981.

Fleischman, Bill, and Al Pearce. *Inside Sports NASCAR Racing: The Ultimate Fan Guide*. Detroit: Visible Ink, 1998.

Fletcher, S.W. *Pennsylvania Agriculture and Country Life, 1840–1940*. Harrisburg: Pennsylvania Historical and Museum Commission, 1955.

Flores-Gonzalez, Nilda. "Paseo Boricua: Claiming a Puerto Rican Space in Chicago." *Centro Journal* 13, no. 2 (Fall 2001): 7–23.

Flores-Pena, Ysamur, and Roberta J. Evanchuk. *Santería Garments and Altars: Speaking Without a Voice*. Jackson: University of Mississippi Press, 1994.

Flory, Richard, and Donald Miller, eds. *Gen X Religion*. New York: Routledge, 2000.

Flynt, J. Wayne. *Poor but Proud: Alabama's Poor Whites*. Tuscaloosa: University of Alabama Press, 1989.

Foerstner, Abigail. *Picturing Utopia: Bertha Shambaugh and the Amana Photographers*. Iowa City: University of Iowa Press, 2000.

Fogarty, Robert S. *Dictionary of American Communal and Utopian History*. Westport, CT: Greenwood, 1980.

Fogel, Edwin M. "The Himmelsbrief." *German American Annals* 10 (1908): 286–311.

———, ed. *Proverbs of the Pennsylvania Germans.* Lancaster: Pennsylvania-German Society, 1929. Reprint, Bern: Peter Lang, 1995.

Foley, Douglas. *Learning Capitalist Culture: Deep in the Heart of Tejas.* Philadelphia: University of Pennsylvania Press, 1990.

Foley, John Miles, ed. *Oral-Formulaic Theory: A Folklore Casebook.* New York: Garland, 1990.

Fone, Byrne. *Homophobia: A History.* New York: Henry Holt, 2000.

Fong, Mary. *Communicating Ethnic and Cultural Identity.* Lanham, MD: Rowman and Littlefield, 2004.

Fong-Torres, Shirley. *San Francisco Chinatown: A Walking Tour.* San Francisco: China Books, 1991.

Fontes, Manuel da Costa. "The Study of the Ballad and Other Portuguese Folk Traditions in North America." *Canadian Ethnic Studies* 23 (1991): 119–39.

Foote, Kenneth. *Shadowed Ground: America's Landscapes of Violence and Tragedy.* Austin: University of Texas Press, 2003.

Forrest, John. *Lord I'm Coming Home: Everyday Aesthetics in Tidewater North Carolina.* Ithaca, NY: Cornell University Press, 1988.

Foster, George M. "What Is Folk Culture?" *American Anthropologist* 55 (1953): 159–73.

Foster, Helen Bradley. *"New Raiments of Self": African American Clothing in the Antebellum South.* Oxford: Berg, 1997.

Foster, Helen Bradley, and Donald Clay Johnson, eds. *Wedding Dress Across Cultures.* Oxford: Berg, 2003.

Fracchia, Charles A. *City by the Bay: A History of Modern San Francisco, 1945–Present.* Los Angeles: Heritage Media, 1997.

Francaviglia, Richard V. "The Mormon Landscape: Definition of an Image in the American West." *Proceedings of the Association of American Geographers* 2 (1970): 59–61.

Francis, Doris. *Will You Still Need Me, Will You Still Feed Me, When I'm 84?* Bloomington: Indiana University Press, 1984.

Franks, Clyda. *Tulsa: Where the Streets Were Paved with Gold.* Charleston, SC: Arcadia, 2000.

Franz, Barbara. "Bosnian Refugees and Socio-Economic Realities: Changes in Refugee and Settlement Policies in Austria and the United States." *Journal of Ethnic and Migration Studies* 29 (2003): 5–25.

Fraser, Walter J., Jr. *Charleston! Charleston! The History of a Southern City.* Columbia: University of South Carolina Press, 1989.

Frazier, Ian. *Great Plains.* New York: Farrar, Straus, and Giroux, 1989.

Freeman, Eileen Elias. *Angelic Healing: Working with Your Angels to Heal Your Life.* New York: Warner Books, 1994.

———. *Touched by Angels.* New York: Warner Books, 1992.

Freeman, James A. *Hearts of Sorrow: Vietnamese-American Lives.* Stanford, CA: Stanford University Press, 1989.

Freeman, Roland. *The Arabbers of Baltimore.* Centerville, MD: Tidewater Press, 1989.

Friday, Karl. "Bushido or Bull: A Medieval Historian's Perspective on the Imperial Army and the Japanese Warrior Tradition." *History Teacher* 27 (1994): 339–49.

Friedman, Martin, ed. *Naives and Visionaries.* Minneapolis, MN: Walker Art Center, 1974.

Fries, Adelaide L. *Customs and Practices of the Moravian Church.* Bethlehem, PA: Moravian Church in North America, 2003.

———. *Distinctive Customs and Practices of the Moravian Church.* Bethlehem, PA: Comenius, 1949.

Friesen, John W., and Virginia Lyons Friesen. *The Palgrave Companion to North American Utopias.* New York: Palgrave, 2004.

Frisch, Michael. *A Shared Authority: Essays on the Craft and Meaning of Oral and Public History.* Albany: State University of New York Press, 1990.

Fritz, Georg. *The Chamorro: A History and Ethnography of the Marianas.* Trans. Elfriede Craddock. Saipan, Commonwealth of the Northern Marianas: Division of Historic Preservation, 1986.

Frommer, Myrna Katz, and Harvey Frommer. *It Happened in Brooklyn: An Oral History of Growing Up in the Borough in the 1940s, '50s and '60s.* New York: Harcourt Brace, 1993.

Frye, Nancy Kettering. "'An Uncommon Woman' in the Age of the Common Man: The Life and Times of Sarah Righter Major." *Pennsylvania Folklife* 46:2 (Winter 1996–1997): 54–70.

Fujita, Stephen S., and David J. O'Brien. *Japanese American Ethnicity: The Persistence of Community.* Seattle: University of Washington Press, 1991.

Fussell, Fred. *Blue Ridge Music Trails: Finding a Place in the Circle*. Chapel Hill: University of North Carolina Press, 2003.

Gage, Mary, and James Gage. *The Art of Splitting Stone: Early Rock Quarrying Methods in Pre-Industrial New England, 1630–1825*. Amesbury, MA: Powwow River Books, 2002.

Gailey, Alan. "The Nature of Tradition." *Folklore* 100 (1989): 143–61.

Gambino, Richard. *Blood of My Blood: The Dilemma of the Italian Americans*. Toronto: Guernica, 1997.

Gambos, Zoltan, ed. *Hungarians in America*. Cleveland, OH: Szabadsag, 1941.

Ganahl, Pat. *Hot Rods and Cool Customs*. New York: Artabras, 1996.

Gannon, Jack R. *Deaf Heritage: A Narrative History of Deaf America*. Silver Spring, MD: National Association of the Deaf, 1981.

Gans, Herbert J. *The Levittowners: Ways of Life and Politics in a New Suburban Community*. New York: Pantheon, 1967.

Garcha, Rajinder. "The Sikhs in North America: History and Culture." *Ethnic Forum: Journal of Ethnic Studies and Ethnic Bibliography* 12, no. 2 (1992): 80–93.

Garcia, Maria Cristina. *Havana USA: Cuban Exiles and Cuban Americans in South Florida, 1959–1994*. Berkeley: University of California Press, 1997.

García, Ofelia, and Joshua A. Fishman, eds. *The Multilingual Apple: Languages in New York City*. New York: Mouton de Gruyter, 2002.

Garcia, Victor Q. "Mexican Enclaves in the U.S. Northeast: Immigrant and Migrant Mushroom Workers in Southern Chester County, Pennsylvania." JSRI Research Report #27. Julian Samora Research Institute/Michigan State University, East Lansing, MI, 1997.

Gardner, Emelyn. *Folklore from the Schoharie Hills, New York*. Ann Arbor: University of Michigan Press, 1937.

Gardner, Howard. *Leading Minds: An Anatomy of Leadership*. New York: Basic Books, 1995.

Garland, Robert. "Greek Drinking Parties." *History Today* 33 (June 1982): 18–21.

Garreau, Joel. *The Nine Nations of North America*. Boston: Houghton Mifflin, 1981.

Garry, Jane, and Hasan El-Shamy, eds. 2005. *Archetypes and Motifs in Folklore and Literature*. Armonk, NY: M.E. Sharpe.

Garvey, Joan B., and Mary Lou Widmer. *Beautiful Crescent: A History of New Orleans*. New Orleans, LA: Garmer Press, 1982.

Gaster, Theodor H. *New Year: Its History, Customs, and Superstitions*. New York: Abelard-Schuman, 1955.

Gastil, Raymond D. *Cultural Regions of the United States*. Seattle: University of Washington Press, 1975.

Gaudet, Marcia, and James C. McDonald, eds. *Mardi Gras, Gumbo, and Zydeco: Readings in Louisiana Culture*. Jackson: University of Mississippi Press, 2003.

Gayton, Anna H. "The 'Festa da Serreta' at Gustine." *Western Folklore* 7 (1948): 251–65.

Geddes, William R. *Migrants of the Mountains: The Cultural Ecology of the Blue Miao (Hmong Njua) of Thailand*. Oxford: Clarendon Press, 1976.

Gedmintas, Aleksandras. *An Interesting Bit of Identity: The Dynamics of Ethnic Identity in a Lithuanian American Community*. New York: AMS Press, 1989.

———. *The Interpretation of Cultures*. New York: Basic Books, 1973.

Gehman, Mary. *The Free People of Color of New Orleans: An Introduction*. New Orleans, LA: Margaret Media, 1994.

Gehres, Eleanor M., Sandra Dallas, Maxine Benson, and Stanley Cuba, eds. *The Colorado Book*. Golden, CO: Fulcrum, 1993.

Geist, Troyd A. *From the Wellspring: Faith, Soil, Tradition; Folk Arts from Ukrainian Culture in North Dakota*. Bismarck: North Dakota Council on the Arts, 1997.

Gelberg, Steven J., ed. *Hare Krishna, Hare Krishna: Five Distinguished Scholars on the Krishna Movement in the West*. New York: Grove Press, 1983.

Geller, Jaclyn. *Here Comes the Bride: Women, Weddings and the Marriage Mystique*. New York: Four Walls Eight Windows, 2001.

George, Victoria, and Alan Dundes. "The Gomer: A Figure of American Hospital Folk Speech." *Journal of American Folklore* 351, no. 91 (January–March 1978): 568–81.

Georges, Eugenia. *The Making of a Transnational Community: Migration, Development, and Cultural Change in the Dominican Republic*. New York: Columbia University Press, 1990.

Georges, Robert A. "Research Perspectives in Ethnic Folklore Studies." *Folklore and Mythology Studies* 7 (1983): 1–23.

———. "Skinnerian Behaviorism and Folklore Studies." *Western Folklore* 49 (1990): 400–405.

Georges, Robert A., and Alan Dundes. "Toward a Structural Definition of the Riddle." *Journal of American Folklore* 76 (1963): 111–18.

Georges, Robert A., and Michael Owen Jones. *Folkloristics: An Introduction.* Bloomington: Indiana University Press, 1995.

Gerlach, Celeste S. *Scherenschnitte from Collections of Early America.* 1978. Reprint, Emmaus, PA: Gerlachs of Lecha, 1982.

Gessler, Diana Hollingsworth. *Very Charleston: A Celebration of History, Culture, and Lowcountry Charm.* Chapel Hill, NC: Algonquin, 2003.

Gibson, Margaret A. *Accommodation Without Assimilation: Sikh Immigrants in an American High School.* Ithaca, NY: Cornell University Press, 1988.

Gillespie, Angus K. *Folklorist of the Coal Fields: George Korson's Life and Work.* University Park: Pennsylvania State University Press, 1980.

Gillespie, Angus K., and Jay Mechling, eds. *American Wildlife in Symbol and Story.* Knoxville: University of Tennessee Press, 1987.

Gilley, Jennifer, and Stephen Burnett. "Deconstructing and Reconstructing Pittsburgh's Man of Steel: Reading Joe Magarac against the Context of the 20th-Century Steel Industry." *Journal of American Folklore* 111 (1998): 392–408.

Gilliland, Mary Kay, Sonja Spoljar-Vrzina, and Vlasta Rudan. "Reclaiming Lives: Variable Effects of War on Gender and Ethnic Identities in the Narratives of Bosnian and Croatian Refugees." *Anthropology of East Europe Review* 13 (1995): 30–39.

Gillis, John R. *A World of Their Own Making: Myth, Ritual, and the Quest for Family Values.* New York: Basic Books, 1996.

Gilmore, Janet C. *The World of the Oregon Fish Boat: A Study in Maritime Folklife.* Ann Arbor, MI: UMI Research Press, 1986.

Gilmore, Robert Karl. *Ozark Baptizings, Hangings, and Other Diversions: Theatrical Folkways of Rural Missouri, 1885–1910.* Norman: University of Oklahoma Press, 1984.

Gimbutas, Marija. *The Civilization of the Goddess.* San Francisco: Harper, 1991.

Gitlitz, David M. *Secrecy and Deceit: The Religion of the Crypto-Jews.* Philadelphia: Jewish Publication Society, 1996.

Gizelis, Gregory. *Narrative Rhetorical Devices of Persuasion in the Greek Community of Philadelphia.* New York: Arno Press, 1980.

Gjerde, Jon. *From Peasants to Farmers: The Migration from Balestrand, Norway, to the Upper Midwest.* New York: Cambridge University Press, 1985.

Glanz, Rudolf. *The Jew in the Old American Folklore.* New York: Waldon Press, 1961.

Glass, Joseph W. *The Pennsylvania Culture Region: A View from the Barn.* Ann Arbor, MI: UMI Research Press, 1986.

Glasser, Ruth. *Aqui me quedo: Puerto Ricans in Connecticut.* Middletown, CT: Connecticut Humanities Council, 1997

Glassie, Henry H. *Folk Housing in Middle Virginia: A Structural Analysis of Historic Artifacts.* Knoxville: University of Tennessee Press, 1975.

———. "Folklore and Geography: Towards an Atlas of American Folk Culture." *New York Folklore Quarterly* 29 (1973): 3–20.

———. *Material Culture.* Bloomington: Indiana University Press, 1999.

———. *Pattern in the Material Folk Culture of the Eastern United States.* Philadelphia: University of Pennsylvania Press, 1968.

———. *The Spirit of Folk Art: The Girard Collection at the Museum of International Folk Art.* New York: Harry N. Abrams, 1989.

———. "Three Southern Mountain Jack Tales." *Tennessee Folklore Society Bulletin* 30 (1964): 78–94.

———. "Tradition." In *Eight Words for the Study of Expressive Culture,* ed. Burt Feintuch, 176–97. Urbana: University of Illinois Press, 2003.

———. "The Variation of Concepts Within Tradition: Barn Building in Otsego County, New York." In *Man and Cultural Heritage: Papers in Honor of Fred B. Kniffen,* ed. H.J. Walker and W.G. Haag, 177–234. Baton Rouge: Louisiana State University School of Geoscience, 1974.

———. *Vernacular Architecture.* Bloomington: Indiana University Press, 2000.

———. "William Houck, Maker of Pounded Ash Adirondack Packbaskets." *Keystone Folklore Quarterly* 12 (1967): 23–54.

Glassman, Carl. "The Russian Jews of Brighton Beach." *Jewish Folklore and Ethnology Review* 10 (1988): 23–27.

Glatfelter, Charles. *Pastors and People: German Lutheran and Reformed Churches in the Pennsylvania Field, 1717–1793.* Vol. 1, *Pastors and Con-*

gregations. Vol. 2, *The History*. Breinigsville: Pennsylvania German Society, 1980–1981.

Glazer, Mark. *A Dictionary of Mexican American Proverbs*. Westport, CT: Greenwood, 1987.

Glazier, Michael, ed. *Encyclopedia of the Irish in America*. Notre Dame, IN: University of Notre Dame Press, 1999.

Glazier, Michael, and Thomas J. Shelley. *The Encyclopedia of American Catholic History*. Collegeville, MO: Liturgical Press, 1997.

Glimm, James York. *Flatlanders and Ridgerunners: Folktales from the Mountains of Northern Pennsylvania*. Pittsburgh: University of Pittsburgh Press, 1983.

Gluck, Sherna Berger, and Daphne Patai, eds. *Women's Words: The Feminist Practice of Oral History*. New York: Routledge, Chapman and Hall, 1991.

Goble, Danney. *Tulsa: Biography of the American City*. Tulsa: Council Oak Books, 1997.

Goff, James R., Jr. *Close Harmony: A History of Southern Gospel*. Chapel Hill: University of North Carolina Press, 2002.

Goffman, Erving. *The Presentation of Self in Everyday Life*. London: Allen Lane, 1969.

Gold, Gerald L., and Marc-Adélard Tremblay, comps. *Communities and Culture in French Canada*. Toronto: Holt, Rinehart and Winston of Canada, 1973.

Gold, Steven. *Refugee Communities: A Comparative Field Study*. Newbury, CA: Sage, 1992.

Goldschmidt, Matti. *The Bible in Israeli Folk Dancing*. Viersen, Germany: Choros Verlag, 2001.

Goldsmith, Robert, ed. *The Bluegrass Reader*. Urbana: University of Illinois Press, 2004.

Goldy, J.M., and A.W. Purdue. *The Making of the Modern Christmas*. Athens: University of Georgia Press, 1986.

Golenbock, Peter. *American Zoom: Stock Car Racing from the Dirt Tracks to Daytona*. London: Macmillan, 1994.

———. *The Spirit of St. Louis: A History of the St. Louis Cardinals and Browns*. New York: HarperEntertainment, 2001.

Golway, Terry. *So Others Might Live: A History of New York's Bravest*. New York: Basic Books, 2002.

Gonzalez, Juan L., Jr. "Asian Indian Immigration Patterns: The Origins of the Sikh Community in California." *International Migration Review* 20, no. 1 (Spring 1986): 40–54.

Goodman, Felicitas D. *How About Demons? Possession and Exorcism in the Modern World*. Bloomington: Indiana University Press, 1988.

Goodman, Philip, ed. *The Rosh Hashanah Anthology*. Philadelphia: Jewish Publication Society, 1970.

Goodwin, Joseph. *More Man Than You'll Ever Be: Gay Folklore and Acculturation in Middle America*. Bloomington: Indiana University Press, 1989.

Goodwin, Marjorie Harness. *He-Said-She-Said: Talk As Social Organization Among Black Children*. Bloomington: Indiana University Press, 1990.

Gopalan V., and Bruce E. Nickerson. "Faith Healing in Indiana and Illinois." *Indiana Folklore* 6 (1973): 33–99.

Goswami, Satsvarupa Dasa. *He Lives Forever: On Separation from Srila Prabhupada*. Port Royal, PA: GN Press, 1979.

Gothic Rock. Cleopatra Records, 1992. Compact disc.

Goulart, Tony P. *The Holy Ghost Festas: A Historic Perspective of the Portuguese in California*. San Jose, CA: Portuguese Heritage Publications, 2003.

Gourd Woman and Eagle Heart. *The Elders Speak: Dakotah and Ojibway Stories of the Land*. Enhanced CD. Bismarck, ND: Makoche Word and the North Dakota Council on the Arts, 1999.

Gracza, Rezsoe, and Margaret Gracza. *The Hungarians in America*. Minneapolis, MN: Lerner Publications, 1969.

Gradén, Lizette. *On Parade: Making Heritage in Lindsborg, Kansas*. Uppsala, Sweden: Acta Universitatis Upsaliensis, 2003.

Gradwohl, David M. "On Vestiges and Identities: Some Thoughts on the Controversy Concerning 'Crypto-Jews' in the American Southwest." *Jewish Folklore and Ethnology Review* 18 (1996): 83–84.

Graham, Andrea, ed. *Neon Quilt: Folk Arts in Las Vegas*. Carson City: Nevada State Council on the Arts, 1994.

Graham, Frank, Jr. *Baseball Wit and Wisdom: The Folklore of a National Pastime*. New York: Scholastic Books, 1965.

Graham, Joe, ed. *Hecho en Tejas: Texas Mexican Folk Arts and Crafts*. Denton: University of North Texas Press, 1991.

Graham, Laurie. *Singing the City: The Bonds of Home in an Industrial Landscape*. Pittsburgh: University of Pittsburgh Press, 1998.

Grant, Gail Paton. "Getting Started: Outfitting the Bride in Seaside." *Canadian Folklore* 15 (1993): 69–81.

Grasmuck, Sherri, and Patricia Pessar. *Between Two Islands: Dominican International Migration.* Berkeley: University of California Press, 1991.

Graves, Alvin R. *Portuguese Californians: Immigrants in Agriculture.* San Jose, CA: Portuguese Heritage Publications, 2004.

Gray, Nada. *Holidays: Victorian Women Celebrate in Pennsylvania.* Lewisburg, PA: Oral Traditions Project, 1983.

Gray, Roland Palmer, ed. *Songs and Ballads of the Maine Lumberjacks.* Cambridge, MA: Harvard University Press, 1925.

Grazian, David. *Blue Chicago: The Search for Authenticity in Urban Blues Clubs.* Chicago: University of Chicago Press, 2003.

Greeley, Andrew. *The Catholic Myth: The Behavior and Beliefs of American Catholics.* 1990. Reprint, New York: Touchstone, 1997.

Green, Archie, ed. *Only a Miner: Studies in Recorded Coal Mining Songs.* Urbana: University of Illinois Press, 1972.

———, ed. *Songs About Work: Essays in Occupational Culture.* Bloomington: Indiana University Press, 1993.

———. *Tin Men.* Urbana: University of Illinois Press, 2002.

———. *Torching the Fink Books and Other Essays on Vernacular Culture.* Chapel Hill: University of North Carolina Press, 2001.

———. *Wobblies, Pile Butts, and Other Heroes: Labor Lore Explorations.* Urbana: University of Illinois Press, 1993.

Green, Henry Alan, and Marcia Kerstein Zerivitz. *Mosaic: Jewish Life in Florida.* Gainesville: University Press of Florida, 1998.

Green, Thomas A., ed. "Folk Drama." Special Issue. *Journal of American Folklore* 94, no. 374 (1981).

———, ed. *Folklore: An Encyclopedia of Beliefs, Customs, Tales, Music, and Art,* 2 vols. Santa Barbara, CA: ABC-CLIO, 1997.

———, ed. *Martial Arts of the World: An Encyclopedia.* Santa Barbara, CA: ABC-CLIO, 2001.

———. "Toward a Definition of Folk Drama." *Journal of American Folklore* 91, no. 361 (July–September 1978): 843–50.

Green, Thomas A., and W.J. Pepicello. "The Folk Riddle: A Redefinition of Terms." *Western Folklore* 38 (1979): 3–20.

Green, Thomas A., and Joseph Svinth, eds. *Martial Arts in the Modern World: Transmission, Change, and Adaptation.* Westport, CT: Praeger, 2003.

Greene, Victor R. *A Passion for Polka: Old Time Ethnic Music in America.* Berkeley: University of California Press, 1992.

Greenway, John. *American Folksongs of Protest.* 1953. Reprint, New York: Octagon, 1970.

Gregory, Hiram F., and Joseph Moran. *"We Know Who We Are": An Ethnographic Overview of the Creole Community and Traditions of Isle Brevelle and Cane River, Louisiana.* Denver, CO: Jean Lafitte National Historical Park and Preserve, U.S. Department of Interior, 1996.

Grele, Ronald J. *Envelopes of Sound: The Art of Oral History.* 2nd ed. Chicago: Precedent Publishing, 1985.

Grenier, Guillermo J., and Alex Stepick III. *Miami Now! Immigration, Ethnicity, and Social Change.* Gainesville: University Press of Florida, 1990.

Greninger, Edwin T. "Thanksgiving: An American Holiday." *Social Science* 54 (1979): 3–15.

Grennan, Sean. *Gangs: An International Approach.* Upper Saddle River, NJ: Prentice Hall, 2000.

Grider, Sylvia Ann. "Conservatism and Dynamism in the Contemporary Celebration of Halloween: Institutionalization, Commercialization, and Gentrification." *Southern Folklore* 53 (1996): 3–15.

———. "The Function of Texas Historical Legends." *Artes Populares* 16–17 (1995): 314–28.

———. "Spontaneous Shrines: A Modern Response to Tragedy and Disaster (Preliminary Observations Regarding the Spontaneous Shrines Following the Terrorist Attacks of September 11, 2001)." *New Directions in Folklore* 5 (October 2001). www.temple.edu/isllc/newfolk/shrines.html. Accessed July 4, 2005.

Griebel, Helen Bradley. "Carroll County Rug Hookers: Morphology of a Craft." *Midwestern Folklore* 17 (1991): 34–55.

Griffin, James B. "Comments on the Late Prehistoric Societies in the Southeast." In *Towns and Temples Along the Mississippi,* ed. David H. Dye and Cheryl Anne Cox, 5–15. Tuscaloosa: University of Alabama Press, 1990.

Griffith, James S. *Beliefs and Holy Places: A Spiritual Geography of the Pimería Alta.* Tucson: University of Arizona Press, 1992.

———. *A Shared Space: Folklife in the Arizona-Sonora Borderlands.* Logan: Utah State University Press, 1995.

———. *Southern Arizona Folk Arts.* Tucson: University of Arizona Press, 1988.

Grimes, Ronald L. *Deeply into the Bone: Re-Inventing Rites of Passage.* Berkeley: University of California Press, 2002.

———, ed. *Readings in Ritual Studies.* Upper Saddle River, NJ: Prentice Hall, 1995.

Grobman, Neil R. "Wycinanki and Pysanky: Forms of Religious and Ethnic Folk Art in the Delaware Valley." Occasional paper. Pittsburgh: Pennsylvania Ethnic Heritage Studies Center, University of Pittsburgh, 1981.

Groce, Nancy. *New York: Songs of the City.* New York: Watson-Guptill, 1999.

Groce, Nora Ellen. *Everyone Here Spoke Sign Language: Hereditary Deafness on Martha's Vineyard.* Cambridge, MA: Harvard University Press, 1985.

Gross, Leonard. *The Golden Years of the Hutterites: The Witness and Thought of the Communal Moravian Anabaptists During the Walpot Era, 1565–1578.* Scottdale, PA: Herald, 1980.

Gross, Paul S. *Hutterite Way: The Inside Story of the Life, Customs, Religion, and Traditions of the Hutterites.* Saskatoon, Canada: Freeman, 1965.

Gross, Steven, and Sue Daley. *Santa Fe Houses and Gardens.* New York: Rizzoli, 2002.

Groth, Paul, and Todd W. Bressi, eds. *Understanding Ordinary Landscapes.* New Haven, CT: Yale University Press, 1997.

Group, Thetis M. *Nursing, Physician Control, and the Medical Monopoly: Historical Perspectives on Gendered Inequality in Roles, Rights, and Range of Practice.* Bloomington: Indiana University Press, 2001.

Gundaker, Grey, ed. *Keep Your Head to the Sky: Interpreting African American Home Ground.* Charlottesville: University of Virginia Press, 1998.

Gura, Philip F., and James F. Bollman. *America's Instrument: The Banjo in the Nineteenth Century.* Chapel Hill: University of North Carolina Press, 1999.

Gurda, John. *The Making of Milwaukee.* Brookfield, WI: Burton and Mayer, 1999.

Gurock, Jeffrey. *When Harlem Was Jewish, 1870–1930.* New York: Columbia University Press, 1979.

Guthrie, George M., ed. *Six Perspectives on the Philippines.* Manila, Philippines: Bookmark, 1971.

Guthrie, Patricia. *Catching Sense: African American Communities on a South Carolina Sea Island.* Westport, CT: Bergin and Garvey, 1996.

Gutierrez, David G. *Walls and Mirrors: Mexican Americans, Mexican Immigrants, and the Politics of Ethnicity.* Berkeley: University of California Press, 1995.

Gutowski, John A. "The Art of Professional Wrestling: Folk Expression in Mass Culture." *Keystone Folklore Quarterly* 17 (1972): 41–50.

Haas, Mary R. "Southeastern Indian Folklore." *Journal of American Folklore* 60 (1947): 403–6.

Haddad, Yvonne Yazbeck, and Jane Idleman Smith, eds. *Muslim Communities in North America.* Albany: State University of New York Press, 1994.

Hafen, P. Jane, and Diane Dufva Quantic, eds. *A Great Plains Reader.* Lincoln: University of Nebraska Press, 2003.

Hafstein, Valdimar T. "The Politics of Origins: Collective Creation Revisited." *Journal of American Folklore* 117 (2004): 300–315.

Hahamovitch, Cindy. *Fruits of Their Labor: Atlantic Coast Farmworkers and the Making of Migrant Poverty, 1870–1945.* Chapel Hill: University of North Carolina Press, 1997.

Hahn, Robert A. *Sickness and Healing: An Anthropological Perspective.* New Haven, CT: Yale University Press, 1995.

Hakala, Joyce. *Memento of Finland: A Musical Legacy.* St. Paul: Pikebone Music, 1997.

Hale, Frederick. *Danes in Wisconsin.* Madison: State Historical Society of Wisconsin, 2005.

Halevy, Schulamith C. "Manifestations of Crypto-Judaism in the American Southwest." *Jewish Folklore and Ethnology Review* 18 (1996): 68–76.

Haley, James L. *Apaches: A History and Culture Portrait.* Norman: University of Oklahoma Press, 1997.

Hall, Edwin S. *The Eskimo Storyteller: Folktales from Noatak, Alaska.* Knoxville: University of Tennessee Press, 1975.

Hall, Gwendolyn Midlo. *Africans in Colonial Louisiana: The Development of Afro-Creole Culture in the Eighteenth Century.* Baton Rouge: Louisiana State University Press, 1992.

Hall, Michael D., and Eugene W. Metcalf, Jr., eds. *The Artist Outsider: Creativity and the Boundaries of Culture.* Washington, DC: Smithsonian Institution Press, 1994.

Hall, Patricia A. "A Case for Folklife and the Local

Historical Society." In *American Material Culture and Folklife*, ed. Simon J. Bronner, 205–20. 1985. Reprint, Logan: Utah State University Press, 1992.

Hall, Patricia, and Charlie Seemann, eds. *Folklife and Museums: Selected Readings*. Nashville, TN: American Association for State and Local History, 1987.

Hall, Stephanie A. *Ethnographic Collections in the Archive of Folk Culture: A Contributor's Guide*. Washington, DC: American Folklife Center, Library of Congress, 1995.

———. "Monsters and Clowns: A Deaf American Halloween." In *Folklife Annual 1990*, ed. James Hardin, 122–31. Washington, DC: American Folklife Center at the Library of Congress, 1991.

Halpert, Herbert. "Chain Letters." *Western Folklore* 15 (1956): 287–89.

Halter, Marilyn. *Between Race and Ethnicity: Cape Verdean American Immigrants, 1860–1965*. Urbana: University of Illinois Press, 1993.

Hamblin, Jacob, and James A. Little. *Jacob Hamblin: His Life in His Own Words*. 1881. Reprint, New York: Paramount Books, 1995.

Hamer, Lynne. "Folklore in Schools and Multicultural Education." *Journal of American Folklore* 113, no. 447 (Winter 2000): 44–69.

Hamill, John. *Tulsa: The Great American City*. Montgomery, AL: Community Communications, 2000.

Hamilton, C. Mark. *Nineteenth-Century Mormon Architecture and City Planning*. New York: Oxford University Press, 1995.

Hamilton, J. Taylor, and Kenneth G. Hamilton. *History of the Moravian Church. The Renewed Unitas Fratrum, 1722–1957*. Bethlehem, PA: Moravian Church in America, 1957.

Hamilton, John D. *Material Culture of the American Freemasons*. Lexington, MA: Museum of Our National Heritage, 1994.

Hamm, Thomas D. *Quakers in America*. New York: Columbia University Press, 2003.

Hammack, David C., Diane L. Grabowski, and John J. Grabowski, eds. *Identity, Conflict and Cooperation: Central Europeans in Cleveland, 1850–1930*. Cleveland: Western Reserve Historical Society, 2002.

Hand, Wayland D., ed. *American Folk Legend: A Symposium*. Berkeley: University of California Press, 1971.

———, ed. *American Folk Medicine: A Symposium*. Berkeley: University of California Press, 1976.

———, ed. *Magical Medicine: The Folkloric Component of Medicine in the Folk Belief, Custom, and Ritual of the Peoples of Europe and America*. Berkeley: University of California Press, 1980.

———, ed. *Popular Beliefs and Superstitions from North Carolina*. The Frank C. Brown Collection of North Carolina Folklore. Vol. 6 and 7. Durham, NC: Duke University Press, 1961, 1964.

Hand, Wayland D., Anna Casetta, and Sondra B. Thiederman, eds. *Popular Beliefs and Superstitions: A Compendium of American Folklore from the Ohio Collection of Newbell Niles Puckett*. 3 vols. Boston: G.K. Hall, 1981.

Handlin, Oscar. *Boston's Immigrants: A Study in Acculturation*. Revised edition. New York: Atheneum, 1971.

Handy, W.C. *Father of the Blues: An Autobiography*. Edited by Arna Bontemps, with a foreword by Abbe Niles. 1941. Reprint, New York: Collier Books, 1970.

Haney, C. Allen, Christina Leimer, and Juliann Lowery. "Spontaneous Memorialization: Violent Death and Emerging Mourning Ritual." *Omega: Journal of Death and Dying* 35, no. 2 (1997): 159–71.

Hannan, Kevin. "Ethnic Identity Among the Czechs and Moravians of Texas." *Journal of American Ethnic History* 15 (1996): 3–31.

Hansen, Gregory. "N.F.S. Grundtvig's Idea of Folklore: Resurrecting Folk-Life Through the Living Word." *Folklore Historian* 12 (1995): 5–13.

Hardy, Don, ed. *Pierced Hearts and True Love: A Century of Drawings for Tattoos*. New York: Drawing Center, 1995.

Harinck, George, and Hans Krabbendam, eds. *Sharing the Reformed Tradition: The Dutch-North American Exchange, 1846–1996*. Amsterdam: VU University Press, 1996.

Harkins, Anthony. *Hillbilly: A Cultural History of an American Icon*. New York: Oxford University Press, 2003.

Harlan, Lane, Robert Hoffmeister, and Ben Bahan. *A Journey into the Deaf-World*. San Diego, CA: DawnSignPress, 1996.

Harley, Gail M. *Hindu and Sikh Faiths in America*. New York: Facts on File, 2003.

Harlow, Francis H. *Two Hundred Years of Historic Pueblo Pottery*. Albuquerque: University of New Mexico Press, 1991.

Harlow, Illana. "The Queens Folklorist: Reflections

on a Folk Arts Program." *New York Folklore Newsletter* 19 (Winter–Spring 1998): 4–5.

Harmetz, Aljean. *On the Road to Tara: The Making of Gone with the Wind.* New York: Harry N. Abrams, 1996.

Harmon, Alexandra. *Indians in the Making: Ethnic Roots and Indian Identity Around Puget Sound.* Berkeley: University of California Press, 1999.

Harmon, Jack. *Texas Missions and Landmarks.* San Antonio: University of Texas Institute of Texan Cultures at San Antonio, 1977.

Harmond, Richard P., and Thomas J. Curran. *A History of Memorial Day: Unity, Discord and the Pursuit of Happiness.* New York: Peter Lang, 2002.

Harris, Lis. *Holy Days: The World of the Hasidic Family.* New York: Touchstone, 1995.

Hart, Donn V. *Riddles in Filipino Folklore: An Anthropological Analysis.* Syracuse, NY: Syracuse University Press, 1964.

Hart, Donn V., and Harriett E. Hart. "The Images of the Catholic Priest in Bisayan Filipino Folklore." *Southern Folklore Quarterly* 40 (1976): 307–41.

Hartsfield, Mariella. *Tall Betsy and Dunce Baby: South Georgia Folktales.* Athens: University of Georgia Press, 1987.

Hasan, Asthma Gull. *American Muslims: The New Generation.* New York: Continuum, 2000.

Haslip-Viera, Gabriel, ed. *Taíno Revival: Critical Perspectives on Puerto Rican Identity and Cultural Politics.* Princeton, NJ: Markus Wiener, 2001.

Hass, Kristin Ann. *Carried to the Wall: American Memory and the Vietnam Veterans Memorial.* Los Angeles: University of California Press, 1998.

Hastings, Scott E., Jr. *The Last Yankees: Folkways in Eastern Vermont and the Border Country.* Hanover, NH: University Press of New England, 1990.

Hatayama, Leslie T. *Righting a Wrong: Japanese Americans and the Passage of the Civil Liberties Act of 1988.* Stanford, CA: Stanford University Press, 1993.

Hatch, Mary Jo, and Michael Owen Jones. "Photocopylore at Work: Aesthetics, Collective Creativity and the Social Construction of Organizations." *Studies in Cultures, Organizations, and Societies* 3 (1997): 263–87.

Hathaway, Rosemary V. "'Life in the TV': The Visual Nature of 9/11 Lore and Its Impact on Vernacular Response." *Journal of Folklore Research* 42 (2005): 33–56.

Haugen, Einar. *The Norwegian Language in America: A Study in Bilingual Behavior.* Bloomington: Indiana University Press, 1969.

Hawk, Tony. *Hawk: Occupation Skateboarder.* New York: ReganBooks, 2001.

Hawley, John Stratton, and Gurinder Singh Mann. *Studying the Sikhs: Issues for North America.* Albany: State University of New York Press, 1993.

Hawley, W.M. *Chinese Folk Designs: A Collection of 300 Cut-Paper Designs Together with 160 Chinese Art Symbols.* New York: Dover Publications, 1971.

Hay, Frederick J. *Goin' Back to Sweet Memphis: Conversations with the Blues.* Athens: University of Georgia Press, 2001.

Hayano, David M. *Poker Faces: The Life and Work of Professional Card Players.* Berkeley: University of California Press, 1982.

Haycox, Stephen W. *Alaska: An American Colony.* Seattle: University of Washington Press, 2002.

Hayden, Dolores. *Building Suburbia: Green Fields and Urban Growth, 1820–2000.* New York: Vintage Books, 2003.

Hayes, Diana L., and Cyprian Davis, eds. *Taking Down Our Harps: Black Catholics in the United States.* Maryknoll, NY: Orbis Books, 1998.

Hays, Samuel P., ed. *City at the Point: Essays on the Social History of Pittsburgh.* Pittsburgh: University of Pittsburgh Press, 1989.

Hazzard-Gordon, Katrina. *Jookin': The Rise of Social Dance Formations in African-American Culture.* Philadelphia: Temple University Press, 1990.

Healey, James C. *Foc's'le and Glory-Hole: A Study of the Merchant Seaman and His Occupation.* New York: Greenwood, 1969.

Heavilin, Barbara, and Charles W. Heavilin, eds. *The Quaker Presence in America: "Let Us Then Try What Love Will Do."* Lewiston, NY: Edwin Mellen Press, 2003.

Hebdige, Dick. *Subculture: The Meaning of Style.* London: Methuen, 1979.

Hecker, Melvin, and Heike Fenton, eds. *The Greeks in America 1528–1977: A Chronology and Fact Book.* Dobbs Ferry, NY: Oceana, 1978.

Hegi, Ursula. *Tearing the Silence: On Being German in America.* New York: Simon and Schuster, 1997.

Heilbut, Tony. *The Gospel Sound: Good News and Bad Times.* New York: Anchor Books, 1975.

Heilman, Samuel C. *Defenders of the Faith: Inside Ultra-Orthodox Jewry.* New York: Schocken, 1992.

———. *When a Jew Dies.* Berkeley: University of California Press, 2001.

Hemphill, Paul. *The Nashville Sound: Bright Lights and Country Music.* New York: Simon and Schuster, 1970.

Hennesey, James J. *American Catholics: A History of the Roman Catholic Community in the United States.* New York: Oxford University Press, 1981.

Henry, Big Boy. *Poor Man's Blues.* CD 9508. Somer's Point, NJ: New Moon Music, 1996.

Henry, Jean M. "'Mrs. O'Leary's Cow': The Rhetorical Folklore and History Surrounding the Great Fire of Chicago." *Midwestern Folklore* 25 (1999): 54–59.

Hereniko, Vilsoni. "Comic Theater of Samoa: An Interview with John Kneubuhl." *Manoa* 5 (1993): 99–106.

Herman, Bernard L. "The Embedded Landscapes of the Charleston Single House." *Perspectives in Vernacular Architecture* 7 (1997): 41–57.

Herman, Daniel Justin. *Hunting and the American Imagination.* Washington, DC: Smithsonian Institution Press, 2001.

Hernández, Jo Farb. "Folklore in Museums: Issues and Applications." In *Putting Folklore to Use*, ed. Michael Owen Jones, 62–75. Lexington: University Press of Kentucky, 1994.

———. "Josep Pujiula i Vila." *Raw Vision* 40 (Fall 2002): 24–29.

———. "Watts Towers." *Raw Vision* 37 (Winter 2001): 32–39.

Herr, John. *John Herr's Complete Works.* Buffalo, NY: Peter Paul and Bro., 1890.

Herrera-Sobek, María. *The Bracero Experience: Elitelore vs. Folklore.* Berkeley: University of California Press, 1979.

———. *The Mexican Corrido: A Feminist Analysis.* Bloomington: Indiana University Press, 1990.

———. *Northward Bound: The Mexican Immigrant Experience in Ballad and Song.* Bloomington: Indiana University Press, 1993.

Herring, J.L. *Saturday Night Sketches: Stories of Old Wiregrass Georgia.* Boston: Gorham, 1918.

Hess, Clarke. *Mennonite Arts.* Atglen, PA: Schiffer, 2001.

Heyck, Denis L., ed. *Barrios and Borderlands: Cultures of Latinos and Latinas in the United States.* New York: Routledge, 1994.

Heylin, Clinton. *From the Velvets to the Voidoids: A Pre-Punk History for a Post-Punk World.* London: Penguin, 1993.

Hickey, Gerald Cannon. *Free in the Forest: Ethnohistory of the Vietnamese Central Highlands, 1954–1976.* New Haven, CT: Yale University Press, 1982.

———. *Shattered World: Adaptation and Survival Among Vietnam's Highland Peoples During the Vietnam War.* Philadelphia: University of Pennsylvania Press, 1993.

———. *Sons of the Mountains: Ethnohistory of the Vietnamese Central Highlands to 1954.* New Haven, CT: Yale University Press, 1982.

Hicks, Michael. *Mormonism and Music: A History.* Urbana: University of Illinois Press, 1989.

Hicks, Robert D. *In Pursuit of Satan: The Police and the Occult.* Buffalo, NY: Prometheus Books, 1991.

Hiiemae, Mall. "Souls' Visiting Time in the Estonian Folk Calendar." In *Folk Belief Today*, ed. Mare Koiva and Kai Vassiljeva, 124–29. Tartu: Estonian Academy of Sciences, 1995.

Hill, Errol. *The Trinidadian Carnival: Mandate for a National Theater.* Austin: University of Texas Press, 1972.

Hills, Matt. *Fan Cultures.* New York: Routledge, 2002.

Hilton, Hope A. *"Wild Bill" Hickman and the Mormon Frontier.* Salt Lake City, UT: Signature Books, 1988.

Hine, Robert V. *California's Utopian Colonies.* Revised edition. Berkeley: University of California Press, 1983.

Hinshaw, John H. *Steel and Steelworkers: Race and Class Struggle in Twentieth-Century Pittsburgh.* Albany: State University of New York Press, 2002.

Hinton, William, and D'Arcy Rahming. *Men of Steel Discipline: The Official Oral History of Black Pioneers in the Martial Arts.* Edited by Jennifer H. Baarman. Chicago: Modern Bu-Jutsu, 1995.

Hisatsune, Kimi Yonemura. *Shinshu in Modern Society.* San Francisco: Department of Buddhist Education, Buddhist Churches of America, 1995.

Hively, Kay, and Albert E. Brumley, Jr. *I'll Fly Away: The Life Story of Albert E. Brumley.* Branson, MO: Mountaineer Books, 1990.

Hockings, Paul, ed. *Principles of Visual Anthropology.* The Hague: Mouton, 1975.

Hodkinson, Paul. *Goth: Identity, Style and Subculture.* Oxford: Berg, 2002.

Hoerig, Karl A. *Under the Palace Portal: Native American Artists in Santa Fe.* Albuquerque: University of New Mexico Press, 2003.

Hofer, Samuel. *The Hutterites: Lives and Images of*

a Communal People. Saskatoon, Saskatchewan, Canada: Hofer, 1998.

Hoffman, Bob. *Weight Training for Athletes.* New York: Ronald, 1961.

Hoffman, David F., Jr. "The Meaning and Function of the Kolo Club 'Marian' in the Steelton, Pennsylvania, Croatian Community." *Keystone Folklore Quarterly* 16 (1971): 115–31.

Hogan, Steve, and Lee Hudson. *Completely Queer: The Gay and Lesbian Encyclopedia.* New York: Henry Holt, 1998.

Hohman, John George. *Pow-wows, or the Long-Lost Friend.* 1820. Reprint, Pomeroy, WA: Health Research, 1971.

Holbrook, Stewart H. *Yankee Loggers: A Recollection of Woodsmen, Cooks, and River Drivers.* New York: International Paper Company, 1961.

Holli, Melvin, and Peter Jones. *Ethnic Chicago.* Grand Rapids, MI: Eerdmans, 1984.

Hollis, Susan Tower, Linda Pershing, and M. Jane Young, eds. *Feminist Theory and the Study of Folklore.* Urbana: University of Illinois Press, 1993.

Holm, Bill. *Northwest Coast Indian Art: An Analysis of Form.* Seattle: University of Washington Press, 1965.

Holmes, Lowell Don, and Ellen Rhoads Holmes. *Samoan Village: Then and Now.* Fort Worth, TX: Harcourt Brace Jovanovich, 1992.

Holmquist, June Drenning, ed. *They Chose Minnesota.* St. Paul: Minnesota Historical Society Press, 1981.

Holtzman, Jon D. *Nuer Journeys, Nuer Lives: Sudanese Refugees in Minnesota.* Boston: Allyn and Bacon, 2000.

Hood, Clifton. *722 Miles: The Building of the Subways and How They Transformed New York.* Baltimore: Johns Hopkins University Press, 1995.

Hood, Ralph W. "When the Spirit Maims and Kills: Social Psychological Considerations of the History of Serpent Handling Sects and the Narrative of Handlers." *International Journal for the Psychology of Religion* 8 (1998): 71–96.

Hook, Wade F. "Religious Regionalism: The Case of Lutherans in the South." *Review of Religious Research* 27 (1985): 77–85.

Hopf, Claudia. *Scherenschnitte, Traditional Papercutting.* Lebanon, PA: Applied Arts Press, 1977.

———. *Scherenschnitte: The Folk Art of Scissors Cutting.* Lancaster, PA: John Baer's Sons, 1971.

Hopkins, Dwight. *Shoes That Fit Our Feet: Sources for a Constructive Black Theology.* Maryknoll, NY: Orbis, 1993.

Hopkins, Jerry. *The Hula.* Hong Kong: APA Productions, 1982.

Horejs, Vit, ed. *Czechoslovakian-American Puppetry.* New York: GOH Productions/Seven Loaves, 1994.

Horell, C. William, Henry Dan Piper, and John W. Voight. *Land Between the Rivers: The Southern Illinois Country.* Carbondale: Southern Illinois University Press, 1974.

Horowitz, David A., ed. *Inside the Klavern: The Secret History of a Ku Klux Klan of the 1920s.* Carbondale: Southern Illinois University Press, 1999.

Horton, Laurel, ed. *Quiltmaking in America: Beyond the Myths.* Nashville: Rutledge Hill Press, 1994.

Hosokawa, Bill. *Nisei: The Quiet Americans.* New York: William Morrow, 1969.

Hostetler, Beulah S. "The Formation of the Old Orders." *Mennonite Quarterly Review* 66, no. 1 (1992): 5–25.

———. "An Old Order River Brethren Love Feast." *Pennsylvania Folklife* 24, no. 2 (Winter 1974–1975): 8–20.

Hostetler, John A. *Amish Society.* 4th ed. Baltimore: Johns Hopkins University Press, 1993.

———. *Hutterite Society.* 1974. Reprint, Baltimore: Johns Hopkins University Press, 1997.

Hostetler, John A., and Gertrude E. Huntington. *The Hutterites in North America.* Fort Worth, TX: Harcourt Brace College Publishers, 1996.

Hovanec, Evelyn A. *Common Lives of Uncommon Strength: The Women of the Coal and Coke Era of Southwestern Pennsylvania 1880–1970.* Uniontown: Coal and Coke Heritage Center, Penn State Fayette, 2001.

Howell, Mark D. *From Moonshine to Madison Avenue: A Cultural History of the NASCAR Winston Cup Series.* Bowling Green, OH: Bowling Green University Popular Press, 1997.

Hubbard, Lester A. "Danish Numskull Stories." *Western Folklore* 19 (1960): 56–58.

Hubka, Thomas C. *Big House, Little House, Back House, Barn: The Connected Farm Buildings of New England.* 1984. Reprint, Hanover, NH: University Press of New England, 2004.

Hudson, Charles. *The Southeastern Indians.* Knoxville: University of Tennessee Press, 1976.

Huffman, Alan. *Ten Point: Deer Camp in the Missis-*

sippi Delta. Jackson: University Press of Mississippi, 1997.

Huffman, Ray. *Nuer Customs and Folk-Lore*. London: Oxford University Press, 1931.

Hufford, David J. "Beings Without Bodies: An Experience-Centered Theory of the Belief in Spirits." In *Out of the Ordinary: Folklore and the Supernatural,* ed. Barbara Walker, 11–45. Logan: Utah State University Press, 1995.

———. "Folk Healers." In *Handbook of American Folklore*, ed. Richard M. Dorson, 306–13. Bloomington: Indiana University Press, 1983.

———. "Folklore Studies Applied to Health." *Journal of Folklore Research* 35 (1998): 295–313.

———. *The Terror That Comes in the Night: An Experience-Centered Study of Supernatural Assault Traditions*. Philadelphia: University of Pennsylvania Press, 1982.

Hufford, Mary T. *American Folklife: A Commonwealth of Cultures*. Washington, DC: American Folklife Center, 1991.

———. *Chaseworld: Foxhunting and Storytelling in New Jersey's Pine Barrens*. Philadelphia: University of Pennsylvania Press, 1992.

———, ed. *Conserving Culture: A New Discourse on Heritage*. Urbana: University of Illinois Press, 1994.

———. "Context." In *Eight Words for the Study of Expressive Culture*, ed. Burt Feintuch, 146–75. Urbana: University of Illinois Press, 2003.

———. *One Space, Many Places: Folklife and Land Use in New Jersey's Pineland National Reserve*. Washington, DC: American Folklife Center, Library of Congress, 1986.

Hufford, Mary, Steven Zeitlin, and Marjorie Hunt. *The Grand Generation: Memory, Mastery, Legacy*. Seattle: University of Washington Press, 1988.

Hughes, Linda A. "Children's Games and Gaming." In *Children's Folklore*, ed. Brian Sutton-Smith, Jay Mechling, Thomas W. Johnson, and Felicia R. McMahon, 93–120. Logan: Utah University Press, 1999.

Humphrey, Theodore C. "A Family Celebrates a Birthday: Of Life and Cakes." In *"We Gather Together": Food and Festival in American Life,* ed. Theodore C. Humphrey and Lin T. Humphrey, 19–26. Ann Arbor, MI: UMI Research Press, 1988.

Humphrey, Theodore C., and Lin T. Humphrey, eds. *"We Gather Together": Food and Festival in American Life*. 1988. Reprint, Logan: Utah State University Press, 1991.

Hunt, Marjorie. *The Stone Carvers: Master Craftsmen of Washington National Cathedral*. Washington, DC: Smithsonian Institution Press, 1999.

Hurd, James P. "Marriage Practices Among the 'Nebraska' Amish of Mifflin County, Pennsylvania." *Pennsylvania Mennonite Heritage* 20, no. 2 (April 1997): 20–24.

Hurh, Won Moo, and Kwang Chung Kim. *Korean Immigrants in America: A Structural Analysis of Ethnic Confinement and Adhesive Adaptation*. Madison, NJ: Fairleigh Dickinson University Press, 1984.

———. "Religious Participation of Korean Immigrants in the United States." *Journal of the Scientific Study of Religion* 19 (1990): 19–34.

Hurley-Glowa, Susan. "Cape Verdean-American Communities in Southern New England." In *American Musical Traditions*. Vol. 2, *African American Music,* ed. Jeff Titon and Bob Carlin, 19–23. New York: Schirmer/Macmillan Reference, 2002.

Hurston, Zora Neale. *Mules and Men*. Philadelphia: J.B. Lippincott, 1935.

Hurt, Douglas R. *The Ohio Frontier: Crucible of the Old Northwest, 1720–1830*. Bloomington: Indiana University Press, 1996.

Hutchinson, Sharon Elaine. *Nuer Dilemmas: Coping with Money, War, and the State*. Berkeley: University of California Press, 1996.

Hutchinson, Sydney. "Pinto Güira and His Magic Bullet: A Dominican Instrument Maker in Corona, Queens." *Voices: The Journal of New York Folklore* 28 (Fall–Winter 2002): 10–15.

Hutton, Ronald. *The Triumph of the Moon: A History of Modern Pagan Witchcraft*. Oxford: Oxford University Press, 1999.

Hyatt, Harry Middleton. *Hoodoo—Conjuration—Witchcraft—Rootwork: Beliefs Accepted by Many Negroes and White Persons, These Being Orally Recorded Among Blacks and Whites*. Hannibal, MO: Memoirs of the Alma Egan Hyatt Foundation, 1970–1974.

Hyde, Clinton M. "Danish-American Theatre." In *Ethnic Theatre in the United States*, ed. Maxine Schweartz Seller, 101–18. Westport, CT: Greenwood, 1983.

Hyman, Colette. *Staging Strikes: Workers' Theatre and the American Labor Movement*. Philadelphia: Temple University Press, 1997.

Hymes, Dell, ed. *Reinventing Anthropology*. New York: Pantheon, 1972.

———. "Toward Ethnographies of Communication: The Analysis of Communication Events." In *Language and Social Context: Selected Readings*, ed. Pier Paolo Giglioli, 21–44. Hammondsworth: Penguin, 1972.

Ichioka, Yuji. *The Issei: The World of the First Generation Japanese Immigrants, 1885–1924.* New York: Free Press, 1988.

———, ed. *Views from Within: The Japanese American Evacuation and Resettlement Study.* Los Angeles: Asian American Studies Center, University of California at Los Angeles, 1989.

Ihde, Thomas, ed. *The Irish Language in the United States: A Historical, Sociolinguistic, and Applied Linguistic Survey.* Westport, CT: Bergin and Garvey, 1993.

Ikeda, Keiko. *A Room Full of Mirrors: High School Reunions in Middle America.* Stanford, CA: Stanford University Press, 1999.

Illick, Joseph E. *American Childhoods.* Philadelphia: University of Pennsylvania Press, 2002.

Indian Bottom Association, Old Regular Baptists. *Songs of the Old Regular Baptists: Lined-Out Hymnody from Southeastern Kentucky.* Vols. 1 and 2. Coproduced by Elwood Cornett, John Wallhausser, and Jeff Todd Titon. Washington, DC: Smithsonian Folkways, 1997, 2004.

Irish Traditional Music in America: Chicago. Rounder Records 6006, 2001. Compact disc.

Irvine, Leslie, and Brian Klocke. "Redefining Men: Alternative Masculinities in a Twelve-Step Program." *Men and Masculinities* 4 (2001): 27–48.

Isajiw, Wsevolod W., ed. *Ukrainians in American and Canadian Society: Contributions to the Sociology of Ethnic Groups.* Jersey City, NJ: M.P. Kots, 1976.

Ivanits, Linda J. *Russian Folk Belief.* Armonk, NY: M.E. Sharpe, 1989.

Ivanov, Viacheslav. *The Russian Orthodox Church of Alaska and the Aleutian Islands and Its Relation to Native American Traditions: An Attempt at a Multicultural Society, 1794–1912.* Washington, DC: Library of Congress, 1996.

Iverson, Peter. *Diné: A History of the Navajos.* Albuquerque: University of New Mexico Press, 2002.

Ives, Edward D. *The Argyle Boom.* Orono, ME: Northeast Folklore Society, 1977.

———. *George Magoon and the Down East Game War: History, Folklore, and the Law.* Urbana: University of Illinois Press, 1988.

———. *Joe Scott, the Woodsman-Songmaker.* Urbana: University of Illinois Press, 1978.

———. *Larry Gorman: The Man Who Made the Songs.* Bloomington: Indiana University Press, 1964.

———. *The Tape Recorded Interview.* 2nd ed. Knoxville: University of Tennessee Press, 1995.

Jablonski, Romona. *The Paper Cut-out Design Book.* Owings Mills, MD: Stemmer House, 1976.

Jackson, Bruce, ed. "Folklore and Feminism." Special issue, *Journal of American Folklore* 100, no. 398 (October–December 1987).

———. *Get Your Ass in the Water and Swim Like Me: Narrative Poetry from Black Oral Tradition.* Cambridge, MA: Harvard University Press, 1974.

———. *Get Your Ass in the Water and Swim Like Me! Narrative Poetry from the Black Oral Tradition.* Rounder Records, CD 2014. 1998.

———. *Killing Time: Life in the Arkansas Penitentiary.* Ithaca, NY: Cornell University Press, 1977.

———. "Prison Folklore." *Journal of American Folklore* 78 (1965): 317–29.

———. "Prison Nicknames." *Western Folklore* 26 (1967): 48–54.

———. *Wake Up Dead Man: Afro-American Worksongs from Texas Prisons.* 1972. Reprint, Cambridge, MA: Harvard University Press, 1999.

Jackson, Bruce, Judith McCulloh, and Marta Weigle, eds. *Folklore/Folklife.* Washington, DC: American Folklore Society, 1984.

Jackson, Dave, and Neta Jackson. *Glimpses of Glory: Thirty Years of Community.* Elgin, IL: Brethren, 1987.

Jackson, David Paul, and Janice A. Jackson. *Tibetan Thangka Painting: Methods and Materials.* Boulder, CO: Shambhala, 1984.

Jackson, Gregory L. "Bi-Lingual German Churches in the Lutheran Church in America." *Journal of German-American Studies* 9 (1975): 11–15.

Jackson, Kenell. "What Is Really Happening Here? Black Hair Among African Americans and in American Culture." In *Hair in African Art and Culture*, ed. Roy Sieber and Frank Herreman, 174–85. New York: Museum of African Art, 2000.

Jackson, Kenneth T. *Crabgrass Frontier: The Suburbanization of the United States.* New York: Oxford University Press, 1985.

———, ed. *Encyclopedia of New York City.* New Haven, CT: Yale University Press, 1995.

———. *The Neighborhoods of Brooklyn.* New Haven, CT: Yale University Press, 1998.

Jacobs, Claude F, and Andrew J. Kaslow. *The Spiritual Churches of New Orleans: Origins, Beliefs, and Rituals of an African-American Religion.* Knoxville: University of Tennessee Press, 1991.

Jacobs, Janet Liebman. *Hidden Heritage: The Legacy of the Crypto-Jews.* Berkeley: University of California Press, 2002.

Jacobs, Leo M. *A Deaf Adult Speaks Out.* 2nd ed. Washington, DC: Gallaudet College Press, 1980.

Jacobs, Lewis, ed. *The Documentary Tradition.* 2nd ed. New York: W.W. Norton, 1979.

Jacobs, Michael. *Complete CB Dictionary.* North Miami, FL: Success, 1978.

Jacoby, Mary Moore, ed. *The Churches of Charleston and the Lowcountry.* Columbia: University of South Carolina Press, 1994.

Jah, Yusuf, and Sister Shah'Keyah. *Uprising.* New York: Simon and Schuster, 1997.

Jalkanen, Ralph J. *The Faith of the Finns: Historical Perspectives on the Finnish Lutheran Church in America.* East Lansing: Michigan State University Press, 1972.

James-Duguid, Charlene. *Work as Art: Idaho Logging as an Aesthetic Moment.* Moscow: University of Idaho Press, 1996.

Janiskee, Robert L. "Resort Camping in America." *Annals of Tourism Research* 17 (1990): 385–407.

Jansen, William Hugh. "The Esoteric-Exoteric Factor in Folklore." In *The Study of Folklore*, ed. Alan Dundes, 43–51. Englewood Cliffs, NJ: Prentice-Hall, 1965.

Janzen, Reinhild Kauenhoven, and John M. Janzen. *Mennonite Furniture: A Migrant Tradition (1766–1910).* Intercourse, PA: Good Books, 1991.

Japanese American Cultural and Community Center. *A Gathering of Joy: Obon Music and Dance Traditions in the United States.* Los Angeles: Japanese American Cultural and Community Center, 1993.

Jemie, Onwuchekwa, ed. *Yo' Mama! New Raps, Toasts, Dozens, Jokes and Children's Rhymes from Urban Black America.* Philadelphia: Temple University Press, 2003.

Jennings, Jan, and Herbert Gottfried. *American Vernacular Interior Architecture, 1870–1940.* New York: Van Nostrand Reinhold, 1988.

Jensen, George H. *Storytelling in Alcoholics Anonymous: A Rhetorical Analysis.* Carbondale: Southern Illinois University Press, 2000.

Jensen, Joan M. *Passage from India: Asian Indians in North America.* New Haven, CT: Yale University Press, 1988.

Jensen, Joli. *Nashville Sound: Authenticity, Commercialization, and Country Music.* Nashville, TN: Vanderbilt University Press, 1997.

Joans, Barbara. *Bike Lust: Harleys, Women, and American Society.* Madison: University of Wisconsin Press, 2001.

Johnson, Geraldine N. "'More for Warmth Than for Looks': Quilts of the Blue Ridge Mountains." *North Carolina Folklore Journal* 30 (1982): 55–84.

———. *Weaving Rag Rugs: A Women's Craft in Western Maryland.* Knoxville: University of Tennessee Press, 1985.

Johnson, Guy B. *Folk Culture on St. Helena Island, South Carolina.* Chapel Hill: University of North Carolina Press, 1930.

Johnson, Hannibal B. *Black Wall Street: From Riot to Renaissance in Tulsa's Historic Greenwood District.* Burnet, TX: Eakin, 1998.

Johnson, Lois, and Margaret Thomas. *Detroit's Eastern Market: A Farmers Market Shopping and Cooking Guide.* Detroit, MI: Wayne State University Press, 2005.

Johnson, Madeleine. *Fire Island: 1650's–1980's.* Mountainside, NJ: Shoreland, 1992.

Jonaitis, Aldona, ed. *Chiefly Feasts: The Enduring Kwakiutl Potlatch.* Seattle: University of Washington Press, 1991.

Jones, Barbara. *Follies and Grottoes.* London: Constable, 1974.

Jones, Bessie, and Bess Lomax Hawes. *Step It Down: Games, Plays, Songs, and Stories from the Afro-American Heritage.* 1972. Reprint, Athens: University of Georgia Press, 1987.

Jones, C.P. "Stigma: Tattooing and Branding in Graeco Roman Antiquity." *Journal of Roman Studies* 77 (1988): 135–55.

Jones, Leroi. *Blues People.* New York: William Morrow, 1963.

Jones, Louis C. "The Little People: Some Irish Lore of Upstate New York." *New York Folklore Quarterly* 18 (1962): 243–64.

———. *Outward Signs of Inner Beliefs: Symbols of American Patriotism.* Cooperstown: New York State Historical Association, 1975.

———. *Three Eyes on the Past: Exploring New York

Folk Life. Syracuse, NY: Syracuse University Press, 1982.

Jones, Loyal. *Faith and Meaning in the Southern Uplands.* Urbana: University of Illinois Press, 1999.

Jones, Michael Owen. "The Concept of 'Aesthetic' in the Traditional Arts." *Western Folklore* 30 (1971): 77–104.

———. *Craftsman of the Cumberlands: Tradition and Creativity.* Lexington: University Press of Kentucky, 2003.

———. *Exploring Folk Art: Twenty Years of Thought on Craft, Work, and Aesthetics.* Ann Arbor, MI: UMI Research Press, 1987. Reprint, Logan: Utah State University Press, 1993.

———. "A Folklorist's Approach to Organizational Behavior (OB) and Organizational Development (OD)." In *Putting Folklore to Use,* ed. Michael Owen Jones, 162–86. Lexington: University Press of Kentucky, 1994.

———. "'For Myself I Like a *Decent,* Plain-Made Chair': The Concept of Taste and the Traditional Arts in America." *Western Folklore* 31 (1972): 27–52.

———. *The Hand Made Object and Its Maker.* Berkeley: University of California Press, 1975.

———. "L.A. Add-ons and Re-dos: Renovation in Folk Art and Architectural Design." In *Perspectives on American Folk Art,* ed. Ian M.G. Quimby and Scott T. Swank, 325–63. New York: W.W. Norton, 1980.

———, ed. *Putting Folklore to Use.* Lexington: University Press of Kentucky, 1994.

———, ed. "Works of Art, Art as Work, and the Arts of Working." Special section, *Western Folklore* 43, no. 3 (July 1984): 172–221.

———. *Why Faith Healing?* Ottawa: National Museums of Canada, 1972.

———. "Why Folklore and Organization(s)?" *Western Folklore* 50 (1991): 29–40.

Jones, Michael Owen, Michael Moore, and Richard Synder, eds. *Inside Organizations: Understanding the Human Dimension.* Newbury Park, CA: Sage, 1988.

Jones, Schuyler. *Tibetan Nomads: Environment, Pastoral Economy, and Material Culture.* Edited by Ida Nicolaisen. Carlsberg Foundation's Nomad Research Project. New York: Thames and Hudson, 1996.

Jones, Steven Swann. "Slouching Toward Ethnography: The Text/Context Controversy Reconsidered." *Western Folklore* 38 (1979): 42–47.

Jones, Suzi, ed. *Pacific Basket Makers: A Living Tradition.* Fairbanks: University of Alaska Museum, for the Consortium for Pacific Arts and Cultures, Honolulu, Hawaii, 1983.

———. *Webfoots and Bunchgrassers: Folk Art of the Oregon Country.* Salem: Oregon Arts Commission and the University of Oregon Museum of Art, 1980.

Jones-Jackson, Patricia. *When Roots Die: Endangered Traditions on the Sea Islands.* Athens: University of Georgia Press, 1987.

Jordan, Rosan A., and Frank A. de Caro. "Women and the Study of Folklore." *Signs* 11, no. 3 (1986): 500–518.

Jordan, Rosan A., and Susan J. Kalcik, eds. *Women's Folklore, Women's Culture.* Philadelphia: University of Pennsylvania Press, 1985.

Jordan, Terry G. *American Log Buildings: An Old World Heritage.* Chapel Hill: University of North Carolina Press, 1985.

———. *Texas Graveyards: A Cultural Legacy.* Austin: University of Texas Press, 1982.

Jordan-Bychkov, Terry G. *The Upland South: The Making of an American Folk Region and Landscape.* Santa Fe, NM: Center for American Places, 2003.

Jorgensen-Earp, Cheryl, and Lori Lanzilotti. "Public Memory and Private Grief: The Construction of Shrines at the Sites of Public Tragedy." *Quarterly Journal of Speech* 84 (1998): 150–70.

Joselit, Jenna Weissman. *The Wonders of America: Reinventing Jewish Culture, 1880–1950.* New York: Hill and Wang, 1994.

Joseph, Nathan. *Uniforms and Nonuniforms: Communication Through Clothing.* New York: Greenwood, 1986.

Joyce, Rosemary. "Pysanky: The Ukrainian Easter Egg in Ohio." *Journal of the Ohio Folklore Society* 5 (1978): 3–9.

Joyner, Charles W. *Down by the Riverside: A South Carolina Slave Community.* Urbana: University of Illinois Press, 1984.

———. *Shared Traditions: Southern History and Folk Culture.* Urbana: University of Illinois Press, 1999.

Juárez, Miguel, Jr. *Colors on Desert Walls: The Murals of El Paso.* El Paso: Texas Western Press, 1998.

Judah, J. Stillson. *Hare Krishna and the Counterculture.* New York: John Wiley and Sons, 1974.

Juhnke, James C. *The Mennonite Experience in America.* Vol. 3, *Vision, Doctrine, War: Mennonite*

Identity and Organization in America 1890–1930. Scottdale, PA: Herald, 1989.

Kalčik, Susan J. "Women's Handles and the Performance of Identity in the CB Community." In *Women's Folklore, Women's Culture,* ed. Rosan A. Jordan and Susan J. Kalčik, 99–108. Philadelphia: University of Pennsylvania Press, 1985.

Kan, Sergei. *Symbolic Immortality: The Tlingit Potlatch of the Nineteenth Century.* Washington, DC: Smithsonian Institution Press, 1989.

Kanahele, George S. *Hawaiian Music and Musicians: An Illustrated History.* Honolulu: University of Hawaii Press, 1979.

———. *Ku Kanaka, Stand Tall: A Search for Hawaiian Values.* Honolulu: University of Hawaii Press, 1993.

Kanlaya, Dara. *Legends in the Weaving.* Bangkok: Group for Promotion of Art and Lao Textiles and the Japan Foundation Asia Center, 2001.

Kapchan, Deborah A. "Performance." In *Eight Words for the Study of Expressive Culture,* edited by Burt Feintuch, 121–45. Urbana: University of Illinois Press, 2003.

Kaplan, Anne R., Marjorie A. Hoover, and Willard B. Moore. *The Minnesota Ethnic Food Book.* St. Paul: Minnesota Historical Society Press, 1986.

Karaczun, Daniel. *Out of This Kitchen: A History of the Ethnic Groups and Their Foods in the Steel Valley.* Pittsburgh: Publassist, 1992.

Kashima, Tetsuden. *Buddhism in America: The Social Organization of an Ethnic Religious Institution.* Westport, CT: Greenwood, 1977.

Kasinitz, Philip. *Caribbean New York: Black Immigrants and the Politics of Race.* Ithaca, NY: Cornell University Press, 1992.

———. "Community Dramatized, Community Contested: The Politics of Celebration in Brooklyn Carnival." In *Island Sounds in the Global City: Caribbean Popular Music and Identity in New York,* ed. Ray Allen and Lois Wilcken, 93–113. Urbana: University of Illinois Press, 1998.

Kassay, John. *The Book of Shaker Furniture.* Amherst: University of Massachusetts Press, 1980.

Kasson, John. *Amusing the Million: Coney Island at the Turn of the Century.* New York: Hill and Wang, 1978.

Kastenbaum, Robert. *On Our Way: The Final Passage Through Life and Death.* Berkeley: University of California Press, 2004.

Kauffman, Henry J. *The American Pewterer: His Techniques and His Products.* Mendham, NJ: Astragal Press, 1994.

———. *Metalworking Trades in Early America: The Blacksmith, the Whitesmith, the Farrier, the Edge Toolmaker, the Cutler, the Locksmith, the Gunsmith, the Nailer, the Tinsmith.* Mendham, NJ: Astragal Press, 1995.

Kauffman, S. Duane. *Mifflin County Amish and Mennonite Story, 1791–1991.* Belleville, PA: Mifflin County Mennonite Historical Society, 1991.

Kaufman, Moises, and Members of the Tectonic Theatre Project. *The Laramie Project.* New York: Vintage Books, 2001.

Kealiinohomoku, Joann W. "Folk Dance." In *Folklore and Folklife: An Introduction,* ed. Richard M. Dorson, 381–404. Chicago: University of Chicago Press, 1972.

Keil, Charles. *Urban Blues.* Chicago: University of Chicago Press, 1966.

Keil, Charles, Angeliki Keil, and Dick Blau. *Polka Happiness.* Philadelphia: Temple University Press, 1992.

Keil, Hartmut, ed. *German Workers' Culture in the United States, 1850 to 1920.* Washington, DC: Smithsonian Institution Press, 1988.

Kein, Sybil, ed. *Creole: The History and Legacy of Louisiana's Free People of Color.* Baton Rouge: Louisiana State University Press, 2000.

Keith, Jennie. *Old People, New Lives: Community Creation in a Retirement Residence.* Chicago: University of Chicago Press, 1982.

Kelker, Henriette A., and David J. Goa. "When Pilgrims Emigrate: The Skaro Pilgrimage to Our Lady." *Ethnologia Europaea* 26 (1996): 27–35.

Keller, Charles M. *Cognition and Tool Use: The Blacksmith at Work.* New York: Cambridge University Press, 1996.

Kelley, Robin D.G. *Race Rebels: Culture, Politics, and the Black Working Class.* New York: Free Press, 1994.

Kelly, Raymond C. *The Nuer Conquest.* Ann Arbor: University of Michigan Press, 1985.

Kemp, Alvin F. "Pennsylvania Dutch Dialect Stories." *Pennsylvania Folklife* 28, no. 2 (1978–1979): 27–33.

Kendon, Adam. *Gesture: Visible Action as Utterance.* Cambridge: Cambridge University Press, 2004.

Kennedy, Billy. *Faith and Freedom: The Scots Irish in America.* Greenville, SC: Ambassador-Emerald, 1999.

Kennedy, Richard, and Lynn Martin. "Hawai'i: Cosmopolitan Culture at the Crossroads of the Pacific." In *1989 Festival of American Folklife*, ed. Frank Proschan, 36–49. Washington, DC: Smithsonian Institution and the National Park Service, 1989.

Keyes, Cheryl L. *Rap Music and Street Consciousness*. Urbana: University of Illinois Press, 2002.

Khandelwal, Madhulika. *Becoming American, Being Indian: An Immigrant Community in New York City*. Ithaca, NY: Cornell University Press, 2002.

Kidd, Kenneth B. *Making American Boys: Boyology and the Feral Tale*. Minneapolis: University of Minnesota Press, 2004.

Kievit, Joyce Ann. "A Discussion of Scholarly Responsibilities to Indigenous Communities." *American Indian Quarterly* 27 (2003): 3–45.

Kim, Illsoo. *New Urban Immigrants: The Korean Community in New York*. Princeton, NJ: Princeton University Press, 1981.

Kim, Sojin. *Chicano Graffiti and Murals: The Neighborhood Art of Peter Quezada*. Jackson: University Press of Mississippi, 1995.

Kimbrough, David L. *Taking Up Serpents: Snake Handlers of Eastern Kentucky*. Macon, GA: Mercer University Press, 2002.

Kinnery, Martha E. "'If Vanquished I Am Still Victorious': Religious and Cultural Symbolism in Virginia's Confederate Memorial Day Celebrations, 1866–1930." *Virginia Magazine of History and Biography* 106 (1998): 237–66.

Kinser, Samuel. *Carnival, American Style: Mardi Gras at New Orleans and Mobile*. Chicago: University of Chicago Press, 1990.

Kirby, Edward. *From Africa to Beale Street*. Memphis: Musical Management, 1983.

Kirkland, James, Holly F. Mathews, C.W. Sullivan III, and Karen Baldwin, eds. *Herbal and Magical Medicine: Traditional Healing Today*. Durham, NC: Duke University Press, 1992.

Kirshenblatt-Gimblett, Barbara. *Destination Culture: Tourism, Museums, and Heritage*. Berkeley: University of California Press, 1998.

———. "The Future of Folklore Studies in America: The Urban Frontier." *Folklore Forum* 16 (1983): 175–234.

———. "Kodak Moments, Flashbulb Memories: Reflections on 9/11." *Drama Review* 47 (2003): 11–48.

———, ed. *Speech Play: Research and Resources for Studying Linguistic Creativity*. Philadelphia: University of Pennsylvania Press, 1976.

Kisslinger, Jerome. *The Serbian Americans*. New York: Chelsea House, 1990.

Kittler, Pamela Goyan, and Kathryn P. Sucher. *Cultural Foods: Traditions and Trends*. Belmont, CA: Wadsworth/Thomson Learning, 2000.

Klassen, Pamela E. *Blessed Events: Religion and Home Birth in America*. Princeton, NJ: Princeton University Press, 2001.

Kleebat, Norman L., and Gerard C. Wertkin. *The Jewish Heritage in American Folk Art*. New York: Universe Books, 1984.

Klees, Fredric. *The Pennsylvania Dutch*. New York: Macmillan, 1950.

Klein, Allen. *Little Big Men: Bodybuilding Subculture and Gender Construction*. Albany: State University of New York Press, 1993.

Klein, Barbro. "Folklore, Heritage Politics and Ethnic Diversity: Thinking About the Past and the Future." In *Folklore, Heritage Politics and Ethnic Diversity: A Festschrift for Barbro Klein*, ed. Pertti Anttonen, Anna-Leena Siikala, Stein R. Mathisen, and Leif Magnusson, 23–36. Botkyrka, Sweden: Multiculture Centre, 2000.

———. *Legends and Folk Beliefs in a Swedish American Community*. 2 vols. New York: Arno, 1980.

Klibanov, A.I. *History of Religious Sectarianism in Russia, 1860s–1917*. Oxford: Pergamon, 1982.

Kloberdanz, Timothy J. "Henry John Deutschendorf, Jr.: The World Knew Him as John Denver." *Journal of the American Historical Society of Germans from Russia* 21, no. 4 (Winter 1998): 1–5.

———. "In the Land of *Inyan Woslata*: Plains Indian Influences on Reservation Whites." *Great Plains Quarterly* 7, no. 2 (Spring 1987): 68–82.

———. "Plainsmen of Three Continents: Volga German Adaptation to Steppe, Prairie, and Pampa." In *Ethnicity on the Great Plains*, ed. Frederick C. Luebke, 54–72. Lincoln: University of Nebraska Press, 1980.

Klymasz, Robert B. *Ukrainian Folklore in Canada*. New York: Arno, 1980.

Knapp, Mary, and Herbert Knapp. *One Potato, Two Potato: The Secret Education of American Children*. New York: W.W. Norton, 1976.

Kneubuhl, Victoria. "Traditional Performance in Samoan Culture: Two Forms." *Asian Theatre Journal* 4 (1987): 166–76.

Kniffen, Fred B. "American Cultural Geography and Folklife." In *American Folklife,* ed. Don Yoder, 51–70. Austin: University of Texas Press, 1976.

———. "Folk Housing: Key to Diffusion." In *Common Places: Readings in American Vernacular Architecture,* ed. Dell Upton and John Michael Vlach, 3–26. Athens: University of Georgia Press, 1986.

Kniffen, F., and H. Glassie. "Building in Wood in the Eastern United States of America." *Geographical Review* 56 (1966): 40–66.

Knight, Nick. *Skinhead.* London: Omnibus, 1982.

Knoke, David, and David Presnky. "What Relevance Do Organizational Theories Have for Voluntary Associations?" *Social Science Quarterly* 65 (1985): 3–20.

Koch, Fred C. *The Volga Germans: In Russia and the Americas, from 1763 to the Present.* University Park: Pennsylvania State University Press, 1977.

Koch, Ronald P. *Dress Clothing of the Plains Indians.* Norman: University of Oklahoma Press, 1990.

Kollin, Susan. *Nature's State: Imagining Alaska as the Last Frontier.* Chapel Hill: University of North Carolina Press, 2001.

Koltyk, Jo Ann. "Self-Documentation of Life in the Old and New Country." *Journal of American Folklore* 106 (1993): 435–49.

Köngäs-Maranda, Elli. "French-Canadian Folklore Scholarship: An Overview." In *Canadian Folklore Perspectives,* ed. Kenneth S. Goldstein, 21–37. St. John's: Memorial University of Newfoundland, 1978.

Konnyu, Leslie. *Hungarians in the U.S.A.* St. Louis, MO: American Hungarian Review, 1967.

Koons, Kenneth E., and Warren R. Hofstra. *After the Backcountry: Rural Life in the Great Valley of Virginia, 1800–1900.* Knoxville: University of Tennessee Press, 2000.

Kopp, Joel, and Kate Kopp. *American Hooked and Sewn Rugs: Folk Art Underfoot.* New York: E.P. Dutton, 1975.

Kornbluh, Joyce L. *Rebel Voices: An IWW Anthology.* Chicago: Charles H. Kerr, 1998.

Korson, George. *Black Rock: Mining Folklore of the Pennsylvania Dutch.* Baltimore: Johns Hopkins University Press, 1960.

———. *Coal Dust on the Fiddle: Songs and Stories of the Bituminous Industry.* Philadelphia: University of Pennsylvania Press, 1943.

———. *Minstrels of the Mine Patch: Songs and Stories of the Anthracite Industry.* 1938. Reprint, Hatboro, PA: Folklore Associates, 1964.

———, ed. *Pennsylvania Songs and Legends.* Philadelphia: University of Pennsylvania Press, 1949.

Koster, Rick. *Texas Blues.* New York: St. Martin's Press, 1998.

Koven, Mikel J. "Folklore Studies and Popular Film and Television: A Necessary Critical Survey." *Journal of American Folklore* 116 (2003): 176–95.

Krajsa, Joseph C., ed. *Slovaks in America.* Middletown, PA: Slovak League of America, 1978.

Krakauer, Jon. *Under the Banner of Heaven: A Story of Violent Faith.* New York: Doubleday, 2003.

Kramer, Frank R. *Voices in the Valley: Mythmaking and Folk Belief in the Shaping of the Middle West.* Madison: University of Wisconsin Press, 1964.

Krause, Bonnie J., and Cynthia R. Houston. "Bits and Pieces: The Southern Illinois Tradition in Rag Rugs." *Mid-America Folklore* 21 (1993): 18–27.

Krauss, Michael. *Native Peoples and Languages of Alaska.* Fairbanks: Alaska Native Language Center, 1982.

Kraybill, Donald B., ed. *The Amish and the State.* Baltimore: Johns Hopkins University Press, 1993.

———. *The Riddle of Amish Culture.* Revised edition. Baltimore: Johns Hopkins University Press, 2001.

Kraybill, Donald B., and Carl F. Bowman. *On the Backroad to Heaven: Old Order Hutterites, Mennonites, Amish, and Brethren.* Baltimore: Johns Hopkins University Press, 2001.

Kraybill, Donald B., and C. Nelson Hostetter. *Anabaptist World USA.* Scottdale, PA: Herald, 2001.

Kraybill, Donald B., and James P. Hurd. *Horse and Buggy Mennonites: Hoofbeats of Humility in a Postmodern World.* University Park: Pennsylvania State University Press, 2006.

Kraybill, Donald B., and Steven M. Nolt. *Amish Enterprise: From Plows to Profits.* Baltimore: Johns Hopkins University Press, 1995.

Kraybill, Donald B., and Marc A. Olshan, eds. *The Amish Struggle with Modernity.* Hanover, NH: University Press of New England, 1994.

Kreider, Jacob L., ed. *Good Tidings: A Quarterly Published by Reformed Mennonite Church.* 2 vols. Lancaster, PA: Graphic Crafts, 1973.

Krell, Roberta. "At a Children's Hospital: A Folklore Survey." *Western Folklore* 39 (1980): 223–31.

Kreneck, Thomas H. *Del Pueblo: A Pictorial History of Houston's Hispanic Community.* Houston, TX: Houston International University, 1989.

Kretzschmar, William A. *Handbook of the Linguistic Atlas of the Middle and South Atlantic States.* Chicago: University of Chicago Press, 1993.

Kreyling, Christine, Wesley Paine, Charles W. Warterfield, and Susan Ford Wiltshire. *Classical Nashville: Athens of the South.* Nashville, TN: Vanderbilt University Press, 1996.

Kriebel, David W. "Powwowing: A Persistent American Esoteric Tradition." *Esoterica* 4 (2002): 16–28.

Kroes, Rob, and Henk-Otto Neuschäfer, eds. *The Dutch in North America: Their Immigration and Cultural Continuity.* Amsterdam: VU University Press, 1991.

Kruckemeyer, Kate. "'You Get Sawdust in Your Blood': 'Local' Values and the Performance of Community in an Occupational Sport." *Journal of American Folklore* 115 (Summer/Fall 2002): 301–31.

Kubose, Gyomay. *American Buddhism: A New Direction.* Chicago: Dharma House, 1976.

Kalčik, Antanas. *Lithuanians in America.* Boston: Encyclopedia Lituanica, 1975.

Kugelmass, Jack. "Wishes Come True: Designing the Greenwich Village Halloween Parade." *Journal of American Folklore* 104 (1991): 443–65.

Kuhlken, Robert, and Rocky Sexton. "The Geography of Zydeco Music." In *The Sounds of People and Places: A Geography of American Folk and Popular Music,* ed. George O. Carney, 63–76. Lanham, MD: Rowman and Littlefield, 1994.

Kuipers, Giselinde. "Media Culture and Internet Disaster Jokes: Bin Laden and the Attack on the World Trade Center." *European Journal of Cultural Studies* 5 (2002): 450–70.

Kuo, Chia-ling. *Social and Political Change in New York's Chinatown: The Role of Voluntary Associations.* New York: Praeger, 1977.

Kurashige, Lon. *Japanese American Celebration and Conflict: A History of Ethnic Identity and Festival in Los Angeles, 1934–1990.* Berkeley: University of California Press, 2002.

Kurath, Hans. *Linguistic Atlas of New England.* Providence, RI: Brown University, 1939–1943.

———. *A Word Geography of the Eastern United States.* Ann Arbor: University of Michigan Press, 1949.

Kurian, George T., Miles Orvell, Johnnella E. Butler, and Jay Mechling, eds. *Encyclopedia of American Studies.* 4 vols. New York: Grolier, 2001.

Kurin, Richard. *Reflections of a Culture Broker: A View from the Smithsonian.* Washington, DC: Smithsonian Institution Press, 1997.

———. *Smithsonian Folklife Festival: Culture of, by, and for the People.* Washington, DC: Smithsonian Institution Press, 1998.

Kuriscak, Steve. *Casino Talk: A Rap Sheet for Dealers and Players.* Los Angeles: Screenwriters Guild, 1985.

Kwiatkowska, Barbara J. "Introduction to the Musical Culture of the Diegueño Indians from San Diego County Reservations in California." *Canadian Folk Music Bulletin* 24 (1990): 14–21.

Kwong, Peter. *The New Chinatown.* New York: Hill and Wang, 1996.

Laatsch, William G., and Charles F. Calkins. "Belgians in Wisconsin." In *To Build in a New Land: Ethnic Landscapes in North America,* ed. Allen G. Noble, 195–210. Baltimore: Johns Hopkins University Press, 1992.

Laba, Martin. "Urban Folklore: A Behavioral Approach." *Western Folklore* 38 (1979): 158–69.

Labov, William. *Language in the Inner City: Studies in the Black English Vernacular.* Philadelphia: University of Pennsylvania Press, 1972.

———. "Rules for Ritual Insult." In *Rappin' and Stylin' Out: Communication in Urban Black America,* ed. Thomas Kochman, 265–314. Urbana: University of Illinois Press, 1972.

Labov, William, and Joshua Waletzky. "Narrative Analysis: Oral Versions of Personal Experience." In *Essays in the Verbal and Visual Arts,* ed. June Helm, 12–14. Seattle: University of Washington Press, 1967.

Lacher, J.H. *The German Element in Wisconsin.* Milwaukee, WI: Steuben Society of America, 1925.

Ladenheim, Melissa, Merrill Oliver, and Catherine Schwoeffermann. *Three Catskill Storytellers.* Binghamton, NY: Roberson Center for the Arts and Sciences, 1986.

Laderman, Carol, and Marina Roseman, eds. *The Performance of Healing.* London: Routledge, 1996.

Laderman, Gary. *Rest in Peace: A Cultural History of Death and the Funeral Home in Twentieth-Century America.* New York: Oxford University Press, 2003.

Lagerquist, L. DeAne. *The Lutherans.* Westport, CT: Greenwood, 1999.

Laguerre, Michael S. *American Odyssey: Haitians in New York City.* Ithaca, NY: Cornell University Press, 1984.

———. *Diasporic Citizenship: Haitian Americans in Transnational America.* New York: Palgrave Macmillan, 1998.

———. *The Global Ethnopolis: Chinatown, Japantown and Manilatown in American Society.* New York: St. Martin's Press, 2000.

Lahickey, Beth, ed. *All Ages: Reflections on Straight Edge.* Huntington Beach, CA: Revelation Books, 1997.

Landau, David. *Piety and Power: The World of Jewish Fundamentalism.* New York: Hill and Wang, 1993.

Landes, Richard, ed. *Encyclopedia of Millennialism and Millennial Movements.* New York: Routledge, 2000.

Landre, Rick, Mike Miller, and Dee Porter. *Gangs: A Handbook for Community Awareness.* New York: Facts on File, 1997.

Lane, Brigitte. *Franco-American Folk Traditions and Popular Culture in a Former Milltown: Aspects of Ethnic Urban Folklore and the Dynamics of Folklore Change in Lowell, Massachusetts.* New York: Garland, 1990.

Langlois, Janet L. "The Belle Island Bridge Incident: Legend Dialectic and Semiotic System in the 1943 Detroit Race Riots." *Journal of American Folklore* 96 (1983): 183–99.

———. "Moon Cake in Chinatown, New York City: Continuity and Change." *New York Folklore Quarterly* 28 (1972): 83–117.

Lanier, Gabrielle M., and Bernard L. Herman. *Everyday Architecture of the Mid-Atlantic: Looking at Buildings and Landscapes.* Baltimore: Johns Hopkins University Press, 1997.

Lapin, Dierdre. *Hogs in the Bottom: Family Folklore in Arkansas.* Little Rock, AR: August House, 1982.

Lapsansky, Emma Jones, and Anne A. Verplanck, eds. *Quaker Aesthetics: Reflections on a Quaker Ethic in American Design and Consumption.* Philadelphia: University of Pennsylvania Press, 2003.

Larson , Gustive O. "Orrin Porter Rockwell—The Modern Samson." In *Lore of Faith and Folly,* ed. Thomas E. Cheney, 179–90. Salt Lake City: University of Utah Press, 1971.

Larson, Mildred R. "Danish Lore in Denmark and at Troy, N.Y." *New York Folklore Quarterly* 10 (1954): 266–73.

Lasansky, Jeannette. *To Draw, Upset, and Weld: The Work of the Pennsylvania Rural Blacksmith, 1742–1935.* Lewisburg, PA: Oral Traditions Project of the Union County Historical Society, 1980.

———. *Willow, Oak, and Rye: Basket Traditions in Pennsylvania.* University Park: Pennsylvania State University Press, 1979.

Lau, Kimberly J., Peter Tokofsky, and Stephen D. Winick, eds. *What Goes Around Comes Around: The Circulation of Proverbs in Contemporary Life.* Logan: Utah State University Press, 2004.

Lavitt, Wendy. *Animals in American Folk Art.* New York: Knopf, 1990.

Law, Rachel Nash, and Cynthia W. Taylor. *Appalachian White Oak Basketmaking: Handing Down the Basket.* Knoxville: University of Tennessee Press, 1991.

Lawless, Elaine J. *A Guide to the Idaho Folklore Archives.* Idaho Folklife Publications No. 1. Boise: Idaho Folklife Center, Idaho Historical Society, 1983.

———. *God's Peculiar People: Women's Voices and Folk Tradition in a Pentecostal Church.* Lexington: University Press of Kentucky, 1988.

———. *Handmaidens of the Lord: Pentecostal Women Preachers and Traditional Religion.* Philadelphia: University of Pennsylvania Press, 1988.

———. "'Your Hair Is Your Glory': Public and Private Symbology of Long Hair for Pentecostal Women." *New York Folklore* 12 (1986): 33–49.

Lawrence, Bruce B. *New Faiths, Old Fears: Muslims and Other Asian Immigrants in American Religious Life.* New York: Columbia University Press, 2002.

Lawrence, Elizabeth Atwood. *Hoofbeats and Society: Studies of Human-Horse Interactions.* Bloomington: Indiana University Press, 1985.

Laws, G. Malcolm, Jr. *Native American Balladry: A Descriptive Study and a Bibliographical Syllabus.* Philadelphia: American Folklore Society, 1964.

Laxalt, Robert. *Sweet Promised Land.* Reno: University of Nevada Press, 1986.

Layman, Emma McCloy. *Buddhism in America.* Chicago: Nelson-Hall, 1976.

Leach, Joseph. *The Typical Texan: Biography of an American Myth.* Dallas: Southern Methodist University Press, 1952.

Leach, Michael, and Therese J. Blockard, eds. *I Like

Being a Catholic: Treasured Tradition, Rituals, and Stories. New York: Doubleday, 2000.

Leadbeater, C.W. *Freemasonry and Its Ancient Mystic Rites.* New York: Gramercy, 1998.

Lears, Jackson. *Fables of Abundance: A Cultural History of Advertising in America.* New York: Basic Books, 1994.

———. *Something for Nothing: Luck in America.* New York: Viking, 2003.

Leary, James P. "Folklore of Michigan Loggers: 1940–1990." In *1991 Festival of Michigan Folklife*, ed. Ruth D. Fitzgerald and Yvonne R. Lockwood, 15–25. East Lansing: Michigan State University Museum, 1991.

———, ed. *So Ole Says to Lena: Folk Humor of the Upper Midwest.* 2nd ed. Madison: University of Wisconsin Press, 2001.

———. *Wisconsin Folklore.* Madison: University of Wisconsin Press, 1999.

Leavitt, Judith. *The Healthiest City: Milwaukee and the Politics of Health Reform.* Madison: University of Wisconsin Press, 1996.

Leder, Hans Howard. *Cultural Persistence in a Portuguese-American Community.* New York: Arno, 1980.

Lee, Melicent. *Indians of the Oaks.* San Diego: San Diego Museum of Man, 1989.

Lehman, Jacob S., ed. *Christianity Defined.* Lancaster, PA: Reformed Mennonite Church, 1926.

Leighton, Ann. *American Gardens of the Nineteenth Century.* Amherst: University of Massachusetts Press, 1987.

Leonard, Karen Isaksen. *Making Ethnic Choices: California's Punjabi Mexican Americans.* Philadelphia: Temple University Press, 1992.

———. *The South Asian Americans.* Westport, CT: Greenwood, 1997.

Leonard, Stephen J., and Thomas J. Noel. *Denver: Mining Camp to Metropolis.* Niwot: University Press of Colorado, 1984.

Lessinger, Johanna. *From the Ganges to the Hudson: Indian Immigrants in New York City.* Boston: Allyn and Bacon, 1995.

Leverette, Marc. *Professional Wrestling: The Myth, the Mat, and American Popular Culture.* Ceredigion, UK: Edwin Mellen Press, 2003.

Levin, Ted, and Ankica Petrovič, comps. *Bosnia: Echoes from an Endangered World: Music and Chant of the Bosnian Muslims.* Smithsonian/Folkways. CD SF 40407. 1993.

Levine, Joseph A. *Synagogue Song in America.* Crown Point, IN: White Cliffs Media, 1989.

Levine, Lawrence W. *Black Culture and Black Consciousness: Afro-American Folk Thought from Slavery to Freedom.* New York: Oxford University Press, 1978.

Levine, Robert M., and Moises Asis. *Cuban Miami.* New Brunswick, NJ: Rutgers University Press, 2000.

Levine, Stephanie Wellen. *Mystics, Mavericks, and Merrymakers: An Intimate Journey Among Hasidic Girls.* New York: New York University Press, 2003.

Lévi-Strauss, Claude. *Structural Anthropology.* Translated by Claire Jacobson and Brooke Grundfest Schoepf. Garden City, NY: Doubleday, 1967.

Levitt, Peggy. *The Transnational Villagers.* Berkeley: University of California Press, 2001.

Levy, Jerrold E. *In the Beginning: The Navajo Genesis.* Berkeley: University of California Press, 1998.

Lewis, David. *When Harlem Was in Vogue.* New York: Penguin, 1997.

Lewis, I.M. *Ecstatic Religion: A Study of Shamanism and Spirit Possession.* 2nd ed. New York: Routledge, 1989.

Lewis, J. Lowell. *Ring of Liberation: Deceptive Discourse in Brazilian Capoeira.* Chicago: University of Chicago Press, 1992.

Lewis, Joanne M. *To Market to Market, An Old-Fashioned Family Story: The West Side Market.* Cleveland Heights, OH: Elandon Books, 1981.

Lewis, Peirce. "Common Houses, Cultural Spoor." In *Re-Reading Cultural Geography,* ed. Kenneth E. Foote, Peter J. Hugill, Kent Mathewson, and Jonathan M. Smith, 82–110. Austin: University of Texas Press, 1994.

———. "Small Town in Pennsylvania." *Association of American Geographers Annals* 62 (1972): 323–51.

Lich, Glen E., and Dona B. Reeves, eds. *German Culture in Texas.* Boston: Twayne, 1980.

Licht, Michael. "Some Automotive Play Activities of Suburban Teenagers." *New York Folklore Quarterly* 30 (1974): 44–65.

Lieberman, Susan Abel. *New Traditions: Redefining Celebrations for Today's Family.* New York: Farrar, Straus and Giroux, 1991.

Liebman, Seymour B. *The Jews in New Spain: Faith, Flame and the Inquisition.* Miami: University of Miami Press, 1970.

Light, Alan, ed. *The Vibe History of Hip Hop*. New York: Three Rivers Press, 1999.

Liley, H.M.I. *Modern Motherhood: Pregnancy, Childbirth, and the Newborn Baby*. New York: Random House, 1969.

Lilly, John, ed. *Mountains of Music: West Virginia Traditional Music from Goldenseal*. Urbana: University of Illinois Press, 1999.

Limón, José. "The Folk Performance of 'Chicano' and the Cultural Limits of Political Ideology." In *"And Other Neighborly Names": Social Process and Cultural Images in Texas Folklore*, ed. Richard Bauman and Roger D. Abrahams, 197–225. Austin: University of Texas Press, 1981.

Linck, Ernestine Sewell, and Joyce Gibson Roach. *Eats: A Folk History of Texas Foods*. Fort Worth: Texas Christian University Press, 1989.

Lindahl, Carl, ed. *American Folktales from the Collections of the Library of Congress*. Armonk, NY: M.E. Sharpe, 2004.

———, ed. *Perspectives on the Jack Tales and Other North American Märchen*. Bloomington: Indiana University Folklore Institute, 2001.

———. "The Presence of the Past in the Cajun Country Mardi Gras." *Journal of Folklore Research* 33 (1996): 101–29.

———, ed. "Southwestern Louisiana Mardi Gras Traditions." Special issue, *Journal of American Folklore* 114, no. 452 (2001).

Lindahl, Carl, and Carolyn Ware. *Cajun Mardi Gras Masks*. Jackson: University Press of Mississippi, 1997.

Linenthal, Edward. *The Unfinished Bombing: Oklahoma City in American Memory*. New York: Oxford, 2001.

Linton, Ralph, and Adelin Linton. *We Gather Together: The Story of Thanksgiving*. New York: Schuman, 1949.

Litwicki, Ellen M. *America's Public Holidays, 1865–1920*. Washington, DC: Smithsonian Institution Press, 2000.

Liubniene, Vilmante, and Mary E. Kelly. "Some Aspects of Lithuanian Folklore in Lithuania and the United States." *Lituanus* 43 (1997): 56–75.

Ljungmark, Lars. *Den stora utvandringen: svensk immigration till USA 1840–1925*. Stockholm: Sveriges Radio, 1965.

Llanes, Jose. *Cuban Americans: Masters of Survival*. Cambridge, MA: Abt Books, 1982.

Lloyd, Timothy. *The Archive of Folk Culture: The National Collection of American and World Folklife*. Washington, DC: American Folklife Center, Library of Congress, 1992.

Lloyd, Timothy Charles. "The Cincinnati Chili Culinary Complex." *Western Folklore* 40 (1981): 28–40.

Lloyd, Timothy Charles, and Patrick B. Mullen. *Lake Erie Fishermen: Work, Identity, Tradition*. Urbana: University of Illinois Press, 1990.

Lobban, Richard. *Cape Verde: Crioulo Colony to Independent Nation*. Boulder, CO: Westview Press, 1995.

Lockwood, William G. "Automotive Folk Art: Street Rods, Custom Cars, and Low Riders." In *1997 Michigan Folklife Annual*, ed. Yvonne R. Lockwood and Marsha MacDowell, 14–22. East Lansing: Michigan State University Press, 1997.

Lockwood, Yvonne R. "Immigrant to Ethnic: Folk Symbols of Identity Among Finnish Americans." In *Folklife Annual 1986*, ed. Alan Jabbour and James Hardin, 92–107. Washington, DC: Library of Congress, 1986.

———. "The Sauna: An Expression of Finnish-American Identity." *Western Folklore* 36 (1977): 71–84. Reprinted in *Folklore and Ethnicity*, ed. Larry Danielson. Los Angeles: California Folklore Society, 1978.

———. *Text and Context: Folksong in a Bosnian Muslim Village*. Columbus, OH: Slavica, 1983.

Lockwood, Yvonne R., and William G. Lockwood. "Finnish American Milk Products in the Northwoods." In *Milk: Beyond Dairy*, ed. Harlan Walker, 232–39. Totnes, England: Prospect Books, 2000.

———. "Pasties in Michigan: Foodways, Interethnic Relations and Cultural Dynamics." In *Creative Ethnicity*, ed. Stephen Stern and John Allan Cicala, 3–20. Logan: Utah State University Press, 1991.

Lomax, Alan. *The Land Where the Blues Began*. New York: Pantheon, 1993.

Long, Amos, Jr. *The Pennsylvania German Family Farm*. Breinigsville: Pennsylvania German Society, 1972.

Long, Patrick Du Phuoc, and Laura Ricard. *The Dream Shattered: Vietnamese Gangs in America*. Boston: Northeastern University Press, 1996.

Longhauser, Elsa, and Harald Szeeman, eds. *Self-Taught Artists of the 20th Century: An American Anthology*. San Francisco: Chronicle Books, 1998.

Loomis, Ormond H. *Cultural Conservation: The*

Protection of Cultural Heritage in the United States. Washington, DC: Library of Congress, 1983.

———. "Organizing a Folklore Museum." In *Handbook of American Folklore*, ed. Richard M. Dorson, 499–506. Bloomington: Indiana University Press, 1983.

Lopata, Helena Znaniecki. *Polish Americans.* New Brunswick, NJ: Transaction, 1994.

Lopreato, Joseph. *Italian Americans.* New York: Random House, 1970.

Lornell, Kip. *Introducing American Folk Music.* Madison, WI: Brown and Benchmark, 1993.

Lornell, Kip, and Charles C. Stephenson, Jr. *The Beat: Go-Go's Fusion of Funk and Hip-Hop.* New York: Billboard, 2001.

Louder, Dean, and Eric Waddell, eds. *French America.* Baton Rouge: Louisiana State University Press, 1992.

Lovato, Andrew Leo. *Santa Fe Hispanic Culture: Preserving Identity in a Tourist Town.* Albuquerque: University of New Mexico Press, 2004.

Lovett, Bobby L. *The African-American History of Nashville, Tennessee: Elites and Dilemmas.* Fayetteville: University of Arkansas Press, 1999.

Lovette, Leland P. *Naval Customs, Traditions and Usage.* 3rd ed. Annapolis, MD: U.S. Naval Institute, 1939.

Lovrich, Frank. "The Dalmatian Yugoslavs in Louisiana." *Louisiana History* 8 (1967): 149–64.

Lowens, Irving. *Music and Musicians in Early America.* New York: W.W. Norton, 1964.

Loza, Steven. *Barrio Rhythm: Mexican American Music in Los Angeles.* Urbana: University of Illinois Press, 1993.

Lucas, Phillip C., John J. Guthrie, Jr., and Gary Monroe, eds. *Cassadaga: The South's Oldest Spiritualist Community.* Gainesville: University Press of Florida, 2000.

Luebke, Frederick C. *Ethnicity on the Great Plains.* Lincoln: University of Nebraska Press, 1980.

Lufkin, Jack. "Patten's Neighborhood: The Center Street Community and the African-American Who Preserved It." *Iowa Heritage Illustrated* 77 (1996): 122–44.

Luhrman, Tanya. *Persuasions of the Witch's Craft: Ritual Magic in Contemporary England.* Cambridge, MA: Harvard University Press, 1989.

Lund, Jens. *Flatheads and Spooneys: Fishing for a Living in the Ohio River Valley.* Lexington: University Press of Kentucky, 1995.

———. *Folk Arts of Washington State: A Survey of Contemporary Folk Arts and Artists in the State of Washington.* Tumwater: Washington State Folklife Council, 1989.

Lyle, Katie Letcher. *Scalded to Death by the Steam.* Chapel Hill, NC: Algonquin, 1983.

Lyons, Arthur, Jr. *Satan Wants You: The Cult of Devil Worship in America.* New York: Mysterious Press, 1988.

Lyons, Patrick D. *Ancestral Hopi Migrations.* Tucson: University of Arizona Press, 2003.

MacDonell, Margaret. *The Emigrant Experience: Songs of Highland Emigrants in North America.* Toronto: University of Toronto Press, 1982.

MacDougall, Pauleena, and David Taylor, eds. *Northeast Folklore: Essays in Honor of Edward D. Ives.* Orono: University of Maine Press and the Maine Folklife Center, 2000.

MacDowell, Betty. 1982. "Religion on the Road: Highway Evangelism and Worship Environments for the Traveler in America." *Journal of American Culture 5*, no. 4 (1982): 63–74.

MacDowell, Marsha L., ed. *African American Quiltmaking in Michigan.* East Lansing: Michigan State University Press, 1997.

———. *Stories in Thread: Hmong Pictorial Embroidery.* East Lansing: Michigan State University Museum, 1989.

MacDowell, Marsha L., and C. Kurt Dewhurst, eds. *To Honor and Comfort: Native Quilting Traditions.* Santa Fe: Museum of New Mexico Press, 1997.

MacGregor, John. *The Discovery of the Art of the Insane.* Princeton, NJ: Princeton University Press, 1989.

Machann, Clinton, ed. *Czech-Americans in Transition.* Austin, TX: Eakin Press, 1999.

Maciel, David R., and Isidro D. Ortiz, eds. *Chicanas/Chicanos at the Crossroads: Social, Economic, and Political Change.* Tucson: University of Arizona Press, 1996.

MacLean, Nancy. *Behind the Mask of Chivalry: The Making of the Second Ku Klux Klan.* New York: Oxford University Press, 1995.

Macleod, David I. *Building Character in the American Boy: The Boy Scouts, YMCA, and Their Forerunners, 1870–1920.* Madison: University of Wisconsin Press, 1983.

MacMaster, Richard K. *The Mennonite Experience in America.* Vol. 1, *Land, Piety, Peoplehood: The*

Establishment of Mennonite Communities in America, 1683–1790. Scottdale, PA: Herald, 1985.

Macneal, Patricia M., Bonelyn L. Kyofski, and Kenneth A. Thigpen, eds. *Headwaters and Hardwoods: The Folklore, Cultural History, and Traditional Arts of the Pennsylvania Northern Tier.* Mansfield, PA: Northern Tier Cultural Alliance, 1997.

MacNeil, Robert, and William Cran. *Do You Speak American?* New York: Talese, 2004.

Mageo, Jeannette Marie. *Theorizing Self in Samoa: Emotions, Genders, and Sexualities.* Ann Arbor: University of Michigan Press, 1988.

———. "The Third Meaning in Cultural Memory—History, Identity, and Spiritual Power in Samoa." In *Cultural Memory: Reconfiguring History and Identity in the Postcolonial Pacific*, ed. Jeanette Marie Mageo, 58–80. Honolulu: University of Hawaii Press, 2001.

Magliocco, Sabina. "The Bloomington Jaycees' Haunted House." *Indiana Folklore and Oral History* 14 (1985): 19–28.

———. *Neo-Pagan Sacred Art and Altars: Making Things Whole.* Jackson: University Press of Mississippi, 2001.

Magliocco, Sabina, and Holly Tannen. "The Real Old-Time Religion: Towards an Aesthetics of Neo-Pagan Song." *Ethnologies* 20 (1998): 175–201.

Magnaghi, Russell M. *Italians in Michigan.* East Lansing: Michigan State University Press, 2001.

Magocsi, Paul Robert. *Our People: Carpatho-Rusyns and Their Descendants in North America.* Toronto: Multicultural History Society of Ontario, 1985.

Magocsi, Paul Robert. "Rusyn-American Ethnic Literature." *Proceedings of the Comparative Literature Symposium* 9 (1978): 503–20.

Magocsi, Paul Robert, and Joshua A. Fishman. "Small Languages and Small Language Communities, XV: Scholarly Seminar on the Codification of the Rusyn Language." *International Journal of the Sociology of Language* 104 (1993): 119–25.

Mahakian, Charles. *History of the Armenians in California.* San Francisco: R and E Research Associates, 1974.

Mails, Thomas E. *The Mystic Warriors of the Plains: The Culture, Arts, Crafts and Religion of the Plains Indians.* New York: Marlowe, 2002.

Maira, Sunaina Marr. *Desis in the House: Indian American Youth Culture in New York City.* Philadelphia: Temple University Press, 2002.

Maizels, John. *Raw Creation: Outsider Art and Beyond.* London: Phaidon, 1996.

Malik, Iftikhar H. *Islam and Modernity: Muslims in Europe and the United States.* London: Pluto, 2004.

Malinowski, Bronislaw. *Magic, Science, and Religion.* Garden City: Doubleday, 1954.

Malone, Bill C. *Country Music USA.* 2nd rev. ed. Austin: University of Texas Press, 2002.

———. *A Scientific Theory of Culture, and Other Essays.* Chapel Hill: University of North Carolina Press, 1944.

Malone, Jacqui. *Steppin' on the Blues: The Visible Rhythm of African American Dance.* Urbana: University of Illinois Press, 1996.

Malpezzi, Frances M., and William M. Clements. *Italian-American Folklore.* Little Rock, AR: August House, 1992.

Mangione, Jerre. *Mount Allegro: A Memoir of Italian American Life.* 1942. Syracuse, NY: Syracuse University Press, 1998.

Mangione, Jerre, and Ben Morreale. *La Storia: Five Centuries of the Italian American Experience.* Reprint, New York: HarperPerennial, 1992.

Manley, Roger, and Mark Sloan. *Self-Made Worlds: Visionary Folk Art Environments.* New York: Aperture, 1997.

Mansfield, Bill. "The Development of the Bright-Leaf Tobacco Auctioneer's Chant." In *Arts in Earnest: North Carolina Folklife*, ed. Daniel W. Patterson and Charles G. Zug III, 102–13. Durham, NC: Duke University Press, 1990.

Mansfield, Stephen. *Lao Hill Tribes: Traditions and Patterns of Existence.* Oxford: Oxford University Press, 2000.

Manuel, Peter. *East Indian Music in the West Indies: Tan-Singing, Chutney, and the Making of Indo-Caribbean Culture.* Philadelphia: Temple University Press, 2000.

Maranda, Pierre, and Elli-Kaija Köngäs Maranda, eds. *Structural Analysis of Oral Tradition.* Philadelphia: University of Pennsylvania Press, 1971.

Marberry, Craig, and Michael Cunningham. *Spirit of Harlem: A Portrait of America's Most Exciting Neighborhood.* New York: Doubleday, 2003.

March, Richard. "The Tamburitza Tradition in the Calumet Region." *Indiana Folklore* 10 (1977): 127–38.

Marcus, Clare Cooper. "Environmental Memories." In *Place Attachment*, ed. Irwin Altman and Setha M. Low, 87–112. New York: Plenum, 1992.

Maresca, Frank, and Roger Ricco. *American Self-Taught: Paintings and Drawings by Outsider Artists.* New York: Knopf, 1993.

Margolis, Maxine L. *Little Brazil: An Ethnography of Brazilian Immigrants in New York City.* Princeton, NJ: Princeton University Press, 1994.

Marks, Stuart A. *Southern Hunting in Black and White: Nature, History, and Ritual in a Carolina Community.* Princeton, NJ: Princeton University Press, 1991.

Marland, Hillary, and Anne Marie Rafferty, eds. *Midwives, Society, and Childbirth: Debates and Controversies in the Modern Period.* New York: Routledge, 1997.

Marling, Karal Ann. *Debutante: Rites and Regalia of American Debdom.* Lawrence: University Press of Kansas, 2004.

Marshall, Howard W. *Merry Christmas! Celebrating America's Greatest Holiday.* Cambridge, MA: Harvard University Press, 2000.

———. *Folk Architecture in Little Dixie: A Regional Culture in Missouri.* Columbia: University of Missouri Press, 1981.

———. "Folklife and the Rise of American Folk Museums." *Journal of American Folklore* 90 (1977): 391–413.

———. *Paradise Valley, Nevada: The People and the Buildings of an American Place.* Tucson: University of Arizona Press, 1995.

———. "Tom Tit Tot: A Comparative Essay on Aa-Th.-Type 500, the Name of the Helper." *Folklore* 84 (1973): 51–57.

Marshall, Howard W., and John Michael Vlach. "Toward a Folklife Approach to American Dialects." *American Speech* 48 (1973): 163–91.

Martin, Ann Smart, and J. Ritchie Garrison, eds. *American Material Culture: The Shape of the Field.* Knoxville: University of Tennessee Press, 1997.

Martin, Lynn, ed. *Folklife Hawai'i.* Honolulu, HI: State Foundation on Culture and the Arts, 1990.

Martin, Philip. *Farmhouse Fiddlers: Music and Dance Traditions in the Rural Midwest.* Mount Horeb, WI: Midwest Traditions, 1994.

———. *Rosemaling in the Upper Midwest.* Mount Horeb: Wisconsin Folk Museum, 1989.

Martindale, Don, ed. *Functionalism in the Social Sciences: The Strengths and Limits of Functionalism in Anthropology, Economics, Political Science, and Sociology.* Philadelphia: American Academy of Political and Social Science, 1965.

Mason, Bruce Lionel. "Moving Toward Virtual Ethnography." *American Folklore Society News* 25, no. 2 (April 1996): 4–6.

Mason, Michael Atwood. *Living Santeria: Rituals and Experiences in an Afro-Cuban Religion.* Washington, DC: Smithsonian Institution Press, 2002.

Massey, Ellen Gray. *Bittersweet Country.* Garden City, NY: Anchor Press/Doubleday, 1978.

Mastick, Patricia. "Dry Stone Walling." *Indiana Folklore* 9 (1976): 113–33.

Mastran, Shelley S., ed. *Your Town: Mississippi Delta.* New York: Princeton Architectural Press for the National Endowment for the Arts, 2002.

Matchak, Stephen. "The North Carolina Wildfowl Decoy Tradition." In *Arts in Earnest: North Carolina Folklife,* ed. Daniel W. Patterson and Charles G. Zug III, 27–46. Durham, NC: Duke University Press, 1990.

Mathew, Biju. *Taxi! Cabs and Capitalism in New York City.* New York: New Press, 2005.

Matsumoto, Valerie J. *Farming the Home Place: A Japanese American Community in California, 1919–1982.* Ithaca, NY: Cornell University Press, 1993.

———. "Japanese American Women and the Creation of Urban Nisei Culture in the 1930s." In *Over the Edge: Remapping the American West,* ed. Valerie J. Matsumoto and Blake Allmendinger, 291–306. Berkeley: University of California Press, 1999.

Matthew, Dennis. *Red, White, and Blue Letter Days: An American Calendar.* Ithaca, NY: Cornell University Press, 2002.

Matthiessen, Peter. *Men's Lives: The Surfmen and Baymen of the South Fork.* New York: Vintage Books, 1988.

Mattson, Mark, and Molefi K. Asante. *The African-American Atlas: Black History and Culture.* New York: Simon and Schuster, 1998.

Mazer, Sharon. *Professional Wrestling: Sport and Spectacle.* Jackson: University Press of Mississippi, 1998.

Mazo, Margarita. "Molokans and Old Believers in Two Worlds: Migration, Change, and Continuity." In *1995 Festival of American Folklife,* edited by Carla Borden, 83–89. Washington, DC: Smithsonian Institution Press, 1995.

McAlister, Elizabeth. *Rara!: Vodou, Power, and Performance in Haiti and Its Diaspora.* Berkeley: University of California Press, 2002.

McCaffrey, Lawrence J. *Textures of Irish America.* Syracuse, NY: Syracuse University Press, 1992.

McCaffrey, Lawrence, Ellen Skerrett, Michael F. Funchion, and Charles Fanning. *The Irish in Chicago.* Urbana: University of Illinois Press, 1987.

McCallum, Brenda. "Songs of Work and Songs of Worship: Sanctifying Black Unionism in the Southern State of Steel." *New York Folklore* 14 (1988): 9–33.

McCarl, Robert. *The District of Columbia Fire Fighters' Project: A Case Study in Occupational Folklife.* Washington, DC: Smithsonian Institution Press, 1985.

McCarthy, William B., ed. *Jack in Two Worlds: Contemporary North American Tales and Their Tellers.* Chapel Hill: University of North Carolina Press, 1994.

McCaurs, Ernest, ed. *The Development of Arab-American Identity.* Ann Arbor: University of Michigan Press, 1994.

McClary, Andrew. *Toys with Nine Lives: A Social History of American Toys.* North Haven, CT: Linnet Books, 1997.

McClenon, James. *Wondrous Events: Foundations of Religious Belief.* Philadelphia: University of Pennsylvania Press, 1994.

McClung, William A. *Landscape of Desire: Anglo Mythologies of Los Angeles.* Berkeley: University of California Press, 2000.

McComb, David G. *Houston: The Bayou City.* Austin: University of Texas Press, 1969.

McCoy, Maureen, and William Silag. "The Italian Heritage in Des Moines." *Palimpsest* 64 (1983): 58–68.

McCracken, Grant. *Big Hair: A Journey into the Transformation of Self.* Woodstock, NY: Overlook, 1996.

———. *Culture and Consumption: New Approaches to the Symbolic Character of Consumer Goods and Activities.* Bloomington: Indiana University Press, 1991.

McCullough, Lawrence E. "An American Maker of Uilleann Pipes: Patrick Hennelly." *Éire-Ireland* 10 (1975): 109–15.

McDannell, Colleen. *Material Christianity: Religion and Popular Culture in America.* New Haven: Yale University Press, 1995.

McDavid, Raven. *Varieties of American English.* Stanford, CA: Stanford University Press, 1980.

McDonald, Marie A. *Ka Lei: The Leis of Hawaii.* Honolulu, HI: Topgallant, 1985.

McDowell, John Holmes. *Children's Riddling.* Bloomington: Indiana University Press, 1979.

———. "Halloween Costuming Among Young Adults in Bloomington, Indiana: A Local Exotic." *Indiana Folklore* 14 (1985): 1–18.

———. *Poetry and Violence: The Ballad Tradition of Mexico's Costa Chica.* Champaign: University of Illinois Press, 2000.

McGowan, Thomas, ed. "Folklore in the Schools." Special issue, *North Carolina Folklore Journal* 26, no. 1 (1978).

McGregory, Jerrilyn. *Wiregrass Country.* Jackson: University Press of Mississippi, 1997.

McGuire, James Patrick. *The Hungarian Texans.* San Antonio: University of Texas Institute of Texan Cultures at San Antonio, 1993.

McGuire, Meredith B. *Pentecostal Catholics: Power, Charisma and Order in a Religious Movement.* Philadelphia: Temple University Press, 1982.

McGuire, Meredith B., and Debra Kantor. *Ritual Healing in Suburban America.* New Brunswick, NJ: Rutgers University Press, 1988.

McIntosh, David S. *Folk Songs and Singing Games of the Illinois Ozarks.* Edited by Dale R. Whiteside. Carbondale: Southern Illinois University Press, 1974.

McIver, Joel. *Extreme Metal.* New York: Omnibus, 2000.

McKee, Harley J. *Introduction to Early American Masonry: Stone, Brick, Mortar and Plaster.* Washington, DC: Preservation, 1973.

McKee, Margaret, and Fred Chisenhall. *Beale Black & Blue: Life and Music on Black America's Main Street.* Baton Rouge: Louisiana State University Press, 1981.

McLaughlin, Valerie. "Czech Tales." *New York Folklore Quarterly* 25 (1969): 202–20.

McMahon, Eileen M. *What Parish Are You From? A Chicago Irish Community and Race Relations.* Lexington: University Press of Kentucky, 1995.

McMurry, Sally. *From Sugar Camps to Star Barns: Rural Life and Landscape in a Western Pennsylvania Community.* University Park: Pennsylvania State University Press, 2001.

McNeil, W.K., ed. *Appalachian Images in Folk and Popular Culture.* 2nd ed. Knoxville: University of Tennessee Press, 1995.

———, ed. *The Charm Is Broken: Readings in Arkansas and Missouri Folklore.* Little Rock, AR: August House, 1984.

———, ed. *Ozark Country*. Jackson: University Press of Mississippi, 1995.

———. *Ozark Mountain Humor: Jokes on Hunting, Religion, Marriage, and Ozark Ways*. Little Rock, AR: August House, 1989.

———, ed. *Southern Folk Ballads*. 2 vols. Little Rock, AR: August House, 1987.

McNeil, W.K., and William M. Clements, eds. *An Arkansas Folklore Sourcebook*. Fayetteville: University of Arkansas Press, 1992.

McNeill, David. *Hand and Mind: What Gestures Reveal About Thought*. Chicago: University of Chicago Press, 1996.

McWhiney, Grady. *Cracker Culture: Celtic Ways in the Old South*. Tuscaloosa: University of Alabama Press, 1989.

McWilliams, Carey. *Factories in the Field*. Santa Barbara, CA: Peregrine, 1972.

Mead, Margaret. *Coming of Age in Samoa: A Psychological Study of Primitive Youth for Western Civilization*. 1928. Reprint, New York: Perennial, 2001.

Mechling, Jay. "'Banana Cannon' and Other Folk Traditions Between Human and Nonhuman Animals." *Western Folklore* 48 (1989): 312–23.

———. "Children's Folklore." In *Folk Groups and Folklore Genres: An Introduction*, ed. Elliott Oring, 91–120. Logan: Utah State University Press, 1986.

———. "Children's Folklore in Residential Institutions: Summer Camps, Boarding Schools, Hospitals, and Custodial Facilities." In *Children's Folklore: A Sourcebook*, ed. Brian Sutton-Smith, Jay Mechling, Thomas W. Johnson, and Felicia R. McMahon, 273–91. Logan: Utah State University Press, 1999.

———. "From archy to Archy: Why Cockroaches Are Good to Think." *Southern Folklore* 48 (1991): 121–40.

———. "Mediating Structures and the Significance of University Folk." In *Folk Groups and Folklore Genres: A Reader*, ed. Elliott Oring, 287–95. Logan: Utah State University Press, 1989.

———. *On My Honor: Boy Scouts and the Making of American Youth*. Chicago: University of Chicago Press, 2001.

———. "Picturing Hunting." *Western Folklore* 63 (2004): 51–78.

Medway, Gareth J. *Lure of the Sinister: The Unnatural History of Satanism*. New York: New York University Press, 2001.

Meinig, D.W., ed. *The Interpretation of Ordinary Landscapes: Geographical Essays*. New York: Oxford University Press, 1979.

———. "The Mormon Culture Region: Strategies and Patterns in the Geography of the American West, 1847–1964." *Annals of the Association of American Geographers* 55 (June 1965): 191–220.

Meley, Patricia M. "Paper Power: A Search for Meaning in the Folded Paper Toys of Pre-Adolescents." *Children's Folklore Review* 11, no. 2 (1989): 3–5.

Menhaden Chanteymen. *Won't You Help Me to Raise 'Em*. CD 220. New York: Global Village, 1991

The Mennonite Encyclopedia. 5 vols. Scottdale, PA: Mennonite Brethren Publishing House, 1955–1990.

Menzer, Joe. *The Wildest Ride: A History of NASCAR*. New York: Simon and Schuster, 2001.

Mercer, Mick. *Hex Files: The Goth Bible*. Woodstock, NY: Overlook Press, 1997.

Merton, Robert K. *Social Theory and Social Structure*. Revised and enlarged edition. New York: Free Press of Glencoe, 1957.

Messerschmidt, Donald A., ed. *Anthropologists at Home: Methods and Issues in the Study of One's Own Society*. Cambridge: Cambridge University Press, 1981.

Methodist Episcopal Church. *Pioneering in Penn's Woods: Philadelphia Methodist Episcopal Annual Conference Through One Hundred Fifty Years*. Philadelphia: Philadelphia Conference Tract Society of the Methodist Episcopal Church, 1937.

Meulder, Walter George. *Methodism and Society in the Twentieth Century*. New York: Abingdon, 1961.

Meyer, B.H. "Fraternal Beneficiary Societies in the United States." *American Journal of Sociology* 6 (March 1901): 646–51.

Meyer, Richard E, ed. *Cemeteries and Gravemarkers: Voices of American Culture*. Logan: Utah State University Press, 1992.

———, ed. *Ethnicity and the American Cemetery*. Bowling Green, OH: Bowling Green State University Popular Press, 1993.

Meyers, Thomas J. *An Amish Patchwork: Indiana's Old Orders in the Modern World*. Bloomington, IN: Quarry Books, 2005.

Michael, Moina. *The Miracle Flower: The Story of the Flanders Fields Memorial Poppy*. Philadelphia: Dorrance, 1941.

Micozzi, Marc S., ed. *Fundamentals of Complemen-*

tary and Alternative Medicine. Philadelphia: Churchill Livingstone, 2001.

Mid-Atlantic Arts Foundation. *Folk Arts and Cultural Traditions of the Delmarva Peninsula.* Baltimore: Mid-Atlantic Arts Foundation, 2003.

Mieder, Wolfgang. *American Proverbs: A Study of Texts and Contexts.* New York: Peter Lang, 1989.

———. *The Politics of Proverbs: From Traditional Wisdom to Proverbial Stereotypes.* Madison: University of Wisconsin Press, 1997.

———, ed. *Wise Words: Essays on the Proverb.* New York: Garland, 1994.

Mieder, Wolfgang, Stewart A. Kingsbury, and Kelsie B. Harder, eds. *A Dictionary of American Proverbs.* New York: Oxford University Press, 1992.

Mijatovic, Elodie Lawton. *Serbian Folk Lore.* 1874. Reprint, Manchester, NH: Ayer, 1968.

Milanovich, Anthony, Stith Thompson, Yvonne J. Milspaw, and Linda Dégh. "Serbian Tales from Blanford." *Indiana Folklore* 4 (1971): 1–60.

Miles, Ann. *From Cuenca to Queens: An Anthropological Story of Transnational Migration.* Austin: University of Texas Press, 2004.

Miles, Clement A. *Christmas Customs and Traditions: Their History and Significance.* 1912. Reprint, New York: Dover Publications, 1976.

Miles of Smiles, Years of Struggle. 16-mm film and video. Produced by Paul Wagner and Jack Santino. South Burlington, VT: California Newsreel, 1983.

Milinaire, Caterine. *Celebrations: From Birth to Death and from New Year's to Christmas.* New York: Harmony Books, 1981.

Miller, Barbara D. "The Disappearance of the Oiled Braid: Indian Adolescent Female Hairstyles in America." In *Hair: Its Power and Meaning in Asian Cultures,* ed. Alf H. Hebeitel and Barbara D. Miller, 259–80. Albany: State University of New York Press, 1998.

Miller, Donald L. *City of the Century: The Epic of Chicago and the Making of America.* New York: Simon and Schuster, 1996.

Miller, Elaine K. *Mexican Folk Narrative from the Los Angeles Area.* Austin: University of Texas Press, 1973.

Miller, John M. *Deer Camp: Last Light in the Northeast Kingdom.* Cambridge, MA: MIT Press, 1992.

Miller, Kerby, and Paul Wagner. *Out of Ireland: The Story of Irish Emigration to America.* Washington, DC: Elliot and Clark, 1994.

Miller, Lorna Touryan, and Donald Eugene Miller. *Survivors: An Oral History of the Armenian Genocide.* Berkeley: University of California Press, 1993.

Miller, Timothy. *American Communes: A Bibliography.* New York: Garland, 1990.

Mills, Gary B. *The Forgotten People: Cane River's Creoles of Color.* Baton Rouge: Louisiana State University Press, 1977.

Milnes, Gerald. *Play of a Fiddle: Traditional Music, Dance, and Folklore in West Virginia.* Lexington: University Press of Kentucky, 1999.

Milspaw, Yvonne J. "Protestant Home Shrines: Icon and Image." *New York Folklore* 12 (1986): 119–36.

Mink, Charles R. "The Ozark Hillbilly: A Vanishing American." *Missouri Folklore Society Journal* 3 (1981): 31–45.

Minton, John. "Creole Community and Mass Communication: Houston Zydeco as a Mediated Tradition." *Journal of Folklore Research* 32 (1995): 1–19.

———. "Houston Creoles and Zydeco: The Emergence of an African-American Urban Style." *American Music* 14 (1996): 480–526.

Mintz, Jerome R. *Hasidic People: A Place in the New World.* Cambridge, MA: Harvard University Press, 1992.

———. *Legends of the Hasidim: An Introduction to Hasidic Culture and Oral Tradition in the New World.* Chicago: University of Chicago Press, 1968.

Minutes of the Annual Meeting of the Old German Baptist Brethren Church from 1778 to 2002. Grand Rapids, MI: Dickinson, 2002.

Mirak, Robert. *Torn Between Two Lands: Armenians in America 1890 to World War I.* Cambridge, MA: Harvard University Press, 1983.

Mirzoeff, Nicholas, ed. *The Visual Culture Reader.* London: Routledge, 2002.

Mishler, Craig. *The Crooked Stovepipe: Athapaskan Fiddle Music and Square Dancing in Northeast Alaska and Northwest Canada.* Urbana: University of Illinois Press, 1993.

Mitchell, Carol. "The Sexual Perspective in the Appreciation and Interpretation of Jokes." *Western Folklore* 36, no. 4 (1977): 303–29.

———. "Some Differences in Male and Female Joke-Telling." In *Women's Folklore, Women's Culture,* ed. Rosan A. Jordan and Susan J. Kalcik, 163–86. Philadelphia: University of Pennsylvania Press, 1985.

Mitchell, George. *Ponce de Leon.* Atlanta, GA: Argonne Books, 1983.

Mitchell, Reid. *All on a Mardi Gras Day: Episodes in the History of New Orleans Carnival.* Cambridge, MA: Harvard University Press, 1995.

Mitchell, Robert D. *Commercialism and Frontier: Perspectives on the Early Shenandoah Valley.* Charlottesville: University Press of Virginia, 1977.

Mitchell, Roger. "Ancestral Spirits and Hitchhiking Ghosts: Syncretism on Guam." *Midwestern Journal of Language and Folklore* 2 (1976): 45–55.

Mitford, Jessica. *The American Way of Death, Revisited.* New York: Knopf, 1998.

Moffat, Michael. *Coming of Age in New Jersey: College and American Culture.* New Brunswick, NJ: Rutgers University Press, 1989.

Moffet, Marian, and Lawrence Wodehouse. *East Tennessee Cantilever Barns.* Knoxville: University of Tennessee Press, 1993.

Molnar, August J. "Hungarian Pioneers and Immigrants in New Jersey Since Colonial Days." In *The New Jersey Ethnic Experience*, ed. Barbara Cunningham, 249–66. Union City, NJ: Wm. H. Wise, 1977.

Monahan, Molly. *Seeds of Grace: Reflections on the Spirituality of Alcoholics Anonymous.* New York: Riverhead Books, 2002.

Montell, William Lynwood. *Ghosts Along the Cumberland: Deathlore in the Kentucky Foothills.* Knoxville: University of Tennessee Press, 1975.

———. *The Saga of Coe Ridge: A Study in Oral History.* Knoxville: University of Tennessee Press, 1970.

———. *Tales from Tennessee Lawyers.* Lexington: University Press of Kentucky, 2005.

Montgomery, Margaret. "A Macedonian Wedding in Indianapolis." *Hoosier Folklore* 7 (1948): 101–4.

Montgomery, Michael, ed. *The Crucible of Carolina: Essays in the Development of Gullah Language and Culture.* Athens: University of Georgia Press, 1994.

Monti, Ralph. *I Remember Brooklyn: Memories from Famous Sons and Daughters.* New York: Birch Lane Press, 1991.

Mook, Maurice A. "The Nebraska Amish of Pennsylvania." *Mennonite Life* 17, no. 1 (January 1961): 27–30.

Moon, Elaine Latzman. *Untold Tales, Unsung Heroes: An Oral History of Detroit's African American Community, 1918–1967.* Detroit, MI: Wayne State University Press, 1994.

Moore, Charles W., Kathryn Smith, and Peter Becker, eds. *Home Sweet Home: American Domestic Vernacular Architecture.* New York: Rizzoli, 1983.

Moore, Jack B. *Skinheads Shaved for Battle: A Cultural History of American Skinheads.* Bowling Green, OH: Bowling Green University Popular Press, 1993.

Moore, Leonard J. *Citizen Klansmen: The Ku Klux Klan in Indiana, 1921–1928.* Chapel Hill: University of North Carolina Press, 1991.

Moore, R. Laurence. *In Search of White Crow.* New York: Oxford University Press, 1977.

Moore, Rudy Ray. *Rudy Ray Moore—Greatest Hits.* Capitol, CD 35735. 1995.

Moore, Willard B., ed. *Circles of Tradition: Folk Arts in Minnesota.* St. Paul: Minnesota Historical Society for the University of Minnesota Art Museum, 1989.

———. "Folklore Research and Museums." In *Handbook of American Folklore*, ed. Richard M. Dorson, 402–8. Bloomington: Indiana University Press, 1983.

———. "Metaphor and Changing Reality: The Foodways and Beliefs of the Russian Molokans in the United States." In *Ethnic and Regional Foodways in the United States: The Performance of Group Identity*, ed. Linda Keller Brown and Kay Mussell, 91–112. Knoxville: University of Tennessee Press, 1984.

———. *Molokan Oral Tradition: Legends and Memorates of an Ethnic Sect.* University of California Publications, Folklore Studies, 28. Berkeley: University of California Press, 1973.

Morawska, Ewa T. *The Maintenance of Ethnicity: A Case Study of the Polish-American Community in Greater Boston.* San Francisco: R and E Research Associates, 1977.

Morgan, David, and Sally M. Promey, eds. *The Visual Culture of American Religions.* Berkeley: University of California Press, 2001.

Morgan, Douglas. *What Do You Do with a Drunken Sailor? Unexpurgated Sea Chanties.* Pomfret, CT: Swordsmith, 2002.

Morgan, Gareth. *Images of Organization.* London: Sage, 1996.

Morgan, Lael, ed. *Alaska's Native People.* Anchorage: Alaska Geographic Society, 1979.

Morgenroth, Lynda. *Boston's Neighborhoods.* Guilford, CT: Globe Pequot, 2001.

Morley, Peter, and Roy Wallis, eds. *Culture and Curing: Anthropological Perspectives on Traditional*

Medical Beliefs and Practices. London: Peter Owen, 1978.

Mormino, Gary R. *Immigrants on the Hill: Italian-Americans in St. Louis, 1882–1982*. Urbana: University of Illinois Press, 1986.

Morris, Ann, ed. *Lift Every Voice and Sing: St. Louis African Americans in the Twentieth Century*. Columbia: University of Missouri Press, 1999.

Morris, Richard A. *Old Russian Ways: Cultural Variations Among Three Russian Groups in Oregon*. New York: AMS Press, 1991.

Morrow, Phyllis, and William Schneider, eds. *When Our Words Return: Writing, Hearing, and Remembering Oral Traditions of Alaska and the Yukon*. Logan: Utah State University Press, 1995.

Mortensen, Enok. *The Danish Lutheran Church in America: The History and Heritage of the American Evangelical Lutheran Church*. Philadelphia: Board of Publication, Lutheran Church in America, 1967.

Moskos, Charles C. *Greek Americans, Struggle and Success*. Englewood Cliffs, NJ: Prentice-Hall, 1980.

Motely, Mary Penick. *The Invisible Soldier: The Experience of the Black Soldier, World War II*. Detroit, MI: Wayne State University Press, 1975.

Moyle, Richard. *Traditional Samoan Music*. Auckland, NZ: Auckland University Press, 1988.

Muir, Helen. *Miami, U.S.A.* Gainesville: University Press of Florida, 2000.

Mukhi, Sunita. *Doing the Desi Thing: Performing Indianness in New York City*. New York: Garland, 2000.

Mullen, Patrick B. *I Heard the Old Fishermen Say: Folklore of the Texas Gulf Coast*. Logan: Utah State University Press, 1988.

———. *Listening to Old Voices: Folklore, Life Stories, and the Elderly*. Urbana: University of Illinois Press, 1991.

———. "The Relationship of Legend and Folk Belief." *Journal of American Folklore* 84 (1971): 406–13.

Mullin, Molly H. *Culture in the Marketplace: Gender, Art, and Value in the American Southwest*. Durham, NC: Duke University Press, 2001.

Murphy, Joseph. *Santeria: African Spirits in America*. Boston: Beacon, 1993.

Murphy, Peter F. *Studs, Tools, and the Family Jewels: Metaphors Men Live By*. Madison: University of Wisconsin Press, 2001.

Murray, Catherine. *A Taste of Memories from the Old "Bush": Italian Recipes and Fond Memories from the People Who Lived in Madison's Greenbush District*. 2 vols. Madison, WI: Greenbush Remembered, 1988, 1990.

Murray-Wooley, Caroline, and Karl Raitz. *Rock Fences of the Bluegrass*. Lexington: University of Kentucky Press, 1992.

Musafar, Fakir. "Kiss of Fire: The ABC's of Branding." *Body Play Quarterly*, no. 1 (1992): 9–18.

Musgrave, Jon. *Egyptian Tales of Southern Illinois*. Marion, IL: Illinoishistory.com, 2000.

Musser, Daniel. *The Reformed Mennonite Church, Its Rise and Progress, with Its Principles and Doctrines*. 2nd ed. Lancaster, PA: Inquirer Printing and Publishing, 1878.

Myerhoff, Barbara. *Number Our Days*. New York: Simon and Schuster, 1978.

Myers, Robert J. *Celebrations: The Complete Book of American Holidays*. Garden City, NY: Doubleday, 1972.

N'Diaye, Diana Baird, and Betty Belanus. "The African Immigrant Folklife Study Project." Center for Folklife and Cultural Heritage, Smithsonian Institution, 2005. www.folklife.si.edu/africa/about.htm.

Nabeel, Abraham, and Andrew Shryock. *Arab Detroit: From Margin to Mainstream*. Detroit, MI: Wayne State University Press, 2000.

Nabokov, Peter. *Native American Architecture*. New York: Oxford University Press, 1989.

Nagamine, Shoshin. *Tales of Okinawa's Great Masters*. Translated by Patrick McCarthy. Boston: Tuttle, 2000.

Narváez, Peter. "Folkloristics, Cultural Studies and Popular Culture." *Canadian Folklore Canadien* 14, no. 1 (1992): 15–30.

———. *Of Corpse: Death and Humor in Folklore and Popular Culture*. Logan: Utah State University Press, 2003.

Narváez, Peter, and Martin Laba, eds. *Media Sense: The Folklore-Popular Culture Continuum*. Bowling Green, OH: Bowling Green State University Popular Press, 1986.

Nash, Jesse W. *Vietnamese Catholicism*. Harvey, LA: Art Review Press, 1992.

Nash, Tom, and Twilo Scofield. *The Well-Traveled Casket: A Collection of Oregon Folklife*. Salt Lake City: University of Utah Press, 1992.

Nathan, Hans. *Dan Emmett and the Rise of Early*

Negro Minstrelsy. Norman: University of Oklahoma Press, 1977.

Nathan, Rebekah. *My Freshman Year: What a Professor Learned by Becoming a Student.* Ithaca, NY: Cornell University Press, 2005.

National Council of Jewish Women, Pittsburgh Section. *By Myself I'm a Book! An Oral History of the Immigrant Jewish Experience in Pittsburgh.* Waltham, MA: American Jewish Historical Society, 1972.

National Council of Negro Women. *The Black Family Reunion Cookbook: Recipes and Food Memories.* New York: Fireside, 1993.

Ndubuike, Darlington Iheonunekwu Iheanacho. *The Struggles, Challenges, and Triumphs of the African Immigrants in America.* New York: Edwin Mellen Press, 2002.

"Neda Jurisich: Hard Work Is Her Prescription for Life." *Down the Road* 6, no. 7 (June 1994): 7–11.

Needham, Maureen, ed. *I See America Dancing: Selected Readings, 1685–2000.* Urbana: University of Illinois Press, 2002.

Neely, Charles. *Tales and Songs of Southern Illinois: Timeless Folklore in Story and Verse.* Menashe, WI: Collegiate Press, 1938.

Neitz, Mary Jo. *Charisma and Community: A Study of Religious Commitment Within the Charismatic Renewal.* New Brunswick, NJ: Transaction, 1987.

Nelson, E. Clifford, ed. *The Lutherans in North America.* Philadelphia: Fortress Press, 1975.

Nelson, Marion. *Norwegian Folk Art: The Migration of a Tradition.* New York: Abbeville, 1995.

Nelson, Pamela B., ed. *Rites of Passage in America: Traditions of the Life Cycle.* Philadelphia: Balch Institute for Ethnic Studies, 1992.

Nelson, Robin. *Toys and Games Then and Now.* Minneapolis, MN: Lerner Publications, 2003.

Nettl, Bruno. *Folk Music in the United States: An Introduction.* 3rd ed. Detroit, MI: Wayne State University Press, 1976.

Nettl, Bruno, and Moravcik, Ivo. "Czech and Slovak Songs Collected in Detroit." *Midwest Folklore* 5 (1955): 37–49.

Neufeld, Peter, Jim Dwyer, and Barry Scheck. *Actual Innocence: Five Days to Execution, and Other Dispatches from the Wrongly Accused.* New York: Doubleday, 2000.

Neulander, Judith S. "New Mexican Crypto-Jewish Canon: Choosing to be 'Chosen' in Millennial Tradition." Special issue, *Jewish Folklore and Ethnology Review* 18 (1996): 19–58.

Neustadt, Kathy. *Clambake: A History and Celebration of an American Tradition.* Amherst: University of Massachusetts Press, 1992.

Nevell, Richard. *A Time to Dance: American Country Dancing from Hornpipes to Hot Hash.* New York: St. Martin's Press, 1977.

Newall, Venetia. *An Egg at Easter: A Folklore Study.* London: Routledge and Kegan Paul, 1971.

Newman, Daisy. *A Procession of Friends: Quakers in America.* Garden City, NY: Doubleday, 1972.

Newman, I.M., J.K. Craword, and M.J. Nellis. "The Role and Function of Drinking Games in a University Community." *Journal of American College Health* 39 (1991): 171–75.

Newman, Simon P. *Parades and the Politics of the Street: Festive Culture in the Early American Republic.* Philadelphia: University of Pennsylvania Press, 1997.

Newton, Esther. *Cherry Grove, Fire Island: Sixty Years in America's First Gay and Lesbian Town.* Boston: Beacon, 1993.

Ngo, Bach, and Gloria Zimmerman. *The Classic Cuisine of Vietnam.* Woodbury, NY: Barron's, 1978.

Nicholas, Mark A. "Mashpee Wampanoags of Cape Cod, the Whalefishery, and Seafaring's Impact on Community Development." *American Indian Quarterly* 26 (2002): 165–97.

Nichols, Bill. *Representing Reality: Issues and Concepts in Documentary.* Bloomington: Indiana University Press, 1991.

Nickell, Joe. *Looking for a Miracle: Weeping Icons, Relics, Stigmata, Visions and Healing Cures.* Amherst, NY: Prometheus Books, 1993.

Nickerson, Bruce. "Is There a Folk in the Factory?" *Journal of American Folklore* 7 (1974): 133–39.

Nicolaisen, W.F.H. "The Folk and the Region." *New York Folklore* 2 (1976): 143–49.

———. "Folklore and Geography: Towards an Atlas of American Folk Culture." *New York Folklore Quarterly* 29 (1973): 3–20.

———. "Language Contact and Onomastics." In *Contact Linguistics. An International Handbook of Contemporary Research.* Vol. 1. Edited by Hans Goebl, 549–54. Berlin: Walter de Gruyter, 1996.

———. "The Mapping of Folk Culture as Applied Folklore." Special issue, "Bibliographic and Special Studies." *Folklore Forum* 8 (1971): 26–30.

———. "Names and Narratives." *Journal of American Folklore* 97 (1984): 259–72.

———. "Onomastic Dialects." *American Speech* 55 (1980): 36–45.

———. "Some Humorous Folk-Etymological Narratives." *New York Folklore* 3 (1977): 1–13.

———. "Surveying and Mapping North American Culture." *Mid-South Folklore* 3 (1975): 35–40.

———. "Variant, Dialect and Region: An Exploration of the Geography of Tradition." *New York Folklore* 6 (1980): 137–49.

Nicoletta, Julie. *Architecture of the Shakers*. Woodstock, VT: Countryman Press, 2000.

Niles, Christina. "The Revival of the Latvian *Kokle* in America." *Selected Reports in Ethnomusicology* 3 (1978): 211–39.

Niles, Susan A. *Dickeyville Grotto: The Vision of Father Mathias Wernerus*. Jackson: University Press of Mississippi, 1997.

Nimer, Mohamed. *The North American Muslim Resource Guide: Muslim Community Life in the United States and Canada*. New York: Routledge, 2002.

Nissenbaum, Stephen. *The Battle for Christmas*. New York: Vintage Books, 1996.

Noble, Allen G, ed. *To Build in a New Land: Ethnic Landscapes in North America*. Baltimore: Johns Hopkins University Press, 1992.

———. *Wood, Brick, and Stone: The North American Settlement Landscape*. 2 vols. Amherst: University of Massachusetts Press, 1984.

Noble, Allen G., and Brian Coffey. "The Use of Cobblestones as a Folk Building Material." *P.A.S.T.: Pioneer America Society Transactions* 9 (1986): 45–51.

Nolt, Steven M. *Foreigners in Their Own Land: Pennsylvania Germans in the Early Republic*. University Park: Pennsylvania State University Press and Pennsylvania German Society, 2002.

———. *A History of the Amish*. Intercourse, PA: Good Books, 1992.

Noonan, Kerry. "May You Never Hunger: Religious Foodways in Dianic Witchcraft." *Ethnologies* 20 (1998): 151–73.

Nordhoff, Charles. *The Communistic Societies of the United States*. 1875. Reprint, New York: Hillary House, 1961.

Nordyke, Eleanor C. *The Peopling of Hawai'i*. 2nd ed. Honolulu: University of Hawaii Press, 1989.

Norris, Karen, and Ralph Norris. *Northwest Carving Traditions*. Atglen, PA: Schiffer, 1999.

Nostrand, Richard L., and Lawrence E. Estaville, eds. *Homelands: A Geography of Culture and Place Across America*. Baltimore: John Hopkins University Press, 2001.

Noyes, Dorothy. "Group." In *Eight Words for the Study of Expressive Culture*, ed. Burt Feintuch, 7–41. Urbana: University of Illinois Press, 2003.

———. *Uses of Tradition: Arts of Italian Americans in Philadelphia*. Philadelphia: Philadelphia Folklore Project, 1989.

Noyes, John Humphrey. *History of American Socialisms*. 1870. Reprint, New York: Dover Publications, 1966.

Nugent, Walter. *Into the West: The Story of Its People*. New York: Vintage Books, 2001.

Nuñez Molina, Mario A. "Community Healing Among Puerto Ricans: Espiritismo as a Therapy for the Soul." In *Healing Cultures: Art and Religion as Curative Practices in the Caribbean and Its Diaspora*, ed. Margarite Fernández Olmos and Lizabeth Paravisini-Gebert, 115–32. New York: Palgrave, 2001.

Nusbaum, Philip. "The Festival Committee of the Minnesota Bluegrass and Old Time Music Association: A Musical Community." *Mid-America Folklore* 25 (1997): 14–35.

———. "The Importance of Storytelling Style Among New York City Taxi Drivers." *New York Folklore Quarterly* 6 (1980): 67–88.

———. *Norwegian-American Music from Minnesota: Old-Time and Traditional Favorites*. St. Paul: Minnesota Historical Society Press, 1989. LP and cassette with essay.

———. "Some Notes on the Construction of the Jewish American Dialect Story." *Keystone Folklore* 23 (1979): 28–52.

———. "Spear Fishing and Spear Fishing Decoy Collecting: Connected, Yet Different Experiential Worlds." *New York Folklore* 19 (1993): 19–41.

———. "Traditionalizing Experience: The Case of Vietnam Veterans." *New York Folklore* 17 (1991): 45–62.

Nusz, Nancy, ed. "Folklife in Education." Special issue, *Southern Folklore* 48, no. 1 (1991).

O'Brien, Donal B. Cruise. *The Mourides of Senegal: The Political and Economic Organization of an Islamic Brotherhood*. Oxford: Clarendon Press, 1971.

O'Connor, Thomas H. *South Boston. My Home Town: The History of an Ethnic Neighborhood*. Lebanon,

NH: Northeastern Univesity Press/University Press of New England, 1994.

O'Hara, Craig. *The Philosophy of Punk: More Than Noise*. San Francisco: AK Press, 1995.

O'Leary, Cecilia Elizabeth. *To Die For: The Paradox of American Patriotism*. Princeton, NJ: Princeton University Press, 1999.

Obidinski, Eugene E., and Helen Stankiewicz Zand. *Polish Folkways in America*. Lanham, MD: University Press of America, 1987.

Odum, Howard W., and Harry Estell Moore. *American Regionalism*. New York: Henry Holt, 1938.

Ogawa, Dannis M. *Kodomo No Tame Ni, for the Sake of the Children: The Japanese American Experience in Hawaii*. Honolulu: University Press of Hawaii, 1978.

Ohrn, Steven, ed. *Passing Time and Traditions: Contemporary Iowa Folk Artists*. Des Moines: Iowa State University Press for the Iowa Arts Council, 1984.

Ohrn, Stephen, and Michael E. Bell, eds. "Saying Cheese: Studies in Folklore and Visual Communication." Special issue, *Folklore Forum* 13 (1975).

Oinas, Felix J., ed. *Folklore, Nationalism, and Politics*. Columbus, OH: Slavica Publishers, 1978.

Oktavec, Eileen. *Answered Prayers: Miracles and Milagros Along the Border*. Tucson: University of Arizona Press, 1995.

Ola, Per, and Emily d'Aulaire. "Now What Are They Doing at That Crazy St. John the Divine?" *Smithsonian* 23, no. 9 (December 1992): 32–44.

Oliver, Paul, ed. 1997. *Encyclopedia of the Vernacular Architecture of the World*, 3 vols. Cambridge: Cambridge University Press.

———. *The Meaning of the Blues*. New York: Collier, 1960.

———. *Savannah Syncopators: African Retentions in the Blues*. New York: Studio Vista, 1970.

———. *Songsters and Saints: Vocal Traditions on Race Records*. New York: Cambridge University Press, 1984.

———. *The Story of the Blues*. Philadelphia: Chilton, 1969.

Olmos, Margarite Fernandez, and Lizabeth Paravisini-Gebert. *Creole Religions of the Caribbean: An Introduction from Voodoo and Santeria, to Obeah and Espiritismo*. New York: New York University Press, 2003.

Olney, Douglas, ed. *Hmong in the West, Observations and Reports*. St. Paul: University of Minnesota Press, 1982.

Olson, James S., and Judith E. Olson. *Cuban Americans: From Trauma to Triumph*. New York: Twayne, 1995.

Olson, Ted. *Blue Ridge Folklife*. Jackson: University Press of Mississippi, 1998.

Oney, Steve. *And the Dead Shall Rise: The Murder of Mary Phagan and the Lynching of Leo Frank*. New York: Pantheon, 2003.

Opie, Iona, and Peter Opie. *The Singing Game*. Oxford: Oxford University Press, 1985.

Oquilluk, William A. *People of Kauwerak: Legends of the Northern Eskimo*. Anchorage: AMU Press, 1973.

Oring, Elliott. "Ethnic Groups and Ethnic Folklore." In *Folk Groups and Folklore Genres*, ed. Elliott Oring, 23–44. Logan: Utah State University Press, 1986.

———, ed. *Folk Groups and Folklore Genres: An Introduction*. Logan: Utah State University Press, 1986.

———. "On the Concepts of Folklore." In *Folk Groups and Folklore Genres: An Introduction*, ed. Elliott Oring, 1–22. Logan: Utah State University Press, 1986.

———. "Three Functions of Folklore: Traditional Functionalism as Explanation in Folkloristics." *Journal of American Folklore* 89 (1976): 67–80.

Orlofsky, Patsy, and Myron Orlofsky. *Quilts in America*. 1974. Reprint, New York: Abbeville Press, 1992.

Orser, W. Edward. *Blockbusting in Baltimore*. Lexington: University Press of Kentucky, 1994.

Orsi, Robert Anthony. *The Madonna of 115th Street, Faith and Community in Italian Harlem, 1880–1950*. New Haven, CT: Yale University Press, 1985.

Orsinger, Trevor J., and Drew F. Orsinger. *The Firefighter's Best Friend: Lives and Legends of Chicago Firehouse Dogs*. Chicago: Lake Claremont Press, 2003.

Ortíz-Gonzalez, Victor M. *El Paso: Local Frontiers at a Global Crossroads*. Minneapolis: University of Minnesota Press, 2004.

Orvell, Miles. *American Photography*. New York: Oxford University Press, 2003.

Osofsky, Gilbert. *Harlem: The Making of a Ghetto*. New York: HarperTorchbooks, 1966.

Ostapchuck, Emily. *Folk Art of Carpatho-Ukraine*. Toronto: P. Ostapchuk, 1957.

Oster, Harry. *Living Country Blues*. Detroit: Folklore Associates, 1969.

Ostler, James, Marian Rodee, and Milford Nahohai. *Zuni: A Village of Silversmiths*. Zuni, NM: Zuni Ashiwi, 1996.

Otto, John Solomon. "Plain Folk, Lost Frontiersmen, and Hillbillies: The Southern Mountain Folk in History and Popular Culture." *Southern Studies* 26 (1987): 5–17.

Owens, William A. *Texas Folk Songs*. Dallas: Southern Methodist University Press, 1976.

Pacini Hernández, Deborah. *Bachata: A Social History of a Dominican Popular Music*. Philadelphia: Temple University Press, 1995.

Pacyga, Dominic A., and Ellen Skerrett. *Chicago, City of Neighborhoods: Histories and Tours*. Chicago: Loyola University Press, 1986.

Padgett, Deborah. *Settlers and Sojourners: A Study of Serbian Adaptation in Milwaukee, Wisconsin*. Brooklyn, NY: AMS Press, 1990.

Padilla, Felix M. "Salsa Music as a Cultural Expression of Latino Consciousness and Unity." *Hispanic Journal of Behavioral Sciences* 11, no. 1 (February 1989): 29–43.

Page, Linda Garland, and Hilton Smith, eds. *The Foxfire Book of Appalachian Toys and Games*. Chapel Hill: University of North Carolina Press, 1993.

Palazzolo, Laurie A. Gomulka. *Horn Man: The Polish American Musician in Twentieth-Century Detroit*. Detroit, MI: Wayne State University Press, 2003.

Palmer, Robert. *Deep Blues*. New York: Viking, 1981.

Pankuch, Jan. *History of the Slovaks in Cleveland and Lakewood*. Translated from Slovak by Rasto Gallo. Cleveland: Czechoslovak Genealogical Society and Western Reserve Historical Society, 2001.

Pap, Leo. *The Portuguese Americans*. Boston: Twayne, 1981.

Papanikolas, Helen Z. *An Amulet of Greek Earth: Generations of Immigrant Folk Culture*. Athens, OH: Swallow, 2002.

———, ed. *The Peoples of Utah*. Salt Lake City: Utah State Historical Society, 1981.

Paranjape, Makarand, ed. *In Diaspora: Theories, Histories, Texts*. New Delhi, India: Indialog, 2001.

Paredes, Américo. *Folklore and Culture on the Texas-Mexican Border*. Edited by Richard Bauman. Austin: CMAS Books, Center for Mexican American Studies, University of Texas at Austin, 1993.

———. *A Texas-Mexican Cancionero: Folksongs of the Lower Border*. Chicago: University of Illinois Press, 1976.

———. *"With His Pistol in His Hand." A Border Ballad and Its Hero*. Austin: University of Texas Press, 1958.

Paredes, Américo, and Richard Bauman, eds. *Toward New Perspectives in Folklore*. Austin: University of Texas Press, 1972.

Paredes, Américo, and Ellen J. Stekert, eds. *The Urban Experience and Folk Tradition*. Austin: University of Texas Press, 1971.

Parsons, William T. *The Pennsylvania Dutch: A Persistent Minority*. Boston: Twayne, 1976.

Patai, Raphael. *On Jewish Folklore*. Detroit: Wayne State University Press, 1983.

Patterson, Daniel W. *The Shaker Spiritual*. 2nd ed. New York: Dover Publications, 2000.

Patterson, George James, Jr. *The Unassimilated Greeks of Denver*. New York: AMS Press, 1989.

Patterson, Paul. "Cowboy Comedians and Horseback Humorists." In *The Golden Log*, ed. Mody C. Boatright, Wilson M. Hudson, and Allen Maxwell, 99–107. Dallas, TX: Southern Methodist University Press, 1962.

Paulsen, Frank Martin. *Danish Settlements on the Canadian Prairies: Folk Traditions, Immigrant Experiences, and Local History*. Ottawa: National Museums of Canada, 1974.

Pawlowska, Harriet. *Merrily We Sing: 105 Polish Folksongs*. Detroit: Wayne State University Press, 1961.

Peachey, Samuel W. *Amish of Kishacoquillas Valley*. Scottdale, PA: Mennonite Publishing House, 1930.

Peacock, Robert. *Paradise Garden: A Trip Through Howard Finster's Visionary World*. San Francisco: Chronicle Books, 1996.

Pearson, Barry Lee. *Virginia Piedmont Blues: The Lives and Art of Two Virginia Bluesmen*. Philadelphia: University of Pennsylvania Press, 1990.

Pearson, Thomas. "Missions and Conversions: Creating the Montagnard-Dega Refugee Community (North Carolina)." Ph.D. diss., University of North Carolina at Chapel Hill, 2001.

Peck, Catherine. "Local Character Anecdotes Down East." *North Carolina Folklore Journal* 39 (1992): 63–71.

Peltz, Rakhmiel. *From Immigrant to Ethnic Culture: American Yiddish in South Philadelphia*. Stanford, CA: Stanford University Press, 1998.

Peña, Manuel. *The Texas-Mexican Conjunto: History*

of a Working Class Music. Austin: University of Texas Press, 1985.

Penland, Paige R. *Lowrider: History, Pride, Culture.* St. Paul, MN: MBI, 2003.

Pennar, Jaan, ed. *The Estonians in America, 1627–1975.* Dobbs Ferry, NY: Oceana, 1975.

Penti, Marsha. "Juhlat. Good Times for Finns." In "Finnish American Folklife," Special issue, *Finnish Americana: A Journal of Finnish American History and Culture* 8 (1990): 12–19.

Pepicello, William, and Thomas A. Green. *The Language of Riddles: New Perspectives.* Columbus: Ohio State University Press, 1984.

Perdue, Charles L., Jr., ed. *Outwitting the Devil: Jack Tales from Wise County, Virginia.* Santa Fe, NM: Ancient City Press, 1987.

Perks, Robert, and Alistair Thomson. *The Oral History Reader.* London: Routledge, 1998.

Pershing, Linda, et al. "A Feminist Retrospective on Folklore and Folkloristics." Special issue, *Folklore Women's Communication* (Special supplement), 1985.

Peter, Karl A. *The Dynamics of Hutterite Society: An Analytical Approach.* Edmonton, Canada: University of Alberta Press, 1987.

Peterson, Bill. *Coaltown Revisited: An Appalachian Notebook.* Chicago: Henry Regnery, 1972.

Peterson, Elizabeth. "American Sports and Folklore." In *Handbook of American Folklore,* ed. Richard M. Dorson, 257–64. Bloomington: Indiana University Press, 1983.

———. *The Changing Faces of Tradition: A Report on the Folk and Traditional Arts in the United States.* Washington, DC: National Endowment for the Arts, 1996.

Peterson, Sally Nina. "Translating Experience and the Reading of a Story Cloth." *Journal of American Folklore* 101 (1988): 6–22.

Pham, Mai. *Pleasures of the Vietnamese Table.* New York: HarperCollins, 2001.

Phillips, Jenny K. *Symbol, Myth and Rhetoric: The Politics of Culture in an Armenian-American Population.* New York: AMS Press, 1989.

Phillips, Susan A. *Wallbangin': Graffiti and Gangs in L.A.* Chicago: University of Chicago Press, 1999.

Phipps, Anne. "The Runaway Patient: A Legend in Oral Circulation and the Media." *Indiana Folklore* 13, nos. 1–2 (1980): 102–11.

Pierce, Donna. *Vivan Las Fiestas!* Santa Fe: Museum of New Mexico Press, 1985.

Pike, Sarah. *Earthly Bodies, Magical Selves: Contemporary Pagans and the Search for Community.* Berkeley: University of California Press, 2001.

Pillsbury, Richard. "The Pennsylvania Homeland." In *Homelands: A Geography of Culture and Place Across America,* ed. Richard L. Nostrand and Lawrence E. Estaville, 24–43. Baltimore: Johns Hopkins University Press, 2001.

Pirkova-Jakobson, Svatava. "Harvest Festivals Among Czechs and Slovaks in America." *Journal of American Folklore* 69 (1956): 266–80.

Pitzer, Donald, ed. *America's Communal Utopias.* Chapel Hill: University of North Carolina Press, 1997.

Pocius, Gerald L. "Lithuanian Landscapes in America: Houses, Yards, and Gardens in Scranton, Pennsylvania." *New York Folklore* 22 (1996): 49–87.

———, ed. *Living in a Material World: Canadian and American Approaches to Material Culture.* St. John's: Institute of Social and Economic Research, Memorial University of Newfoundland, 1991.

———. *A Place to Belong: Community Order and Everyday Space in Calvert, Newfoundland.* Athens: University of Georgia Press, 1991.

Polanyi, Livia. *Telling the American Story.* Cambridge, MA: MIT Press, 1989.

Polk, Patrick Arthur. *Haitian Vodou Flags.* Jackson: University Press of Mississippi, 1998.

Pollitzer, William S. *The Gullah People and Their African Heritage.* Athens: University of Georgia Press, 1999.

Pollock, Della. *Telling Bodies, Performing Birth: Everyday Narratives of Childbirth.* New York: Columbia University Press, 1999.

The Popovich Brothers of South Chicago. VHS. Directed by Jill Godmilow. Chicago: Facets Multimedia, 2000 (available at http://Folkstreams.net).

Portelli, Alessandro. *The Death of Luigi Trastulli and Other Stories: Form and Meaning in Oral History.* Albany: State University of New York Press, 1991.

Porter, Bernard H. "Truck Driver Lingo." *American Speech* 17 (1942): 102–5.

Posen, I. Sheldon. *You Hear the Ice Talking: The Ways of People and Ice on Lake Champlain.* Plattsburgh, NY: Clinton-Essex-Franklin Library System, 1986.

Posey, Darrell A., and Graham Dutfield. *Beyond Intellectual Property: Toward Traditional Resource Rights for Indigenous Peoples and Local Communities.* Ottawa: International Development Research Centre, 1996.

Posey, Sandra Mizumoto. "The Body Art of Brotherhood." In *African-American Fraternities and Sororities: The Legacy and the Vision*, ed. Tamara L. Brown, Gregory S. Parks, and Clarenda M. Phillips, 269–94. Lexington: University Press of Kentucky, 2005.

Poulton, Hugh. *Who Are the Macedonians?* Bloomington: Indiana University Press, 1995.

Pound, Louise. *Nebraska Folklore*. Lincoln: University of Nebraska Press, 1959.

Powers, Willow Roberts. *Navajo Trading: The End of an Era*. Albuquerque: University of New Mexico Press, 2001.

Pozzetta, George E., ed. *Folklore, Culture, and the Immigrant Mind*. New York: Garland, 1991.

Prabhupada, A.C. Bhaktivedanta Swami, et al. *The Higher Taste: A Guide to Gourmet Vegetarian Cooking and a Karma-Free Diet*. Los Angeles: Bhaktivedanta Book Trust, 2001.

Prashad, Vijay. *The Karma of Brown Folk*. Minneapolis: University of Minnesota Press, 2000.

Prebish, Charles S. *American Buddhism*. North Scituate, MA: Duxbury, 1979.

Preston, Cathy Lynn. "Feminist Approaches to Folklore." In *American Folklore: An Encyclopedia*, ed. Jan Harold Brunvand, 246–49. New York: Garland, 1996.

Preston, Dennis R. "Where Are the Dialects of American English at Anyhow?" *American Speech* 78 (Fall 2003): 235–54.

Preston, Michael J. "The English Literal Rebus and the Graphic Riddle Tradition." *Western Folklore* 41 (1982): 104–38.

Pribichevich, Stoyan. *Macedonia: Its People and History*. University Park: Pennsylvania State University Press, 1982.

Price, H. Wayne, and William D. Walters Jr. "Barn Raising at Metamora: A Photographic Essay." *Material Culture* 21 (1989): 47–56.

Primm, James Neal. *Lion of the Valley: St. Louis, Missouri, 1764–1980*. 3rd ed. St. Louis: Missouri Historical Society Press, 1998.

Prioli, Carmine. "The Harkers Island Work Boat: Draft Horse of the Carolina Sounds." *North Carolina Folklore Journal* 43 (1996): 120–27.

Prioli, Carmine, and Ed Martin. *Hope for a Good Season: The Ca'e Bankers of Harkers Island*. Winston-Salem, NC: Down Home Press, 1998.

Pritchett, Wendell. *Brownsville, Brooklyn: Blacks, Jews and the Changing Face of the Ghetto*. Chicago: University of Chicago Press, 2002.

Propp, Vladimir. *Morphology of the Folk Tale*. 2nd ed. Translated by Laurence Scott and revised by Louis A. Wagner. Austin: University of Texas Press, 1968.

Prosterman, Leslie. *Ordinary Life, Festival Days: Aesthetics in the Midwestern County Fair*. Washington DC: Smithsonian Institution Press, 1995.

Prpic, George. *The Croatian Immigrants in America*. New York: Philosophical Library, 1971.

———. *South Slavic Immigration in America*. Boston: Twayne, 1978.

Puckett, John L. *Foxfire Reconsidered: A Twenty-Year Experiment in Progressive Education*. Urbana: University of Illinois Press, 1989.

Puckett, Newbell Niles. *Folk Beliefs of the Southern Negro*. 1925. Reprint, New York: Dover, 1926.

Pula, James S. *Polish Americans: An Ethnic Community*. New York: Twayne, 1995.

Pullum, Stephen Jackson. *Foul Demons, Come Out! The Rhetoric of Twentieth-Century American Faith Healing*. Westport, CT: Praeger, 1999.

Puskás, Julianna. *Ties That Bind, Ties That Divide: 100 Years of Hungarian Experience in the United States*. New York: Homes and Meier, 2000.

Queens Council on the Arts. *The International Express: A Guide to Communities Along the #7 Train*. New York: Queens Council on the Arts, 2005.

Quimby, Ian M.G., and Scott T. Swank, eds. *Perspectives on American Folk Art*. New York: W.W. Norton, 1980.

Quinlin, Michael. *Irish Boston*. Guilford, CT: Globe Pequot, 2004.

Quinn, John Philip. *Gambling and Gambling Devices*. 1912. Reprint, Las Vegas, NV: Gambler's Book Club, 1979.

Rabinowicz, Tzvi M., ed. *Encyclopedia of Hasidism*. New York: Jason Aronson, 1996.

Rabinowitz, Joan, ed. *Asian Festivals of Washington State: Hmong New Year*. Seattle: Ethnic Heritage Council, Jack Straw Productions, Washington State Arts Commission, 2004.

Radcliffe-Brown, A.R. *Structure and Function in Primitive Society*. New York: Free Press, 1965.

Radner, Joan Newlon, ed. *Feminist Messages: Coding in Women's Folk Culture*. Urbana: University of Illinois Press, 1993.

Rafferty, Milton D. *The Ozarks: Land and Life*. 2nd ed. Fayetteville: University of Arkansas Press, 2001.

Ragsdale, John G. *Dutch Ovens Chronicled: Their*

Use in the United States. Fayetteville: University of Arkansas Press, 1991.

Ralbovsky, Martin. *Lords of the Locker Room.* New York: Wyden, 1974.

Ramirez, Frank, comp. *The Love Feast.* Elgin, IL: Brethren, 2000.

Randolph, Vance. *Down in the Holler: A Gallery of Ozark Folk Speech.* Norman: University of Oklahoma Press, 1979.

———. *Ozark Folksongs.* 4 vols. Columbia: University of Missouri Press, 1980.

———. *Ozark Mountain Folks.* New York: Vanguard, 1932.

———. *Roll Me in Your Arms* and *Blow the Candle Out: "Unprintable" Ozark Folksongs and Folklore.* 2 vols. Edited by G. Legman. Fayetteville: University of Arkansas Press, 1992.

———. *We Always Lie to Strangers: Tall Tales from the Ozarks.* New York: Columbia University Press, 1951.

Raphael, Ray. *The Men from the Boys: Rites of Passage in Male America.* Lincoln: University of Nebraska Press, 1988.

Rapping, Elayne. *The Culture of Recovery: Making Sense of the Self-Help Movement in Women's Lives.* Boston: Beacon, 1996.

Rasmussen, Anne K. "The Music of Arab Detroit: A Musical Mecca." In *Musics of Multicultural America: A Study of Twelve Musical Communities*, ed. Kip Lornell and Anne K. Rasmussen, 73–100. New York: Schirmer, 1997.

Raspa, Richard. "The CEO as Corporate Myth-Maker: Negotiating the Boundaries of Work and Play at Dominos Pizza Company." In *Symbols and Artifacts: Views of the Corporate Landscape,* ed. Pasquale Gagliardi, 273–79. Berlin: Walter de Gruyter, 1990.

———. "Folklore Expression in the Auto Industry." *Southern Folklore* 46 (1989): 71–89.

Rau, John E. "Czechs in South Dakota." In *To Build in a New Land: Ethnic Landscapes in North America*, ed. Allen G. Noble, 285–306. Baltimore: Johns Hopkins University Press, 1992.

RavenWolf, Silver. *HexCraft: Dutch Country Magick.* St. Paul: Llewellyn, 1997.

Re, Vittorio. *Michigan's Italian Community: A Historical Perspective.* Detroit, MI: Wayne State University, Office of International Exchanges and Ethnic Programs, 1981.

Reagon, Bernice Johnson. *If You Don't Go, Don't Hinder Me: The African American Sacred Song Tradition.* Lincoln: University of Nebraska Press, 2001.

———. *We'll Understand It Better By and By: Pioneering African-American Gospel Composers.* Washington, DC: Smithsonian Institution Press, 1992.

Red Shirt, Delphine. *Bead on an Anthill: A Lakota Childhood.* Lincoln: University of Nebraska Press, 1998.

Redekop, Calvin. *Mennonite Society.* Baltimore: Johns Hopkins University Press, 1989.

Redfield, Robert. "The Folk Society." *American Journal of Sociology* 52, no. 4 (1947): 293–308.

———. *The Little Community and Peasant Society and Culture.* Chicago: University of Chicago Press, 1967.

Redford, Dorothy Spruill, with Michael D'Orso. *Somerset Homecoming: Recovering a Lost Heritage.* New York: Doubleday, 1988.

Rehberger, Dean. "Visions of the New Mexican in Public Pageants and Dramas of Santa Fe and Taos, 1918–1940." *Journal of the Southwest* 37 (1995): 450–69.

Reichmann, Eberhard. *Hoosier German Tales: Small and Tall.* Indianapolis: German-American Center and Indiana German Heritage Society, 1991.

Reid, Jon, and Cynthia Reid. "A Cross Marks the Spot: A Study of Roadside Death Memorials in Texas and Oklahoma." *Death Studies* 25 (2001): 341–56.

Reider, Jonathan. *Canarsie: The Jews and Italians of Brooklyn Against Liberalism.* Cambridge, MA: Harvard University Press, 1985.

Reimensnyder, Barbara L. *Powwowing in Union County: A Study of Pennsylvania German Folk Medicine in Context.* New York: AMS Press, 1982.

Rennick, Robert M. "The Folklore of Curious and Unusual Names (A Brief Introduction to the Folklore of Onomastics." *New York Folklore Quarterly* 22 (1966): 5–14.

Renoff, Richard, and Stephen Reynolds, eds. *Proceedings of the Conference on Carpatho-Ruthenian Immigration.* Cambridge, MA: Harvard Ukrainian Research Institute, 1975.

Rettig, Lawrence L. *Amana Today: A History of the Amana Colonies from 1932 to the Present.* South Amana, IA: Amana Society, 1975.

Reuss, Richard. "That Can't Be Alan Dundes, Alan Dundes Is Taller than That: The Folklore of Folklorists." *Journal of American Folklore* 87 (1974): 303–17.

Reuter, Mark. *Sparrow's Point: Making Steel.* New York: Simon and Schuster, 1988.

Reynard, Elizabeth. *Narrow Land: Folk Chronicles of Old Cape Cod.* Chatham, MA: Chatham Historical Society, 1985.

Reynolds, Margaret C. *Plain Women: Gender and Ritual in the Old Order River Brethren,* ed. Simon J. Bronner. University Park: Pennsylvania State University Press, 2001.

Rice, George. *Toys and Games from Times Past and Still Enjoyed Today.* Nashville, IN: American Folk Toys, 2000.

Rice, Lee M., and Glenn R. Vernam. *They Saddled the West.* Centreville, MD: Cornell Maritime Press, 1975.

Rich, Linda G., Joan Clark Netherwood, and Elinor B. Cahn. *Neighborhood: A State of Mind.* Baltimore: Johns Hopkins University Press, 1982.

Rich, Paul. "Researching Grandfather's Secrets: Rummaging in the Odd Fellows and Masonic Attics." *Journal of American Culture* 20 (1997): 139–46.

Richards, Rand. *Historic San Francisco: A Concise History and Guide.* San Francisco: Heritage House, 1991.

Richardson, Keith P. "Polliwogs and Shellbacks: An Analysis of the Equator Crossing Ritual." *Western Folklore* 36 (1977): 154–59.

Riches, Suzanne Volmar. "Threads Through a Patchwork Quilt: The Wedding Shower as a Communication Ritual and Rite of Passage for the Mormon Woman." Ph.D. diss., University of Utah, 1987.

Richman, Irwin. *Borscht Belt Bungalows: Memories of Catskill Summers.* Philadelphia: Temple University Press, 2003.

Ricourt, Milagros, and Ruby Danta. *Hispanas de Queens: Latino Panethnicity in a New York City Neighborhood.* Ithaca, NY: Cornell University Press, 2003.

Riddle, Ronald. "Music Clubs and Ensembles in San Francisco's Chinese Community." In *Eight Urban Musical Cultures,* ed. Bruno Nettl, 223–59. Urbana: University of Illinois Press, 1978.

Riebsame, William E., general ed. *Atlas of the New West: Portrait of a Changing Region.* New York: W.W. Norton, 1997.

Riedmann, Peter. *Hutterite Confession of Faith: Translation of the 1565 German Edition of Confession of Our Religion, Teaching, and Faith by the Brothers Who Are Known as Hutterites.* Edited and translated by John Friesen. Scottdale, PA: Herald, 1999.

Rieff, David. *Going to Miami: Exiles, Tourists and Refugees in the New America.* Gainesville: University Press of Florida, 1999.

Riesman, David. *The Lonely Crowd: A Study of the Changing American Character.* New Haven, CT: Yale University Press, 1960.

Riggins, Stephen Harold. "If Work Made People Rich: An Oral History of General Farming, 1905–1925." *Midwestern Folklore* 17 (1991): 73–109.

Riggio, Milla, ed. "Trinidad and Tobago Carnival: Special Edition." Special issue, *Drama Review* 42, no. 3 (Fall 1998).

Rikoon, J. Sanford. "On the Politics of the Politics of Origins: Social (In)Justice and the International Agenda on Intellectual Property, Traditional Knowledge, and Folklore." *Journal of American Folklore* 117 (2004): 325–36.

———. *Threshing in the Midwest, 1820–1940: A Study of Traditional Culture and Technological Change.* Bloomington: Indiana University Press, 1988.

Riley, Michael. "Mexican American Shrines in Southern Arizona: A Postmodern Perspective." *Journal of the Southwest* 34, no. 2 (1992): 206–31.

Rippberger, Susan J. *Pledging Allegiance: Learning Nationalism at the El Paso-Juárez Border.* New York: Routledge, 2002.

Rippley, La Vern J. *The German-Americans.* Lanham, MD: University Press of America, 1984.

Ritchie, Donald A. *Doing Oral History.* New York: Twayne, 1995.

Rivera-Batiz, Francisco, and Carlos Santiago. *Puerto Ricans in the United States: A Changing Reality.* Washington, DC: National Puerto Rican Coalition, 2000.

Rivera, Raquel Z. *New York Ricans from the Hip Hop Zone.* New York: Palgrave, 2003.

Roach, Joseph. "Carnival and the Law in New Orleans." *Drama Review* 37, no. 3 (1993): 42–75.

Robbins, Thomas, and Susan Palmer, eds. *Millennium, Messiahs, and Mayhem: Contemporary Apocalyptic Movements.* New York: Routledge, 1997.

Robbins, Walter L. "Wishing and Shooting in the New Year Among the Germans in the Carolinas." In *American Folklife,* ed. Don Yoder, 257–79. Austin: University of Texas Press, 1976.

Roberts, J.A.G. *China to Chinatown: Chinese Food in the West.* London: Reaktion Books, 2002.

Roberts, Joan I. *Feminism and Nursing: An Historical Perspective on Power, Status, and Political Activism in the Nursing Profession.* Westport, CT: Praeger, 1995.

Roberts, John M., and Michael J. Forman. "Riddles: Expressive Modes of Interrogation." *Ethnology* 10 (1971): 509–33.

Roberts, Leonard, ed. *Sang Branch Settlers: Folksongs and Tales of a Kentucky Mountain Family.* Austin: University of Texas Press, 1974.

———, ed. *South from Hell-fer-Sartin: Kentucky Mountain Folk Tales.* Lexington: University of Kentucky Press, 1955.

Roberts, Peter. *Anthracite Coal Communities.* New York: Arno Press, 1970.

Roberts, Warren E. "Folk Crafts." In *Folklore and Folklife: An Introduction,* ed. Richard M. Dorson, 233–52. Chicago: University of Chicago Press, 1972.

———. *Log Buildings of Southern Indiana.* Bloomington, IN: Trickster Press, 1996.

———. *Viewpoints on Folklife: Looking at the Overlooked.* Ann Arbor, MI: UMI Research Press, 1988.

Robinson, John A. "Personal Narratives Reconsidered." *Journal of American Folklore* 94 (1981): 58–85.

Robinson, Rowland. *Danvis Tales.* Edited by David Budbill. Hanover, NH: University Press of New England, 1995.

Roche, Judith, and Meg McHutchison, eds. *First Fish, First People: Salmon Tales of the North Pacific Rim.* Seattle: University of Washington Press, 2003.

Rochford, E. Burke. *Hare Krishna in America.* New Brunswick, NJ: Rutgers University Press, 1985.

Rodriguez, Joseph. *East Side Stories: Gang Life in East L.A.* New York: Powerhouse Books, 1998.

———. *Nuestro Milwaukee: The Making of the United Community Center.* Madison: Wisconsin Humanities Council, 2000.

Rodriguez, Nestor P. "Economic Restructuring and Latino Growth in Houston." In *In the Barrios: Latinos and the Underclass Debate,* ed. Joan Moore and Raquel Pinderhughes, 101–27. New York: Russell Sage Foundation, 1993.

Roeber, A.G. *Palatines, Liberty, and Property: German Lutherans in Colonial British America.* Baltimore: Johns Hopkins University Press, 1993.

Roeder, Beatrice A. *Chicano Folk Medicine from Los Angeles, California.* Berkeley: University of California Press, 1988.

Rogers, Nicholas. *Halloween: From Pagan Ritual to Party Night.* New York: Oxford University Press, 2002.

Rogers, Robert. *Destiny's Landfall: A History of Guam.* Honolulu: University of Hawaii Press, 1994.

Rogosin, Donn. *Invisible Men: Life in Baseball's Negro Leagues.* New York: Atheneum, 1983.

Rohe, Randall E. "The Evolution of the Great Lakes Logging Camp, 1830–1930." *Journal of Forest History* 30 (January 1986): 17–28.

Romalis, Shelly. *Pistol Packin' Mama: Aunt Molly Jackson and the Politics of Folksong.* Urbana: University of Illinois Press, 1998.

Rooks, Noliwe M. *Hair Raising: Beauty, Culture, and African American Women.* New Brunswick, NJ: Rutgers University Press, 1996.

Rooney, John F., Jr., Wilbur Zelinsky, and Dean R. Louder, eds. *This Remarkable Continent: An Atlas of United States and Canadian Society and Cultures.* College Station: Texas A&M University Press, 1982.

Rooth, Anna Birgitta. *The Alaska Expedition 1966: Myths, Customs and Beliefs Among the Athabascan Indians and the Eskimos of Northern Alaska.* Lund, Sweden: Gleerup, 1971.

Rosales, Francisco, and Barry J. Kaplan, eds. *Houston: A Twentieth Century Urban Frontier.* Port Washington, NY: Associated Faculty Press, 1983.

Rosenberg, Bruce E. *Can These Bones Live? The Art of the American Folk Preacher.* Urbana: University of Illinois Press, 1988.

Rosenberg, Neil V. *Bluegrass: A History.* Urbana: University of Illinois Press, 1985.

———, ed. *Transforming Tradition: Folk Music Revivals Examined.* Urbana: University of Illinois Press, 1993.

Rosenberger, Homer Tope. *Mountain Folks: Fragments of Central Pennsylvania Lore.* Lock Haven, PA: Annie Halenbake Ross Library, 1974.

———. *The Pennsylvania Germans, 1891–1965.* Lancaster: Pennsylvania German Society, 1966.

Rosengarten, Dale. *Row upon Row: Sea Grass Baskets of the South Carolina Lowcountry.* Columbia: McKissick Museum, University of South Carolina, 1987.

Rosenthal, Alan, ed. *New Challenges for Documentary.* Berkeley: University of California Press, 1988.

Ross, Steven J. *Workers on the Edge: Work, Leisure, and Politics in Industrializing Cincinnati, 1788–1890.* New York: Columbia University Press, 1985.

Rossiter, Phyllis. *A Living History of the Ozarks.* Gretna, LA: Pelican, 1992.

Rothenberg, Daniel. *With These Hands: The Hidden World of Migrant Farmworkers Today.* Berkeley: University of California Press, 1998.

Rothman, Hal, ed. *The Culture of Tourism, the Tourism of Culture: Selling the Past to the Present in the American Southwest.* Albuquerque: University of New Mexico Press, 2003.

———. *Neon Metropolis: How Las Vegas Started the Twenty-First Century.* New York: Routledge, 2002.

Rothman, Hal K., and Mike Davis, eds. *The Grit Beneath the Glitter: Tales from the Real Las Vegas.* Berkeley: University of California Press, 2002.

Roucek, Joseph S. *The Czechs and Slovaks in America.* Minneapolis, MN: Lerner Publications, 1967.

Royce, Anya Peterson. *Ethnic Identity: Strategies of Diversity.* Bloomington: Indiana University Press, 1982.

Rubin, Arnold, ed. *Marks of Civilization: Artistic Transformations of the Human Body.* Los Angeles: Museum of Cultural History, University of California, Los Angeles, 1988.

Rubin, Ruth. *Voices of a People: The Story of Yiddish Folksong.* 2nd ed. New York: McGraw-Hill, 1973.

Ruby, Jay, ed. *A Crack in the Mirror: Reflexive Perspectives in Anthropology.* Philadelphia: University of Pennsylvania Press, 1982.

Ruck, Rob. *Sandlot Seasons: Sport in Black Pittsburgh.* Urbana: University of Illinois Press, 1987.

———. *The Tropic of Baseball: Baseball in the Dominican Republic.* Lincoln: University of Nebraska Press, 1999.

Runcie, John F. "Truck Drivers' Jargon." *American Speech* 44 (1973): 200–209.

Rupp, Leila J. *A Desired Past: A Short History of Same-Sex Love in America.* Chicago: University of Chicago Press, 2002.

Russell, Charles. *Self-Taught Art: The Culture and Aesthetics of American Vernacular Art.* Jackson: University Press of Mississippi, 2001.

Russell, Tony. *The Blues: From Robert Johnson to Robert Cray.* New York: Schirmer, 1997.

Ruth, John Landis. *The Earth Is the Lord's: A Narrative History of the Lancaster Mennonite Conference.* Scottdale, PA: Herald, 2001.

Rutherford, Susan. *A Study of American Deaf Folklore.* Burtonsville, MD: Linstok, 1993.

Rutledge, Paul J. *The Vietnamese Experience in America.* Bloomington: Indiana University Press, 1992.

Ryan, Dennis P. *A Journey Through Boston's Irish History.* Charleston, SC: Arcadia, 1999.

Ryden, Kent C. *Landscape with Figures: Nature and Culture in New England.* Iowa City: University of Iowa Press, 2001.

———. *Mapping the Invisible Landscape: Folklore, Writing, and the Sense of Place.* Iowa City: University of Iowa Press, 1993.

Sabin, Roger, ed. *Punk Rock: So What! The Cultural Legacy of Punk.* New York: Routledge, 1999.

Sachs, Steven L. *Street Gang Awareness: A Resource Guide for Parents and Professionals.* Minneapolis, MN: Fairview Press, 1997.

Sacks, Howard L., and Judith Rose. *Way Up North in Dixie: A Black Family's Claim to the Confederate Anthem.* Washington, DC: Smithsonian Institution Press, 1993.

Sacks, Maurie, ed. "The Jewish Catskills." Special issue, *Jewish Folklore and Ethnology Review* 19, nos. 1–2 (1997).

Safford, Carleton, and Robert Bishop. *America's Quilts and Coverlets.* New York: E.P. Dutton, 1972.

Sajna, Mike. *Buck Fever: The Deer Hunting Tradition in Pennsylvania.* Pittsburgh: University of Pittsburgh Press, 1990.

Salaman, R.A. *Dictionary of Leather-Working Tools, c. 1700–1950.* New York: Macmillan, 1985.

Salamone, Frank A., ed. *Encyclopedia of Religious Rites, Rituals, and Festivals.* New York: Routledge, 2004.

Salemink, Oscar. *The Ethnography of Vietnam's Central Highlanders: A Historical Contextualization, 1850–1990.* Honolulu: University of Hawaii Press, 2002.

———, ed. *Viet Nam's Cultural Diversity: Approaches to Preservation.* New York: United Nations Educational, Scientific, and Cultural Organization, 2001.

Salmons, Joseph. "On the Social Function of Some Southern Indiana German-American Dialect Stories." *Humor: International Journal of Humor Research* 1 (1988): 159–75.

Saloutos, Theodore. *The Greeks in the United States.* Cambridge, MA: Harvard University Press, 1964.

Salsi, Lynn, and Frances Eubanks, comps. *The Crystal Coast.* Charleston, SC: Arcadia, 2000.

Salvador, Mari Lyn. *Festas Acoreanas: Portuguese Religious Celebrations in California and the Azores.* Oakland, CA: Oakland Museum, 1981.

Samuelson, Sue. "A Review of the Distinctive Genres of Adolescent Folklore." *Children's Folklore Review* 17 (1995): 13–32.

———, ed. *Twenty Years of the Department of Folklore and Folklife at the University of Pennsylvania: A Dissertation Profile, 1962–1982.* Philadelphia: Department of Folklore and Folklife, University of Pennsylvania, 1983.

Samuelson, Sue, and Ray Kepner. "Bocce Ball Meets Hacky-Sack: A Western Pennsylvania Independence Day Gathering." *Keystone Folklore* 3 (1984): 26–35.

Sanavaiana, Carole. "Where Spirits Laugh Last." In *Clowning as Critical Practice: Performance Humor in the South Pacific*, ed. William Mitchell, 192–218. Pittsburgh: University of Pittsburgh Press, 1992.

Sánchez , George J. *Becoming Mexican American: Ethnicity, Culture and Identity in Chicano Los Angeles, 1900–1945.* New York: Oxford University Press, 1995.

Sandelowski, Margarete. *Devices and Desires: Gender, Technology, and American Nursing.* Chapel Hill: University of North Carolina Press, 2000.

Sanders, Clinton R. *Customizing the Body: The Art and Culture of Tattooing.* Philadelphia: Temple University Press, 1989.

Sanders, Sara L., ed. *English in the Southern United States.* Cambridge: Cambridge University Press, 2003.

Sandler, Gilbert. *The Neighborhood: The Story of Baltimore's Little Italy.* Baltimore: Bodine, 1974.

Sandmel, Ben. *Zydeco!* Jackson: University Press of Mississippi, 1999.

Sandoval, Isabelle Medina. "Abraham's Children of the Southwest." *Jewish Folklore and Ethnology Review* 18 (1996): 77–82.

Santino, Jack. *All Around the Year: Holidays and Celebrations in American Life.* Urbana: University of Illinois Press, 1994.

———. "Catholic Folklore and Folk Catholicism." *New York Folklore* 8 (1982): 93–106.

———, ed. *Halloween and Other Festivals of Death and Life.* Knoxville: University of Tennessee Press, 1994.

———. *Miles of Smiles, Years of Struggle: Stories of Black Pullman Porters.* Urbana: University of Illinois Press, 1989.

———, ed. *New Old-Fashioned Ways: Holidays and Popular Culture.* Knoxville: University of Tennessee Press, 1996.

———. *Signs of War and Peace: Social Conflict and the Use of Public Symbols in Northern Ireland.* New York: Palgrave, 2001.

———, ed. *Spontaneous Shrines and the Public Memorialization of Death.* New York: Palgrave Macmillan, 2006.

Sapoznik, Henry. *Klezmer! Jewish Music from Old World to Our World.* New York: Schirmer, 1999.

Saran, Parmatma, and Edwin Eames, eds. *The New Ethnics: Asian Indians in the United States.* New York: Praeger, 1980.

Sarna, Jonathan, and Ellen Smith, eds. *The Jews of Boston.* Boston: Combined Jewish Philanthropies of Boston, 1995.

Sato, Ikuya. "Play Theory of Delinquency: Toward a General Theory of 'Action.'" *Symbolic Interaction* 11 (1988): 191–212.

Satzewich, Vic. *The Ukrainian Diaspora.* London: UCL Press, 2000.

Savage, Jon. *England's Dreaming: Anarchy, Sex Pistols, Punk Rock, and Beyond.* New York: St. Martin's Press, 1992.

Saville-Troike, Muriel. *The Ethnography of Communication: An Introduction.* 3rd ed. New York: Basil Blackwell, 2003.

Savishinsky, Joel S. *Breaking the Watch: The Meanings of Retirement in America.* Ithaca, NY: Cornell University Press, 2000.

Savoy, Ann Allen. "Cajun and Zydeco: The Musics of French Southwest Louisiana." In *American Roots Music,* ed. Robert Santelli, Holly George-Warren, and Jim Brown, 104–25. New York: Harry N. Abrams, 2001.

Schechner, Richard. *The Future of Ritual: Writings on Culture and Performance.* New York: Routledge, 1993.

Schechter, Harold. *The Bosom Serpent: Folklore and Popular Art.* Iowa City: University of Iowa Press, 1988.

Scher, Philip W. "Copyright Heritage: Preservation, Carnival and the State in Trinidad." *Anthropological Quarterly* 75 (2002): 453–84.

Scheuner, Gottlieb. *Inspirations—History: The His-*

tory of the Inspiration, trans. Janet Zuber. Amana, IA: Amana Church Society, 1978.

Schindler, Henri. *Mardi Gras: New Orleans.* Paris: Flammarion, 1997.

Schlabach, Theron F. *The Mennonite Experience in America.* Vol. 2, *Peace, Faith, Nation: Mennonites and Amish in Nineteenth Century America.* Scottdale, PA: Herald, 1988.

Schloss, Joseph. *Making Beats: The Art of Sample-Based Hip-Hop.* Middletown, CT: Wesleyan University Press, 2004.

Schmidt, Alvin J. *Fraternal Organizations.* Westport, CT: Greenwood, 1980.

Schmidt, Leigh Eric. "The Easter Parade: Piety, Fashion, and Display." In *Religion and American Culture: A Reader,* ed. David G. Hackett, 249–69. New York: Routledge, 1995.

Schneider, Paul. *The Enduring Shore: A History of Cape Cod, Martha's Vineyard and Nantucket.* New York: Henry Holt, 2000.

Schneider, William. *. . . So They Understand: Cultural Issues in Oral History.* Logan: Utah State University Press, 2002.

Schoemaker, George. "Made in Heaven: Marriage Confirmation Narratives Among Mormons." *Northwest Folklore* 7 (1989): 38–53.

Schorr, Thelma, with Maureen Shawn. *100 Years of American Nursing: Celebrating a Century of Caring.* Philadelphia: Lippincott, Williams and Wilkins, 1999.

Schrager, Sam. "The Stories That Communities Tell." *Oregon Historical Quarterly* 97 (1996): 212–29.

———. *The Trial Lawyer's Art.* Philadelphia: Temple University Press, 1999.

Schrum, Wesley, and John Kilburn. "Ritual Disrobement at Mardi Gras: Ceremonial Exchange and Moral Order." *Social Forces* 75, no. 2 (December 1996): 423–58.

Schultz, Albert J. *The Voices of Eden: A History of Hawaiian Language Studies.* Honolulu: University of Hawaii Press, 1994.

Schwartz, David G. *Suburban Xanadu: The Casino Resort on the Las Vegas Strip and Beyond.* New York: Routledge, 2003.

Schwartz, Scott. *Faith, Serpents, and Fire: Images of Kentucky Holiness Believers.* Jackson: University Press of Mississippi, 1999.

Schwarzenegger, Arnold, and Bill Dobbins. *The New Encyclopedia of Modern Bodybuilding.* New York: Simon and Schuster, 1998.

Schwieder, Dorothy. *Iowa: The Middle Land.* Ames: Iowa State University Press, 1996.

Sciorra, Joseph. "Return to the Future: Puerto Rican Vernacular Architecture in New York City." In *Representing the City: Ethnicity, Capital, and Culture in the 21st Century Metropolis,* ed. Anthony D. King, 60–92. New York: New York University Press, 1996.

Sciorra, Joseph, and Martha Cooper. "'We're Not Here Just to Plant. We Have Culture.' An Ethnography of the South Bronx *Casita Rincon Criollo.*" *New York Folklore* 20 (1994): 19–41.

Scott, Stephen E. *An Introduction to Old Order and Conservative Mennonite Groups.* Intercourse, PA: Good Books, 1996.

———. "The Old Order River Brethren." *Pennsylvania Mennonite Heritage* 1 (1978): 13–22.

———. *Why Do They Dress That Way?* Intercourse, PA: Good Books, 1986.

Seckar, Alvena V. "Slovak Wedding Customs." *New York Folklore Quarterly* 3 (1947): 189–205.

Seeger, Mike. *Talking Feet: Buck, Flatfoot and Tap.* Berkeley, CA: North Atlantic Books, 1992.

Seelye, John. *Memory's Nation: The Place of Plymouth Rock.* Chapel Hill: University of North Carolina Press, 1998.

Selassie, Bereket H. "Washington's New African Immigrants." In *Urban Odyssey: A Multicultural History of Washington D.C.,* ed. Francine Curro Cary, 264–75. Washington, DC: Smithsonian Institution Press, 1996.

Seligson, Marcia. *The Eternal Bliss Machine: America's Way of Wedding.* New York: William Morrow, 1973.

Serrin, William. *Homestead: The Glory and Tragedy of an American Steel Town.* New York: Random House, 1992.

Sewell, Ernestine P., and Joyce Gibson Roach. *Eats: A Folk History of Texas Food.* Fort Worth: Texas Christian University Press, 1989.

The Shakers: Hands to Work, Heart to God. DVD. Directed by Ken Burns. Los Angeles: Paramount Home Video, 2004.

Shambaugh, Bertha M.H. *Amana That Was and Amana That Is.* Iowa City: State Historical Society of Iowa, 1932.

Shankar, Lavina D., and Rajini Srikanth, eds. *A Part, Yet Apart: South Asians in Asian America.* Philadelphia: Temple University Press, 1998.

Shannon, William V. *The American Irish.* New York: Macmillan, 1966.

Shapiro, Ellen. *The Croatian Americans.* New York: Chelsea House, 1989.

Shay, Frank. *American Sea Songs and Chanteys.* New York: W.W. Norton, 1948.

———. *A Sailor's Treasury.* New York: W.W. Norton, 1951.

Sheehan, Elizabeth. "'Fields of Greens': Hmong Gardens, Farms and Land Ownership in America: Constructing Environment and Identity in the Carolinas." *Lao Study Review* 1 (December 2003). On-line journal at http://home.vicnet.net.au/~lao/laostudy/garden.htm.

Shelemay, Kay Kaufman. *Let Jasmine Rain Down: Song and Remembrance Among Syrian Jews.* Chicago: University of Chicago Press, 1998.

Shellans, Herbert. *Folk Songs of the Blue Ridge Mountains.* New York: Oak, 1968.

Shelton, Beth Anne, Robert D. Bullard, Joseph R. Feagin, and Nestor Rodriguez. *Houston: Growth and Decline in a Sunbelt Boomtown.* Philadelphia: Temple University Press, 1989.

Sherman, Josepha. *A Sampler of Jewish American Folklore.* Little Rock, AR: August House, 1992.

Sherman, Sharon R. *Chain-Saw Sculptor: The Art of J. Chester "Skip" Armstrong.* Jackson: University Press of Mississippi, 1995.

———. *Documenting Ourselves: Film, Video, and Culture.* Lexington: University of Kentucky Press, 1998.

Shifflet, Crandall A. *Coal Towns: Life, Work and Culture in Company Towns of Southern Appalachia, 1880–1960.* Knoxville: University of Tennessee Press, 1991.

Shils, Edward. *Tradition.* Chicago: University of Chicago Press, 1981.

Shirky, James M. "A Missouri Dunkard Community." *Missouri Folklore Society Journal* 2 (1980): 27–45.

Shoemaker, Alfred A. *Christmas in Pennsylvania: A Folk-Cultural Study.* 1959. Reprint, Mechanicsburg, PA: Stackpole, 1999.

———. *Eastertide in Pennsylvania: A Folk-Cultural Study.* 1960. Reprint, Mechanicsburg, PA: Stackpole, 2000.

Shoemaker, Henry W. *A Forgotten People: The Pennsylvania Mountaineers.* Altoona, PA: Tribune, 1922.

———. *Thirteen Hundred Old Time Words of British, Continental or Aboriginal Origins, Still or Recently in Use Among Pennsylvania Mountain People.* Altoona, PA: Times Tribune, 1930.

Shope, Bradley. "Urdu Poetry in Queens." *Urban Folk* (Spring 2003): 8–11.

Shorto, Russell. *The Island at the Center of the World: The Epic Story of Dutch Manhattan and the Forgotten Colony That Shaped America.* New York: Vintage Books, 2005.

Shuldiner, David. *Of Moses and Marx: Folk Ideology and Folk History in the Jewish Labor Movement.* Westport, CT: Bergin and Garvey, 1999.

Sider, Gerald. *Culture and Class in Anthropology and History: A Newfoundland Illustration.* Cambridge: Cambridge University Press, 1986.

Siegel, Helene. *The Totally Picnic Cookbook.* Berkeley, CA: Ten Speed Press, 1996.

Sifakis, Carl. *The Encyclopedia of Gambling.* New York: Facts on File, 1990.

Sikes, Gini. *8 Ball Chicks: A Year in the Violent World of Girl Gangsters.* New York: Doubleday, 1997.

Silverman, Deborah Anders. *Polish-American Folklore.* Urbana: University of Illinois Press, 2000.

Simeone, William E. *Rifles, Blankets and Beads: Identity, History, and the Northern Athapaskan Potlatch.* Norman: University of Oklahoma Press, 1995.

Simeone, William E., and James W. VanStone. *"And He Was Beautiful": Contemporary Athapaskan Material Culture in the Collections of the Field Museum of Natural History.* Chicago: Field Museum of Natural History, 1986.

Simmons, Marc. *New Mexico.* Albuquerque: University of New Mexico Press, 1976.

Simmons, William S. *Spirit of the New England Tribes: Indian History and Folklore, 1620–1984.* Hanover, NH: University Press of New England, 1986.

Simons, Elizabeth Radin. *Student Worlds/Student Words: Teaching Writing Through Folklore.* Portsmouth, NH: Boynton/Cook, 1990.

Simpson, Georgiana Kennedy. *Navajo Ceremonial Baskets: Sacred Symbols, Sacred Space.* Summertown, TN: Native Voices, 2003.

Simpson, Thelma Pake, and Rebecca Willis Sanders. *Kith and Kin of Eastern Carteret County.* Morehead City, NC: Carteret County Historical Society, 1997.

Siskind, Janet. "The Invention of Thanksgiving: A Ritual of American Nationality." *Critique of Anthropology* 12 (1992): 167–91.

Skal, David. *Death Makes a Holiday: A Cultural History of Halloween.* New York: Bloomsbury, 2002.

Skelton, Tracey, and Gill Valentine, eds. *Cool Places:*

Geographies of Youth Cultures. London: Routledge, 1998.

Slatta, Richard W. *Cowboys of the Americas.* New Haven, CT: Yale University Press, 1990.

Slim, Hugo, and Paul Thompson. *Listening for a Change: Oral Testimony and Community Development.* Philadelphia: New Society Publishers, 1995.

Slobin, Mark, ed. *American Klezmer: Its Roots and Offshoots.* Berkeley: University of California Press, 2002.

Slovenz-Low, Madeline. "On the Tail of the Lion: Approaches to Cross-Cultural Fieldwork with Chinese-Americans in New York." In *Creative Ethnicity: Symbols and Strategies of Contemporary Ethnic Life,* ed. Stephen Stern and John Allan Cicala, 55–71. Logan: Utah State University Press, 1991.

Smidchens, Guntis. "Latvian Folk History and Family Stories in America." *Lituanus: Baltic States Quarterly of Arts and Sciences* 33, no. 3 (Fall 1987): 62–72.

Smith, Anna Deavere. *Fires in the Mirror.* New York: Anchor Books, 1993.

Smith, Dennis. *Report from Engine Co. 82.* New York: Warner Books, 1999.

Smith, Elmer Lewis. *The Amish Today: An Analysis of Their Beliefs, Behavior and Contemporary Problems.* Allentown, PA: Schlecters, 1961.

Smith, Elmer Lewis, John G. Stewart, and M. Ellsworth Kyger. *The Pennsylvania Germans of the Shenandoah Valley.* Allentown, PA: Schlecter's, 1964.

Smith, Kathryn Schneider, ed. *Washington at Home: An Illustrated History of Neighborhoods in the Nation's Capital.* Northridge, CA: Windsor, 1988.

Smith, Richard D. *Can't You Hear Me Callin': The Life of Bill Monroe.* Boston: Little, Brown, 2000.

Smith, Shawn Michelle. *American Archives: Gender, Race, and Class in Visual Culture.* Princeton, NJ: Princeton University Press, 1999.

Snyder, Robert. *The Voice of the City: Vaudeville and Popular Culture in New York.* New York: Oxford University Press, 1989.

Snyder-Grenier, Ellen M. *Brooklyn: An Illustrated History.* Philadelphia: Temple University Press, 1996.

So Sabi: Cape Verdean Music from New England. CD. Rounder Records, 1999.

Sobol, Joseph Daniel. *The Storytellers' Journey: An American Revival.* Urbana: University of Illinois Press, 1999.

Sokolov, Raymond. *Fading Feast: A Compendium of Disappearing American Regional Foods.* Rev. ed. Jaffrey, NH: Godine, 1998.

Sollors, Werner, ed. *Theories of Ethnicity: A Classical Reader.* New York: New York University Press, 1996.

Sommer, Robert. *Farmers Markets of America: A Renaissance.* Santa Barbara, CA: Capra Press, 1980.

Sommers, Laurie Kay. *Festa, Fe, y Cultura: Celebrations of Faith and Culture in Detroit's Colonia Mexicana.* East Lansing: Michigan State University Museum and Casa de Unidad, 1995.

Song, Bang-Song. *The Korean-Canadian Folk Song: An Ethnomusicological Study.* Ottawa: National Museums of Canada, 1974.

Souter, Gerry, and Janet Souter. *The American Fire Station.* Osceola, WI: MBI, 1998.

Southard, Bruce. "Where Is 'Down East'?" *American Speech* 4 (2000): 377–80.

Southern, Eileen. *The Music of Black Americans: A History.* New York: W.W. Norton, 1971.

Soyer, Daniel. *Jewish Immigrant Associations and American Identity in New York, 1880–1939.* Cambridge, MA: Harvard University Press, 1997.

Spann, M. Graham. "NASCAR Racing Fans: Cranking Up an Empirical Approach." *Journal of Popular Culture* 36 (2002): 352–60.

Speck, Frank G. "Some Outlines of Aboriginal Culture in the Southeastern States." *American Anthropologist* 9 (1907): 287–95.

Spencer, Jon Michael. *Black Hymnody: A Hymnological History of the African-American Church.* Knoxville: University of Tennessee Press, 1992.

Spencer, Thomas M. *The St. Louis Veiled Prophet Celebration: Power on Parade, 1877–1995.* Columbia: University of Missouri Press, 2000.

Spergel, Irving A. *The Youth Gang Problem: A Community Approach.* New York: Oxford University Press, 1995.

Spicer, Rosamund B., and Ross N. Crumrine, eds. *Performing the Renewal of Community: Indigenous Easter Rituals in North Mexico and Southwest United States.* Lanham, MD: University Press of America, 1997.

Spickard, Paul R. *Japanese Americans: The Formation and Transformations of an Ethnic Group.* New York: Twayne, 1996.

Spitz, Marc, and Brenden Mullen. *We Got the Neutron Bomb: The Untold Story of L.A. Punk*. New York: Three Rivers Press, 2001.

Spitzer, Nicholas R. "Mardi Gras in L'Anse de Prien Noir: A Creole Community Performance in Rural French Louisiana." In *Creoles of Color of the Gulf South*, ed. James H. Dormon, 87–127. Knoxville: University of Tennessee Press, 1996.

Spradley, James P., and David W. McCurdy, eds. *The Cultural Experience: Ethnography in Complex Society*. Chicago: Science Research Associates, 1972.

Sprigg, June. *Shaker Design*. New York: Whitney Museum of American Art, 1986.

St. Johns, Adela Rogers. *Final Verdict*. Garden City, NY: Doubleday, 1962.

Stahl, Sandra D. *Literary Folkloristics and the Personal Narrative*. Bloomington: Indiana University Press, 1989.

Stanley, David, and Elaine Thatcher, eds. *Cowboy Poets and Cowboy Poetry*. Urbana: University of Illinois Press, 2000.

Starr, Kevin, and Richard J. Orsi, eds. *Rooted in Barbarous Soil: People, Culture, and Community in Gold Rush California*. Berkeley: University of California Press, 2000.

Starr, S. Frederick. *Inventing New Orleans: Writings of Lafcadio Hearn*. Jackson: University Press of Mississippi, 2001.

Starrs, Paul F. *Let the Cowboy Ride: Cattle Ranching in the American West*. Baltimore: Johns Hopkins University Press, 1998.

Stavans, Ilan. *Spanglish: The Making of a New American Language*. New York: Rayo, 2003.

Stayer, Jonathan R. "An Interpretation of Some Ritual and Food Elements of the Brethren Love Feast." *Pennsylvania Folklife* 34, no. 2 (Winter 1984–1985): 61–70.

Stegner, Wallace. *Mormon Country*. New York: Duell, Sloan, and Pearce, 1942.

Stein, Howard F. *American Medicine as Culture*. San Francisco: Westview, 1990.

Stein, Lou. *San Diego County Place Names*. San Diego: Tofua, 1975.

Stein, Stephen J. *The Shaker Experience in America: A History of the United Society of Believers*. New Haven, CT: Yale University Press, 1992.

Steltzer, Ulli. *A Haida Potlatch*. Seattle: University of Washington Press, 1984.

Stern, Stephen, and John Allan Cicala, eds. *Creative Ethnicity: Symbols and Strategies of Contemporary Ethnic Life*. Logan: Utah State University Press, 1991.

Steward, Samuel M. *Bad Boys and Tough Tattoos: A Social History of the Tattoo with Gangs, Sailors, and Street-Corner Punks, 1950–1965*. New York: Harrington Park Press, 1990.

Stewart, Edward C., and Milton J. Bennett. *American Cultural Patterns: A Cross-Cultural Perspective*. Yarmouth, ME: Intercultural Press, 1991.

Stewart, Susan. "Rational Powwowing: An Examination of Choice Among Medical Alternatives in Rural York County, Pennsylvania." *Pennsylvania Folklife* 26, no. 1 (1976): 12–17.

Stick, David. *The Outer Banks of North Carolina 1584–1958*. Chapel Hill: University of North Carolina Press, 1958.

Stilgoe, John R. *Common Landscape of America, 1590 to 1845*. New Haven, CT: Yale University Press, 1982.

Still, Bayard. *Milwaukee: The History of a City*. Milwaukee, WI: North American Press, 1948.

Stitt, Michael J. "Conversational Genres at a Las Vegas '21' Table." *Western Folklore* 45 (1986): 278–89.

Stokker, Kathleen. *Keeping Christmas: Yuletide Traditions in Norway and the New Land*. St. Paul: Minnesota Historical Society Press, 2000.

Stolarik, M. Mark. *Growing Up on the South Side: Three Generations of Slovaks in Bethlehem, Pennsylvania, 1880–1976*. Lewisburg, PA: Bucknell University Press, 1985.

Stoller, Eleanor. "Sauna, Sisu, and Sibelius: Ethnic Identity Among Finnish Americans." *Sociological Quarterly* 37, no. 1 (1996): 145–75.

Stoller, Paul. *Money Has No Smell: The Africanization of New York City*. Chicago: University of Chicago Press, 2002.

Stone, Lisa, and Jim Zanzi. *Sacred Spaces and Other Places: A Guide to Grottos and Sculptural Environments in the Upper Midwest*. Chicago: School of the Art Institute of Chicago Press, 1993.

Stora-Sandor, Judith. "From Eve to the Jewish American Princess: The Comic Representation of Women in Jewish Literature." In *Semites and Stereotypes: Characteristics of Jewish Humor*, ed. Avner Ziv and Anat Azjdman, 131–41. Westport, CT: Greenwood, 1993.

Stoval, DeeDee. *Picnic*. North Adams, MA: Storey Books, 2001.

Strom, Yale. *The Hasidim of Brooklyn: A Photo Essay.* New York: Jason Aronson, 1993.

Stroud, Hubert B. *The Promise of Paradise: Recreational and Retirement Communities in the United States Since 1950.* Baltimore: Johns Hopkins University Press, 2001.

Stryker, Susan, and Jim Van Buskirk. *Gay by the Bay: A History of Queer Culture in the San Francisco Bay Area.* San Francisco: Chronicle Books, 1996.

Stuempfle, Stephen. *The Steelband Movement: The Forging of a National Art in Trinidad and Tobago.* Philadelphia: University of Pennsylvania Press, 1995.

Sturken, Marita, and Lisa Cartwright. *Practices of Looking: An Introduction to Visual Culture.* New York: Oxford University Press, 2001.

Suleiman, Michael W., ed. *Arabs in America: Building a New Future.* Philadelphia: Temple University Press, 1999.

Sullivan, C.W., III. "Johnny Says His ABCs." *Western Folklore* 46 (1987): 36–41.

———. "Knowing What Children Believe: Believing What Children Know." *Children's Folklore Review* 19 (1996): 19–24.

Sunstein, Bonnie Stone, and Elizabeth Chiseri-Strater. *Fieldworking: Reading and Writing Research.* Upper Saddle River, NJ: Prentice Hall, 1997.

Suter, John W., ed. *Working with Folk Materials in New York State: A Manual for Folklorists and Archivists.* Schenectady: New York Folklore Society, 1994.

Suter, Scott Hamilton. *Shenandoah Valley Folklife.* Jackson: University Press of Mississippi, 1999.

———. *Tradition and Fashion: Cabinetmaking in the Upper Shenandoah Valley, 1850–1900.* Dayton, VA: Shenandoah Valley Folk Art and Heritage Center, 1996.

Suttles, Wayne, ed. *Handbook of North American Indians.* Vol. 7, *Northwest Coast.* Washington, DC: Smithsonian Institution Press, 1990.

Sutton-Smith, Brian. *The Folkgames of Children.* Austin: University of Texas Press, 1972.

———. *Toys as Culture.* New York: Gardner Press, 1986.

Sutton-Smith, Brian, and Elliott M. Avedon, eds. *The Study of Games.* 1971. Reprint, Huntington, NY: Robert E. Krieger, 1979.

Sutton-Smith, Brian, and Dianna Kelly-Byrne, eds. *The Masks of Play.* West Point, NY: Leisure Press, 1984.

Sutton-Smith, Brian, Jay Mechling, Thomas W. Johnson, and Felicia McMahon, eds. *Children's Folklore: A Source Book.* 1995. Reprint, Logan: Utah State University Press, 1999.

Svinth, Joseph R. *Getting a Grip: Judo in the Nikkei Communities of the Pacific Northwest, 1900–1950.* Guelph, Ontario: EJMAS, 2003.

Svoboda, Terese. "Oral Poetry and Nuer Children." *The Lion and the Unicorn: A Critical Journal of Children's Literature* 4, no. 2 (Winter 1980–1981): 10–29.

Swain, Carol M. *The New White Nationalism in America.* Cambridge: Cambridge University Press, 2002.

Swan, James A. *The Sacred Art of Hunting: Myths, Legends and the Modern Mythos.* Minocqua, WI: Willow Creek, 1999.

Swank, Scott T. *Arts of the Pennsylvania Germans.* New York: W.W. Norton, 1983.

———. *Shaker Life, Art, and Architecture: Hands to Work, Hearts to God.* New York: Abbeville Press, 1999.

Swanson, Catherine, and Philip Nusbaum, eds. "Occupational Folklore and the Folklore of Working." Special issue, *Folklore Forum* 11, no. 1 (1978): 1–65.

Swanson, Lynne. "Celebrating Midsummer in Brevort." In *1996 Michigan Folklife Annual,* ed. Ruth D. Fitzgerald and Yvonne R. Lockwood, 22–28. East Lansing: Michigan State University Museum, 1996.

Swanton, John R. "Aboriginal Culture of the Southeast." *Annual Report of the Bureau of American Ethnology* 42 (1924–1925): 673–726.

———. *The Indians of the Southeastern United States.* Washington, DC: Smithsonian Institution Press, 1946.

———. *Tlingit Myths and Texts.* St. Clair Shores, MI: Scholarly Press, 1976.

Sweet, David C., Kathryn Wertheim Hexter, and David Beach, eds. *The New American City Faces Its Regional Future: A Cleveland Perspective.* Columbus: Ohio University Press and Swallow Press, 1999.

Sweezy, Nancy. *Raised in Clay: The Southern Pottery Tradition.* Chapel Hill: University of North Carolina Press, 1994.

Swetnam, George. *Pittsylvania Country.* New York: Duell, Sloan and Pearce, 1951.

Swierenga, Robert P., ed. *The Dutch in America: Im-*

migration, Settlement, and Cultural Change. New Brunswick, NJ: Rutgers University Press, 1985.

Swigart, Leigh, and Vera Viditz-Ward. *Extended Lives: The African Immigrant Experience in Philadelphia.* Philadelphia: Balch Institute for Ethnic Studies, 2001.

Swora, Maria Gabrielle. "Narrating Community: The Creation of Social Structure in Alcoholics Anonymous Through the Performance of Autobiography." *Narrative Inquiry* 11 (2001): 363–84.

Synan, Vinson. *Century of the Holy Spirit: 100 Years of Pentecostal and Charismatic Renewal, 1901–2001.* Nashville, TN: Nelson Reference, 2001.

———. *The Holiness-Pentecostal Tradition: Charismatic Movements in the Twentieth Century.* Grand Rapids, MI: W.B. Eerdmans, 1997.

Taft, Robert. *The Byzantine Rite: A Short History.* Collegeville, MN: Liturgical, 1992.

Takaki, Ronald. *Strangers from a Different Shore: A History of Asian Americans.* Rev. ed. Boston: Back Bay Books, 1998.

Tales from Arab Detroit. VHS. Directed by Joan Mandell. Los Angeles: Olive Branch Productions, 1995.

Tallant, Robert. *Voodoo in New Orleans.* New York: Pelican, 1983.

Tallmadge, William. "Baptist Monophonic and Heterophonic Hymnody in Southern Appalachia." *Yearbook for Inter-American Musical Research* 11 (1975): 106–36.

Tangherlini, Timothy R. "Los Angeles Intersections (Folklore and the City)." *Western Folklore* 58 (1999): 99–106.

———. "Remapping Koreatown: Folklore, Narrative and the Los Angeles Riots." *Western Folklore* 58 (1999): 149–73.

Tashjian, Dickran, and Ann Tashjian. *Memorials for Children of Change: The Art of Early New England Stonecarving.* Middletown, CT: Wesleyan University Press, 1974.

Tava, Rerioterai. *Niihau: The Traditions of a Hawaiian Island.* Honolulu, HI: Mutual, 1989.

Taylor, Archer. *English Riddles from Oral Tradition.* Berkeley: University of California Press, 1951.

———. *The Proverb.* Cambridge, MA: Harvard University Press, 1931. Reprint, Hatboro, PA: Folklore Associates, 1962. Reprint, with an introduction and bibliography by Wolfgang Mieder. Bern, Germany: Peter Lang, 1985.

Taylor, Archer, and Bartlett Jere Whiting. *A Dictionary of American Proverbs and Proverbial Phrases, 1820–1880.* Cambridge, MA: Harvard University Press, 1958.

Taylor, David A. *Documenting Maritime Folklife: An Introductory Guide.* Washington, DC: Library of Congress, 1992. www.loc.gov/folklife/maritime/top.html.

Taylor, John Martin. *Hoppin' John's Lowcountry Cooking.* New York: Houghton Mifflin, 2000.

Taylor, Lonn, and Ingrid Maar, comps. *The American Cowboy.* Washington, DC: American Folklife Center, Library of Congress, 1983.

Teague, David W. *The Southwest in American Literature and Art: The Rise of a Desert Aesthetic.* Tucson: University of Arizona Press, 1997.

Teal, Donn. *The Gay Militants.* New York: St. Martin's Press, 1971.

Terrell, Bob. *The Music Men: The Story of Professional Gospel Quartet Singing in America.* Asheville, NC: Bob Terrell, 1990.

Teske, Robert T. "The Eikonostasi Among Greek Philadelphians." *Pennsylvania Folklife* 23 (Autumn 1973): 20–30.

———, ed. *Wisconsin Folk Art: A Sesquicentennial Celebration.* Cedarburg, WI: Cedarburg Cultural Center, 1997.

Tezla, Albert, ed. *The Hazardous Quest: Hungarian Immigrants in the United States, 1895–1920.* Budapest, Hungary: Corvina Books, 1993.

Thatcher, Kevin, ed. *How to Build Skateboard Ramps: Halfpipes, Boxes, Bowls, and More.* San Francisco: High Speed, 2001.

Thévoz, Michel. *Art Brut.* New York: Rizzoli, 1976.

They Do Not from the Truth Depart, in Word or Work, in Hand or Hearts: Sabbathday Lake in 1800, 1900, and 2000. New Gloucester, ME: United Society of Shakers, 2000.

This Is Neo-Goth. Cleopatra Records, 2003. Compact disc.

Thiselton-Dyer, T.F. *Folk-Lore of Women.* Chicago: A.C. McClurg, 1906.

Thomas, G. Scott. *The United States of Suburbia: How the Suburbs Took Control of America and What They Plan to Do with It.* Amherst, NY: Prometheus Books, 1998.

Thomas, William I., and Florian Znaniecki. *The Polish Peasant in Europe and America.* 5 vols. Boston: Richard G. Badger, 1918–1920.

Thompson, Charles D., Jr. *The Old German Baptist Brethren: Faith, Farming, and Change in the Vir-*

ginia Blue Ridge. Urbana: University of Illinois Press, 2005.

Thompson, Hunter S. *Hell's Angels: A Strange and Terrible Saga.* New York: Modern Library, 1999.

Thompson, Jerry. *My Life in the Klan.* New York: Putnam, 1982.

Thompson, M.R. *Sikh Belief and Practice.* London: Edward Arnold, 1985.

Thompson, Paul. *The Voice of the Past.* 3rd ed. Oxford: Oxford University Press, 2000.

Thompson, Stith. *The Folktale.* New York: Dryden, 1946.

———.*Motif-Index of Folk-Literature,* 6 vols. Revised and enlarged edition. Bloomington: Indiana University Press, 1955.

———, ed. *Tales of the North American Indians.* Bloomington: Indiana University Press, 1966.

Thoreau, Henry David. *Cape Cod,* ed. Joseph J. Moldenhauer. Princeton, NJ: Princeton University Press, 2004.

Thorne, Barrie. *Gender Play: Boys and Girls in School.* New Brunswick, NJ: Rutgers University Press, 1993.

Thornton, Francis Beauchesne. *Catholic Shrines in the United States and Canada.* New York: Wilfred Funk, 1954.

Thornton, Russell. *American Indian Holocaust and Survival: A Population History Since 1492.* Norman: University of Oklahoma Press, 1987.

Thrasher, Fredric M. *The Gang: A Study of 1,313 Gangs in Chicago.* Chicago: University of Chicago Press, 1927.

Thursby, Jacqueline S. *Mother's Table, Father's Chair: Cultural Narratives of Basque American Women.* Logan: Utah State University Press, 1999.

Tiger, Lionel. *Men in Groups.* 2nd ed. New York: Marion Boyars, 1984.

Tillis, Steve. *Rethinking Folk Drama.* London: Greenwood, 1999.

Tilney, Philip V.R. "The Immigrant Macedonian Wedding in Ft. Wayne." *Indiana Folklore* 3 (1970): 3–34.

Tinker, Hugh. *The Banyan Tree: Overseas Emigrants from India, Pakistan and Bangladesh.* New York: Oxford University Press, 1977.

Titon, Jeff Todd. *Early Downhome Blues: A Musical and Cultural Analysis.* 2nd ed. Chapel Hill: University of North Carolina Press, 1995.

———. *Old-Time Kentucky Fiddle Tunes.* Lexington: University Press of Kentucky, 2001.

———. *Powerhouse for God: Speech, Chant, and Song in an Appalachian Baptist Church.* Austin: University of Texas Press, 1988.

———. "'The Real Thing': Tourism, Authenticity, and Pilgrimage Among the Old Regular Baptists at the 1997 Smithsonian Folklife Festival." *The World of Music* 41, no. 3 (1999): 115–39.

———. "Text." *Journal of American Folklore* 108 (1995): 432–48.

Todd, Jan. *Muscle Beach: Birthplace of Modern Fitness.* Syracuse, NY: Syracuse University Press, 2005.

Toelken, Barre. *The Dynamics of Folklore.* Revised and expanded edition. Logan: Utah State University Press, 1996.

———. "Folklore and Reality in the American West." In *Sense of Place: American Regional Cultures,* ed. Barbara Allen and Thomas Schlereth, 14–27. Lexington: University Press of Kentucky, 1990.

———. "The Folklore of Academe." In *The Study of American Folklore: An Introduction,* ed. Jan Harold Brunvand, 502–28. 3rd ed. New York: W.W. Norton, 1986.

———. "The Yellowman Tapes, 1966–1997." *Journal of American Folklore* 111 (1998): 381–91.

Toews, Paul. *The Mennonite Experience in America.* Vol. 4, *Mennonites in American Society, 1930–1970: Modernity and the Persistence of Religious Community.* Scottdale, PA: Herald, 1996.

Tolzmann, Don Heinrich. *Cincinnati's German Heritage.* Bowie, MD: Heritage Books, 1994.

———. *The German-American Experience.* Amherst, NY: Humanity Books, 2000.

Toop, David. *Rap Attack: African Rap to Global Hip Hop.* 3rd ed. London: Serpent's Tail, 2000.

Travers, Len. *Celebrating the Fourth: Independence Day and the Rites of Nationalism in the Early Republic.* Amherst: University of Massachusetts Press, 1997.

Trommler, Frank, and Joseph McVeigh, eds. *America and the Germans: An Assessment of a Three-Hundred-Year History.* Philadelphia: University of Pennsylvania Press, 1985.

Trotter, Joe. *Black Milwaukee: The Making of an Industrial Proletariat.* Urbana: University of Illinois Press, 1984.

Truumees, Eevi, and Emmi Bajars, eds. *Estonian Americans: Seabrook, New Jersey, 1949–1999.* Bridgeton, NJ: Bill Adams Printing, 1999.

Tuan, Yi-Fu. *Space and Place: The Perspective of Ex-*

perience. Minneapolis: University of Minnesota Press, 1977.

Tucker, Elizabeth. "'I Saw the Trees Had Souls': Personal Experience Narratives of Contemporary Witches." In *Creativity and Tradition in Folklore*, ed. Simon J. Bronner, 141–52. Logan: Utah State University Press, 1992.

Tucker, Richard K. *The Dragon and the Cross: The Rise and Fall of the Ku Klux Klan in Middle America*. Hamden, CT: Archon Books, 1991.

Tullos, Allen, ed. *Long Journey Home: Folklife in the South*. Chapel Hill, NC: Southern Exposure, 1977.

Turner, E.S. *A History of Courting*. New York: E.P. Dutton, 1955.

Turner, Edith. *The Hands Feel It: Healing and Spirit Presence Among a Northern Alaska People*. Dekalb: Northern Illinois University Press, 1996.

Turner, Kay. *Beautiful Necessity: The Art and Meaning of Women's Altars*. New York: Thames and Hudson, 1999.

Turner, Lorenzo Dow. *Africanisms in the Gullah Dialect*. 1949. Reprint, Columbia: University of South Carolina Press, 2002.

Turner, Patricia A. *I Heard It Through the Grapevine: Rumor in African-American Culture*. Berkeley: University of California Press, 1993.

Turner, Richard Brent. *Islam in the African-American Experience*. Bloomington: Indiana University Press, 2003.

Turner, Tom. *Sierra Club: 100 Years of Protecting Nature*. New York: Abrams, in association with the Sierra Club, 1991.

Turner, Victor. *The Anthropology of Performance*. New York: PAJ, 1986.

———, ed. *Celebration: Studies in Festivity and Ritual*. Washington, DC: Smithsonian Institution Press, 1982.

Tweed, Thomas A. *Our Lady of the Exile: Diasporic Religion at a Cuban Catholic Shrine in Miami*. New York: Oxford University Press, 1997.

Twining, Mary A., and Keith E. Baird, eds. *Sea Island Roots: African Presence in the Carolinas and Georgia*. Trenton, NJ: Africa World Press, 1991.

Twining, Mary Arnold, ed. "The New Nomads: Art, Life, and Lore of Migrant Workers in New York State." Special Issue, *New York Folklore* 13, nos. 1–2, 1987.

Twitchell, James B. *Lead Us into Temptation: The Triumph of American Materialism*. New York: Columbia University Press, 1999.

Tyler, Ron, ed. *Handbook of Texas*. 6 vols. Austin: Texas State Historical Association, 1966.

Udall, Sharyn Rohlfsen. *Contested Terrain: Myth and Meanings in Southwest Art*. Albuquerque: University of New Mexico Press, 1996.

Uhl, Lauren, and Tracy L. Coffing. *Pittsburgh's Strip District: Around the World in a Neighborhood*. Pittsburgh: Historical Society of Western Pennsylvania, 2003.

Ulrich, Laurel Thatcher. *A Midwife's Tale: The Life of Martha Ballard, Based on Her Diary, 1785–1812*. New York: Vintage Books, 1990.

Umble, Diane Zimmerman. *Holding the Line: The Telephone in Old Order Mennonite and Amish Life*. Baltimore: Johns Hopkins University Press, 1996.

Upton, Dell, ed. *America's Architectural Roots: Ethnic Groups That Built America*. Washington, DC: Preservation Press, 1986.

Urban, Peter. *The Karate Dojo: Traditions and Tales of a Martial Art*. Rutland, VT: Charles E. Tuttle, 1967.

Uther, Hans-Jörg. *The Types of International Folktales: A Classification and Bibliography Based on the System of Antti Aarne and Stith Thompson*, 3 vols. Helsinki: Suomalainen Tiedeakatemia/ Academia Scientiarum Fennica, 2004.

Valdez, Al. *Gangs: A Guide to Understanding Street Gangs*. 3rd ed. San Clemente, CA: Law Tech, 2000.

Vale, V., and Andrea Juno, eds. *Re/Search #12: Modern Primitives, An Investigation of Contemporary Adornment and Ritual*. San Francisco: Re/Search Publications, 1989.

Valentine, Bill. *Gangs and Their Tattoos: Identifying Gangbangers on the Street and in Prison*. Boulder, CO: Palladin Press, 2000.

Van, Dang Nghiem. "The Flood Myth and the Origin of Ethnic Groups in Southeast Asia." *Journal of American Folklore* 106 (1993): 304–37.

Van Auken, Lance, and Robin Van Auken. *Play Ball! The Story of Little League Baseball*. University Park: Pennsylvania State University Press, 2001.

van Buren, Tom, and Leonardo Iván Domínguez. *Quisqueya en el Hudson: Dominican Music in New York*. CD (SFWCD 40495). Washington, DC: Smithsonian Folkways Recordings, 2004.

Van Gennep, Arnold. *The Rites of Passage*. Translated by Monika B. Vizedom. Chicago: University of Chicago Press, 1961.

Van Maanen, John. *Tales of the Field: On Writing*

Ethnography. Chicago: University of Chicago Press, 1988.

Van Reenan, Antanas J. *Lithuanian Diaspora: Königsberg to Chicago.* Lanham, MD: University Press of America, 1990.

Van Rosenstiel, Helene. *American Rugs and Carpets: From the Seventeenth Century to Modern Times.* New York: William Morrow, 1978.

Van Tassel, David, and John J. Grabowski, eds. *The Encyclopedia of Cleveland History.* Bloomington: Indiana University Press, 1987.

Varacalli, Joseph A., Salvatore Primeggia, Salvatore J. LaGumina, and Donald J. D'Elia, eds. *The Saints in the Lives of Italian Americans: An Interdisciplinary Investigation.* Stony Brook, NY: Forum Italicum, 1999.

Várdy, Steven Béla. *The Hungarian Americans.* Boston: Twayne, 1985.

———. *The Hungarian Americans: The Hungarian Experience in North America.* New York: Chelsea House Publishers, 1990.

Various Artists—Ethnic and Immigrant Communities. *New York: Global Beat of the Boroughs.* Smithsonian Folkways Recordings, CD (SFW404932001).

Vassilikos, Vassilis. *And Dreams Are Dreams.* Translated by Mary Kitroëff. New York: Seven Stories, 1996.

Vaughn-Roberson, Courtney Ann. *City in the Osage Hills: The History of Tulsa, Oklahoma.* Boulder, CO: Pruett, 1984.

Veblen, Thorstein. *The Theory of the Leisure Class.* 1899. Reprint, New York: Penguin, 1994.

Vecoli, Rudolph J., ed. *Italian Immigrants in Rural and Small Town America. Essays from the Fourteenth Annual Conference of the American Italian Historical Association.* Staten Island, NY: American Italian Historical Association, 1987.

Velez, Gonzalo. "Filipinos in New Jersey." In *The New Jersey Ethnic Experience,* ed. Barbara Cunningham, 198–210. Union City, NJ: Wm. H. Wise, 1977.

Veličkov, Aleksandăr. "Some Bulgarian-American Cultural Societies and Organizations Between the Two World Wars." *Bulgarian Historical Review* 22 (1994): 88–100.

Vellinga, Marcel. "Drawing Boundaries: Vernacular Architecture and Maps." *Traditional Dwellings and Settlements Review* 14 (2003): 21–32.

Venturi, Robert, Denise Scott Brown, and Steven Izenour. *Learning from Las Vegas: The Forgotten Symbolism of Architectural Form.* Cambridge, MA: MIT Press, 2000.

Victor, Jeffrey S. *Satanic Panic: The Creation of a Contemporary Legend.* Chicago: Open Court, 1993.

Vidan, Aida. *Embroidered with Gold, Strung with Pearls: The Traditional Ballads of Bosnian Women.* Cambridge, MA: Milman Parry Collection of Oral Literature, 2003.

Vigil, James Diego. *Barrio Gangs: Street Life and Identity in Southern California.* Austin, TX: University of Texas Press, 1988.

———. *A Rainbow of Gangs: Street Cultures in the Mega-City.* Austin: University of Texas Press, 2002.

Vigil, Vicki Blum. *Cleveland Cemeteries: Stone, Symbols and Stories.* Cleveland, OH: Gray and Company, 1999.

Vila, Pablo. *Crossing Borders, Reinforcing Borders: Social Categories, Metaphors and Narrative Identities on the U.S.-Mexico Frontier.* Austin: University of Texas Press, 2000.

———, ed. *Ethnography at the Border.* Minneapolis: University of Minnesota Press, 2003.

Villa, Raúl Homero, and George J. Sánchez, eds. *Los Angeles and the Future of Urban Cultures.* Baltimore: Johns Hopkins University Press, 2005.

Villarino, José, and Arturo Ramírez. *Chicano Border Culture and Folklore.* San Diego, CA: Marin, 1992.

Viluoja, Eha. "Beliefs and Legends About the Dead in Estonian Folk Tradition." *Artes Populares* 16–17 (1995): 835–39.

Vincent, John. *Old Age.* London: Routledge, 2003.

Vinitzky-Seroussi, Vered. *After Pomp and Circumstance: High School Reunion as an Autobiographical Occasion.* Chicago: University of Chicago Press, 1998.

Viramontes, Helena Maria. *Under the Feet of Jesus.* New York: Plume/Penguin, 1995.

Vlach, John Michael. *The Afro-American Tradition in Decorative Arts.* Athens: University of Georgia Press, 1990 [1978].

———. *Barns.* New York: W.W. Norton, 2003.

———. *By the Work of Their Hands: Studies in Afro-American Folklife.* Ann Arbor, MI: UMI Research Press, 1991.

———. *Charleston Blacksmith: The Work of Philip Simmons.* Rev. ed. Columbia: University of South Carolina Press, 1992.

———. "The Concept of Community and Folklife

Study." In *American Material Culture and Folklife*, ed. Simon J. Bronner, 63–75. Logan: Utah State University Press, 1992.

———. "Folklife and the Tangible Text." In *100 Years of American Folklore Studies*, ed. William M. Clements, 18–20. Washington, DC: American Folklore Society, 1988.

———. *Plain Painters: Making Sense of American Folk Art*. Washington, DC: Smithsonian Institution Press, 1988.

Vlach, John Michael, and Simon J. Bronner, eds. *Folk Art and Art Worlds*. 1986. Reprint, Logan: Utah State University Press, 1992.

Vogel, Morris J. *Cultural Connections: Museums and Libraries of Philadelphia and the Delaware Valley*. Philadelphia: Temple University Press, 1991.

Von Gwinner, Schnuppe. *The History of the Patchwork Quilt: Origins, Traditions, and Symbols of a Textile Art*. West Chester, PA: Schiffer, 1988.

Vosler, Ronald J. *Lost Shawls and Pig Spleens: Folklore, Anecdotes, and Humor of the Germans from Russia in the Dakotas*. Fargo: Germans from Russia Heritage Collection, North Dakota State University Libraries, 2002.

———. *Not Until the Combine Is Paid and Other Jokes: From the Oral Traditions of Germans from Russia in the Dakotas*. Fargo: Germans from Russia Heritage Collection, North Dakota State University Libraries, 2001.

Voth, Norma Jost. *Festive Breads of Easter*. Scottdale, PA: Herald, 1980.

Vrga, Djuro J., and Frank J. Fahey. *Changes and Socio-Religious Conflict in an Ethnic Minority Group: The Serbian Orthodox Church in America*. San Francisco: R and E Research Associates, 1975.

Vujnovich, Milos M. *Yugoslavs in Louisiana*. Gretna, LA: Pelican, 1974.

Wachs, Eleanor. *Crime Victim Stories: New York City's Urban Folklore*. Bloomington: Indiana University Press, 1988.

Wacker, Grant. *Heaven Below: Early Pentecostals and American Culture*. Cambridge, MA: Harvard University Press, 2003.

Wacker, Peter O. "Folk Architecture as an Indicator of Culture Areas and Culture Diffusion: Dutch Barns and Barracks in New Jersey." *Pioneer America* 5 (1973): 37–47.

Wade, Edwin L. "The Ethnic Art Market in the American Southwest, 1880–1980." In *Objects and Others: Essays on Museums and Material Culture*, ed. George W. Stocking, Jr., 167–91. Madison: University of Wisconsin Press, 1985.

Wagner, Edith. *The Family Reunion Sourcebook*. New York: McGraw-Hill, 1999.

Wahlman, Maude Southwell. *Signs and Symbols: African Images in African-American Quilts*. New York: Studio Books, 1993.

Waldman, Carl. *Atlas of the North American Indian*. New York: Facts on File, 2000.

Walker, Barbara, ed. *Out of the Ordinary: Folklore and the Supernatural*. Logan: Utah State University Press, 1995.

Walker, Robert Harris. *Cincinnati and the Big Red Machine*. Bloomington: Indiana University Press, 1988.

Walker, Tom, ed. *Folk Arts and Cultural Traditions of the Delmarva Peninsula: An Interpretive Resource Guide*. Baltimore: Mid-Atlantic Arts Foundation, 2003.

Walko, M. Ann. *Rejecting the Second Generation Hypothesis: Maintaining Estonian Ethnicity in Lakewood, New Jersey*. New York: AMS Press, 1989.

Wallace, Carol. *All Dressed in White: The Irresistible Rise of the American Wedding*. New York: Penguin, 2004.

Wallhauser, John. "I Can Almost See Heaven from Here." *Katallagete* (Spring 1983): 2–10.

Walls, Robert E. "Green Commonwealth: Forestry, Labor, and Public Ritual in the Post–World War II Pacific Northwest." *Pacific Northwest Quarterly* 87 (1996): 117–29.

———. "Logger Poetry and the Expression of Worldview." *Northwest Folklore* 5 (1987): 15–45.

Walser, Robert. *Running with the Devil: Power, Gender, and Madness in Heavy Metal Music*. Hanover, NH: Wesleyan University Press. 1993.

Walter, E.V. *Placeways: A Theory of the Human Environment*. Chapel Hill: University of North Carolina Press, 1988.

Ward, Daniel Franklin. *Personal Places: Perspectives on Informal Art Environments*. Bowling Green, OH: Bowling Green State University Popular Press, 1984.

Ward, Fay E. *The Cowboy at Work: All About His Job and How He Does It*. Norman: University of Oklahoma Press, 1987.

Ward, Martha. *Voodoo Queen: The Spirited Lives of Marie Laveau*. Jackson: University Press of Mississippi, 2004.

Ware, Carolyn. "Croatians in Southeastern Louisiana: An Overview." *Louisiana Folklore Miscellany* 11 (1996): 67–86.

Warner, Sam Bass. *Greater Boston: Adapting Regional Traditions to the Present.* Philadelphia: University of Pennsylvania Press, 2001.

Warner, William W. *Beautiful Swimmers: Watermen, Crabs, and the Chesapeake Bay.* Boston: Little, Brown, 1976.

———. *Distant Water: The Fate of the North Atlantic Fisherman.* New York: Penguin Books, 1984.

Warren, Kennedy. *Big Steel: The First Century of the United States Steel Corporation, 1901–2001.* Pittsburgh: University of Pittsburgh Press, 2001.

Warshaver, Gerald. "Urban Folklore." In *Handbook of American Folklore,* ed. Richard M. Dorson, 162–71. Bloomington: Indiana University Press, 1983.

Warzeski, Walter C. *Byzantine Rite Rusins in Carpatho-Ruthenia and America.* Pittsburgh: Byzantine Seminary Press, 1971.

"Washington, D.C.: It's Our Home." In *2000 Smithsonian Folklife Festival Program Book,* ed. Carla M. Borden, 12–37. Washington, DC: Smithsonian Center for Folklife and Cultural Heritage, 2000.

Watson, Steven. *The Harlem Renaissance: Hub of African-American Culture, 1920–1930.* New York: Pantheon, 1996.

Waugh, Earle H., Baha Abu-Laban, and Regula B. Qureshi, eds. *The Muslim Community in North America.* Edmonton, Canada: University of Alberta Press, 1983.

Waugh, Earle H., Sharon McIrvin Abu-Laban, and Regula Burckhardt Qureshi, eds. *Muslim Families in North America.* Edmonton, Canada: University of Alberta Press, 1991.

Waugh, Thomas, ed. 1984. *"Show Us Life": Toward a History and Aesthetics of the Committed Documentary.* Metuchen, NJ: Scarecrow, 1984.

Weaver, Martin G. *Mennonites of Lancaster Conference.* 1931. Reprint, Ephrata, PA: Eastern Mennonite Publications, 1993.

Weaver, William Woys. *Country Scrapple: An American Tradition.* Mechanicsburg, PA: Stackpole, 2003.

Weaver-Zercher, David, ed. *Writing the Amish: The Worlds of John A. Hostetler.* University Park: Pennsylvania State University Press, 2005.

Webb, Robert Lloyd. *Ring the Banjar: The Banjo in America from Folklore to Factory.* Cambridge, MA: MIT Museum, 1984.

Webber, Philip E. *Kolonie-Deutsch: Life and Language in Amana.* Ames: Iowa State University Press, 1993.

———. *Pella Dutch: The Portrait of a Language and Its Use in One of Iowa's Ethnic Communities.* Ames: Iowa State University Press, 1988.

Weber, David J. *Myth and the History of the Hispanic Southwest.* Albuquerque: University of New Mexico Press, 2002.

Weeks, Jeanne D., and Donald Treganowan. *Rugs and Carpets of Europe and the Western World.* New York: Weathervane, 1969.

Weeks, Linton. *Memphis: A Folk History.* Little Rock, AR: Parkhurst, 1982.

Weems, Mickey. "The Circuit: Gay Men's Techniques of Ecstasy." In *Manly Traditions: The Folk Roots of American Masculinities,* ed. Simon J. Bronner, 171–207. Bloomington: Indiana University Press, 2005.

Weems, Robert E., Jr. *Desegregating the Dollar: African American Consumerism in the Twentieth Century.* New York: New York University Press, 1998.

Weider, Lawrence D. *Language and Social Reality: The Case of Talking the Convict Code.* Hawthorn, NY: Mouton, 1974.

Weigle, Marta, and Peter White. *Folklore of New Mexico.* Albuquerque: University of New Mexico Press, 2003.

———. *The Lore of New Mexico.* Albuquerque: University of New Mexico Press, 1988.

Weiler, Lloyd M. "An Introduction to Old Order Mennonite Origins in Lancaster County, Pennsylvania: 1893 to 1993." *Pennsylvania Mennonite Heritage* 16, no. 4 (October 1993): 2–13.

Weinstein, Deena. *Heavy Metal: The Music and Its Culture.* Boulder, CO: Da Capo, 2000.

Weisberg, Barbara. *Talking to the Dead: Kate and Maggie Fox and the Rise of Spiritualism.* San Francisco: HarperSanFrancisco, 2004.

Weiser, Francis X. *The Christmas Book.* New York: Harcourt, Brace, 1952.

Weiser, Frederick S. "The Clothing of the 'White Top' Amish of Central Pennsylvania." *Pennsylvania Mennonite Heritage* 21, no. 3 (July 1998): 2–10.

———. "Handlumpe, Naameduch, and Kelleduch: Embroidered Textiles Among 'Nebraska Amish.'" *Der Reggeboge: Journal of the Pennsylvania German Society* 21, no. 1 (1987): 23–31.

Weitz, Rose. *Rapunzel's Daughters: What Women's Hair Tells Us About Women's Lives.* New York: Farrar, Straus and Giroux, 2004.

Welch, Charles E., Jr. *Oh! Dem Golden Slippers: The Story of the Philadelphia Mummers.* Rev. ed. Philadelphia: Book Street Press, 1991.

Welch, Charles E., Jr. "Oh, Dem Golden Slippers: The Philadelphia Mummers Parade." *Journal of American Folklore* 79, no. 314 (October–December 1966): 523–36.

Weller, Worth H. *Under the Hood: Unmasking the Modern Ku Klux Klan.* North Manchester, IN: DeWitt Books, 1998.

Wells, Keiko. "Shin Buddhist Song Lyrics Sung in the United States: Their History and Expressed Buddhist Images (1) 1898–1939." *Pacific and American Studies* 2 (2002): 75–99.

———. "Shin Buddhist Song Lyrics Sung in the United States: Their History and Expressed Buddhist Images (2) 1936–2001." *Pacific and American Studies* 3 (2003): 41–64.

Welsch, Roger L. *Shingling the Fog and Other Plains Lies.* Lincoln: University of Nebraska Press, 1980.

———. *Tall-Tale Postcards: A Pictorial History.* New York: A.S. Barnes, 1976.

———. *A Treasury of Nebraska Pioneer Folklore.* Lincoln: University of Nebraska Press, 1966.

Wenger, A. Grace. *Frontiers of Faithfulness: The Story of the Groffdale Mennonite Church.* Leola, PA: Groffdale Mennonite Church, 1992.

Wepman, Dennis, Ronald B. Newman, and Murray B. Binderman. *The Life: The Lore and Folk Poetry of the Black Hustler.* Philadelphia: University of Pennsylvania Press, 1976.

Wertheimer, Jack. *A People Divided: Judaism in Contemporary America.* Hanover, NH: Brandeis University Press, 1993.

Wertkin, Gerard C., ed. *Encyclopedia of American Folk Art.* New York: Routledge, 2004.

———. *The Four Seasons of Shaker Life: An Intimate Portrait of the Community at Sabbathday Lake.* New York: Simon and Schuster, 1986.

Wertsman, Vladimir. *The Armenians in America, 1618–1976: A Chronology in Fact and Book.* Dobbs Ferry, NY: Oceana, 1978.

Wessinger, Catherine. *How the Millennium Comes Violently: From Jonestown to Heaven's Gate.* New York: Seven Bridges Press, 2000.

West, John O. *Mexican-American Folklore.* Little Rock, AR: August House, 1988.

Westkott, Marcia. "Powwowing in Berks County." *Pennsylvania Folklife* 19, no. 2 (1969–1970): 2–9.

Westmacott, Richard. *African-American Gardens and Yards in the Rural South.* Knoxville: University of Tennessee Press, 1992.

Weston, George. *Boston Ways: High, By, and Folk.* 3rd ed. Boston: Beacon, 1974.

Wetherington, Mark. *The New South Comes to Wiregrass Georgia: 1860–1910.* Knoxville: University of Tennessee Press, 1994.

Whatley, Mariamne H., and Elissa R. Henken. *Did You Hear About the Girl Who . . . ? Contemporary Legends, Folklore, and Human Sexuality.* New York: New York University Press, 2003.

Whayne, Jeannie M. "What Is the Mississippi Delta? A Historian's Perspective." *Arkansas Review* 30 (1999): 3–9.

Whisker, James B. *Pennsylvania Silversmiths, Goldsmiths and Pewterers, 1684–1900.* Lewiston, PA: E. Mellen Press, 1993.

Whisnant, David E. *All That Is Native and Fine: The Politics of Culture in an American Region.* Chapel Hill: University of North Carolina Press, 1983.

White, Marilyn M. "Family Reunions: Preservation, Protection, and Renewal." In *1994 Festival of Michigan Folklife*, edited by Ruth D. Fitzgerald and Yvonne R. Lockwood, 14–20. East Lansing: Michigan State University, 1994.

White, Sid, and Sam Solberg, eds. *Peoples of Washington State.* Pullman: Washington State University Press, 1989.

Whiteford, Andrew Hunter. *Southwestern Indian Baskets and Their Makers.* Santa Fe, NM: School of American Research Books, 1988.

Wicker, Christine. *Lily Dale: The True Story of the Town that Talks to the Dead.* San Francisco: HarperSanFrancisco, 2003.

Wiggins, William H., Jr. "The Black Folk Church." In *Handbook of American Folklore*, ed. Richard M. Dorson, 145–54. Bloomington: Indiana University Press, 1983.

———. "'In the Rapture': The Black Aesthetic and Folk Drama." *Callaloo: Journal of African American and African Arts and Letters* 2 (1978): 103–11.

———. *O Freedom! Afro-American Emancipation Celebrations.* Knoxville: University of Tennessee Press, 1987.

Wiggins, William H., Jr., and Douglas DeNatale, eds. *Jubilation! African American Celebrations in the*

Southeast. Columbia, SC: McKissick Museum, 1993.

Wigginton, Eliot, ed. *The Foxfire Book.* Garden City: Anchor Press/Doubleday, 1972.

———. *Foxfire: 25 Years.* Garden City, NY: Anchor Books, 1991.

Wilcken, Lois. "Spirit Unbound: New Approaches to the Performance of Haitian Folklore." In *Caribbean Dance from Abakuá to Zouk: How Movement Shapes Identity*, ed. Susanna Sloat, 114–23. Gainesville: University Press of Florida, 2002.

Wildhaber, Robert. "Folk Atlas Mapping." In *Folklore and Folklife: An Introduction*, ed. Richard M. Dorson, 479–96. Chicago: University of Chicago Press, 1972.

Wilgus, D.K. "The Text Is the Thing." *Journal of American Folklore* 86 (1973): 241–52.

Wilhelm, Gene. "Folk Settlements in the Blue Ridge Mountains." *Appalachian Journal* 5 (1978): 204–45.

———. "Material Culture in the Blue Ridge Mountains." In *Culture, Form and Place: Essays in Cultural and Historical Geography,* ed. Kent Mathewson, 197–256. Baton Rouge: Louisiana State University Press, 1993.

Williams, Bruce T. *Coal Dust in Their Blood: The Work and Lives of Underground Coal Miners.* New York: AMS Press, 1991.

Williams, Michael Ann. *Great Smoky Mountains Folklife.* Jackson: University Press of Mississippi, 1995.

———. *Homeplace: The Social Use and Meaning of the Folk Dwelling in Southwestern North Carolina.* Athens: University of Georgia Press, 1991.

Williams, Raymond Brady, ed. *A Sacred Thread: Modern Transmission of Hindu Traditions in India and Abroad.* Chambersburg, PA: Anima, 1992.

Williamson, J.W. *Hillbillyland.* Chapel Hill: University of North Carolina Press, 1995.

Willis, Clint, ed. *Firefighters: Stories of Survival from the Front Lines of Firefighting.* New York: Thunder's Mouth, 2002.

Willis, John C. *Forgotten Time: The Yazoo-Mississippi Delta After the Civil War.* Charlottesville: University Press of Virginia, 2000.

Willoughby, David. *The Super Athletes.* New York: A.S. Barnes, 1970.

Wilmshurst, W.L. *The Meaning of Masonry.* New York: Gramercy, 1995.

Wilson, Charles Reagan, and William Ferris, eds. *Encyclopedia of Southern Culture.* Chapel Hill: University of North Carolina Press, 1989.

Wilson, Chris. *The Myth of Santa Fe: Creating a Modern Regional Tradition.* Albuquerque: University of New Mexico Press, 1997.

Wilson, Chris, and Paul Groth, eds. *Everyday America: Cultural Landscape Studies After J.B. Jackson.* Berkeley: University of California Press, 2003.

Wilson, William A. "Freeways, Parking Lots, and Ice Cream Stands: The Three Nephites in Contemporary Society." *Dialogue: A Journal of Mormon Thought* 21 (1988): 13–26.

———. "On Being Human: The Folklore of Mormon Missionaries." *New York Folklore* 8, nos. 3–4 (1982): 5–27.

———. "'We Did Everything Together': Farming Customs of the Mountainwest." *Northwest Folklore* 4 (1985): 23–30.

Winston, Mary Ellen, and Holly Garrison. *The New York Cabbie Cookbook: More Than 120 Authentic Homestyle Recipes from Around the Globe.* Philadelphia: Running Press, 2003.

Wise, Marc F. *Truck Stop.* Jackson: University Press of Mississippi, 1995.

Wishart, David J., ed. *The Great Plains Encyclopedia.* Lincoln: University of Nebraska Press, 2005.

Wittlinger, Carlton O. *Quest for Piety and Obedience: The Story of the Brethren in Christ.* Nappanee, IN: Evangel Press, 1978.

Wojcik, Daniel. *The End of the World As We Know It: Faith, Fatalism, and Apocalypse in America.* New York: New York University Press, 1997.

———. *Punk and Neo-Tribal Body Art.* Jackson: University Press of Mississippi, 1995.

Wolensky, Kenneth, Nicole Wolensky, and Robert P. Wolensky. *Fighting for the Union Label: The Women's Garment Industry and the ILGWU in Pennsylvania.* University Park: Pennsylvania State University Press, 2002.

Wolfe, Charles. *The Devil's Box: Masters of Southern Fiddling.* Nashville: Country Music Foundation Press and Vanderbilt University Press, 1997.

———. *Tennessee Strings: The Story of Country Music in Tennessee.* Knoxville: University of Tennessee Press, 1977.

Wolfenstein, Martha. *Children's Humor: A Psychological Analysis.* 1954. Reprint, Bloomington: Indiana University Press, 1978.

Wolters, Richard A. *Living on Wheels.* New York: E.P. Dutton, 1973.

Wong, Jade Snow. *Fifth Chinese Daughter.* Seattle: University of Washington Press, 1989.

Wood, Charles Roger. *Down in Houston: Bayou City Blues.* Austin: University of Texas Press, 2003.

Wood, Joseph S. *The New England Village.* Baltimore: Johns Hopkins University Press, 1997.

Wood, Roger. *Down in Houston: Bayou City Blues.* Austin: University of Texas Press, 2003.

Wooden, Wayne S., and Randy Blazak. *Renegade Kids, Suburban Outlaws: From Youth Culture to Delinquency.* Belmont, CA: Wadsworth, 2001.

Working Americans Program, Smithsonian Bicentennial Festival of American Folklife. *Ring Like Silver, Shine Like Gold: Folklore in the Labor Press.* Washington, DC: Smithsonian Institution Press, 1976.

Workman, Mark E. "The Differential Perception of Popular Dramatic Events." *Keystone Folklore* 23 (1979): 1–10.

———. "Dramaturgical Aspects of Professional Wrestling Matches." *Folklore Forum* 10 (1977): 14–20.

Wright, Dorothy. *The Complete Book of Baskets and Basketry.* New York: Charles Scribner's Sons, 1977.

Wright, Jim. *Fixin' to Git: One Fan's Love Affair with NASCAR's Winston Cup.* Durham, NC: Duke University Press, 2002.

Wright, Robert L., ed. *Irish Emigrant Ballads and Songs.* Bowling Green, OH: Bowling Green Universty Popular Press, 1975.

Wright, Robin K., ed. *A Time of Gathering: Native Heritage in Washington State.* Seattle: Burke Museum and University of Washington Press, 1990.

Wright, Sharon D. *Race, Power, and Political Emergence in Memphis.* New York: Garland, 2000.

Writers' Program of the Work Projects Administration in the State of Texas. *Houston: A History and Guide.* Houston, TX: Anson Jones Press, 1942.

Wrobel, Paul. *Our Way: Family, Parish, and Neighborhood in a Polish-American Community.* Notre Dame, IN: University of Notre Dame Press, 1979.

Wust, Klaus. *The Virginia Germans.* Charlottesville: University Press of Virginia, 1969.

Wyaco, Virgil, Carroll L. Riley, and J.A. Jones, eds. *A Zuni Life: A Pueblo Indian in Two Worlds.* Albuquerque: University of New Mexico Press, 1998.

Wyatt, Sherry Joines. "Feeding the Farm Family: Domestic Outbuildings and Traditional Food Ways in the Blue Ridge." *Chronicle of the Early American Industries Association* 55, no. 3 (September 2002): 85–94.

Wyckoff, Daryl D. *Truck Drivers in America.* Lexington, MA: Lexington Books, 1979.

Yablonsky, Lewis, and Jonathan J. Brower. *The Little League Game.* New York: Times Books, 1979.

Yamanouchi, Tayeko. *Ways of Worship.* Philadelphia: Friends World Committee, Philadelphia Yearly Meeting, 2001.

Yamauchi, Lois A., Andrea K. Ceppi, and Jo-Anne Lau-Smith. "Teaching in a Hawaiian Context: Educator Perspectives on the Hawaiian Language Immersion Program." *Bilingual Research Journal* 24 (2000): 385–403.

Yanagisako, Sylvia Junko. *Transforming the Past: Tradition and Kinship Among Japanese Americans.* Stanford, CA: Stanford University Press, 1985.

Yañez, Richard. *El Paso del Norte: Stories on the Border.* Reno: University of Nevada Press, 2003.

Yeh, Chiou-Ling. "In the Traditions of China and in the Freedom of America: The Making of San Francisco's Chinese New Year Festivals." *American Quarterly* 56 (2004): 395–420.

Yip, Christopher L. "California Chinatowns: Built Environments Expressing the Hybridized Culture of Chinese Americans." In *Hybrid Urbanism: On the Identity Discourse and the Built Environment,* ed. Nezar Al Sayyad, 67–82. Westport, CT: Praeger, 2001.

Yocom, Margaret R. "'Awful Real': Dolls and Development in Rangeley, Maine." In *Feminist Messages: Coding in Women's Culture,* ed. Joan Radner, 126–54. Urbana: University of Illinois Press, 1993.

———. "'Cut My Teeth on a Spud!'—Rodney Richard, Mad Whittler from Rangeley, Maine." *Chip Chats* 41, no. 1 (1994): 17–19.

———. "Exuberance in Control: The Dialogue of Ideas in the Tales and Fan Towers of Woodsman William Richard of Phillips, Maine." In *Northeast Folklore: Essays in Honor of Edward D. Ives,* ed. Pauleena MacDougall and David Taylor, 265–95. Orono: University of Maine Press and the Maine Folklife Center, 2000.

———. "'Just Call Me Sandy, Son': Poet Jeep Wilcox's Tribute to Sandy Ives." In *Northeast Folklore: Essays in Honor of Edward D. Ives,* ed. Pauleena MacDougall and David Taylor, 265–95. Orono: University of Maine Press and the Maine Folklife Center, 2000.

Yoder, Don, ed. *American Folklife.* Austin: University of Texas Press, 1976.

———, ed. *Discovering American Folklife: Essays on Folk Culture and the Pennsylvania Dutch.* Harrisburg, PA: Stackpole, 2001.

———. "Folk Cookery." In *Folklore and Folklife: An Introduction,* ed. Richard M. Dorson, 325–50. Chicago: University of Chicago Press, 1972.

———. "Folk Costume." In *Folklore and Folklife: An Introduction,* ed. Richard M. Dorson, 295–323. Chicago: University of Chicago Press, 1972.

———. "Folk Medicine." In *Folklore and Folklife: An Introduction,* ed. Richard M. Dorson. Chicago: University of Chicago Press, 1972.

———. "The Folklife Studies Movement." *Pennsylvania Folklife* 13, no. 3 (July 1963): 43–56.

———. *Groundhog Day.* Harrisburg, PA: Stackpole, 2003.

———. "Harvest Home." In *Discovering American Folklife: Essays on Folk Culture and the Pennsylvania Dutch,* 227–46. Harrisburg, PA: Stackpole, 2001.

———. "Hohman and Romanus: Origins and Diffusion of the Pennsylvania German Powwow Manual." *American Folk Medicine: A Symposium,* edited by Wayland D. Hand, 235–48. Berkeley: University of California Press, 1976.

———. "Official Religion vs. Folk Religion." *Pennsylvania Folklife* 15 (1965–1966): 36–52.

———. *The Pennsylvania German Broadside: A History and Guide.* University Park: Pennsylvania State University Press, 2005.

———. "Toward a Definition of Folk Religion." *Western Folklore* 33 (1974): 2–12.

Yoder, Don, and Thomas E. Graves. *Hex Signs: Pennsylvania Dutch Barn Symbols and Their Meanings.* Harrisburg, PA: Stackpole, 2000.

Young, Karl. "The Origin of the Easter Play." *Publications of the Modern Language Association of America* 29 (1914): 1–58.

Yow, Valerie Raleigh. *Recording Oral History: A Practical Guide for Social Scientists.* Thousand Oaks, CA: Sage, 1994.

Yung, Judy. *Unbound Feet: A Social History of Chinese Women in San Francisco.* Berkeley: University of California Press, 1995.

Zabytko, Irene. *When Luba Leaves Home.* Chapel Hill, NC: Algonquin, 2003.

Zdatny, Steven. "The Boyish Look and the Liberated Woman: The Politics and Aesthetics of Women's Hairstyles." *Fashion Theory* 1 (1997): 367–98.

Zeitlin, Steven J., and Ilana Beth Harlow. *Giving a Voice to Sorrow: Personal Responses to Death and Mourning.* New York: Perigree, 2001.

Zeitlin, Steven J., Amy J. Kotkin, and Holly Cutting Baker, eds. *A Celebration of American Family Folklore.* Cambridge, MA: Yellow Moon Press, 1992.

Zelinsky, Wilbur. *The Cultural Geography of the United States.* Englewood Cliffs, NJ: Prentice-Hall, 1973.

———. *Exploring the Beloved Country: Geographic Forays into American Society and Culture.* Iowa City: University of Iowa Press, 1994.

———. "Geography." In *Pennsylvania: A History of the Commonwealth,* ed. Randall M. Miller and William Pencak, 389–410. University Park: Pennsylvania State University Press, 2002.

———. "Globalization Reconsidered: The Historical Geography of Modern Western Male Attire." *Journal of Cultural Geography* 22 (2004): 83–134.

———. "North American Vernacular Regions." *Annals of the Association of American Geographers* 70 (1980): 1–16.

Ziegler, Rebecca. "'Strangers and Exiles': Narratives from the Brethren." *Folklore and Mythology Studies* 1 (1977): 23–36.

Ziff, Bruce, and Pratima V. Rao, eds. *Borrowed Power: Essays on Cultural Appropriation.* New Brunswick, NJ: Rutgers University Press, 1997.

Zinkin, Harold, and Bonnie Hearn. *Remembering Muscle Beach: Where Hard Bodies Began—Photographs and Memories.* Los Angeles: Angel City, 1999.

Zipes, Jack, trans. 2003. *The Complete Fairy Tales of the Brothers Grimm.* 3rd ed. New York: Bantam.

Zug, Charles G., III. *Turners and Burners: The Folk Potters of North Carolina.* Chapel Hill: University of North Carolina Press, 1986.

Zumwalt, Rosemary. *American Folklore Scholarship: A Dialogue of Dissent.* Bloomington: Indiana University Press, 1988.

Internet Sources

American Folklife Center. Library of Congress. www.loc.gov/folklife.

American Folklore Society. www.afsnet.org.

Arab American Institute. www.aaiusa.org.

Association of Senegalese in America. www.asaweb.org.

Bartis, Peter, and Stephanie Hall, comps. *Folklife Sourcebook: A Directory of Folklife Resources in the United States.* www.loc.gov/folklife/source.

Boston Irish Reporter. www.bostonirish.com.

Center for Great Plains Studies, University of Nebraska-Lincoln. www.unl.edu/plains.

Center for Southern Folklore. www.southernfolklore.com.

Church of Jesus Christ of Latter-Day Saints. www.lds.org.

City Lore. www.citylore.org.

"Community Roots: Selections from the Local Legacies Project." American Folklife Center, Library of Congress. www.loc.gov/folklife/roots.

Core Sound Waterfowl Museum website. "Traditional Craftsmen." Designed by Vanda Lewis and Casey Amspacher; updated April 15, 2005, by Vision IPD .www.coresound.com.

Di Loreto, Camille. "Italian American Experience." www.virtualitalia.com/italamer/.

Sicilian Culture. www.sicilianculture.com.

"Folklore and Education Section of the American Folklore Society." American Folklore Society. www.afsnet.org/sections/education.

Folklore Archives. Walter P. Reuther Library of Labor and Urban Affairs. Wayne State University. www.reuther.wayne.edu/collections/hefa_1731-wsu.htm.

Greek Orthodox Diocese of America. www .goarch .org.

International Society for Krishna Consciousness. www.iskcon.org.

"Italian Neighborhoods." www.italianneighborhoods.com.

Latvians Online. www.latviansonline.com.

Lithuanian American Community, Inc. www.javlb.org.

Maine Folklife Center. www.umaine.edu/folklife.

Maklink. www.maklink.com.

National Museum of Industrial History. www.nmih.org.

Sabbathday Lake Shaker Village. www.shaker.lib.me.us.

Sacred Dance Guild. "What Is Sacred Dance?" www.sacreddanceguild.org.

Southern Folklife Collection. Manuscripts Department. Wilson Library. University of North Carolina at Chapel Hill. www.lib.unc.edu/mss/sfc1.

"Spiritualism: Pathway of Light." National Association of Spiritualist Churches. www.nsac.org/spiritualism/index.htm.

"Tradition Bearers." Rivers of Steel National Heritage Area. www.riversofsteel.com.

Traditional Arts Program, California Academy of Sciences. www.calacademy.org/research/anthropology/tap/index.htm.

Veterans History Project. A Project of the American Folklife Center at the Library of Congress. www.loc.gov/folklife/vets/.

World Intellectual Property Organization. "Traditional Cultural Expressions (Folklore)." www.wipo.int/tk/en/folklore/index.html.

General Index

Cultural Group Index

~~~ ~~~

A

Acadian communities, **1:**137–40;
  2:444–45
Adolescents
  courtship, **1:**229–30
  dialect, **1:**305–6
  gangs, **2:**467–73; **4:**1136–39
  humor, **1:**3
  legend tripping, **1:**4, 5; **2:**694–95
  music-song, **2:**358–62
  oral tradition, **1:**4
  performance, **1:**3–4, 5
  skateboarders, **4:**1133–36
  Straight Edge, **4:**1189–90
  students, **4:**1191–92
  subversive play, **1:**4–5
African American communities,
  1:8–11
  Afro-Dominican culture, **1:**312
  American South, **4:**1152, 1153–55
  Appalachia, **1:**36–37
  Atlanta, **1:**54–57
  automobiles, **1:**61
  background, **1:**8–9
  banjo, **1:**65–67, 95
  baskets-basketry, **1:**78, 79, 80, 170,
    171
  Black English, **1:**305
  blues music, **1:**101–5, 152–53,
    174–75, 289–90; **2:**604;
    3:762–63; **4:**1217
  branding, **1:**107, 108, 124–26
  Brooklyn, **1:**127, 129, 130
  Cape Cod, **1:**140, 142
  Carolina, Down East, **1:**152–53
  Charleston-Lowcountry South
    Carolina, **1:**170, 171, 172,
    173
  Chicago, **1:**174–75, 177
  Cincinnati, **1:**204, 205
  Cleveland, **1:**206–7, 209
  coastal Carolina plain region, **1:**210,
    212

African American communities
  (continued)
  Creoles (Louisiana), **1:**138–40,
    237–40
  cultural transformation, **1:**10;
    3:1030
  dance, **1:**262, 266–68
  death-funerals, **1:**281–82
  Delmarva-Eastern Shore Region,
    1:287
  Denver, **1:**291, 293
  Des Moines, **1:**295, 296
  Detroit, **1:**297, 298, 302–3
  foodways, **2:**534
  gangs, **2:**468, 469, 470, 718
  gardens, **2:**476
  gospel music, **2:**501–2
  Gullah-Geechee community, **1:**170,
    171, 172, 173; **2:**529–35
  Harlem, **2:**552, 554–57
  Juneteenth, **2:**430–31
  Ku Klux Klan, **2:**669–72
  legends, **2:**692
  Los Angeles, **2:**718
  Midwest, **3:**793, 795, 796
  Milwaukee, **3:**807–8
  Mississippi River Delta, **1:**289–91
  Muslims, **3:**845–46
  Nashville, **3:**857
  New Orleans, **3:**871–72, 873
  old-time music, **3:**915–16
  performance, **1:**9–10, 314–15
  proverbs, **3:**998
  race relations, **1:**237–39; **2:**664,
    666, 669–72
  railroaders, **3:**1028, 1030
  religion, **1:**9–10, 314–15
  slavery ancestry, **2:**529–31, 541
  toasts-dozens, **2:**607–8;
    4:1227–30
  Washington, D. C., **4:**1270–71
Agriculture. *See* Farmers
Arab communities
  background, **1:**41–42

Arab communities *(continued)*
  community locations, **1:**41–44, 301
  cultural diversity, **1:**40–42
  cultural preservation, **1:**44
  dance, **1:**43–44
  folk art, **1:**43
  foodways, **1:**43
  music-song, **1:**42–43
  oral tradition, **1:**42–43
  religion, **1:**40, 42–43
Armenian communities
  background, **1:**47
  community locations, **1:**47–48, 49
  cultural preservation, **1:**49
  foodways, **1:**49
  immigration, **1:**47–48
  music, **1:**49
  religious traditions, **1:**47, 48–49
Asian communities. *See specific
  ethnicity*
Azorean community. *See* Portuguese-
  speaking communities

B

Bangladesh community. *See* South
  Asian communities
Basque communities
  community locations, **1:**81–82
  cultural preservation, **1:**81–82, 83
  festivals, **1:**82
  traditions, **1:**82–83
Belgian community. *See* Netherlands
  Dutch and Belgian communities
Bhutan community. *See* South Asian
  communities
Bikers
  contemporary culture, **1:**89
  Harley-Davidson, **1:**87, 88
  outlaw clubs, **1:**87–89; **2:**469
Birth
  cultural groups, **1:**89–90, 92
  cultural knowledge, **1:**90–91
  hospital experience, **1:**91–92

Geographical Index